RETURN TO
JOHN OLIVER LIBRARY
530 EAST 41st AVE,
VANCOUVER, B.C.

D0460992

797.1   COP /
SAI
The Sailing book

RETURN TO
JOHN OLIVER LIBRARY

The Sailing Book

VANCOUVER PUBLIC SCHOOLS

This book may be kept until the last date
stamped below.

DUE	DUE	DUE	DUE
NOV 12 9D			
Summer '89			
St JAN 5 1992			
JUN 10 1994 ST			

SLIP

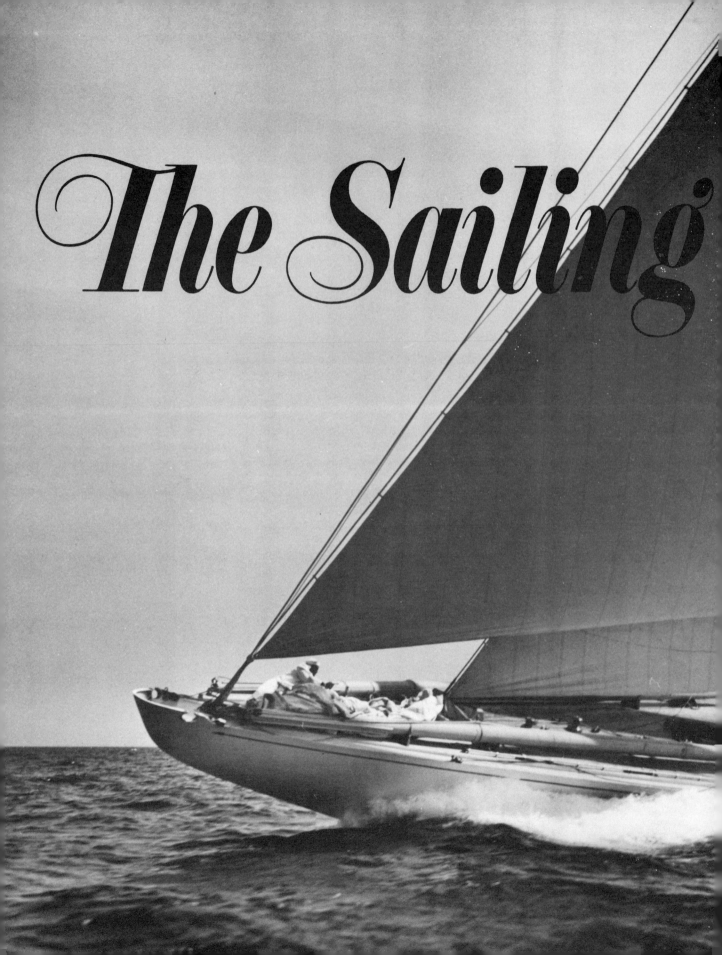

The Sailing

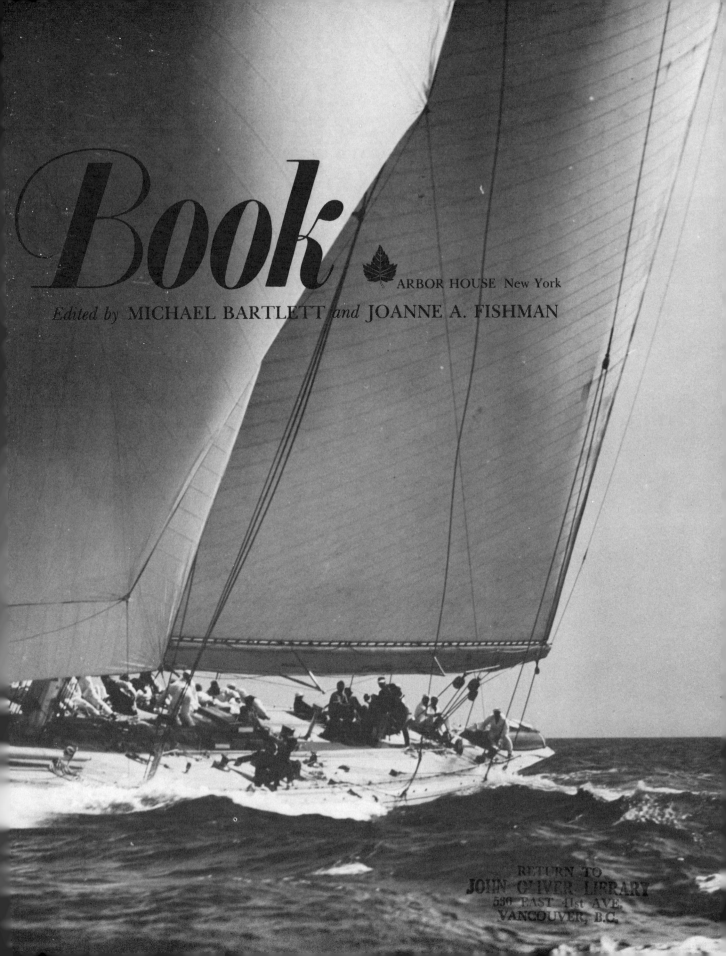

Book

ARBOR HOUSE New York

Edited by *MICHAEL BARTLETT and JOANNE A. FISHMAN*

RETURN TO
JOHN OLIVER LIBRARY
530 EAST 41st AVE.
VANCOUVER, B.C.

OTHER BOOKS BY MICHAEL BARTLETT
The New 1969 Golfer's Almanac

Bartlett's World Golf Encyclopedia

The Golf Book

The Tennis Book

Copyright © 1982 by Michael Bartlett and Joanne A. Fishman

All rights reserved, including the right of reproduction in whole or in part in any form.
Published in the United States of America by Arbor House Publishing Company and in
Canada by Fitzhenry & Whiteside, Ltd.

Library of Congress Catalogue Card Number: 81-71663
ISBN: 0-87795-369-4
MANUFACTURED IN THE UNITED STATES OF AMERICA
10 9 8 7 6 5 4 3 2 1

This book is printed on acid free paper. The paper in this book meets the guidelines for permanence and
durability of the Committee on Production Guidelines for Book Longevity of the Council on Library Resources.

Designed by Antler & Baldwin, Inc.

For Betsy, Shannon, Jenny and Kate—
and
For Lew, David, and Lee—
our favorite crews

Contents

Part II: THE GREAT RACES

Part III: THE ART OF SAILING

Part IV: BEFORE THE WIND

Part V: THE RECORDS

Acknowledgments

The following acknowledgments constitute an extention of the copyright page.

—"Mother Sea" ("The Gray Beginnings") from *The Sea Around Us* by Rachel Carson. Copyright © 1950, 1951, 1961 by Rachel Carson; renewed 1978 by Roger Christie. Reprinted by permission of Oxford University Press, Inc.

—"The Ancients and Sailing," by Samuel Eliot Morison from *Spring Tides.* Copyright © 1965 by Samuel Eliot Morison. Reprinted by permission of Curtis Brown, Ltd.

—"The Story of the Ship," by Alan Villiers from *Oceans of the World.* Copyright © 1963 by Alan Villiers. Reprinted by permission of the author and Museum Press Ltd., London, England.

—"The Sea," by Jan de Hartog from *A Sailor's Life.* Copyright © 1955, 1956 by Jan de Hartog and Littra A.G. Copyright © 1955 by The Curtis Publishing Co. Reprinted by permission of the author.

—"Landfall," by Samuel Eliot Morison from *Admiral of the Ocean* Sea. Copyright © 1942 by Samuel Eliot Morison; copyright renewed 1970 by Samuel Eliot Morison. Reprinted with permission of Little, Brown & Company in association with the Atlantic Monthly Press.

—"The Pilot of the Pinta," by Joshua Slocum from *Sailing Alone Around the World.* Reprinted by permission of Volvo Penta, Sweden.

—"The Great Barrier Reef," by Alistair Maclean from *Captain Cook.* Copyright © 1972 by Alistair Maclean. Reprinted by permission of Doubleday and Company, Inc. and William Collins Sons and Company, Ltd., London.

—"My 65th Birthday," by Sir Francis Chichester from *Gypsy Moth Circles the World.* Copyright © 1967 by Sir Francis Chichester. Reprinted by permission of Hodder and Stoughton Limited and Coward, McCann and Geoghegan.

—"Halfway," Reprinted from *Kon-Tiki* by Thor Heyerdahl. Copyright © 1950 by Thor Heyerdahl. Published in the United States by Rand McNally & Co., and reprinted with its permission.

—"Sailing on the Roof of the World," by Tristan Jones from *The Incredible Voyage.* Copyright © 1977 by Sheed Andrews and McMeel, Inc. Subsidiary of Universal Press Syndicate, Kansas City. Reprinted by permission of the publisher.

—"Grim Landfall," is reprinted from *Ice Bird,* The First Single-Handed Voyage to Antarctica, by David Lewis, with the permission of W.W. Norton & Company, Inc. Copyright © 1975 by David Lewis.

—"The Ultimate Storm," by William A. Robinson from *To The Great Southern Sea.* Published by Harcourt Brace Jovanovich, Inc. and reprinted with the permission of the author.

—"Shipwreck," is reprinted from *Two Against Cape Horn* by Hal Roth, with the permission of W.W. Norton & Company, Inc. Copyright © 1978 by Hal Roth.

—"North Atlantic Storm," from *Alone Against the Atlantic* by Gerry Spiess with Marlin Bree. Copyright © 1981 by Gerald F. Spiess and Marlin Bree. All rights reserved. Used with the permission of the publisher, Control Data Publishing, Minneapolis, MN.

—"Alain Colas: A Legend Lost At Sea," by William Oscar Johnson. The following article is reprinted courtesy of *Sports Illustrated* from the January 8, 1979 issue. Copyright © 1979 Time Inc., A Legend Lost At Sea," by William Oscar Johnson.

—"An Ordeal of Grandeur," by Webb Chiles from *Storm Passage.* Copyright © 1977 by Webb

Chiles. Reprinted by permission of Times Books, a division of Quadrangle/The New York Times Book Co., Inc.

—"1866: The Start of It All," by Alfred Loomis from *Ocean Racing.* Copyright © 1936 by Alfred L. Loomis. Published by William Morrow and Company. Reprinted by permission of Jason Aronson, Inc.

—"The America's Triumph," from *White Sails Shaking* by Ira Henry Freeman. Copyright © 1948 by The Macmillan Co. Copyright © 1962 by Ira Henry Freeman and reprinted by his permission. Article originally extracted from The London *Times,* August 25, 1851.

—"The Fisherman's Cup Races: Last Act" is reprinted from *Wanderer* by Sterling Hayden, with the permission of W.W. Norton & Company, Inc. Copyright © 1977, 1963 by Sterling Hayden.

—"On The Starboard Tack to Bermuda," by Herbert L. Stone from *The Best of Yachting.* Copyright © 1967 by Charles Scribner's Sons. Reprinted by permission of Jason Aronson, Inc.

—"The Southern Cross: Sydney to Hobart Race," by Edward Heath from *A Course of My Life.* Copyright © 1976 by Edward Heath. Reprinted with the permission of Stein and Day Publishers and Sedgwick & Jackson, Ltd.

—"The Southern Ocean Racing Conference," by Michael Levitt from *Nautical Quarterly.* Adapted from an article in *Nautical Quarterly* #3 and reprinted with the permission of the publisher.

—"Let De Boat Walk," by Bob Payne from *Sail* Magazine, June, 1979. Reprinted with the permission of the author and *Sail* Magazine.

—"The Ultimate Race," by Joanne A. Fishman from The New York *Times.* Copyright © 1981 by The New York Times Company. Reprinted by permission.

—"Grimalkin, An Orderly Boat, A Disorderly Storm," is reprinted from *Fastnet: Force 10* by John Rousmaniere, with the permission of W.W. Norton & Company, Inc. Copyright © 1980 by John Rousmaniere.

—"Freedom of the Dream," from *Fastnet: One Man's Voyage* by Roger Vaughan. Reprinted with the permission of PEI Books, Inc. Copyright © 1980 by Roger Vaughan.

—"Navigation," by Carleton Mitchell from *Passage East.* Reprinted by permission of the author.

—"Less Weight and More Speed," by Meade Gougeon and Tyrus Knoy from *Sailboat Design Yesterday, Today and Tomorrow.* Copyright © by Meade Gougeon and Tyrus Knoy. Reprinted by permission of the authors.

—"The Aerodynamics of Sails: Nature As A Guide," by Manfred Curry from *Yacht Racing: The Aerodynamics of Sail,* Fifth Edition, Translated by Charles E. Curry and Robert W. Atkinson. Copyright © 1948 by Manfred Curry; copyright renewed 1976 by Maria

Pfister-Curry. (New York: Charles Scribner's Sons, 1948). Reprinted with the permission of Charles Scribener's Sons.

—"On Sails," by Ted Hood from *Racing With Cornelius Shields and the Masters.* Copyright © 1974, 1964 by Prentice Hall, Inc. Reprinted with the permission of the author.

—"Formula For Success" is reprinted from *Wind and Strategy* by Stuart Walker, with the permission of W.W. Norton & Company, Inc. Copyright © 1973 by W.W. Norton & Company, Inc.

—"Racing," by Uffa Fox from *According to Uffa.* Published in the United States by St. Martin's Press and in the United Kingdom by Newnes. Reprinted with the permission of the publishers and the author.

—"The Heavies—North, Turner, Hood and Melges," is reprinted from *No Excuse To Lose, Winning Yacht Races* with Dennis Conner, as told to John Rousmaniere, with the permission of W.W. Norton & Company, Inc. Copyright © 1978 by Dennis Conner and John Rousmaniere.

—"Turner and Jobson In Conversation," by Ted Turner and Gary Jobson from *The Racing Edge.* Copyright © 1979 by Rutledge Books, Inc. Reprinted with permission of Simon & Schuster, a Division of Gulf + Western Corporation.

—"September Hurricane," by Adlard Coles from *Heavy Weather Sailing.* Reprinted with permission of the author and John de Graff, Inc., Clinton Corners, New York 12514.

—"The Sirens," by Homer from *The Odyssey,* translated by S.A. Butcher and Andrew Lang. Introduction by John A. Scott (New York: Macmillan, 1930). Reprinted with permission of Macmillan Publishing, Co. Inc.

—"Sea Law," from *Mutiny On The Bounty* by Charles Nordhoff and James Norman Hall. Copyright 1932, 1940 by Little, Brown and Co.; copyright renewed 1960, 1968. Reprinted by permission of Little, Brown & Company, in association with Atlantic Monthly Press Books.

—"Sharks In The Boatyard," from *White Sails Shaking* by Ira Henry Freeman. Copyright © 1948 by Macmillan Company and 1962 by Ira Henry Freeman. Extracted from "The Cruise of the Snark," by Jack London.

—"The Story of Sailing," by James Thurber from *My World—and Welcome To It.* Copyright © 1942 James Thurber; copyright © 1970 Helen W. Thurber and Rosemary T. Sauers. From *My World—And Welcome To It,* published by Harcourt Brace Jovanovich, Inc. Reprinted by permission of the author.

—"About Figaro," by William Snaith from *On The Wind's Way.* Copyright © 1973 by William Snaith. Reprinted by permission of G.P. Putnam's Sons.

—"Cyrano: The First Cruise," by William F. Buckley, Jr. from *Airborne: A Sentimental Journey.* Copyright © 1970, 1972, 1976 by William F. Buckley, Jr. Originally appeared in *The New Yorker.* Reprinted by permission of Macmillan Publishing Co. and Wallace & Sheil Agency, Inc.

—"The Hunting of Hewlish," by Sam Nicholson from *Omni* Magazine. Copyright © 1980 by Omni Publications International Ltd. Reprinted by permission of the author and the Barbara Bova Literary Agency.

—"The Chains of Possession," by Ernest K. Gann from *Song of the Sirens.* Copyright © 1968 by Ernest K. Gann. Reprinted by permission of the author and the author's agents, Scott Meredith Literary Agency, Inc., 845 Third Ave., New York, N.Y. 10022.

Foreword

by **DENNIS CONNER**

THERE is a place for this book in the library of anyone who has an interest in the sea, whether that interest is the result of years of competition, of occasional cruising or a vicarious experience shared by the landbound. These selections gives a true feeling of what it is like to be out on the ocean.

Over the past twenty years I have sailed extensively and had numerous adventures on the sea. For me, it was particularly revealing to compare some of my experiences to those of others in similar situations. For instance, reading William Robinson's account of "The Ultimate Storm," I could empathize with him when he keeps saying to himself that the barometer must start to go down, but instead the wind continues rising and rising. And I could understand his relief that he was out there in a well-designed boat that had been tested in the tank at Stevens Institute and had a very strong rudder.

His boat had been built for this, otherwise he would have been in trouble. I remembered that I had felt the same way about *Williwaw* during the calamitous storm in the 1979 Fastnet Race. Then, I too was thankful my boat had been built with a little extra strength compared to the standard state-of-the-art boats.

Anyone who goes out on the ocean has his own private level of fear, just as everyone's vision of reality is slightly different. You will become scared out there at a different point than I, and I don't know who would scare first, you or I. But anyone who has known that feeling of "What am I doing out here?" will be able to relate to the half a dozen or so excellent stories in this collection that illustrate how man copes with fear and the sea's fury.

I also found Hal Roth's account of being shipwrecked particularly revealing. Most shipwreck stories have a happy ending: the owner digs his boat off and floats away to safety. But Roth's account was honest. He didn't gloss over the seriousness of his problems, not the least of which was a panic-stricken crewman, but instead sought to solve them.

If you enjoy reading historic sea adventures, there are the absorbing passages by Joshua Slocum, Sir Francis Chichester and Thor Heyerdahl as well as several fictional classics. And if you like reading about adventures you didn't even know were possible, there is Tristan Jones' remarkable account of "Sailing on the Roof of the World."

A singular classic, both technically and as literature in its own right, is Manfred Curry's *"The Aerodynamics of Sails."* Anyone who is genuinely interested in the professional, technical approach to winning races should study this work. The Uffa Fox selection is also excellent; like

Curry, Fox too was ahead of his time. And if you follow the advice Stuart Walker gives in "Formula for Success" and use his checklist, you will win numerous sailboat races without doing anything else.

Because of my interest in navigation, I found the selection on navigation by Carleton Mitchell fascinating. It was revealing to learn how navigational tools, such as the taffrail log, evolved; what a "knot" really is and how we came to use that as a term for speed rather than miles per hour.

Those who love racing will especially enjoy the selections on the first ocean race and the first America's Cup race right through to the best accounts of contemporary racing stories. And for insight into what some at the leading edge of the

sport are like, there is my description of "The Heavies"—which still seems to hold up after a number of years—as well as the article "Turner and Jobson in Conversation." With the latter, it was fun for me to relive some of Gary Jobson and Ted Turner's thoughts on the America's Cup because they brought to mind what it was like to win and how Turner's approach differed from mine.

In all, when reading through a collection of stories such as this, one realizes people have been thinking about the sea and telling stories about it for probably as long as civilization has existed. This tends to put man's relationship with the sea in perspective—and provide fine entertainment as well.

The Siren Call

by **JOANNE A. FISHMAN**

EVER since the day 6,000 years or so ago when the first person conceived of stretching a piece of fabric or animal skin across a frame and lifting it up on a boat to catch the wind, carrying him up the Nile or Tigres or Euphrates rivers, man has been sailing.

Sailing became a means of trade and transport, exploration and discovery, and the route to gold and glory belonged to those with the fastest boats and superior knowledge, those who had best mastered the art of sailing. This era ended in the 19th century when steam engines, and later gasoline engines, replaced sails. But men continued to go to sea in boats with sails, this time for the fun of it. The sport of sailing, which began a little over a century ago as the great sailing ships were progressively being abandoned, has now evolved from a pastime for the wealthy into a popular form of recreation. Today sailors race 27,000 miles around the world for the pure thrill of it. In the summer, lakes, bays and rivers across the country are dotted with sailboats.

In the past decade, the art of sailing has taken a quantum jump with the discovery of new materials and construction techniques for both hulls and sails. Sails, for instance, are being constructed of synthetic fibers and plastics and designed by computers into precise airfoils.

Those sailmakers, designers, builders and sailors at the leading edge of the sport are creating boats that are lighter and stronger and that sail faster and closer to the wind than ever before. The America's Cup races have been the focal point for much of this innovation. And with boats such as the series of catamarans called *Patient Lady,* which have defended the Little America's Cup, American sailors also have pioneered the development of powerful, solid wingsails (rigid airfoils) and the use of carbon fiber.

Speed on the race course is the driving force behind all this research and development. Going fast under sail is fun, as well; thus, the meteoric rise in popularity of the sailboard—a cross between a sailboat and a surfboard that can reach twenty-five and thirty knots and is relatively inexpensive. At the other end of the racing spectrum, huge seventy-six-foot grand prix yachts now log bursts of speed of thirty and thirty-five knots. And the latest gossamer-light *Patient Lady* easily outraces the wind, reaching speeds of thirty knots in a fifteen or twenty knot breeze.

Beyond the race course the applications of the new sailing technology are just beginning to be tapped as sailing now seems to be coming full circle. Futuristic dreams and plans for harnessing the wind to help propel commercial ships are coming off the drawing boards and becoming a reality, accelerated by the end of cheap fuel.

When we scan the horizon twenty years from now, we may see ships with sails unlike anything we have ever seen before—some with solid wingsails, others with soft synthetic sails. And these sails will be automatically trimmed, and furled or unfurled, depending on the wind direction and velocity, by microcomputers on the ship's bridge.

Japan is already using this technology. Looking like a starship with two rectangular wingsails rising from its deck, the Japanese freighter *Shin Aitoku Maru* now plies the Sea of Japan. Its sail-assisted power accounts for a fifteen percent savings in fuel consumption. And the same Japanese concern already has built a scale model for a sail-assisted supertanker. Such ships are light years away from the days only a century ago when the majestic square riggers coursed the world's sea lanes propelled by acres of billowing canvas and trimmed with lines of hemp by men of iron.

When confronted with the vast span of time and diversity of purpose that sailing encompasses, one quickly realizes it is impossible to compress all the classics into one volume—or even two or three for that matter. Our intent was to include classic works, as well as stories of adventure and those that offer insight into the skill of sailing. But beyond that we wanted to follow the elemental thread that has linked man to the sea throughout the millennia.

The boats may have changed, but man's relationship to the sea remains the same. From that first sailor in ancient Egypt or Sumeria to the millions who sail small boats and yachts today, the sea has provided a constant challenge. And as William Snaith writes, "Every man should have a point on the scale from which to measure the events of his life, something constant and unchanging against which to reckon his highs and lows . . . The North Atlantic is constant enough; lord knows, it is a steadfast adversary . . . The sea has not changed since 'in the beginning' when as the first task on that mighty third day, it was divided from the dry places. It is the dry places that have changed."

At sea, there may be moments of terror and fear and loneliness at times, but there also is great beauty, exhilaration and joy. There is a sense of adventure, as nothing that deals with the wind and the water can ever be truly predictable and certain. And there is the spirit of freedom that cuts to the core of man's existence, the moments of magic when one feels in tune with the eternal mysteries and the infinite source of life on earth.

Common to sailors of all epochs is, as historian Samuel Eliot Morison describes it, "the soul of the eternal sailor, who can never bear to stay ashore as long as he has a ship, and willing shipmates to share the danger and the ecstasy of rolling over the multitudinous seas 'laden with suffering,' if you will, but refreshing the soul of man as nothing else, short of religion, can do."

The material in this collection seemed to fall naturally into four categories: Challenging the Sea, The Great Races, The Art of Sailing and Before the Wind. The last is a mixture of fiction and non-fiction ranging from "The Sirens" of Homer's *Odyssey* to Ernest K. Gann's "Song of the Sirens," a song heard by sailors throughout the ages.

As a fitting complement to the fine writing, we add the pictures of Stanley Rosenfeld, the esteemed marine photographer.

We are indebted to the New York Yacht Club not only for the use of its magnificent library but also for the assistance of its librarian, Sohei Hohri. When he arranged for us to use the library, Vic Romagna, a member of the club's America's Cup Committee, observed that "most people think the gem of the New York Yacht Club is the America's Cup. In reality, it is Mr. Hohri." He is right.

We also would like to thank Dan Fales, executive editor of *Motor Boating & Sailing Magazine,* for his helpful guidance.

Finally, we want to thank Diane Kiffin and Rebecca Leopold for their meticulous research efforts and work on the manuscript.

And now, climb aboard, take the helm and cast off on a literary voyage in search of the "soul of the eternal sailor" that lies deep within us all.

Joanne A. Fishman

PART I

CHALLENGING THE SEA

"In the artificial world of his cities and towns, man often forgets the true nature of his planet . . . The sense of all these things comes to him most clearly in the course of a long ocean voyage, when he watches day after day the receding rim of the horizon, ridged and furrowed by waves; when at night he becomes aware of the earth's rotation as the stars pass overhead; or when, alone in this world of water and sky, he feels the loneliness of his earth in space. And then, as never on land, he knows the truth that his world is a water world, a planet dominated by its covering mantle of ocean, in which the continents are but transient intrusions of land above the all-encircling sea."

—Rachel Carson from *The Sea Around Us.*

Mother Sea

by RACHEL CARSON

In her classic work, The Sea Around Us, *Rachel Carson helps us see clearly how we derive from the primal waters that covered the evolving earth. It is this link which explains man's compelling need to challenge, explore, conquer and sometimes succumb to the mystery and might of the sea. In the following introductory chapter, Rachel Carson proves why sailing, in every sense of the word, is an* elemental *experience.*

And the earth was without form, and void;
and darkness was upon the face of the deep,
—GENESIS

BEGINNINGS are apt to be shadowy, and so it is with the beginnings of that great mother of life, the sea. Many people have debated how and when the earth got its ocean, and it is not surprising that their explanations do not always agree. For the plain and inescapable truth is that no one was there to see, and in the absence of eyewitness accounts there is bound to be a certain amount of disagreement. So if I tell here the story of how the young planet Earth acquired an ocean, it must be a story pieced together from many sources and containing whole chapters the details of which we can only imagine. The story is founded on the testimony of the earth's most ancient rocks, which were young when the earth was young; on other evidence written on the face of the earth's satellite, the moon; and on hints contained in the history of the sun and the whole universe of star-filled space. For although no man was there to witness this cosmic birth, the stars and the moon and the rocks were there, and, indeed, had much to do with the fact that there is an ocean.

The events of which I write must have occurred somewhat more than 2 billion years ago. As nearly as science can tell, that is the approximate age of the earth, and the ocean must be very nearly as old. It is possible now to discover the age of the rocks that compose the crust of the earth by measuring the rate of decay of the radioactive materials they contain. The oldest rocks found anywhere on earth—in Manitoba—are about 2.3 billion years old. Allowing 100 million years or so for the cooling of the earth's materials to form a rocky crust, we arrive at the supposition that the tempestuous and violent events connected with our planet's birth occurred nearly 2.5 billion years ago. But this is only a minimum estimate, for rocks indicating an even greater age may be found at any time.

The new earth, freshly torn from its parent sun, was a ball of whirling gases, intensely hot, rushing through the black spaces of the universe on a path and at a speed controlled by immense forces. Gradually the ball of flaming gases cooled. The gases began to liquefy, and Earth became a molten mass. The materials of this mass eventually became sorted out in a definite pattern: the heaviest in the center, the less heavy surrounding them, and the least heavy forming the outer rim. This is the pattern which persists today—a central sphere of molten iron, very nearly as hot as it was 2 billion years ago, an intermediate sphere of semiplastic basalt, and a hard outer shell, relatively quite thin and composed of solid basalt and granite.

The outer shell of the young earth must have been a good many millions of years changing from the liquid to the solid state, and it is believed that, before this change was completed, an event of the greatest importance took place—the formation of the moon. The next time you stand on a beach at night, watching the moon's bright path across the water, and conscious of the moon-drawn tides, remember that the moon itself may have been born of a great tidal wave of earthly substance, torn off into space. And remember that if the moon was formed in this fashion, the event may have had much to do with shaping the ocean basins and the continents as we know them.

There were tides in the new earth long before there was an ocean. In response to the pull of the sun, the molten liquids of the earth's whole surface rose in tides that rolled unhindered around the globe and only gradually slackened and diminished as the earthly shell cooled, congealed and hardened. Those who believe that the moon is a child of Earth say that during an early stage of the earth's development something happened that caused this rolling, viscid tide to gather speed and momentum and to rise to unimaginable heights. Apparently the force that created these greatest tides the earth has ever known was the force of resonance, for at this time the period of the solar tides had come to approach, then equal, the period of the free oscillation of the liquid earth. And so every sun tide was given increased momentum by the push of the earth's oscillation, and each of the twice-daily tides was larger than the one before it. Physicists have calculated that, after five hundred years of

such monstrous, steadily increasing tides, those on the side toward the sun became too high for stability, and a great wave was torn away and hurled into space. But immediately, of course, the newly created satellite became subject to physical laws that sent it spinning in an orbit of its own about the earth. This is what we call the moon.

There are reasons for believing that this event took place after the earth's crust had become slightly hardened, instead of during its partly liquid state. There is to this day a great scar on the surface of the globe. This scar or depression holds the Pacific Ocean. According to some geophysicists, the floor of the Pacific is composed of basalt, the substance of the earth's middle layer, while all other oceans are floored with a thin layer of granite, which makes up most of the earth's outer layer. We immediately wonder what became of the Pacific's granite covering, and the most convenient assumption is that it was torn away when the moon was formed. There is supporting evidence. The mean density of the moon is much less than that of the earth (3.3 compared with 5.5), suggesting that the moon took away none of the earth's heavy iron core, but that it is composed only of the granite and some of the basalt of the outer layers.

The birth of the moon probably helped shape other regions of the world ocean besides the Pacific. When part of the crust was torn away, strains must have been set up in the remaining granite envelope. Perhaps the granite mass cracked open on the side opposite the moon scar. Perhaps, as the earth spun on its axis and rushed on its orbit through space, the cracks widened and the masses of granite began to drift apart, moving over a tarry, slowly hardening layer of basalt. Gradually the outer portions of the basalt layer became solid and the wandering continents came to rest, frozen into place with oceans between them. In spite of theories to the contrary, the weight of geologic evidence seems to be that the locations of the major ocean basins and the major continental land masses are today much the same as they have been since a very early period of the earth's history.

But this is to anticipate the story, for when

the moon was born there was no ocean. The gradually cooling earth was enveloped in heavy layers of cloud, which contained much of the water of the new planet. For a long time, its surface was so hot that no moisture could fall without immediately being reconverted to steam. This dense, perpetually renewed cloud covering must have been thick enough that no rays of sunlight could penetrate it. And so the rough outlines of the continents and the empty ocean basins were sculptured out of the surface of the earth in darkness, in a Stygian world of heated rock and swirling clouds and gloom.

As soon as the earth's crust cooled enough, the rains began to fall. Never have there been such rains since that time. They fell continuously, day and night, days passing into months, into years, into centuries. They poured into the waiting ocean basins, or, falling upon the continental masses, drained away to become sea.

That primeval ocean, growing in bulk as the rains slowly filled its basins, must have been only faintly salt. But the falling rains were the symbol of the dissolution of the continents. From the moment the rains began to fall, the lands began to be worn away and carried to the sea. It is an endless, inexorable process that has never stopped—the dissolving of the rocks, the leaching out of their contained minerals, the carrying of the rock fragments and dissolved minerals to the ocean. And over the eons of time, the sea has grown ever more bitter with the salt of the continents.

In what manner the sea produced the mysterious and wonderful stuff called protoplasm we cannot say. In its warm, dimly lit waters, the unknown conditions of temperature and pressure and saltiness must have been the critical ones for the creation of life from nonlife. At any rate, they produced the result that neither the alchemists with their crucibles nor modern scientists in their laboratories have been able to achieve.

Before the first living cell was created, there may have been many trials and failures. It seems probable that, within the warm saltiness of the primeval sea, certain organic substances were fashioned from carbon dioxide, sulphur, nitrogen, phosphorus, potassium and calcium. Per-

haps these were transition steps from which the complex molecules of protoplasm arose—molecules that somehow acquired the ability to reproduce themselves and begin the endless stream of life. But at present no one is wise enough to be sure.

Those first living things may have been simple microorganisms rather like some of the bacteria we know today—mysterious borderline forms that were not quite plants, not quite animals, barely over the intangible line that separates the nonliving from the living. It is doubtful that this first life possessed the substance chlorophyll, with which plants in sunlight transform lifeless chemicals into the living stuff of their tissues. Little sunshine could enter their dim world, penetrating the cloud banks from which fell the endless rains. Probably the sea's first children lived on the organic substances then present in the ocean waters, or, like the iron and sulphur bacteria that exist today, lived directly on inorganic food.

All the while the cloud cover was thinning, the darkness of the nights alternated with palely illumined days, and finally the sun for the first time shone through upon the sea. By this time, some of the living things that floated in the sea must have developed the magic of chlorophyll. Now they were able to take the carbon dioxide of the air and the water of the sea and of these elements, in sunlight, build the organic substances they needed. So the first true plants came into being.

Another group of organisms, lacking the chlorophyll but needing organic food, found they could make a way of life for themselves by devouring the plants. So the first animals arose, and from that day to this, every animal in the world has followed the habit it learned in the ancient seas and depends, directly or through complex food chains, on the plants for food and life.

As the years passed, and the centuries, and the millions of years, the stream of life grew more and more complex. From simple, one-celled creatures, others that were aggregations of specialized cells arose, and then creatures with organs for feeding, digesting, breathing, reproducing. Sponges grew on the rocky bottom of the sea's edge and coral animals built their habitations in warm, clear waters. Jellyfish swam and drifted in the sea. Worms evolved, and starfish, and hard-shelled creatures with many-jointed legs, the arthropods. The plants, too, progressed, from the microscopic algae to branched and curiously fruiting seaweeds that swayed with the tides and were plucked from the coastal rocks by the surf and cast adrift.

During all this time, the continents had no life. There was little to induce living things to come ashore, forsaking their all-providing, all-embracing mother sea. The lands must have been bleak and hostile beyond the power of words to describe. Imagine a whole continent of naked rock, across which no covering mantle of green had been drawn—a continent without soil, for there were no land plants to aid in its formation and bind it to the rocks with their roots. Imagine a land of stone, a silent land, except for the sound of the rains and winds that swept across it. For there was no living voice, and no living thing moved over the surface of the rocks.

Meanwhile, the gradual cooling of the planet, which had first given the earth its hard granite crust, was progressing into its deeper layers; and as the interior slowly cooled and contracted, it drew away from the outer shell. This shell, accommodating itself to the shrinking sphere within it, fell into folds and wrinkles—the earth's first mountain ranges.

Geologists tell us that there must have been at least two periods of mountain building (often called "revolutions") in that dim period, so long ago that the rocks have no record of it, so long ago that the mountains themselves have long since been worn away. Then there came a third great period of upheaval and readjustment of the earth's crust, about a billion years ago, but of all its majestic mountains the only reminders today are the Laurentian hills of eastern Canada and a great shield of granite over the flat country around Hudson Bay.

The epochs of mountain building only served to speed up the processes of erosion by which the continents were worn down and their crumbling rock and contained minerals returned to the sea. The uplifted masses of the mountains were prey to the bitter cold of the upper atmosphere, and under the attacks of frost and snow and ice the rocks cracked and crumbled away. The rains beat with greater violence upon the slopes of the hills and carried away the substance of the mountains in torrential streams. There was still no plant covering to modify and resist the power of the rains.

And in the sea, life continued to evolve. The earliest forms have left no fossils by which we can identify them. Probably they were soft-bodied, with no hard parts that could be preserved. Then, too, the rock layers formed in those early days have since been so altered by enormous heat and pressure, under the foldings of the earth's crust, that any fossils they might have contained would have been destroyed.

For the past 500 million years, however, the rocks have preserved the fossil record. By the dawn of the Cambrian period, when the history of living things was first inscribed on rock pages, life in the sea had progressed so far that all the main groups of backboneless or invertebrate animals had been developed. But there were no animals with backbones, no insects or spiders, and still no plant or animal had been evolved that was capable of venturing onto the forbidding land. So for more than three-fourths of geologic time the continents were desolate and uninhabited, while the sea prepared the life that was later to invade them and make them habitable. Meanwhile, with violent tremblings of the earth and with the fire and smoke of roaring volcanoes, mountains rose and wore away, glaciers moved to and fro over the earth, and the sea crept over the continents and again receded.

It was not until Silurian time, some 350 million years ago, that the first pioneer of land life crept out on the shore. It was an arthropod, one of the great tribe that later produced crabs and lobsters and insects. It must have been something like a modern scorpion, but, unlike some of its descendants, it never wholly severed the ties that united it to the sea. It lived a strange life, half-terrestrial, half-aquatic, something like that of the ghost crabs that speed along the beaches today, now and then dashing into the surf to moisten their gills.

Fish, tapered of body and stream-molded by the press of running waters, were evolving in Silurian rivers. In times of drought, in the drying pools and lagoons, the shortage of oxygen forced them to develop swim bladders for the storage of air. One form that possessed an air-breathing lung was able to survive the dry periods by burying itself in mud, leaving a passage to the surface through which it breathed.

It is very doubtful that the animals alone would have succeeded in colonizing the land, for only the plants had the power to bring about the first amelioration of its harsh conditions. They helped make soil of the crumbling rocks, they held back the soil from the rains that would have swept it away, and little by little they softened and subdued the bare rock, the lifeless desert. We know very little about the first land plants, but they must have been closely related to some of the larger seaweeds that had learned to live in the coastal shallows, developing strengthened stems and grasping, rootlike holdfasts to resist the drag and pull of the waves. Perhaps it was in some coastal lowlands, periodically drained and flooded, that some such plants found it possible to survive, though separated from the sea. This also seems to have taken place in the Silurian period.

The mountains that had been thrown up by the Laurentian revolution gradually wore away, and as the sediments were washed from their summits and deposited on the lowlands, great areas of the continents sank under the load. The seas crept out of their basins and spread over the lands. Life fared well and was exceedingly abundant in those shallow, sunlit seas. But with the later retreat of the ocean water into the deeper basins, many creatures must have been left stranded in shallow, landlocked bays. Some of these animals found means to survive on land. The lakes, the shores of the rivers, and the coastal swamps of those days were the testing grounds in which plants and animals either became adapted to the new conditions or perished.

As the lands rose and the seas receded, a strange fishlike creature emerged on the land, and over the thousands of years its fins became legs, and instead of gills it developed lungs. In the Devonian sandstone, this first amphibian left its footprint.

On land and sea the stream of life poured on. New forms evolved; some old ones declined and disappeared. On land the mosses and the ferns and the seed plants developed. The reptiles for a time dominated the earth, gigantic, grotesque and terrifying. Birds learned to live and move in the ocean of air. The first small mammals lurked inconspicuously in hidden crannies of the earth as though in fear of the reptiles.

When they went ashore, the animals that took up a land life carried with them a part of the sea in their bodies, a heritage which they passed on to their children and which even today links each land animal with its origin in the ancient sea. Fish, amphibian and reptile, warm-blooded bird and mammal—each of us carries in our veins a salty stream in which the elements sodium, potassium and calcium are combined in almost the same proportions as in seawater. This is our inheritance from the day, untold millions of years ago, when a remote ancestor, having progressed from the one-celled to the many-celled stage, first developed a circulatory system in which the fluid was merely the water of the sea. In the same way, our lime-hardened skeletons are a heritage from the calcium-rich ocean of Cambrian time. Even the protoplasm that streams within each cell of our bodies has the chemical structure impressed upon all living matter when the first simple creatures were brought forth in the ancient sea. And as life itself began in the sea, so each of us begins his individual life in a miniature ocean within his mother's womb, and in the stages of his embryonic development repeats the steps by which his race evolved, from gill-breathing inhabitants of a water world to creatures able to live on land.

Some of the land animals later returned to the ocean. After perhaps 50 million years of land life, a number of reptiles entered the sea about 170 million years ago, in the Triassic period. They were huge and formidable creatures. Some had oarlike limbs by which they rowed through the water; some were web-footed, with long, serpentine necks. These grotesque monsters disappeared millions of years ago, but we remember them when we come upon a large sea turtle swimming many miles at sea, its barnacle-encrusted shell eloquent of its marine life. Much later, perhaps no more than 50 million years ago, some of the mammals, too, abandoned a land life for the ocean. Their descendants are the sea lions, seals, sea elephants and whales of today.

Among the land mammals, there was a race of creatures that took to an arboreal existence. Their hands underwent remarkable development, becoming skilled in manipulating and examining objects, and along with this skill came a superior brain power that compensated for what these comparatively small mammals lacked in strength. At last, perhaps somewhere in the vast interior of Asia, they descended from the trees and became again terrestrial. The past million years have seen their transformation into beings with the body and brain and spirit of man.

Eventually man, too, found his way back to the sea. Standing on its shores, he must have looked out upon it with wonder and curiosity, compounded with an unconscious recognition of his lineage. He could not physically reenter the ocean as the seals and whales had done. But over the centuries, with all the skill and ingenuity and reasoning powers of his mind, he has sought to explore and investigate even its most remote parts, so that he might reenter it mentally and imaginatively.

He built boats to venture out on its surface. Later he found ways to descend to the shallow parts of its floor, carrying with him the air that, as a land mammal long unaccustomed to aquatic life, he needed to breathe. Moving in fascination over the deep sea he could not enter, he found ways to probe its depths, he let down nets to capture its life, he invented mechanical eyes and ears that could recreate for his senses a world long lost, but a world that, in the deepest part of his subconscious mind, he had never wholly forgotten.

And yet he has returned to his mother sea only on her own terms. He cannot control or change the ocean as, in his brief tenancy of earth, he has subdued and plundered the continents. In the artificial world of his cities and towns, he often forgets the true nature of his planet and the long vistas of its history, in which the existence of the race of men has occupied a mere moment of time. The sense of all these things comes to him most clearly in the course of a long ocean voyage, when he watches day after day the receding rim of the horizon, ridged and furrowed by waves; when at night he becomes aware of the earth's rotation as the stars pass overhead; or when, alone in this world of water and sky, he feels the loneliness of his earth in space. And then, as never on land, he knows the truth that his world is a water world, a planet dominated by its covering mantle of ocean, in which the continents are but transient intrusions of land above the surface of the all-encircling sea.

The Story of the Ship

by ALAN VILLIERS

Alan Villiers first went to sea in square-rigged ships at the age of fifteen. Although he later sailed on everything from Arab dhows to a nuclear merchantman, his heart always remained with the majestic sailing ships. Here he relates, from Oceans of the World, *the development of the square riggers and concludes with a stirring soliloquy that serves as an enduring epitaph to the ships he loved.*

THERE was a tremendous difference between Commodore Byron's frigate *Dolphin* and Captain Cook's ex-collier *Endeavour,* but both were excellent ships. The *Dolphin* was a fighting ship, her bulwarks and upper sides pierced with gunports through which, when opened, cannon thrust their noisy snouts to belch iron balls as necessary. She could carry her fighting needs and the requirements of her large crew, and that was all. Her lean hull, with its fine underwater lines, could not take the ground, as seamen say. That is, she had to be afloat, properly supported in the sea, or she would fall over.

Any ship provided for him, said Cook, "must be of a construction that will bear to take the ground"—i.e., stand upon the shallow sea bed, not fall over and wreck itself on it—"and of a size which, in case of necessity, may be safely and conveniently laid on shore to repair any accidental damage. These properties are not to be found in ships of war of forty guns, or frigates, nor in East India Company's ships, nor in large three-decked West India ships, nor, indeed, in any other but North country ships such as are built for the coal trade."

How right he was proved to be when the *Endeavour,* sailing for the first time inside the long labyrinth of the Great Barrier Reef off the northeast coast of Australia, struck on a reef and had to be grounded for repairs. Cook made her sound again, hove her off the beach and sailed back to England. As a coal carrier trading on the east coast of England, the *Endeavour* had to be able to sit on the mud flats while her coal was unloaded. An awkward, almost clumsy little thing to look at—she was less than four hundred tons—she was a slow sailer but immensely safe, for her tubby hull shook off the assaults of the sea like a barrel and her decks were safe to work on even in the wildest storm. But they were horribly exposed. She must have been a very uncomfortable ship in far southern latitudes. She had a straight, unprotected upper deck, and even what passed as her quarterdeck had no shelter at all. Her helmsman and her watchkeepers stood in the open and took what came. She was a ship for the toughest of the tough seafarers of those days, from her captain downwards.

At that time, all these seagoing wooden ships were rigged in much the same way—English, Dutch, French, Spaniards, Baltic, Portuguese. Hull forms might differ greatly, but much the same sail plan drove the lot. There were huge cargo carriers such as the carracks of Portugal and the East Indiamen, big sea wagons whose principal function was to sail to India somehow, gorge themselves with cargo there and then somehow sail back again. If they took a year for one voyage it didn't matter, so long as they got home at all. They had to be able to fight when need be. Most of them looked more like fighting ships than the passenger-cargo liners which they were. Their bulwarks and 'tween decks were pierced for guns and they carried big crews to fight: there is a record of one group of sixteen of them which, pretending to be ships of the line, opened up on a French fleet and scared them off.

These East Indiamen were the Cunarders of their day except in the matter of speed (which didn't count): the West Indiamen were smaller, Atlantic copies of them. There were also tramps, ships not built for any special trade but able to bring timber and hemp and turpentine from the Baltic, wine in tuns from France and Spain, coals from Newcastle, wool to Flanders, dried and salt fish from Newfoundland, timber and tobacco from Virginia.

There were a surprising lot of these ships. Ships and trade made more trade and slowly improved living conditions for everyone.

Most of these ships were three-masters of the old school—full-rigged ships—built of wood as solidly as possible, with one mast well forward, another in the center of the ship (more or less) and a third mast somewhere aft. The two more important masts—always the fore and main—were made of three separate spars. The lower spar was always a very solid piece of tree, stepped—that is, standing firmly—on the keelson, on the inside of the bottom of the ship. It rose through the deck high enough to carry a yard from which a large square sail was set. Above this lower mast was another, secured by a

rather cumbersome arrangement. This was called the topmast. As the centuries rolled by, a third and lighter piece of mast was fitted to the top of the topmast. This was the topgallant.

On each of these masts a square sail was set from a yard smaller than that on the lower mast. All these yards hoisted and lowered for the convenience of setting and taking in sail. The yards were swung by ropes and tackles called braces, to trim the sails for shifts of wind or alterations of course. The bowsprit still carried a spritsail, but now it spread triangular sails called jibs as well. These were set as they are aboard yachts today, by hauling the pointed head up towards a convenient place on the foremast.

Other such triangular sails took up the space between the masts, and behind the mizzen—always a much shorter mast than the main—was an improved lateen. This sail set entirely behind the mast, where it could be swung across easily. It was a very useful sail to maneuver the ship and to help the steering.

A great tracery of rope rigging of all shapes and sizes had long been evolved to support and control the masts and sails. This appeared most complicated to the landsmen of those times, and still does today. Essentially, it was simple. Every rope was there for a definite purpose. It was placed one way, led one way, had its own name and its own spot on deck. A sailor could step from one ship to another and be perfectly at home within ten minutes. He "knew the ropes" on the blackest night as well as the fairest day: he could "hand, reef and steer," which means that he could make all the necessary knots and splices in cordage; handle sail in the wildest gale on the highest yard and, with his shipmates, keep on fighting the sail until it was secured; and he could stand his "trick" at the wheel.

Both officers and seamen were extremely conservative. Their calling made them so. Any experiment with ships was also with their lives. Having evolved an efficient ship which could survive at sea and make useful voyages, they were against change—*all* change, even for the better. They liked square sails because yards were more manageable than lateens. As ships increased in size, square sails increased with them, far beyond the point of practicability for any other sort of sail. When they became too large, square or oblong sails could be divided into two by halving the sail and setting the two halves on separate yards. The lateen could never be subdivided like that.

As ships grew, masts were built up higher. Sails were set higher and higher—royals, skysails, moonrakers. Square sails could be extended in area in good sailing winds (like the Trades) by adding extension pieces to them, called studding sails. The size of the lateen could be increased only by lowering the yard and lashing an extra piece to the end of it, then changing to a larger sail. This was very awkward, caused a great deal of work and loss of way while it was being done and, moreover, there was a definite limit to the size of the sail that could be carried. So the rule was square sails for ocean voyaging, right from medieval days until the end of the deep-sea sailing era. A sailing-ship sailor from a Cape Horner of the early 1950s (when only two such ships were still sailing) could step back aboard the old *Mayflower* and, within an hour, workout the complications of her Elizabethan rig, "hand, reef and steer" aboard her just as in his modern ship. (Some did: or I could never have sailed that replica.) As for frigates, ships of the line, East Indiamen and West Indiamen, any square-rigger man could take the lot in his stride.

True, he might find conditions aboard somewhat irksome were he really called upon to step back through the centuries. Matters like food and accommodation and the general treatment of seamen could be very annoying indeed, for the deep-sea sailor was considered expendable right until the twentieth century. His food was appalling and his quarters what he might make of some below-decks hutch in an insanitary, wet and ill-ventilated (or else too well-ventilated) part of the stinking ship. He might be flogged, ducked from the yardarm or keelhauled, if he had bad officers. He could die of scurvy at sea, or fever ashore, and no one bother about him. His wages were a pittance. Worst of all, he could be press-ganged—seized and forcibly enlisted—into the navy in time of wars, real or impending, and as far as he was concerned the navy

was even worse than the merchant service. At least in East Indiamen, if he survived a voyage, he could draw his pay and leave on return to his home port. In the navy he was lucky if he had either pay or leave while war lasted.

In the old days, the seaman was far more subject to shipwreck and drowning. Overloaded East Indiamen foundered, got on rocks or lee shores and broke to pieces, were sometimes seized by enemies or pirates. After every severe storm, the east coast of England was littered with the wrecks of poor little North Sea traders driven up there, and the flaxen-haired bodies washed up on the beaches for weeks.

The way of the sea was hard.

It was almost as hard, as first iron, then steel, took the place of wood in ship construction both for hulls and then masts and yards, for the size of big sailing ships doubled and trebled while crews were cut down. As the ships were stronger, they stayed longer at sea and made more difficult voyages, habitually fighting a way to the westwards past Cape Horn on Chilean and Peruvian voyages and passages between Europe and the west coast of North America. Where the wooden ships had been slow and high and (unless they sank or hit the land) reasonably safe to work aboard, these steel ships were long and low and raced through the seas like half-tide rocks, spilling men overboard, throwing them from their bowsprits, which dug too often right into the sea. They were laden heavily down, and they fought their way at sea from voyage beginning to voyage end: as a result, they were wet and uncomfortable, and could be dangerous.

In the old days, the easygoing East Indiamen reduced sail at night and took no risks (except of getting ashore, perhaps). If the principal reason for this was to allow the old captain (and his important passengers) a good night's sleep, the seamen benefited also, for there were plenty of them to cope with the extra work of reducing sail at night and setting it again next morning.

This sloppy way of sailing came to an end before the days of iron ships. Easygoing voyaging was based on monopoly. In England, for example, there was only the one East India Company: so long as its cargoes reached the market at all, they were immensely profitable. The company controlled that trade more or less as it liked. There were fortunes for all. A captain could retire with a fortune after three voyages, if he looked after things properly. Owners did even better. The riches of the East still came by what amounted to parcel trade. They were for the rich who could afford high prices. The change from a high-priced parcel trade and a rigidly controlled, profiteering monopoly to cheap bulk and free trade was a shock which owners, masters and seamen alike put off as long as possible. Seafaring nations fought wars to maintain things as they were.

All this was knocked on the head forever by the clipper ship from the new United States of America, which not only cut in on established trades and upset monopolies but began positively to hustle ships as they had never been hurried before. The Americans drove their lean, lithe and heavily sparred tall ships *day and night* from voyage beginning to voyage end.

This was new: it had to be met. What the Americans could do the Scots and English could do likewise, if not better. This was the era of the wonderful clipper races when, instead of shortening down their slow-moving charges, gorging themselves with their rich passengers on a splendid nine-course dinner and varied wines before turning in for a good night's sleep, masters lean and lithe and tall like their ships catnapped in deck chairs on their reeling poops while they drove their magnificent ships to get every last knot out of them, to make them shift nonstop over the colossal distance between the tea ports of China and the auction marts of London faster than man had ever moved anything across the seas before.

Drive and race, and let the gale howl in the strong rigging! Drive and keep on driving! Short-cut through the islands of the China and the Java Seas, dodge among the reefs (maybe hit one sometimes: that was too bad), cut down the miles, step up the speed, and the devil take the hindmost.

The London market loved this. A big bonus awaited the first master to land new season's

Majestic in their full panoply of sail, great square-rigged cargo ships like this once dominated the oceans and engaged in thrilling races for profit and glory.

teas. This was the wonderful era when ships like the *Ariel* and the *Taeping,* sailing from their China port together, raced sixteen thousand miles, never seeing one another again until both came storming up the English Channel at the end, like the magnificent ocean yachts they were. On they raced, streaking past the steamships as they raced neck and neck, pyramids of white sails leaning gracefully upon the sea as the glorious hulls, spray covered, spume to the mastheads, tore up-channel in the grandest sailing spectacle ever seen by man. The steamships men turned to cheer them as they were overhauled. Crowds gathered on the Channel cliffs and beaches to admire the sight as these glorious, impeccable thoroughbreds came racing by.

For all felt that these were the quintessence of sailing-ship evolution. These were wonderful and heart-stirring ships, produced by man. These were the ultimate development, at least of fast sailing-ships in the China trade.

There were other clippers—plenty of them. They raced out to California in the gold rush and again to Australia when gold was discovered there, powerful big two-thousand tonners like the wonderful *James Baines, Lightning, Champion of the Seas*—ships which claimed runs of four hundred miles and more a day, and cut the sailing time to Australia from five to six months to two.

But it was all in vain.

While the graceful *Taeping* and *Ariel* stormed westwards past Good Hope, ten thousand lean, dark hands were tearing at the Egyptian sand five thousand miles away, digging a canal through the narrow neck of land joining Africa to Asia— this time a canal for oceangoing ships, which would not silt up and be forgotten. The year was 1866. Three years afterwards, the modern Suez Canal was opened. This was doom to the clipper ships. No matter how beautifully they were designed or how strongly rigged and bravely sailed, they could not hope to stand up to competition through this short cut they could not use.

It was no use to them. Going through the canal would not benefit them. For the way of sail on the oceans could never be through that ditch. It was strictly for steamships.

There were deep-sea, cargo-carrying sailing ships for ninety years after that: but they were big steel cargo carriers, bulk movers of coal, grain, lumber, nitrates, guano. For another fifty years after Suez, they fought the steamships: for thirty years there were owners to back them who thought they still might win. As late as the first decade of the twentieth century, big, engineless sailing ships were still being built in Scotland and in Germany. German, French, British, American, and Scandinavian sailers did their best to carry on in world trades.

The Americans concentrated for years on the fore-and-aft rig, developing large schooners for their own coastwise and the transpacific trades. Three-, four- and five-masters became six-masters—even one seven. The schooners were economical and useful vessels. There were trades such as soft coal from Virginia ports which they suited, and in these they managed to make a living for many years after steamships should have ousted them. In the end, the big schooners were put out of business by towed barges and road transport.

These schooners could be sailed with a working crew of one man a mast plus a large steam donkey engine to lighten the heavy jobs of hoisting their sails, getting the anchor up and so on. In the Pacific, the trade winds suited them almost ideally for the run to Australia. But when it came to real world-circling sailing, they were greatly inferior to square rig despite the fact that, size for size, square-riggers required three times the crew.

The one seven-masted schooner built was so big and clumsy she could scarcely get out of her own way. She made few voyages and drove up on the coast of the Scilly Islands the first time she tried to cross the North Atlantic.

Square-rigged ships were very useful bulk carriers in certain trades, particularly coal from Newcastle, NSW, across the South Pacific with the strong westerly winds of the Roaring Forties (the sailors' name for those areas where the wind was frequently roaring) and then back again with nitrates from Chile or guano from Peru, before the southeast trade winds. Many big ships sailed from Australia to Chilean ports in better than tramp-steamer times.

But that was in vain too. The trade left them, principally because of the unfortunate perversity of the miners in New South Wales, who went on strike so often that even their best customers had to look for their coal elsewhere. Then some scientist discovered how to extract nitrate from the air.

The last of the big sailing ships survived in two last trades—between Germany and the west coast of South America, and from South Australian outports to northwest Europe with grain. Some of these German ships were as outstanding in their way as the best of the clippers ever were. The Germans were the most powerful, the strongest and the most consistently well-sailed big sailing ships there ever were. The Hamburg five-masted, full-rigged ship *Preussen* of 1902—the only such ship built—averaged better than 7 knots throughout her entire seagoing life and could do 17½ in a gale. Unlike the clippers with their parcel cargoes, she carried eight thousand tons. Unlike them too, she had a comparatively small crew—forty-two all told. Many a thousand-ton clipper had that many able seamen.

The *Preussen* was so fast that in the end her own speed killed her. A cross-Channel steamer, unable to believe that she was doing better than twelve knots, tried to cut across her bows one day off Dover in 1910. Too late she realized her error: she smashed into the *Preussen* and knocked her headgear and her foremast down. Handicapped in this way, the five-master drove ashore: a gale came up and finished her.

What was it really like to sail in such ships? There was a great exhilaration, a superb sense of satisfaction and achievement in handling one of these engineless Cape Horn ships on a voyage, say, from South Australia nonstop to the United Kingdom. I have been in a big sailing ship which did it in eighty-three days—sixteen thousand miles at an average speed of eight knots carrying fifty-six hundred tons of bagged wheat, with a crew of four men and twenty boys. I have done it in my own small, full-rigged ship from Tahiti, as part of a voyage round the world.

Day after day the ship, alone in the wild immensity of the endless sea, rushes on before the gale. The wind screams, the sea rises. Will it continue to rise and overwhelm the ship? For all such ships are vulnerable if imperfectly sailed. I can name twenty stout steel four-masters and ships missing down there. I know the beautiful clipper *Ariel* sailed under in the end. I know there is ice: I know that despite a good chronometer checked by radio time signals, a rotating modern log, a perfect sextant and the best of government-sponsored nautical tables, navigation can still go wrong.

I know my limitations. I walk the reeling poop, I cling beneath the weather cloth lashed in mizzen or jigger rigging, as stinging hail lashes out of the night. Before the bow rushes a roll of foam so wide and white that it throws up light—the only light we have, for the ship sails blacked out save for the binnacle's fitful and uncertain gleam. At the wheel, two lads strain to keep the ship running truly upon her course—within a compass point each side, at best—while the seas rage, lifting high astern as if intent upon one thing only, to fall upon and utterly destroy my running ship, to sweep her end for end, flood her from bulwark to bulwark, drive her down in her headlong way.

Shall I heave to, stop? Will this great wind rise to such strength that I cannot sail before it, or, shifting quickly, so twist the sea that instead of running in long parallel crests it will become a snarling, tossed-up maelstrom in which no running ship can live? Heave to! Heave to! the coward in me shouts: heave to while you have the chance!

For the hove-to ship will lie in safety, shoulder to the sea like an albatross asleep, yielding, no longer fighting for her head and speed, no longer in danger of being overwhelmed. There is sea room. I can drift for days, and the drift will be in the right direction.

The masts roll, toss, lurch like forest giants in the torment of a hurricane. Somewhere high aloft, I can hear the cries of the boy crew as they fight to save the remnants of a blown-out sail and, even against the agonizing tumult of the screaming wind, I can hear the frightful thunderous cannonade of blown-out canvas, hear the murderous and demoniacal shriek of torn, strong wire lashing in the wind.

The ship runs on, flinging her masts now as if she seeks deliberately to toss them out of her and, with them, to hurl those boys into the sea. It is horrible how much more loudly the wind screams and the sea rises, when one has command.

Heave to!

Yet I know the wind *should* ease. I have already hove to three times in the weeks of that wild run. To heave to I lose time, prolong the danger, give in, if only for the moment—or all night. At the wind's slightest easing, I will pay off again and let the ship drive before the wind. She is well snugged down. She still steers and handles well. No fatal weight of water yet breaks over her. . . .

Whatever decision is made is mine and mine alone. All lives aboard are in my hands.

I have three ribs broken by being flung across the poop earlier that day. I have cat-napped twenty minutes in the past three gale-filled days.

But the ribs are lashed up tightly. Down there, sleep is for the dead.

I look to windward—no hope there! No sign of any easing! The storm howls, screams, roars, bellows with ear-jambing might as if it never could make any other sound and all silence has departed from the world for ever. I look aloft. The boys are winning—no serious damage. A blown-out sail can be replaced in the morning. I look along the deck. The long bowsprit rearing high above some great comber of a sea that passes beneath the vessel with a hiss and snarl and lash of gale-blown spume points the way ahead, a single storm jib out there straining like a black iron triangle.

A sudden break—I see a star! A star to windward: heave to be damned! Drive on, drive on! Let her go!

We shall have five-thousand more miles of this, and worse, perhaps, but to all of us it is the most satisfying, challenging, most adventurous and reddest-blooded calling in all the world. We envy no land-lubbers with their soft dry beds. We envy no one.

Not a man or boy aboard would change that calling then for a million dollars. One feels that one can keep the ship's head up, fighting, only with one's mind and alert eyes.

Let her go! I'm glad I'm here!

The Sea

by JAN DE HARTOG

After a lifetime of crossing the oceans in every kind of boat, Jan de Hartog attempted to translate his understanding in the form of a diary he kept for a young boy who wanted to be a sailor. In the following section de Hartog defines the "personality" of the oceans and seas.

Sunrise

HOWEVER bewildered, homesick or seasick the young sailor may be, he will forget himself for a few moments when he watches his first sunrise at sea.

There is something about a ship emerging from the night that cannot be equaled by any dawn ashore. Night at sea is closer to the origin of the earth than it is on land. There are few dangers that can be called real; the coast and its rocks are far away; other ships are well lit and easily spotted; the night itself hides no burglars, ghosts or cats on the prowl to tinge the darkness with terror. There is nothing but the darkness, in which an occasional wave swishes past, or a burst of spray shimmers green on starboard, red on the port side.

Dawn at sea breaks high in the sky: a faint flush on the highest peaks of the clouds. Then the miracle starts that never fails to make man humble: the momentous occurrence of the earth's creation. One moment, darkness is upon the face of the deep and the spirit of God moves upon the waters; the next moment, there is light. The young sailor will see the light and feel, more than he understands, why God called the light Day and the darkness Night, and rested.

Dawn at sea is short. Within a matter of minutes, after the first cloud's peak's being touched by the light, the newborn day starts to foretell the weather, or to reveal the lookout asleep; within a quarter of an hour, Paradise has been created and lost, man has fallen and the gates of Paradise have closed behind him until tomorrow's dawn.

If the young sailor can keep alive within himself that moment's awe for the miracle of Creation, he will fall asleep after his first watch with the certainty that he'll be all right.

North Sea

When I was young, the North Sea was the biggest sea I knew, and terrifying in its might. To the youngsters of the east coast of England, the North Sea is a friend; to the ones on its opposite shores, it is wrought with menace, a never-relenting enemy. Young English boys potter around lustily with little boats and rickety old

31

yachts in the shelter of their island; on the eastern shores of the North Sea, it is another matter.

For the prevailing winds in the North Sea are westerly, and gales are frequent and sudden. Furthermore, the eastern shores are sown with banks and shifting shoals, so, apart from courage, the young yachtsman needs a solid knowledge of navigation to go playing around in the great gray open.

The North Sea, more than any other sea I know, belongs to the fishermen, a great many of whom are Dutch. They are among the toughest and most antique of their kind. Some of them still wear their local costumes and pray to tribal gods. I sailed with them as a boy; so to me the North Sea stood for seasickness, cold, wet clothes, sore hands, homesickness and the icy wrath of Yahweh. I shall never be able to give an objective description of the North Sea for that reason. There I have known my first fears and joys; my earliest dreams of love and adventure have been circled over by mewing seagulls in a pale blue sky, and my first anticipations of eternal damnation have been shivered out in the peak of a rusty trawler as the relentless hordes of the horses of the Apocalypse came thundering by from horizon to horizon.

To the young sailor who passes through the North Sea on his way elsewhere, it will come as a surprise. The waves are steep, short and aggressive; the currents are strong and navigation becomes tricky because of the shoals of fishermen and the intense traffic, which turns the Channel into a village main street on Fair Day. The fishermen are worse in their disdain for intruders than anywhere else. If they show lights at all at night, they show the wrong ones; and as a lot of fishing is done in pairs (two drifting luggers dragging a net between them), one should take great care not to pass between the two. For trouble on the North Sea is about the worst to be got anywhere.

On summer days, the North Sea can give a wonderful somnolent feeling of security that is dangerous. Lighthouses and lightships swing their transparent scythes through the stars, garlands of colored lights festoon the distant shores, and the faint glow of towns lights up the haze afar. Yet those visions of a better world and eternal peace should be considered as highly suspect. Somewhere a gale is brewing, waiting to pounce with all the shrieks of hell, and there is little leeway to the east.

My most poignant memory of the North Sea in later years was a Christmas Eve over the Dogger Bank. I sat with the wireless operator in his cubicle on the boat deck and we listened in to the divine services of all the countries around the shores. There came a moment when they blended: prayers from Denmark, songs from Germany, bells from Holland, carols from England, sermons from Scotland and a faint icy tinkling of handbells, shaken by children in the snow outside some Norwegian village church. I have never felt nearer to God and His benevolent bewilderment than at that moment.

If the Mediterranean is the cradle of man's culture, the Atlantic the backdrop to his daring, and the Pacific his lonely road through space, the North Sea is the mirror of Christianity's young struggle and melodious hope.

Mediterranean
This is a magnificent sea. It combines everything one dreamed of as a boy: the deep blue water, the crystalline depths, the hot sun, the white clouds over distant mountains. Every shore bears the trace of antiquity: in the south, the Dark Ages loom from the forbidding hilltops, and on deserted beaches the antlike silhouettes of a man and a donkey trudge wearily along the surf. In the north, the orange and dark green of fir-grown cliffs and the skyline of snowcapped mountains give the sailor lost in this dream a feeling of being offered all the riches of the earth at once, like Jesus.

The keynote to the Mediterranean shores is ripeness. The fruit is bigger; the flowers, heavy with scent, bloom forever; enormous crickets rattle like dice and prehistoric fish rise gaping and monstrous within sight like in an aquarium. The people are ripe too; the centuries of strife are past; now they sit or loiter, amongst the cozy rubble of discarded cultures, and play games with giant iron marbles. They rarely sing, always

Ceramco New Zealand, skippered by Peter Blake, was one of the top-seeded entries in the 1981–82 Whitbread Round the World Race.

quarrel, never fight; their life is punctuated by the slow-swinging clatter of the wooden bead curtains that keep out the flies; and they exert a tremendous tidal pull towards their careless, lazy existence.

The offshore dangers, apart from the reefs and rocks, are sudden violent winds that have romantic names like *mistral, sirocco* and *tramontane*. They come literally like bolts from the blue and, in the case of the mistral, its violence is never quite realized because of the bright blue sky and the dazzling visibility. The waves are short and steep, and there are some regions marked in red on the pilot charts where crosscurrents and confused swell can sink ships without a trace. The dangers at sea are the reflection of the dangers ashore; the little islands set gemlike in the evening sky are, like the happy ripeness of life on land, offered as a temptation. To be young and a sailor in the Mediterranean is to feel like a god on Olympus. On going ashore, one feels like shedding one's cloak of immortality and turning into a swan. When Ulysses had himself tied to the mast after blocking the ears of his crew to the sirens' song, he wrote a most important addition to the Notices to Mariners, Mediterranean.

Atlantic

There is a South Atlantic and there is a North Atlantic, but only the northern one is unique. The South Atlantic is a watered-down version of the Pacific and the Indian Ocean. It is neither the sea on which every point of the compass holds a different promise, like the Indian Ocean, nor man's nearest experience to eternity, like the Pacific. It is like the big square in a provincial town, smaller than others and bigger than some. It looks and feels as if it were a substitute for something; apart from the trade winds and the doldrums, the South Atlantic is just any sea until one reaches the Roaring Forties.

The trades, so the young sailor will find, make him uneasy, they just cannot be true. For the same wind to blow at the same strength from the same direction forever is, strangely enough, the very reverse of relaxing. The doldrums, im-

portant in the days of sail, have now lost their menace, except to lifeboats.

It is only in the North Atlantic that man is forever faced by Oceanus in his might. Not one day is the same: gales of incredible violence, days of supernatural glassy calm, red skies, green skies, blue skies and the fantastic northern lights make the sailor realize he is fighting an alien element.

It is not for nothing that, of all the great explorers, Columbus is the most famous, for ever since antiquity the Atlantic has been the threshold to the edge of the world. All fantastic stories, from sea serpents to the Aldebaran and Atlantis, have come from the Atlantic, and no one who has not sailed that incredible sea knows what it means to be a sailor. All other oceans have their schedule: the Indian Ocean has a bad period and a good one; the Pacific gives ample warning of its mood; even the Mediterranean harbors few surprises to the experienced navigator. Only the Atlantic is completely and utterly unpredictable, despite all the solemn studies written about her character that try to make sense of her streaks of madness and her incomparable moments of majesty. All the adjectives used to describe the sea since the beginning of man's consciousness can be applied to the Atlantic. The only way to predict her aspect for tonight is to write all those adjectives on separate bits of paper, roll them into little balls, put them in a tin, shake them and let the cabin boy draw. It may be *azure* and it may be *fickle;* it may be *terrifying* and it may be *pewter;* the only safe ones are *deep* and *wet*.

To those reared on the North Atlantic, every sea change will be a holiday.

Pacific

Years ago I described in my first novel a sailor's impression on rounding the Horn and facing the Pacific for the first time in his life. I said that the waves were different, for behind them surged twenty-five thousand miles of loneliness, and that every crew emerging into the waste of the silent ocean had a difficult time overcoming the archaic terror of man's futility in the universe. After reading the book, several old sailors wrote to me saying that for the first time they had found the Pacific truthfully described.

Yet I had never been there. All I had done was to look at a sixpenny globe atlas and realize how big it was. I have been there since and found that I was right; there is indeed something about the Pacific that makes it different from any other ocean on our planet. The description I provided as a young man was not a flash of genius; every sailor facing a waste of water which he knows to be the Pacific falls under the spell of the sixpenny globe of his childhood.

There are things man is unable to forget. To look at a photograph of a sphinx may make it look like one of a set of iron log supports; once one sets eyes on the real thing, one is assailed by the concentrated awe of hundreds of generations of spectators. The same goes for the Taj Mahal, Napoleon's tomb and Washington's spectacles. It is the magic of the countless that does its eerie work; and the Pacific, biggest ocean of the world, is the most tinged with mankind's imagination. It is a place where vessels vanish and are perhaps still sailing between water and wind. It is a desert full of ghosts, and on its trailless plain more dreams and memories course than there are shooting stars in an August night. For beyond the silver horizon lies modern man's new paradise; the islands.

People who have actually been there rarely dream about living on a Pacific island. They are not fragments of paradise; they are outsize cradles. If modern man thinks of a return to the satin and the faint smell of powder of babyhood as bliss, the Pacific islands are indeed the answer. To lie on his back, pint sized, facing the lazy choice between his toes and the dangling rattle, is the real image of man in the South Pacific paradise. For the guitar-strumming beauties in their grass skirts are oddly sexless once one sets eyes on them, and the eternal song of the surf underneath the tropical sky has the disadvantage that it is eternal. On these conditions, bliss is the best working description of hell I can think of.

The ocean itself, however, will give the young sailor an unforgettable experience. By its sheer size, it brings home to him the tempo of life at sea. To sail for weeks upon weeks without anything in sight but the water, the sky and the snub nose of his vessel slowly rising and falling will set him musing in his diary about things he has so far ignored because of his eager expectancy of land to be sighted at dawn. He will write, "I wonder whether perhaps I am idealizing Maggie," which is the first step on the road that took the great philosophers of mankind out of sight of the footslogging army.

When at last land is sighted, and the pilot or the harbor master climbs on board, he will have the strangest experience of all: he will feel an inexpressible mixture of relief and regret.

Indian Ocean

There are two Indian Oceans: one between November and April and one between May and October. The two are so different that the Indian Ocean frequently becomes the cause of heated quarrels in fo'c'sles and messrooms, when those who know it contradict one another with the violence of conviction. In the Arabian Sea, for instance, winds are mainly southwest from June to August, reaching gale force on eight to ten days a month. From November to April, light to moderate northeasterly winds prevail. Between Suvadiva, south of the Maldive Islands, and the west coast of Sumatra, light to moderate winds between west and northwest cradle the sailor on a sea of turquoise between November and April, whereas from May to October, he is buffeted and maddened by squalls and calms from the south. This goes for the whole of the Indian Ocean in varying degrees, and the contrasts are so strong as to be hard to believe. There are months in which one might as well be sailing the North Atlantic, snarling and gray, with low ragged clouds, and there are months of such unearthly beauty that it has taken Conrad a lifetime to describe it.

The young sailor entering the Indian Ocean in the good period will realize that he has never known there were so many brilliant stars in the sky. The whole night dome, of dark blue velvet, seems to have turned into one colossal Milky Way, and the Milky Way itself is a dazzling furrow ploughed through the universe. The sea has an oily quality that is not encountered anywhere else on earth. It breathes slowly like a sleeper with a long cradling swell, and the ship's wake mirrors the Milky Way. Strange, luminous shapes glide silently underneath the glassy surface, squids rise like fiery rockets from the depths, and occasionally, in very still nights, the young sailor will feel as if touched by a magic wand and turn into Sinbad, when in the darkness a whale roars or a dolphin splashes.

The Indian Ocean in the calm season is a sea of dreams. To stand on the bridge at night and watch the world makes the sailor feel young and immortal. His future is brilliant, his past fortunate, his sweetheart the greatest stroke of luck any man ever had, and they say that women show their breasts in Bali. He will think of leading the life of a planter; he will look forward to all his boyhood books of adventure coming true; above all, he will be happy to be himself.

Then, when the land of promise is first discerned by a strange nutty smell, he will head for those waiting for him with a completely guileless mind. The magic will last until he either sails home in the gale season, or sights the white miracle of Aden. Until then, the rug he bought will be Persian, the brass idol gold, the Javanese rice picker sculptured in teak a work of art and the earrings of conscience will be jade. Seldom will a man have brought home more junk, and a better notion of the richness of life.

Ice

On the pilot charts of the oceans is found a red line, along which is printed: "Extreme limit of drifting ice." Further north, or south as the case may be, there is a second red line: "Extreme limit of Polar pack ice." Between these two lines lies a ghostly region.

No one who has not sailed these regions can quite imagine what they are like, for not only is the sea totally different from anywhere else, the sky changes also. It may run through all the colors, from rose to dark orange with a greenish hue, like the copper chimney of an old-fashioned ship's stove when it is heated.

There are many sailors who talk about the sea as if it had a personality and were subject to moods, like the early God of the Old Testament. I defy anyone sailing in the ghostly region of icebergs and floes to endow the sea with any manlike emotion. The sailor moving slowly among the icebergs, his little ship and its little noise lost in stark eternity, will, after a few days, feel creep over him the awe of the dawn of creation. For even the word *day* doesn't apply here any more. He will move either in a perpetual variation of misty dawn and hazy dusk or in an eternal night; and when aurora borealis raises its world-large frayed standard of victory, older than the sea itself, the sailor can truly say that he has seen, if not the edge of his world, at least its Bethlehem.

The Arctic regions are not interesting; for no man can call their effect on him "interesting." It is crushing, it is evaporating, it plays havoc with the ego and makes the ties of love and comradeship seem as flimsy as gossamer threads, at the mercy of the evening breeze. One impression is supreme: man has no business there, and in the great white silence a lesson is put to him which he is unable to grasp. The young sailor may come across some older officer or seaman who seems different from those around him. Calmer perhaps, less emotional about big things, and overshadowed by a faint sadness that yet is not dark. Chances are that his companion has sailed the Arctic route during the war. For to have witnessed man hunting man in the Arctic changes the survivor for life.

At college, the pupil is taught rules about icebergs and how to avoid them, but not until he has felt their cold radiation and heard his voice echoed by the first substance of the earth will he know what lies in store for him when the cry goes up from the mast: "Ice!"

Fish

The sea, to the sailor, is a surface, and he hates everything that reminds him that there is anything more to it. So fish and sailors don't get on well together. Unless he is a fisherman and takes a commercial interest in the denizens of the deep, he acknowledges their existence, if pressed, and leaves it at that. Unlike birds, fish are no harbingers: they are reminders.

The reason why Miss Carson's admirable book *The Sea Around Us* is not as popular with sailors as the ladies who compose the reading bags for the Merchant Navy seem to suppose is that, in a way, Miss Carson's book is a printed fish. Next time you go on a sea voyage, take it with you and read it in your bunk. Ten to one that by the end of the first chapter, your hair will stand on end and you will be unable to fall asleep, even with the light on; for Miss Carson has contrived to make you aware of the unechoing depths underneath your mattress.

Yet fish are very interesting creatures and extremely intelligent. Any underwater hunter who stalks his prey with Aqua-lungs, frog feet and a portable harpoon will tell you how intelligent they are, for they usually get away. There is many a tale in the lore of the sea about intelligent fish. There was a white dolphin off the coast of Australia that used to follow the ships in and became so popular with the sailors that a law was passed to protect it. It met its end by being cut in half by the propeller of a Turk, and everyone who had ever been welcomed by its playful leaps mourned its passing.

Dolphins are magnificent fish. Anyone who has ever seen them leap and play around the ship has stared at them in wonder. Shelley wrote a poem about them; I had my ears boxed for them by Bosun Jongman of the *Loppersum* when I was lookout on duty. Apart from the dolphin, there are hundreds of thousands of different fish in the seas of the world, but the less said about them the better. Every man will see for himself. There are two kinds of fish, however, that must be talked about, because they rank high in the sailors' imagination.

First, the whale, which, ever since Jonah, is supposed to have a little apartment inside, complete with potbellied stove, cuckoo clock and Lutheran prints. Every cabin boy is told the story of the famous Finn who dropped overboard, was swallowed by a whale and spat out again on the beach of Monte Carlo. Some say he was green when he came out, others say red; in any case, he

was raving mad and and an obvious liar anyhow, as the whale's gullet is not made for man. The fo'c'sle fantasies about whales, however extravagant they may be, are always friendly. Even the fact that a whale, when maddened by torture, will attack a boat does not change the sailor's opinion of the mammal. The people in those boats only got what they asked for. Whalers, for that reason, are not popular at sea.

The shark, on the contrary, embodies all that is evil. Scientists, divers, and big-game fishermen, all assure us that sharks only very rarely eat human flesh, because they don't like the taste. "Very rarely," however, will do for the sailor. The scientists may disagree; the sailor is convinced that sharks do eat sailors and everything else that drops overboard: bottles, caps, and the scraps of discarded love letters. When a shark is caught and hoisted on board ship, as occasionally happens on long voyages, the aft deck turns into a slaughterhouse. The men go berserk in a prehistoric orgy of fury and blood and rip out the animal's stomach to see what is inside. At those moments, the jolly old tars are not lovable. When the orgy is over, there is a bewildered sense of shame and they pretend that the slaughter has had a purpose. They will cut out the spine to turn it into a walking stick for a father-in-law; I have seen a grim, fat bosun struggle for weeks with a bit of corrugated iron skin, trying to make a handbag.

There are fish, no bigger than a finger, who come in shoals and strip a man who falls overboard down to his skeleton within five minutes. There are fish . . .

Well, there are fish.

On Seeing

You may have been at sea for years without ever really looking at it. Many a landsman would be surprised to know that, after one cruise of a fortnight, he has a better picture in his mind of the sea than many a sailor; for he has been a passenger, and the sailor on the bridge or on the lookout is on duty. When a sailor scans the sea, he is looking for something or at something, rarely at the sea itself.

I had this brought home to me when I sailed as a junior seaman on a Dutch fishing smack, out for herrings on the North Sea. The ship was buckled and rusty; the captain, a stolid man given to long prayers before the meals, which consisted of fish, with stewed pears on Sundays. It was the first trip of the season.

In Holland, a reward and much publicity awaits the fisherman who brings home the first herring of spring. Life on board our fishing smack, ordinarily hustling enough, was a frenzy this time. On all the trawlers and luggers of the herring fleet, men were driven to exhaustion by their skippers, eager to catch the reward. It was before the invention of the shoal detector, and no aircraft circled over the fishing grounds to guide our fleet. Fishing was still in the stage it had been in on the Sea of Galilee when Jesus spoke to the crowds from a boat.

Despite the race for the prize, the trip was a normal commercial proposition. No captain would dream of turning for home without his holds being full; so the ship that caught most in the shortest time, and was nearest home, was the winner. An impartial observer could have told us before we set out that we hadn't a hope. The ship was slow, with a blunt bow which it pushed into the waves like a cow its muzzle into the hay. If the engine turned at more than half its maximum revolutions, the whole ship shook and rivets snapped in the hull. Yet we were full of hope and the captain was full of certainty according to his prayers. At every mealtime, after we had slumped down on the wooden benches in the poky fo'c'sle, covered with the scales of fish, our hands clumsy things unable to move, the captain addressed God as if He were in his service. He was not downright critical, yet he made it plain that if he was not going to catch the first herring this spring, he would have to think again on the matter of religion. We listened to his prayers, dazed with the singing in the ears that exhaustion brings.

Then the morning came when the boy in the masthead yelled, "Over starboard, skipper! Two points above the beam, starboard!" We all looked. There went the lucky trawler, a white moustache in front of her bows, heading for home, flying a flag from her mast as big as a house, blowing her hooter with a white plume followed by a triumphant shriek.

The captain scowled at the winner, and we waited for him to speak, but he said nothing. He only set his jaw, and we knew that God had it coming. That mealtime, at noon, he said, "Silence." After a long, motionless silence, in which we stared at him with our hands folded, he said, "Amen."

During the days that followed, it dawned on us as we hauled in the meager catch that the skipper believed in God no longer. Never since have I seen a man so steeped in damnation. He was not an intelligent man; his rebellion had nothing to do with reason. He stalked the bridge and the deck, his hands clasped behind his back, his head jutting out, as Adam must have stalked in Paradise after it turned into a hostile jungle. None of us understood why he should have finished with God this time, considering that he had never caught the first herring in spring. There was no reason. He had been stricken by the moment of darkness that awaits every man in his time.

The effect on the ship of his brooding, depressing at first, grew frightening. Men started to grumble, the cook burned the meals and snarled when anyone dared to remark on it. The engineer, who had concentrated on pistons and tappets so far, and to whom the catch meant little, stopped singing while oiling the engine and no longer tried to cheer the morning table with his jokes. In the end, the captain's silence spread over the ship like a shadow. The only human sound to be heard was the mate's Gregorian chant at the hauling in of the nets.

The sun was shining all the time, it was a lovely spring. Yet I have never known a trip to last so long. When, finally, the holds were full, every man had secretly decided not to sail with the captain again. The last catch was hauled in during the evening; we turned for home and sailed into the night.

The next morning, at sunrise, most of us were still on deck packing the last herrings of the trip into the barrels. The sun rose out of a misty horizon, the sea was calm, the eastern sky opened like a flower. The morning star still sparkled coldly on the edge of the darkness, but from the sea rose the promise of spring. The first man who looked at it did not look away. In the end we all looked, knife in hand. When the sun came out, our scale-covered oilskins glistened like armor. Then the captain came out into the dawn, stood still and gazed.

The ship plodded on in the slow swell. As the colors faded in the sky, we washed, took off our oilskins and sat down in the fo'c'sle for the morning meal. The captain folded his hands and said, "For what we are about to receive, O Lord, make us truly thankful." Then he took his fork and speared a fish.

"Stop me if you know this one," said the engineer.

Landfall

by SAMUEL ELIOT MORISON

Tom Wolfe and others may think they pioneered a new kind of firstperson journalism, but they could take a page from Samuel Eliot Morison's uncanny account of Columbus reaching America (specifically one of the Bahamas, the island of San Salvador). From sextant readings to speeches by Columbus himself, Morison lets us be there for the final and significant discovery of the New World.

*Et potestas eius a mari usque ad mare,
et a fluminibus usque ad fines terrae.*

And his dominion shall be from sea even to
sea,
and from the river even to the ends of the
earth.

ZECHARIAH 9: 10

SUN set under a clear horizon about 5: 30, every man in the fleet watching for a silhouette of land against its red disk; but no land was there. All hands were summoned as usual, and after they had said their evening prayers and sung the *Salve Regina,* "which all seamen are accustomed to say and sing in their own fashion," Columbus from the sterncastle made his men a little speech, reminding them of the grace Our Lord had shown them in conducting them so safely and prosperously with fair winds and a clear course, and in comforting them with signs of better things to come; and he urged the night watch to keep a particularly sharp lookout on the forecastle, reminding them that although he had given orders to do no night sailing after reaching a point seven hundred leagues from the Canaries, the great desire of all to see land had decided him to carry on that night. Hence all must make amends for this temerity by keeping a particularly good watch, and looking sharp for land; and to him who first sighted it he would then and there give a silk doublet, in addition to the annuity of 10,000 maravedis that the Sovereigns had promised. The gromet then sang his little ditty for changing the watch and turned the *ampolleta,* boatswain Chachu bellowed out the Castilian equivalent to "Watch below lay belo-o-w!" and the men took their stations with eyes well peeled.

During the eleven and a half hours since sunrise, with a brisk trade wind and the heaviest following sea of the entire voyage, the fleet had made seventy-eight miles, an average of almost seven knots. At sunset, it breezed up to gale force, until the vessels were tearing along at nine knots. At the same time, Columbus ordered the course changed from west-southwest back to the original west. Why he did this, nobody has explained. I suspect that it was simply a desire to prove that he was right. He had begun the voyage by steering a course due west for Japan, and so he wished to pick up land on a due west course. I have known commanders, good seamen too, who are like that. Or the change may have been just a hunch. If so, it was a good one, for the west-southwest course would have missed Guanahaní, and put the fleet next day in a dangerous position with the long, shelterless shore of Long Island under its lee. Common prudence would have made Columbus heave to for the night, since shoals and rocks invisible by moonlight might lie ahead. *María*'s pilot, Peralonso Niño, is said to have so advised him; but the Captain General felt that this was no time for common prudence. He had promised the men to turn back if land were not made within three days, and he intended to make all possible westing in this gale of wind. So the signal was made for *oeste!*

Anyone who has come onto the land under sail at night from an uncertain position knows how tense the atmosphere aboard ship can be. And this night of October 11–12 was one big with destiny for the human race, the most momentous ever experienced aboard any ship in any sea. Some of the boys doubtless slept, but nobody else. Juan de la Cosa and the Pinzons are pacing the high poops of their respective vessels, frequently calling down to the men at the tiller a testy order—keep her off damn your eyes must I go below and take the stick myself?—pausing at the break to peer under the main course and sweep the western horizon, then resting their eyes by looking up at the stars. Consultation as to whether or not to shorten sail; Martín Alonso perhaps confiding to Pilot Cristóbal García that he doesn't like carrying sail this way in a gale of wind with possible shoals ahead, but if that crazy Genoese can carry sail, we can carry sail; *Pinta* can stand it better than that Galician tub, and heave to quicker if anything shows up, and I want one of you men of Palos to win that *albricias*, d'ye see? Lookouts on the forecastles and in the roundtops talking low to each other—Hear anything? Sounds like breakers to me—nothing but the bow wave you fool—I tell you we won't sight land till Saturday, I dreamt it, and my dreams—you and

your dreams, here's a hundred maravedis says we raise it by daylight. . . . They tell each other how they would have conducted the fleet—The Old Man should never have set that spritsail, she'll run her bow under—if he'd asked my advice, and I was making my third voyage when he was playing in the streets of Genoa, I'd have told him. . . . Under such circumstances, with everyone's nerves taut as the weather braces, there was almost certain to be a false alarm of land.

An hour before moonrise, at 10:00 P.M., it came. Columbus, standing on the sterncastle, thought he saw a light, "so uncertain a thing that he did not wish to declare that it was land," but called Pedro Gutiérrez to have a look, and he thought he saw it too. Rodrigo Sánchez was then appealed to, "but he saw nothing because he was not in a position where he could see anything." One guesses that Rodrigo was fed up with false alarms, and merely stuck his head out of the companionway to remark discouragingly that he didn't see nothing; no, not a thing. The light, Columbus said, "was like a little wax candle rising and falling," and he saw it only once or twice after speaking to Gutiérrez.

At this juncture, one of the seamen, named Pedro Yzquierdo, a native of Lepe, thought he saw a light and sang out, *"Lumbre! Tierra!"* Pedro de Salcedo, Columbus's page boy, piped up with "It's already been seen by my master," and Columbus, who heard the cry, snubbed the man with, "I saw and spoke of that light, which is on land, some time ago."

What was this feeble light resembling a wax candle rising and falling, which Columbus admits that only a few besides himself ever saw? It cannot have been a fire or other light on San Salvador, or any other island; for, as the real landfall four hours later proves, the fleet at 10:00 P.M. was at least thirty-five miles off shore. The 400,000 candlepower light now on San Salvador, 170 feet above sea level, is not visible nearly so far. One writer has advanced the theory that the light was made by Indians torching for fish—why not lighting a cigar?—but Indians do not go fishing in three thousand fathoms of water thirty-five miles offshore at night in a gale of wind. The sentimental school of thought would have this light supernatural, sent by the Almighty to guide and encourage Columbus; but of all moments in the voyage, this is the one when he least needed encouragement, and he had laid his course straight for the nearest land. I agree heartily with Admiral Murdock, "the light was due to the imagination of Columbus, wrought up to a high pitch by the numerous signs of land encountered that day." Columbus admitted that only a few even thought they saw it. Anyone who has had much experience trying to make night landfalls with a sea running knows how easy it is to be deceived, especially when you are very anxious to pick up a light. Often two or three shipmates will agree that they see "it," then "it" disappears, and you realize that it was just another illusion. There is no need to criticize Columbus's seamanship because he sighted an imaginary light; but it is not easy to defend the fact that for this false landfall, which he must have known the next day to have been imaginary, he demanded and obtained the annuity of 10,000 maravedis promised by the Sovereigns to the man who first sighted land. The best we can say in extenuation is to point out that glory rather than greed prompted this act of injustice to a seaman; Columbus could not bear to think that anyone but himself sighted land first. That form of male vanity is by no means absent from the seafaring tribe today.

At 2:00 A.M., October 12, the moon, past full, was riding about seventy degrees high over Orion on the port quarter, just the position to illuminate anything ahead of the ships. Jupiter was rising in the east, Saturn had just set and Deneb was nearing the western horizon, toward which all waking eyes were directed. There hung the Square of Pegasus, and a little higher and to the northward Cassiopeia's Chair. The Guards of Polaris, at fifteen degrees beyond "feet," told the pilots that it was two hours after midnight. On speed the three ships, *Pinta* in the lead, their sails silver in the moonlight. A brave trade wind is blowing and the caravels are rolling, plunging and throwing spray as they cut down the last invisible barrier between the Old World and the New. Only a few moments now, and an era that began in remotest antiquity will end.

Rodrigo de Triana, lookout on *Pinta*'s forecastle, sees something like a white sand cliff gleaming in the moonlight on the western horizon, then another, and a dark line of land connecting them. *"Tierra! Tierra!"* he shouts, and this time land it is.

Martín Alonso Pinzón, after a quick verification, causes a lombard already loaded and primed to be fired as the agreed signal, and shortens sail in order to wait for the flagship. As soon as *Santa María* approached (remembered *Pinta*'s steward many years later), Columbus called out, "Señor Martín Alonso, you have found land!" and Pinzón replied, "Sir, my reward is not lost," and Columbus called back, "I give you 5,000 maravedis as a present!"

By Columbus's reckoning, the land was distant about six miles. The fleet had made sixty-five miles in the eight and a half hours since sunset, an average better than seven and one half knots; according to our reckoning, they were very near latitude twenty-four degrees north, longitude seventy-four degrees twenty minutes west when Rodrigo sang out.

As the fleet was heading straight for a lee shore, Columbus wisely ordered all sail to be lowered except the *papahigo*, which, as Las Casas explains, was the main course without bonnets; and with the main yard braced sharp and port tacks aboard, *Santa María*, *Pinta* and *Niña* jogged off and on until daylight. When they appeared to be losing the land, they wore around to the starboard tack, so the net result was a southerly drift at a safe distance from the breakers, during the remaining two and a half hours of moonlit night. The windward side of the island today is strewn with the wrecks of vessels that neglected this precaution.

This first land of the Western Hemisphere sighted by Columbus, or by any European since the voyages of the Northmen, was the eastern coast of one of the Bahamas now officially named "San Salvador or Watlings Island." Other candidates there have been for this honor: the Grand Turk, Cat Island, Rum Cay, Samana Cay and Mayaguana. But there is no longer any doubt that the island called Guanahaní, which Columbus renamed after Our Lord and Savior, was the present San Salvador or Watlings. That alone, of any island in the Bahamas, Turks or Caicos groups, fits Columbus's description. The position of San Salvador and of no other island fits the course laid down in his journal, if we work it backward from Cuba.

San Salvador is a coral island about thirteen miles long by six wide; the twenty-fourth parallel of latitude and the meridian of seventy-four degrees thirty minutes west of Greenwich cross near its center. The entire island, except for a space of about one and three-quarter miles on the west or leeward side, is surrounded by dangerous reefs. By daylight, Columbus's fleet must have drifted to a point near the Hinchinbrooke Rocks off the southeastern point. Making sail and filling away, they sought an opening through the reef barrier where they might safely anchor and send boats ashore. And the first gap that they could have discovered, one easy to pick out with a heavy sea running, was on the western shore about five miles north of Southwest Point. Here, rounding a prominent breaking ledge now called Gardiner Reef, the caravels braced their yards sharp and entered a shallow bay (Long or Fernandez), protected from winds between north by east around to south by west. Off a curving beach of gleaming coral sand, they found sheltered anchorage in five fathoms of water.

Somewhere on this beach of Long or Fernandez Bay took place the famous landing of Columbus, often depicted by artists, but never with any respect for the actual topography. Las Casas's abstract of the journal, and Ferdinand Columbus, who had the journal before him when he wrote the biography of his father, are the unique sources for this incident. Fitting together the two, we have this description:

> Presently they saw naked people, and the Admiral went ashore in the armed ship's boat with the royal standard displayed. So did the captains of *Pinta* and *Niña*, Martín Alonso Pinzón and Vicente Yáñez his brother, in their boats, with the banners of the Expedition, on which were depicted a green cross with an *F* on one arm and a *Y* on the other, and over each his or her

crown. And, all having rendered thanks to Our Lord kneeling on the ground, embracing it with tears of joy for the immeasurable mercy of having reached it, the Admiral arose and gave this island the name *San Salvador.* Thereupon he summoned to him the two captains, Rodrigo de Escobedo secretary of the armada and Rodrigo Sánchez of Segovia, and all others who came ashore, as witnesses; and in the presence of many natives of that land assembled together, took possession of that island in the name of the Catholic Sovereigns with appropriate words and ceremony. And all this is set forth at large in the testimonies there set down in writing. Forthwith the Christians hailed him as Admiral and Viceroy and swore to obey him as one who represented Their Highnesses, with as much joy and pleasure as if the victory had been all theirs, all begging his pardon for the injuries that through fear and inconstancy they had done him. Many Indians having come together for that ceremony and rejoicing, the Admiral, seeing that they were a gentle and peaceful people and of great simplicity, gave them some little red caps and glass beads which they hung around their necks, and other things of slight worth, which they all valued at the highest price.

At this point, Las Casas begins to quote the *palabras formales* ("exact words") of the Admiral, as we may now fairly style Columbus. So we may gather, as well as words can convey, the impression made by this branch of the American Indians on the vanguard of the race that would shortly reduce them to slavery, and exterminate them:

> In order that we might win good friendship, because I knew that they were a people who could better be freed and converted to our Holy Faith by love than by force, I gave to some of them red caps and to some glass beads, which they hung on their necks, and many other things of slight value, in which they took much pleasure; they remained so much our friends that it was a marvel; and later they

came swimming to the ships' boats in which we were, and brought us parrots and cotton thread in skeins and darts and many other things, and we swapped them for other things that we gave them, such as little glass beads and hawks' bells. Finally they swapped and gave everything they had, with goodwill; but it appeared to us that these people were very poor in everything. They go quite naked as their mothers bore them; and also the women, although I didn't see more than one really young girl. All that I saw were young men, none of them more than 30 years old, very well made, of very handsome bodies and very good faces; the hair coarse almost as the hair of a horse's tail and short; the hair they wear over their eyebrows, except for a hank behind that they wear long and never cut. Some of them paint themselves black (and they are of the color of the Canary Islanders, neither black nor white), and some paint themselves white, and others red, and others with what they have. Some paint their faces, others the whole body, others the eyes only, others only the nose. They bear no arms, nor know thereof; for I showed them swords and they grasped them by the blade and cut themselves through ignorance; they have no iron. Their darts are a kind of rod without iron, and some have at the end a fish's tooth and others, other things. They are generally fairly tall and good looking, well made. I saw some who had marks of wounds on their bodies, and made signs to them to ask what it was, and they showed me how people of other islands which are near came there and wished to capture them, and they defended themselves. And I believed and now believe that people do come here from the mainland to take them as slaves. They ought to be good servants and of good skill, for I see that they repeat very quickly all that is said to them; and I believe that they would easily be made Christians, because it seemed to me that they belonged to no religion. I, please Our Lord, will carry off six of them at my departure to Your Highnesses, so that

they may learn to speak. I saw no beast of any kind except parrots in this island.

Saturday, October 13: At daybreak there came to the beach many of these men, all young men as I have said, and all of good stature, very handsome people. Their hair is not kinky but loose and coarse like horsehair; and the whole forehead and head is very broad, more so than any other race that I have seen, and the eyes very handsome and not small, and themselves not at all black, but of the color of the Canary Islanders; nor should anything else be expected, because this is on the same latitude with the island of Ferro in the Canaries. Their legs are very straight, all in a line; and no belly, but very well built. They came to the ship in dugouts which are fashioned like a longboat from the bole of a tree, and all in one piece, and wonderfully made (considering the country), and so big that in some came 40 or 45 men, and others smaller, down to the size that held but a single man. They row with a thing like a baker's peel and go wonderfully [fast], and if they capsize all begin to swim and right it and bail it out with calabashes that they carry. They brought skeins of spun cotton, and parrots and darts and other trifles that would be tedious to describe, and gave all for whatever was given to them.

In his Letter to the Sovereigns, which was promptly printed at Barcelona and widely distributed throughout Europe in a Latin translation, Columbus lays stress on the gentleness and generosity of the natives:

They are so ingenuous and free with all they have, that no one would believe it who has not seen it; of anything that they possess, if it be asked of them, they never say no; on the contrary, they invite you to share it and show as much love as if their hearts went with it, and they are content with whatever trifle be given them, whether it be a thing of value or of petty worth. I forbade that they be given things so worthless as bits of broken crockery and of green glass and lace-points, although when they could get them, they thought they had the best jewel in the world.

Unfortunately, this guilelessness and generosity of the simple savage aroused the worst traits of cupidity and brutality in the average European. Even the Admiral's humanity seems to have been merely political, as a means to eventual enslavement and exploitation. But to the intellectuals of Europe, it seemed that Columbus had stepped back several millennia and encountered people living in the Golden Age, that bright morning of humanity which existed only in the imagination of poets. Columbus's discovery enabled Europeans to see their own ancestors, as it were, in a "state of nature," before Pandora's box was opened. The "virtuous savage" myth, which reached its height in the eighteenth century, began at Guanahaní on October 12, 1492. As Peter Martyr, who first gave it currency, wrote of these Indians, and as Richard Eden translated him in 1555:

> And surely if they had receaued owre religion, I wolde thinke their life moste happye of all men, if they might therwith enioye their aunciente libertie. A fewe thinges contente them, hauinge no delite in such superfluites, for the which in other places men take infinite paynes and commit manie vnlawfull actes, and yet are neuer satisfied, whereas many haue to muche, and none inowgh. But emonge these simple sowles, a fewe clothes serue the naked: weightes and measures are not needefull to such as can not skyll of crafte and deceyte and haue not the vse of pestiferous monye, the seede of innumerable myscheues. So that if we shall not be ashamed to confesse the truthe, they seeme to lyue in that goulden worlde of the whiche owlde wryters speake so much: wherin men lyued simplye and innocentyle without inforcement of lawes, without quarrellinge Iudges and libelles, contente onely to satisfie nature, without further vexation for knowledge of thinges to come.

These Indians of the Bahamas, and indeed all whom Columbus encountered on his first voyage, belonged to the so-called Taino culture of the Arawak language group. Their ancestors had emigrated to the Antilles from the mainland of South America, and within a century of Columbus's voyage had branched out from Haiti, overrunning Cuba, Jamaica and the Bahamas, pushing back or enslaving an earlier and more primitive tribe known as the Siboney. The Tainos were fairly advanced in civilization, growing corn, yams and other roots, making cassava bread from yucca, spinning and weaving cotton, making a fine brown pottery adorned with grotesque heads, and various ornaments and utensils of shell, living in huts made of a wooden frame and palm thatch. The broad, low forehead that Columbus remarked was due to a process of artificially flattening the skulls of infants by pressing them between boards.

Columbus's frame of reference, it is interesting to note, was partly African and partly classical. He expected to find kinky-haired blacks such as he had encountered on the coast of Guinea, because Aristotle taught that people and products on the same latitude were similar; but he reflected that being on the same latitude as Ferro—a mistake of three degrees forty-one minutes—it was not surprising to find them of the same brown color as the Guanches, the primitive inhabitants of the Canaries. The word that he used for their canoes, *almadias,* was what the Portuguese used for the dugouts of West Africa; and the trading goods that he brought, Venetian glass beads, brass rings, red caps and the small round bronze bells used in falconry, were exactly what the Portuguese had found to be in most demand among the Negroes.

Although the Tainos had driven back the primitive hunter folk, their only weapon, a short spear or dart with a fish-tooth or fire-hardened wooden point, was insufficient to cope with the Caribs, who occasionally raided them from the Caribbee Islands. Much less were they prepared to resist domination by the Spaniards. And it is clear from the concluding sentences of Columbus's journal for October 12 that on the very day of discovery the dark thought crossed his mind that these people could very easily be enslaved. On October 14 he noted, "These people are very unskilled in arms . . . with fifty men they could all be subjected and made to do all that one wished." It is sad but significant that the only Indians of the Caribbean who have survived are those who proved both willing and able to defend themselves. The Tainos, whom Columbus found so gentle and handsome and hospitable, are long since extinct.

Guanahaní, the native name of this island, means the *iguana,* a reptile now extinct there. Columbus described it as "very big and very level and the trees very green, and many bodies of water, and a very big lake in the middle, but no mountain, and the whole of it so green that it is a pleasure to gaze upon." The island is honeycombed with salt lagoons, the largest of which is only a few hundred yards from the beach where Columbus landed; and the highest hill on the island is only 140 feet above sea level. Later, after exploring the northern part, Columbus noted groves of trees, the most beautiful he had ever seen, "and as green and leafy as those of Castile in the months of April and May." Visitors to San Salvador and the other Bahamian islands find Columbus's descriptions of nature extravagant, and are inclined to accuse him of laying it on thick to impress the Sovereigns.

Any land looks good to seamen after a long and perilous voyage, and every woman fair; but Columbus's description of the Bahamas was not extravagant for 1492. At that time, they were highly fertile and covered with a dense growth of tropical hardwood, which the Indians had cleared but slightly to plant gardens. In the late eighteenth century, the English colonists (many of them loyalist refugees from the United States) caused a large part of the forest to be cut down in order to grow sea island cotton. This exhausted the soil, and hurricanes stripped the island at not infrequent intervals. When cotton culture ceased to pay, the fields were abandoned, and today such parts of the islands as the Negroes do not use for their potato patches and pasturage are covered with a scrubby second growth and ruins of old plantation houses. Large trees for making dugout canoes of the size that

Columbus described no longer exist. Near an inland lagoon of San Salvador, we were shown a surviving grove of primeval forest which for lushness and beauty merits Columbus's praise, and this grove harbors a variety of tropical woodpecker that must once have had a wider forest range. Skeletal remains of other birds which could only have lived among dense foliage have been discovered on the island by naturalists.

All day Saturday, October 13, the caravels lay at anchor in Long Bay with a swarm of canoes passing back and forth, while the Spaniards in turn took shore leave, wandered into the natives' huts, did a little private trading for the curios that all seamen love and doubtless ascertained that the girls of Guanahaní were much like others they had known. Columbus, who ever had an eye for "improvements," reported that he found "a quarry of stones naturally shaped, very fair for church edifices or other public uses." Three centuries elapsed before anyone thought to build a church at San Salvador, and then it was found easier to fashion the soft coral rock into rectangular blocks; the outcrop that Columbus saw at Hall's Landing just north of his landing place, partly underwater and curiously split into squares like flagstones, is still unquarried.

The Admiral was busy gathering such information as he could from signs and gestures; his Arabic interpreter was of no use in this neck of the Indies. On Saturday night, he decided that no time must be lost, he must press on to Japan. But first San Salvador must be explored. On Sunday morning the three ships' boats took the Admiral north along the leeward coast "to see the other side, which was the eastern side, what was there, and also to see the villages; and soon I saw two or three, and the people all came to the beach, shouting and giving thanks to God. Some brought us water; others, things to eat. Others, when they saw that I did not care to go ashore, plunged into the sea swimming and came aboard, and we understood that they asked us if we had come from Heaven. And one old man got into the boat, and others shouted in loud voices to all, men and women, "Come and see the men who come from Heaven, bring them food and drink." Many came and many women, each with something, giving thanks to God, throwing themselves flat and raising their hands to Heaven, and then shouting to us to come ashore; but I was afraid to, from seeing a great reef of rocks which surrounded the whole of this island, but inside it was deep and a harbor to hold all the ships in Christendom, and the entrance of it very narrow."

This was the place now known as Grahams Harbor, formed by the reefs that surround the island coming together in an inverted *V*. At three or four places, the reefs rise high enough to form cays, and beside one of these on the western side, Green Cay, is a good boat channel with seven feet of water. Here, rather than the alternate High Reef channel, which is difficult for a stranger to find, was probably where the boats entered. "Inside there are some shoal spots," Columbus correctly observed, "but the sea moves no more than within a well." The smooth water inside these coral-reef harbors is always a pleasant surprise to mariners.

Glenn Stewart's yacht lay quietly and safely in Grahams Harbor during a heavy norther in January, 1930.

Columbus's boats rowed across the harbor, about two miles to the eastward, where they found a rocky peninsula that thrusts out from the northern side of San Salvador, half of it almost an island, and "which in two days could be made an island," suitable for a fortress. Since Columbus's visit, the sea has here broken a narrow channel that one can wade across at low water. Someone, probably the English, took up Columbus's suggestion that the place was a natural fortress, for Dr. Cronau found an iron cannon there in 1891. After inspecting the harbor, the boats returned to the vessels at their anchorage in Long Bay, a row of some twenty miles going and coming; and in the early afternoon the fleet made sail for Cipangu.

So ended forty-eight hours of the most wonderful experience that perhaps any seamen have ever had. Other discoveries there have been more spectacular than that of this small, flat sandy island that rides out ahead of the American continent, breasting the trade winds. But it was there that the ocean for the first time "loosed the chains of things" as Seneca had prophesied, gave up the secret that had baffled Europeans since they began to inquire what lay beyond the western horizon's rim. Stranger people than the gentle Tainos, more exotic plants than the green verdure of Guanahaní have been discovered, even by the Portuguese before Columbus; but the discovery of Africa was but an unfolding of a continent already glimpsed, whilst San Salvador, rising from the sea at the end of a thirty-three-day westward sail, was a clean break with past experience. Every tree, every plant that the Spaniards saw was strange to them, and the natives were not only strange but completely unexpected, speaking an unknown tongue and resembling no race of which even the most educated of the explorers had read in the tales of travelers from Herodotus to Marco Polo. Never again may mortal men hope to recapture the amazement, the wonder, the delight of those October days in 1492 when the New World gracefully yielded her virginity to the conquering Castilians.

The Pilot of the Pinta

by CAPTAIN JOSHUA SLOCUM

At the age of forty-five, Joshua Slocum was a man adrift, a sailing ship master unable to find work in the age of steam. Then an old captain in Boston gave him a vintage oyster sloop named Spray. *With* Spray, *Slocum journeyed into history in 1889, becoming the first man to sail around the world alone. In his classic account of that epic voyage,* Sailing Alone Around the World, *Slocum becomes delirious during a gale and hallucinates that he is not alone on ship.*

I set sail from Horta early on July 24. The southwest wind at the time was light, but squalls came up with the sun, and I was glad enough to get reefs in my sails before I had gone a mile. I had hardly set the mainsail, double-reefed, when a squall of wind down the mountains struck the sloop with such violence that I thought her mast would go. However, a quick helm brought her to the wind. As it was, one of the weather lanyards was carried away and the other was stranded. My tin basin, caught up by the wind, went flying across a French schoolship to leeward. It was more or less squally all day, sailing along under high land; but rounding close under a bluff, I found an opportunity to mend the lanyards broken in the squall. No sooner had I lowered my sails when a four-oared boat shot out from some gully in the rocks, with a customs officer on board, who thought he had come upon a smuggler. I had some difficulty in making him comprehend the true case. However, one of his crew, a sailorly chap, who understood how matters were, while we palavered jumped on board and rove off the new lanyards I had already prepared, and with a friendly hand helped me "set up the rigging." This incident gave the turn in my favor. My story was then clear to all. I have found this the way of the world. Let alone be without a friend, and see what will happen!

Passing the island of Pico, after the rigging was mended, the *Spray* stretched across to leeward of the island of St. Michael's, which she was up with early on the morning of July 26, the wind blowing hard. Later in the day she passed the Prince of Monaco's fine steam-yacht bound to Fayal, where, on a previous voyage, the prince had slipped his cables to "escape a reception" which the padres of the island wished to give him. Why he so dreaded the "ovation" I could not make out. At Horta they did not know. Since reaching the islands, I had lived most luxuriously on fresh bread, butter, vegetables and fruits of all kinds. Plums seemed the most plentiful on the *Spray,* and these I ate without stint. I had also a Pico white cheese that General Manning, the American consul general, had given me, which I

48

supposed was to be eaten, and of this I partook with the plums. Alas! by nighttime I was doubled up with cramps. The wind, which was already a smart breeze, was increasing somewhat, with a heavy sky to the southwest. Reefs had been turned out, and I must turn them in again somehow. Between cramps, I got the mainsail down, hauled out the earings as best I could and tied away point by point, in the double reef. There being sea room, I should, in strict prudence, have made all snug and gone down at once to my cabin. I am a careful man at sea, but this night, in the coming storm, I swayed up my sails, which, reefed though they were, were still too much in such heavy weather; and I saw to it that the sheets were securely belayed. In a word, I should have laid to, but did not. I gave her the double-reefed mainsail and whole jib instead, and set her on her course. Then I went below, and threw myself upon the cabin floor in great pain. How long I lay there I could not tell, for I became delirious. When I came to, as I thought, from my swoon, I realized that the sloop was plunging into a heavy sea, and looking out of the companionway, to my amazement I saw a tall man at the helm. His rigid hand, grasping the spokes of the wheel, held them as in a vise. One may imagine my astonishment. His rig was that of a foreign sailor, and the large red cap he wore was cockbilled over his left ear, and all was set off with shaggy black whiskers. He would have been taken for a pirate in any part of the world. While I gazed upon his threatening aspect, I forgot the storm, and wondered if he had come to cut my throat. This he seemed to divine. "Señor," said he, doffing his cap, "I have come to do you no harm." And a smile, the faintest in the world, but still a smile, played on his face, which seemed not unkind when he spoke. "I have come to do you no harm. I have sailed free," he said, "but was never worse than a *contrabandista*. I am one of Columbus's crew," he continued. "I am the pilot of the *Pinta* come to aid you. Lie quiet, señor captain," he added, "and I will guide your ship tonight. You have a *calentura,* but you will be all right tomorrow." I thought what a very devil he was to carry sail. Again, as if he read my mind, he exclaimed: "Yonder is the *Pinta* ahead; we

must overtake her. Give her sail; give her sail! *Vale, vale, muy vale!*" Biting off a large quid of black twist, he said: "You did wrong, captain, to mix cheese with plums. White cheese is never safe unless you know whence it comes. *Quien sabe,* it may have been from *leche de Capra* and becoming capricious—"

"Avast, there!" I cried. "I have no mind for moralizing."

I made shift to spread a mattress and lie on that instead of the hard floor, my eyes all the while fastened on my strange guest, who, remarking again that I would have "only pains and *calentura,*" chuckled as he chanted a wild song:

High are the waves, fierce, gleaming,
High is the tempest roar!
High the seabird screaming!
High the Azore!

I suppose I was now on the mend, for I was peevish, and complained: "I detest your jingle. Your Azore should be at roost, and would have been were it a respectable bird!" I begged he would tie a rope yarn on the rest of the song, if there was any more of it. I was still in agony. Great seas were boarding the *Spray,* but in my fevered brain I thought they were boats falling on deck, that careless draymen were throwing from wagons on the pier to which I imagined the *Spray* was now moored, and without fenders to breast her off. "You'll smash your boats!" I called out again and again, as the seas crashed on the cabin over my head. "You'll smash your boats, but you can't hurt the *Spray.* She is strong!" I cried.

I found, when my pains and *calentura* had gone, that the deck, now as white as a shark's tooth from seas washing over it, had been swept of everything movable. To my astonishment, I saw now at broad day that the *Spray* was still heading as I had left her, and was going like a racehorse. Columbus himself could not have held her more exactly on her course. The sloop had made ninety miles in the night through a rough sea. I felt grateful to the old pilot, but I marveled some that he had not taken in the jib. The gale was moderating, and by noon the sun was shining. A meridian altitude and the distance on the patent log, which I always kept towing, told me that she had made a true course throughout the twenty-four hours. I was getting much better now, but was very weak and did not turn out reefs that day or the night following, although the wind fell light; but I just put my wet clothes out in the sun when it was shining, and lying down there myself, fell asleep. Then who should visit me again but my old friend of the night before, this time, of course, in a dream. "You did well last night to take my advice," said he, "and if you would, I should like to be with you often on the voyage, for the love of adventure alone." Finishing what he had to say, he again doffed his cap and disappeared as mysteriously as he came, returning, I suppose, to the phantom *Pinta*. I awoke much refreshed, and with the feeling that I had been in the presence of a friend and a seaman of vast experience. I gathered up my clothes, which by this time were dry, then, by inspiration, I threw overboard all the plums in the vessel.

July 28 was exceptionally fine. The wind from the northwest was light and the air balmy. I overhauled my wardrobe, and bent on a white shirt against nearing some coasting packet with genteel folk on board. I also did some washing to get the salt out of my clothes. After it all I was hungry, so I made a fire and very cautiously stewed a dish of pears and set them carefully aside till I had made a pot of delicious coffee, for both of which I could afford sugar and cream. But the crowning dish of all was a fish hash, and there was enough of it for two. I was in good health again, and my appetite was simply ravenous. While I was dining, I had a large onion over the double lamp stewing for a luncheon later in the day. High living today!

In the afternoon, the *Spray* came upon a large turtle asleep on the sea. He awoke with my harpoon through his neck, if he awoke at all. I had much difficulty in landing him on deck, which I finally accomplished by hooking the throat halyards to one of his flippers, for he was about as heavy as my boat. I saw more turtles, and I rigged a burton ready with which to hoist them in; for I was obliged to lower the mainsail whenever the halyards were used for such purposes, and it was no small matter to hoist the large sail again. But the turtle steak was good. I found no fault with the cook, and it was the rule of the voyage that the cook found no fault with me. There was never a ship's crew so well agreed. The bill of fare that evening was turtle steak, tea and toast, fried potatoes, stewed onions; with dessert of stewed pears and cream.

Sometime in the afternoon I passed a barrel buoy adrift, floating light on the water. It was painted red and rigged with a signal staff about six feet high. A sudden change in the weather coming on, I got no more turtle or fish of any sort before reaching port. July 31 a gale sprang up suddenly from the north, with heavy seas, and I shortened sail. The *Spray* made only fifty-one miles on her course that day. August 1 the gale continued, with heavy seas. Through the night, the sloop was reaching, under close-reefed mainsail and bobbed jib. At 3:00 P.M. the jib was washed off the bowsprit and blown to rags and ribbons. I bent the jumbo on a stay at the night heads. As for the jib, let it go; I saved pieces of it, and, after all, I was in want of pot rags.

On August 3 the gale broke, and I saw many signs of land. Bad weather having made itself felt in the galley, I was minded to try my hand at a loaf of bread, and so rigging a pot of fire on deck by which to bake it, a loaf soon became an accomplished fact. One great feature about ship's cooking is that one's appetite on the sea is always good—a fact that I realized when I cooked for the crew of fishermen in the before mentioned boyhood days. Dinner being over, I sat for hours reading the life of Columbus, and as the day wore on I watched the birds all flying in one direction, and said, "Land lies there."

Early the next morning, August 4, I discovered Spain. I saw fires on shore, and knew that the country was inhabited. The *Spray* continued on her course till well in with the land, which was that about Trafalgar. Then keeping away a point, she passed through the Strait of Gibraltar, where she cast anchor at 3:00 P.M. of the same day, less than twenty-nine days from Cape Sable. At the finish of this preliminary trip, I found myself in excellent health, not overworked or cramped, but as well as ever in my life, though I was as thin as a reef point.

Two Italian barks, which had been close alongside at daylight, I saw long after I had anchored, passing up the African side of the strait. The *Spray* had sailed them both hull down before she reached Tarifa. So far as I know, the *Spray* beat everything going across the Atlantic except the steamers. All was well, but I had forgotten to bring a bill of health from Horta, and so when the fierce old port doctor came to inspect, there was a row. That, however, was the very thing needed. If you want to get on well with a true Britisher, you must first have a deuce of a row with him. I knew that well enough, and so I fired away, shot for shot, as best I could. "Well, yes," the doctor admitted at last, "your crew are healthy enough, no doubt, but who knows the diseases of your last port?"—a reasonable enough remark. "We ought to put you in the fort, sir!" he blustered. "But never mind. Free pratique, sir! Shove off, coxswain!" And that was the last I saw of the port doctor.

But on the following morning, a steam launch, much longer than the *Spray,* came alongside—or as much of her as could get alongside—with compliments from the senior naval officer, Admiral Bruce, saying there was a berth for the *Spray* at the arsenal. This was around at the new mole. I had anchored at the old mole, among the native craft, where it was rough and uncomfortable. Of course I was glad to shift, and did so as soon as possible, thinking of the great company the *Spray* would be in among battleships such as the *Collingwood, Barfleur* and *Cormorant,* which were at that time stationed there, and on board all of which I was entertained, later, most royally.

" 'Put it thar!' as the Americans say," was the salute I got from Admiral Bruce, when I called at the admiralty to thank him for his courtesy of the berth, and for the use of the steam launch which towed me into dock. "About the berth, it is all right if it suits, and we'll tow you out when you are ready to go. But, say, what repairs do you want? Ahoy the *Hebe,* can you spare your sailmaker? The *Spray* wants a new jib. Construction and repair, there! Will you see to the *Spray?* Say, old man, you must have knocked the devil out of her coming over alone in twenty-nine days! But we'll make it smooth for you here!" Not even Her Majesty's ship the *Collingwood* was better looked after than the *Spray* at Gibraltar.

Later in the day came the hail: "*Spray* ahoy! Mrs. Bruce would like to come on board and shake hands with the *Spray.* Will it be convenient today?" "Very!" I joyfully shouted. On the following day, Sir F. Carrington, at the time governor of Gibraltar, with other high officers of the garrison, and all the commanders of the battleships, came on board and signed their names in the *Spray*'s logbook. Again there was a hail, "*Spray* ahoy!" "Hello!" "Commander Reynold's compliments. You are invited on board H.M.S. *Collingwood,* 'at home' at 4:30 P.M. Not later than 5:30 P.M." I had already hinted at the limited amount of my wardrobe, and that I could never succeed as a dude. "You are expected, sir, in a stovepipe hat and a claw-hammer coat!" "Then I can't come." "Dash it! come in what you have on; that is what we mean." "Aye, aye, sir!" The *Collingwood*'s cheer was good, and had I worn a silk hat as high as the moon, I could not have had a better time or been made more at home. An Englishman, even on his great battleship, unbends when the stranger passes his gangway, and when he says "at home," he means it.

That one should like Gibraltar would go without saying. How could one help loving so hospitable a place? Vegetables twice a week and milk every morning came from the palatial grounds of the admiralty. "*Spray* ahoy!" would hail the admiral. "Hello!" "Tomorrow is your vegetable day, sir." "Aye, aye, sir!"

I rambled much about the old city, and a gunner piloted me through the galleries of the rock as far as a stranger is permitted to go. There is no excavation in the world, for military purposes, at all approaching these of Gibraltar in conception or execution. Viewing the stupendous works, it became hard to realize that one was within the Gibraltar of his little old Morse geography.

Before sailing, I was invited on a picnic with the governor, the officers of the garrison and the commanders of the warships at the station; and

RETURN TO
JOHN OLIVER LIBRARY
530 EAST 41st AVE.
VANCOUVER, B.C.

a royal affair it was. Torpedo boat Number 91, going twenty-two knots, carried our party to the Morocco shore and back. The day was perfect—too fine, in fact, for comfort on shore, and so no one landed at Morocco. Number 91 trembled like an aspen leaf as she raced through the sea at top speed. Sublieutenant Boucher, apparently a mere lad, was in command, and handled his ship with the skill of an older sailor. On the following day, I lunched with General Carrington, the governor, at Line Wall House, which was once the Franciscan convent. In this interesting edifice are preserved relics of the fourteen sieges which Gibraltar has seen. On the next day, I supped with the admiral at his residence, the palace, which was once the convent of the Mercenaries. At each place, and all about, I felt the friendly grasp of a manly hand, that lent me vital strength to pass the coming long days at sea. I must confess that the perfect discipline, order and cheerfulness at Gibraltar were only a second wonder in the great stronghold. The vast amount of business going forward caused no more excitement than the quiet sailing of a well-appointed ship on a smooth sea. No one spoke above his natural voice, save a boatswain's mate now and then. The Honorable Horatio J. Sprague, the venerable United States consul at Gibraltar, honored the *Spray* with a visit on Sunday, August 24, and was much pleased to find that our British cousins had been so kind to her.

The Great Barrier Reef

by **ALISTAIR MACLEAN**

While known to large audiences as the author of super-thriller adventures like Where Eagles Dare, Ice Station Zebra *and* The Guns of Navarone, *Alistair Maclean is a student of the sea and author of a biography of Captain Cook, one of history's great explorers, who mapped new worlds for England during the eighteenth century. Here is Maclean's account of Cook's remarkable journey through Australia's Great Barrier Reef.*

THE *Endeavour* did not remain long in the vicinity of Queen Charlotte Sound. Both the ship and all aboard were in excellent condition and Cook was in no mind to linger. They had done all that had been asked of them to do and now they were free to return to England. There were three possible routes home, so Cook called his usual democratic council of officers and, as usual, made up his mind in his own way.

They could go home by Cape Horn, but that was a long and dangerous passage. Cook doubted whether the cordage, now long past its best, could stand up to the storms they could almost certainly expect off the cape, and food supplies, now running low, were judged insufficient for the length of the voyage and, besides, the southern winter was coming on.

They could have gone via the Cape of Good Hope, but this involved the appalling prospect of the *Endeavour,* which, at the best of times, could only sail into the wind with the greatest of difficulty, beating for endless weeks against the prevailing westerlies before reaching the cape. This would again involve the question of food supplies. And, besides, Tasman had already done that voyage and Cook wasn't a man much given to following in the footsteps of others.

The third choice, the one Cook finally made, was the inevitable one. For Cook, it must have been irresistible, for it involved a fresh achievement, a new discovery, an exploration of the only great stretch of land still left unexplored in the temperate world—the east coast of Australia. As far as Cook was aware, no European except Tasman had ever seen or set foot on the eastern side of the continent: this was a challenge after his heart. (In point of fact, what Cook did not know —and died not knowing—was that he himself was the first discoverer, for neither Tasman nor he ever learned that Van Diemen's Land, which Tasman had visited, was the island we now call Tasmania and quite detached from the Australian mainland.) And when they reached the north of Australia they could head for the Dutch East Indies, where, Cook knew, they could obtain provisions in quantity.

53

The *Endeavour* left New Zealand on April 1. Cook's intention was to head straight for Van Diemen's Land—Tasman had left an accurate enough fix on its position—but contrary gales blew them far to the north of their intended route and when they did sight land it was Australia and not Tasmania: just as gales had caused Cook to miss the Foveaux Strait between South Island and Stewart Island, so now more gales caused him to miss Bass Strait between Australia and Tasmania. As far as Cook was concerned, he thought he'd just sighted land some way further up the same coast as Tasman had seen.

It is worth noting, perhaps, that by a remarkable coincidence Cook's attitude to the Bass Strait was as ambivalent as Tasman's to Cook Strait. Tasman, in his charts, showed North and South islands joined together but in his journal expressed the private belief that there probably was a strait separating the two: Cook, in his chart, showed Australia and Tasmania as being joined together but in *his* journal expressed the private belief that there was probably a strait separating the two.

Almost certainly, the *Endeavour* was already in Bass Strait when Lieutenant Hicks first sighted Australia on April 21. The location of this landfall—Point Hicks Hill—is not precisely known, but it is believed to be a hill behind a promontory now known as Cape Everard.

Cook moved along the coast, at first in an easterly then in a northerly direction, looking for a suitable harbor. They could see smoke at frequent intervals and from this they assumed that the area was inhabited, although there were no people to be seen. After a week of sailing north, they found what seemed an eminently suitable harbor and put into it. Here they met their first aborigines, nearly black in color, quite different from the Polynesians and the Maoris. Some were hostile, but not nearly as hostile as the Maoris had been. Some were indifferent—Cook relates with astonishment that two canoe loads of aborigines, busy fishing, paid no attention whatsoever as the *Endeavour* moved in but displayed total indifference, which one cannot regard as other than totally astonishing, as it was quite impossible that they had ever seen such a ship in

their lives before. None of the aborigines offered any kind of welcome. All of them, it was observed, carried "short scimitars"—the famous boomerangs.

Water was obtainable and the bay teemed with fish, to such an extent that Cook called the place Stingray Harbour, but there was no meat to be had, no fresh fruit and no vegetables—the aborigines knew nothing of the art of cultivation, which clearly made them a much more backward race than the Maoris of the Bay of Plenty, who had developed the art to a considerable degree. But one thing did abound in a profusion that delighted the hearts of Banks, Solander and the other scientists—plants. They found hundreds there that were totally unknown in Europe, so many in fact that Cook was constrained to change his mind about Stingray Harbour and give it instead that name that was to be the most famous—and with the introduction of the convict settlements, the most infamous—in early Australian history: Botany Bay.

They sailed on May 6. About nine miles to the north, they passed the entrance to another harbor, which Cook called Port Jackson, hazarding the opinion that it might prove a safe anchorage. It is as well, perhaps, for Cook's peace of mind that he died without knowing that he had just passed up the most magnificent harbor in the world: Sydney.

For the next five weeks, the *Endeavour* sailed up the coast in remarkably fine weather. Cook was in his element. He had his difficulties to cope with, of course, such as when someone cut off part of the ears of his clerk, Mr. Orton, when he was in a drunken stupor (the culprit was never discovered) and, later, when coping with the mazy intricacies, the rocks and shoals and reefs too innumerable to count, of the Great Barrier Reef. But in the main, he was doing what he best loved to, making a splendid series of charts and christening everything in sight—the numbers of isles, bays, sounds, heads and capes that Cook named is almost beyond belief. It is another facet of his character that he must have had a remarkably inventive mind: he never once seems to have been at a loss for a name.

At 11:00 P.M. on the night of June 11, the

Endeavour grounded on an underwater coral reef with an impact that shook every timber in the ship. She was held there, fast, immovable, and it was immediately apparent that the damage was of a very serious nature, for great amounts of water at once started gushing into the stricken ship. To make matters worse, she had not only grounded on the top of the tide—a circumstance which ships' captains dread above all others—but the heavy swell beyond the reef was breaking as it crossed the reef and was continually pounding the stranded vessel—not heavily, but severely enough to increase the risk of extending the damage already sustained to the bottom.

The pumps were manned but could not cope with the inflow of water. As the tide receded, the *Endeavour* developed a list, which put a further strain on the already damaged timbers. The more the tide went out, the greater the angle of list became. The mainland was twenty miles away. A sudden storm and the ship might be torn off the rocks, tearing more timbers in the process, and founder: and there weren't enough boats to carry the complement of the vessel to safety.

It had all the makings of a desperate situation, but such are the situations that the Captain Cooks of this world are born for. He had the ship lightened as much as possible by throwing overboard about fifty tons of material—the boatswain's and carpenter's condemned stores, firewood, stone and iron ballast from the hold, even the guns—although those were carefully buoyed for later recovery. At the same time, he had anchors put aboard the pinnace, and taken and dropped some distance from the *Endeavour* so that with the aid of capstan and windlass they could kedge the vessel into deeper water. One can imagine the sheer backbreaking labor involved in all this: the continuous pumping, the transport of the heavy anchors and, especially, the removal of the fifty tons of ballast from the hold. By eleven o'clock the following morning, the time of the next high tide, almost every man on board was in a state of exhaustion.

The tide came and went and still she was stuck fast. Cook retained his remarkable calm. He knew that the night tides on that coast were considerably higher than the day tides. At the same time, he did question the wisdom of trying to get her off at all—for all they knew it was only the coral reef on which the *Endeavour* rested that prevented her from sinking like a stone. Cook decided to risk it. If she started to sink quickly, he would try to kedge her back on to the reef at once; if she got off and made water only comparatively slowly, he would try to sail her to the coast, beach her there, break her up and build a smaller boat from her timbers and sail in that to the East Indies. *Indomitable* is hardly a word that one would apply to Captain Cook if one could find a better one.

In the event, neither of those courses had to be followed. At high tide that night, with every possible hand on the windlasses attached to the anchor ropes—and most of the others at the pumps—the *Endeavour* was pulled clear. To the astonishment—and relief—of all, not only did she not sink, she now made even less water than she had done before. (What had happened, as they discovered later, was that a large chunk of coral had broken off as she'd been hauled free and had partially plugged the hole.)

Cook decided to plug the hole some more—to fother it, as it was called. A rope was passed under the ship and attached to a sail which was covered with oakum and wool. This was pulled under the ship, and when it came to the hole, water pressure jammed it in position, an operation which reduced incoming water to a relative trickle, although the pumps still had to be manned.

Cook dispatched boats to reconnoiter the coast to find a suitable spot where the *Endeavour* could be careened and the gash in the bottom repaired. And now luck had turned to Cook's side, for a boat returned saying that it had found a suitable river estuary on the coast, some little way to the north. Cook took the *Endeavour* there, and despite the fact that he had to wait three days, because of adverse winds, to enter the river, and even then grounded twice, eventually they found a perfect anchorage not more than twenty feet from the riverbank.

Cook had the ship lightened of all stores and ballast to enable her to be warped as far as possible up the beach. The damage was serious enough—much of the underwater sheathing had been stripped off and four planks were gone, but there was nothing the resourceful carpenters and blacksmiths couldn't cope with: their greatest difficulty was that they could work only at low tide, when the timbers were exposed.

Here, for the first time, they managed to establish a degree of rapport with the aborigines. They were, unlike the Polynesians, a shy, reserved, almost timorous people, although they did share to a marked degree the Tahitians' predilection for lifting things that didn't belong to them. Materially, Cook reckoned, they were the poorest people on earth—they had almost literally nothing: but Cook was astute enough to suggest that they probably led happier and more carefree lives than Europeans did.

This semitropical region—it must be remembered that Cook was now only fifteen degrees from the Equator—was a naturalist's joy. It teemed with wildlife and fish of all kinds. Mussels and turtles there were in abundance. There were scores of tropical varieties of birds. Here they saw their first crocodiles, their first flying foxes, their first dingoes, their first wallabies, their first kangaroos.

The scientists would dearly have loved to remain there for an indefinite period, but Cook would have none of it. Although the *Endeavour* had been well enough patched up, she was still in a basically unsatisfactory state and the nearest shipyard facilities were at Batavia, Java, in the Dutch East Indies—and Cook didn't even know how to get there, for there was as yet no proof that a passage existed between northern Australia and New Guinea. Further, he had only three months' provisions left. Worst of all, if he delayed too long, the southeast trades would change to the northwest trades and it would take the *Endeavour* forever to battle her way to Batavia against a head wind. So Cook left on August 6, having named their temporary port the Endeavour River. (The city that now stands on that site is called Cooktown.)

They moved on north—but very circumspectly indeed. There were more shoals, reefs, rocks and islets than ever. It took Cook a whole week to get through a particularly bad section which he christened the Labyrinth. The dangers were so great that at nighttime it was impossible to move at all. During the day, the pinnace, constantly sounding, went ahead of the *Endeavour,* while on the ship Cook himself was at the masthead, guiding and instructing all day long.

Even after the Labyrinth had been safely traversed, Cook's troubles with the Barrier Reef continued for over another week. At one point, thoroughly exasperated with the painfully slow progress they were making—it took them sixteen days to cover what a modern ship would easily do in one, although it has to be borne in mind, of course, that Cook was the first man ever to navigate through those infinitely treacherous seas—he took advantage of a gap in the Barrier Reef and broke through to the open ocean beyond.

But the distance between the land and the Barrier Reef steadily began to widen—the reef kept steadily north while the land was now tending west of north. Cook became acutely unhappy. Not only was he not now in a position to chart the course, but, much more seriously, if he stood too far out to sea and if there really was a strait between Australia and New Guinea he might miss it altogether and find himself sailing somewhere off the shores of New Guinea. Cook had no option. He turned and headed back in through the Great Barrier Reef—and in the process he almost lost the *Endeavour* on another coral reef.

However, his troubles on those, the worst and most hazardous waters he had ever encountered or was to encounter, were almost over. He closed in on land, and eventually it could be seen from the masthead that the mainland on the left had become so narrow that the sea could be seen on the other side. A little longer and there was no land at all on the port side. Cook had reached the northernmost tip of Australia and through a strait which he now named the Endeavour Strait had found a passageway through to the East Indies.

To this cape he gave the name of Cape York: the same name has since been given to the entire peninsula. There was one last thing that Cook did not neglect to do before he left Australia, just as he hadn't neglected to perform this duty in New Zealand and many Pacific islands: he took formal and ceremonial possession of it in the name of the crown. "New South Wales" he called it and referred to the eastern part of the Australian continent: in effect, he was claiming it all. It is rather a staggering thought that in the space of a few short months one man should add both New Zealand and Australia to the British crown.

Instead of heading directly for Batavia, Cook had to satisfy his insatiable curiosity and go and see for himself how far New Guinea lay to the north of Cape York—it had to be remembered that no one in the Western world had known until then whether Australia and New Guinea were one or not. More accurately, it is believed that some knew that Torres had indeed found a strait between New Guinea and Australia but were keeping the knowledge to themselves. One of those was reported to be Alexander Dalrymple, who had hoped to command the *Endeavour* himself and achieve fame by finding the Torres Strait. This information he had given to Banks, who had passed it on to Cook, who apparently distrusted the information as much as he distrusted Dalrymple. It is one of the more exquisite ironies of fate that it was to be Cook who, on his next and even greater voyage, was to demolish Dalrymple's dream of the Great Southern Continent.

Because of dangerous reefs, and waters so shallow that at times it was almost impossible to keep New Guinea in sight, Cook, with his typical perseverance, finally succeeded in effecting a landing. The natives of the Gulf of Papua, however, turned out to be so uncompromisingly hostile that Cook pursued the matter no further. He headed the *Endeavour* east, traversed the lengths of the Arafura and Timor seas and stopped briefly at the island of Suva, at that time under the control of the Dutch East India Company. Here Cook was hospitably received, being permitted to buy quantities of fresh meat, fruit and vegetables. The *Endeavour* reached Java Head on September 22, but so contrary were the winds and currents that she was unable to reach Batavia until October 10, the first civilized town they had

seen since leaving Rio de Janeiro almost two years previously.

Cook had already collected all the journals and diaries of his officers and men, and these, along with his own journals and the many charts he had drawn, he dispatched to the Admiralty in London by means of a Dutch ship, the *Kronenburg*. Cook's covering letter makes rather astonishing reading. Although he had no illusions as to the value of his charts—"the latitude and longitude of few parts of the world are better settled than these"—he is most extraordinarily deprecating about the importance of his discoveries. He seems almost apologetic about his failure to discover the Great Southern Continent, and, as for his other activities, he says: "The discoveries made in this voyage are not great," a quite remarkable statement from a man who had just annexed New Zealand and Australia for the British crown.

Cook, in his letter, is most complimentary about all his officers and men and equally so about the scientists. In the nature of things, there must have been some who were less than perfect, but Cook makes no mention of them: it is a mark of the man's fundamental generosity of nature. In all his letters, Cook permitted himself the expression of only one small piece of self-satisfaction: "I have the satisfaction to say that I have not lost one man by sickness during the whole voyage."

That was true. If one does not include epilepsy and alcoholic poisoning under the normal definition of sickness, then his statement is accurate—the others who had died had been drowned or perished from exposure, compounded by the consumption of large quantities of rum, in the snows of Tierra del Fuego. But that ever so slightly self-satisfied statement must remain as the saddest sentence that Cook ever wrote. From the health point of view, his troubles were only then beginning: it is ironic to reflect that after this epic world-girdling voyage he arrived in Batavia, that first outpost of civilization, with all his crew in perfect health, and yet when the *Endeavour* sailed from there it did so in the condition of a hospital ship.

Batavia (since the Dutch lost control of the

East Indies after the Second World War the town has been known as Djakarta) was at that time almost certainly the most unhealthy place in the world. The Dutch had built it on a flat low-lying plain after the model of one of their cities in Holland—almost every main street had its own canal running alongside it. But what worked in the cool northern climes of Amsterdam did not work in the steamy, enervated air of the tropics. The canals were filthy beyond belief, full of every imaginable type of refuse and sewage and were quite stagnant. They were therefore the ideal breeding ground for mosquitoes, germs and viruses of a large—and largely lethal—number of tropical diseases. Malaria, naturally, was everywhere, but dysentery appears to have been the chief killer. Banks maintains—and we have no reason to disbelieve him, he had an accurate and scientific mind—that out of every hundred troops who came out from Holland for garrison duty fifty would be dead at the end of the year, twenty-five in hospital and not more than ten fully fit for duty. Such appalling figures seem quite incredible, but no less a person than Cook himself bears him out: when he left Batavia, Dutch captains told him that he, Cook, could consider himself very lucky that half his crew were not dead.

When, repairs completed, the *Endeavour* sailed from Batavia just after Christmas, she had already lost seven of her complement and over forty were so seriously ill that they were unable to help work the ship. And the rest of the crew, Cook wrote, were in poor condition. The seven who died were the surgeon himself, Tupia and his servant, the astronomer Green's servant, and three seamen. Banks became critically ill and saved himself only by taking to the cooler and fresher air of the mountains and dosing himself with large quantities of quinine.

When Cook left Batavia for Cooktown he must—one assumes—have done so with heart-felt relief, confident that the worst lay behind. But the horrifying worst was yet to come. The journals for that ten-week trip between Batavia and the Cape of Good Hope make appalling reading. Four weeks out from Batavia a marine died, and within the next week ten more had died also, including Green, the astronomer, and Parkinson, the natural history draftsman. In the following month of February, twelve more members of the crew died, which meant that in that one—comparatively—brief voyage from the Indies to Africa one-quarter of the original ship's company died. At one particularly desperate stage in that voyage, there were only twelve people fit to work the ship, and even they were in a poor state of health.

Cook himself appears to have remained marvelously immune to sickness, and this may well have been the case: he does appear to have been possessed of an iron constitution. Equally well, he too may have been ill, but neither shown it nor mentioned it: when he had his right hand almost blown off by a gunpowder flask when surveying the Newfoundland coast or, later, when he was critically ill with a gallbladder infection, he does not at any time refer to his own sufferings.

The *Endeavour* arrived at Cape Town on March 14. Those who were still very seriously ill—there were about thirty of them—were put ashore to hospital. That meant that Cook was now without half his original crew and that there were less than twenty left aboard capable of working the ship. Fortunately, Cook was able to engage fresh crew in Cape Town to help him sail the *Endeavour* back to England.

Three more of the *Endeavour's* crew died while in hospital. In mid-April, Cook brought his sick aboard and sailed for England: some were still very ill men indeed, one to such an extent that he died even before they cleared Table Bay. On the way home, Lieutenant Hicks also died—he had been a consumptive for a long time. And then on July 12, 1771, two years and eleven months after sailing, the *Endeavour* was home again.

My Sixty-fifth Birthday

by SIR FRANCIS CHICHESTER

For most people the age of sixty starts to bring the cessation of adventure and rigorous activity. Francis Chichester, on the other hand, set off in Gipsy Moth IV *at age sixty-four to circle the world alone. It was a tumultuous but successful effort which earned him knighthood from Queen Elizabeth II. En route Chichester observed another milestone, his sixty-fifth birthday, and celebrated—in style.*

SEPTEMBER 17 brought my sixty-fifth birthday. I had a big time with a fresh-water wash, followed by opening Sheila's birthday present, a luxurious and most practical suit of silk pajamas. I shed a tear to think of her kindness and love, and all the happiness we have had together since 1937. I started celebrating my birthday by drinking a bottle of wine given me by Monica Cooper and other members of our map-making firm for a birthday present. That was at lunchtime. In the evening I wrote in my log:

"Well here I am, sitting in the cockpit with a champagne cocktail, and I have just toasted Sheila and Giles with my love. Full rig, smoking, smart new trousers, black shoes, etc. The only slipup is that I left my bowtie behind, and have had to use an ordinary black tie. I have

carried this 'smoking' (my green velvet designed and built by Scholte before I met Sheila in 1937) six times in *Gipsy Moth III* across the Atlantic, intending to dine in state one night, but this is the first time I have worn it in a *Gipsy Moth*. No dining in state, either. I don't get hungry in these eighty-five-degree Fahrenheit heats until the middle of the night, or early morning. But why worry, with my bottle of the best presented by my own yacht club, the Royal Western Yacht Club, by that old satyr Terence (I always expect him to pull a pipe from some hidden pocket and start serenading Cupid), my dear Coz's brandy to make the cocktail, a lovely calm evening, hammering along at a quiet seven knots on, extraordinary pleasure, a calm, nearly flat, sea. I will turn on some of the music Giles recorded for me. I meant to ask him to get a recording of Sheila and himself talking together, but forgot, which is not surprising, because the amount of thinking and planning for the voyage was unbelievable. A thousand items to remember or see to.

"This must be one of the greatest nights of my life—right in the middle of this wonderful venture—just passed by 100 miles the longest six-day run by any singlehander that I know of, and a great feeling of love and goodwill towards my family and friends. What does it matter if they are not here? I would not love them as I do in their absence, or at least I would not be aware of that, which seems to be what matters.

"People keep at me about my age. I suppose they think that I can beat age. I am not that foolish. Nobody, I am sure, can be more aware than I am that my time is limited. I don't think I can escape aging, but why beef about it? Our only purpose in life, if we are able to say such a thing, is to put up the best performance we can —in anything, and only in doing so lies satisfaction in living.

"Is it a mistake to get too fond of people? It tears me to shreds when I think of Sheila and Giles being dead. On the other hand, I keep on thinking of the happiness and pleasure I have had at various times with them, usually when doing something with them. That first voyage home from America with Sheila, just the two of us, keeps on recurring to me, all the little episodes, and the joy and comradeship of it. The same with the third passage back, with Giles. I wonder if I shall ever enjoy anything as much. I see that action appears a necessary ingredient for deep feeling. This sort of venture that I am now on is a way of life for me. I am a poor thing, incomplete, unfulfilled without it.

"It is too dark to see any more. Think of me —as the sky darkens, music playing, the perfect sail, and still half a bottle of the satyr's champagne to finish.

"Darkness came, alas, a bit too quickly— sudden nightfall is one of the bad features of the tropics. I love those long northern twilights."

For all that darkness came too soon, that was a magic evening. I had much to celebrate, not only my birthday, but my record run of the previous week. How often does a sailing man sit drinking champagne while his craft glides along at seven knots? The horizon looked a clean straight line, and the departing sun suffused some clouds with an orange glow. The moon was on its back above the sun's exit. That, I think, was about the first time on the voyage that I was at all sentimental—up to then it seemed to have been all technics and worry. It seems odd that it should take about three weeks of a voyage before one can

begin to enjoy it, but so it is, or seemed so then to me.

I could have done without a celebration hangover at 2:00 A.M., when a sharp squall of wind laid *Gipsy Moth* over on her side. I staggered out of my bunk with difficulty, as I was on the lee side of the boat and was still pretty full of brandy and bonhomie. I started looking for clothes, getting the best footholds I could at the side of the boat and on the bunk, but with a shot of panic in my vitals I realized that this was a serious emergency; there was no time for clothes. I grabbed a lifeline harness and put that on as I climbed into the cockpit. *Gipsy Moth* was pressed over on her side, with the sails dipping in the water and out of control of the self-steering gear. No wonder at that, because after I had released the self-steering gear from the tiller, I could not move the tiller even with a tiller line to help. The situation was serious, because if she went over further and the sails got completely below the water, the companion being wide open, the water could easily rush in there and the boat founder. *Gipsy Moth* was carrying every square foot of sail I had been able to set. I let go the mizzen staysail (350 square feet) with a run, and hauled it into the cockpit, which it half filled, until I could get at the mainsheet and pay off the main boom. Slowly the boat righted, and I was able to turn her downwind and engage the self-steering gear again to control her. This enabled me to get forward to drop the big 600-square-foot genoa. That left the staysail genoa and the mainsail. After the squall eased, I waited a few minutes because of the heavy rain, and by 0317 I had added the big jib and the mizzen. I was tempted to reset the mizzen staysail, but did not want to be turned out again that night for another shemozzle with the boat out of control, so left it down. As I turned in again, I made a note that I must devise a better arrangement for the tiller lines.

I was woken by the boom banging and the sails slatting in a calm, with *Gipsy Moth* headed nearly east. There were tropical showers drifting about, an overcast sky and a glassy look about the sea surface. But it looked finer ahead. My leg started hurting me again, and I wondered, did I

Sir Francis Chichester, navigator, map publisher and solo aviator, began sailing after the age of fifty. He organized and won the first singlehanded trans-Atlantic race in 1960, and then went on to become the first person to sail alone around the world with only one stop.

sprain it, or pull the old strain, hauling on the halyards during the night? I comforted myself by thinking that perhaps it was due simply to the champagne.

I felt no inclination to put away my glad rags of the previous night, but it had to be done, so I tidied up. Then I decided to bake some bread, made the dough and got the Primus under the oven going. It was not all that successful, for a series of squalls followed the calm, and perhaps the yeast jibbed at so much movement. I did the actual baking job at a mean angle of heel of thirty degrees.

My noon position on September 18 put me six degrees north, twenty-three degrees forty minutes west within six miles of exactly the same great-circle distance from Plymouth as is Newport, Rhode Island. In the 1964 Singlehanded Transatlantic Race, it took me thirty days to cover this distance, and now it had taken twenty-two days. That was a good thought, in spite of the squally, uneven weather. But I was still in the Doldrums and there was no sign of the tropical rain showers coming to an end. They could be seen in every direction. It was very tedious, the endless changing of the helm and trim before and after each squall. I was up and down to the deck all day, as each squall went through, like a damned jack-in-the-box. Of course, it was the pounding and bashing in a rough sea which I had to worry about; I didn't think that wind would damage the gear. I was feeling the physical strain of the incessant changing of sails at intervals throughout the day and night and cursed having a boat so much bigger than I had wished for, which was causing me the extra labor.

That night I found a Mother Carey's chicken (Wilson's stormy petrel) on the deck and moved it to a more comfortable berth on the weather side where it was more level than down on the lee side and the bird had more to hold on to. It felt woolly, and was a game chick, always good for an attempted peck. It flew off the deck in the end but seemed unhappy. A flying fish landed near me as I was working on the foredeck.

On September 19, I was headed by a southerly wind, and I was only able to make good a track of east-southeast. I could have done a little better on the other tack, but I preferred to make easting in preparation for being pushed westwards by the southeast trade wind, which I was due to reach at any moment.

Early in the morning of September 20, I decided to tack, and, after I had finished the tack, I spent half an hour trimming the sails and the self-steering gear. *Gipsy Moth* was hard on the wind to a twenty-two-knot breeze. I was having a lot of trouble trying to keep her headed close to the wind. *Gipsy Moth* was pounding severely, and every now and then a succession of three or four waves would knock her head closer to windward until she ended up pointing dead into wind, and stopped. At 10:40 that morning, I reckoned that I had sailed into the southeast trade-wind belt at last. I set a 300-foot jib in place of the storm jib. I complained in the log:

"I must be very feeble as it seems such a big effort; also I find it a great disadvantage having completely lost balance control in my feet. Anyway, enough for the ship for a while and now a turn for the Inner Man. A lovely fine day, blue and white; what a wonderful change."

In the evening, I set the mainsail in place of the trysail for the southeast trade wind. It was a lovely evening, and lovely sailing. *Gipsy Moth* was now on the wind doing 5½ knots, and headed S by W. It was now that I experienced one of the big setbacks of the voyage.

Let me explain the situation. From where I was then at four degrees north and twenty-one degrees west, the old clipper way curved slightly westward down through the South Atlantic to Ilha da Trinidade, from where the curve changed gently to the southeast, passing close to Tristan da Cunha Island to reach the Greenwich meridian at forty degrees south. The distance along this route from where I was to where the clipper way passed south of the Cape of Good Hope was roughly five thousand miles or 7.14 knots for seven hundred hours. The first fifteen hundred miles of this clipper way passed through the southeast trade-wind belt. Southeast was the direction of the cape, so both the clippers and *Gipsy Moth* would be hard on the wind for at least the first fifteen hundred miles. I had felt quite sure that this was one point of sailing on which *Gipsy Moth* would excel, and I had checked that she would sail nearly as close to the wind as a twelve-meter in a thirty-knot wind in the comparatively smooth water of The Solent. I had based my plans for a 100-day attempt on sailing much closer to the wind in this belt than the clippers could have done. In other words, I had planned to cut the corner and save no less than eight hundred miles on the way down to the cape. I trimmed up the ship carefully to sail as close as possible to the southeast wind. The wind had dropped to a gentle and ideal breeze and the sea had moderated. The waves were now quite small —ripples, I felt like calling them—but I found that they made *Gipsy Moth* hobbyhorse in such a way that three waves in succession would each knock ¾ knot off the speed. The first wave would cut the speed down from 5½ knots to 4¾, the second to 4 knots and the third to 3¼ knots. If there was a fourth or fourth and fifth they would bring the yacht up head to wind and it would stop dead. The only way of avoiding this with the self-steering gear in control was to head off the wind another twenty degrees. This meant that I could not sail any closer to the wind than the clippers, and the plan that I had set so much store on collapsed in ruins. This hobbyhorsing was the first of *Gipsy Moth*'s nasty tricks that I was to suffer from on the voyage.

It was a tiresome and trying period of the voyage. If I kept *Gipsy Moth* going fast on the wind, she slammed damnably into the seas, which worried me for the safety of her hull. Yet I had to keep going as fast as I could if I was not to fall hopelessly behind the clippers. I could make no good radio contacts, and I had trouble trying to charge the batteries. I could not get a good charge into them. At night I was troubled by cramp in my legs which would hit me after I had been asleep about two hours, and would let go only if I stood up. This meant that I never got more·than about two hours' sleep at a time. It was hot, and I sweated profusely; I wondered if my body might be losing too much salt. I decided to drink half a glassful of seawater a day to put back salt.

On the morning of September 21, I awoke to find the ship headed east with all the sails aback. While I was asleep, hobbyhorsing must have brought the ship's head up into the wind, and after she had stopped, she must have fallen back on the other tack. I released the main boom so as to let the mainsail come over completely and slowly wore the ship round downwind back on to her course. At noon, I saw a tanker, the last ship I was to see for two months. This was at two degrees nineteen minutes north, twenty-one degrees forty-three minutes west. She was the *African Neptune.* She turned and followed me, and came close up to leeward. I am always apprehensive when a steamer comes near the yacht in the open sea. If she comes up to windward of the boat, she takes all the wind away and the yacht loses control. The ship drifts slowly downwind, and the rolling yacht is liable to damage her crosstrees and rigging against the side of the ship, as happened to David Lewis in the 1960 Singlehanded Transatlantic Race. However, the *African Neptune* was well navigated and I need not have worried. The captain asked me if there was anything he could help me with by way of luxuries, etc., which I thought nice and kind of him. At the time, I was trying to make the bilge pump in the cockpit work, and I had the pieces scattered around. On seeing the ship approach, I went below to dig out my "number" GAKK, a hoist of flags; also a signaling lamp and a loud hailer. I tried speaking to them with the signaling lamp, but they took no notice of that. After the steamer had disappeared in the distance, I tackled the bilge pump again. There was a lot of bilge water due to seas washing over the deck and

swilling down the navel pipe, where the anchor chain emerges at the deck. I feared that I should have to dip the bilge water out with a bucket if I could not repair the pump. In the end, I discovered the trouble, which was that one of the rubber flap valves in the bilge pump was not fitting properly. I fixed this up, and the pump worked. Puffed up with my success, I then had a go at the beer keg. It was terrible in that heat to think of all the beer in the keg lying inaccessible. I looked for an air lock or a kink in the pipe down to the keg in the keel but could find nothing wrong there. I came to the conclusion that the CO_2 cylinder had leaked and there was no pressure to force the beer up.

That evening I logged:

"What I cannot understand is why I almost never have an appetite. Here it is 9:00 P.M. and 1¼ hours after dark, and I don't feel the least hungry. I had only two slices of wholemeal with trimmings for breakfast, one slice and one Ryvita with dates and cheese for lunch. Nothing for tea."

I crossed the line on September 22. That was fascinating. I went up to try for some sun shots at local noon, and first I was looking for the sun's reflection in the mirror of my sextant to the southward, as usual. I was amazed to find it in the northeast, then realized that I had overtaken the sun, sailing southward, and that it would pass to the northward of me. I started "shooting." As the sun passed the meridian, I had to swirl round as fast as I could—one minute I was facing northeast, and it seemed only seconds later that I was facing northwest. It is very difficult shooting in these conditions, because the way of telling if you are measuring to the sea vertically in line with the sun is to swing the sextant gently, like a pendulum, until you find the direction in which the height of the sun above the horizon is least. This pendulum sweep moves the sun's image in a flat arc above the horizon, and you must decide where the sun's image "kisses" the horizon.

For some days, I had been having a private race with the sun, which was on its way south for the northern winter. I won by the narrow margin

Sir Francis Chichester at the helm of Gypsy Moth V.

of twenty-two miles because the subsolar point—the point vertically beneath the sun on the earth's surface—was twenty-two miles north of the equator at noon that day. I stowed away my North Atlantic charts and fished out a set for the South Atlantic. It was a thrill changing from one ocean to another.

Navigating with the sun passing nearly overhead, it was wise to get some star sights as well, and, fortunately, I had a fine, starry night. I was wondering what *was* the bright star near Canopus, when I noticed it moving! How awesome those satellites are—I mean, the thought that man has put them up there! I think it is the star-like brightness which is most impressive.

It was now that *Gipsy Moth*'s second vicious habit began to take effect. Now and then when the wind eased, I would log that I was having some lovely sailing, but, alas, a few minutes or hours later there was sure to be a complaint about the difficulty of keeping *Gipsy Moth* to her heading. The log is littered with entries such as "*Gipsy Moth* keeps on edging up to the wind and slowing up then"; "I feel she is too much heeled, laboring and pinned down"; "The self-steering could not settle down and keep to a heading: too much weather helm"; "I see she is sailing too free now; I must have another go at her, drat it!"; "I could not stand the violent slamming which built up when the wind increased above twenty knots and the forty-degree heel is pretty excessive"; "I think the vane must be slipping in some of the big bumps"; "*Gipsy Moth* is sailing sixty-five degrees off the true wind." (She ought to have been sailing within fifty degrees of the true wind at the most.)

From now on, except when the wind dropped and the sea moderated, I had an almost endless struggle trying to keep *Gipsy Moth* to a heading close-hauled. I thought at the time that it was due to the self-steering gear being unable to hold the tiller. Eventually, however, I discovered the trouble. I was standing on the deck one day looking forward, when the wind increased suddenly in a puff from twenty knots to twenty-five knots. The boat heeled over more, and to my astonishment, I saw the bows slide over the water downwind about thirty degrees. It was like a knife spreading butter, sliding over a piece of bread. What had plagued and puzzled me became quite clear; there was a critical angle of heel for the boat. If the hull came a degree or two more upright, it would start griping up to windward and slowing up. If, however, the hull heeled over a degree or two more than this critical angle, the forepart of the boat slid off to leeward; the boat, lying more on its side, had quite different sailing characteristics, and would romp off at great speed on a heading thirty degrees downwind. On this heading, *Gipsy Moth* went at racing speed, but of course this was unfortunate if the heading I wanted was thirty degrees different. When I did discover this trick, it explained something else which had puzzled me. Normally, when sailing hard on the wind, if you want to ease off five or ten degrees, the drill is to slack the mainsail sheet, and the heading will at once ease off a few degrees downwind. With *Gipsy Moth IV,* it was necessary to do exactly the opposite; to head a few degrees *away* from the wind, it was necessary to harden in the sails! What happened was that this changed the angle of heel, and she would romp off downwind at a great pace.

On September 23, I lunched off my first crop of cress grown on the premises, and very good it was too, with Barmene, some mayonnaise, a little garlic and some raisins. I was determined to grow some more cress but was worried by the appalling lethargy which seemed to swamp me. Anything that required remembering and doing twice daily (watering cress, for instance) seemed a burden. It was hot, too hot to stay on deck long during the heat of the day, and pretty hot below—eighty-three degrees at 5:00 P.M. It would have been nice below if I could have opened the skylights, but spray showered in at once. Added to all this, I found it a treble burden

to do anything at all at a constant angle of heel between twenty and thirty degrees. I refreshed myself by pouring buckets of seawater over me in the cockpit.

I could not stand the violent slamming which built up when the wind increased above twenty knots, and the forty-degree angle of heel was excessive. But I told myself that I had got to get used to this, for these southeast trades are no zephyrs.

I decided to sort out my fruit, to remove anything that had gone bad. I found that I still had seven oranges, twelve apples, thirteen lemons and about a dozen grapefruit (but I forgot to count the grapefruit). Very little had gone bad. The fruits were in good nets, each piece wrapped in its own bit of tissue paper.

I tried, and failed, to call up Cape Town. The Cape Town operator said that he could hear me at Strength 2, and I could hear him faintly at times, but then a woman started a very loud, strident talk, which drowned everything.

There were good moments too, though. The night of September 23–24 was lovely, and I felt that I could stay in the cockpit all night. *Gipsy Moth* was sailing beautifully, making 6⅔ knots. The moon's shadow was a perfect curve on the well-setting mainsail, and the water was smooth-ish, which meant little slamming. I reckoned that we should be on the wind for another 1,250 miles.

I had a triumph in getting my old electric clock to go again. I first had this clock in *Gipsy Moth II* in 1957, and it wintered each year in my bedroom at home. But it had stopped going. I turned the pressurized silicone spray into the regulating hole at the back and gave the works full blast. That started it again, and I hoped that it might have a new lease of life. I thought of Joshua Slocum and his one-handed clock which he boiled in oil.

September 24 was the end of my fourth week at sea. I had sailed 3,887 miles at an average speed of 138.6 miles per day. I broke my usual rule of not drinking until evening. It was a maddening day of setting and resetting sails, and I could not get *Gipsy Moth* to hold the course I wanted. In the end in disgust, I left her to it and went below to have a late lunch, or early tea, of a gin and lime and my last bit but one of the Scottish cheddar, some of the best cheese I have ever come across. I finished the fresh butter. I had kept the English brand till last, and none of it ever went rancid, which I thought pretty amazing in the tropics.

I had more trouble with the self-steering. The tiller line stranded, and I fitted a new one with some difficulty—it was like trying to control a half-broken horse without a bridle. I tinkered with the corner block, trying to improve the lead, but the difficulty was that as soon as I got on to the end of the counter, *Gipsy Moth* would first try to shake me off, bucking to shake my teeth loose, then she would bring herself up into the wind until I had to make a rush for the tiller to avoid getting aback or in irons. I tallowed the tiller lines where they were chafing most, and wished I had thought of this before. I tried again to contact Cape Town by radio, but again a powerful woman's voice on the Cape Town frequency blotted out everything.

On Sunday, September 25, I was woken suddenly by the table clock capsizing on my belly. This stirred me into getting to work. *Gipsy Moth* was lying quietly, and although there were some heavy black clouds about, they were only a few. I unreefed the mainsail and set the genoa staysail in place of the smaller one. Then I tackled a job that I'd been dodging for some time—the eggs.

I could not stand it any longer; either the cause of that stink would have to go overboard, or I should. So I turned out the box and found sundry smashed ones, which had reached a nearly audible state of putridity. I was worried about my eggs. The beeswax coating which a friend had proposed for some of them seemed a big failure; the yolks were stuck to the shell inside, and some of the eggs had black spots, which I took for mildew, inside. However, I had an omelet from what I could get out of two, and it seemed pretty fair. The trouble with eggs is that one's imagination makes one feel sick at the suggestion of a bad egg, though it may be quite hale and hearty in fact. I tidied up the box, throwing out all broken or obviously bad ones, and hoped for the best.

The wind at this time seemed to blow up to Force 6 or so every night; I noticed that the barometer would drop two or three millibars in the afternoon and then rise again after dark. On that Sunday night, it blew up in the usual way, and I wondered if my full rig would ride it out. The going became "slammy" with a wind increase from twenty to twenty-four knots, but I decided that this was due to a black cloud passing overhead, and that the blow would not last long. It was a pity to disarrange the rig if it could be avoided. So I left things as they were, and all was well. The change in temperature as we sailed south was noticeable, and I began sleeping under a woolen blanket.

It was not comfortable sailing in the strong winds. Big "slams" would slow the boat right down, and then she would pinch up to windward as if the self-steering had been "forced." I thought, indeed, that this was what was happening, and I would go and give the self-steering a downwind twitch. I felt that I needed both a monkey and an elephant for supplementary crew —the monkey to tackle things when *Gipsy Moth* was heeled to thirty-five degrees or more, and the elephant to take the helm when it got out of control in a squall.

On Monday night (September 26), I had just settled nicely in my berth, absorbed by Maigret and *La Grande Perche,* when there was a big bang astern. A big sail flap followed, and I thought that something in the self-steering gear had burst. I got on deck as fast as I could, but it was no weather to be there without a safety belt. I was relieved to find that it was only a tiller line that had broken. I robbed one of the spinnaker-pole guys, and rigged that hoping that the old rope had just perished and that the new rope would hold. It was quite a long job, in a strong wind and rough sea, but I got it done and got back to my berth feeling so sleepy that I could hardly keep my eyes open. I was not allowed to sleep for long —*Gipsy Moth* was getting such a bashing that I could not stand it. I went on deck again and dropped the mainsail, and then I did manage to get a bit of rest.

I got up after a couple of hours, intending to go on deck and get the mainsail up again, but I decided to have a cup of hot chocolate first. The wind increased to twenty-five knots while I sipped my chocolate, so I hoisted the small stay-sail and left the main down. That morning might have seen the end of the voyage as far as I was concerned, for I had a narrow escape in a nasty, though rather absurd, accident. The weather continued dirty, and *Gipsy Moth* was much thrown about. I went to the head (lavatory) and the door was twice thrown open, and I pushed it shut. Without warning, the door burst open again, smashed back downhill from behind me, and the handle struck me a crack on the forehead, sending my spectacles flying. The blow cut my head about two inches above my eye and left me feeling nearly stunned. Amazingly, the spectacles were not damaged, and some dabbing with disinfectant seemed all that the cut needed. But my escape seemed a miracle—supposing that handle had caught me on the eye, after smashing through my glasses!

My big event next day was a shave. I could not use the mirror in the head, because there was no means of keeping myself in position for shaving when *Gipsy Moth* was heeled over. So I used a bucket, sitting in the lounge with a hand mirror. I mention this because some think that it is only a matter of picking up a razor to shave when sailing and wonder why yachting men are so slovenly!

The heavy-duty bearings in the self-steering gear seemed to be clanking a lot, and I worried a good deal about the gear. There was so much of it to go wrong.

In spite of the efforts I had made to sort out my eggs, all was not well in the egg box. I couldn't stand the smell in the saloon, so I humped the box to the cockpit and found a niche for them in the afterhatch. Fourteen dozen eggs, apart from whether they are bad, make quite a lumpy package to handle gingerly in roughish going. I believe that this big package (too big) was dropped en route to the boat or before sailing, and that the smell came mostly if not wholly from cracked eggs. Those eggs survived only a few days longer. The smell grew worse and worse, and finally I dumped the lot in the ocean and watched the box dwindle to a speck as we

sailed on. It isn't often one has to throw away the best part of fourteen dozen eggs. They were a loss.

Winding up the story of my eggs, I have got a little ahead of events. An odd thing happened in the afternoon after my shave. I decided to pump the bilge to check that the pump was working. I didn't expect to pump more than a few strokes, for I glance at the bilges regularly, and there was hardly any water there when I looked that morning. I began pumping more or less automatically and went on in a sort of daydream, until suddenly I became aware that I had been pumping for a long time. I thought that maybe one of the pump valves was not working properly and that I was just pumping the same water to and fro, so I went forward to hunt for a stick to poke the end of the pipe. I found water running out of the head! I must have left the inlet seacock turned on when I gave up trying to shave there, and transferred myself, razor and shaving things to the cabin. The open seacock had been quietly filling up the boat ever since.

On my thirty-second day out (September 28), I was 1,940 miles from where I should cross the Greenwich meridian at forty degrees south. *Cutty Sark,* on her thirty-second day, was 1,900 miles from where she crossed the meridian. So I figured that the *Cutty Sark* was only some forty miles ahead of me after thirty-two days. The weather grew much colder, and I began wearing woolen shirt and trousers below deck. I felt that the Antarctic was creeping up!

After my encouraging calculation about the *Cutty Sark* on September 28, the 29 began badly, with the discovery that the port aft settee locker was well flooded. I decided that this was due to the main boom flogging during a sail change which had caused the boom downhaul to draw an eyebolt partly from the deck. The mishap was a pity, because the locker was full of books, and they were all messed up. I took the precaution of pumping the bilge again, and found it took thirty-five strokes to clear it. I hoped that it was water from the heads which had not found its way aft when I had pumped out the day before.

After this work with the pump, I noticed that I kept having to hitch up my pants. I measured my waist, and found that it was down to 30¾ inches—pretty ladylike, I thought. I had certainly lost weight, which didn't surprise me, but I wished that I could find more appetite for food. I enjoyed some of my meals, but there were many days when I had more or less to force myself to eat. I stood myself a gin, which was a mistake, for I found that gin usually seemed to bring a squall and hard work on deck.

This gin ran true to form, bringing a gale from 160 degrees, roughly south-southeast, and a horrible sea. The gale came at me from where I wanted to go, so there was not much that I could do about it for a while. I tried to stay in my bunk but was forced out by cramp in my right leg. Wary of the troubles that seem to be in store when I drink gin (or champagne) on board, I gave myself a brandy, hot, "with" for a change. I can't remember what Jorrocks meant by "with," but I think it was sugar and lemon. Anyway, mine was a very good drink to hearten a fellow. The gale moderated a bit, but there was still a rough sea, and we jogged along under reefed mizzen and spitfire jib. The brandy stimulated me to do some deckwork, and I greased and oiled two winches which had refused to work during the night. I also fixed another cord to the self-steering gear. This was most necessary work, for the winches and the self-steering gear had given me hell in a shemozzle during the night. What happened was that I did not think it would pay to tack, so I turned in, to be awakened by the flap when the boat tacked herself. In the darkness, the rattle and flap was enough to panic an elephant. I whipped on a lifeline harness round my waist, but had no time to dress, and arrived on deck barefooted in pajamas. As the headsails were aback, I decided to accept the situation and leave the yacht on the port tack. Neither winch would work. Then the self-steering gear jibed. The steering oar lay hard over to one side, and my most herculean hauling couldn't center it. I had to fiddle with tiller lines to get the boat sailing again while I dealt with the self-steering. This was difficult, because while the self-steering was connected to the tiller, the load on the tiller was very great, and it was hard to cope by using tiller lines. And all the time, I was struggling with torches, my powerful one, to try to see what was wrong with the self-steering, and an ordinary one for the usual deckwork. At some time during all this, an empty bottle, left on the cockpit seat to dry for paraffin storage, was knocked off on to my toe (it gave me a black toe). This last incident did me good, for it emphasized the absurdity of taking it all too seriously. But I could scarcely be surprised at losing weight.

Halfway

by THOR HEYERDAHL

In 1947, Norwegian anthropologist Thor Heyerdahl and five companions set sail from the port of Callao in Peru on a balsa raft christened Kon-Tiki. *Their goal: to duplicate the forty-three-hundred-mile journey between Peru and Polynesia which Kon-Tiki made in the fifth century. Heyerdahl and company made the trip in just about one hundred days, and, at the halfway mark, he set down these thoughts.*

THE weeks passed. We saw no sign either of a ship or of drifting remains to show that there were other people in the world. The whole sea was ours, and, with all the gates of the horizon open, real peace and freedom were wafted down from the firmament itself.

It was as though the fresh salt tang in the air, and all the blue purity that surrounded us, had washed and cleansed both body and soul. To us on the raft, the great problems of civilized man appeared false and illusory—like perverted products of the human mind. Only the elements mattered. And the elements seemed to ignore the little raft. Or perhaps they accepted it as a natural object, which did not break the harmony of the sea but adapted itself to current and sea like bird and fish. Instead of being a fearsome enemy, flinging itself at us, the elements had become a reliable friend which steadily and surely helped us onward. While wind and waves pushed and propelled, the ocean current lay under us and pulled, straight toward our goal.

If a boat had cruised our way on any average day out at sea, it would have found us bobbing quietly up and down over a long, rolling swell covered with little white-crested waves, while the trade wind held the orange sail bent steadily toward Polynesia.

Those on board would have seen, at the stern of the raft, a brown-bearded man with no clothes on, either struggling desperately with a long steering oar while he hauled on a tangled rope, or, in calm weather, just sitting on a box dozing in the hot sun and keeping a leisurely hold on the steering oar with his toes.

If this man happened not to be Bengt, the latter would have been found lying on his stomach in the cabin door with one of his seventy-three sociological books. Bengt had further been appointed steward and was responsible for fixing the daily rations. Herman might have been found anywhere at any time of the day—at the masthead with meteorological instruments, underneath the raft with diving goggles on checking a centerboard, or in tow in the rubber dinghy, busy with balloons and curious measuring apparatuses. He was our technical chief and responsible for meteorological and hydrographical observations.

Knut and Torstein were always doing something with their wet dry batteries, soldering irons and circuits. All their wartime training was required to keep the little radio station going in spray and dew a foot above the surface of the water.

Every night they took turns sending our reports and weather observations out into the ether, where they were picked up by chance radio amateurs who passed the reports on to the Meteorological Institute in Washington and other destinations. Erik was usually sitting patching sails and splicing ropes, or carving in wood and drawing sketches of bearded men and odd fish. And at noon every day, he took the sextant and mounted a box to look at the sun and find out how far we had moved since the day before. I myself had enough to do with the logbook and reports and the collecting of plankton, fishing and filming. Every man had his sphere of responsibility, and no one interfered with the others' work. All difficult jobs, like steering watch and cooking, were divided equally. Every man had two hours each day and two hours each night at the steering oar. And duty as cook was in accordance with a daily roster. There were few laws and regulations on board, except that the night watch must have a rope round his waist, that the lifesaving rope had its regular place, that all meals were consumed outside the cabin wall and that the "right place" was only at the farthest end of the logs astern. If an important decision was to be taken on board, we called a powwow in Indian style and discussed the matter together before anything was settled.

An ordinary day on board the *Kon-Tiki* began with the last night watch shaking some life into the cook, who crawled out sleepily on to the dewy deck in the morning sun and began to gather flying fish. Instead of eating the fish raw, according to both Polynesian and Peruvian recipes, we fried them over a small Primus stove at the bottom of a box which stood lashed fast to the deck outside the cabin door. This box was our kitchen. Here there was usually shelter from the southeast trade wind which regularly blew on

to our other quarter. Only when the wind and sea juggled too much with the Primus flame did it set fire to the wooden box, and once, when the cook had fallen asleep, the whole box became a mass of flames which spread to the very wall of the bamboo cabin. But the fire on the wall was quickly put out when the smoke poured into the hut, for, after all, we had never far to go for water on board the *Kon-Tiki.*

The smell of fried fish seldom managed to wake the snorers inside the bamboo cabin, so the cook usually had to stick a fork into them or sing "Breakfast's ready!" so out of tune that no one could bear to listen to him any longer. If there were no sharks' fins alongside the raft, the day began with a quick plunge in the Pacific, followed by breakfast in the open air on the edge of the raft.

The food on board was above reproach. The cuisine was divided into two experimental menus, one dedicated to the quartermaster and the twentieth century, one to Kon-Tiki and the fifth century. Torstein and Bengt were the subjects of the first experiment and restricted their diet to the slim little packages of special provisions which we had squeezed down into the hole between the logs and the bamboo deck. Fish and marine food, however, had never been their strong suit. Every few weeks, we untied the lashings which held down the bamboo deck and took out fresh supplies, which we lashed fast forward of the bamboo cabin. The tough layer of asphalt outside the cardboard proved resistant, while the hermetically sealed tins lying loose beside it were penetrated and ruined by the seawater which continually washed round our provisions.

Kon-Tiki, on his original voyage across the sea, had no asphalt or hermetically sealed tins; nevertheless, he had no serious food problems. In those days, too, supplies consisted of what the men took with them from land and what they obtained for themselves on the voyage. We may assume that, when Kon-Tiki sailed from the coast of Peru after his defeat by Lake Titicaca, he had one of two objectives in mind. As the spiritual representative of the sun among a solely sun-worshiping people, it is very probable that he ventured straight out to sea to follow the sun itself on its journey in the hope of finding a new and more peaceful country. An alternative possibility for him was to sail his rafts up the coast of South America in order to found a new kingdom out of reach of his persecutors. Clear of the dangerous rocky coast and hostile tribes along the shore, he would, like ourselves, fall an easy prey to the southeast trade wind and the Humboldt Current, and, in the power of the elements, he would drift in exactly the same large semicircle right toward the sunset.

Whatever these sun worshipers' plans were when they fled from their homeland, they certainly provided themselves with supplies for the voyage. Dried meat and fish and sweet potatoes were the most important part of their primitive diet. When the raftsmen of that time put to sea along the desert coast of Peru, they had ample supplies of water on board. Instead of clay vessels, they generally used the skin of giant bottle gourds, which was resistant to bumps and blows, while even more adapted to raft use were the thick canes of giant bamboos. They perforated through all the knots in the center and poured water in through a little hole at the end, which they stopped with a plug or with pitch or resin. Thirty or forty of these thick bamboo canes could be lashed fast along the raft under the bamboo deck, where they lay shaded and cool with fresh seawater—about seventy-nine degrees Fahrenheit in the Equatorial Current—washing about them. A store of this kind would contain twice as much water as we ourselves used on our whole voyage, and still more could be taken by simply lashing on more bamboo canes in the water underneath the raft, where they weighed nothing and occupied no space.

We found that after two months, fresh water began to grow stale and have a bad taste. But by then one is well through the first ocean sea, in which there is little rain, and has arrived in regions where heavy rain showers can maintain the water supply. We served out a good quart of water per man daily, and it was by no means always that the ration was consumed.

Even if our predecessors had started from land with inadequate supplies, they would have managed well enough as long as they drifted across the sea with the current, in which fish abounded. There was not a day on our whole voyage on which fish were not swimming round the raft and could not easily be caught. Scarcely a day passed without flying fish, at any rate, coming on board of their own accord. It even happened that large bonitos, delicious eating, swam on board with the masses of water that came from astern and lay kicking on the raft when the water had vanished down between the logs as a sieve. To starve to death was impossible.

The old natives knew well the device which many shipwrecked men hit upon during the war —chewing thirst-quenching moisture out of raw fish. One can also press the juices out by twisting pieces of fish in a cloth, or, if the fish is large, it is fairly simple matter to cut holes in its side, which soon become filled with ooze from the fish's lymphatic glands. It does not taste good if one has anything better to drink, but the percentage of salt is so low that one's thirst is quenched.

The necessity for drinking water was greatly reduced if we bathed regularly and lay down wet in the shady cabin. If a shark was patrolling majestically round about us and preventing a real plunge from the side of the raft, one had only to lie down on the logs aft and get a good grip of the ropes with one's fingers and toes. Then we got several bathfuls of crystal-clear Pacific pouring over us every few seconds.

When tormented by thirst in a hot climate, one generally assumes that the body needs water, and this may often lead to immoderate inroads on the water ration without any benefit whatever. On really hot days in the tropics, you can pour tepid water down your throat till you taste it at the back of your mouth, and you are just as thirsty. It is not liquid the body needs then, but, curiously enough, salt. The special rations we had on board included salt tablets to be taken regularly on particularly hot days, because perspiration drains the body of salt. We experienced days like this when the wind had died away and the sun blazed down on the raft without mercy. Our water ration could be ladled into us till it squelched in our stomachs, but our throats malignantly demanded much more. On such days, we added from 20 to 40 percent of bitter, salt seawater to our freshwater ration and found, to our surprise, that this brackish water quenched our thirst. We had the taste of seawater in our mouths for a long time afterward but never felt unwell, and, moreover, we had our water ration considerably increased.

One morning, as we sat at breakfast, an unexpected sea splashed into our gruel and taught us quite gratuitously that the taste of oats removed the greater part of the sickening taste of seawater!

The old Polynesians had preserved some curious traditions, according to which their earliest forefathers, when they came sailing across the sea, had with them leaves of a certain plant which they chewed, with the result that their thirst disappeared. Another effect of the plant was that in an emergency they could drink seawater without being sick. No such plants grew in the South Sea islands; they must, therefore, have originated in their ancestors' homeland. The Polynesian historians repeated these statements so often that modern scientists investigated the matter and came to the conclusion that the only known plant with such an effect was the coca plant, which grew only in Peru. And in prehistoric Peru, this very coca plant, which contains cocaine, was regularly used both by the Incas and by their vanished forerunners, as is shown by discoveries in pre-Inca graves. On exhausting mountain journeys and sea voyages, they took with them piles of these leaves and chewed them for days on end to remove the feelings of thirst and weariness. And over a fairly short period, the chewing of coca leaves will even allow one to drink seawater with a certain immunity.

We did not test coca leaves on board the *Kon-Tiki,* but we had on the foredeck large wicker baskets full of other plants, some of which had left a deeper imprint on the South Sea islands. The baskets stood lashed fast in the lee of the cabin wall, and as time passed, yellow shoots and green leaves of potatoes and coconuts shot up higher and higher from the wickerwork. It was like a little tropical garden on board the wooden raft.

When the first Europeans came to the Pacific islands, they found large plantings of sweet potatoes on Easter Island and in Hawaii and New Zealand, and the same plant was also cultivated on the other islands, but only within the Polynesian area. It was quite unknown in the part of the world which lay farther west. The sweet potato was one of the most important cultivated plants in these remote islands where the people otherwise lived mainly on fish, and many of the Polynesians' legends centered round this plant. According to tradition, it had been brought by no less a personage than Tiki himself, when he came with his wife Pani from their ancestors' original homeland, where the sweet potato had been an important article of food. New Zealand legends affirm that the sweet potato was brought over the sea in vessels which were not canoes but consisted of "wood bound together with ropes."

Now, as is known, America is the only place in the rest of the world where the potato grew before the time of the Europeans. And the sweet potato Tiki brought with him to the islands, *Ipomoea batatas,* is exactly the same as that which the Indians have cultivated in Peru from the oldest times. Dried sweet potatoes were the most important travel provisions both for the seafarers of Polynesia and for the natives in old Peru. In the South Sea islands the sweet potato will grow only if carefully tended by man, and, as it cannot withstand seawater, it is idle to explain its wide distribution over these scattered islands by declaring that it could have drifted over four thousand sea miles with ocean currents from Peru. This attempt to explain away so important a clue to the Polynesians' origin is particularly futile, seeing that philologists have pointed out that on all the widely scattered South Sea islands the name of the sweet potato is *kumara,* and *kumara* is just what the sweet potato was called among the old Indians in Peru. The name followed the plant across the sea.

The closer we came into contact with the sea and what had its home there, the less strange it became and the more at home we ourselves felt. And we learned to respect the old primitive peoples who lived in close converse with the Pacific and therefore knew it from a quite different standpoint from our own. True, we have now estimated its salt content and given tunnies and dolphins Latin names. They had not done that. But, nevertheless, I am afraid that the picture the primitive peoples had of the sea was a truer one than ours.

There were not many fixed marks out here at sea. Waves and fish, sun and stars, came and went. There was not supposed to be land of any sort in the forty-three hundred sea miles that separated the South Sea islands from Peru. We were therefore greatly surprised when we approached one hundred degrees west and discovered that a reef was marked on the Pacific chart right ahead of us on the course we were following. It was marked as a small circle, and, as the chart had been issued the same year, we looked up the reference in *Sailing Directions for South America*. We read that "breakers were reported in 1906 and again in 1926 to exist about 600 miles southwestward of Galapagos Islands, in latitude 6° 42′ S., longitude 99° 43′ W. In 1927 a steamer passed one mile westward of this position but saw no indication of breakers, and in 1934 another passed one mile southward and saw no evidence of breakers. The motor vessel 'Cowrie,' in 1935, obtained no bottom at 160 fathoms in this position."

According to the chart, the place was clearly still regarded as a doubtful one for shipping, but, as a deep-draft vessel runs a greater risk by going too near a shoal than we should with a raft, we decided to steer straight for the point marked on the chart and see what we found. The reef was marked a little farther north than the point we seemed to be making for, so we laid the steering oar over to starboard and trimmed the square sail so that the bow pointed roughly north and we took sea and wind from the starboard side. Now it came about that a little more Pacific splashed into our sleeping bags than we were accustomed to, especially as at the same time the weather began to freshen considerably. But we saw to our satisfaction that the *Kon-Tiki* could be maneuvered surely and steadily at a surprisingly wide angle into the wind, so long as the wind was still on our quarter. Otherwise, the sail swung round, and we had the same mad circus

business to get the raft under control again.

For two days and nights, we drove the raft north-northwest. The seas ran high and became incalculable as the trade wind began to fluctuate between southeast and east, but we were lifted up and down over all the waves that rushed against us. We had a constant lookout at the masthead, and when we rode over the ridges the horizon widened considerably. The crests of the seas reached six feet above the level of the roof of the bamboo cabin, and, if two vigorous seas rushed together, they rose still higher in combat and flung up a hissing watery tower which might burst down in unexpected directions. When night came, we barricaded the doorway with provision boxes, but it was a wet night's rest. We had hardly fallen asleep when the first crash on the bamboo wall came, and, while a thousand jets of water sprayed in like a fountain through the bamboo wickerwork, a foaming current rushed in over the provisions and on to us.

"Ring up the plumber," I heard a sleepy voice remark, as we hunched ourselves up to give the water room to run out through the floor. The plumber did not come, and we had a lot of bathwater in our beds that night. A big dolphin actually came on board unintentionally in Herman's watch.

Next day, the seas were less confused, as the trade wind had decided that it would now blow for a time from due east. We relieved one another at the masthead, for now we might expect to reach the point we were making for late in the afternoon. We noticed more life than usual in the sea that day. Perhaps it was only because we kept a better lookout than usual.

During the forenoon, we saw a big swordfish approaching the raft close to the surface. The two sharp pointed fins which stuck up out of the water were six feet apart, and the sword looked almost as long as the body. The swordfish swept in a curve close by the man at the helm and disappeared behind the wave crests. When we were having a rather wet and salty midday meal, the carapace, head and sprawling fins of a large sea turtle were lifted up by a hissing sea right in front of our noses. When that wave gave place to two others, the turtle was gone as suddenly as it had appeared. This time too we saw the gleaming whitish green of dolphins' bellies tumbling about in the water below the armored reptile. The area was unusually rich in tiny flying fish an inch long, which sailed along in big shoals and often came on board. We also noted single skuas and were regularly visited by frigate birds, with forked tails like giant swallows, which cruised over the raft. Frigate birds are usually regarded as a sign that land is near, and the optimism on board increased.

"Perhaps there is a reef or a sandbank there all the same," some of us thought. And the most optimistic said: "Suppose we find a little green grassy island—one can never know since so few people have been here before. Then we'll have discovered a new land—Kon-Tiki Island!"

From noon onward, Erik was more and more diligent in climbing up on the kitchen box and standing blinking through the sextant. At 6:20 P.M. he reported our position as latitude six degrees forty-two minutes south by longitude ninety-nine degrees forty-two minutes west. We were one sea mile due east of the reef on the chart. The bamboo yard was lowered and the sail rolled up on deck. The wind was due east and would take us slowly right to the place. When the sun went down swiftly into the sea, the full moon in turn shone out in all its brilliance and lit up the surface of the sea, which undulated in black and silver from horizon to horizon. Visibility from the masthead was good. We saw breaking seas everywhere in long rows, but no regular surf which would indicate a reef or shoal. No one would turn in; all stood looking out eagerly, and two or three men were aloft at once.

As we drifted in over the center of the marked area, we sounded all the time. All the lead sinkers we had on board were fastened to the end of a fifty-four-thread silk rope more than five hundred fathoms long, and, even if the rope hung rather aslant on account of the raft's leeway, at any rate the lead hung at a depth of some four hundred fathoms. There was no bottom east of the place, or in the middle of it, or west of it. We took one last look over the surface of the sea, and, when we had assured ourselves that we could safely call the area surveyed and free

from shallows of any kind, we set sail and laid the oar over in its usual place, so that wind and sea were again on our port quarter.

And so we went on with the raft on her natural free course. The waves came and went as before between the open logs aft. We could now sleep and eat dry, even if the heaving seas round us took charge in earnest and raged for several days while the trade wind vacillated from east to southeast.

On this little sailing trip up to the spurious reef, we had learned quite a lot about the effectiveness of the centerboards as a keel, and when, later in the voyage, Herman and Knut dived under the raft together and salved the fifth centerboard, we learned still more about these curious pieces of board, something which no one has understood since the Indians themselves gave up this forgotten sport. That the board did the work of a keel and allowed the raft to move at an angle to the wind—that was plain sailing. But when the old Spaniards declared that the Indians to a large extent "steered" their balsa rafts on the sea with "certain centerboards which they pushed down into the chinks between the timbers," this sounded incomprehensible both to us and to all who had concerned themselves with the problem. As the centerboard was simply held tight in a narrow chink, it could not be turned sideways and serve as a helm.

We discovered the secret in the following manner: the wind was steady and the sea had gone down again, so that the *Kon-Tiki* had kept a steady course for a couple of days without our touching the lashed steering oar. We pushed the recovered centerboard down into a chink aft, and in a moment the *Kon-Tiki* altered course several degrees from west toward northwest and proceeded steadily and quietly on her new course. If we pulled this centerboard up again, the raft swung back on to her previous course. But if we pulled it only halfway up, the raft swung only halfway back on her old course. By simply raising and lowering the centerboards, we could effect changes of course and keep to them without touching the steering oar.

This was the Incas' ingenious system. They had worked out a simple system of balances by which pressure of the wind on the sail made the mast the fixed point. The two arms were respectively the raft forward of and the raft aft of the mast. If the aggregate centerboard surface aft was heavier, the bow swung freely round with the wind; but if the centerboard surface forward was heavier, the stern swung round with the wind. The centerboards which are nearest the mast have, of course, the least effect on account of the relation between arm and power. If the wind was due astern, the centerboards ceased to be effective, and then it was impossible to keep the raft steady without continually working the steering oar. If the raft lay thus at full length, she was a little too long to ride the seas freely. As the cabin door and the place where we had meals were on the starboard side, we always took the seas on board on our port quarter.

We could certainly have continued our voyage by making the steersman stand and pull a centerboard up and down in a chink instead of hauling sidewise on the ropes of the steering oar, but we had now grown so accustomed to the steering oar that we just set a general course with the centerboards and preferred to steer with the oar.

The next great stage on our voyage was as invisible to the eye as the shoal which existed only on the map. It was the forty-fifth day at sea; we had advanced from the seventy-eighth degree of longitude to the one hundred-eighth and were exactly halfway to the first islands ahead. There were over two thousand sea miles between us and South America to the east, and it was the same distance on to Polynesia in the west. The nearest land in any direction was the Galapagos Islands to east-northeast and Easter Island due south, both more than five hundred sea miles away on the boundless ocean. We had not seen a ship, and we never did see one, because we were off the routes of all ordinary shipping traffic in the Pacific.

But we did not really feel these enormous distances, for the horizon glided along with us unnoticed as we moved and our own floating world remained always the same—a circle flung up to the vault of the sky with the raft itself as center, while the same stars rolled on over us night after night.

When the sea was not too rough, we were often out in the little rubber dinghy taking photographs. I shall not forget the first time the sea was so calm that two men felt like putting the balloonlike little thing into the water and going for a row. They had hardly got clear of the raft when they dropped the little oars and sat roaring with laughter. And, as the swell lifted them away and they disappeared and reappeared among the seas, they laughed so loud every time they caught a glimpse of us that their voices rang out over the desolate Pacific. We looked around us with mixed feelings and saw nothing comic but our own hirsute faces; but as the two in the dinghy should be accustomed to those by now, we began to have a lurking suspicion that they had suddenly gone mad. Sunstroke, perhaps. The two fellows could hardly scramble back on board the *Kon-Tiki* for sheer laughter and, gasping, with tears in their eyes they begged us just to go and see for ourselves.

Two of us jumped down into the dancing rubber dinghy and were caught by a sea which lifted us clear. Immediately we sat down with a bump and roared with laughter. We had to scramble back on the raft as quickly as possible and calm the last two who had not been out yet, for they thought we had all gone stark staring mad.

It was ourselves and our proud vessel which made such a completely hopeless, lunatic impression on us the first time we saw the whole thing at a distance. We had never before had an outside view of ourselves in the open sea. The logs of timber disappeared behind the smallest waves, and, when we saw anything at all, it was the low cabin with the wide doorway and the bristly roof of leaves that bobbed up from among the seas. The raft looked exactly like an old Norwegian hayloft lying helpless, drifting about in the open sea—a warped hayloft full of sunburned bearded ruffians. If anyone had come paddling after us at sea in a bathtub, we should have felt the same spontaneous urge to laughter. Even an ordinary swell rolled halfway up the cabin wall and looked as if it would pour in unhindered through the wide-open door in which the bearded fellows lay gaping. But then the crazy craft came up to the surface again, and the vagabonds lay there as dry, shaggy, and intact as before. If a higher sea came racing by, cabin and sail and the whole mast might disappear behind the mountain of water, but just as certainly the cabin with its vagabonds would be there again next moment. The situation looked bad, and we could not realize that things had gone so well on board the zany craft.

Next time we rowed out to have a good laugh at ourselves we nearly had a disaster. The wind and sea were higher than we supposed, and the *Kon-Tiki* was cleaving a path for herself over the swell much more quickly than we realized. We in the dinghy had to row for our lives out in the open sea in an attempt to regain the unmanageable raft, which could not stop and wait and could not possibly turn around and come back. Even when the boys on board the *Kon-Tiki* got the sail down, the wind got such a grip on the bamboo cabin that the raft drifted away to westward as fast as we could splash after her in the dancing rubber dinghy with its tiny toy oars. There was only one thought in the head of every man—we must not be separated. Those were horrible minutes we spent out on the sea before we got hold of the runaway raft and crawled on board to the others, home again.

From that day, it was strictly forbidden to go out in the rubber dinghy without having a long line made fast to the bow, so that those who remained on board could haul the dinghy in if necessary. We never went far away from the raft, thereafter, except when the wind was light and the Pacific curving itself in a gentle swell. But we had these conditions when the raft was halfway to Polynesia and the ocean, all dominating, arched itself round the globe toward every point of the compass. Then we could safely leave the *Kon-Tiki* and row away into the blue space between sky and sea.

When we saw the silhouette of our craft grow smaller and smaller in the distance, and the big sail at last shrunken to a vague black square on the horizon, a sensation of loneliness sometimes crept over us. The sea curved away under us as blue upon blue as the sky above, and where they met all the blue flowed together and became one. It almost seemed as if we were suspended in space. All our world was empty and blue; there was no fixed point in it but the tropical sun, golden and warm, which burned our necks. Then the distant sail of the lonely raft drew us to it like a magnetic point on the horizon. We rowed back and crept on board with a feeling that we had come home again to our own world—on board and yet on firm, safe ground. And, inside the bamboo cabin, we found shade and the scent of bamboos and withered palm leaves. The sunny blue purity outside was now served to us in a suitably large dose through the open cabin wall. So we were accustomed to it and so it was good for a time, till the great, clear blue tempted us out again.

It was most remarkable what a psychological effect the shaky bamboo cabin had on our minds. It measured eight by fourteen feet, and to diminish the pressure of wind and sea it was built low so that we could not stand upright under the ridge of the roof. Walls and roof were made of strong bamboo canes, lashed together and guyed, and covered with a tough wickerwork of split bamboos. The green and yellow bars, with fringes of foliage hanging down from the roof, were restful to the eye as a white cabin wall never could have been, and, despite the fact that the bamboo wall on the starboard side was open for one-third of its length and roof and walls let in sun and moon, this primitive lair gave us a greater feeling of security than white-painted bulkheads and closed portholes would have given in the same circumstances.

We tried to find an explanation for this curious fact and came to the following conclusion. Our consciousness was totally unaccustomed to associating a palm-covered bamboo dwelling with sea travel. There was no natural harmony between the great rolling ocean and the drafty palm hut which was floating about among the seas. Therefore, either the hut would seem entirely out of place among the waves, or the waves would seem entirely out of place round the hut wall. So long as we kept on board, the bamboo hut and its jungle scent were plain reality and the tossing seas seemed rather visionary. But from the rubber boat, waves and hut exchanged roles.

The fact that the balsa logs always rode the seas like a gull, and let the water right through aft if a wave broke on board, gave us an unshakable confidence in the dry part in the middle of the raft where the cabin was. The longer the voyage lasted, the safer we felt in our cozy lair, and we looked at the white-crested waves that danced past outside our doorway as if they were an impressive movie, conveying no menace to us at all. Even though the gaping wall was only five feet from the unprotected edge of the raft and only a foot and a half above the waterline, yet we felt as if we had traveled many miles away from the sea and occupied a jungle dwelling remote from the sea's perils once we had crawled inside the door. There we could lie on our backs and look up at the curious roof which twisted about like boughs in the wind, enjoying the jungle smell of raw wood, bamboos and withered palm leaves.

Sometimes, too, we went out in the rubber boat to look at ourselves by night. Coal black seas towered up on all sides, and a glittering myriad of tropical stars drew a faint reflection from plankton in the water. The world was simple—stars in the darkness. Whether it was 1947 B.C. or A.D. suddenly became of no significance. We lived, and that we felt with alert intensity. We realized that life had been full for men before the technical age also—in fact, fuller and richer in many ways than the life of modern man. Time and evolution somehow ceased to exist; all that was real and that mattered were the same today as they had always been and would always be. We were swallowed up in the absolute common measure of history—endless, unbroken darkness under a swarm of stars.

Before us in the night, the *Kon-Tiki* rose out of the seas to sink down again behind black masses of water that towered between her and us. In the moonlight, there was a fantastic atmosphere about the raft. Stout, shining wooden logs fringed with seaweed, the square, pitch black outline of a Viking sail, a bristly bamboo hut with the yellow light of a paraffin lamp aft— the whole suggested a picture from a fairy tale rather than an actual reality. Now and then the raft disappeared completely behind the black

seas; then she rose again and stood out sharp in silhouette against the stars, while glittering water poured from the logs.

When we saw the atmosphere about the solitary raft, we could well see in our mind's eye the whole flotilla of such vessels, spread in fan formation beyond the horizon to increase the chances of finding land, when the first men made their way across this sea. The Inca Tupak Yupanqui, who had brought under his rule both Peru and Ecuador, sailed across the sea with an armada of many thousand men on balsa rafts, just before the Spaniards came, to search for islands which rumor had told of out in the Pacific. He found two islands, which some think were the Galapagos, and, after eight months' absence, he and his numerous paddlers succeeded in toiling their way back to Ecuador. Kon-Tiki and his followers had certainly sailed in a similar formation several hundred years before, but, having discovered the Polynesian islands, they had no reason for trying to struggle back.

When we jumped on board the raft again, we often sat down in a circle round the paraffin lamp on the bamboo deck and talked of the seafarers from Peru who had had all these same experiences fifteen hundred years before us. The lamp flung huge shadows of bearded men on the sail, and we thought of the white men with the beards from Peru whom we could follow in mythology and architecture all the way from Mexico to Central America and into the northwestern area of South America as far as Peru. Here this mysterious civilization disappeared, as by the stroke of a magic wand, before the coming of the Incas and reappeared just as suddenly out on the solitary islands in the west which we were now approaching. Were the wandering teachers men of an early civilized race from across the Atlantic, who in times long past, in the same simple manner, had come over with the westerly ocean current and the trade wind from the area of the Canary Islands to the Gulf of Mexico? That was indeed a far shorter distance than the one we were covering, and we no longer believed in the sea as a completely isolating factor.

Many observers have maintained, for weighty reasons, that the great Indian civilizations, from the Aztecs in Mexico to the Incas in Peru, were inspired by sporadic intruders from over the seas in the east, while all the American Indians in general are Asiatic hunting and fishing peoples who in the course of twenty thousand years or more trickled into America from Siberia. It is certainly striking that there is not a trace of gradual development in the high civilizations which once stretched from Mexico to Peru. The deeper the archaeologists dig, the higher the culture, until a definite point is reached at which the old civilizations have clearly arisen without any foundation in the midst of primitive cultures.

And the civilizations have arisen where the current comes in from the Atlantic, in the midst of the desert and jungle regions of Central and South America, instead of in the more temperate regions, where civilizations, in both old and modern times, have had easier conditions for their development.

The same cultural distribution is seen in the South Sea islands. It is the island nearest to Peru, Easter Island, which bears the deepest traces of civilization, although the insignificant little island is dry and barren and is the farthest from Asia of all the islands in the Pacific.

When we had completed half our voyage, we had sailed just the distance from Peru to Easter Island and had the legendary island due south of us. We had left land at a chance point in the middle of the coast of Peru to imitate an average raft putting to sea. If we had left the land farther south, nearer Kon-Tiki's ruined city Tiahuanaco, we should have got the same wind but a weaker current, both of which would have carried us in the direction of Easter Island.

When we passed one hundred ten degrees west, we were within the Polynesian ocean area, inasmuch as the Polynesian Easter Island was now nearer Peru than we were. We were on a line with the first outpost of the South Sea islands, the center of the oldest island civilization. And when at night our glowing road guide, the sun, climbed down from the sky and disappeared beyond the sea in the west with his whole spectrum of colors, the gentle trade wind blew life into the stories of the strange mystery of Easter Island. While the night sky smothered all concept of

time, we sat and talked and bearded giants' heads were again thrown upon the sail.

But far down south, on Easter Island, stood yet larger giants' heads cut in stone, with bearded chins and white men's features, brooding over the secret of centuries.

Thus they stood when the first Europeans discovered the island in 1722, and thus they had stood twenty-two Polynesian generations earlier, when, according to native tradition, the present inhabitants landed in great canoes and exterminated all men among an earlier population found on the island. The primitive newcomers had arrived from the islands farther west, but the Easter Island traditions claim that the earliest inhabitants, and the true discovers of the island, had come from a distant land *toward the rising sun.* There is no land in this direction but South America. With the early extermination of the unknown local architects, the giant stone heads on Easter Island have become one of the foremost symbols of the insoluble mysteries of antiquity. Here and there on the slopes of the treeless island their huge figures have risen to the sky, stone colossi splendidly carved in the shape of men and set up as a single block as high as a normal building of three or four floors. How had the men of old been able to shape, transport and erect such gigantic stone colossi? As if the problem was not big enough, they had further succeeded in balancing an extra giant block of red stone like a colossal wig on the top of several of the heads, thirty-six feet above the ground. What did it all mean, and what kind of mechanical knowledge had the vanished architects who had mastered problems great enough for the foremost engineers of today?

If we put all the pieces together, the mystery of Easter Island is perhaps not insoluble after all, seen against a background of raftsmen from Peru. The old civilization has left on this island traces which the tooth of time has not been able to destroy.

Easter Island is the top of an ancient extinct volcano. Paved roads laid down by the old civilized inhabitants lead to well-preserved landing places on the coast and show that the water level round the island was exactly the same then as it is today. This is no remains of a sunken continent but a tiny desolate island, which was as small and solitary when it was a vivid cultural center as it is today.

In the eastern corner of this wedge-shaped island lies one of the extinct craters of the Easter Island volcano, and down in the crater lies the sculptors' amazing quarry and workshop. It lies there exactly as the old artists and architects left it hundreds of years ago, when they fled in haste to the eastern extremity of the island, where, according to tradition, there was a furious battle which made the present Polynesians victors and rulers of the island, whereas all grown men among the aboriginals were slain and burned in a ditch. The sudden interruption of the artists' work gives a clear cross section of an ordinary working day in the Easter Island crater. The sculptors' stone axes, hard as flint, lie strewn about their working places and show that this advanced people was as ignorant of iron as Kon-Tiki's sculptors were when they were driven in flight from Peru, leaving behind them similar gigantic stone statues on the Andes plateau. In both places, the quarry can be found where the legendary white people with beards hewed blocks of stone thirty feet long or more right out of the mountainside with the help of axes of still harder stone. And in both places, the gigantic blocks, weighing many tons, were transported for many miles over rough ground before being set up on end as enormous human figures, or raised on top of one another to form mysterious terraces and walls.

Many huge unfinished figures still lie where they were begun, in their niches in the crater wall on Easter Island, and show how the work was carried on in different stages. The largest human figure, which was almost completed when the builders had to flee, was sixty-six feet long; if it had been finished and set up, the head of this stone colossus would have been level with the top of an eight-floor building. Every separate figure was hewn out of a single connected block of stone, and the working niches for sculptors round the lying stone figures show that not many men were at work at the same time on each figure. Lying on their backs with their arms bent

and their hands placed on their stomachs, exactly like the stone colossi in South America, the Easter Island figures were completed in every minute detail before they were removed from the workshop and transported to their destinations round about on the island. In the last stage inside the quarry, the giant was attached to the cliff side by only a narrow ridge under his back; then this too was hewn away, the giant meanwhile being supported by boulders.

Large quantities of these figures were just dragged down to the bottom of the crater and set up on the slope there. But a number of the largest colossi were transported up and over the wall of the crater, and for many miles round over difficult country, before being set up on a stone platform and having an extra stone colossus of red tuff placed on their heads. This transport in itself may appear to be a complete mystery, but we cannot deny that it took place or that the architects who disappeared from Peru left in the Andes Mountains stone colossi of equal size, which show that they were absolute experts in this line. Even if the monoliths are largest and most numerous on Easter Island, and the sculptors there had acquired an individual style, the same vanished civilization erected similar giant statues in human shape on many of the other Pacific islands, but only on those nearest to America, and everywhere the monoliths were brought to their final site from out-of-the-way quarries. In the Marquesas, I heard legends of how the gigantic stones were maneuvered, and, as these corresponded exactly to the natives' stories of the transport of the stone pillars to the huge portal on Tongatabu, it can be assumed that the same people employed the same method with the columns on Easter Island.

The sculptors' work in the pit took a long time but required only a few experts. The work of transport each time a statue was completed was more quickly done but, on the other hand, required large numbers of men. Little Easter Island was then both rich in fish and thoroughly cultivated, with large plantations of Peruvian sweet potatoes, and experts believe that the island in its great days could have supported a population of seven or eight thousand. About a thousand men were quite enough to haul the huge statues up and over the steep crater wall, while five hundred were sufficient to drag them on further across the island.

Wearproof cables were plaited from bast and vegetable fibers, and, using wooden frames, the multitude dragged the stone colossus over logs and small boulders made slippery with taro roots. That old civilized peoples were masters in making ropes and cables is well known from the South Sea islands and still more from Peru, where the first Europeans found suspension bridges a hundred yards long laid across torrents and gorges by means of plaited cables as thick as a man's waist.

When the stone colossus had arrived at its chosen site and was to be set up on end, the next problem arose. The crowd built a temporary inclined plane of stone and sand and pulled the giant up the less steep side, legs first. When the statue reached the top, it shot over a sharp edge and slid straight down so that the footpiece landed in a ready-dug hole. As the complete inclined plane still stood there, rubbing against the back of the giant's head, they rolled up an extra cylinder of stone and placed it on the top of his head; then the whole temporary plane was removed. Ready-built inclined planes like this stand in several places on Easter Island, waiting for huge figures which have never come. The technique was admirable but in no way mysterious if we cease to underestimate the intelligence of men in ancient times and the amount of time and manpower which they had at their command.

But why did they make these statues? And why was it necessary to go off to another quarry four miles away from the crater workshop to find a special kind of red stone to place on the figure's head? Both in South America and in the Marquesas Islands, the whole statue was often of this red stone, and the natives went great distances to get it. Red headdresses for persons of high rank were an important feature both in Polynesia and in Peru.

Let us see first whom the statues represented. When the first Europeans visited the island, they saw mysterious "white men" on shore and, in contrast to what is usual among peoples of this kind, they found men with long flowing beards, the descendants of women and children belonging to the first race on the island, who had been spared by the invaders. The natives themselves declared that some of their ancestors had been white, while others had been brown. They calculated precisely that the last-named had immigrated from elsewhere in Polynesia twenty-two generations before, while the first had come from eastward in large vessels as much as fifty-seven generations back (i.e., ca. A.D. 400–500). The race which came from the east were given the name "long-ears," because they lengthened their ears artificially by hanging weights on the lobes so that they hung down to their shoulders. These were the mysterious "long ears" who were killed when the "short ears" came to the island, and all the stone figures on Easter Island had large ears hanging down to their shoulders, as the sculptors themselves had had.

Now the Inca legends in Peru say that the sun-king Kon Tiki ruled over a white people with beards who were called by the Incas "big ears," because they had their ears artificially lengthened so that they reached down to their shoulders. The Incas emphasized that it was Kon-Tiki's "big ears" who had erected the abandoned giant statues in the Andes Mountains before they were exterminated or driven out by the Incas themselves in the battle on an island in Lake Titicaca.

To sum up: Kon-Tiki's white "big ears" disappeared from Peru westward with ample experience of working on colossal stone statues, and Tiki's white "long ears" came to Easter Island from eastward skilled in exactly the same art, which they at once took up in full perfection, so that not the smallest trace can be found on Easter Island of any development leading up to the masterpieces on the island.

There is often a greater resemblance between the great stone statues in South America and those on certain South Sea islands than there is between the monoliths on the different South Sea islands compared with one another. In the Marquesas Islands and Tahiti, such statues were known under the generic name *Tiki,* and they represented ancestors honored in the islands' history who, after their death, had been ranked as gods. And therein undoubtedly may be found the explanation of the curious red-stone caps on the Easter Island figures. At the time of the European explorations, there existed on all the islands in Polynesia scattered individuals and whole families with reddish hair and fair skins, and the islanders themselves declared that it was these who were descended from the first white people on the islands. On certain islands, religious festivals were held, the participators in which colored their skins white and their hair red to resemble their earliest ancestors. At annual ceremonies on Easter Island, the chief person of the festival had all his hair cut off so that his head might be painted red. And the colossal red-stone caps on the giant statues on Easter Island were carved in the shape which was typical of the local hairstyle; they had a round knot on the top, just as the men had their hair tied in a little traditional topknot in the middle of the head.

The statues on Easter Island had long ears because the sculptors themselves had lengthened ears. They had specially chosen red stones as wigs because the sculptors themselves had reddish hair. They had their chins carved pointed and projecting, because the sculptors themselves grew beards. They had the typical physiognomy of the white race, with a straight and narrow nose and thin sharp lips, because the sculptors themselves did not belong to the Indonesian race. And when the statues had huge heads and tiny legs, with their hands laid in position on their stomachs, it was because it was just in this way the people were accustomed to make giant statues in South America. The sole decoration of the Easter Island figures is a belt which was always carved round the figure's stomach. The same symbolic belt is found on every single statue in Kon-Tiki's ancient ruins by Lake Titicaca. It is the legendary emblem of the sun-god, the rainbow belt. There was a myth on the island of Mangareva according to which the sun-god had taken off the rainbow which was his magic belt and climbed down it from the sky on to Mangareva to people the island with his white-skinned children. The sun was once regarded as

the oldest original ancestor in all these islands, as well as in Peru.

We used to sit on deck under the starry sky and retell Easter Island's strange history, even though our own raft was carrying us straight into the heart of Polynesia, so that we should see nothing of that remote island but its name on the map. But so full is Easter Island of traces from the east that even its name can serve as a pointer.

Easter Island appears on the map because some chance Dutchman "discovered" the island one Easter Sunday. And we have forgotten that the natives themselves, who already lived there, had more instructive and significant names for their home. This island has no less than three names in Polynesian.

One name is *Te-Pito-te-Henua,* which means "navel of the islands." This poetical name clearly places Easter Island in a special position in regard to the other islands farther westward and is the oldest designation for Easter Island according to the Polynesians themselves. On the eastern side of the island, near the traditional landing place of the first "long ears," is a carefully tooled sphere of stone which is called the "golden navel" and is in turn regarded as the navel of Easter Island itself. When the poetical Polynesian ancestors carved the island navel on the east coast and selected the island nearest Peru as the navel of their myriad islands further west, it had a symbolic meaning. And when we know that Polynesian tradition refers to the discovery of their islands as the "birth" of their islands, then it is more than suggested that Easter Island of all places was considered the "navel," symbolic of the islands' birthmark and as the connecting link with their original motherland.

Easter Island's second name is Rapa Nui which means "Great Rapa," while Rapa Iti or "Little Rapa" is another island of the same size which lies a very long way west of Easter Island. Now, it is the natural practice of all peoples to call their first home "Great————," while the next is called "New————" or "Little————," even if the places are of the same size. And on Little Rapa the natives have quite correctly maintained traditions that the first inhabitants of the island came from Great Rapa, Easter Island, to the eastward, nearest to America. This points directly to an original immigration from the east.

The third and last name of this key island is *Mata-Kite-Rani,* which means "the eye (which) looks (toward) heaven." At first glance this is puzzling, for the relatively low Easter Island does not look toward heaven any more than the other loftier islands—for example, Tahiti, the Marquesas or Hawaii. But *Rani,* heaven, had a double meaning to the Polynesians. It was also their ancestors' original homeland, the holy land of the sun-god, Tiki's forsaken mountain kingdom. And it is very significant that they should have called just their easternmost island, of all the thousands of islands in the ocean, "the eye which looks toward heaven." It is all the more striking seeing that the kindred name *Mata-Rani,* which means in Polynesian "the eye of heaven," is an old Peruvian place name, that of a spot on the Pacific coast of Peru opposite Easter Island and right at the foot of Kon-Tiki's old ruined city in the Andes.

The fascination of Easter Island provided us with plenty of subjects of conversation as we sat on deck under the starry sky, feeling ourselves to be participators in the whole prehistoric adventure. We almost felt as if we had done nothing else since Tiki's days but sail about the seas under sun and stars searching for land.

Sailing on the Roof of the World

by TRISTAN JONES

In one of the more offbeat sailing feats every attempted, Tristan Jones tried to negotiate both the world's lowest (the Red Sea) and highest bodies of water. Middle East politics kept him from the Red Sea, but in 1974 he did manage eventually to haul a boat to Peru's Lake Titicaca, almost thirteen thousand feet above sea level, set sail and enjoy an unusual experience.

N EW Year's morning, 1974! On board *Sea Dart,* perched on top of an ancient Ford truck parked in the town plaza of Puno, I woke with the first light of dawn, put the kettle on the stove and clambered down to shake my Quechua friend Salomon, who was sleeping off the effects of a bottle of *chicha* consumed straight after our arrival. I had not bothered to undress the night before, for the temperature in those parts, even during the southern summer, plunges from eighty degrees at 5:00 P.M. to below zero just an hour after the sun sets. I had slept in all my arctic gear and covered the berth with three thick blankets. Nevertheless, I had awakened often with the cold and lack of breath. This was caused by the shortage of oxygen at that height, which is 40 percent less than at sea level. The second phenomenon caused by this lack of oxygen was the time it took for the kettle to boil for morning tea!

All around the muddy plaza, Indians were rising from their sleep in the open. They come into Puno with small bundles of produce to sell, and they stay, sleeping in the freezing air, until the last tiny potato or piglet is sold, then return to their homes, which Salomon told me might be anything up to a hundred miles away. Some of them come in by truck, but most of them walk for days across the bitterly cold, wide-open plain of the altiplano.

By the time we had eaten breakfast, a great crowd of Indians, silent, barefoot and very dirty, had gathered in front of the shabby but impressive cathedral and were gazing expressionlessly at *Sea Dart* and the truck. We were too conspicuous to escape the vigilance of the local constabulary for long, so we set off, wheezing and dripping oil, down to the small jetty on the lake. Having smuggled my way across Peru, there was only one thing in my mind apart from the immense satisfaction of having reached such a remote target, and that was to get the hell out and gone from Puno before the Peruvian customs figured out what had happened. So far, so good, but the stir that our appearance had excited all along the route would surely, sooner or later, put the vultures on my tail. Once I'd actually sailed on the lake, that would not be of such great importance; moreover, I knew that once I was on the lake, they would have to run to catch me, especially if I was near Bolivian waters.

As we crawled in and out of potholes, through a heavy downpour which caused the roads to stream with floodwaters, I was thinking that the way down from the lake back to the Pacific would be comparatively simple. From Guaqui, in Bolivia, at the southern end of the lake, a railroad runs across the Andes into Chile and to the Pacific coast port of Antofagasta. I would, after I had cruised the lake for a few weeks, load the boat on the train and head down to Chile, back into the Pacific, then store up, either for a fast, easy run up the Humboldt Current to Panama, or, if funds were sufficient, across the Pacific for Australia, and then on, after a spell down under, back home to England.

Suddenly I was shaken out of my reverie, for there was the lake, with great black thunderclouds streaming overhead and sheet lightning forking down on the far horizon. But even in the dim gloom of the thunderstorm, it looked more beautiful than any other water in the world. The shoreline consisted of a short, broken-down jetty, a few miserable adobe huts huddled at one end with rainwater streaming off their thatched red roofs, an ancient steamcrane and a shed, but to me it looked more heavenly than the Grand Canal at Venice and more impressive than the Thames at Tower Bridge. The tiny, whitewashed adobe church at the end of the jetty looked more magnificent than the Notre Dame; the small flotilla of ragged little Indian sailing vessels hugging each other along the jetty seemed more majestic than the whole power and glory of all the navies in the world combined.

I jumped off the truck and started to run to the lake shore, but the lack of oxygen soon brought me up short, panting. Salomon stared after me as if I had gone crazy, then he laughed and shouted, *"Bueno, muy bueno!"* I kept walking to the water's edge and, with all my arctic gear on, walked right into the freezing water of Lake Titicaca until it came up to my waist. Then I bent and cupped my hands, drinking in the clear, fresh water, giving thanks to God for letting me survive all the dangers and perils of the last few years long enough to live this moment. As I straightened up, the thunderheads in the distance faded and a bright rainbow, sharper and more vivid than any I had ever seen before, arched across the lake, bridging the sky from the peak of Sorata to the gleaming silver heights of Illampu, way over in the south, more than one hundred miles away. Bands of brilliant color curved across the heavens, framing the Island of the Sun.

I stood in the cold floodwater, oblivious to the iciness in my seaboots, no longer weary with effort, no longer worried about shortage of money, no longer breathless with lack of oxygen. Sunbeams streamed through the rain clouds in golden shafts, illumining green, green islands, where before there had been only dark gray, shadowy smudges. As the clouds rolled apart, they revealed the bluest water in the world, and small green parrots flew overhead like emeralds thrown up into the sky. Then my legs and feet started to ache with pain and numbness.

I sloshed my way back to *Sea Dart's* cabin and changed into dry pants and boots, then walked over to the harbormaster's office, trying to look as confident as I could before a crowd of gawping Indians. They just stood there in the rain, the water pouring off their blankets. Salomon was the only one grinning. *"Bien hecho, amigo inglés!* he crowed. "Well done!"

Half an hour later, *Sea Dart* was afloat in the lake and Salomon was helping me raise the small mainmast and set up the standing rigging. As the rain recommenced, we rigged the sails, hoisted the burgee of the Royal Naval Sailing Association, and there she was, ready for the off, the world's highest burgee, at 12,850 feet above the ocean!

I looked around the jetty. Beyond a netted enclosure, I spied two gray launches, one with a small gun mounted on its bow. I grabbed Salomon's arm and thumbed at them over my shoulder.

"Navy or customs?"

"Navy, *amigo,* but you got no problems. On one boat the gun doesn't work, on the other the engine is buggered. Anyway, they are too busy pissing about policing the town; there's rumors of a revolution in the air!" Again he managed to spit, grin, fart, belch and scratch all at the same time.

Then I got the motor out of its unopened wrappers and rigged it up to move the boat out alongside the jetty. Unfortunately, because of the lack of oxygen and the watery gasoline, it would not start! I'd had the motor ever since Panama and never used it once. Now, it was useless on the lake, so I stowed it away in its wrapper. I had a long sweep oar, and I sculled her around to a berth which the harbormaster arranged for me after his palm had been suitably crossed.

It was raining as Salomon and I waded through two-foot-deep cataracts in the streets on our way to the town bar. We both agreed that *Sea Dart* had beaten the rainy flood season and the Andes snowmelt by only a matter of hours. I paid Salomon $200; the extra we agreed should go towards a new oil sump for his truck, plus a bottle or two of *chicha* for the terrible trip back down to the coast when the rains finally stopped in March. There followed an emotional farewell scene, during which Salomon made a curious remark: *"Amigo inglés, cuidado con los Aymaras!"* "Careful with the Aymaras!" Several weeks later, I found out what he meant. But that afternoon, despite the floods and chaos, we were happy, and by the time I rolled back onboard *Sea Dart* I was in fine fettle, ready to sail off in the morning.

That night, with the oil lamp lit and the tiny cabin cozily warm from the heat of the kerosene stove and after a good, hot meal of bullybeef and potatoes, I lay down and listened to the rain strumming on the coach roof. I had no charts for the lake, for at that time none existed, but I had garnered a little information from Adolph Bandelier's *The Island of Titicaca* in the British Museum Reading Room. In the morning, God willing, I would take off and hide myself away from the prowling customs officials of Peru. I had just over one hundred dollars; I was three hundred miles from the Pacific and two thousand miles from the Atlantic, but I had over three thousand square miles of fresh water to get lost in. Also, I had time to write and restock my depleted coffers.

It takes a few weeks to become accustomed to the lack of oxygen at the altitude of the lake, and I often woke with a tight chest, gasping for breath. Then I would lie thinking of all I had overcome and endured to reach this magic lake; and sometimes it all seemed like a dream. The first night afloat in Lake Titicaca was like that, and I had little sleep. I was fully awake at the first crack of false dawn; with the kettle singing slowly on the stove, I went out into the clear, freezing dawn to let go of the mooring lines.

As I sculled *Sea Dart* with the long oar over the stern out of Puno in the darkness of the early dawn, I did not know that I was about to enter a world of superstition and fear, black magic and wonder, from which I would emerge only after a harrowing eight months. All I could think about was reaching the broad, sweeping miles of high, totora-reed water meadows and there hiding myself and my boat from the Peruvian customs!

By the time the sun rose over the black masses of the high Cordillera Real away to the east; by the time the mountain peaks had changed color to gray and the lake water to startling turquoise under a low-lying mist; I was well out into the lake, with a slight southwest wind. As I crowded sail and headed for the strange, low, floating islands of the Uro Indians, islands which, like living animals, move up and down with the lake water level, islands which support one of the most primitive and pitiful tribes on earth, I thought of what I had learned thus far of the history of the lake.

The Spanish conquistadores first arrived on the shores of Lake Titicaca in 1535, after subjecting the Quechua Indians of Ecuador and Peru. Pizarro and his tiny band enjoyed incredible luck, sailing south from Panama at the precise time when the Holy Child Current had reversed the north-flowing Humboldt. Instead of struggling against the strong Humboldt in their awkward ships, they made a fast passage to Cape Santa Elena, where they landed horses, guns and stores.

The arrival of the Spanish centuries later on the same current which brought the mighty god Kon-Tiki-Vira-Cocha, the creator of plains and mountains, struck terror into the hearts of the Incas. The periodical change in direction of the current was in itself, to the superstitious Incas, evidence of the wrath of Kon-Tiki. This legendary white, bearded god had, according to their legends, after bringing light to the world of darkness, disappeared into the ocean, "walking away across the waters with his band of saints."

Now came these other bearded white beings, perhaps the sons of Kon-Tiki, on the same current as the god himself. This was the mighty current which, when Kon-Tiki wished, changed direction, turning the sea blood red and killing all the fish in the waters. (In the nineteenth century, this phenomenon was called by English seamen "the Callao Painter" because the ships' hulls were turned blood red by the discoloration caused by the millions of dead organisms in the water.) Then the climate would change, earthquakes and disasters would occur throughout the lands of the empire, from the hot jungle shores of northern Ecuador to the cold, barren wastes of Chile. The wind and the rain would lash the mountain fastnesses with unbounded fury, flooding the lowlands, destroying the crops so that hunger and famine stalked the land every seven years. (Shades of Egypt!)

Then, relenting, Kon-Tiki had ordered the first Inca, Manco Capac, to build grain storages throughout the empire, thus establishing an iron hold over all the tribes. Now these strange men, white and bearded like Kon-Tiki himself, with their terrifying thunderbolts and four-legged monsters had stepped ashore at the same place where, the Indian storytellers later told me, Manco Capac himself had first stepped ashore!

In trembling awe, carefully concealed by a great show of pomp, the Inca king, Atahualpa, was carried in a magnificent litter to Cajamarca to meet the sons of Kon-Tiki. Word of the arrival of these gods had been carried swiftly to him for a thousand miles along the imperial highways. Atahualpa was accompanied by a mighty army of fierce warriors: the Quechua, stern and disciplined; the sly Oruro, fastest runners in the empire; and the murderous Aymara.

With incredible courage, Pizarro thrust the Holy Bible of his God into the sacred hands of Atahualpa, who haughtily cast the object into the dust and thereby sealed the fate of South America. In that moment, the whole of Ecuador, Peru, Bolivia and great tracts of Chile and Argentina fell into Pizarro's hands.

With his two hundred bold spirits, the Spanish commander, the bastard son of an Andalusian peasant, seized the Inca by the golden scruff of his neck and drove his assembled minions into screaming retreat. Then, after holding the emperor for ransom, he strangled him with a garrote.

Immense mountain ranges, fertile valleys, towns and cities, half a continent, roaring rivers and dusty deserts, as well as unimaginable treasures of gold, silver, tin and lead fell into the grasping hands of Spain. For the Andes, Indian time stopped from the moment of Atahualpa's seizure until now.

So fell the first, and most efficient, fascist corporate state the world has ever known. Ever since Atahualpa's death, the Andes Indian has mourned him and awaits his return.

Such were my thoughts as I headed out for my first sail on the lake. I was heading toward the unknown, for in their zeal to get to the gold and silver of Bolivia, the conquistadores had bypassed the islands, leaving them practically unexploited.

For centuries now, they had remained almost in the same state they had been in when Atahualpa died.

It was now mid-February, 1974 and the rainy season was more than half over. Our exploration of the Colla coast and the islands of Soto, Amantani, and (for want of any other name) Alpha, Baker and Wight had found *Sea Dart*, Huanapaco and me alternately soaked in bitterly cold showers and perspiring in hot sunshine. Now, as we left Taquila to head for the Island of the Sun, we were seen off by all the able-bodied people. The men wore their best caps, woolen and long, like a stocking with a bobble or pompon on the end. They had their fiesta clothes on, brilliant woven belts of llama wool and black llama-wool trousers. Banging tambourines, they lined up along the miniature port and, with the *kena* flutes piping, played for all they were worth. The women and girls kept a discreet distance, laughing and joking among themselves. One of the prettiest looked long and hard at Huanapaco, who, of course, pretended not to notice. The women wore black mantillas, *licllas* they call them, fastened across the breast with a beautiful ornamental pin either of gold or silver, the *putu*, their most treasured possession. This was the only time in eight months on the lake that I ever saw Indians actually change their clothes. Even for one of the frequent fiestas, they put their magnificent sequined dancing costumes, together with devils' masks and all the other paraphernalia, straight on top of their filthy rags.

Soon the morning breeze picked up *Sea Dart* and sent her dancing over the short chop of Lake Titicaca, heading south towards the Island of the Sun. While cruising the Colla coast, we had encountered some very wild storms indeed, with savage winds blasting down from the frozen Andes peaks onto the sun-baked altiplano, where the difference in temperature between the sunny and shady spots was as much as seventy degrees! I was glad that I had curved the mast in order to spill the wind quickly, for often these devil winds would come out of a clear, sunny, blue sky, with absolutely no warning whatsoever. One minute *Sea Dart* would be ghosting along in a zephyr and the next be almost heeled over flat in a gust of a hundred miles an hour or more. It was exciting, exhilarating sailing, even though I was always short of breath, especially when working the sheets. When the going was steady, it was gravy-sailing, and, to the amusement of Huanapaco, I would whoop and sing at the pure joy of sailing free on the wind across the roof of the world, bound for the Island of the Sun, the legendary Inca birthplace of the world!

Now that *Sea Dart* was out of Peruvian waters, she was safe from the 50 percent import tax on her value, the iniquitous toll demanded by the rubber-stamp caesars of Lima. She was, at the Island of the Sun, not yet officially in Bolivia, although she was in Bolivian waters, for there were no entry facilities until Tiquina, well inside Bolivian territory.

Before sailing through the Strait of Tiquina, which separates the two parts of Lake Titicaca like the stem of an hourglass, into two semiequal halves, Chucuito and Unimarca, I intended to explore the coastline of the Island of the Sun. The rain showers were becoming less frequent, the sun shone brilliantly in the daytime, the winds were easing off and I still had enough food supplies to live, though modestly.

For eight days, we worked our way around the island and its nearby neighbors, Kochi, Pallaya, Chuyu and Lauassani, small islands which support nothing but birds, mainly *chocas*. Huanapaco and I would sound the depths in the early morning from five until nine, before the wind had risen and while the lake was like a smooth sheet of glass, with the early-morning mist suspended thinly above it and the other islands seeming, in the distance, to hang in thin air, as in Chinese paintings. Huanapaco dipped the lead to the bottom and sang out the depths while I sculled the boat this way and that in the time-honored "square search" method. Often I would look up and see, far away in the distance to the north, islands beyond the horizon, Soto and Amantani, apparently hanging upside down on the indistinct horizon, for it was impossible to see where the lake and the sky met. This was the fata-morgana phenomenon, caused by the refraction of light waves by differences of temperature. The last times I had seen it were off Madagascar and Sicily.

About ten o'clock, the wind would slowly increase, and during this time we would lay off, quite close to the island, which is, all around, very steep-to (the lake water is deep right up to the shores). I would set to work with the sextant and hand-bearing compass, fixing the different headlands and peaks in their correct relation to one another on the chart and calling out the numbers, in my turn, to Huanapaco, who would make note of them neatly on the chart.

Hove to, bobbing up and down in the short seas off the Island of the Sun, at early afternoon we would take turns making a midday meal. I would usually make fish and chips, while Huanapaco would come up with a Quechua concoction of totora reed roots, green peppers and oca. By now I had run out of tea, except for a tiny amount which I was hoarding for use in case of a disaster.

From two in the afternoon until four, we would sail round to the next anchorage. This was usually not far. We would arrive there at the full blaze of the sun. On the shore off the anchorage, there would usually be a stream or a small waterfall where we could bathe and relieve ourselves of some of the ever-increasing livestock on our heads and bodies brought on board by visiting Indian fishermen and smugglers. There was no way we could refuse them aboard. They were very conscious of the rules of hospitality, and word passed quickly around the lake. We had many interesting, sometimes funny, chats with the smugglers, who worked under sail, sliding through the Tiquina Strait at night under the noses of the Bolivian navy, carrying meat, flour, coca and sugar to Peru and returning with clothes, *chicha,* beer, radios and textiles. It is estimated that in 1973, 70 percent of Bolivia's imports were smuggled in and 50 percent of its exports were smuggled out! Most of this trade took place in the frontier waters of Titicaca, under sail! Very often a sailboat, with a great lugsail, would appear on the horizon, becalmed in the dawn. She would work her way in, come alongside, and the crew would greet us like lost friends, especially the Quechua boats from the north. They had heard of the strange "gringo" with the even stranger boat, which, like a bird, could actually sail *into* the wind. They would pull up, shouting my Quechua name, *"Macchu Cuito,"* and we would spend an hour or more gossiping through Huanapaco in the clear limpid light which the lake, like a golden chalice, held cupped in its liquid hand until the sun rose over Copacabana Peninsula, forcing us to seek the shadows.

At dusk we would make another meal. The wind would drop, silence would descend all around us, except for the rustling of the reeds. Huanapaco would wrap his poncho around himself and fall asleep; I would light the oil lamp and work on the chart or write up my log. After that, I would work on a magazine article to send off when we again returned to the twentieth century.

About nine o'clock, after listening to the world outside and far below us over the radio, I would warm up the cabin with the kerosene stove and turn in.

Sometimes in the afternoon, after anchoring the boat safely, we would climb to the heights of a nearby island. Often this was to survey the surrounding area, but many times I would clamber up the steep, rocky mountainside and collapse, exhausted, at the top with the lack of oxygen. The view was astounding. Whenever the sun shone, which now was almost all day, the scenery from the heights of Titicaca was magnificent. We could see mountains, far to the east and north, 350 miles apart; and it seemed that we could just reach out with our hands and touch them, the air was so clear. Sweeping away at our feet, the azure blue lake stretched on into the far distance, dotted with islands, most of them surrounded by beds of reeds, glistening emerald and gold as the breeze riffled across them. Far below in the bay, *Sea Dart,* like a tiny toy, bobbed in the wavelets, her red ensign fluttering on the stern, scaring the storks and dipper birds, who loved to perch on the masthead and shit all over the topsides when there was no one on board.

At this height, there were two very obvious phenomena; the first was the effect of the sun's rays on color, which was much more dazzling in the sunshine and subdued in the shade. The difference between light and shade was much sharper than at sea level, and I came to the conclusion that a painter would find the color contrast on the lake even more intense than van Gogh found the country around Arles.

Another not so obvious effect in the thin, clean air was the difficulty in judging distance. As a navigator of small craft for many years, I can normally gauge a distance, especially from seaward, to within a few yards, even at six or seven miles' range. But up on Titicaca, I found myself very often fooled, underestimating distances by anything up to three miles! It seems that the abnormal angle of the light rays, together with the magnifying effect of the clear, clean, dry air, causes this. When surveying, I had frequently to pace the distance between two points of land, or actually sail between two islands to log the distance between them, instead of just taking a sextant angle.

The clearest night skies I have ever seen anywhere were over the lake. Out in the ocean, well clear of the land, perhaps a thousand miles out, the skies are crammed with stars, but on Titicaca there was hardly room for the black sky among the stars! The bright planets and all the major stars were like small moons, their rotundity clearly delineated. The manmade satellites were immediately obvious, like taxicabs on the Epsom Downs course on Derby day. There were literally a million bodies in the sky. I cannot think of any finer place for an observatory to be erected. Many a time, I would go topsides and be struck with wonder at the display of the heavens, beautiful beyond words, awe-inspiring in its magnificence. When the moon rose, I could see every crater and every blemish on its ravaged face.

Grim Landfall

by DAVID LEWIS

Having been born in the Southern Hemisphere, David Lewis would eventually leave the warmer environs of Raratonga and Australia and strike out to attempt the first single-handed voyage to Antarctica. He and his boat, Ice Bird, *survived capsizing, cold and torturous maneuvering around ice floes and icebergs which were, as he details here, full of menace and marked with an eerie beauty.*

Caution—the mariner should exercise great care in navigating the area covered by this work.
                    Antarctic Pilot, p. 2

AS if our change of course had been a signal, the wind now switched into the south-southwest, slowing our southward progress to a crawl and driving us even farther to the east. Good sights were obtained on the twenty-second, which depressingly placed us a long way north. We should be well clear of the South Shetland Islands as yet, and were certainly still a long way north of the Antarctic Peninsula proper, but very soon I must begin to exercise caution lest land be nearer than anticipated—either through bad guesswork as to the error of the wristwatch or through the compass deviation (caused by the twisted pram hood frame) being different on this southerly heading.

The day's log shows a natural preoccupation with the weather conditions. "Snow lying in cockpit. Hard put to hold to windward against lop, so grossly undercanvassed." By 7:00 P.M. "Almost becalmed. Snowing heavily. Shut-in feeling from restricted visibility." Then came the swish of speeding forms, arching half-seen through the swirling snow. They were Commerson's dolphins, small, beautiful black-and-white denizens of Tierra del Fuegan waters and Drake Passage, that gave notice by their presence that my navigation was not so far out, after all.

The last remark set down that evening points to a certain depression—"sick of waterlogged mattresses"—but earlier entries had struck an unusually positive note. "Mended worst rents in my anorak. Mercy to be able to use fingers. Periods of acute pain less often. Hot coffee, first hot drink for a month (since water rationing)—forgot how comforting. Primus burners very dodgy."

Most revealing, however, was this sentence. "Plans for refit maturing." For the very first time, I was thinking beyond gaining safety and even to my long-set goal, the continuation of the voyage.

Another day of repeated snow showers followed, with the skies remaining leaden until midnight, when away to the southward there opened a window beyond the edge of the cloud roof into a sunset-sunrise that was all clear golden light. The wind was variable but mostly easterly, falling very light again during the afternoon. This was the day chosen by Sniffy and Snuffy, after a week spent in our company, to swim off westward. And with them, circling and darting in their wake, went the flock of ice birds that had been with us for so long. This was a break indeed, for, in some illogical way, I knew intuitively that they would not return. I was unable to shake off the fanciful feeling that they were ocean spirits of the drifting snow who, having escorted us safe across the waste and brought us near to land, were departing now their task was ended.

That night I slept soundly, tired out with so much hand steering, and awoke on the morning of the twenty-fourth to find that *Ice Bird* had turned around and was heading back in her tracks. Such are the trials of singlehanded sailing. Because of the capricious breezes and this reversal of course, I found, when I worked out our position at noon, that we had only made eighteen miles in the past twenty-four hours. On the credit side, my fingers were now capable of handling the heavy brass sextant—instead of only the light plastic one— and, with this more accurate instrument available, I had more confidence in my navigation.

Hoped-for stronger winds showed no signs as yet of setting in. In fact, before nine that evening, except for the occasional expiring puff, the wind had died away altogether and the silence of the sea was broken only by the swishing of the sails, as the ship rolled, and the clatter of the blocks against the coach roof. Three pintados on the water bobbed and curtsied to each other and flung up spray with their threshing wings in some private display ritual of their own. By midnight, even the slatting sails and the blocks were still, but at 3:00 A.M. a snowstorm ushered in an easterly wind, which gradually steadied and strengthened, as I sat keeping watch as best I could (ice, as well as land, might now be near) through the brief hours of darkness.

I tried to sort out what I had read and been told about this fascinating Antarctic Peninsula, which could not be so very far beneath the horizon. It was a nine-hundred-mile-long projection of the otherwise almost circular Antarctic continent, geologically and geographically a mirror image of the Andes of South America. The ice-choked Weddell Sea forbade all seaborne access on the east, but the western coast, which we were to approach, washed by the Bellingshausen Sea, was much indented and fringed with islands and could be reached for a time in summer.

But even this accessible side, judging by the *Antarctic Pilot,* was rather like the Himalayas transported to sea level, with its peaks rising sheer to ten thousand feet. "It is nearly all glacier covered," the *Pilot* (p. 131) says, "except the most precipitous peaks and cliffs, some of which form part of the coastline, the remainder of the coast consists chiefly of glacier faces."

Mr. Edward Bransfield, RN, of the sealing brig *Williams,* was the first to discover the peninsula (and very possibly the first to see any part of Antarctica) when, on January 30, 1820, in sixty-three degrees sixteen minutes south latitude, "the haze clearing," land unexpectedly appeared to the southwest. On November 16 that same year, the American sealer Nathanial Palmer in the little *Hero* "got over under the land" at sixty-three degrees forty-five minutes south. (Unaccountably, the Americans have clung stubbornly to the myth, which they well know to be nonsense, that Palmer was the original discoverer.)

These gallant captains were also ruthless exploiters. A year after Bransfield's voyage, ninety-one sealing vessels were active in these waters: by 1822, fur seals had become almost extinct. The whales were more resistant, though a century and a half of continuous hunting in the Antarctic seas have so depleted stocks that only two nations, the Russians and the Japanese, little to their credit, are still carrying on mopping-up operations on any significant scale.

Expeditions to the peninsula have been legion. Of special relevance to the area we were nearing was the British Captain John Biscoe's 1832 landing on Anvers Island, which he thought part of the mainland, and de Gerlache's correction of this error in the *Belgica* in 1898, by the discovery of the strait that bears his name.

Much later on, between 1934 and 1937, the British three-masted schooner *Penola* under J. R. Rymill, recharted the better part of the west coast. Of special significance to me was the fact that this extensive survey was carried out in a tiny gaff-rigged semiopen boat that had been brought to the Antarctic aboard *Penola*. If I remember correctly what its owner, Quentin Riley, told me some years ago in Essex, its overall length was either twenty or twenty-one feet. Seeing that this cockleshell had wandered at will among the icebergs and rocks of this coast for months, why could not I do likewise? At any rate, it should have been possible, had *Ice Bird* still possessed her mast and motor.

I got up and opened the main hatch, for the transparent dome was plastered with snow. Pulling myself up by the pram hood frame, I strained my eyes ahead. It was no use. Nothing but slanting lines of fast-falling snow.

Back inside the cabin, my mind returned to the desolate place where we hoped to find shelter. Even its isolation had not sufficed to keep it out of the unedifying stream of power politics. The peninsula is claimed by Argentina, Britain and Chile. The United States and the USSR also have bases but have sensibly held aloof from what has been, from the World War II years at least, something in the nature of an international circus act. Glancing through the record almost at random, we find:

1942: Argentine ship *Primero de Mayo* takes formal possession of Deception Island.

1943: H.M.S. *Caernarvon Castle* obliterates Argentine marks of sovereignty on Deception Island and hoists British flag.

1943: Argentine ship *Primero de Mayo* removes British emblems at Deception Island and repaints Argentine flag.

1943–44: British expedition removes Argentine emblems from Deception Island.

1951–52: Argentine-British armed clash at Hope Bay.

1953: British remove Argentine and Chilean huts from Whaler's Bay and H.M.S. *Bigbury Bay* patrols Deception Island waters.

Ultimately, nature itself took a hand in the Deception Island dispute and a volcanic eruption blew up the British and Chilean bases there, leaving the Argentinian one almost intact. In any case, by then the custom is said to have developed (and I will not vouch for the truth of the story) of base commanders delivering their official protests in rotation and afterwards being entertained at monumental parties. These parties so disrupted the work of the various national stations that the signing of the 1959 Antarctic Treaty, whereby all territorial claims were put in cold storage for thirty years, became inevitable.

At least the area was peaceful enough now, I thought, calculating that the treaty still had more than twenty years to run. A good thing too. The Antarctic presented obstacles enough to the lone seafarer without any additional naval complications.

By six o'clock on the morning of January 25, I could no longer stay awake. Continuing to maintain a lookout seemed pointless, since it was still snowing so heavily that, despite the daylight, visibility was nil. The unattended yacht went bowling along southward with a fair easterly breeze abeam.

The sun was shining when I woke at nine and the white-flecked sea was a deep blue—and floating upon it, glittering with such brilliance that my eyes hurt to look upon them, were three sugar-icing bergs. They lay in a line from east-southeast to west-northwest across our course. One was tabular, another castellated and the third weather worn and undulating.

Time to steer from the cockpit. Wearing my driest "hand socks" under the windproof but not waterproof canvas overmitts that I had been carefully husbanding for the occasion, and with fully impervious Marlin jacket zipped up over the recently repaired anorak, I was reasonably warm. Soon, a school of blackfish surfed by down the wave faces. Then bergy bits, some as big as small coasters, began to appear ahead and a good lookout became more than ever necessary. Around noon, we passed through the line and, the wind continuing to freshen, quickly left astern the three bergs with their inconspicuous but potentially lethal attendants.

The elderly staysail burst around four o'clock. I reluctantly unearthed from the forepeak the last remaining big headsail that I had been saving for the final approach. It was an old-fashioned sail called a footing staysail, specially made to fit *Isbjorn*'s shortish foremast and never before used. I hoisted it with two knots in the head and set off again. It drew well. "Going like hell," the log records.

Still the wind kept on increasing, until a northeast Force 8 gale was blowing by evening, when I reefed the new staysail, "cold, wet, anxious." Midnight, and I lowered the mainsail altogether, for, to my dismay, a strong Force 8 gale had by then developed. We continued southeastward under the storm trysail alone.

By the time that I got below, my hands were in agony. Minutes later, the pain eased and I battened down fully, then listened dully as volleys of spray exploded against the steel hull and the wind's howl became a scream in the squalls. There was no way of keeping a lookout for ice in these conditions. I crept miserably and fearfully into my chilled sleeping bag, more tired than I realized, because, for the first time ever, I went sound asleep in a gale.

Astonishingly, I did not wake until eight the next morning, January 26, Australia Day. The gale was still blowing but was down a little to Force 8. The cabin temperature was a cheerless minus two degrees Centigrade. Beyond the thirty-foot seas amongst which the yacht labored, gaps in the cloud wrack revealed icefields sweeping up to vast snow mountains and, nearer, a jagged, snow-streaked rocky pinnacle and a jumble of pallid tabular bergs. Far from feeling triumphant at this first sight of land for almost three months—land which I had thought never to see again—I was appalled at the forbidding prospect. After one jaundiced look, I retired to the damp warmth of my sleeping bag and pulled it firmly over my head.

Prudence soon brought me to life again. We were closing the coast fast. By midday, the truly gigantic scale of the icebergs in the foreground and of the ice plateaus and mountains behind was beginning to become apparent (though I was to continue to underestimate the vastness of the country, consistently believing we were closer inshore than we were—with dire consequences

to my pilotage). The wind had continued to decline but the seas were still huge, if less dangerous, and the sun was only intermittently visible. Sun sights at this juncture were so important that I hove to to take them. Even so, I was repeatedly jarred against the pram hood frame as I struggled for balance, and the resulting observations were poor ones.

I committed myself to an option. "Land is Brabant or Anvers Island. My bet (before working sight) is Anvers," I wrote. Sure enough, the latitude line, sixty-four degrees twenty-one minutes south did confirm it as being the west coast of the one-thousand-square-mile Anvers Island, on whose southern shore Palmer Station was situated. With such rapidity did the weather moderate that we were periodically becalmed from four-thirty that afternoon onwards.

Now I really did appreciate the magnificent panorama—sixty miles of ice cap and glacier topped by serrated summits two miles high. A truly enormous berg appeared to be grounded off what I (correctly) took to be Cape Alberto de Monaco, the southwest corner of Anvers, that we were slowly nearing, and which we must round to reach Palmer. The Anvers snowfields appeared, for all the world like level sheets of fog, filling and hiding the valleys, above which soared the lofty summits, culminating in nine-thousand-foot Mount Français, the highest point of the island.

I sat in the cockpit choked with emotion. Close alongside, parties of penguins called "ark, ark" as they porpoised out of the water, landing with a succession of little plops. I was still gazing out upon the scene when the light began to fade with evening. The sky above Anvers was a pastel green and the jagged Graham Coast ranges farther southward turned pale gold. A waning moon hung over the empty land. The ice cliffs of the great bergs turned from blue to mauve to violet and then deep purple. We stood on southeastwards towards an island that I had identified from the chart—only to find next morning that it was really just an iceberg.

The growing daylight revealed my error by 4:30 or so. I took the helm then and continued steering mostly from the cockpit all day; except in the flat calms that alternated monotonously with short-lived northeasterly and easterly wind flurries.

The rounding of Cape Alberto de Monaco would be attended with some hazard, the *Pilot* book warned. The cape itself was "fringed with islands and rocks, frequently with gigantic icebergs grounded between them, extending about seven and a half miles southwestward." (p. 159) Except for a tongue of moraine forming part of the shore of Arthur Harbor, where Palmer Station was sited, the Anvers coastline consisted entirely of one-hundred- to two-hundred-foot ice cliffs.

I wished, for a moment, that we were still making for the Argentine Islands described in the same work (p. 174) as possessing *"a peculiar luxuriance of vegetation . . . moss covering as much as an acre."* (My italics.) Then I recalled their formidable rocky defenses and was glad enough to forgo this mossy demiparadise. The safest route round the cape, I decided, bearing in mind the fickle breeze and our pathetic rig, was outside Joubin Islands at the apex of the extensive fringe of foul ground off Monaco proper. (I was wrong. The inshore route would have been better.)

Tension mounted very high off the first of the Joubins, which we reached about 11:30 after some six hours at the tiller, for the breeze died away completely, leaving the shoreward-setting current free to bear the helpless yacht down upon the snowcapped islet. She had drifted perilously near when a swirl of snowflakes signaled a welcome breath of wind and we ghosted clear of the danger. A little farther on, the track lay hard by an echoing wave-worn cavern, scooped from the base of a three-hundred-foot berg where, even on this calmest of days, surf boomed and thundered, and the passing *Ice Bird* was rocked by the scend.

All afternoon, we continued threading our way among fantastically weathered, grounded bergs and rocky shoals, sometimes passing within a biscuit toss of cold stone or colder blue ice, from time to time, crunching through lines of brash with many a jarring thump. "With no engine or proper sail it was hell," I wrote afterwards, without any exaggeration, for at any mo-

ment during those slow dragging hours a stray current could have grounded and wrecked us. Those anxious hours stretched well into the afternoon, so that it was 5:30 before the Joubins, and their parent cape, had been rounded. Palmer base was eight miles away across a stretch of skerry-studded water.

It might well have been on the moon, so utterly unattainable was it. For it lay dead in the teeth of the easterly wind which, unfortunately, was now the prevailing one, and *Ice Bird*'s ability to tack to windward was minimal and might even prove nonexistent. The sail area was not only totally inadequate, it was also ill balanced. The footing staysail was so large in proportion to the tiny trisail doing duty as a main, that the first gust to break each calm blew the bow round, pivoting the yacht downwind. Not until she had slowly gathered way could I persuade her to swing reluctantly back to windward again, by which time she had lost the better part of the ground so painfully gained earlier. By the same token, the bow was readily knocked to leeward by the slap of the short inshore waves.

I was very tired, for I had been steering for thirteen and a half hours in the chill open air. An elementary mistake in applying magnetic variation, which could well have had fatal consequences, brought sharply home to me the unreliability of my weary brain. Rest and sleep were obviously essential. But where in these tidal waters, surrounded by so many dangers, could it be managed? Anchoring was out of the question; it was far too deep, each islet and shoal was the tip of an underwater pinnacle rising sheer from fifty-fathoms. Safety was so very near. After all the trials we had been through, were we to be wrecked on the very threshold? Exhausted and utterly unnerved, I burst into tears.

Hot coffee—with a generous addition of rum—and a cold snack revived my spirits a little. I took a chance, having no real alternative, and dozed for two hours while *Ice Bird* drifted becalmed. When I awoke at ten, feeling rather better, there was wind again, but the light had grown too dim to sail safely any longer, so I lowered the big staysail, leaving the yacht to forereach slowly under her trisail alone.

One of the unpredictable sudden changes of Antarctic weather now took a hand. Gale-force gusts, easterly, unfortunately, set in shortly after midnight and drove us towards a fanged huddle of skerries overlooked by a double-spired cathedrallike iceberg. I wore round (jibed) on to the port tack and, still under trisail, began to win clear, heading southeastward away from Anvers Island.

As the iceberg receded, I was electrified at the sight of Palmer Station's tantalizingly inaccessible light shining brightly across the intervening miles. Perhaps they had a motorboat that could tow me in? We were moving farther away every minute. I hurriedly let off a flare, which, predictably at that range, accomplished nothing more than burning my fingers.

The violent gusts coalesced into a gale that increased until it was howling, snow laden, down from the mountain defiles at a good sixty knots. The waves were steep but no more than five feet high, for the nearby land gave shelter. In company with a small drifting berg, *Ice Bird* forereached in the direction of the snow-covered Wauwermans Islands off the entrance to Gerlache Strait, which separates Anvers Island from the mainland. The strait is nearly five miles across but, search as I would, once the gaunt buttresses had emerged into the light of a sickly dawn, not one solitary sign of a break could be detected in that sheer mountain wall.

The desire to sleep had again become overpowering. The dangers were obvious, for, although the gale had begun to ease, *Ice Bird* was still moving much too fast for safety. The visibility (it was now 3:00 A.M. on the twenty-eighth) was reasonable but insufficient to detect perils an hour or more ahead. The best I could do was to come about, head towards reasonably open water, and refrain from emptying my bladder before slumping down on to the bunk. Sure enough, the discomfort soon woke me, and once again, but the third time, I slept more soundly and did not awaken until half-past nine. I jumped up, but too late to have been of any use because a jagged rock skerry was even then slipping by only fifty yards abeam. A narrow escape indeed. I dare not doze again.

By eleven that morning, we were once more lying becalmed off the familiar twin-spired berg and its accompanying cold, wet rocks—two hundred yards to windward of where we had been at eleven o'clock the evening before. Little change occurred until two in the afternoon, when a relatively steady northeast breeze set in that bore the yacht across under Anvers—and into a tide race among the Outcast Islands, which, the *Pilot* book advised (p. 160), not very helpfully, "should be given a wide berth." It was a great relief eventually to be through the islands and to be painfully, ever so slowly gaining ground tacking towards Palmer.

The breeze continued to hold. Around ten that evening, a misty drizzle set in, cloaking the dangerous rocks from my view. There was obviously no hope of making port that night, the base being still three miles away upwind. There were two alternatives. Either heave to for the night where we were, or stand out eastwards into the mist on a long tack, the return leg of which should bring us into Arthur Harbor. I chose the second alternative and came very close, in consequence, to losing my ship and my life.

With the steadier wind, I could go below, for *Ice Bird* was now able to steer herself quite well on the wind with the tiller loosely lashed. My jerseys and flying suit beneath the impervious Marlin jacket and trousers were quite as soaked with my own sweat as were my feet, for I had been continuously "wet suited" in full outdoor gear for some days. Of more practical moment, my overmitts and wool gloves were also soaked —from sleet and from handling wet sheets on our frequent tacks. A month earlier and my hands could never have stood it. Now I could repeatedly spend minutes at a time in the chilled, wet darkness of the cockpit, before my fingers drove me inside the cabin again.

There was, fortunately, not a trace of the overwhelming sleepiness I had felt the night before. Perhaps it was the generous tots of overproof rum that I kept drinking to keep myself warm. The rum certainly did counteract wind chill and helped me to stay alert, and I must have consumed all of half a bottle that night. I well know that all this is contrary to accepted ideas on physiology, but these are possibly oversimplified and, moreover, take little account of the body's sometimes altered reactions in conditions of extreme stress.

Monday, January 29. Forty minutes past midnight. All at once, we seemed to have become surrounded by masses of bergy bits. Peering through the murk, I became aware of a loom which took form as the ghostly outline of an enormous berg, the source of the bergy bits. I came about with all speed. Several times in the next few minutes, *Ice Bird* brought up hard against growlers and I blessed her steel hull. They soon fell astern, but she had repeatedly to plow through crackling brash ice that gave out a delicate musical tinkling. Hearing things again, I thought, but the explanation, I heard later, was a natural one. Air bubbles trapped ten thousand years ago in the glacier were being released as the ice melted in the sea.

With dawn close at hand and the wind at last fair for Palmer, came the moment of deadliest peril. I was in the cabin when all of a sudden I felt *Ice Bird* lift under me. We were close under the land; this just could not be happening to us. As these incredulous thoughts shot through my mind, I was leaping for the cockpit and the tiller. As I reached it, a swelling crest broke roaring all about us and I realized that we were in breakers over a rocky shoal. Three times, the seven-ton yacht was picked up bodily and surfed forward through the white, frothing turmoil while I clung to the tiller, at every second expecting the keel to strike and the adventure—and my life—to end among jagged rocks in freezing water: within a mile of safety.

The six-foot-deep keel must have passed over the rocks with no more than inches to spare. I was still trembling with reaction when the increasing light at 2:30 A.M. enabled me to round Lichfield Island into Arthur Harbor and enter sheltered water for the first time since leaving Half Moon Bay three months before.

The gallant little yacht had come sixty-one hundred nautical miles from Sydney in 14½ weeks. Since being dismasted 8½ weeks ago, she had traversed twenty-five hundred miles at a creditable average (especially allowing for the many days without sail) of forty-one miles a day.

The buildings of Palmer Antarctic Station (sixty-four degrees forty-six minutes south, sixty-four degrees two minutes west.) were silhouetted clearly now against a tremendous looming background of ice piedmont. Torgersen Island passed to port, alive with tiny dinner-jacketed figures stumbling over rocks that were ochre red with krill-stained droppings and acrid with the smell of a penguin rookery. There was a rock-built pier in front of the station, made fast to which was a converted minesweeper that later proved to be Jacques Cousteau's *Calypso*. What a little ship, I thought, to venture into these waters. Then I laughed at my own reaction. *Ice Bird* was no more than twice as long as her capacious outboard dinghy.

I dropped anchor within ten yards of the sleeping motor vessel. Then, fearing the patent anchor might drag on the glacier-smoothed bottom of the sound, I called out.

"Is anyone awake? Do you mind if I tie up alongside?" The saloon door crashed open and a very startled figure appeared. I threw him a line and made fast. The first singlehanded voyage to Antarctica had been accomplished.

The Ultimate Storm

by WILLIAM A. ROBINSON

A New England shipbuilder who had moved to Tahiti after World War II, William A. Robinson had an ambitious goal. He wanted to cross the Southern Ocean in the track of the great square-riggers and follow the Humboldt Current northward. Then he ran into the ultimate storm. His superb description of the fear as well as the exultation of surviving the storm's fury in his seventy-foot brigantine Varua *give this account, from* To the Great Southern Sea, *a lasting place in the literature of the sea.*

AHEAD of us still lay a thousand miles of Roaring Forties, part of it with 10 percent of gales or more. But we were now on the chart of the easternmost part of the South Pacific. Our destination, Valdivia, was over on the far edge, a much more explicit goal than an abstract compass course. The albatross, which had vanished during the fog, were back, among them a new variety that was black on top and had a black design under the shoulder. I looked forward to the simple problem of the Roaring Forties, uncomplicated by ice, as something of a rest cure. Such is the innocence and perennial optimism of the sailor.

At dark, the wind whipped out of the northeast in a heavy squall. The barometer was falling fast. Still obsessed with carrying on to the limit to regain some of our lost time, I held on to the mainsail and nursed the ship until midnight, when the squall had not abated and it was apparent that this was another gale, again from the theoretically nonexistent northeast quadrant. In the glow of the masthead light, we got the big sail down safely and secured it with extra lashings. Number 3 had long since been taken off. Now number 2 was sent down to the saloon for repairs to the tack, which had started to open up again. Really bad weather was always the sign for us to make repairs to our two "expendables."

We carried on into the early morning hours under fore and main staysails, making fair time, thinking it was just another northeast gale, not knowing it was to be the culminating storm experience of my life. Anything I had previously seen was child's play compared with what was in store for us during the next forty-eight hours.

We were lying to under our fore staysail and lower main staysail, both of which were built for riding out gales. We lay on the port tack heading five or six points off the wind, forging slowly ahead and making visible leeway. Sometime around 3:30 A.M., when there was enough light for me to see the size and weight of the seas, I put out the oil bags. The effect of the slick on the breaking crests was at once apparent, but even under the two small storm staysails we were sailing too fast, leaving the oil astern. This was temporarily corrected by hauling the fore staysail somewhat to windward, increasing the leeway but stopping the forward motion. The seas were as big as any I had ever seen, perhaps thirty to thirty-five feet, and breaking heavily. We rode beautifully, taking hardly any water on deck.

All went well until sometime after daybreak, when the seas reached such height and steepness that our sails were blanketed when in the trough and subjected to a terrific blast on the crest. When the wind began to tear off whole chunks of sea from the crests and hurl them across our deck into the sails, I took them off.

We put extra lashings around all the sails. Everything else was already snug and secure. Boats and rope cage had all the lashings that could be passed through the ringbolts. Storm covers were on all hatches. There is never loose gear on deck.

Finding her natural drift, with wheel lashed amidships, *Varua* fell off several points and drifted slowly downwind with the seas on her quarter, driven and steadied by the wind on her bare masts and yards. In spite of the increasing wind and sea, she was easier and drier than she had been before, and the oil slick was obviously more effective.

The barometer had fallen half an inch in a few hours. The speed with which wind and sea built up was amazing. The familiar moan of the gale in the rigging increased to a new high-pitched wail. But *Varua* was taking care of herself well, so I worked off my nervous energy doing two jobs I had been putting off: cleaning the engine-room bilge suction and taking up a section of floor to retrieve a lost wrench.

Gradually during the day the gale shifted from northeast to north, but slowly enough so that the seas shifted with it. The ship continued to handle herself nicely, coming up gradually as the wind shifted, keeping it on her quarter. The oil seemed to reduce the power of the breaking crests so that no solid water came aboard. The barometer had stopped its downward rush at 29.50 and was leveling off. The sea was the most impressive I had ever experienced, but the whole thing had developed so fast I was convinced it would blow itself out in a matter of hours.

I was wrong. As night fell, both wind and sea were worse, and I began to feel uneasy. The barometer now remained steady. Oil bags were renewed just before dark, with foul-smelling but effective fish oil that had been aboard ever since 1945 when we left Gloucester. We also had two small drums of heavy coconut oil from Tahiti to experiment with, but it had solidified from the cold and was useless.

Nothing was said, but all of us gathered that evening in the saloon. The ship underwent increasingly violent gyrations and had that cello-like tremble throughout that goes with real gale winds. Through the cabin windows—buried deep one moment, carving great arcs across the sky the next—we caught a glimpse now and then of the growing moon, momentarily visible between flying clouds. I could not help thinking, as I felt the seas crash outside, of the fragile fabric that made up this small ship—man and his little toy—pitted against what was outside. What was more vulnerable, what more dependent upon each individual part? I turned on the radio to drown out the noise of the storm and, surprisingly, it functioned perfectly. We listened to South American music. We made jokes about South American weather and laughed too loudly at our jokes.

At 9:00 P.M., I wrote in the log that "the storm is at its worst." Again I was wrong. From then on things got worse instead of better. The ship jarred more heavily from breaking crests, in spite of the oil. The shriek of wind and the vibration of the whole structure increased—but my confidence that the ship could take care of herself was still unshaken.

At 11:00 P.M., I told the others to try to get some rest, and lay down for a fitful nap myself, only to be awakened a half hour later by a jarring crash as if we had been struck by a pile driver. It was obvious that *Varua* was in trouble now and needed help. Putting on oilskins, I went to the wheel.

As soon as my eyes had become adjusted to the blackness of the night, I could see what was happening. The mechanical action of the rolling seas, now towering incredibly steep and high, had overcome her natural downwind drift. Nearing the top of a sea, the wind blast would heel her over, get a grip on her forward top hamper and start to drive her downwind as before. Then the crest would strike her on the quarter, counteracting the wind. Finally, falling down the steep back side of the sea, cut off from the wind, she would slide broadside to. This was final, dangerous proof of what I had always feared: that letting a ship take her natural drift would not work when conditions produced a disproportionately high, steep sea.

To satisfy my curiosity once and for all, I left her this way a little longer to find out if it was true that "a good ship left alone will always take care of herself." The seas were so huge and concave at this point that the whole upper third seemed to collapse and roar vertically down on us. Our oil had little or no effect now, as the surface water was all being blown to leeward. After feeling the shock of two or three of the more moderate seas crashing down on us, I felt I had carried my scientific investigation far enough. I unlashed the wheel and with no effort at all ran her off downwind before one of the real monsters chanced to break on us. I am convinced that, although her hull structure might have withstood the battering, boats and everything else on deck would have been swept away, and most likely masts as well.

Realizing at last that this was building toward the ultimate conditions I had never yet encountered, I ran *Varua* off dead before it. In choosing to run as a final emergency tactic, I was going against all the books. I thanked my stars we did not have a sea anchor out, for nothing in the world outside of being moored to an island would have held her head into the wind and seas that were now running.

The seas were white phosphorescent avalanches that I felt towering over my head astern but did not see until they burst down on us and swept by on either side. Although under bare poles, *Varua* picked up speed and began running six or seven knots, dangerously, but steering beautifully. We at once put out drags and slowed her down to about three knots, which still left her

with good rudder control. It took a seventy-five-fathom, two-inch-diameter Manila line which we dragged in a big bight, plus four seventy-five-foot mooring lines of the same size, each dragging its big eye splice, plus about a hundred fathoms of assorted lines of smaller size.

Moving slowly ahead as we now were, we could lay an oil slick right along our path and astern. Sometimes, to my astonishment, the wind picked up so much surface water that it even carried some of our oil ahead of us. Conditions being extreme, we kept two oil bags on each side, lashed outboard to the channels so that they could not be thrown by the seas, and pumped oil steadily through a toilet down below. It is difficult to say how much good it did, but it seemed to me that the seas broke less frequently on us than at a little distance to either side, and less heavily.

It was 11:30 P.M. when I took the wheel and began to run. It was noon the following day before a tendency to abate made it safe to turn the ship over to Tino. During those 12½ hours, we fought a battle so crucial that had any one of the great breaking seas caught us off balance we would have been swept. At the very least, this would have meant the loss of boats.

Shifting imperceptibly from north to northwest, the storm reached a peak at around 2:00 A.M. It is banal to use the term *hurricane* as it is so misused, particularly in the accounts of sailing craft. But I have experienced several recorded hurricanes in my life, both on land and at sea, and this was worse than any of them. Before the wind had reached its peak, there had been a whole new set of shrieks and howls in the rigging and fittings. I now learned something entirely new: that when the wind exceeds a certain point, most of these noises stop, and this was more ominous than ever.

From time to time, I began to hear what I thought was thunder—a hollow booming that reverberated through the night—not realizing at first that it was the sound of great seas breaking. But these were seas greater by far than any I had ever before seen.

With all our drags astern, and bare poles, we sailed our steady three or four knots through the water—except when the crests passed under us and we rode them at breathtaking speed. When I spoke of the culminating experience of a life of voyaging, this is what I had in mind. When a fifty-ton, seventy-foot vessel surfboards shudderingly down the face of a great sea on its breaking crest, you have experienced something.

At these times, she was going downhill at such a steep angle that when she reached the bottom she would bury her bowsprit before rising: an excellent object lesson, for if she had been carrying any sail, or even running under bare poles without drags, she would probably have gone right on down.

This was now a fight to save the ship—the final great test which *Varua* had been built to survive. I remembered the design days, bent over the drafting table with Starling Burgess.

"Her rudder must be above all worry," I had said, and that had been easy—a simple matter of engineering.

And when all the other details had been surmounted, there remained the last, the most important of all.

"She must be able to run before it with safety in any weather."

It was against prevailing opinion to choose as a last resort to run with great breaking seas, but I knew instinctively that there would come a point when you could no longer hold her into it, either by drags, sea anchors, riding sails or any other means. When that point was reached, it would probably be too late to turn and run.

I remembered our anxious trips to Stevens Institute with the hull model for tank testing. Special apparatus had been devised to simulate following seas. At first, her stern had been more conventional; but she had a tendency to pull the following seas over on top of her and even to broach to. Little by little, the stern was changed and the rest of the underwater lines accordingly, until one day we had a model that did not disturb the form of the following sea, that did not trip, that ran true before it at all speeds. We called it her "double chin" stern.

Varua had always performed beautifully, but she had never fought for her life before. Starling Burgess is dead now, so he will never know. I like to think that his spirit was there watching, for *Varua* met her test like the thoroughbred she is, running true and clean. Never once that night or the following morning did she make a false move, or fail to lift when she should, or fail to respond to every move of the wheel.

That night was the only time I have felt acute danger of being bodily injured by a sea. There was a double Manila line around my waist, made fast to the bitts beside me, so I could hardly have been washed overboard. But if I were beaten unconscious by a breaking sea and the ship broached to out of control, it would amount to the same thing. The danger in these seas lay in the fact that they were unnaturally short compared to their towering, almost perpendicular height. They had built up so incredibly fast against the old easterly sea that they had had no time to lengthen out.

There was fear in the air that night as the great, blazing hollow crests hung over my head blotting out half the sky. My body tried to shrink down into the steering well for shelter. My hands spun the wheel instinctively to maintain control and keep the keel exactly in line with the sea as we made the trembling rush on the crest.

From time to time, the others passed up mugs of hot soup through the six-inch compass hole in the after side of the chart house. Someone would shout through the hole the latest barometer reading, as I tried to gulp the soup between seas before the wind siphoned it away into the air. The work at the wheel was physically and nervously exhausting, not only from the strenuous exertion, but from the sheer weight of wind, which seemed of only slightly less substance than the sea itself. The dark, low-ceilinged sky seemed to press upon me. There was a feeling of continuity about the gale, of timelessness. In a sort of coma, I steered automatically down the face of the great breaking seas. Everything combined to produce weariness—except my growing confidence in *Varua*.

Sometime around three o'clock in the morning, before daybreak, a sea larger than any of the others broke just as our stern started to lift to it. Tino and Zizi had taken turns pumping oil out through the forward toilet. Possibly there was a

William A. Robinson, left, and a Tahitian crewman aboard Varua, *the seventy-foot brigantine in which Robinson crossed the Southern Ocean in the track of the square riggers.*

lull in the slick just then, as the men changed shifts. More probably, this sea was just so big that nothing could stop or soften it. I had felt it building up in the ominous calm after two or three other great seas had lifted us, and began to tense myself some time before it struck. We had several times been swept by broken water as crests carried us along, or by a cross-sea that came in from the wrong direction, but not by one of the main seas.

This time we were under one of the boomers. As *Varua* lifted on the body of the wave, the breaking crest hung high overhead, and as it

broke I braced myself as low as I could get in the well, holding the wheel in a viselike grip. It crashed on me with a tremendous blow, burying the entire after part of the ship under solid water but pouring off on either side by the time it got past the chart house. I remember hoping just as it hit me on the back that no big fish was lurking in the crest.

Even under the tremendous power exerted by this sea, *Varua* continued to respond to the helm and held straight on her course dead before it. A moment later came the shouted report through the slot in the compass hole that everything was all right below. Water had spurted through hatches that had always been tight, but that was all.

I had felt that my physical endurance might fail. The immersion in ice water brought me out of my fatigue with a vengeance. And when I saw how the ship handled herself with her whole after part immersed under the weight of a great sea, I felt a spiritual lift that released in me the extra forces that we call up to carry us through times of great crisis. I was probably still as cold and bone weary as it is possible to get, but the relief from the ultimate crisis made things seem almost agreeable.

Again and again that night, I asked myself why I was there—and had no better answer than that perhaps this was the very thing that had drawn me into this voyage: an unexpressed urge to experience a real Cape Horn gale. We were not off Cape Horn, but we were close enough for this to be the real thing. And along with the fear that was in the air that night was the exultation that came with the knowledge that the ship would always respond, and that wind of this force could not go on forever, and that I could go on and on, instinctively meeting each sea as it came until the storm was over . . . and perhaps to know this was the reason I was there.

By daybreak, the glass was rising slowly and by 10:00 A.M. I would have let Tino take her. He came and crouched by me, on the other side of the wheel, but was too appalled by the size of the seas to take the responsibility. They were still destructive, the wind in the squalls still screamed, but things were appreciably better. Not until noon would he take her alone. By this time, the destructive force was obviously slackening, although there was still plenty of danger.

The gale had started in the northeast. It had piled up the worst seas from northwest at the height of its fury. Now it had shifted to west. One had to decide which seas were the worst and meet them, allowing the lesser ones to hit us off balance. And as the wind eased, some of the seas got out of control, becoming what I call "crazy seas," which tower up into a huge pyramid and break quite unpredictably. You could not meet one of these crazy seas as you did the more con-

ventional ones—you just hoped you weren't there.

It was 5:00 P.M. when we started to get the drags in, a simple matter of heaving them in one at a time. At 6:00 P.M., we tried the main staysail on her to feel out the seas under way, leaving two or three drag lines still out and keeping on with the oil. A little later, we added the fore staysail and were able to sail our course with the seas on our quarter, seas that were now lengthening out and losing their punch. We hauled in the last of the drags and went on our way, undamaged, but smelling to high heaven of fish oil, sailing in seas that were still greater than any I had previously experienced, but that now, by comparison, seemed perfectly safe. The wind was around to southwest now, and as we resumed our regular watches we were able to steer our course for Patagonia.

Released from captivity just before dark, when the crests were no longer dangerous, eleven-year-old Piho scrambled out at once into the steering well demanding permission to bathe in the rain. Her brown body was covered by only a scrap of red *pareu* around her middle. I don't suppose it would have hurt her, but the thought of it made me shudder in my woolens, boots and two suits of oilskins. I sent her below to bathe, where it was somewhat warmer, but a little later as I was going through my own ritual preliminary to turning in, I wondered if perhaps a bath in the rain, no matter how cold, was to Piho what my shave was to me. For tense and tired as I was, I let down slowly, bathing, shaving, eating leisurely with Ah You at the gimbal table—savoring to the full the exquisite satisfaction of peace after storm before going contentedly to my berth.

The morning after the storm, Tino let me sleep right through my dawn watch. There was a wonderful unspoken understanding between Tino and myself. He was supposed to wake me at 3:00 A.M. every morning for my watch, although he never did. Normally, I would wake up anyway, but when I was behind in sleep, I would get an extra half hour or so before my built-in alarm system began to function. Later, when I had the wheel during the day, I would repay him by letting him oversleep his nap. This particular morning, I slept right on until the smell of breakfast filtered vaguely through to my subconscious. The whole day was vague, as a matter of fact. It was nothing very much as days went, with an unpleasant squally wind; but it was a fair wind at last, from southwest, and we were all under that strange, light-headed intoxication that comes after great fatigue—content with the realization that we and the ship had surpassed ourselves in what was probably the greatest test of our lives. We had between us that extra something that creates an unspoken bond between people who have come through a great ordeal together.

During the hours of trial, I had thought of nothing but security, comfort—even of quitting the sea forever and using *Varua* as a houseboat. Now, after a good night's sleep, the dual nature of the seafarer asserted itself, and I realized that probably never, in any other life, would I feel as fit as I did now.

By midday, we must have been sailing as fast as we ever did. With the wind in the southwest, on our quarter, all our sails pulled to the greatest advantage. That is, all except Number 3, which was down in the saloon being reinforced and which could not have been carried anyway, for the wind must have been near gale force, although we were still too numb from the great storm to feel it.

Looking back, I realize that we were carrying practically full sail under conditions that would have had us shortened way down before the storm. Already we referred to it as *the* storm, and always would. Most of the time, we had been driving as usual in the direction of the Horn. It was a relief to be racing at top speed toward Valdivia for a change, under conditions that were at last ideal for our brigantine rig with its tremendous lifting power.

Night came and we were still flying. The following seas carried us with them, but they were longer now and did not feel dangerous. They were still the seas from our storm, but spread out more. On my first night watch, I was conscious enough to realize vaguely that something magnificent was occurring—Sibelius's

Night Ride kept running round and round in my head—but I was still in a semicomatose state and only half noticed how fast the phosphorescence was flying past the racing hull. We must have been sailing even faster than during the night of February 2, when we made our record run of 233 miles, for when noon came the next day, February 8, we had run 240 miles, and this will, without doubt, remain the greatest day's run of my life.

It is ironic that during the only twenty-four-hour period of the voyage in which we had the weather of the fairy stories, I was still in such a state of numbness from the experience we had been through that it hardly registered. Of the first twelve hours, I remember very little except a lot of violent motion which interfered with our effort to scrub the fish-oil smell from the ship down below. And at night there was *Night Ride*.

It was only on the following morning when I took the wheel from Tino and waited for the dawn that it really began to register. When it was light enough to see, I realized that here at last was the southern ocean of literature: "The Brave West Winds roaring fresh behind us and the mile-long seas breaking high . . ." But even so, I was not prepared for the 240 miles when I laid down our noon position, so little so that I took additional sights and rechecked the previous day's figures as well, to be sure it was true.

These two great runs that *Varua* made are probably not records compared with the big ocean-racing yachts with their mountain of sail nursed by large crews, but considering how undersparred and undercanvased *Varua* is, to allow me to sail her with two men, I think it is going some. And in both cases, we were sailing east, or nearly so, and the period from noon to noon was sixteen minutes less than twenty-four hours due to the time we gained on the sun. These two days, plus two more on which we did respectively 202 and 170 miles, were the only days on the entire voyage when we were able to run free on our course. It is interesting to speculate that had it been possible to maintain the 211-mile average of these four days with really fair winds, we might have sailed from Rapa to Corral over the 3,800-mile route originally planned in just eighteen days.

Filled with elation at the fantastic day's run we had made, we even forgot to resent the squalls and fine, cold driving rain that plagued us all the following night.

After this, I realized we had nothing to fear from the southern ocean any more. We were well clear of the ice limits. Ahead lay several five-degree squares with 10 percent and 12 percent gales—but no gale could ever frighten us after our storm. We were well into our last thousand miles, putting our destination within grasp. One can get one's mind around a few hundred miles. In the thousands, it is better not to think, but to live from day to day. Now there was the growing mystery and excitement of approaching landfall. The little necklace of tiny circles on the chart representing noon positions had crept across the empty spaces, sometimes going in the right direction, sometimes not, until now the thin chain had almost reached Chile. Two or three more would complete the circuit.

The next day was beautiful and we made a fine run. The wind was back in the northwest. For the second time since we entered southern latitudes, the sky was clear. At noon the thermometer was up to sixty-one degrees Fahrenheit and by midafternoon to sixty-five degrees Fahrenheit. I kept repeating in the log "beautiful day," ignoring the big noon halo around the sun, for I was through worrying about signs. After a good sleep, I got out the books on the Cape Horners again. We felt like Cape Horners now. It had been uncanny how we had been constantly forced in the direction of the Horn. Tino had started referring to it as our Cape Horn voyage, and soon the others followed suit. If it had not been for Ah You's condition and the nearness of the approaching event, I think we might have taken the line of least resistance and sailed on around.

Relaxing in the sun on the transom at the foot of the companionway, I reread the saga of the last of the great Cape Horners that had passed this way in the twilight of the great days of sail, and especially of the Finnish fleet of Gustaf Erickson. These ships were the culmination of the knowledge man had stored up over the ages in building and rigging great ocean sailers. Like *Varua,* they had met their great test in these waters. The lucky ones made a fast passage to the Horn and home. The others fell by the wayside dismasted, perhaps driven under, or kept a rendezvous at night with ice and oblivion like the *Kobenhavn.* Perhaps the lucky ones were those that never came home, for they were spared the ignominy of ending their days as coal hulks, or the ultimate disgrace of the breakup yards.

Our trail had followed the route of these last great windjammers. The names ran clearly through my memory: the *Herzogin Cecilie, Grace Harwar, Lawhill, Olivebank, Penang* and all the others. I could almost imagine the ghosts of the great ships booming along before their westerly gales. Our gales had all been easterly; perhaps the westerlies had died with the windjammers.

Thinking of the crews who sailed them down these latitudes—cold and wet for weeks—I realized that they would have considered our mild hardships a life of luxury, eased as they were by hot meals, dry clothes, good quarters and a warm galley to retreat to.

As I read, I glanced up through the companionway at little Piho at the wheel, steering the ship through green seas that still ran high, her pigtails escaped from under her oversize yellow sou'wester hat. I could almost hear the vanished crews turning over in their graves to cry out in horror at this final insult of an eleven-year-old Tahitian girl alone on deck steering a sailing ship through the Roaring Forties.

That night, we had one more wild ride, as usual to the accompaniment of the fine steady rain that prevails in these parts. Vaguely defined squalls built up the wind, now in the northwest, to the danger point for the upper staysails. Number 3 was furled at daybreak to preserve it, while I tried to carry Number 2 on through, expecting the wind to ease up with the sun. But the clew let go at 4:30 A.M., and this perenially expendable sail was again brought down to the saloon for repairs. Both Tino and Zizi had shaved at 4:00 A.M. while waiting around for orders as I debated taking off the topsail. By 5:00 A.M., they were sewing on Number 2. I was struck by the fact that our unnatural hours had become so habitual that nobody thought anything of them.

There was the usual slack period shortly after sunrise. Number 2 was repaired by then, so Tino went aloft and bent it again. Before the wind came back full force, it was set and drawing once more. Our run could not equal the other two record days, but it was good for 202 miles noon to noon, after which the wind shifted suddenly back to southwest after rather startling barometer gyrations, and it fell calm and that was the end of our "westerlies" passage.

Even Ah You recovered now, with the calm, easy motion and the thought of approaching landfall. The weeks of dismal sickness were gone and the future was bright again. She put on a gaily colored *pareu,* combed her long hair and with shining eyes, got out the guitar and sang Paumotu songs.

There were two days of light, shifting breezes and calms, and crazy seas and the voyage was almost done. *Varua* was a beehive of activity, the two girls singing down below as they waxed and polished and prepared the ship for landfall. Zizi, inspired by their example, fell to and cleaned the galley as it had never been cleaned before. Work done, Tino and Zizi would sit together at the wheel talking endlessly, with the enthusiasm of Tahitians, who are never bored. They had been nearly five thousand miles to-gether now and were still not talked out. To our great joy, we caught our first fish since leaving Tahiti, an enormous tuna. We ate fish for breakfast, lunch, and supper—raw, boiled, baked, fried.

The albatross were leaving us now. Only one was left and he seemed to be as reluctant to leave us as we were to see him go. Those great birds are in truth the "Friend of the Cape Horner." The last I saw of him he was floating disconsolately and disheveled on the sea—perhaps waiting for wind to help him take off.

On February 13, when we were five thousand miles out and had only three hundred to go to Port Corral, our old enemy the northeaster came back at us for a last effort. To the end, it would have been easier to go around the Horn. It was a brisk, rainy twenty-four-hour gale. We knew all its tricks, except the weird sea it produced blowing against a huge southwest swell, but it drove us south again to make our landfall far down on the rugged islands off the Patagonian coast. When this last brief gale blew itself out there was no wind left, and we were becalmed only a day's sail from land. The shore birds were all around us. We were avid to see the coast and impatiently started the engine and went on to make landfall under power over an undulating sea that was as smooth as patent leather.

Shipwreck

by HAL ROTH

Hal and Margaret Roth, veteran sailors, left California in their thirty-five-foot sloop to sail through the archipelago on the southwest coast of South America, one of the most remote places on earth, and then continue around Cape Horn. But only twenty-four miles from the Horn, a violent storm wrecked their yacht on a desolate, rocky shore. Hal Roth's account, from Two Against Cape Horn, *is a singular story of courage and resourcefulness.*

THE first feeling the shipwreck gave me was one of incredulity. "It can't happen to me," I muttered as I bit my lip. "Wrecks only happen to other people, because *my* preparations and *my* seamanship are too perfect." Yet poor *Whisper* lay wounded on a rocky beach on an uninhabited islet twenty-four miles north-northwest of Cape Horn. At high tide, the yacht was one-third full of water, and the pounding of the hull against the cannonball-sized rocks was no myth.

Each incoming wave picked up the vessel a little and dropped her as the water receded, slamming the yacht down on the beach. The hull creaked and groaned and shivered. It was awful. I thought of all the places Margaret and I and *Whisper* had been together—French Polynesia, Rarotonga, Samoa, Kusaie, Japan, the Aleutian Islands, Alaska, the Queen Charlotte Islands, the Galapagos, Peru. . . . We had had a few dangerous moments but *Whisper* had always come through. But now, stupid fool, I had let her down. The mighty captain had allowed his vessel to drag ashore in a heavy westerly gale. The whole thing was monstrous and inconceivable.

Shipwrecked! Obviously, the anchors had gotten fouled and were useless. Could I lay out another anchor on a long warp? I looked out into the inky night. Bursts of frigid spray slapped me in the face like shotgun pellets as the waves broke on the stony beach where *Whisper* lay thumping. At that moment, another barrage of williwaws exploded down the mountains of Isla Bayly. The moan of the wind quickly increased to a baritone wail. There was no possibility of launching a dinghy and putting out an anchor until the wind eased.

According to the angle-of-heel indicator we lay at fifty degrees to starboard. The visibility was terrible, but by waving a flashlight around I could dimly see that we were on the edge of an islet with smooth water only a few yards to leeward. Maybe we would blow or bump our way across. But as soon as I thought of this, I knew we would never move to the quiet water beyond the islet because the yacht was so firmly aground. Indeed, the starboard deck almost touched the beach, which was composed of smooth, roundish stones eight inches or so in diameter. There were hundreds, no thousands of these stones that clattered together when a wave rolled in, and again a moment later when the water ran out. It was hard to look around because of the flying water and the steep angle of heel of the yacht. It took a good deal of hanging on to keep from falling over the side.

If only I could row an anchor out to windward while the tide was still flooding. . . . I wondered how many shipwrecked mariners had muttered those words?

To keep from getting increasingly soaked with cold water as the waves broke over the yacht, I went back inside and slammed shut the hatch. Below, I found water rising inside the hull. We had no doubt been holed or stove in on the starboard side where the yacht was pounding. The date was April 29; the time was 1930. We still had two and a half hours to high water. I made a quick calculation with the tidal tables and worked out that the water would rise less than two feet, not enough to swamp or submerge the vessel.

It was impossible to walk around inside *Whisper* because of the angle of heel. We climbed from handhold to handhold. All the loose gear tended to fall toward the low side, which was soon a couple of feet deep in the water. I thought of the women chatting quietly about dinner half an hour earlier. Now we had to shout to talk above the noise of the wind, the waves and the pounding of the hull. Everything had happened so quickly that I was only vaguely aware that a new chapter in my life had begun. I knew that hard times lay ahead.

There were four of us on board. My wife Margaret, dear Margaret, was as steady as a pillar of stone and completely dependable when the going was hard. Eve—the photographer's wife—had sailed with us for a few days in California at an earlier time. She seemed sensible, calm and thoughtful, full of ideas, and she was always willing to pitch in and help. I had no idea how she would react in a crisis.

I knew less about Adam, her husband. He was a big, well-built man with a huge beard and a deep bass voice. A talented filmmaker, he was smart, his mind was logical, and he spoke well. In the last few days, I had learned that he knew little about sailing and was hesitant about helping with the yacht and various chores unless I directed him step by step. Although he wanted to learn about long-distance sailing, he considered any sort of detail work—making eye splices and whipping the ends of a halyard, for instance—as "women's work" and "boring" and simply refused to do it, which I thought odd. How Adam would act when the going got tough was anybody's guess. I hoped for the best.

We were in a nasty situation. Yet it was far from hopeless. Fortunately, the yacht was being battered by relatively small waves because the opposite shore of Seagull anchorage was only a mile and a half away. With limited fetch, the waves had little time to build up. The accident had occurred about three and a half hours after low water, and what waves there were had shoved us well up on the beach. This meant that we would be high and dry at low water. It would be easier to work on the yacht but harder to get the vessel down to the water to refloat her. Patching the hull and hauling the yacht into the water were not my concerns just then, because the refloating would need calmer conditions.

Our biggest problem was exposure and cold. The diesel stove was submerged in salt water; the cabin was soon to be one-third full of thirty-nine-degrees-Fahrenheit water. All of us, however, were warmly dressed in woolens, oilskins, boots, hats and gloves. Most of the bedding was dry. The yacht was cold, but she gave us protection from the wind.

"We'll stay here until morning," I announced. "Let's turn in and get some rest."

Adam and Eve crowded into the quarter berth, which was on the high side of the yacht. Margaret and I managed to nap on the port saloon berth, which had a large canvas lee cloth. I firmed up the one-burner Taylor kerosene cabin heater, which happened to be on the port side. I climbed into the angled saloon berth, intermeshed my oilskinned limbs with Margaret's and managed to doze a little. The heating-stove flue didn't work too well because of the high wind. I wondered whether I should get up and shut off the stove. "It is better to die of asphyxiation and be warm, or to be cold and alive?" The stove hissed away and I fell asleep pondering the question.

I awoke from time to time because my position was so cramped. In the night, the tide fell and the water drained from inside the vessel. The pounding of the hull on the beach stopped. The silence was wonderful. I climbed outside. Though the wind was still strong, the spray was gone. I took a flashlight and dropped to the beach. I wanted to see where we were and I was curious about the land, but the low clouds made the night very dark and my sea-boots slipped on the mossy rocks. The walking was treacherous. I went back to the yacht to wait for daylight. The others were still asleep.

At first light, I dropped to the beach again and walked around the yacht. Except for a chunk torn from the bottom of her rudder, *Whisper* seemed in good condition. The entire port side was perfect and looked as if the vessel had just come from a shipyard. The damage, however, was underneath the starboard side, on which she lay. I was amazed to discover that the second anchor we had dropped the night before was up on the beach higher than *Whisper*. In fact, the anchor had been blown or carried by the water across the end of the islet to the extremity of the nylon cable, which was stretched tightly downwind. Think of the power of a storm to do that!

We were on Isla Diana, a scimitar-shaped islet about one mile long and a quarter of a mile wide on the west side of Seagull anchorage. The islet was only about ten or twelve feet above the sea. There were no trees, only large clumps of tall, coarse-leaved tussock grass. Across from us to the west and south rose the brown and withered mountains and hills of the main Wollaston Islands. Patchy snow lay near the heights.

It was impossible to prepare anything to eat on board, so we took a Primus stove and some food to the lee side of the islet. The wind kept blowing out the Primus, so we got the yacht's dinghy and dragged it around the islet for a windbreak. Margaret cooked hot cereal and made coffee. I took a couple of pictures of *Whisper*.

After eating, Adam and I walked along the slippery beach stones to the opposite end of the islet to have a look at our general situation. While we were picking our way across the rocks, Adam suddenly stopped and turned toward me.

"What are our chances, Hal?" he blurted out. "I mean, do you think we'll ever get out of this?"

I had been so busy thinking about the wreck that I hadn't paid much attention to Adam. Now, when I looked closely at him, my heart sank. He was shaking in his boots. His eyes had become slits and he was almost crying. Instead of looking at me when he spoke, Adam looked at the ground. During World War II and the Korean War, I had seen what fear could do to a man. The stranding of the vessel was bad enough. To be obliged to deal with a terrified photographer who had an acute case of the browns was trouble indeed.

"The yacht is finished," he said. "We don't even have a radio. How much food is there? I want an inventory of the food right away. We must count the cans."

"Relax," I said. "Margaret and I have done a lot of mountaineering. We know how to live out in the wilds. The yacht is extremely well provisioned and we have enough food for at least two months. If necessary, we can supplement the food with shellfish. We may have to find some fresh water."

"Water?" said Adam nervously. "How much is there? How many days will it last? How much can we have each day? Let's sound the tanks right away."

I tried to reassure him. "I think we can get the yacht off," I said. "At least we're going to try hard. When the wind drops, we're going to run out a couple of anchors, move a lot of stones and see if we can turn the bow toward the water. At high tide, we may be able to slip a couple of driftwood timbers under the starboard side. Then at the next low tide when the hull is empty of water, we'll try to bolt a plywood patch on the hull. We may have to work in the water a little. I have a thick rubber wet suit . . ."

"Work in the water?"

I saw that Adam was horrified. It was clear that he wanted nothing more to do with the yacht. His idea of heaven just then would have been for the clouds to open and a helicopter to land and whisk him to the Cabo de Hornos Hotel in Punta Arenas, 188 miles to the northwest.

Back on the yacht, Eve and Margaret had taken more food ashore and we all had a hot lunch on the beach. Then, while I worked inside to expose the hull damage, I asked Adam to take the dinghy and row out an anchor. The wind had dropped and the job was easy. I told him exactly what I wanted, but when I looked out later, I saw that he had put the anchor out to the south, not the west. A fifteen-minute job had taken two hours and instead of securing the anchor warp to the port bow cleat to help pull the yacht toward deep water, Adam had put the warp on the starboard stern cleat, which meant that he was tying the yacht to the land. Maybe on purpose. Poor Adam was wandering about in a daze.

We had thousands of feet of new 16-mm film and two cameras on board. "How about taking some footage of the wreck and what we're doing?" said Margaret to Adam during the afternoon. "After all, a photographer doesn't have this opportunity every day."

"You're entirely right," said Adam in his deep bass voice. "We must start on a systematic shooting schedule and chronicle every aspect of this experience. We need a lot of good sequences."

Adam talked eloquently, but he took no photographs—then or in the days to follow. Later, he climbed into the yacht where I was working. He was looking for something and began to pick up things from the high, dry side and let them fall into the water on the low side of the saloon or the galley. He took a large plastic jar with all my taps and dies and drills from a tool drawer that I had open. His eyes were searching for something else, so he simply dropped these irreplaceable tools into the salt water. I gasped. I could hardly believe what I had seen. At first I was angry, but as I moved closer to shout at him, I saw that Adam's eyes were glazed and that he was breathing heavily. He was sick with fear and not in control of himself. Instead of anger, I began to feel sorry for him.

I took Margaret aside and spoke to her privately. "Adam is pretty upset," I said. "He's in a bad way. We're going to have to set up a camp on shore and forget about *Whisper*."

Margaret had been watching Adam on her own and she agreed with me.

I gathered everyone together and spoke in strong terms for Adam's benefit. "Tomorrow morning, if the wind is down, Margaret and I will take the fiberglass dinghy and row across the hundred yards or so to Isla Grevy, the next island, to see about setting up a camp in the grove of trees that Adam and I spotted this morning on our walk. I know from reading that Indians and seal hunters have lived in the Wollastons, and I believe we'll find water and shelter. We can make a tent with the sails from *Whisper*. Tonight, we'll stay on the yacht, but by moving a few things, we can be more comfortable. It's possible that we may see a patrol vessel or a fishing boat. In addition, I think there's another Chilean navy lookout station south of us. I don't know whether it's on Isla Hermite, Herschel or Deceit, but we may find something. So everybody cheer up. Let's all have a whisky and then some dinner."

The next morning, Margaret and I rowed across to Peninsula Low on Isla Grevy. We found a good-sized rivulet of fresh water, and in walking through the trees we discovered the remains of an old campsite. A conical tent of some kind had once been arranged over a framework of poles. The tent was long gone, but the framework was good enough for us to throw a sail over for shelter. The camp was about thirty or forty feet above the water; a walk of one hundred fifty feet to the north took us to the eastern edge of the peninsula, where we had an excellent view north and northeast into Bahía Nassau and of Isla Navarino in the distance beyond. Lots of wild celery grew near the camp. Margaret saw mussels that uncovered at low tide.

During the next few days, we rowed several dozen loads of sails, bedding, bunk cushions, tools, line, water jugs, dishes and pots and pans to the camp, which gradually became quite deluxe. We lashed three sails around the existing tent framework to make a serviceable tepee, which we floored with sail bags and the sun awning. Then came cushions and mattresses, followed by blankets and sleeping bags. We had two kerosene stoves and a pressure kerosene lantern. There were several hundred cans of food plus larger containers of flour, rice, sugar, noodles and spaghetti. We dug a shallow ditch around the tent to drain off water and gradually improved the tent with props and lines until it was quite weatherproof. I am sure the sailmaker would have been amazed to have seen what we had done with his handiwork.

Eve worked especially hard collecting mussels, which she steamed, fried, curried or made into delicious soup. She hauled water from the rivulet and gathered wild celery. At first, her husband wanted a big nightly campfire until we convinced him that wet wood would make a smoky fire, besides being a lot of trouble to get going and keep up. Adam liked the camp but he still acted nervously. He slept at least ten hours a night and spent hours writing furiously in a notebook. We repeatedly asked him to use the movie cameras, but nothing happened.

It is not my purpose to mock Adam and to make sarcastic comments on his behavior, but simply to observe that when fear grips a man it changes him and he becomes wretched and useless. Adam was the biggest person in the party, and he should have been the strongest. Fear bled his strength away and he became the weakest.

We tried to assign Adam little jobs. Not much seemed to interest him, however, until Margaret got the idea of giving him the rifle and making him the camp hunter. Adam was a good shot and disappeared for hours on hunting expeditions. He brought back big kelp geese, which Eve cooked in the pressure cooker. The meat was dark brown, something like turkey, and it tasted delicious. The trouble was that the thirty-thirty rifle was much too powerful for birds. The big slugs tended to destroy the creatures instead of merely killing them, as a shotgun would have. Nevertheless, we were glad for the additional food, even if it was in small pieces.

Working to set up the camp and running it was a full-time job and a half. Collecting naturally occurring food may sound romantic, but it takes an unbelievable amount of time and patient effort unless you are a local native and have learned to do it from childhood on. We saw lots of clamshells along certain beaches, but we had no rake, which I thought of making from a deck brush and a row of copper nails.

The weather was surprisingly mild. A few days were stormy, but in general the wind and cold were minimal. Maybe we were getting used to Cape Horn living. Of course, once on land we tended to ignore sea conditions.

We spent many hours rowing back and forth to the wreck and carrying things across the slippery rocks. The round trip was about two miles or so, but part of the way was through kelp, whose long, heavy stalks and leaves would get wrapped around the oars. The person rowing would have to stop, unship the fouled oar, slide it out of the kelp (or cut the leaves away) and then reship the oar and begin again. It was always easier to go around kelp patches even if it meant a long detour.

One morning when Margaret and I started out for the wreck, I got the idea of rowing along the outside—the northwest side—of Isla Diana to avoid the heavy kelp. The wind was calm and I thought we might see something new along the beach. We started out well, but the kelp was thicker than I had foreseen and the rowing quickly became impossible. Every two or three strokes I had to unship the oars to clear them. All of a sudden, gusts of wind from the southwest began to blow at us and to push the dinghy away from shore. I redoubled my rowing efforts, but I only got the oars fouled twice as fast. At first our position was merely annoying, but it quickly grew alarming. Here we were in a tiny dinghy only eight feet long getting blown away from land! I threw out an anchor at once, but it didn't hold in the slippery kelp. I had read somewhere about Indian women mooring canoes by tying to bunches of kelp, so I knelt in the bow of the dinghy, grabbed three or four thick kelp branches and passed a line around them. The line slipped from the slimy stalks. I tried a second time. The line slipped again.

All this while the wind was increasing—say, to thirty knots. Not a great deal, but in a small dinghy even a little is a lot. We were gradually losing ground and getting blown to sea. I looked shoreward to see if there was any chance of help.

Adam and Eve stood watching us, not knowing what to do. I tried to wave to them to send us a float or the inflatable dinghy on a long line, but the notion didn't occur to them in spite of my earnest gestures. I remember so well thinking of two expert sailing friends in San Francisco and wishing that one of them had been on the beach to help us.

Margaret and I were rapidly getting blown away from shore. What to do? I glanced behind us. Fortunately, there was another islet about a mile to leeward. Whether we would be able to make our way there, however, and to land in one piece were questions that I couldn't answer or even think about. Already, we were skimming along downwind in swells higher than the dinghy's freeboard. I found that by keeping the stern exactly parallel to the swells, we went along in fairly good fashion. I steered by using the oars as drags, digging one in a little to turn the vessel slightly. It was a delicate business and my heart was in my mouth because if we had gotten broadside to the waves, we would have capsized at once, and certainly would have perished in the frigid water. Margaret sat perfectly still in the sternsheets and gave me directions as we steered across the swells toward the islet.

The sea got lumpier and we raced downwind. I was afraid that we would be swamped any second. Finally, as we got near the islet, and close to the rocks and small breaking waves on the lee shore, Margaret spied a little sheltered place past a tiny bit of land. We avoided several rocks, managed to steer past a stone ledge, touched bottom, jumped out and quickly ran the dinghy high up on the shore. I almost wilted from nervous excitement. If there hadn't been an islet to leeward, we would have been blown out to sea east of Cape Horn.

During my life, I have been lucky to sidestep death many times, but this was the most providential. As I guided the dinghy by selectively dragging the oars, I remember thinking of a book by John Muir in which he described the first ascent of Mount Ritter in California's Sierra Nevada in 1871. Muir had been climbing for hours, and he finally got into a situation in which he could neither go up nor come down. He clung high on the side of the mountain with his arms outstretched while noisy ravens chattered nearby. "Not yet, not yet," he cried. "I'm not carrion yet."

"Not yet, not yet," I mumbled to myself. "We're still alive, even though we passed through the shadow . . ."

Margaret and I walked around and around the little islet—its name was Islote Otter, we later found out—for the next eight hours to keep warm. We ate some mussels from tidal pools and collected tiny red berries from bushes. At dusk, the wind dropped and we were able to launch the dinghy and row back to the grounded yacht for a load of gear. We then returned to the camp on Peninsula Low and stumbled into the tent in the dark. Adam and Eve had put out the camp light and had gone to bed. Eve got up to fix us something to eat.

"We thought you had bedded down for the night," she said.

"Bedded down?" said Margaret. "Bedded down in what? If we had bedded down on the islet, we'd have died of exposure."

Seagull anchorage was discovered in April, 1839 by the 110-ton New York pilot schooner *Seagull,* which was part of the U.S. Navy exploring expedition led by Charles Wilkes. Unfortunately, a few days later the *Seagull* left Bahía Orange on a routine voyage and got into a furious gale. The *Seagull* (two officers and fifteen men) was never seen again. In November, 1855, W. Parker Snow, the energetic captain of the eighty-eight-ton missionary schooner *Allen Gardiner,* anchored in Bahía Gretton and took a ship's boat into Seagull anchorage. Snow noticed a deserted wigwam and he walked ashore at the precise site of *Whisper*'s emergency camp on Peninsula Low. During the same week, Snow and the *Allen Gardiner* went through a five-day hurricane plus squalls that almost tore his schooner apart. He lay with two big anchors out, one on 540 feet of chain.

> During the night of the third day of its prevalence, I was on deck when a furious squall of hail and wind, similar to a tornado, burst upon us with a force like the blow of an enormous sledgehammer.

The little ship trembled again; you could hear every part of her move under that tremendous blast, and I might easily fancy her a living thing shuddering with the apprehension of the wrath and power of those terrible elements she was calmly striving to resist. On that wild coast, near that dark and frowning land, during that inky night relieved occasionally by fitful gleams of a strange and peculiar light, with the large hail pelting upon one like showers of bullets, I could not but feel deeply anxious.

Louis-Ferdinand Martial, in charge of the 1882–83 French scientific mission, visited Seagull anchorage to chart the region and discovered that Victoria Channel ran between Isla Bayly and land to the north. Martial named the separate land Isla Grevy, "in honor of the first magistrate of the Republic." In 1923, the artist-adventurer Rockwell Kent sailed to the area in a small chartered boat from Ushuaia.

All four of these visitors—Wilkes, Snow, Martial and Kent—found Indians living and working on the islands. A little seal hunting, fishing and shellfish and crab gathering supported the people in subsistence fashion. The account by Rockwell Kent is charming. Kent even contrived to baptize the half-breed offspring of an Argentine ex-prison inspector and a Yaghan woman.

We in the *Whisper* party thought it a pity that the lives of the Indians had been so tampered with by the missionaries and white settlers. The Indians were all dead—gone forever. We would have liked to have seen them and to have learned from them how to live off the land.

Adam and Eve and Margaret and I began to make reconnaissance hikes to the west and north of the island. Two of us went out on each clear day to see if we could find any people or structures or shipwrecks or a campsite closer to Peninsula Hardy or Isla Navarino.

The land was severe, but it had redeeming qualities. Isla Grevy was mostly open and rocky, with handsome light brown coloring. Parts of the island were boggy and you had to watch your footing to keep from stepping into little pockets of sphagnum moss. Our routes climbed through flats of matted brush and dwarf wind-blasted trees. In protected canyons and draws along the shores, we walked through luxuriant thickets of evergreen beeches twenty-five to forty feet high. These small forested areas always had water, tall grasses, wild celery and thick topsoil. In every one we visited, we saw traces of Indian campsites.

We found no animals. The only land birds were a brown mockingbird type about ten inches long with white horizontal lines above and below the eyes. Along the shores, we scared up lots of steamer ducks, which would rush off, madly flapping away, and leave wakes of foam behind. I was never sure who was startled more—the steamer ducks or I. We saw many kelp geese about the size of small turkeys. The females were a hard-to-see mottled brown. The males stood out in white dress with specks of black. If you saw a male, you could be sure that a female was nearby, but it took hard looking to spot her. We noticed a few brown ducks, some sea gulls and black cormorants with white breasts.

Along much of the shoreline of Grevy were large rounded boulders covered with slippery moss. Half in and out of the water, the big rocks guarded the shore like tank traps and made walking extremely hazardous. The combination of the boulders and masses of nearby offshore kelp made any small-boat work unthinkable.

From heights on the island, we looked out across at Peninsula Hardy, eight miles to the west. With a sky of blue, the water was blue too, and the sunny Pacific seemed lovely. Below us, at our feet, lay Bahía Beaufort, which was wide open to the southwest swell; even from a distance, the water had a feeling of power and purpose. From the north end of Grevy, we could see across the thirteen miles of Bahía Nassau toward the snowy slopes of Isla Navarino, which shimmered in the blue haze of distance.

By now a week had passed. I removed a heavy twelve-volt storage battery from the wreck and took my English Aldis signaling lamp to the lookout point past the camp. The powerful light was visible for fifteen miles—perhaps more—so we signaled from time to time toward Isla Navarino, which we knew had some ranches on it. Eve got the idea of spreading a sail on nearby dark trees in case a plane flew over. I began to work on a sailing rig for the dinghy.

On the ninth morning, Margaret and I started rowing to the yacht when we saw Adam and Eve run through camp. Adam had my Olin flare gun and began to shoot red and white flares, all of which fizzled out after rising only a foot or two. We hurried to the lookout point and saw a Chilean torpedo vessel about three miles to the northeast.

I grabbed the Aldis lamp and called up the Chilean vessel. She stopped at once and I signaled our identity and condition. Margaret had the binoculars and reported that a rubber boat was being launched. Adam was whooping with joy.

"I'm glad to see the Chileans too," said Eve, "but I'm a little sad that our camping experience is over. I would have liked to have explored a little more."

Twenty minutes later, an officer and three Chilean sailors waded ashore. I ran up to the man in charge and apologized for his wet legs and feet.

"Oh it's nothing," he said, his face all aglow. "These patrols are a bore. Rescuing someone is the most exciting thing that's happened to us in years."

North Atlantic Storm

by **GERRY SPIESS**

To sail alone in a tiny boat into the teeth of a North Atlantic storm can seem like riding through the biblical Valley of Death. Most accounts of storms focus on wind and waves, the skill required to survive, the coolheadedness of the sailors. Few convey as graphically internal terror and helplessness as the following encounter with the forces of nature aboard a stubby ten-foot sailboat.

Woe to him that is alone when he falleth; for he hath not another to help him up.

Ecclesiastes 4:10

AFTER four days of gradually worsening weather, the Atlantic had finally erupted into violence. Long lines of waves advanced out of the south and the east simultaneously; when they met, they crested and broke in towers of roaring, churning foam. The peaks were larger than any I had ever seen—some were as tall as *Yankee Girl*'s mast.

Braced inside the cabin, I was at the mercy of the sea. There was nothing I could do against the shifting, blinding walls of water that surrounded us. They came with the sound of freight trains and broke over the boat like thunder. Again and again *Yankee Girl* reeled as if she had been hit with a giant sledgehammer.

It was the fourteenth day of my voyage and the third day of the storm. Three days of booming waves and shrieking winds, of never-ending motion and aching fatigue.

When the wind had begun to shift from its easterly position, I had hoped that it would continue to veer around to the west. Instead, it had swung to the south and was now blowing across the Gulf Stream at speeds of over forty knots. The changing wind and the stream's current were locked in a deadly battle. The stream wanted to flow one way; the gale wanted to push another.

The resulting cross waves, some of which were fifteen feet tall, were coming about eight to ten seconds apart. I had to listen for them, for I could see nothing out my portholes. *Yankee Girl* was closed up like a coffin with me inside.

Her movement through the water was frighteningly erratic. Rather than climbing up the face of each wave and then surging down its back into the trough, she rose and fell with a *whump,* then rose abruptly and fell again.

When the storm began, I had tried strapping myself down with my seat belt. But while that had held my trunk secure, my arms and legs had flopped up and down and my head had been jerked from side to side. Finally, I had crawled up into the bow, turned sideways and wedged my knees against the navigation box and my head between my first-aid kit and a sail bag. This dampened my side-to-side motion, but I still had to brace my arm against the ceiling to keep from being slammed up and down.

I was in constant pain. In the beginning, I had been able to open the hatch, kneel there for a moment and then slowly straighten my back. But now this was no longer possible. My muscles were sore beyond belief, and my hips were badly bruised.

Inside the tiny cabin the air was stuffy and hot. When I did manage to fall into an exhausted sleep, I awoke almost immediately, gasping for breath. Then I would slide the hatch back a few inches, risking a faceful of water for the fresh air I so desperately needed.

Water was leaking in around the closed hatch and through the tiller opening. The blue ripstop nylon flap fastened around the tiller where it came through the transom kept pulling loose. Whenever a wave slammed against the stern, water spurted in through the open flap and sprayed the inside of the boat like a fire hose.

I tried to solve this problem by stuffing sponges into the gaps around the tiller. I also put towels around the hatch and secured it more tightly by hammering a screwdriver in on one side and jamming my ballpoint pen into the other. These emergency measures helped—a little. The water still came in, but with less force.

I was continually sponging out the inside of the cabin. I would begin by mopping water from my foul-weather gear, the seat cushions and the cabin sides. Then I would reach as far as I could into the footwell, laboriously moving and replacing each piece of gear. When my sponge was saturated, I would stop and listen to the waves crashing around the boat. A momentary hush meant that I had a little less than ten seconds in which to unscrew the inspection port in the transom, shove the sponge out, squeeze it, yank my arm back inside and seal up the port again. If I miscalculated—even by a split second—the next wave surged up my sleeve and soaked me to the waist.

I was using an old meat baster to bail out the bilges. I would insert it down below, pump the tube full of water and then shoot the water into my portable head—the one-gallon plastic jug, complete with screw top, in which I relieved myself during these stormy conditions. When the jug was full of bilge water, I'd pause again to gauge the waves. Then I'd quickly pull out the screwdriver and ballpoint pen I'd wedged in around the hatch, unfasten the hatch and slide it forward a few inches. After checking for cross waves, I'd open it just wide enough to allow me to poke my head and shoulders out and empty the jug.

Sometimes, in the intervals between waves, I'd find myself staring at the seascape. I had never before seen anything like it. Despite my pain, my overwhelming sense of fatigue and the knowledge that I was in great danger, I could not help but marvel at its fierce beauty.

Everywhere I looked the ocean was streaked with foam, for the gale-force winds were literally ripping the tops off of the highest waves. The clouds were so low that they seemed to be riding the surface of the water. I was in another world, a world of screaming winds and mountainous waves, a world that was totally indifferent to me. I felt its enormous power—and my utter powerlessness.

All of my careful planning had come to this: three days of being tossed about by the Atlantic like an insignificant speck. I could do nothing but wait out the storm, hoping it would end before I became exhausted beyond the point of return —or before *Yankee Girl* sustained irreparable damage.

My dream had turned into a nightmare.

Hours passed, but the storm showed no signs of abating. Meanwhile, I got on with the business of staying alive—and keeping my tiny boat afloat.

As I dumped another jug of bilge water, I decided to take a few seconds and resecure the fastenings on the nylon tiller flap. Too much water was still coming in. Holding tightly to the hatch coaming with one hand, I bent over the transom and grabbed the flap.

I became so engrossed in what I was doing that I forgot to pay attention to the waves.

Suddenly there was a terrible silence.

I looked up to see a solid wall of green water towering over me. It was more than seventeen feet in height—taller than my mast—and it was heading right for *Yankee Girl* and her wide-open hatch.

I ducked down into the cabin and frantically slammed the hatch shut—just as the wave broke over the boat. There was no time to lock the hatch, so I braced myself against it and held it with every ounce of my strength.

It was wrenched out of my hands.

With incredible fury and force, the water poured in. I was knocked back against the bulkhead. Stunned, I watched as the water continued to rush in—more water than *Yankee Girl* had ever taken on. I felt as if I were in a dream, a horrible dream in which everything moved in slow motion and there was no escape.

Somehow, my adrenaline took over. I scrambled up, dumping a lapful of water, and literally tore at the hatch. Under my desperate clawing, it moved an inch at a time until finally it closed, shutting off the deluge.

I shook my head to clear it. Then, groggily, I surveyed the cabin. What I saw nearly caused me to panic. There was water everywhere—from the bunk on down.

I had to get it out as quickly as I could. With every lurch and roll of the boat, more of my provisions and gear were becoming saturated. I knew that, under constant exposure to salt water, my cans of food would start to rust—along with my butane cylinders.

At first with a tin can and then with the baster, I bailed. And bailed.

It was like trying to empty the ocean with a spoon.

Several hours later, on the brink of total exhaustion, I sat down to rest. Only then did I notice that I was sopping wet. My clothes were clinging to me, pasted against my body by a combination of sweat and salt water.

Piece by piece, I began to peel them off.

I hadn't undressed in days, and I wasn't prepared for what I saw in the dim light of the cabin.

I had been immersed in water for so long that my outer layer of skin had simply dissolved. As I toweled myself off, it fell away in slimy masses.

But that wasn't the worst of it. The skin on my groin had turned a fiery red, and it itched horribly. I knew what that meant, and I dreaded it: I was in the initial stages of a fungus infection. Under the best conditions, with proper care and treatment, it took days or even weeks for this type of infection to clear up. I would carry it with me all the way to England—*if* I reached England.

I reached for my talcum powder and began dusting myself with both hands. For a moment, I let go of my hold on the boat.

That was my second unforgivably careless act of the day.

The rogue wave caught us broadside. I was thrown down violently, and my head struck the side of the cabin. My shoulder broke off the towel rack, and my hip hit the gas tank hard enough to leave a dent in it.

I lay on my back with my eyes closed for a few seconds, not daring to move. When I opened them again, I found myself staring straight out the starboard ports.

I was lying on the *side* of the cabin.

We had capsized!

Instinctively, I scrambled upward, trying to get my weight on *Yankee Girl*'s high side. Meanwhile, things kept falling toward me—my hand compass, foul-weather gear, bags of batteries and more of the ubiquitous grapefruit.

After what seemed like ages, I was up.

The scene was one of sheer pandemonium. Gear was flying through the air, and water was pouring in through the hatch on *Yankee Girl*'s submerged port side.

I threw my weight on top of the bunk and pushed.

Come on, Girl, I pleaded. *Come on. Over.*

I had to right her—now. If another wave hit while we were capsized, she might roll all the way over and we could lose the mast.

Suddenly, blessedly, *Yankee Girl* popped upright. The half-ton of supplies below her waterline had levered her mast up out of the water.

I didn't even have time to breathe a word of thanks. First, I had to find out whether my boat had sustained any damage on deck. As I listened to the wave pattern, I peered out a porthole.

Part of my gear was floating away.

I slide back the hatch and gazed out over *Yankee Girl* and the surrounding water. The six empty gasoline cans I had lashed to the side of the cabin were gone, literally torn away by the force of the knockdown. So was the sea anchor. I watched helplessly as they drifted out of reach.

There was nothing I could do to save them. Even in good weather they would have been difficult to recover. The loss of the sea anchor didn't bother me that much—I was almost glad to see it go—but I did mind seeing my gasoline containers bobbing off into the distance. They had been part of my backup flotation system, and I had counted on using them if *Yankee Girl*'s hull were ever damaged.

A hundred pounds of emergency flotation, gone forever.

With growing anxiety, I glanced around at the back of the boat. Had my little Evinrude been torn off its bracket? Had I lost that too? No—I could see it bouncing along behind the transom. At least I still had my motor. Whether it worked, after the beating it had taken, was a question I wasn't yet ready to face.

I looked down at my hands. They were trembling. My adrenaline reserves were nearly used up. I felt myself slipping backward into the hatch

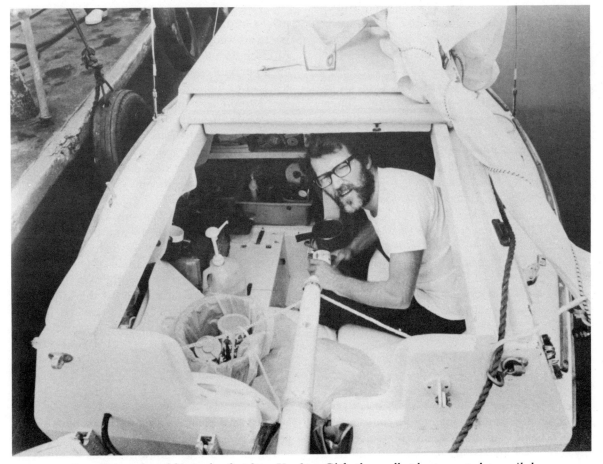

Gerry Spiess aboard his twelve-foot-long **Yankee Girl,** *the smallest boat ever to have sailed across the North Atlantic Ocean.*

and gripped the rails hard, gritting my teeth.

I had never been so frightened in my life.

At that moment, I wanted more than anything to give up—to get away from the agony, to escape the fear. I wanted to close my eyes and open them again and be *somewhere else*—back home in Minnesota, in safety and security, with my family and friends.

I bowed my head. I would cry out to God for his help.

But then, surprisingly, I found myself hesitating.

I was here of my own choosing. Would it be right to ask God to save me, to get me out of a situation I'd entered into freely?

I shook my head. God had given me all of the resources I needed to survive this storm and any other that came along. It was up to me to use them—and not to ask for more.

Instead of pleading for help, I said a prayer of thanks. I was alive, and my boat was whole. That was enough.

With my last ounce of energy, I forced myself below the pitching deck once more. Then I locked the hatch and squatted down in the wet, steamy cabin.

Night was falling. In the howling, shrieking storm, I would try to sleep.

"Hey, there's a gas station!" I shouted excitedly. "That's just what we need!"

It sat like a gleaming oasis at the side of the road. I turned the wheel of my car and slowed down.

At last, a gas station! After all those miles! I smiled in relief.

But as I pulled in beside the pumps, I sensed that there was something wrong. Something dreadfully, terribly wrong . . .

I awoke with a start. My teeth were chattering, and I was lying in a pool of perspiration.

There *was* something wrong—with me. I was losing control of my mind.

This had been going on for most of the night. I would fall into an exhausted sleep, and my subconscious would take over—trying to lift me up and away, out of my predicament and my fear.

The gas station had been the latest in a series of escape routes my mind had fabricated. Earlier, there had been a park—green and inviting—and before that a rest stop. But each time I had begun to pull off the road, I had awakened, shivering, to find myself back in the boat. The noise, the cloying stuffiness, the constant racking motion and the darkness—*these* were reality. Not the road, or the car, or the sun shining brightly overhead or the trees waving in the wind.

I rubbed my face, feeling the salt and the sweat and the stubble of my beard.

Rather than helping me, my dreams were making me feel even more miserable. For I knew that there was no place to stop and rest—not here, in the middle of the Atlantic, in a storm that wouldn't end.

I was suffocating. Once again, I had jammed myself into the forepeak as far as I could go, with my head wedged into a narrow *V* between bags of clothing and my legs drawn up against my chest, braced against the bulkhead. It seemed as if I had to fight for every breath.

I could hear the sounds of *Yankee Girl* rushing madly through the night. As she careened down one mountainous wave after another, the Evinrude banged against the stern and wind shrieked up the slot of the bare mast. I pressed my sleeping bag against my ears to shut out the relentless din.

I had been lying on my right arm. Now, slowly, I tried to move it—and groaned aloud. Every muscle in my body was sore, and my head ached from the insidious smell of gasoline. The firey red splotches where my skin had been rubbed off burned and itched at the same time.

Coughing and gasping, I reached for the overhead ventilator. I was acting more out of desperation than sea sense, for even as I screwed it open, water blasted through it with the force of a fire hydrant. I closed it again as quickly as I could and wiped the salt water from my face and eyes.

At least that had brought me back to my senses.

I stared at the luminous hands of my wristwatch, pale green beneath the moisture-fogged crystal. It was 3:00 A.M.

I had to think for a moment before I realized that it would soon be dawn. I was not looking forward to another day. Instead, I found myself hoping that night would last forever, that I could continue to hide under the blanket of darkness.

The waves kept coming, rumbling and thundering like locomotives. Suddenly, one broke, slamming us sideways. It was then that I heard the noise I had been dreading.

Cr-a-a-a-a-ck!

It came from somewhere beneath me, near the stem.

Grabbing my flashlight, I crawled forward. With growing apprehension, I started pulling gear from the forepeak and shoving it behind me.

I had to get down to the keel.

Fears raced through my mind. Had *Yankee Girl* finally succumbed to the pressures of the storm? Had that last wave wounded her in some way? *Was she breaking up?*

Bracing myself against her side, I hunched forward and played the light on her glue lines. This was the point where a fracture was most likely to occur. I ran the beam down one side of her stem in the forward compartment and up the other; in her white-painted bilge, a crack would be immediately visible.

Nothing.

Was my mind playing tricks on me again?

No. I *had* heard the noise. It *had* been real.

I could feel the perspiration dripping down my forehead as I searched further. Incredibly, there were no cracks, and the forward bilge was dry.

I placed my hands on the plywood planking and felt for signs of "oilcanning"—the flexing back and forth that would indicate a weakness or fracture. But even as we plunged down another wave and my breath was jolted out of me, I could feel no movement.

I *knew* I had heard a crack, the sound of breaking wood!

There had to be a problem *somewhere*; I just hadn't found it yet. Perhaps there was a split under the keel which hadn't worked its way through to the bilge.

Without being conscious of what I was doing, I reached for my life jacket.

In all of the hours I'd spent aboard *Yankee Girl*, I hadn't thought once of donning my life jacket. But now, it appeared, it was time.

If *Yankee Girl* were seriously damaged, I'd have to survive in a swamped boat. I knew that my little girl would never sink, but my life jacket would provide an extra measure of safety.

It would give me a chance to save *Yankee Girl* —if I didn't die first of cold and exposure.

I braced my foot against the side of the cabin and my back against the dented gas tank. As the next cross wave struck, I imagined that I felt the plywood flex inward.

Methodically, instinctively, I began going through emergency procedures.

I pulled out my air bags, inflated them, and tied them to both sides near the stern. I thought briefly about the empty gasoline containers fastened along the side of *Yankee Girl*'s cabin—and then remembered that they'd been torn away yesterday, when we'd capsized. The air bags would have to do.

Afterward I sat and stared at my EPIRB. An orange-and-yellow transmitter about the size of a half-gallon milk carton, my Emergency Position Indicating Radio Beacon was my final card. When—if—I switched it on, it would send out a continuous tone which would be heard by aircraft on a monitored frequency. They in turn would report it to the Coast Guard, who would request a ship in my area to pick me up.

I shuddered. Even if I did call for help, how would anyone rescue me under these conditions? Trying to get from my boat to a towering steel ship would be more dangerous than staying on board *Yankee Girl*. I visualized a huge black hull, looming fifty feet above me, plunging and wallowing alongside—and, with a final roll, crushing my little plywood vessel.

I could imagine how hard it would be to maneuver a ship in this storm. Moreover, it was highly possible that its crew wouldn't be trained in this kind of rescue attempt.

The odds were not in my favor.

But what would happen if a ship were to come along *right now* and ask, "Do you want to be brought aboard?" What would I do? What would I say?

Sitting in the darkness, I debated with myself. I would have to make a sensible decision—that was clear. But what *was* the best thing to do under these circumstances? I didn't know.

And, finally, what if a ship were to pull up alongside and say, "There's a hurricane coming—the storm is going to get a lot worse"? What then?

I fingered my life jacket, pondering the alternatives.

On the one hand, I was determined not to give up just because I was frightened and miserable. On the other, though, I wanted to act intelligently. Would it be reasonable to stay in the middle of this terrible storm with a hurricane on the way? Would it be worth the risk? Or would it be better to give up my dream, to let myself be rescued by a ship and go back home?

I shook my head, hard. Again I was losing my grip on reality.

For there was no ship. There would be no ship. I was alone, in the here and now, and all I could do was hope to survive.

Alain Colas: a Legend Lost at Sea

by WILLIAM OSCAR JOHNSON

On November 5, 1978 Alain Colas set sail from France's Brittany coast in what is called The Rum Race, four thousand miles, single-handed, to Point-à-Pitre, Guadeloupe. He never arrived and an extraordinary life —in sailing and human terms—ended. In this moving piece of reportage from Sports Illustrated, *William Oscar Johnson illuminated the rare spirit of a daring sailor.*

ALAIN Colas is missing at sea. An intensive search has been conducted by planes and ships across a vast wedge of the North Atlantic. His last official radio contact was with a French radio station on the afternoon of November 16, from a location thought to be north and west of the Azores. Colas was barely thirty-five, yet he was already a man whose life contained the stuff of legend. He was one—some say Number 1—of a breed so unique that most folks can only approximate in dreams what he did in real life. He was a single-handed ocean sailor, one of the few who make blue-water voyages alone, relying on the wind for power, their wits for company. And even among these extraordinary few, Colas stood apart, exuding an aura of isolation. There was a hint of the fever of obsession about him, although he tended to keep it under precise control.

No man ever looked more like a sailor than Colas. He had black, curly hair, and he affected the thick muttonchop sideburns of a nineteenth-century mariner. His face was seamed with sun-squint lines and he walked with a limp, the result of a sailing accident. The limp gave him an Ahab-like mystique.

Colas spoke with disdain about life in modern cities, indeed, years ago he had fled Paris for the South Seas. He was married to a beautiful Tahitian who gave him a daughter four years ago and twin sons last summer.

Colas, who had turned thirty-five on September 16, had traveled one hundred thirty thousand miles under sail, five times around the planet, when he was lost at sea. For some fifty thousand of those miles—close to two years, in total time—he was alone, including two transatlantic races from Plymouth, England, to Newport, Rhode Island. Colas won the 1972 race, sailing the three thousand-plus miles in a record twenty days, thirteen hours and fifteen minutes, which sliced nearly six full days off the previous best time. Colas's *Pen Duick IV* was first among the 55 boats entered that year, and in 1976, the next running of the event, he was third out of 125 starters. On this occasion, he was at the helm of the controversial *Club Méditerranée*, the 236-foot four-masted schooner which he designed. It was, and is, the largest sailing ship to be built since before World War I, and he sailed it alone across the Atlantic in one of the worst seasons of storms in memory. In another of his celebrated single-handed voyages, Colas circumnavigated the globe in 168 days, 57 days better than the record set by Sir Francis Chichester in *Gipsy Moth III.*

In early November, Colas was off once more; when last seen he was alone again at the helm of the trusty old trimaran *Manureva* he had twice sailed around the world. This time, he was heading across the treacherous Atlantic on a race of four thousand-odd miles, starting at Saint-Malo on the north coast of France; his destination was Pointe-à-Pitre on Guadeloupe in the French West Indies.

Although Colas was alone on his boat, he wasn't exactly alone on that reach of ocean. No fewer than thirty-seven other solitary sailors had left Brittany with him on the morning of November 5 in a new transatlantic race for single-handers called La Route du Rhum. The name comes from the course: roughly the reverse of the route sailed by clippers and schooners whose holds were loaded with barrels of rum. It is something of an upstart event in that the British have pretty much held the franchise for such races with the *London Observer*'s eighteen-year-old Plymouth-Newport event. The French also trod on yachting tradition by offering money as a reward—$45,000 for first prize and lesser sums for other places. The winner of the Plymouth-Newport race receives a twelve-inch silver plate.

The Rum Race is about half again as long as Plymouth-Newport, and while the starting field for the inaugural event was mainly French, it also attracted such world-class sailing loners as Chay Blyth of Great Britain, Michael Birch of Canada and Philip Weld of the United States. The most optimistic entrants predicted that the winner would complete the race in three weeks. But Colas was more meditative about the course. He thought that the mean and unpredictable weather in the Atlantic in November, plus the tough windward tack into the prevailing westerlies during the first third of the race,

would mean no one could reach Guadeloupe in less than twenty-five days—or not until November 30.

Sailing the ocean alone is a romantic notion. It sounds like simplicity itself, a mere matter of a brave man with a strong hand on the tiller and a sharp eye on the stars putting canvas to wind. Single-handed ocean sailing has the ring of an ultimate reduction of life's complexities, an escape to personal purity, a consummate human adventure.

Unfortunately, this isn't quite the case. Adventure and romance are there, certainly, but the single-handed sailor is far from being a free child of nature. One may view him as a man who should express himself in poetry, but to whom, in fact, the jargon of modern technology is more suitable. The single-handed ocean racer is almost as much a product of the space age as an astronaut is.

A month before the race, Colas was in Brittany, supervising the overhaul of the *Manureva.* The name is Tahitian: it translates into *L'Oiseau du Voyage* in French, *The Bird of Travel* in English. Parts of the boat were scattered about a cluttered machine shop near Saint-Malo. Colas watched intently through a welding mask as a mechanic blazed away at a section of the rudder. Colas said something in French, removed the mask and switched to English. "This has come to be like auto racing," he said, "so technical and so much demand for precision to the last detail. We are very close to airplane techniques in design, shaping the surfaces to put up the least resistance. Turn an airplane upside-down and you have a boat, you see?" He looked around at the disarray of the machine shop, then sighed. "The race itself is almost a minor point. It is the preparation that rates first, the attention to each technicality."

He spoke quickly in French to the proprietor of the shop, then limped out into a radiant October morning. He climbed into his car. "Let's go have a look at the old girl," he said. "She and I have been separated for most of a year now."

He careened over stony hills on narrow roads and pulled into a boatyard at the village of

Trinité-sur-Mer. There, perched on pilings above the receding tide, sat *Manureva.*

The trimaran looked nothing at all like a bird of travel. Indeed, she resembled nothing quite so much as a great steel water spider, a bizarre contraption painted grayish blue. Still, she was oddly graceful, an interlocking arrangement of two large pontoons attached to a center hull by struts and beams. She looked to be more cousin to a lunar lander than to the *Pequod.* The two needlelike masts were of a light new alloy. Everything else was made of a stainless-steel alloy that was the best stuff available when the boat was built ten years ago. *Manureva* was thirty-five feet wide and almost seventy feet long.

"She's a racing machine," Colas said admiringly. Then he shrugged. "But she is ten years old now and there are many boats in the race that are bigger and made of all the newest stuff. There'll be bigger boats and younger chaps than I. Perhaps this old girl is already outmoded and gone past her day. But with the right skirt and a little makeup, she will look as fine as the new girls who will be running with her."

Colas went aboard, followed by a worker who furiously took notes as Colas dictated what was still to be done.

Manureva was a racing machine, all right, stripped of excess weight and creature comfort. The metal struts were punched with holes to lighten weight. For the skipper, there was a cramped little cockpit filled with stacks of charts and navigational instruments. A plastic dome offered minimal protection from storms. Inside the bare metal of the hull was a narrow cabin containing a galley with a gas heating plate and a bunk mattress fitted into a box to keep the sleeper from being tossed out of bed in heavy seas. One had to bend almost double to move about.

Colas looked into this dark hole with affection. "This was my home for many months, really for years," he said. "I'm as comfortable in there as if it was a snug little house with a hearth and a parlor."

Although the sea and a boat reflected all the warmth of home to Colas, it wasn't too long ago that they were alien to him; few sailors were born with less seawater in their veins. He grew up in the hills of Burgundy, the son of a man whose livelihood was literally made of earth—his father was a potter and a ceramics manufacturer in the village of Clamecy. "He takes a handful of clay and turns it into whatever you might think of," Colas said.

As a boy, the only water sport Colas attempted was kayaking on the local river. He attended the University of Dijon, then the Sorbonne. It was there that restlessness struck.

"I began to crave a more thorough life. I wanted more colors, more sun, more open ways," Colas said. In 1966, he left what he called "the polluted skies of Paris" and flew to Australia to become a lecturer in French at the University of Sydney. It was there, at twenty-two, that he discovered the sea. "My friends were sailors and racing enthusiasts and they took me out in a keelboat one afternoon. It was love at first sight. I went to the library and got every book on sailing that I could carry. I learned a mainsail from a helm and, gradually, I became a good crewman."

In December of 1967, Eric Tabarly came to Australia for the Sydney-Hobart Race. Tabarly was a celebrated French sailor, winner of the 1964 Plymouth-Newport Race and, although Colas was crewing on another boat, the two men became friends. When the race was over, Colas joined Tabarly's crew and sailed for New Caledonia.

This first cruise was almost Colas's last: they were caught at sea by Hurricane Brenda's 100-mph winds and thirty-five-foot waves. With sails shredded and rigging snarled, the boat barely made the harbor afloat. But it was adventure enough to hook Colas on sailing, and by 1968 he was back in France on the Breton coast, where Tabarly was building a trimaran for that year's Plymouth-Newport Race.

Tabarly had become entranced with the idea of a multihulled racer, with none but the barest essentials. He figured it could cross the Atlantic in the faintest of winds, yet hold its own to windward in heavy stuff. The result was a prototype that critics said looked like a floating tennis court. In the spring of 1968, there was a rash of strikes throughout France and the boat was

Alain Colas at the helm of **Club Mediterranee.** *The two hundred thirty-six-foot, four-masted schooner is the largest ship of its kind in the world.*

barely finished in time for the race. Tabarly named her *Pen Duick IV,* after a black sea swallow of Brittany, and set sail. Barely out of Plymouth Harbor, he collided with a freighter and limped back in for repairs. He took off again and the automatic steering broke down. Tabarly gave it up and went back to France.

Although out of the race, Tabarly nonetheless figured the time was right to cross the Atlantic. Then he would go through the Panama Canal and cruise the Pacific. Colas signed on as crew. They had a good year, putting in at such romantic spots as Tahiti, Hawaii and Samoa, setting a batch of records along the way.

Tabarly was not entirely comfortable with a multihull, however, and he decided to sell *Pen Duick IV.* While in Los Angeles, he scrawled a crude for-sale sign and stuck it to the mast.

There were no bidders. But Colas had come to love the freakish-looking craft and wanted it. To raise the money, he began cruising the Pacific in an old schooner, the *Naragansett,* working as a free-lance journalist and photographer. By 1970, he had made enough money for a down payment, and Tabarly agreed to sell *Pen Duick IV* for $50,000. Now she belonged to Colas—on credit. He used her as his journalist's workboat. "I roamed the Pacific for stories," he said. "And always I was gaining knowledge of the boat, sailing with fewer people, until I knew that one day I would go it all alone."

In the fall of 1971, Colas was in Tahiti, gripped with a new obsession: he would sail in the 1972 Transatlantic Race. A solo journey home to France, a mere fourteen-thousand-mile jaunt, would be just the thing to get him in shape. It was about that time that Colas met a Tahitian named Teura Krause.

"She was very dark and very Tahitian and we were close from our first meeting," Colas said. "She became my wife, but that is not a good enough word. We are life companions. I had to hurry to make the starting line at Plymouth, but we didn't feel like parting. So we sailed together.

"But she suffered seasickness beyond belief. Also, a pack of thirty or forty sharks followed us for days, dashing in to snap and attack anytime we made any move near the water. Finally, after a twenty-four day passage out of Darwin into Maurice-La-Reunion, in the Indian Ocean, Teura flew on ahead and I was left to make my first major single-handed passage."

Teura left him in mid-December and Colas made his last landfall at Mauritius, on December 16, 1971. He sailed nonstop past Madagascar, around the Cape of Good Hope, and up the coast of Africa to the north coast of France without ever putting a foot on land. He averaged 125 miles a day and made the trip in sixty-six days.

At the boatyard in Brittany last fall, as he gazed pensively at the familiar lines of the former *Pen Duick IV,* Colas said, "We have sailed some lovely miles alone, the old girl and I, but I don't go out on the ocean for the sake of being on my own. Solitude isn't what I seek. I must have a sense of purpose behind a solitary sail, and that overcomes the solitude. There are loners of the sea, men who wish not to speak to others and who avoid all ports of call because that is the cut of their personality. I felt that old Joshua Slocum, our spiritual father, as the first man to do a single-handed circumnavigation, was the one who treasured his aloneness. I don't know that he actually disliked people, but I think the old captain was a bona fide loner. But for me, a single-handed sail is part of an idea that leads to something other than solitude itself."

Whatever the purpose behind a single-handed sail, solitude is as intrinsic to the game as the sea itself. And as Colas went on to say about his colleagues, "We are a special brand of sport maniacs who derive our pleasure from our own lonely actions instead of performing in a gymnasium or a pool or a stadium. Our sport involves long hardships and strange times, but it makes us very happy."

Whether its main appeal is hardship or happiness, solitary ocean racing as an organized sport is not yet twenty years old. It had its inception in 1960 when five boats left Plymouth bound for New York, three thousand-odd miles away. The largest boat that year was Chichester's *Gipsy Moth III,* at thirty-nine feet considered a possibly unmanageable handful for a man at sea alone. Chichester won the race in forty days and 13½ hours. Over the years, the number of single-handed sailors has increased, the boats have grown longer and lighter and computers are used in navigating and weather forecasting. But while the technology has changed greatly since the days of the clipper ships, human beings have changed hardly at all. At sea alone, they are as susceptible today to strange visitations and hallucinations as they were a century ago.

Slocum, the celebrated nineteenth-century salt, was the first and perhaps still the greatest of the world's lone circumnavigators. Slocum spent more than three years on a voyage that began on April 24, 1895, when he headed out of Boston in his thirty-five-foot sloop, *Spray.* He sailed forty-six thousand miles in all, and during much of the trip, Slocum, who was fifty-one when he started out, indulged in countless hours of conversation with a cheerful, bearded fellow who periodically appeared on *Spray* to help with navigation—a courteous man who introduced himself as the pilot of Columbus's *Pinta,* which had sailed the seas some four hundred-odd years earlier.

Such hallucinations are not uncommon. During the 1972 Plymouth-Newport Race, a medical survey was taken to study the mental, emotional and physical effects of the race on several of the entrants. Through logbooks and interviews, they reported impressions of their lonely journeys. One man recalled that throughout the trip he had heard "the usual high-pitched voices" in his rigging calling "Bill! Bill!" Another said that after fifty-six continuous hours at the helm, he noticed that his father-in-law had appeared at the top of the mast, where he was quietly sitting. The sailor didn't find this surprising or unusual. Another competitor reported that he was lying on his bunk when he heard a man at the helm putting the boat onto another tack. When he went on deck to investigate, the man passed him in the passageway coming down. They didn't speak and he didn't recognize the man, but when he checked the bearing, he found that the boat had, indeed, been put about and the course changed. Still another sailor reported that, on his thirty-third day at sea alone, he was raising his sails when he noticed a baby elephant in the sea and thought, "My, what a strange place to put a baby elephant." A few minutes later, he saw that it wasn't a baby elephant at all but a Ford automobile. Later he realized that in fact it had been a whale.

The single most serious problem is the shortage of sleep. Each sailor handles it in his own way. Some never sleep more than an hour at a time. Others, like Colas, would doze off for three hours at a stretch, with automatic-steering vanes set to hold course. But with sleep always uncertain, half-world sensations arise. "My mind was completely separated from my body," one sailor reported. "I just used my body to get around the boat."

Then come the terrors of storms, and almost as fearsome, calm. Some of the logbook entries dealt with the suffocating frustration of a perfectly windless sea. One man wrote, "I feel like a prisoner in a well-stocked cell, but with no one around to tell me the date of the termination of my sentence." Another kept logging the word *becalmed,* writing it larger and larger each day until, finally, the single word BECALMED covered two full pages.

The changes in mood of men alone at sea are enormous, ranging from highs where they sing and dance hornpipes all alone, to blackest depressions. During the early hours of the 1968 race, one sailor inscribed in his log some noble lines from "The Sea" by Louis MacNeice:

Incorrigible, ruthless,
It rattled the shingly beach of my childhood. . . .

A day later the same man scribbled darkly, "I must be nuts!"

In spite of this, most single-handed sailors say that the sense of isolation is neither frightening nor uncomfortable. One sailor said, "There is an intimate and complex relationship with the natural environment and the creatures that inhabit the sea and the air, so that the lone sailor never feels abandoned or rejected." Colas said last year, "There is no sense of being an infinitesimal, helpless speck in the universe when you are sailing in solitude. This is because you become the center of your own universe, you give birth to your own island, to your own nation when you sail alone. Soon enough, you sail her right out of the ocean and into your own small circle of being. Perhaps that is too existential, but that is the way it comes to seem."

What about fear? "Not a factor," Colas said. "Fear is a result of the unknown. An awareness of danger is not fear. I have many times felt my heart jump into my mouth at the sight of a mighty mountain of the sea hovering over me and my little boat. But I know we will climb up that steep wall and reach the top and slide down unharmed. We know things, so we need not fear. We know this earth is not a disk and that we may not sail to the edge and fall off. We know a storm is not Neptune shaking his trident and aiming his wrath directly at a poor sailor at sea. We know storms are caused by cold air moving in over hot air. What we know, we do not fear—and we know much these days."

Is religion an essential companion to the single-handed sailor? "Ah, well, that may depend," said Colas. "I am deeply Christian; I was raised as a Catholic. But perhaps I have read too much of Ralph Waldo Emerson and the transcendentalists, and perhaps they are too much to my liking. I believe man's fate is in his own hands. It is good to have religion, but I know that God will not be coming down to help me rig a genoa, and thus I get a good hold of the sail by myself. There are times when I might be thankful to see God there with me in the cockpit on a black and tumultuous night, but I know that I cannot count on that. He is not too reliable that way, I think, and therefore I must be perfectly reliable alone."

To Colas, the true exhilaration in the life of a single-handed sailor lay in its stark contrast with the ordinary perceptions that most men come to take for granted. "This kind of sailing is a way of knowing yourself a little better and of enjoying life more intensely," he said. "The risk sharpens you, and being deprived of so many things makes you sensitive to the true wonders of life when you return. You rediscover how wonderful it is to be close to people again. The deprivation of social warmth for so many weeks sharpens the sensations of friendship and of love, and you have never known before how immensely important people are to you, how warm they are and how necessary."

After the voyage to Brittany, Colas had mastered himself and the eccentricities of *Pen Duick IV* at sea and was well prepared for the shorter trip between Plymouth and Newport. His boat was well known, partly because of Eric Tabarly's former ownership and partly because of the records it had set in the Pacific. But Colas was relatively unknown and, he was definitely not the favorite.

The boat to beat was a radically new 128-footer called *Vendredi 13* (Friday the Thirteenth), bankrolled for $250,000 by French film director Claude Lelouch. It would be skippered by Jean-Yves Terlain, a veteran single-hander. *Vendredi 13* was a three-master designed to churn steadily through heavy windward seas; Colas's boat, by contrast, was meant to pick up faint breezes and skim the surface.

As the weather worked out, *Pen Duick IV* was the perfect boat. *Vendredi 13* stuck to the sea as if it were glued when winds were light—and a good part of the voyage was made in whispering breezes. Colas finished twelve hours ahead of Terlain. When reporters asked the victor if he had experienced any trouble, Colas shrugged and smiled. "After sixty-six days, what is another twenty?" he said.

Spartan quarters aside, Colas had lived in style at sea. He was well stocked with Camembert, Pont l'Evêque and Livarot cheese, pâté

from his home village and tripe à la mode de Caen. "I bring a special Burgundian approach to provisions," he said. "I always cook three meals a day at sea, always. I keep some hardtack stuff to put in the pockets of my oilskins for long hours at the helm, and I have some tinned foods on hand, but I like to travel with fresh things. Cabbage keeps for months, and I bring eggs and onions, which are known as sailor's caviar. I always bring garlic, because how can you cook without garlic? And I bring a few bottles of wine, because how can you cook without wine? Sitting at my little stove, browning nicely my onions and stirring up the fragrances of home with a wooden spoon—these things warm you up in many ways. And even though it may sound indulgent, it is not. I consider myself as a machine, a bit of mechanical equipment, and just as an engine works better on excellent petrol, so does a man."

One form of petrol Colas never used was liquor. "It is too dangerous at sea," he said. "I am always flabbergasted at the amount of weight our English friends sometimes take along in ale and grog. Whoever must enhance his perception of life with this extra stimulant, he has a poor grasp of things." (Colas's attitude toward alcohol is in the minority among single-handed sailors: Sir Francis Chichester rarely left port without a great store of whisky and beer, and a few years ago an Australian dentist may have set quite another kind of transatlantic record by guzzling twenty-three dozen cans of beer in a thirty-day voyage.)

After the 1972 Plymouth-Newport victory, Teura told the press, "Up to now, we haven't had the money to get married—everything has gone into the boat. So we had to win for our marriage, for our future, for everything." And the victory did bring Colas more than a silver plate. He got book contracts and endorsements in France, where single-handed racing is a surprisingly popular sport. One of his books sold two hundred thousand copies, the money giving him further freedom to sail as he wished.

What Colas did next was to circumnavigate the world alone in his trimaran (then renamed *Manureva*). He departed Saint-Malo in Brittany in September of 1973, sailed around Africa to

Sydney, continued across the Pacific, around Cape Horn and back to Saint-Malo. He believed that any man who could negotiate the treacherous straits at Cape Horn would achieve a special and praiseworthy goal.

"Cape Horn is to sailing as the Eiffel Tower is to Paris," he once wrote, "[it is] the most beautiful page in the history of the sea."

The first leg of the trip, 14,640 nautical miles to Sydney, took him just seventy-nine days, beating all single-handed records. He arrived in Australia on November 27, 1972, laid over for a month, then set out across the Pacific five days after Christmas. His boat carried a collection of books, letters and logbooks by captains and crewmen who had circumnavigated a century before. "I was rubbing minds with the ancient mariners," said Colas. "Their ideas and their words, the mythology they created, were my companions, and I was greatly affected by them and their ideas."

One idea that came to be a compulsion during the second half of the voyage was an increasingly desperate desire for speed. "I was driving the boat as hard as she could be driven day after day," Colas said, "and soon the complexion of the trip changed. I was obsessed, spurred to sail faster. An idea was growing inside of me, and on the one hundred sixtieth day at sea, it peaked like a child in a mother's belly. I was pregnant with the idea for a new and faster boat."

The round-the-world trip was a success: 30,067 miles in a record 168 days.

Back in France in the spring of 1974, Colas began to design a massive ship that he would sail alone in the 1976 Plymouth-Newport Race. He was still thinking speed. "Those ancient mariners knew the secret," he said, "but I knew something was missing on my modern boat. What? It was length. When I rounded Cape Horn, I topped eighteen knots in the best conditions, but I wanted a boat that could do more. I wanted to design a boat that could do twenty-nine knots and sustain a steady twenty to twenty-one knots day after day."

Colas began organizing the project. He made dozens of sales talks to potential sponsors, contacted steel and sail companies, tested model hulls in wind tunnels and water tanks. About $1 million was needed. He gave lectures to raise money (from $1,000 to $1,800 per appearance), wrote more books and sold films made during his voyages. He convinced a steel company to give him 150 tons of raw iron ore in return for a TV documentary covering the building of the ship. He induced French naval architect Michel Bigoin to work with him on the hull design. And, ultimately, the great ship began to take shape.

She would be a four-master, with masts 105 feet tall. Each of her four mainsails measured 1,035 square feet, each of her four foresails 2,205 square feet, and there was a 1,071-square-foot spinnaker—a combined sail area of 14,031 square feet. The hull was 236 feet long, longer than a Boeing 747, with a 36-foot beam, a draft of 18 feet and a displacement of 280 tons. Much of her rigging would be so far away from Colas at the helm that he would need TV cameras and computers to monitor the condition of the sails.

Finally, Colas got a major sponsor. The Club Méditerranée, the global resort firm based in Paris, decided to give $600,000, the cost of the rough hull. Colas would name his *grand bateau Club Méditerranée.*

"They gave more than money," he said. "They gave trust and countless hours of commitment by their best men. They no longer own the boat; she is all mine and I could name her *Alain Colas II* if I wished. But she'll remain *Club Méditerranée.* They did not waver in their faith in me—even after I did that bloody stupid thing on a joyride."

The accident happened on May 19, 1975, in the tranquil harbor of La Trinité sur Mer. Colas and Teura, some friends and a couple of crew members were returning from a day's sailing aboard *Manureva.* "It was only an afternoon joyride, and my concentration was not complete," Colas said. "I did not have my sheath knife at my belt, as I always do at sea, and I only had a small folding knife in my pocket. We were charging through the boats and moorings in the harbor because the mainsail had gotten wedged at the top of the mast, and I felt we should slow down. I jumped forward to put down the anchor. The big hook fell over, 100 pounds or more, and I turned on my left foot to return to the helm. Ordinarily, I would be watching the anchor line snake out, but this time I did not. My right foot was above the uncoiling line. A loop sprang up and lassoed my foot above the ankle.

"It sawed swiftly through the skin, sliced the muscle, bit through the bone, and by the time I managed to get my knife out of my pocket and the blade opened I could no longer see my foot. Only the naked end of the tibia bone where it had been cut through. The knife cut the running line very briskly, but by then all that was attached to my foot was the Achilles tendon. I fished the foot up by the tendon and I knew enough to press the artery in my knee to slow down the rush of blood.

"The major reaction I had at the moment was one of annoyance. The boat was still moving quickly and I had to give orders. I was annoyed that I could not use my hands to give signals, because I had to continue pressing the artery. And there was the severed foot itself to hold against my leg. I had to keep my balance on my one good foot and keep giving orders to bring the boat to a standstill.

"A friend was there who had had medical experience during the war in Algeria. He put on a tourniquet and kept me from spilling too much more blood. My wife played the part of a siren with her screams and woke up the village. An ambulance came and sped me to a tiny hospital forty miles away. The surgeon there didn't know what else to do but some ax work further up the leg to get it organized for a later fitting of wood perhaps. I wanted none of that.

"Eventually we were able to raise Professor Jean-Vincent Bainvel in Nantes, a specialist in orthopedics, along with a colleague in cardiology well acquainted with the lacework of veins and arteries. We raced to Nantes, which is about eighty-five miles away, and by the time they put me in the operating room, it had been eight hours since the foot was pulled off. I was extremely fit and they decided to give it a go—to reattach the foot where it belonged."

The operation lasted seven hours and involved an intricate stitching of lengths of vein and arteries from other parts of Colas's body into the leg and severed foot. Over the next seven months, there were twenty-two more operations involving skin grafts, and further work on the circulatory system. Miraculously, Colas kept his foot. It was almost as numb and stiff as if it were indeed made of wood, but it was alive and well in its own way.

"I have never wanted to be a surgical hero," said Colas. "I'd rather be a sailing hero. But I prefer my own foot to an artificial construction. One gets to like one's own things, you know. And it has also added a rather impressive new weather-forecasting aid to my sailing. The foot is very sensitive to any change in the humidity—I find it as reliable as a barometer in most cases. Sometimes more reliable."

The trauma of the accident was short-lived: Colas's obsession with the building of his new boat took over almost immediately. On the second day after his foot was "spliced back," as he put it, Colas signed a contract to begin construction of the hull. For the next several months, he masterminded all of the initial construction from his hospital bed. "The project literally pulled me out of bed," he said. "One year and one week after the accident, I was making final preparations to start the race in my dream boat."

Club Méditerranée had indeed been built and fitted out in the year, and it was an incredible racing machine. But the British race sponsors found it rather an irritation. Bitter arguments arose over the entry of such a behemoth. The British insisted that Colas sail his beast on a fifteen-hundred mile qualifying run instead of the five hundred miles required of the other entrants. Colas had no trouble: he finished the fifteen hundred miles in just over six days.

The sponsors searched for other ways to disqualify him, according to Colas, but their rules put no limits on size, and nothing could be done. (Since then, race rules have been changed and no boat longer than fifty-six feet is allowed.) The Route du Rhum has no limitation on maximum size, a policy Colas endorsed. "I believe there should never be a limit to the audacity of this sport," he said.

For the 1976 Newport Race, Colas wore a special boot to keep more of his weight supported by the knee instead of by the still-weak foot. Although his makeshift circulatory system was beginning to function, it was far from perfect.

"One artery and one vein were back at work," Colas said, "but the vein was not doing its cleansing job very well. I could hardly totter more than seven hours out of every twenty-four in a standing position. The other seventeen hours, I had to keep the foot in a higher position than the leg to allow it to drain and circulate the blood properly. On board ship during the race, I had to pace my efforts carefully. When I had been standing too long and still had work to do about the boat, I simply had to crawl."

The 1976 race was the roughest ever run. The weather in the Atlantic was savage, with winds and storms battering the entire field. Of the 125 starters, 37 boats retired and 5 sank; two men were lost. Some sailors reported winds up to eighty knots. Sails were popped off, masts snapped, automatic steering gear fouled. Through these days of tempest, Colas hobbled about his huge vessel, setting sails manually as the regulations required, fighting to make headway and at the same time keep his sails from being blown out. But he, too, fell victim to the terrible weather and was forced to put in at Newfoundland to repair his sails.

It all proved to be part of a bitter experience for Colas. "There was—and is—nothing that can go faster across the ocean under sail than my four-masted old girl. Nothing," he said. "But it was a very hard year on the Atlantic. My adversities were many. Some newsmen were reporting that I was running second to my old friend Eric Tabarly. Unfortunately, I believed that. Actually, it turned out that I was two days ahead of him; had I known that, I wouldn't have stayed so long in Newfoundland."

But Tabarly had finished first in his seventy-three-foot ketch *Pen Duick VI*. He was exhausted after twenty-three days, twenty hours and twelve minutes on the raging Atlantic, most of it with his self-steering rudder out of whack. *Club Méditerranée* glided into Newport out of a heavy mist in an elapsed time of twenty-four days, three hours and thirty-six minutes, which included Colas's

layover time. He was second man in, but he was assessed a fifty-eight hour penalty, dropping him to third. It was claimed that he had illegally taken passengers aboard when he left the boatyard in Newfoundland to return to the racecourse.

The loss of the race was a blow to Colas, but he maintained a proud posture in discussing the outcome. "I have nothing to prove," he said. "I have my own contentment."

Colas returned to Tahiti in 1976, where he carried paying passengers on joyrides aboard *Club Méditerranée.* But he hadn't retired from racing, and when the Route du Rhum was announced early in 1978, Colas was one of the first entrants.

"I love to race and I ache when I am too long away from a race," he said. "But don't forget, I must work for my boats. Sailing has been a sport too much for the sons of rich men. There has never been enough professionalism in it. And professionalism is the truest democracy. If there were more money in racing—sponsors and money prizes as in the Rum Race—then a poor young man could participate in his sport just as the rich do."

As for his hopes, he said shortly before leaving, "My boat and I, we sail at a good pace. And we are good in all weather. I think it will take twenty-five days to finish, but others say three weeks or only eighteen days. Well, good on them, if they can do it. When I arrive, if I find some others have made harbor sooner than I, I shall say, 'Bravo to you!' And then I shall continue on and sail my old girl home to Tahiti. It will be the boat's third trip around the world. She has earned a rest and I must spend more time with my family.

"If I am first across the line I will say, 'Bravo, old *Manureva*, bravo!—and I shall still set sail with her for home. I will feel that I am a winner either way."

At about 4:00 P.M. last November 16, the Saint-Lys radio station on the French coast near Bordeaux received a message from Alain Colas. It was quite cheerful and optimistic. He was west of the Azores, proceeding nicely, he said. The operator warned him that his signal was weak and full of interference, suggesting that his battery was failing. That was his last known message.

The night of the sixteenth, a storm hit the area where Colas had been. Winds rose to more than 50 mph, with waves cresting at twenty-five feet or so. The conditions were bad, but not critically so for a man of Colas's experience. That night, ham-radio operators in Lisbon, Portugal, and Ostender, Norway, heard a Mayday distress signal and a call for "immediate assistance" from an unknown vessel at sea.

The winner of the Route du Rhum, the Canadian Michael Birch, arrived in Guadeloupe on November 29. After four thousand miles of ocean racing, his margin of victory was just three hundred yards over Michel Malinovsky of France. Philip Weld of Gloucester, Massachu-

setts, was third. One by one, the other boats appeared at Pointe-à-Pitre. The last two arrived on December 9. Only Colas was missing.

On December 1, the French Navy dispatched four planes—two to the Azores, two to Guadeloupe—to start a concentrated, twelve-hour-a-day search for *Manureva* and Colas. They crisscrossed some two million kilometers of ocean, flying alternately at six thousand feet and fifteen hundred feet. There was no sign of boat or debris.

The search planes were recalled and the French Naval Ministry canceled the search December 28 after covering a 5-million-square-kilometer area in 450 hours of flying time. Little hope remains. It now seems likely that the sea has claimed Alain Colas.

An Ordeal of Grandeur

by WEBB CHILES

Storm Passage *is Webb Chiles's account of a thirty-eight-thousand-mile solo circumnavigation in his thirty-seven-foot cutter* Egregious. *Here, as he approaches Tahiti in 1976, the thirty-three-year-old sailor captures the poignancy of the moment when the dream of a lifetime is about to be fulfilled.*

Day 279 • May 26

A CONSTANT, dismal slow rain yesterday was broken only by squalls of harder rain. At 8:00 P.M. I hove to, letting us head on a course of about 110 degrees until 4:00 A.M. It was one of the most unpleasant nights I have spent at sea, with the sails rattling and *Egregious* being thrown about by the waves. Although there was almost no visibility and I told myself our course was a safe one, I got up every thirty minutes and peered into the oblivion of rain, always half expecting Tahiti to be looming over us.

At 4:00 A.M., I donned my foul-weather gear and resolutely turned us north. Sunrise would not be until 6:30, but I did not think there was any possibility we could hit anything before then. I remained in the cockpit anyway.

Not long before dawn, the sky cleared partially, and a few diluted stars were visible; an omen that during the day I might be able to get some sun sights. At that point, after three hundred miles of dead reckoning, which included a night of drifting becalmed in circles, several deliberate course changes and several hours of the boat's yawing eighty to ninety degrees in squalls, I felt as much lost as I ever have at sea; much more lost than found.

When daylight came—euphemism if ever there was one, because the insipid pallid cast that turned the rethickening clouds one infinitesimal shade of gray lighter than they had been bore only the most remote family resemblance to true daylight—something of a sister's neighbor's mother's brother-in-law's dog to daylight, if even that is not indeed too close a relationship. Anyway, when daylight came, I sat poised in the companionway, sextant in one hand, stopwatch in another, awaiting any brief shadow of a silhouette of the sun. At 9:10, I was rewarded by a three-second glimpse of my prey, but it was gone before I could lift the sextant to my eye.

The steady rain had ceased, but heavy squalls still passed once or twice an hour. That I welcomed this as a considerable improvement is an apt commentary on the relativity of value systems.

Egregious swooped north at a minimum of

seven knots and often more; too much more for my liking, as I kept a close eye on the leech of the mainsail, where the leech cord had broken during the night. Before my next circumnavigation, I may replace or repair the self-steering vane, but I will definitely experiment with twin headsails for self-steering on a run, a concept that before this voyage I ignorantly disdained. The saving in stress on the mainsail, the rigging and my nerves would be well worth whatever disadvantages such a system might entail.

As the morning wore on, I occasionally saw off the port bow an outline with a sharpness of edge and constancy of position that made me think it might be land rather than cloud; but I was far from certain. Then, at 10:30, the sun was dimly visible through several layers of overcast for two intervals of not more than fifteen seconds each, and I grabbed two of the quickest sights ever taken.

I worked them out eagerly at the chart table. Both resulted in a position line that put Tahiti only ten miles away. I returned to the deck and looked for my questionable land. The horizon cleared to the northwest, and there was no question any longer: it was land and we were found.

The location of the island off the port bow, when I had expected it to appear to starboard, was somewhat puzzling, until after another hour the solution appeared in the form of the high mountains of Tahiti only three miles to starboard. Visibility had been so limited to the northeast that we had been sailing along the Tahitian coast for fifteen miles without the least sign of those seven-thousand-foot heights, and my first sight of land had been Moorea, although it was smaller and farther away.

By noon, long after our position had definitely been established, the sky cleared to the north and the sun shone brightly. And the wind died to the lightest of zephyrs. More and more of Tahiti became visible; a dim jade jewel shrouded in mist and clouds, with mysterious valleys and a line of waves crashing on the reef offshore, as we ghosted up the passage between the islands.

Self-steering was not possible, so I held the helm while the sky darkened again. A great black line formed behind us and marched slowly up our desultory wake: five miles, I think, five more miserable miles—less than one hour of average sailing—and we would be in. Then the squall swallowed us. Our speed leaped from one knot to eight, almost wrenching the tiller from my grasp. It was just such a squall which struck us when we left Papeete on December 23, 1974. I have learned something in circumnavigating: this time I have my foul-weather gear on.

Fortunately, it passed over us in ten minutes; unfortunately, it took all the wind with it.

By 3:30 P.M. we were a quarter-mile off the pass at Papeete, having slowly glided by the unnecessary warning of a wrecked ship on the reef at the northwest corner of the island. I could feel no wind; there was no sign of wind on the horizon, not a single cat's-paw anywhere; the boat speed registered zero. Only by dropping a piece of paper over the side and watching it drift aft inch by inch could I tell we were moving.

For more than an hour we sit there, bow deliberately kept offshore because I think we might have to spend another night at sea. With only five minutes of wind, we would be in the harbor. But another hour passes, and we drift another one hundred yards offshore; the sky remains still, the sea flat and leaden. Not only are we to have one more night at sea, it is to be spent in such dangerous proximity to the land that I must not sleep. I gaze enviously at the yachts at anchor along the quay and at the automobiles driving along the shore.

Smoke rises lazily straight up from a hillside above the town. Low clouds sit motionless on the high slopes of Tahiti and Moorea. To the east, limp sails are lowered on a ketch, and an engine is started. I am tempted to ask for a tow but cannot bring myself to do it. We are only a few hundred yards short of a circumnavigation completely under sail. *Egregious* has been towed only twice, and then only inside harbors to boatyards. We will wait. Fish leap, breaking the glassy surface of the sea, and one of them catches my attention and directs it west, where a faint outline of wind darkens the water on the horizon.

Steadily, that line of darker water moves east and as it finally reaches us, I bring *Egregious* about, trim her sails and square off for the pass.

I am not yet certain I will actually attempt to go in, but I want to see how well we can sail on that course. The boat speed hovers around four knots, and I decide to continue on; then it drops to three and I weaken. Then back to four, up to five. The buoys are coming nearer, as are the waves breaking on the reef. If we are to sheer away, we must do so now.

I have no time to consider the voyage, which has now covered more than thirty-three thousand miles and 279 days and which will come to total thirty-eight thousand miles and 312 days when I return to San Diego in October, completing the circumnavigation San Diego-Auckland-Papeete-San Diego in 203 sailing days, not far off my original estimates and a world record for a solo circumnavigation in a monohull; no time to remember the disappointments of the early damage when I thought Cape Horn would remain ever elusive; no time to recall the beauty of moonlight on the sea, or the power of the albatross, or the freezing cold of the Horn, or the great storms of the Forties, the capsizes, the leak, the ever-increasing exhaustion of bailing, the struggle to survive and the moments when I did not think I would, the coast of Tasmania at dawn, or Cyclone Colin, the near wrecks on the approach to Auckland. I did not think, then, of my friend on Antares, whom I had often felt during these past months has been back in his home, his voyage successfully completed, hoping mine would be, too. I did not think that later that night I would row out on the black waters of Papeete harbor and look back at *Egregious* as I had a year and a half before; that from inside the cabin the trees seen through the companionway and the mad crowing rooster on shore would be the same. I did not think that for the first time I was entering a harbor without having immediately to look for a boatyard. I did not have time to understand that the voyage really was only moments from being over.

I did think of Suzanne. Even for me, it is odd not to know if I am going to marry a woman or never see her again. And I think of Mary. And of Bach. The "Little Fugue" plays merrily in my mind as the breakers are abeam.

Then we are through. We are inside the har-bor. The circle is closed. The dream fulfilled. The vow to myself kept. I have sailed around the world alone.

I have reserved my final judgment on *Egregious*. Even now I am uncertain whether to be angry I had as much trouble with her as I did, or grateful I did not have more. Few boats have ever been sailed harder and she did not kill me. Quite. I have come to expect her always to be broken and always to survive. She is a boat to love and a boat to hate. The words uttered first in anger remain true in tranquillity: she *is* a beautiful bitch.

Briefly I consider the future and wonder what an obsessed man does when he has fulfilled his obsession.

When he was a young man, Saint Augustine prayed, "God, make me pure—but not yet." There will be other commitments and other voyages for me, including another solo rounding of Cape Horn—after all, who, having visited hell, would not, given the opportunity, return to see if it really was as bad as he remembered. But, like Saint Augustine, I say "Not yet." For the moment, I have no ambition beyond lying in the sun like a lizard and swimming tomorrow in the warm sea off Maeva Beach. I know I will tire of indolence, that having lived on the edge of life, I can never return for long to something less. The intensity is too intoxicating. But not yet.

I do not delude myself that I have conquered the sea; it is enough to have faced it. And I am more proud that I continued to struggle against defeat than of my ultimate victory. To struggle was in my control; victory in that of chance.

Resurgam, I said, and now I must learn the Latin for "I have risen." "Time and chance and Cape Horn: I am still coming at you," I said, and I kept coming until Cape Horn was mine; and for one brief moment in my life, time and chance subdued. "Victory or death," I said, and though death often seemed the more likely, finally it is victory. Wind and waves of torment cease, and for a while they have. Sail to the limit, and I sailed beyond. "An ordeal of grandeur," I said, and it was. It truly was.

THE VOYAGES OF EGREGIOUS

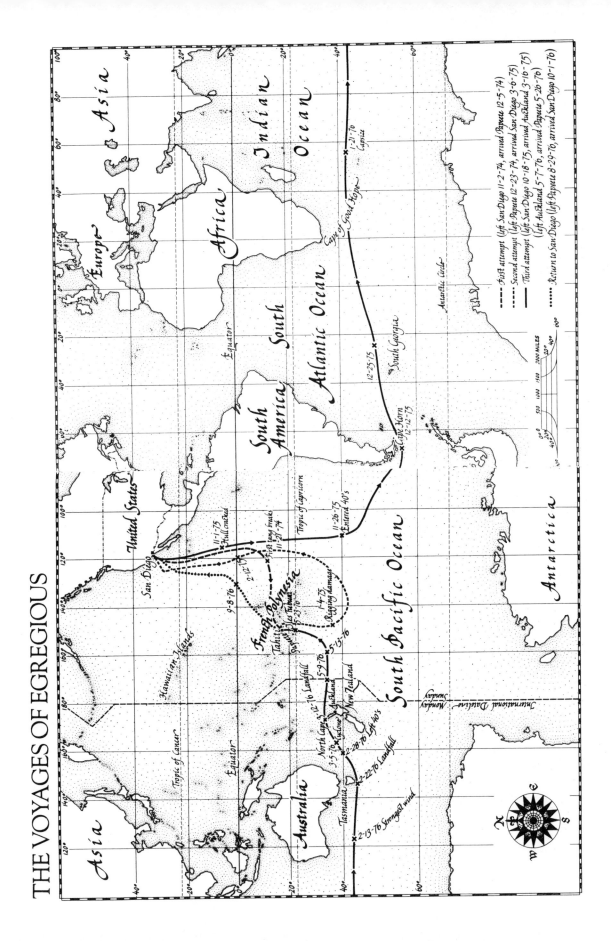

In Auckland, Suzanne and I attended an exhibit of Chinese art. One of the objects was a figure holding aloft thirty-two concentric spheres, only the outer half-dozen of which were visible, all carved from a single piece of ivory. The satisfaction of the artist upon completing carving all thirty-two spheres and knowing that each—even the innermost, which would never be seen—was perfect, is the same as that of a man who completes a solo circumnavigation, who fulfills any dream, even though no one else knows.

I smile to myself as *Egregious* sails slowly across the dusky harbor; and behind the sea-etched face of the man, a small boy grins because he has made his dream come true.

Egregious man, boat, voyage, life.

The fool smiles and sails on.

PART II

THE GREAT RACES

"Off Cowes were innumerable yachts, and on every side was heard the hail:

'Is the America first?' The answer, 'Yes.' 'What's second?' The reply,
'Nothing.'"

—unsigned from The London Times, August 25, 1851.

1866: The Start of It All

by ALFRED F. LOOMIS

In 1866 men of wealth pitted their pride in a race from America to England which saw tragedy and battles against the onslaughts of the Atlantic. Vesta, Henrietta *and* Fleetwing *went at it in the first tranatlantic race and this was the result.*

IN 1866, American yachting was on the up-and-up. The Civil War was over. Pleasure boats were being launched from stocks that for years had felt only the heavy keels of merchantmen and war vessels. The forty-eight-foot sloop *Alice,* newly built at Portsmouth, New Hampshire, sailed from Boston to England in nineteen days and a few hours, bettering by two days the historic transatlantic passage of the *America,* fifteen years before. Longshore racing engaged the sporting attention of the affluent. Bragging and boasting filled the air.

Two New York yachts of equal size but of diverse design were believed by their respective owners to be the best that money could build. *Vesta,* a centerboard schooner 105 feet in length to a beam of 25 feet and a draft of 7 feet 6 inches, with the centerboard up, could take the measure of any keel yacht afloat. So said Pierre Lorillard, who had had her built that June. She had defeated the keel schooner *Henrietta* in a hard breeze, racing from Sandy Hook around Cape May Lightship and return. She had won from other famous yachts in a spotty two-hundred-mile event in Long Island Sound. Mr. Lorillard may not have been a slangy man, but he hadn't the slightest shadow of a doubt that *Vesta* could put out and take it.

Modified superiority, said George and Franklin Osgood, owners of the keel schooner *Fleetwing,* built the year before to a length of 106 feet 7 inches, a beam of 23 feet 11 inches, and a draft of 11 feet 11 inches. When you talk about defeating the *Henrietta,* don't forget that *Fleetwing* had done it with a rounder margin. *Fleetwing* could strut her stuff in anything from a flat calm to a hurricane, and the Messrs. Osgood had money that spoke to the same purpose.

Ridiculous, alleged the owner of the *Vesta.* *Fleetwing* had won from *Henrietta* in a drifting match, whereas *Vesta* had trounced her in a gale of wind, with *Vesta*'s jibboom carried away, sails torn and lashings parted. That's how hard it blew. And she could do the same to *Fleetwing.*

Of course, opined the Osgood brothers, if a race were judged by the amount of gear that let go, *Vesta* was a dangerous contender. But if the payoff took place at the finish line, it could be demonstrated that *Fleetwing* was the better boat.

Very well then, let's get down to brass tacks. Here's money that says the *Vesta* can whip the

Fleetwing in an ocean race. How much? Say, $30,-000. Agreed. And this being the month of October, shall we leave the issue in doubt till spring? Not by a long shot. Start the race in December, when there's wind enough for both. Again agreed. And shall the course be from Sandy Hook to Cape May, or where? From Sandy Hook to the Isle of Wight, England, so that a man may get a run for his money. Shake on that and sign a contract.

So—or just about so—the great race of 1866 originated. It was an epic plan—three thousand miles of deepwater racing in the severest season of the year, when gales raged and green seas broke and the strongest ships were liable to founder. History does not relate why the parties of the first and second parts—fire-breathing, wallet-slapping sportsmen that they were—did not see fit to enter themselves as well as their yachts in this epochal contest. Perhaps family ties or business interests kept them home. Perhaps they had a Roman emperor's taste for combat. Whatever we may suppose in these days of personal participation in rugged sport, the originators of the first transatlantic race stayed ashore and permitted others to represent their interests afloat.*

Not so James Gordon Bennett, Jr., owner of the very schooner that had been defeated by the *Vesta* and the *Fleetwing*. His *Henrietta*, 107 feet over all, 22 feet in beam, and drawing 11 feet 6 inches of water, had been built in 1861 and had

---

*In an article published in 1869 in *All the Year Round*, a weekly journal conducted by Charles Dickens, these enlightening statements were made: "Some difficulty was experienced in securing seamen to cross the Atlantic in such vessels and in such weather. The men were willing enough to engage, but their mothers, wives and sweethearts interfered and persuaded them not to sign articles. Moved by such feminine solicitations, the picked crew of the *Henrietta* deserted her a few days before the start, and their places had to be supplied by a lot of landlubbers, few of whom could climb a mast. . . . Invitations to prominent yachtsmen were declined for various reasons and the gentlemen who finally served in this capacity were almost all volunteers. . . . From this time [seven o'clock of the morning of the start] no communication was permitted between the yachts and the shore; partly to prevent any further difficulties in regard to the crews; and partly because several kind but frightened friends had conceived the idea of subpoenaing some of the yachtsmen as witnesses in trials of which they knew nothing in order to preserve them from the perils of the sea."

seen service in the war. She had been places, and the son of the owner of the spicy *New York Herald* could gather together $30,000 to make it a three-cornered race. Ninety thousand in all, and the winner take the pot. Bennett would be aboard to take it.

Proposition accepted, and a new agreement drawn and signed by all. This was to be more than a yacht race. It was to be the Great Race of 1866. A fortune to the winner. Glory enough for all. Read about it in the *Herald* and the *Times*. Step up Broadway to Lafayette Hall and place your wagers. *Fleetwing* is the favorite with odds at four to three. One to three, if you want a safe bet, that *Vesta*, the centerboarder, will trail the fleet.

Henrietta? A little better than the *Vesta*, but young Bennett certainly asked for punishment when he horned into a two-boat match. On the *Fleetwing*, we give you as skipper old Dick Brown, who sailed the *America* to eternal glory in '51. You can have Bully Samuels, ranting, roaring ex-skipper of the Liverpool packet *Dreadnought*, on the *Henrietta*. But she will have her owner too, and you know how it is with divided authority. Bennett a kid of twenty-five? Well, all the worse for *Henrietta*, and what does a clipper ship captain know about a rich man's plaything? . . . But they say now that Dick Brown has backed out because *Fleetwing*'s clearance papers were issued in her navigator's name. That may even the chances, and it will be a good race anyway. The Great Race of 1866.

Tuesday they started, the eleventh of December. From an anchorage off Stapleton, Staten Island, the three schooners, their rigs cut down a little—only a little—in deference to the stormy season, towed astern of tugs to Sandy Hook. The New York Yacht Club, superintending the start, chartered the steamer *River Queen* to give the yachts a send-off. There were few if any yachts among the attending vessels, for in those days, even more than now, yachtsmen saw the wisdom of hauling out in winter months. But there were yachtsmen in the excursion fleet, and their keen eyes hit upon a curious point of similarity between the *Vesta* and the *Henrietta*. The spacious cockpits of these two had been decked over, making them flush-deckers abaft the main companionway. Though green water might sweep their decks, though their crews might have to stand miserably in the lee of weather cloths to keep out of the wind's icy blast, the *Vesta* and the *Henrietta* would be safer in a bitter chance. A pity the *Fleetwing* hadn't taken the same precaution, for the seas would be big out there, and cruel and hungry.

Well, here was hoping. At least the hardy lads weren't taking chances with balloon canvas. The agreement stipulated that only working sails, storm sails and small topsails might be carried. Plus square sails, as an afterthought. They'd get to the Needles, Isle of Wight, with that assortment, minus what they blew away.

Conditions could not have been more perfect for the start. At 1:00 P.M. when the signal was given, the wind was west-northwest, blowing fresh, and the sea, even in the lee of the Long Island shore, was making up. *Fleetwing* got the start, with *Vesta* close upon her and *Henrietta* last. All carried plain sail and in addition *Henrietta* and *Fleetwing* had gaff topsails above their mainsails. Within a few minutes, *Vesta* set her topsails and the others hung up square sails, all running dead off on east-southeast, packet-ship fashion, to gain an offing. With her centerboard up, *Vesta* set the pace, and when last seen by the eyes of stay-at-homes, led *Henrietta* by half a mile and *Fleetwing* by twice that distance. At this time, with three thousand miles to go, it was, of course, anybody's race.

So now as Captain George Dayton of the *Vesta* congratulates himself for having kept his square sail below, and as Captains Samuels and Thomas assure themselves that it will be a different story when the wind draws abeam, let us inquire into the personnel of each racing yacht. Understand first, however, that these are not racing machines. They are twice as big and carry three times as many men as modern yachts which trust themselves to Neptune's tender mercies.

Aboard the *Vesta* were George Lorillard, a brother of the owner, and Stuart Taylor, as judges. These were her only amateurs. Besides Captain Dayton, there were First Officer Hodg-

son and twenty-two other officers and men—a total complement of twenty-six.

On *Henrietta* were Bennett (who had been loudly cheered at the start for being "the only man who goes in his own boat"); Lawrence R. Jerome and A. M. Knapp, as judges for the other boats; Steve Fisk, the first seagoing newspaper correspondent; the redoubtable Captain Samuel Samuels; Sailing Master Lyons, and a crew of twenty-four—thirty men in all.

Fleetwing carried Robert Center and Ernest Staples, of the New York Yacht Club, as judges, and was commanded by Captain Thomas, late of the packet ship *New York,* First Mate Brown (not the immortal Dick), Sailing Master Crandall, and a crew of twenty—twenty-five all told. Lucky for the crew that Ernest Staples was aboard. Despite his valiant efforts, not all were to survive the Great Ocean Race of 1866.

Darkness shut in with *Henrietta* and *Vesta* beam to beam and *Fleetwing* trailing. Next day, each boat was lost to the view of the others, and from then on imagination rather than ocular evidence was to supply the spur that kept the yachtsmen up to racing pitch. As we cannot hold them all in sight, let us follow them individually across the glowering Atlantic. *Henrietta* first, since her record is most complete and since her skipper, Bully Samuels, was a man to stir the admiration of any sailor.

At 8:00 P.M. Samuels shook off the *Vesta,* which had been annoying him, he says, by keeping too close, and at midnight when the wind worked to the westward with heavy squalls, he jibed to the port tack on an easterly course. With all canvas set, he drove through squalls of sleet and snow, and when day broke, dark and lowering, the wind freshened and in the puffs blew really hard. By noon, when there was every prospect of a gale, the ship was running at close to ten knots, and had tucked away 225 miles by observation.

At ten o'clock that night, the topsails and flying jib were taken in, and at the change of the watch, working in darkness and nipping cold, the crew double-reefed the mainsail. But the gale held off and at the end of a day of sail drill, during which the reefs had been shaken out and the topsails had been set, hauled and set again too often for enumeration in the log, the yacht was sailing fast in a northerly, snow-filled breeze. So it went through the third, fourth and fifth days of the race, Samuels driving her, the foremast hands doubting whether yachting was a pleasure, and the *Henrietta* reaching north and east on the steamship route across the Grand Banks of Newfoundland. Various ships, sail and steam, were sighted and signaled. On Sunday, there was divine service in the cabin, with the reading of prayers and lesson for the day, and "one of Jay's sermons," and by midnight the ship was running in the trough of the sea and fairly burying herself. These are Samuels's words, to which he added, "This is yachting in earnest." Yes, particularly the reading of one of Jay's sermons!

But the run to noon on Monday was the best yet, with 280 miles to *Henrietta*'s account, and by noon of Tuesday she had chalked up another 250 miles and was tumbling downhill, more than halfway to the Needles. Despite shifts of wind, high seas and wearying handling of canvas, the captain stated the ship to be in perfect order and all hands in the best of spirits and condition.

All but one, who was unmentioned by the captain. It appears from the story subsequently published in the *London Times* that in the hurly-burly of reefing, shaking out reefs, jibing to the starboard tack as the wind whipped into the southwest, and whatnot, the carpenter built up a good case of psychological jitters. Here is how the eyewitness's story goes:

The southwest wind freshened after noon [of the 18th], and at 4:00 P.M. it blew a regular gale. The mainsail was furled and three reefs taken in the foresail and the jibs taken in. Even with this small spread of canvas, the yacht was driven nine miles an hour. On deck, the rain and spray shut in the vessel like a watery curtain. Below, the pitching and tossing rendered it impossible to sleep. A bucket of water was placed near the stove to extinguish the fire should the necessity arise. The deadlights leaked unexpectedly and uncomfortably. Holes were bored in the stateroom floors to let out water should the skylights be broken in. The servants were dashed about the cabins as if shot from invincible [invisible?] catapults. The guests had enough to do to hold themselves inside their berths. . . . Just at midnight, the struggling yacht was struck by a tremendous sea that burst over the quarter, struck full upon the foresail and then fell heavily upon the deck, staving in the yacht's boat. Simultaneously, the carpenter rushed wildly into the cabin, pale with alarm, and shouted, "Mr. Bennett, we must heave her to; she is opening up forward, sir!" With great good sense, nobody stirred save Mr. Bennett, who quietly informed Captain Samuels of the carpenter's report. As quietly, the captain came down from the deck and examined the supposed leak, which turned out to be nothing but the bilgewater oozing through the line planking [ceiling?] near the cook's berth. The gale strengthened, however, and at last the captain decided that the *Henrietta* could be driven no longer. Preparations were made to heave to, which is simply laying the ship head to the wind under close canvas so that she rides as if at anchor. The storm trysails happened to be stored in the cabin, and as the sailors came silently down, coiled the tackle and carried the sail up on the deck, the scene reminded one of the bringing forth of a pall for a funeral. A pause in a race like this seemed the burial of all our hopes. Nevertheless, it was some consolation to be informed by Captain Samuels that in his thirty years' experience he had never seen a vessel that could face a gale so long. . . .

So they hove to, and Bully Samuels, omitting mention of the carpenter's jitters, refers affectionately to the *Henrietta* in his log as "the little plaything. Well may her owner feel proud of her." The captain was no psychologist—I take it, at least, that in those days a master of sail began with the premise that he would judge sea conditions with entire objectivity and be guided only by wisdom and experience—and it is reasonable to suppose that he saw no link between the carpenter's panic and his own decision to heave to "the little plaything." But what a revelation is there in the reporter's story and in the captain's characterization! According to the ship's log, the heavy sea came aboard not at midnight, but at 8:40, and by 11:00 P.M. the sky had cleared, the moon shining beautifully the rest of the night. As I picture it, the carpenter introduced hysteria which blurred the reporter's perceptions and which, in inducing the indomitable Samuels to think of a rugged oceangoing yacht as a little plaything, caused him to heave to his able ship.

Sometime that night when the moon shone and the *Henrietta* rocked "lazily and pleasantly," the *Vesta*, a centerboarder, less seaworthy, crossed her course and overtook her, scudding under a reefed foresail at better than eight knots.

Not until 5:00 A.M., when it was nearly calm, did the *Henrietta* set a single-reefed foresail and jibs. At 9:00 A.M., the wind freshened, the square sail was set and, again in the captain's words, the ship stepped off again. Thirteen hours wasted because a carpenter, frightened by a breaking sea, mistook agitated bilgewater for an inundating torrent!

This was the climax of the race so far as *Henrietta* was concerned. *Vesta*, which had sharply shifted course to run dead off before the gale—*Vesta*, which might have sunk with all hands had she attempted to heave to—from then on, *Vesta* led the way across the wind-swept ocean. Ofttimes in modern racing, a skipper does as Samuels did—that is, he carries on to what he believes to be the limit of a boat's endurance and then heaves to, only to learn later that another skipper, not many miles away, has obtusely failed to recognize dire exigency and has blithely continued to spin out the wavering, watery miles.

Of *Vesta*'s log there is little that is now available. For the day ending at noon of the nineteenth, the record reads: "Heavy gale of wind from S.S.W., vessel scudding for eight hours. Distance run, 222 miles. Lat. 50–56; Long. 36–04." *Vesta* was then ninety miles due north and

a couple of miles east of *Henrietta*'s dead-reckoning position. Twenty-four hours later, she had increased her lead from two to eighty miles, and the two yachts, sailing converging courses, were only forty-six minutes of latitude apart. A day now in which *Vesta* reported light northwesterly weather and *Henrietta* noted southerlies, and the latter's noon position is only twenty-five miles from the leader's. ("Everybody on deck like turtles in the sun.") These relative positions are maintained for two days more, and if a skysail-yarder had sailed between them, her lookout, training his gaze now northeast to the *Vesta* and now southwest to the *Henrietta*, would have called it *Vesta*'s race.

So it would have been had the contest ended with the landfall. At 6:55 of Christmas Eve, *Vesta* made the lights of the Scilly Isles. Fifty minutes later, *Henrietta* picked them up. But there were still two hundred miles to go up Channel to the Needles, and in poor pilotage *Vesta* threw away the ascendency that she had gained and held in mid-Atlantic driving. In maneuvers not revealed, the centerboarder lost time in weathering the dangerous group of islets that constitutes England's bristling welcome from the sea. In a freshening southwesterly, *Henrietta* brought land abeam at 10:00 P.M., unknowing that off there to leeward *Vesta* was dropping fast astern. The Bennett schooner romped at thirteen knots up Channel, ticking off the Lizard, Eddystone, Start Point and Portland Bill like clockwork, and at forty minutes after noon of Christmas Day picked up the pilot who would take them in to Cowes. Stepping aboard, he set off a chorus of cheers with the word that 'Enrietta was the first boat in, and a good 'un. At 3:45 P.M. she passed the Needles with everything set and going her best, and so won the race in the phenomenal time of thirteen days, twenty-one hours and forty-five minutes.

But what of the *Fleetwing*, with her open cockpit, unreported by racing yacht or merchant vessel since the evening of December 12? Here are extracts from her log, as printed in the *New York Herald* in the first month of 1867:

Thursday, Dec. 13.—During this day pleasant breeze from N.W. 8 P.M., *Vesta* bearing N. by W. 6:30 A.M., wind N.N.E., carried away jibboom. 7 A.M., in squaresail and light sails. Lat. by observation, 41–27, Long., 63–26; distance run, 249 miles. Wind, N.W.

Friday, Dec. 14.—Commences with pleasant gale from N.N.E. 3:30 P.M., squally with snow; two reefs in the mainsail. 8 P.M., more moderate; out all reefs; set light sails. . . .

And so, with no incident to Wednesday the nineteenth, the day *Henrietta* hove to and *Vesta* scudded out ahead. *Fleetwing* had chosen a more southerly route than her competitors, and had lost time and distance as the days rolled by. She was now slanting up on her great circle course, feeling the influence of the east-going Gulf Stream and ready with a break of luck to wipe out her disadvantage. But catastrophe overtook her. The log reads:

Wednesday, Dec. 19.—This day commences with a light breeze from S.S.W. 2 P.M., in all light sails, gale increasing with heavy sea. 7 P.M., blowing a gale; running under two-reef foresail and forestaysail. 9 P.M., shipped a sea, which washed six of the crew out of the cockpit; hove to for five hours under two-reef foresail. 2 A.M., kept off; latter part moderate, wind hauling to west; set squaresail. Lat. 47–20, Long. 37–27. Distance run, 199 miles.

So the sea reached in and claimed its own— four seamen and two quartermasters. . . . And the latter part was moderate with the wind hauling into the west. There might not have been even this repressed statement in the log if Ernest Staples had not been there to save the ship. Bereft of helmsmen, *Fleetwing* lay beaten in the sea. Broaching to, she thrust her bowsprit into its savage breast and snapped off her jibboom. If she had been a centerboarder with no outside ballast . . . Staples jumped to the wheel, from which two spokes were horribly missing, and wrested her from the ocean's angry might. Two men of eight who had been washed out of the

false security of the cockpit hauled themselves aboard. Nothing was ever seen of the other six. Lost overboard in the black of night, there was no hope from the beginning that they would be saved. But the *Fleetwing* fulfilled humane demands and her surviving crew went through the ritual of search, their shouts unanswered. Then she carried on.

An interesting sidelight on this tragic happening has been furnished me by Captain George H. Crandall, a state pilot of Rhode Island, whose father, James, was the regular summer skipper of the *Fleetwing*. For the race, Captain Thomas, a "square-rigged commander," was given command, but Captain Crandall shipped as sailing master. In the words of his son, "As I recall father's story of that eventful day aboard the *Fleetwing*, Captain Crandall and Mate Beebe, his summer mate, had been on deck several hours. Captain Crandall had suggested to Captain Thomas that they let *Fleetwing* come to, as we say, as it would appear that it had been a very hard struggle to keep the heavy sea from sweeping the decks nearly all that day. I think I can remember father saying that Mate Beebe and he had just surrendered the watch to the oncoming crew, consisting of two sailing masters, and that he and Mate Beebe had just left the deck and were on the ship's stairs leading to the cabin when a tremendous sea came aboard which listed the yacht in such a manner that the upper rigging shrouds lay in the water, and only for the fact that the *Fleetwing* had extra-high hatch coaming and very tight-fitting skylights, it's doubtful if they would have saved her, for Captain Crandall and Mate Beebe crept on their hands and knees from aft forward through the cabins to a hatchway forward, placed the ship under short sail and let her lay to for about nine hours until conditions were more favorable."

It is said in an early story of the contest that with heart of grace gone from the passage, *Fleetwing* was out of the race from this time forward; but there is little in the record to substantiate this statement.

Despite the hours of search, *Fleetwing* turned in 199 miles that fatal day. The next gave her 260 miles with all sail set in a westerly gale. On other days, she made good 232, 215 and 270 miles, and, shorthanded though she was, *Fleetwing* tore past the Scilly Isles less than seven hours behind the *Henrietta*. Reefed down in another gale, she roared up Channel, and crossed the finish line at midnight of Christmas Day, only eight hours and fifteen minutes behind the winner.

Fleetwing finished second, for *Vesta*, which had not hove to, which had lost nobody and nothing, missed her way at the Needles through the error of a local pilot, and took last place forty minutes later.

It was indeed a great race, this race of '66, with tragedy and elemental savagery contributing to its greatness. Four times since—in the Transatlantic Race of 1870, in the Fastnet Race of 1931, in the Bermuda Race of 1932 and in the race to Norway in 1935—have men's lives paid tribute to the sea. But ever since in a score of ocean races have seamanship and dogged determination and inscrutable luck mirrored the greatness of the historic match between *Henrietta*, *Fleetwing* and *Vesta*.

AUTHOR'S NOTE: Just before this chapter went to press, correspondence with John D. McClearn, of Liverpool, Nova Scotia, disclosed this pertinent information. In 1916, McClearn's father purchased the schooner *Vesta*, then fifty years old, and had her sailed from Long Island Sound to Liverpool, where she was loaded with lumber for a voyage to New York. It was her last voyage. Mr. McClearn has sent me a quotation from the *Liverpool Advance* of July 26, 1916, which tells the poignant story. It follows:

"Among marine happenings of recent date an incident connected with the loss of the schooner *Vesta*, appears, from some points of view, of more than usual interest.

"The *Vesta*, on a voyage from this port to New York, sprang a leak last Friday when a few miles to the eastward of Seal Island and in spite of all efforts of her crew, by five o'clock that afternoon her deck was awash, and the ship's company were compelled to take to the small dory.

"The sea was somewhat rough, and the fog was dense, and when the five men, with some food and water, were in the boat, it appeared evident that their safety would be seriously jeopardized by taking another passenger.

"So the master bid adieu to the dog, a splendid animal

that had accompanied him on previous voyages, remarking as he left the ship, 'It's no use, Prince, I'll have to leave you,' and Prince, as Captain Evans believes, understanding every word that was said, made no effort to get into the boat but quietly took his accustomed place on the compass box, as if resigned to his fate.

"The dory with all its five passengers reached shore at Pubnico at seven o'clock the following morning, where Captain Evans with heavy heart took train for Liverpool.

"On Saturday as the fishing schooner *Don* of Pubnico was making for land an object was discovered, which on nearer approach was found to be part of the deckhouse of a small vessel, and seated on top of it, but in an exceedingly exhausted and bedraggled condition was Prince, who had evidently managed with great difficulty to maintain a precarious position there.

"The dog was promptly rescued and was taken to Pubnico, whence news of his safety was sent to his master here, and today Prince comes, a passenger by the H. & S. W. Railway, reflecting deeply, no doubt, upon the dangers of those who go down to the sea in ships.

"The *Vesta* and cargo were owned by the McClearn Co., Ltd., of this town. The crew lost all their effects."

The America's Triumph

UNSIGNED

Southampton and Cowes were congested with thousands of visitors that week in August, 1851. Latecomers lugged baggage through the streets long after midnight, vainly seeking shelter. The great race to be run on the morrow was the inauguration of international yacht racing.

A syndicate headed by John C. Stevens, first commodore of the New York Yacht Club (the Brother Jonathan of the following report) had commissioned George Steers to design the ninety-three-foot schooner America *expressly to challenge the finest English yachts in their home waters.*

The whole venture was marked by typical Yankee dash. Builder William Brown demanded $30,000 for his work, but volunteered to forfeit every penny if the America *turned out less than the fastest yacht in the world. Stevens then offered a wager of 10,000 guineas on his* America *against any yacht of any size, but there were no takers. "Things have come to a pretty pass,"* moaned the Times *correspondent at Cowes for the race. Here is his colorful account of that first contest for the "America's Cup."*

Cowes, Saturday night, Aug. 25, 1851

IN the memory of man, Cowes never presented such an appearance as upon last Friday. There must have been upwards of 100 yachts lying at anchor in the roads; the beach crowded from Egypt to the piers—the esplanade in front of the club thronged with ladies and gentlemen and with the people inland, who came over in shoals with wives, sons and daughters for the day. Booths were erected all along the quay, and the roadstead was alive with boats, while from the sea and shore arose an incessant buzz of voices, mingled with the splashing of oars, the flapping of sails and the hissing of steam from the excursion vessels preparing to accompany the race. Flags floated from the beautiful villas which stud the wooded coast, and ensign and burgee, rich with the colors of various clubs, or the devices of the yachts, flickered gaily out in the soft morning air.

The windows of the houses which commanded the harbor were filled from the parlor to the attic, and the old salts on the beach gazed moodily on the low black hull of the Yankee and spoke doubtfully of the chances of her competitors.

Among the visitors were many strangers—Frenchmen en route for Havre, Germans in quiet wonderment at the excitement around them, and Americans already triumphing in the anticipated success of their countrymen. The cards containing the names and colors of the yachts describe the course merely as being "round the Isle of Wight"; the printed program stated that it was to be "round the Isle of Wight, inside of Noman's Buoy and Sandhead Buoy and outside the Nab." The distinction, it will be seen, might have been productive of larger consequences than could be imagined.

The following yachts were entered, being named in the order in which they were placed from Cowes Castle, the first named being the nearest. They were moored in a double line. No time allowed for tonnage:

Name	Type	Tons	Owner
Beatrice	schooner	161 tons	Sir W. P. Carew, Bart.
Volante	cutter	48	J. L. Craigie
Arrow	cutter	84	T. Chamberlayne
Wyvern	schooner	205	Duke of Marlborough
Ione	schooner	75	Almon Hill
Constance	schooner	218	Marquis of Conyngham
Titania	schooner	100	R. Stephenson
Gipsy Queen	schooner	160	Sir H. B. Hoghton, Bart.
Alarm	cutter	193	J. Weld
Mona	cutter	82	Lord Alfred Paget
America	schooner	170	J. C. Stevens
Brilliant	schooner	392	G. H. Ackers
Bacchante	cutter	80	B. H. Jones
Freak	cutter	60	W. Curling
Stella	cutter	65	R. Frankland
Eclipse	cutter	50	H. S. Fearson
Fernande	schooner	127	Major M. Martyn
Aurora	cutter	47	Mr. Le Merchant

The mist that hung over the fields and woods from sunrise was carried off about nine o'clock by a very gentle breeze from the westward, which veered around a little to the south soon afterwards, and the morning became intensely warm. At 9:55, the preparatory gun was fired from the clubhouse battery, and the yachts were soon sheeted from deck to topmast with clouds of canvas, huge gaff topsails and balloon jibs being greatly in vogue, and the *America* evincing her disposition to take advantage of her new jib by hoisting it with all alacrity. The whole flotilla not in the race were already in motion, many of them stretching down towards Osborne and Ryde to get a good start of the clippers.

Of the list above given, the *Titania* and the *Stella* did not start, and the *Fernande* did not take her station (the latter was twice winner in 1850 and once this year; the *Stella* won once last year). Thus, only fifteen started, of which seven were schooners, including the *Brilliant* (three-masted schooner) and eight cutters. At ten o'clock, the signal gun for sailing was fired, and before the smoke had well cleared away, the whole of the beautiful fleet was under way, moving steadily to the east with the tide and a gentle breeze. The start was effected splendidly, the yachts breaking away like a field of racehorses. The only laggard was the *America,* which did not move for a second or two after the others.

Steamers, shore boats and yachts of all sizes buzzed along on each side of the course and spread away for miles over the rippling sea—a sight such as the Adriatic never beheld in all the pride of Venice; such, beaten though we are, as no other country in the world could exhibit; while it is confessed that anything like it was never seen, even here, in the annals of yachting.

Soon after they started, a steamer went off from the roads with the members of the sailing committee. The American minister, Mr. Abbott Lawrence, and his son, Colonel Lawrence, attaché to the American legation, arrived too late for the sailing of the *America,* but were accommodated on board the steamer and went round the island in her; and several steamers, chartered by private gentlemen or for excursion trips, also accompanied the match.

The *Gipsy Queen,* with all her canvas set and in the strength of the tide, took the lead after starting, with the *Beatrice* next, and then with little difference in order, the *Volante, Constance, Arrow* and a flock of others. The *America* went easily for some time under mainsail (with a small gaff topsail of a triangular shape, braced up to the truck of the short and slender stick which serves as her main-topmast), foresail, forestaysail and jib; while her opponents had every cloth set that the club regulations allow. She soon began to creep up on them, passing some of the cutters to windward. In a quarter of an hour, she had left them all behind, except the *Constance, Beatrice* and the *Gipsy Queen,* which were well together, and went along smartly with the light breeze. Once or twice the wind freshened a little, and at once the *America* gathered way and passed ahead of the *Constance* and the *Beatrice.* Another puff came, and she made a dart to pass the *Gipsy Queen,* but the wind left her sails, and the little *Volante* came skimming past her with a stupendous jib, swallowing up all the wind that was blowing.

As the glorious pageant passed under Osborne House, the sight was surpassingly fine, the whole expanse of the sea from shore to shore being filled, as it were, with a countless fleet, while the dark hull of the *Vengeance* in the distance of Spithead, towered in fine relief above the tiny little craft that danced around her—the green hills of Hampshire, the white batteries of Portsmouth and the picturesque coast of Wight forming a fine framework for the picture. As the *Volante* passed the *America,* the patriotic were delighted, but the nautical cognoscenti shook their heads and said that the triumph would be short lived; the breeze was freshening, and then the sprightly cutter must give way, though she was leading the whole squadron at the time.

At 10:30, the *Gipsy Queen* caught a small draught of wind and ran past the *Volante,* the *Constance, America, Arrow* and *Alarm* being nearly in line. At 10:45, the breeze freshened again for a short time, and the *America* passed the *Arrow, Constance* and *Alarm* but could not shake off the *Volante* nor come up to the *Gipsy Queen,* and exclamations were heard of "Well, Brother Jonathan is not going to have it all his own way," etc.

Passing Ryde, the excitement on shore was very great, and the great *Ichthyosaurus*-like pier was much crowded; but the *America* was forging ahead and lessening the number of her rivals every moment. The Sandheads were rounded by the *Volante, Gipsy Queen* and the *America* without any perceptible change in point of time at eleven o'clock, the last being apparently to leeward. Again the wind freshened, and the fast yachts came rushing up before it, the run from the Sandheads being most exciting and well contested. Here, one of the West India mail steamers was observed paddling her best to come in for some of the fun, and a slight roll inwards began to impart a livelier motion to the yachts and to render amateurs, whether male or female, ghastly looking and uncomfortable. The yachts were timed off Noman's Land buoy, and the character of the race at this moment may be guessed from the result:

Volante	11 hours	7 minutes	0 seconds
Freak	11	8	20
Aurora	11	8	30
Gipsy Queen	11	8	45
America	11	9	0
Beatrice	11	9	15
Alarm	11	9	20
Arrow	11	10	0
Bacchante	11	10	15

The other six were staggering about in the rear, and the *Wyvern* soon afterwards hauled her wind and went back towards Cowes. At this point, the wind blew somewhat more steadily, and the *America* began to show a touch of her quality. Whenever the breeze took the line of her hull, all her sail set as flat as a drumhead, and without any careening or staggering, she walked along past cutter and schooner, and, when off Brading, had left every vessel in the squadron behind her—a mere ruck—with the exception of the *Volante,* which she overtook at 11:30, when she very quietly hauled down her jib, as much as to say she would give her rival every odds, and laid herself out for the race round the back of the island.

The weather showed symptoms of improvement, so far as yachting was concerned; a few seahorses waved their crests over the water, and the high lands on shore put on their fleecy nightcaps of cloud, and the horizon looked delightfully threatening; and now the Yankee flew like the wind, leaping over, not against, the water, and increasing her distance from the *Gipsy Queen, Volante* and *Alarm* every instant.

The way her sails were set evinced a superiority in the cutting which our makers would barely allow; but, certain it is, that while the jib and mainsails of her antagonists were bellied out, her canvas was as flat as a sheet of paper. No foam, but rather a water jet, rose from her bows; and the greatest point of resistance—for resistance there must be somewhere—seemed about the beam, or just forward of her mainmast, for the seas flashed off from her sides at that point every time she met them. While the cutters were thrashing through the water, sending spray over their bows, and the schooners were wet up to the foot of the foremast, the *America* was dry as a bone.

She had twenty-one persons on her deck, consisting of the owners, crew, cook and steward, a Cowes pilot named Underwood and some seamen who had been lent her by the *Surprise,* a London-built schooner yacht now at Cowes Road. They nearly all sat aft, and when the vessel required any handling, crouched down on the deck by the weather bulwarks.

The *Gipsy Queen,* when a little past Brading, seemed to have carried away her foresail sheets, but even had it not been so, she had lost all chances of success. The *America,* as the wind increased, and it was now a six-knot breeze at least, hauled down her wee gaff-topsail and went away under mainsail, foresail and forestaysail, so that it required the utmost the steamer could do to keep alongside of her. This was her quickest bit of sailing, for on rounding the east point of the island, it was necessary to beat to the westward in order to get along the back of the Wight. At 11:37, the *Arrow, Bacchante, Constance* and *Gipsy Queen* stood away to the north to round the Nab, imagining most probably that it was requisite to do so, as the usual course certainly is to go outside the lightship, though the cards did not specify it on this occasion.

The *America* and most of the other yachts kept their course round the Foreland, and by Bembridge. She ran past the white and black buoys at a tremendous rate, and at 11:47 tacked to the west and stood in towards the Culver cliffs, the nearest yacht being at least two miles to leeward or astern of her. She was not very quick in stays on this occasion, and it would seem she was not very regular in the maneuver, sometimes taking a minute, sometimes thirty seconds, to perform it. At 11:58, she stood out again to the

southeast, and, having taken a stretch of a mile or so, went about and ran in towards Sandown. The breeze died off at this point, and, to keep the cutters and light craft off, the *America* hoisted her gaff-topsail and jib once more.

Under Shanklin Chine, the set of the tide ran heavily against her, but still there was nothing to fear, for her rivals were miles away, some almost hull down. While running under Dunnose at 12:-58, her jibboom broke short off. It may be remembered she procured the spar of Ratsey of Cowes, but no blame attaches to him, for not only did he recommend Messers. Stevens to take a yellow spar instead of a white one they selected, but the boom was broken by mismanagement on the part of the men when straining on it with the windlass, and did not snap from the action of the sail. The accident threw her up in the wind and gave the advantage of about a quarter of an hour to her opponents while she was gathering in the wreck. But it was of little use to them.

Looking away to the east, they were visible at a great distance, standing inshore or running in and out most hopelessly astern, the *Aurora, Freak* and *Volante,* in spite of light winds and small tonnage, being two or three miles behind. The wind fell off very much for more than an hour, and it was but weary work stretching along the coast against a baffling tide, every moment making the loss of her jib of greater consequence to the *America.*

Soon after three o'clock, the *Arrow* managed to run on the rocks to the east of Mill Bay, and the sailing committee's steamer, the *Queen, Her Majesty,* an excursion boat, and the *Alarm* at once made in to her assistance. They ran down to the ledge of rocks with a hawser, steamed away as hard as possible and, after some twenty or thirty minutes, towed off the poor little *Arrow,* which won but the other day at the Ryde Regatta, in such a condition that she nevermore was fit for sea. She put about and went off towards the Nab, with the intention of returning to Cowes; and the *Alarm,* which might have had a chance with Brother Jonathan in a heavy seaway, kept her company in the same direction, having generously run down to aid her.

The *America* at this time was some miles

A photograph of a modern lithograph of the ninety-three-foot schooner America *which beat the finest English yachts in a race around the Isle of Wight to win the ornate silver trophy later known as the America's Cup.*

ahead and, as the breeze freshened, from west-southwest half west, slipped along on her way, making tacks with great velocity and stood well up to windward. Her superiority was so decided that several of the yachts wore, and went back again to Cowes in despair; and, for about a half hour, the New York boat increased her distance every second, the *Aurora, Freak* and *Volante* keeping in a little squadron together—tack for tack—and running along close under the cliffs. This was rather unfortunate in one respect, for, in going about, the *Freak* fouled the *Volante* and carried away her jibboom; and the boatmen's pet became thereby totally disabled and lost the small glimpse of fortune which the light winds might have given her.

Meanwhile, minute after minute, the Yankee was gaining ground, and at 3:30 was flying past St. Lawrence towards Old Castle, while the *Bacchante* and *Eclipse,* which had been working along honestly and steadily, were about two and a half miles to leeward behind her. Further away still were visible five or six yachts, some hull down, some dipped further still, digging into the tideway as hard as they could and lying into the wind as well as their sails might stand it.

The *America* had, by this time, got the wind on her quarter, having gone round Rockenend, and thus having a tolerably fair course from the south to northwest up to the Needles, the wind being light and the water somewhat broken. The persons on board the steamers were greatly astonished at seeing ahead of the *America,* after she had rounded the Rockenend, a fine cutter, with jib and foresail together, bowling away with all speed, as if racing away for her life, and it was some time before they could be persuaded she was not the *Aurora;* but she was in reality the *Wildfire,* forty-two tons, Mr. F. Thynne of the Royal Cork Club, which was taking a little share in the match to herself and had passed the end at 3:40. The *America,* however, bore straight down for the cutter, which was thoroughly well sailed, and passed her after a stern chase of more than an hour, though the *Wildfire* when first sighted must have been two and a half miles ahead of the schooner. At 5:40, the *Aurora,* the nearest yacht, was fully seven and a half miles astern, the *Freak* being about a mile more distant and the rest nowhere.

The *America* was at this time close to the Needles, upon which she was running with a light breeze all in her favor. Two of the excursion steamers ran into Alum Bay, and anchored there to see the race round the Needles. While waiting there in intense anxiety for the first vessel that should shoot round the immense pillars of chalk and limestone which bear the name, the passengers were delighted to behold the *Victoria and Albert,* with the royal standard at the main and the Lord Admiral's flag at the fore, steaming round from the northwest, followed by the *Fairy* and the little dockyard tender. Her Majesty, the Prince and the royal family were visible by the aid of a glass from the deck of the steamers. The royal yacht went past the Needles, accompanied by the *Fairy,* at 5:35, but quickly returned, and at 5:45 lay off Alum Bay. The *Fairy* was signaled to proceed round the Needles to bring tidings of the race and at once started Ariel-like on her errand.

Soon after the royal yacht anchored, a boat put off from her, in the stern sheets of which were Prince Albert and the Prince of Wales, who wore his white sailor's dress and tarpaulin hat. They landed, attended by two gentlemen, on the beach under the cliff at Alum Bay with the aid of the boatmen, and it was some time before the saunterers from the steamboats, who were climbing up towards the heights, were aware of the presence of such distinguished visitors. They proceeded a short way up the narrow, winding patch which leads to the heights, but a wet drizzle drifted before the wind and rendered the walk unpromising, and the royal party soon returned to the beach, the young prince dancing down the shelving road with boyish vivacity. After a stay of eight or ten minutes, the royal party returned to the yacht. The *Fairy,* which had returned to signal, again stood out past the Needles, but all doubt and speculation, if any there could have been, was soon reproved by the appearance of the *America,* hauling her wind round the cliff at 5:50. The breeze fell dead under the shore, and the *America* lowered her foresail and forestaysail, so as to run before it. All the steamers weighed and accompanied her, giving three cheers as she passed, a compliment which owners and crew acknowledged with uncovered heads and waving hats. At 6:04, the *Wildfire* rounded the Needles and bore away after the schooner, which by this time had got almost in a line with the *Victoria and Albert.*

Though it is not usual to recognize the appearance of Her Majesty on such occasions as a racing match, no more indeed than a jockey would pull up his horse to salute the Queen when in the middle of his stride, the *America* immediately lowered her ensign—blue with white stars—the commodore took off his hat, and all his crew, following his order and example, remained with uncovered heads for some minutes, till they had passed the yacht—a mark of respect to the Queen not the less becoming because it was bestowed by republicans. The steamers, as she passed on, renewed their cheering, and the private battery of some excellent gentlemen at the Crow's Nest opened fire with a royal salute as the *Victoria and Albert* slowly steamed alongside the *America.*

On turning towards the Needles at 6:30, not a sail was in sight, but the breeze was so very light that all sailing might be said to have finished, and it was evident that the *America* had won the cup, unless some light cutter ran up with a breeze in the dusk and slipped past her. The steamers, including the *Tourist,* which astonished the natives by steaming through the still water at the rate of some fifteen or sixteen miles an hour, returned towards Cowes, and the royal yacht, having run close by the *America* under half steam for a short distance, went on towards Osborne. Off Cowes were innumerable yachts, and on every side was heard the hail:

"Is the *America* first?"

The answer, "Yes."

"What's second?"

The reply, "Nothing."

As there was no wind, the time consumed in getting up from Hurst Castle to the winning flag was very considerable, the *America*'s arrival first not having been announced by gunfire till 8:37. The *Aurora,* which slipped up very rapidly after rounding the Needles, in consequence of her light tonnage and a breath of wind, was signaled at 8:45, the *Bacchante* at 9:30, the *Eclipse* at 9:45, the *Brilliant* at 1:20 A.M. August 23. The rest were not timed.

Thus, the *America* made good all her professions, and the Messers. Stevens were presented by the Royal Yacht Squadron with the well-won cup.

The Fishermen's Cup Races: Last Act

by STERLING HAYDEN

One of sailing's most famous rivalries was between Captain Angus Walters out of Lunenberg, Nova Scotia, in Bluenose *and Captain Ben Pine of Goucester in* Gertrude L. Thebaud. *They raced officially and unofficially for nearly twenty years. In 1938 Sterling Hayden, sailor and later actor, acted as* Thebaud's *navigator and mastheadman, and wrote this account.*

OUT of Gloucester, a week before the first race, forty men and one tall ship bound on a trial run. Pitted against the clock. Against some wind as well—ragged brawling wind blowing a southeast gale. Storm warnings fly beneath a dull gray sky, and leaves skirmish. (Out on the Banks, no dories will work this day, and up in Boston, girls clutch skirts and hats go tumbling to leeward.)

Half past ten, says a belfry clock. Captain Ben Pine stands by the wheel. You would swear he was part of his ship—in spite of the blue-vested suit, the brown felt hat and a red bow tie. More like a coach he looks than like a racing-schooner skipper.

A motor launch tows the *Thebaud* free of the wharves and holds her head to the wind. "You can set your mainsail now," Ben says softly. Forty men to the halyards—peak to starboard, throat to port. Twenty men to a side—to lay back haul-ing, grunting at first, then gasping. Big new halyards an inch and a half in a diameter. The canvas flogs. All over the harbor you hear it. (Plenty of empty seats in Gloucester's schools. Plenty of hooky players hiding out in wharves.)

"Now go ahead on your foresail." Ben spits in his hands and paces in front of the wheel, feeling the wind and gauging the heft of the ship. Putting pieces together like an artist, working with wood and wind, buoys and rocks and anchored vessels, painting a wind-blown scene.

"Run up your jumbo and jib." His voice edged now, the coach look lost. The decks a tangle of gear: of mooring warps, gaskets, lifts, sheets, runners, tackles and halyards. (Paid for by townsmen who donated money or labor, by riggers and shipwrights and sailmakers who worked for almost nothing.) Ben spits as he gauges and measures. The towline is gone, and the bow cants fast to starboard. She starts to move through the water. Most skippers would be content to run for the open sea, but not Ben Pine.

Cordage bites into grooved oak rails. Like an iron-capped lance, her bowsprit flies toward Sherm Tarr's office window. A sharp puff rams home in her sails and lays the vessel over. Her rail smokes. Dead toward the dock she goes. Anyone who doesn't know schooners would swear something is wrong.

She goes now. Better than ten she goes. Up aloft, you hear a deep rumbling roar—and the hissing of spray. Square in mid-channel lies an old-time sailing vessel—a brigantine with a lascar crew, hailing from Ceylon. Her name stands out—*Florence C. Robinson.*

With a thrust of his fist, Ben orders a man aloft. Up he goes on the run till he reaches the masthead, where he heaves himself over the hounds, breathing hard, and goes to work with the topsail. "Stand by!" Ben's voice betrays his calm. One final look—full circle—with an arm flung wide for balance. Now he claws at the wheel, fighting it over. "Helm's alee!" For the first time, he really yells out.

She slashes into the wind. Canvas booms and sheet blocks dance under booms. Straight into the eye of the wind. (Not six feet separate her from the queer brig with the crew all wrapped in skirts and blankets—tumbling up on deck in response to a shipmate's warning.)

She passes across the wind, flung down to port. "Leggo your main sheet, boys." Ben is right where he wants to be. "Clear that coil—now let her run to the knot." The sheet runs snaking out till the knot fetches up in the block.

She swings toward the harbor entrance, and all around the harborside spurts of white stab from whistles—a pleasant sound, on a southeast day with rain.

Half a mile inside the breakwater she really begins to pitch, though the force of the wind is blunted. Both topsails are set. Down in the galley, they're mixing hot water with rum, butter and cinnamon.

Up aloft you hang on. Beyond the breakwater the wild Atlantic growls. Plumes of spray pounce on lighthouse windows. Your mainmasthead is six feet higher than where Jack Hackett lives, thirty feet away. His voice is high and loud. "Oh dyin' Jaysus, boy, if she catches one o' them seas just right she'll pitch us clear to Newfoundland!" Up here, you feel the motion more. You feel her reach out over a sea and hang; then down she goes with a sickening rush, and the second after the crash your mast goes buckling forward with a sideways motion. You wonder how wood can take it. (This goes on for an hour and more. Then both topsails are furled so as not to do any damage.)

Boudreau comes up from the galley, wiping his lips, leaning in to the weather rail, shoulders hunched. His yellow oilskins shine. He rests one knee on the deck and jams one booted leg out stiff against a hatch as he watches the vessel go. Low in the water she flies; two feet of sifting water conceal her rail. Her long bow threads through breaking seas, reaching high, plunging down, always with the roar in the shrouds. He thrashes his arms and screams: "Fourteen, goddamn it, boys, fourteen she goes, or I hope to die with a hard-on!"

Ben by the lee of the wheel, fondling the spokes, feeling her go—knee deep in water. Satisfied.

Captain Angus Walters swung his big saltbanker *Bluenose* in past the Boston lightship, strapped her down and sent her rampaging up harbor in time for a welcoming luncheon thrown by the governor on behalf of the Commonwealth. Those who were there pronounced it a dandy affair: plenty of dames, plenty of booze, plenty of platitudes. Captain Angus wasn't there. He stayed by his vessel instead. "Let 'em spout," he barked. "I'm gettin' ready to race."

The mayor of Gloucester passed the word to the better saloons down on Duncan Street that he expected a little decorum, a little restraint . . . during the racing. When they heard this, the boys in the red jackboots and the checked shirts smiled. Saloon keepers are smart: by the time the *Bluenose* arrived there wasn't a piece of movable furniture in a single waterfront bar.

October came in like a lamb, mewed for a few days, roared like a lion for the better part of two weeks, then trailed off into November. The first two races were sailed in moderate winds and sunshine. *Thebaud* took the first one by thirty seconds, and *Bluenose* waltzed off with the second. During the scheduled three-day hiatus that followed, Gloucester got down on its knees and prayed for a living gale. While Gloucester was busy praying, Angus Walters took advantage of the moonless midnight hours to scan the weather forecasts and juggle around with his ballast.

When the Clerk of the Weather predicted a breeze of wind—into the *Bluenose* went an extra ton or two of pig-iron ballast. When the clerk called for light airs—back on the wharf went the pigs. Pretty clever. It was also against the rules that governed the races. But Captain Elroy Proctor of the Master Mariners Association and Miss Ray Adams, Ben Pine's partner, were pretty clever too. They sprinkled a layer of sand over the ballast pile, and Angie was caught red-handed. "Some cute," said Gloucester. What Angus said did not appear in the *Gloucester Times.* Everybody shrugged. After all, the little Lunenburger was more than just a crack racing skipper: he was renowned as a dairyman, and, like all businessmen, he wanted to win and to hell with your goddamn rules.

The day of the third race dawned with rain and a driving easterly gale. All but one of the *Thebaud*'s crew smiled, and I was the one who didn't. The reason was simple enough: only the day before, I had been turned from masthead-man to navigator because my predecessor had got all but lost in the second race. To make things worse, Captain Pine was in the hospital with a sinus attack.

A cannon on the Coast Guard boat let go with a puff of smoke and the race was on. Both schooners hit the starting line going twelve knots and the Canadian pulled ahead. Captain Cecil Moulton hung to the *Thebaud*'s wheel with his boots full of water and his cap rammed down on his eyes. We averaged thirteen and a half to the first mark, where forty brawny Gloucestermen lay back chanting and straining on swollen manila sheets. "Haul, you bastards, haul!" cried Harry the cook, buried waist deep in the hatch, clutching his derby in one hand, a mug of rum in the other.

The *Bluenose* tore past the plunging buoy two lengths ahead of us and swung hard on the wind. Her long black snout, streaming spray, reached over a steep sea, then fell like a maul into the trench beyond. Her scarred old timbers shuddered. Her spars pitched hard against their tracery of shrouds. High far aloft, her foretopmast backstay parted and the wire rained down on deck. Fiery Angus—never a man noted for

patience—laid down on the wind-honed waters a savage barrage of four-letter words.

With this stay gone, they were forced to strike their big jib topsail. The smaller *Thebaud* forced by to windward, slogging her way uphill now, through charging white-plumed seas. This was the windward leg. Fifteen miles away, dead into the eye of the wind, lay a small white buoy. The visibility was about two hundred yards at best—less in the squalls, of course. Back and forth the two great wagons tacked, sawing away at the base course. When they came about, you could hear the flogging of canvas halfway to Scollay Square. I'm all right, I kept reassuring myself, so long as the wind doesn't shift. If we can't find the buoy, they'll not blame me too much, what with this horsing around, first to the southeast, then to the northeast—with Christ knows what for a current setting beneath the keel. But if the wind should haul and we run for the mark—and I have to conjure a fixed course —what in hell then?

The wind hauled. I pored over the chart, gauging and guessing and praying. I crossed myself twice, exhaled with resignation and called out to Cecil: "Let her go east by south and a quarter south."

"East by south and a quarter south it is!" his voice came through the hatch. I wished I were Irving Johnson. I wished myself back on the masthead, where there was nothing to do but curse, work and spit downwind—all the while thinking how tough you were. I took the binoculars and made my way forward past the prone bodies of thirty men—half of whom were skippers of lesser craft. I climbed halfway up the lee fore rigging, locked my legs through the ratlines and smoked. For forty minutes, she blazed a trail with her rail buried deep in foam. The harder I looked, the less I saw. Either that, or there were buoys everywhere: dozens of baby buoys bouncing around plunging like pistons between helmeted seas.

"That's it, isn't it, Hayden?" Cooney the sailmaker called from his place in the bows.

"I think so," I called back calmly, seeing nothing yet, stealing a glance at him, from under my binoculars. The *Bluenose* was far astern. The buoy lay dead ahead. If Cecil hadn't knocked her off a touch, we might have run it down. You lucky bastard, I muttered under my breath; and, swinging down to the deck, I sauntered aft, looking the world in the eye, vindicated, my belly afire with pride.

Rounding the mark, we flew downwind like a gull, bound for the finish line. The Coast Guard boat, with its cargo of seasick race committeemen, had quit and run for the cover of Boston. We clocked ourselves across the line. But fishermen are casual about some things. Nobody knew for certain whether we should leave the marker to port or starboard; so we finished twice for good measure, then jogged along slowly, the gang all on their feet, tired—but not too tired to line the rail and give three cheers when the big Queen of the North Atlantic came booming down on the line.

A late October day and the racing is finished, forever. Five thousand people are gathered under the Gloucester sun, with Legion and high-school bands, with the governor himself on hand, along with half a dozen subgovernors, surplus mayors and councilmen. Natives mingle with tourists in for the day, newsmen audit the scene with cameras and pencils and cabled microphones. This is an occasion: it marks the formal dedication of the big, new red-brick fish pier, financed in part by the PWA—with greetings from FDR.

Moored to the dock in the place of honor lie the two great racing schooners, victor and vanquished: *Bluenose* and *Thebaud.* The former had retained her title as champion of the North Atlantic, taking the last two races by a wide margin in what Gloucester called with contempt "New York Yacht Club weather." Both ships are dressed in flags this hot and windless day, and the traffic on Main Street is snarled. Tomorrow

*Racing home to port—*Bluenose *and* Gertrude L. Thebaud *head for Gloucester, Massachusetts in one of the last great races between these famous fishing schooners.*

it will all be over and the saloons will blossom with tables and chairs and benches.

A politician speaks. Hear him now, a comical cutout figure, full of brass, tempered in booze, bursting with plans for the future—his future: "And so, friends, we are met this glorious fall day, not just to dedicate this marvel of brick and mortar, but to pay our respects to those men, living and dead, who for more than three hundred years have gone down to the terrible sea in frail barks to reap from it a harvest of fish. Now, friends, and fellow citizens of this great commonwealth, and our neighbors from across the gulf, it is altogether fitting that—"

From the fish hold of the *Bluenose* comes the sound of a trumpet muted by three-inch pine. A journalist stalks through the mob. His shirt is drenched and he harbors a terrible thirst as he swings to the deck of the *Bluenose*. Fishermen guard each hatch, for the party below is by invitation only—given by the crews of the schooners in their own honor, and maybe that of the press. No one else is welcome.

He shows his card: Tom Horgan, Associated Press. They give him a nod and down the ladder he goes to the cavernous hold. Here ninety men are assembled out of the sun, away from the politicians and tourists, the kids and the wives. They're assembled this day to bury some hatchets and kill a few kegs of rum. Up and down this cave, long bundles of sail are spread, with flags nailed to the inner hull. Hymie Rodenhauser, one of the *Bluenose*'s mastheadsmen, straddling a keg in a cradle, is blasting loose with his trumpet. A bedlam of laughter and singing and wild gesticulations seen through a pall of smoke.

Horgan is handed a cup. He raises his fist. "To the *Bluenose!* I say we drink to this ship!" A hand is slammed on his back. "I say we pretty damn well better drink to this ship, Tom, or else get our ass knocked off." The man who says this is pleasantly drunk. His head is large, with a domed brow and bright eyes, a big nose that leads to an upturned mouth. His hands are those of an artist. His name is Lawrence Patrick Joseph O'Toole ("Of the South Boston O'Tooles," he says). Along this coast he is a legend; if you want him any time, look down on T Wharf, where he

hangs out, living with Horgan sometimes, or with any one of a thousand friends. People like to have him around because he makes them happy. He doesn't drive a car and he is always broke, and the worse things are, the more he laughs, painting away at his pictures of people and ships, or carving a figurehead.

Tom Horgan drains his cup. "Larry, you miserable bastard, why aren't you up on the dock making a speech or something?" O'Toole looks around and places a finger to his lips. "Sh-h-h," he whispers, "to the health of the poor old *Thebaud.*" Their cups meet. A man comes by with a pail full of rum. It slops when he ladles it out. O'Toole scoops deep with his cup.

Now they edge their way to a corner where a friend sits mute on a blown-out stays'l. "All right," says Tom, "I shall now propose a toast: To the best damn man to sail out of Gloucester in many a fucked-up year."

"Hear! Hear!" says O'Toole. "That's right."

The friend seems a little embarrassed. "Oh no," he smiles with a deprecatory nod, "don't say that."

"Whaddaya mean, 'Oh no'? You know who said that? Ben Pine said that. Don't be so goddamned modest."

"Then, I drink to Ben," says the friend, killing what's left in his cup.

A figure bursts into the hold, blowing the cook's tin whistle. "All right you bassards, up, up, everybo'y up on the goddamn deck! Hear me? The governor's gonna make us his honorin' speech, an' the mayor wants every friggin' one o' you on th' deck . . . An' leave the booze down here . . . An' no more friggin' noise! Hear?"

No one moves. "Drink up!" roars O'Toole. You can hear the Legion band playing the National Anthem. All rise. When the anthem expires, they sit—among them, three friends: Horgan, O'Toole and Hayden.

Requiem. Midnight. The dock is deserted, the flags make an arch in the rigging, and the night around is cool, calm and clear. Aloft on the *Thebaud*'s mainmast, a man lies flat in the crosstrees, staring up at the stars. His legs are crossed at the ankles, one fist is full of a halyard. Up past the head of the pier, the streetlights blink when crossed by nodding branches.

(We approach this man . . . gently . . . intent on asking some questions . . . on probing his mind just a little.)

"Hey. [*softly*] Hey, you on a mainmast-head—"

"Yes?"

"You're sober, we trust."

"I'm sober enough."

"Where, if you don't mind the asking, where will you go from here, now that the racing is ended?"

"Oh hell," he sighs heavily, "I don't have the least idea." His eyes keep staring up.

"They say that, during the course of the races, you really distinguished yourself."

"Do they?"

"Yes. [*A rustling of paper is heard*] Yes, they do. We quote from the *Boston Post,* dated October 24, 1938: The mettle of the *Thebaud*'s crew was tested when a block on the end of the main gaff began tearing out under the pressure of wind-tautened wet canvas. Sterling W. Hayden, the youngest and tallest of the Gloucesterman's crew, went inching out along the spar to secure the block along with Jack Hackett. The two men struggled there on this perilous perch, clinging against the blast of the gale, and—"

A hand is raised in the darkness. "Stop. That's enough."

"But there's more."

"I know; I read it all right, don't worry about that; made me feel good, I admit."

"Well, of course. [*Now a further rustling is heard*] And how about this? Again from the *Post* —under a big headline at the top of the second page, next to a picture of a face, close-up and grinning, showing some wind-tossed hair. THE-BAUD SAILOR LIKE MOVIE IDOL. Gloucester Youth, 22, Born Sea Rover . . . Fine Masculine Specimen . . . Neat seamanship may decide the victor of the fishermen's races, but when it comes to masculine pulchritude, Sterling W. Hayden, tall, blond, and lithe, wins by 100 fathoms over fellow members of both crews. He stands straight as a ramrod and is six feet five inches tall . . . More than a few of the scores of women who viewed the vessels yesterday at the fish pier inquired as to his identity . . .' "

"They did, eh?"

That's what it says in the paper.

The figure sweeps to an upright position and strikes a match off a shackle. "Yeah, yeah. I read that one, too. They shouldn't print stuff like that." Oh? why not?

"Because it makes you feel embarrassed. Besides, it's not even true."

What do you mean?

"Never you mind what I mean."

On the Starboard Tack to Bermuda

by HERBERT L. STONE

Since 1906, when Frank Maier's Tamerlane *won the initial contest, the Bermuda Race has been a fixture among the world's major sailing competetors. The 1932 event had all the elements which make for excitement—a ship in flames and a record time.*

THE story of this year's Bermuda Race has many sides. First, there was the record-breaking drive of three days in a hard sou'wester and heavy seas, with all hands carrying on without a letup to smash their way to St. David's Head in faster time than it had ever been done before in a Bermuda Race. Then there was the unfortunate burning of one of the entries, the schooner *Adriana,* and the gallant rescue of all but one of her crew by the British cutter *Jolie Brise,* which Bobby Somerset, commodore of the Royal Ocean Racing Club, had sailed across for the race. Finally, there was the long anxious wait for the stragglers that found the going too heavy, or suffered minor casualties that delayed them long after the leaders had finished and brought them in with weary crews.

It was a hard race, chiefly because it was a fast race. Not that there was much to do in the way of sail handling. The boats, at least the leaders, sailed on one tack from Montauk all the way to St. David's Head. But to drive any little boat

625 sea miles in three days, with wind and sea forward of the beam, means wet work and slamming through heavy seas at an average of nearly eight and three-quarter knots for the entire distance. After the first two hours the speed of the leading yachts did not once fall below eight knots. Often it was over nine. Only those who have sailed ocean races realize how wet a little ship can get when driven at this speed into a rough sea. Decks were washed constantly, cockpits were filled frequently, while getting about on deck was always precarious. Skylights were battened down and the air below was foul, while many stomachs labored no less than the boats. Sights for navigation were difficult until the last day, and cooking on most of the racers was a lost art or of a very sketchy character. In other words, it was a race one was glad to have sailed in, but gladder still to finish.

Highland Light set a pace that will hardly be beaten by a boat of this size in this race. She sailed so fast that she arrived at the finish before the tug had established the line. The race committee had hardly camped out at St. David's Lighthouse, expecting at least a twenty-four-hour wait for the first boat, before the tall, slim sails of the Boston cutter lifted off Northeast Breaker. She beat up the last six miles to the finish like a cup racer off Newport, going like a train of cars, with everything set that would draw. Just under nine knots she had made from start to finish. The nearest approach to this mark was in the race of 1909 when the schooner *Amorita* covered the course from Sandy Hook to St. David's in seventy-eight hours nineteen minutes and fifteen seconds. Though the latter course is forty-five miles longer than the one from Montauk, *Amorita* was a much larger yacht, one hundred feet in length, and her average speed only eight and one-half knots against eight and three-quarters for the much smaller *Highland Light.*

Twenty-seven yachts started in the race, an exceptionally creditable showing for a year when economic conditions are as stringent as in this. Fourteen of these were in the larger Class A, and twelve in Class B. A last minute entry was the schooner *Adriana.* As she was too large to fit in any of the regular classes, she was allowed to start in a special class, racing against the best corrected time of the fleet.

The caliber of the fleet was exceedingly high, and interest was heightened by the entry of two British yachts from the Royal Ocean Racing Club, Bobby Somerset's *Jolie Brise,* which raced here in 1926 when she was owned by E. G. Martin, and the *Lexia,* a new boat last year, owned by Major T. P. Rose-Richards, and a contestant in the last Fastnet Race. Both had crossed the Atlantic by way of the West Indies to take part in the Bermuda Race. Then there were two Bermuda boats at the starting line, our old friend the *Dainty,* with a new jib-headed ketch rig and sailed by Alfred Darrell, and the ketch *Zena* sailed by Wilfred Darrell. In the fleet, also were six new yachts, sailing their first race and of which very little was known as to their speed capabilities. These were the schooner *Barlovento,* owned by P. S. duPont 3rd; the schooner *Brilliant,* Walter Barnum, owner; and the *Mandoo,* built for D. S. Berger, all in Class A. In the smaller class the newcomers were the schooner *Sonny,* Albert D. Phelps, owner; the yawl *Ayesha,* built for John R. Hogan; and the new Wells cutter, *Cyclone,* just down from Nova Scotia, where she was built.

All in all, it was a brave fleet that shoved off that gray afternoon from Montauk Point, where the starting line had been moved from off New

London, shortening the course by some twenty miles. The change did not provoke much enthusiasm, for it meant getting under way in the early forenoon and, as the wind was fair, a wait of several hours off the Long Island headland for the starting gun at 3:10 P.M., with all hands impatient to be on their way.

The fresh westerly breeze of the forenoon had backed to sou'west by west as starting time approached and the sky clouded over with a hard, leaden aspect to windward, giving a hint of the rain and wind to follow.

By starting time the wind had eased off a bit, but the direction was fair so that the fleet could lay the course, southeast by south, with started sheets. Frank Paine had *Highland Light* on the line at the gun and he, along with *Grenadier* and *Barlovento,* probably got what honors there were at the start. The adverse tide played hob with the starting plans of many of the other skippers. But the start does not mean much in a race of this length. George Roosevelt's *Mistress* got away late, but with everything drawing hard, she started to overhaul the boats ahead of her in short order, gradually working up with the leaders. *Jolie Brise* got away with the leaders, breaking out a big, tanned jib topsail that pulled her along in good style. *Lexia* had the wrong combination of head sails and dropped back until a big genoa jib was substituted for the three first used, when she began to move properly.

Five minutes after the large class was away, Class B started. *Dorade,* last year's Transatlantic and Fastnet Race winner, stepped out in the lead, followed by Philip LeBoutillier's *Viking,* and Jay Well's new *Cyclone.* These three soon caught and passed the laggards of Class A. By nightfall, the fleet was strung out with *Highland Light* leading, closely pressed by *Barlovento, Grenadier, Teragram, Brilliant* and *Malabar X.* At this time the wind was moderate and the sea fairly smooth.

With the coming of darkness, the wind began to harden, with now and then a spatter of rain. Sometime before midnight a hard squall swept the fleet, bringing light sails down on deck in a hurry. On some boats, mainsails were lowered, only to be set again when the heft of the squall had passed, leaving the wind more to the westward. From this point on the boats really began to step out, reeling off the knots with the regularity of a steamer. Gradually the wind backed to sou'west and hardened, while the sea began to make up rapidly. It was blowing, perhaps, twenty miles an hour, and up to twenty-five or thirty in the puffs, but on the whole it was remarkably steady, except for occasional squalls. It was too much, with the wind forward of the beam, for light sails, and the fleet had all it could stagger under with lowers, while mainsails were reefed or foresails stowed on some of the boats. The smaller craft, of course, suffered more in this respect than the larger ones, although all had more breeze at times than they wanted.

It was about three o'clock on the morning of the first night out that *Adriana* burned. A tile heating stove in the cabin became overheated and set fire to a locker containing oilskins and hemp rigging. When discovered, it burst out fiercely, and when extinguishers failed to make any impression on it, the cabin was shut tight and distress flares were burned. The watch on *Jolie Brise,* some three miles ahead, saw a rocket (a Very pistol was used, I think) and Bobby Somerset immediately turned back to give aid, burning flares to show that the distress signals had been seen. On reaching the burning yacht, Somerset decided to go alongside and take off the crew, as to launch a boat would have been too slow and dangerous an undertaking. With rare seamanship, *Jolie Brise* was ranged alongside the *Adriana* to leeward, and as the two vessels came together with the heave of the sea, those on the now-blazing yacht jumped to the British boat, being helped aboard by the latter's crew. *Jolie Brise* was forereaching at about four knots as she went by.

Clarence Kozlay, at the wheel of *Adriana,* keeping her under control until his ten shipmates were rescued, delayed too long. When he jumped it was too late and he fell into the water between the two vessels. In the darkness he was swept away and drowned, the first fatality in these races since they were inaugurated.

Jolie Brise had her rail and stanchions smashed when the yachts came together. After cruising about for several hours in a vain attempt

to find Kozlay, she bore off and started back to Montauk, where the ten rescued men were landed early Monday morning. Somerset, of course, abandoned the race and went to Bristol, Rhode Island, for repairs to his damaged ship. It was a gallant piece of work executed with rare skill and courage.

It blew hard the second day out. Noon positions showed that the leaders had done from 175 to 180 miles in the 21 hours since the start. Thereafter the pace was to be even faster. The Gulf Stream brought its usual confused sea, but the squalls, except in rare instances, carried nothing vicious, though some of the boats shortened down for a few of them. By noon the second day, runs of from 212 to 222 nautical miles for the 24 hours were hung up by the larger yachts, the latter figure being turned in by the *Brilliant.* It was wonderful going, but wet and uncomfortable, particularly below. There was not much to do on deck but sit and steer as the boats drove to the southeast, with now and then a pull on the sheets as the wind backed a bit more. The third day brought hardly any slackening of the pace, and many runs of over 200 miles were recorded. While the wind eased off a trifle, the sea was smoother and steering was easier.

At this time *Highland Light* was some twenty-five miles ahead of the fleet, with Bermuda almost within sight at noon. She tore down on the Northeast Breaker buoy, marking the corner of the outlying reef, and hardened her sheets for the beat up to the finish. She crossed the line at 3:34:43 p.m. (Bermuda time), less than three days after the start. *Mistress,* well sailed all the way, was her closest competitor. She shaved the buoys around the reef to finish at 7:20:51 p.m. In sight, behind her, came *Barlovento* and *Malabar X,* followed by *Teragram* and *Brilliant,* with *Grenadier* and *Water Gipsy* treading on the latter's heels. It was a stirring finish with only one hour and ten minutes separating these six schooners. Three hours later *Lexia* finished, in a softening wind, and about 1:30 a.m., the little *Dorade,* first in her class by a margin of ten hours. She had, as always sailed a fine race.

Malabar X, sailed by her former owner, John

Alden, passed *Barlovento* on the short beat up from Kitchen Shoals buoy, getting the gun five minutes and twenty-two seconds before the du-Pont schooner. So far, she had saved her time on all those ahead of her. But there were others with larger handicaps still out. Would they beat her time? Neither *Teragram* nor *Brilliant* did it, but *Grenadier* was in sight, and dangerous. It was dark when the last named crossed the line, shortly before nine o'clock, with over an hour's allowance on *Malabar*. It was going to be close—a matter of minutes only—perhaps of seconds. With no communication with the shore, the crews of neither boat knew which had won, or if perhaps some other smaller yacht would slip in during the night to save her time. It was only when they dropped anchor in Hamilton Harbor the next morning that the actual standing was known. *Malabar X* had saved her time, but only by three minutes and seventeen seconds on *Grenadier*. It was one of the closest finishes in the long record of Bermuda races. *Water Gipsy,* hard driven all the way, took third place on corrected time and *Teragram* was fourth. *Highland Light,* in spite of her record-breaking run of seventy-one hours, thirty-five minutes, forty-three seconds,

Ketches and schooners head for the line at the start of the 1932 Bermuda Race.

had to be content with fifth place on corrected time.

In Class B, the little *Twilight,* with an allowance of seventeen hours thirty-three minutes, figured winner of second place, with the new yawl *Ayesha* third and the *Viking* fourth. So close were the boats in this class that only five minutes separated third and fifth place in the final standing. It was a great race—perhaps the fastest that will ever be sailed for years to come. (Ed. note—record broken in 1956.)

Of the unfortunate tragedy, with the loss of a well-known and much-liked yachtsman, most of the crews knew nothing until they finished, except those on *Mandoo* and *Sonny,* both of which stood by the burning yacht when they sighted her, after the crew had been taken off by *Jolie Brise.* But with the universal regret at the occurrence went admiration and praise for Somerset and his crew, who, by their prompt and efficient action, upheld the best traditions of the sea.

In view of the many conflicting reports regarding the adventures of the *Curlew,* the following explanation, given by the yawl's navigator and approved by her crew, is published as an authorized account of the facts—an account which her crew feel they owe to yachtsmen and to the government authorities for the concern and inconvenience inadvertently caused by them, and in an effort to clear up the unpleasant publicity which followed.

The crew of the *Curlew* entered the race admittedly green to ocean racing, but they had experienced three years of coastwise cruising in their boat and had full confidence in her, as well as a realization of the rigors of ocean racing, for which the boat was adequately equipped. Rumors of *Curlew*'s unfitness for the race reached the committee before the start of the race, and the committee's inspection was, therefore, doubly rigid. The boat was declared sound and properly equipped. That this inspection was not faulty was borne out by the fact that the boat withstood two weeks of hard weather without leaking, and her crew returned in good health, with ample food and water remaining. During the two weeks' interval, her experience might

have been that of any boat of forty-six feet overall length under the prevailing conditions.

For the first three days *Curlew* did well, reaching a latitude of one hundred miles north of Bermuda, but being driven to leeward and to the eastward by the fresh head wind and steep seas. All on board lent willing hands to reduce canvas in the squalls and the boat behaved well. On the fourth day, those who were in or near Bermuda will recall, it blew very hard from the southwest. *Curlew*'s crew estimated the velocity at forty mph. In these conditions, under reduced canvas, *Curlew* was driven farther to the eastward, as it was anticipated would be the lot of the smaller boats by those who had already reached Bermuda. Added to these circumstances was the eastward set of the currents around Bermuda, which navigators making landfalls on the third day estimated to be between one and two knots. The net result of adverse wind and current brought *Curlew,* at the end of the fourth day, to the latitude of Bermuda, but one hundred miles to the eastward.

Under reduced canvas, *Curlew* could not hope to beat against the strong southwesterly, high seas, and adverse current; so they tacked north and south, awaiting a shift of wind, meanwhile being carried to leeward about one mile per hour. For three days there was no let up in the wind, and *Curlew,* being carried to leeward about thirty miles per day, reached a position two hundred miles east of Bermuda. Overdue, and with only one week of their vacation remaining, the crew decided to ease sheets and sail for the steamer lanes and home. At the end of the eighth day *Curlew* turned in a good run of one hundred sixty miles, and then the wind dropped. Had they waited one more day they would have made Bermuda about the same time that *Spanish Rose* came in.

The calm was followed by some nasty weather over the Fourth of July weekend which made it impossible for them to get to the westward, but allowed them to make nothing toward the Atlantic steamer lanes where they hoped to be reported.

On the twelfth day out, they reached the steamer lane and sighted four tramp steamers in the distance. Flags were hoisted but were not distinguished. Distress signals were considered, but not being in distress and not wishing to create a needless sensation, they were not used. On the thirteenth day, a landfall was made on Davis South Shoal Buoy, south of Nantucket, and a course was laid for Newport. It was then that the Coast Guard sighted *Curlew* and hove alongside, advising that a search was being made for her and found that she needed no assistance.

BERMUDA RACE
Starting from Montauk Point, June 25, 1932

CLASS A

YACHT AND OWNER	ELAPSED TIME	CORRECTED TIME
Malabar X, R. I. Gale, John G. Alden	75:42:29	69:48:48
Grenadier, H. A. and S. Morss	76:47:28	69:52:04
Water Gipsy, William McMillan	76:57:52	70:57:04
Teragram, George W. Mixter	76:13:24	71:33:24
Highland Light, F. C. Paine	71:35:43	71:35:43
Brilliant, Walter Barnum	76:42:07	71:37:21
Mistress, G. E. Roosevelt	75:10:51	72:10:24
Barlovento, P. S. duPont III	75:47:51	72:15:18
Lexia, Major T. P. Rose-Richards	80:08:26	76:14:48
Vamarie, Vadim Makaroff	89:28:11	77:31:15
Discovery, J. H. Nichols	98:37:46	91:43:00
Mandoo, D. S. Berger	97:10:58	92:13:22
Sea Witch, E. S. Parsons	123:35:15	116:04:39
Jolie Brise, Robert Somerset	Withdrew	

CLASS B

YACHT AND OWNER	ELAPSED TIME	CORRECTED TIME
Dorade, R. Stephens, Jr.	81:33:33	72:11:10
Twilight, Edw. S. Bradford, Jr.	98:09:55	80:36:10
Ayesha, John R. Hogan	97:56:33	82:10:46
Sonny, Albert D. Phelps	95:08:40	82:11:55
Viking, P. LeBoutillier	91:24:26	82:15:52
Malabar V, Herbert Parsons	94:53:17	82:56:21
Duckling, Chas. H. Atwater	119:00:08	99:12:47
Zena, C. H. Masters	127:35:15	105:22:14
Amberjack II, Paul D. Rust, Jr.	Withdrew	
Cyclone, F. Jay Wells	Withdrew	
Dainty, Alfred A. Darrell	Withdrew	
Curlew, David Rosenstein	Withdrew	

The Southern Cross: Sydney to Hobart Race

by **EDWARD HEATH**

Edward Heath, the former prime minister of the United Kingdom, is also an avid sailor who didn't get into the sport until he was fifty. Since then he has numerous racing accomplishments to his credit, not the least of which was his record-setting run in the 1969 Sydney-Hobart Race.

AS we sailed up the river Derwent towards Hobart, I could feel the tension growing. The wind, which had been some twenty-five to thirty knots across the deck as we came out of Storm Bay at the entrance to the river, had been steadily dropping. Now it was light and looked like dropping away altogether. Were we to be denied our victory so close to the line? It is the moment every racing sailor fears.

The tension was understandable. It was only at one o'clock that afternoon, as we were crossing Storm Bay, that my navigator heard on the local Tasmanian radio that if we were across the line by six o'clock that evening, we would win the twenty-fifth Sydney-Hobart Race. Until then, we had not thought we had a chance. According to the news, very few boats were already in the dock. In fact, only three big boats, including Sir Max Aitken's British boat *Crusade,* which had fought a running battle with Alan Bond's Australian boat *Apollo* all the way down the coast,

were home. But three others were reported moving upriver, including the second boat for the British team, Arthur Slater's *Prospect of Whitby.* Now here we were, only a few hundred yards from the finishing line at the entrance to the dock, with the wind behind us, our light floater spinnaker up, and only the merest breeze.

I was at the helm myself, the other five members of the crew around me in the stern. I had told them that as we were in a winning position, we had better freshen ourselves up after more than four days at sea and make ourselves look as seamanlike as possible. The quickest and easiest way of doing this was to put on our white and blue oilies, which the weather and summer heat made neither necessary nor bearable. But at least we would sail—or drift—into Hobart looking respectable.

As we moved slowly ahead, I took a moment to glance to each side of us. The docks were crowded with people peering towards us. Behind them were rows and rows of cars stretching back up the hillsides. The sun shone on the clean, white buildings. I could see what was presumably the committee boat waiting at what must be the finishing line itself. Even at that distance, I could sense the excitement of the crowds.

The wind became lighter still and I realized that the boat was being gently headed towards the riverbank to the south. All the time, I was trying to counter this, easing her along so that we would still be able to hit the finishing line. I could feel the crew becoming more and more apprehensive, and when we were some 150 yards away from the committee boat, I realized that we would not be able to reach it without jibing. Reluctantly, I gave the order, "Prepare to jibe!" So strung up were the crew, that the two helmsmen, who normally stood in the cockpit as the afterguard, leaped forward, to the astonishment of the foredeck hands, and ran to seize the spinnaker pole to jibe the boat. As one of the foredeck crew said afterwards: "They had never been up there before, and I don't suppose they will ever be up there again."

I could almost hear the crowd draw in its breath as they watched us jibe so close to the finishing line. None of us would claim afterwards that it was the best jibe that we had ever done, or that it resembled in any way our normal drill, but it served its purpose, which was all that mattered.

With the wind lightened still further, I gently moved the tiller over and we continued our progress towards the line. It seemed to take an interminable time, but as we inched forward, everthing in view became clearer and clearer. We could see the tops of the masts of the boats already in. We could begin to see individual faces among the crowd; then we were coming up to the committee boat. The excitement increased.

At last, we found ourselves crossing the finishing line. And as we did so, all bedlam broke loose. Every car within range was hooting its horn, the crowds cheered and the sirens went. Everything happened so quickly. The launch came alongside to tow us into the dock. We dropped the spinnaker. The tension on the boat suddenly collapsed. We found ourselves laughing with joy. I had a lump in my throat. In almost the smallest boat of the lot, we had won the Sydney-Hobart Race.

We tied up alongside the big boats already in. The British on *Crusade* burst into some familiar nautical songs appropriate to the occasion. The crowds surging along the dock seemed to enjoy their somewhat bawdy flavor. It is said that

in his excitement a member of another British crew promptly climbed the mast of his boat, exposing his bottom as he went. That we never saw, for on *Morning Cloud* we were busy trying to realize that our victory was real. I took a glance around the boat to find that Owen Parker was already quietly getting the spinnaker sheets and guys off the deck and stowing sails, quite oblivious to the welcome which was about to descend upon us.

First to come on board was a representative of the local Tasmanian brewery bringing a large case of canned beer. We were—and still are—a dry boat, so this went down well. Cans were popping all over the place. Then we were invaded by the television cameras and the press photographers, all wanting pictures of different groupings at the same moment. By this time it had become rather a scrum on board.

Having got through all that and thinking I would relax in the cockpit with the rest of the crew for a few moments, I found our third visitor had arrived. He was a tall, well-dressed young man who stood smartly in front of me and said: "Sir, the governor presents his compliments and is delighted you are able to stay with him at Government House. He has asked me to tell you that he is expecting you there for dinner tonight, quarter to eight for eight o'clock—black tie." And with that request, I knew that the British and all their traditions were still firmly ensconced in that faraway part of Australia. We really had come home!

After thanking him, I pulled myself together and said: "In that case, I must find my baggage." The Australians, with that helpful efficiency of which we had already had a great deal of experience, had collected all our baggage in Sydney and flown it, free of charge, down to Hobart. The governor's ADC had already discovered the shed on the dock where it had been stacked. He promptly led me along there only to find that of all the crews of the seventy-nine-strong fleet, mine was the only suitcase which had gone astray.

There was nothing for it but to go to Government House as I was. That night, I dined there with the governor, his family and friends, in whites with the dark blue *Morning Cloud* sailing sweater. It must be the first and probably the last time that a sailor home from the sea has dined there in such a garb.

Dinner over, I rejoined the crew in their celebrations, now in the Yacht Club in Hobart. All of them appeared to be giving television interviews with what seemed reckless impunity. They were celebrating not only a sailing victory, they were celebrating a successful gambling operation. For unknown to me, they had joined in the betting which had taken place on the race, and so confident were they of *Morning Cloud,* that they had put their money on our own boat. They were busy spending the profits.

Eventually, the parties broke up. It was a late night, or, rather, an early morning. But who could blame us? The Sydney-Hobart Race is one of the three great ocean-racing classics of the world—and, some would say, very often the toughest. After a long, fast spinnaker run, we had come through an Antarctic gale. The first race, in 1945, had been won by John Illingworth, who was British. We were the first British to win it since, and we had done so our first time out. Whatever happened in the future, this was something no one could ever take away from us or from *Morning Cloud.*

Boxing Day, December 26, 1969, was a glorious day, with the hot sun shining out of a bright blue sky. Sydney harbor looked magnificent, a gentle breeze just ruffling the water. Eleven o'clock on Boxing Day is the traditional time for the start of the Sydney-Hobart Race, but long before that, the mass of boats carrying spectators was beginning to muster all the way along the harbor from the starting line to the Heads, through which the competing boats had to pass out into the southern Pacific. On the balconies of the houses along the waterfront, looking over innumerable bays, people were grouping in parties to toast the boats as they went past. The sides of the hills were covered with people, as many as half a million some said, waiting with excitement for the long race to begin. It was a splendid, bustling, colorful scene, worthy of a great occasion.

After being driven down to *Morning Cloud,* I said good-bye to the driver, who had been looking after me for the previous ten days. As we gazed at the boats preparing for the race, I said to him: "How wonderful it all is. What confidence everyone seems to have here in Australia. Tell me, why is it?" To which this young man, who had a wife and family and who had been telling me he was in the process of buying a new home, replied, quite simply: "Because, sir, out here we know that tomorrow will always be better than today." What confidence! Six months later in June 1970, I led the Conservative Party into a general election campaign with a manifesto entitled "A Better Tomorrow." Little did my Australian driver know that he was to be the inspiration for that campaign.

I had always known that it would not be possible for me to sail on *Morning Cloud* for all four races of the Southern Cross in Australia because Parliament was sitting well into December. When I arrived in Sydney, the boats were on the last leg of the two-hundred-mile race. At the airport, I immediately got into a small private plane which had been lent to me and flew off to find the fleet. By this time, it was widely spread. But after flying low over a considerable area, we spotted *Morning Cloud* heading for home, but not very well placed. It had taken the crew longer to get acclimatized than they had expected. They had also found the seas off Sydney difficult to handle.

I was more fortunate than I expected. In the first short race, *Morning After,* one of the three British boats, had become entangled with a New Zealand boat at one of the marks. It was decided to sail the race again, even though it meant having two short races in rapid succession. I was there for both of these. Fairly quickly, we got used to the new conditions, no tides to worry about and a rather long heaving swell outside the harbor. In the second short race, we had an exciting finish. As we came up towards the finishing line, we gradually overtook a New South Wales one-tonner, *Boambillie,* much bigger than ourselves. With our floater spinnaker up on a close reach in a light breeze, we finally passed them only a short distance from the line. We were exuberant. As the Australians crossed the line, they stood together on deck and cheered *Morning Cloud.* True sportsmanship. This put us all in fine fettle for the Sydney-Hobart Race.

The next few days were spent preparing her for the big race. I wanted her ready in every detail by Christmas Eve, no matter how late we worked on her. The only exception was to be the fresh meat and vegetables. Sammy Sampson was commissioned to bring these on board shortly before we left our moorings. There was no room for an icebox down below and we knew that fresh food would not keep for very long in that heat.

By early evening on Christmas Eve, *Morning Cloud* was ready to race thirty-six hours later. We knew we could have an enjoyable Christmas Day. We spent it at the home of Tryg Halvorsen, overlooking Sydney harbor. Tryg, an Australian of Norwegian extraction, had himself won the Sydney-Hobart four times. Now he was going as navigator on *Apollo,* one of the big Australian boats. We ate our Christmas dinner with all the usual festivities. After spending the afternoon talking over the race, we had a cup of tea and went to take leave of our host. As I left, Tryg Halvorsen followed me to the door and said: "I have been watching you racing out here and I think you might well pull this off. But you will only do it if you go right out early on and stay right out. Good luck." And he was gone.

We looked in at the berths on the way back to our hotel just to make sure that *Morning Cloud* was untouched. The whole marina was an amazing bustle of activity. The crews of all the other boats appeared to be rushing around trying to get ready in time. Alan Bond's large new boat *Apollo* had only recently come into her berth. Seeing me on the pontoon, he beckoned me aboard and invited me to have a look round. I went below to find joiners and carpenters still busy putting in the basic furnishings. On deck, I commented on the size of the spinnaker poles and asked him how she went downwind. "I don't know," he said. "We have not tried them yet. If the wind stays we will have to take her down the sound in the morning and run up towards the starting line to find out." There seemed to be chaos everywhere, but at

the same time complete confidence that on the day it would be all right.

There was nothing more for us to do. We had a quiet dinner on Christmas evening, an early night and a sound sleep. After a good breakfast, we went down to the boat.

The race was started from a frigate by the Australian prime minister John Gorton. Although there was a record entry of seventy-nine boats, of which we were the smallest, there was plenty of room to maneuver on the starting line. What caused me some alarm looking ahead was to see some four thousand boats of the spectator fleet stretching right along the harbor, obviously ready to move in on us once we were under way. The starting line itself was most effectively policed; not a launch was allowed near it. Spectators were biding their time. The thought of tacking with seventy-eight other boats, surrounded by four thousand more of every size and kind filled with rumbustious Australians out for a jolly, made me wonder whether we would ever get out of the harbor without colliding with one of them or being hit by some enthusiast.

We made a good start, just a second to spare. We had long practiced this operation and we were proud of our drill. I was at the helm, Anthony Churchill, the navigator, was doing the timing and checking our position in relation to the line, Owen Parker was looking after the tactical situation as a whole. In a small boat, we were so near each other that it was possible to have very close coordination without anyone needing to raise his voice.

Once over the line, we were on the wind going down the harbor, tacking once or twice as we got near the Heads. The fleet of spectator boats turned out to be extraordinarily well disciplined. They were careful to keep out of our way, not to take our wind and not to come immediately across our bows. It only needed a quick indication that we were about to tack for them to get out of the way altogether. Going through the Heads, we could see tens of thousands of people massed on the hill slopes with a splendid view of the fleet as it departed.

Once through the Heads and in a true north-northeasterly wind, we got the big spinnaker up and went out to sea. Quite soon, we were away from the difficult slop at the entrance to the harbor and moving on a long ocean swell. The breeze strengthened to about twenty knots, the sun shone with an occasional white cloud in the sky and we were happily on our way.

We had given a lot of thought as to whether or not we should stay fairly close to the coast or go right out to sea. The direct line from Sydney to Hobart, the rhumb line as it is called, runs between ten and twenty miles off the coast. It is, of course, the shortest route. On the other hand, we thought that by keeping in we might well lose the wind at night. By going out, we should be taking a longer course, but we hoped we would also hold the wind better. More than that, we were in search of the "set," or current, to help us on our way down the coast.

Quite early on we had heard about this "set," but I was astonished when I reached Australia to find out how little precise information there seemed to be about it. I do not think our Australian friends and competitors were withholding the information from us; it was just that they could not really tell us from their own experience much about it. At first, we understood that it ran south, but there were some who said that in certain conditions it ran north. This depended on the strength of the prevailing wind and for how long it had been blowing. As we had had northeasterlies and northwesterlies for some time, it seemed to us there was a good chance it would be flowing south. Most people we talked to thought that it was to be found roughly along the hundred-fathom line. This posed a certain problem for us because our depth meter went no deeper than fifty fathoms. We had to judge where the hundred-fathom line was by dead reckoning.

We were told of two other ways by which we could recognize the set. The temperature of the water, which was normally sixty-nine degrees Fahrenheit at that time of the year, would be up to seventy-two degrees. For this purpose, many Australian boats carried a thermometer in some part of their hull which could easily be read. As we had nothing of this kind, we attached a thermometer to a line and dipped it overboard regu-

larly every half hour. Secondly, bluebottles—little blue jellyfish—could be seen floating in this warm water. If we succeeded in finding the set flowing south, we would be sailing with up to a two-knot current, which would improve our position enormously. So we sailed out to find the set.

Our search took us about sixty miles offshore. Our thermometer never rose much above seventy degrees and only occasionally did we see bluebottles, but once out there, we were convinced that we had a powerful current behind us. This was confirmed by our navigator when he compared the plots he had worked out from his daily reckoning with the results of the sights from his astronavigation. Indeed, we could never have stayed so far out from shore had we not had astronavigation to help us. I was fortunate in having three members of the crew, Anthony Churchill, Sammy Sampson and Jean Berger, all capable of using the sextant and making a good job of it. This is really vital for the Sydney-Hobart Race. There is only one radio station between Sydney and Hobart, that on the northeasterly point of Tasmania, and it is not particularly strong. It can be helpful as a check on either dead reckoning or astronavigation, but there is no other radio station with which it can be used as a direction-finding instrument to provide a fix, or position. Boats with no one on board capable of astronavigation would have to keep reasonably close to the coast to check their position.

Under the racing instructions, all boats had to report their position three times a day, essentially for safety reasons should the weather get really rough, as it frequently does in the Sydney-Hobart Race. In the first race twenty-five years previously, in which there were only nine competitors, eight boats who hove to in a gale were not heard of for a long period. The only skipper who battled on was John Illingworth, who emerged as British victor. Since then, the race has always gone to Australians, except for one occasion when the New Zealanders triumphed.

The radio-control vessel moved down the course in the middle of the fleet. Calling over the names of seventy-nine boats in order and recording their positions took quite a time on each occasion, but it enabled us to plot our competitors' places on the chart, to see how well they were doing and to judge the sort of conditions under which they were sailing. In this way, we watched the battle of the giants which was going on close inshore between *Crusade* and *Apollo*. On occasions, we suspected that information was being provided for tactical reasons so as to influence other boats. One position given by *Morning After* showed her to be further out to sea than we were in *Morning Cloud*. Was this, we wondered, a plot to get us still further away from the coast? We listened eagerly to the next reports only to hear with some relief that *Morning After* was safely back near the coast again. Useful and interesting information was also often passed with the navigation report. On the second day out, one boat described seeing a small group of killer whales. Later on, we were to see another group ourselves. We had heard many stories of the damage they can do to small boats, either intentionally by attacking, or by coming up under their keel and overturning them. We watched them keenly and with some apprehension, but after half an hour or so they moved off in the other direction.

We could not help noticing that some of the larger boats were missing from the evening six o'clock reports. "Ah!" we said to ourselves "It's cocktail time on *Crusade*. Think of the fun they must be having." Reporting also had its humorous moments. On one occasion, after the navigator on *Prospect of Whitby* had given his position, the control boat commented: "Thank you *Prospect of Whitby*. That puts you plumb over Alice Springs. I hope you enjoy the rabbit shooting there." No doubt *Prospect*'s navigator wished he could have been spared this Australian wit.

In my view, this reporting system, extremely efficiently organized, should be introduced to other ocean races. It is, of course, a controversial matter. There is the overall expense of having a control boat moving all the time with the fleet. There is the individual expense of installing long-distance radio on each boat. However, if ocean racing is to be efficiently organized, this general cost ought to be met, and I do not be-

lieve that the cost of a radio as a proportion of the cost of an ocean-racing boat is such as to deter any skipper from installing one. The other argument is more concerned with seamanship and the tactics of sailing. "Why should we reveal our course and our tactics to our competitors?" asked many skippers. Indeed, there is much to be said for this point of view. Against it must be set the safety advantages and the fact that it makes the sport much more interesting both for those taking part and for those interested ashore. In Australia, the positions of boats are broadcast over the radio after each reporting session so that the public at large can follow the contest closely. This in itself musters support for the sport. This reporting system is much better organized on a compulsory rather than a voluntary basis. Voluntary reporting is a safety precaution for those who take part in it. There is a disadvantage, however. Some boats' positions are given away to others who do not reveal their own. In Britain, more thought needs to be given to this aspect of ocean racing.

Having got our spinnaker up, we sped along at between seven and eight knots. At times, *Morning Cloud* planed over the long waves, and to Owen Parker's excited cries of, "This is a big one. Come along ole gal!" she reached ten knots and then went off the clock. From time to time, after a long run, we jibed, keeping all the time the same distance out to sea.

We kept our big spinnaker up continuously for sixty-seven and a half hours, the longest run that any of us can ever have had. Then, towards breakfast time on the fourth day out, the wind gradually became lighter. We changed over to the floater spinnaker, but soon there was no breeze left to fill even that. It drooped woefully. We were becalmed. Now and again came a puff. The wind appeared to be moving round the compass. We tried a light headsail, but after a short time, this light, fluky breeze backed and we made another attempt with the floater. Again, after a while, the puff disappeared and all around us was calm. Yet none of us had the feeling we had often experienced in the English Channel and in the Irish Sea during the Fastnet Race the previous August that the calm had come to stay for hours.

We sensed that we were on the point of a drastic wind change. It worried us.

We had listened to the weather forecasts all the way down the coast. From Sydney onwards, they had said that a strong wind might come in from the south. Recently, our navigator had picked up the broadcasts from Tasmania. Those north of us were saying the wind would come in from the southwest. In Tasmania, they were forecasting a blow from the southeast. Which was it to be? If it were to come in from the southeast, it would suit us admirably. From our way-out position, we could tack in towards Tasmania on the wind, and with a bit of luck we should finish up not far north of the entrance to the Derwent River, on which Hobart stands. Meanwhile, other boats close inshore would be short-tacking right down the Tasmanian coast. If the wind were to come in from the southwest, the inshore boats would benefit. We would be faced with a long tack of twenty hours or more, which would put us somewhere near the northeast tip of Tasmania, whilst the inshore boats would have got down to the river estuary. That would be the price we would have to pay for the advantages of having gone so far offshore.

We waited, and gradually the wind filled in. It seemed an interminable wait, but in fact it could not have lasted more than an hour and a half. Then from the Antarctic across the Tasman Sea came the gale.

Until then, it had been one of the most enjoyable experiences of sailing we had ever had. The weather had been perfect. When not on watch, we could lie, sunbathing, on the deck, but in the evenings it was pleasantly cool. With little heel on the boat while running, work in the galley was easy. We had got through our fresh food during the first two days and then moved on to tinned and packaged foodstuffs. Our small cabin was only some ten feet long and, at its widest point, nine feet across. But no one felt cramped and there were no wet clothes around the place to worry about.

Now, suddenly, everything changed.

The wind blew from the southeast. Thank heaven for that. If it held from that direction and we could keep the boat going through the heavy sea, we ought to make reasonable time to the Tasmanian coast.

As the wind got up, we changed our headsails and began to reef the main—the dial was registering thirty-five to forty knots, gusting to more than fifty. By this time, we were down to our Number 5 headsail, with mainsail reefed to its numbers, battling our way through a heavy sea. On deck, the crew on watch were getting soaked from the waves breaking over the boat and with the spray. The clouds got lower, visibility became poor and, indeed, was reduced almost to zero as it began to rain or, rather, hail. Hailstones flew at our faces like bullets. And the cold—never before had I known such bitter cold. We were now nearly five hundred miles further south than Sydney. The light disappeared much earlier and soon it was dark.

Down below, life was far from easy. Cooking in our small galley was almost impossible as we heeled so far to starboard—not that anyone much wanted to eat. Everyone's clothes were soaked. There was little room to get them out of the way. Then, to our alarm, we found water steadily mounting in the bilges until it was well over the cabin floor. Where was it coming from? We could find no obvious answer to the question. The hull still appeared sound enough. Had the keel bolts worked loose, letting in the water? And, if so, how secure was our keel? Or was the water seeping through from some other point?

We worked the pump, but it seemed to be ineffective. Was the heavy heel of the boat keeping the water in the bilges away from the hose? On inspection, this seemed to be the case. There was only one answer. That was to bail and keep on bailing as long as the storm lasted. I set to with one of the crew off watch, and we kept at it continuously. That presented its own problems. To get rid of the buckets of water, we had to open the hatch over the companionway. If we were unlucky enough to do so as a wave washed over the boat, more water came below, splashing over the bunks, the galley and the chart table. Soon, everything below was as wet as on deck. Bailing kept down the water in the cabin. The storm got worse. Both boat and crew were taking a heavy pounding.

We were working on our usual system of changing watch every four hours. Two of the crew were on each watch, and the navigator and myself were always available and joined them from time to time. At one stage in the race, we did two hours ourselves so that each watch in turn could have a clear six hours' sleep. Now I decided to change the system again. The driving wind and bitter cold made conditions in the cockpit so bad that no helmsman could do a complete watch. His crew, huddled down beside him, was in a wretched position. I changed the helmsmen round so that they did one hour on and three hours off. Even an hour in those conditions was almost unbearable. As an emergency system it worked, but it made other crew duties more difficult.

That night, after twelve hours of the storm, we came up to the Tasmanian coast at the Freycinet Peninsula. This was rather further north than I had hoped, but the crew thought we had done well. Then we had to beat down the coast until we could turn up the estuary into Storm Bay, a distance of some sixty miles.

The storm continued, but as dawn came it seemed slowly to be blowing itself out. We were able to get a larger headsail up. As the sea went down, we appeared to take less water on board and the intervals between bailing out *Morning Cloud* grew longer.

We could see the coast clearly. The landmark we were seeking is known colloquially as the Organ Pipes, a high rock formation dropping vertically down to the sea in hollow half-pipe-like formation. The wind comes over the top and siphons down with increasing speed. This was one of the things Tryg Halvorsen had warned us about on Christmas Day. "Either keep right in close alongside," he said, "or keep right out. If you do anything else, you will risk being knocked flat by the wind coming down the Pipes." There was no point in trying to get in under them. We decided to keep right out and, with the wind now from the south, we came into Storm Bay. It was then that we heard we stood a chance of winning. The rest of the story I have already told.

When we crossed the finish line, we had been at sea for a few minutes over four-and-a-

quarter days. When this time had been corrected to allow for our handicap rating, it amounted to three days, four hours, twenty-five minutes and fifty-seven seconds. This put us fifty-one minutes, twenty-two seconds ahead of the next boat, Arthur Slater's *Prospect of Whitby.* Allowing that we probably sailed some seven hundred miles from Sydney to Hobart, this gave us just under four-and-a-half seconds a mile in hand over the whole race. Not much! A bad tack, a poor bit of drill or a wrong decision in the navigation could easily have cost us this.

The hospitality in Tasmania was tremendous. Our hosts almost managed to prevent us from getting on with the task of getting the boat ready to ship her back to England. When we did dismantle her, we found that the keel bolts had indeed worked slightly loose. We could just see daylight between the keel and the hull, but this did not explain the amount of water we had taken on board. It was only when we examined her again back home that we found the water had been coming in through the gutter round the top of the cockpit lockers. A slight modification and all was well. We also found that the clevis pin, a pin which passes through the forestay to hold it on the bow of the boat, was bent like a crooked finger and had just held. Had it given way, the forestay would have gone, and with it the mast.

The presentation of the trophies by the governor in a packed City Hall was a great occasion. For *Morning Cloud,* we received nine trophies, including a replica of the Sydney-Hobart trophy. All of this, Qantas kindly flew home for us.

In a short speech, Max Aitken said it was the most efficiently organized race in which he had ever taken part. With that we all agreed. In my few words, I emphasized the favorable impact such a contest could have on Anglo-Australian relationships in particular, and on commonwealth friendship in general. I felt that perhaps the Australians no longer regarded us as being quite such a decadent people after all. Alas, our success was not sufficient for the British to win the Southern Cross Cup as a team. If *Morning Cloud* had been in the team instead of the reserve boat, the cup would have been ours.

After these celebrations, I flew off to Canberra to spend a day with John Gorton, the Australian prime minister, and his wife and family at their home. Then I flew on to Indonesia.

In Djakarta, I had my first talks with the new president and the foreign minister. There was no doubt about the friendliness of the government towards the British, the desire to see our firms reestablished in Indonesia and the wish to put an end to the differences between Indonesia, Malaysia and Singapore. A year earlier, I had spoken to the Press Club in Canberra, outlining the Conservative plans for a resumption of our role in the Far East should we be returned to power. The president had no objection to this from the Indonesian point of view; indeed, he welcomed it as a contribution to the stability of the area.

For me, this visit provided a new personal interest. It was in Djakarta that I started to collect Chinese porcelain and ceramics, in particular celadon. Both the then ambassador and the British Council representative were well-informed enthusiasts about this subject. In January, 1970, Indonesia was only just beginning to be recognized as a repository of much Chinese craftsmanship, the result of being an export market for southern China for several hundred years. Two or three local collectors had been exploring some of the multitude of islands making up that country. There they found treasures still in everyday household use. Very often, these were bought on a communal basis, the total payment being a small boat or some other item useful to the village community. Apart from a number of small celadon cups and jars, I was able to buy for just a few pounds a beautiful Swatow bowl (made about 1590), some nineteen inches across, which we carefully protected and brought home. A few months later, when I became prime minister, it rested on the table in the hall of my flat at 10 Downing Street. Every time I looked at it, there seemed to me to be something particularly romantic about its story. Fashioned by some loving potter in southern China more than 350 years ago, it had then followed the pattern of trade to the Indonesian islands. There it was used by some family day in and day out until discovered by a dealer searching for treasures and brought

back to the capital of the newly established independent country. From there, it traveled halfway across the world by the most modern form of transport, finally to rest on the table of the prime minister of Britain. How could any potter have foreseen such a future for his bowl? Alas, in the move from 10 Downing Street to my home four years later, it was smashed. I was heartbroken. And so ended the story of that precious Ming bowl.

In Singapore, the prime minister, Lee Kuang Yew, was as stimulating as ever and anxious for me to see the tremendous developments which had taken place on the island since my last visit four years earlier. Massive new housing projects had been completed, large modern hotels had sprung up, and the vast industrial estate was well under way. It was all exciting, but it did not prevent me from driving out to my favorite haunt, the orchid farm to the north of the island. There you can not only see almost any variety of orchid growing in the open, you can also have them sent to your friends all over the world. You choose your blooms and in less than thirty-six hours they can be adorning a room in London.

My first visit to Hong Kong followed. If Singapore was exciting, Hong Kong was breathtaking. Never having given it much thought before, but having in my mind a picture of a somewhat barren rock rather like Gibraltar, with slums smothering new territory on the mainland, I was taken aback by the beauty of the setting, the splendor of the skyline, the extent of the modern development and the efficiency of the organization. Above all, I was impressed by the way in which more than 2.5 million refugees had been absorbed into the life of such a tiny entity, housed mostly in high flats provided for them, and their other needs met. A visit to some of the few remaining slums on the side of a hill near the sea, with water trickling down through them, showed what still remained to be done. This cannot diminish the remarkable success which the island has already had. In the course of three days, I was able to meet not only the various organizations concerned with the politics and administration of the island, but also a large number of individuals, many of whom have remained my friends. Nor must I forget the Hong Kong Yacht Club, which gave me a most friendly welcome and always remained in touch with me. I was glad that in 1975 Hong Kong was able to enter a team in the Admiral's Cup races at Cowes.

In Hobart many had pressed me—apparently not attributing undue weight to my political responsibilities—to sail on *Morning Cloud* in the Hobart-Auckland Race, which was starting early in January. "Then," they said, invitingly, "you can take the boat to Hong Kong and race from Hong Kong to Manila in March." This I was also urged to do in the Hong Kong Yacht Club. After Manila, it was suggested we could sail across the Pacific through the Panama Canal and take part in the Transatlantic Race, arriving in England just in time for Cowes Week. To all these sailors, this seemed a rather obvious and enjoyable season's racing. Work—and perhaps politics—is indeed the curse of the sailing classes!

And so we flew home just in time for the Boat Show. It was there, with the crew in the cockpit of the sister ship of *Morning Cloud,* that we did one of the best, and certainly one of the most enjoyable, television broadcasts in which I have ever taken part—Sports Night with Coleman. It must have been the first time that ocean racing had ever been put in such a high spot on television. Perhaps we were beginning to make an impact?

The Southern Ocean Racing Conference

by MICHAEL LEVITT

The Southern Ocean Racing Conference is a six-race series that is sailed during the winter in Florida and Bahamian waters. It has become the top competition for offshore racing yachts in the United States. Here Michael Levitt, managing editor of Nautical Quarterly, *gives an in-depth look at the 1978 "Southern Circuit"—the evolution, of the races and the grand prix boats, as well as a look at some of the sailors that play this high-powered sport.*

AS long as there's a winter, there will be an SORC. The Southern Ocean Racing Conference has become the choicest contest in American ocean racing because of when and where it is sailed: in February, the butt end of the year in most of the United States; and in Florida, where the weather is decidedly civilized in the shortest month and where sailors can navigate around, through and occasionally under the challenging river that runs in the Atlantic Ocean, the Gulf Stream. It is this river of warm water, which travels north at speeds from zero to four knots while varying its eddies and meanders by the minute, that makes the six-race SORC series so special.

In northern climes, men do strange things in February. Melville's Ishmael was so far gone he was affected in November, but what he said ex-presses the feeling well: "Whenever it is a damp, drizzly November in my soul; whenever I find myself involuntarily pausing before coffin ware-houses, and bringing up the rear of every funeral I meet; and especially whenever my hypos get such an upper hand of me that it requires a strong moral principle to prevent me from deliberately stepping into the street, and methodically knocking people's hats off—then, I account it high time to get to sea as soon as I can. This is my substitute for pistol and ball. . . . I quietly take to the ship."

Men have been "taking to the ship" for decades in winter in Florida. In the teens and twenties, there were a few races for the very rich to liven up the holiday lassitude aboard the family yacht in company with other like-minded and like-moneyed men. Some of these contests became established features—the Lipton Cup, which dates back to 1929; the St. Petersburg-Havana Race, which started in '30; and the Miami-Nassau Race, which was first sailed in '34. That first Nassau race was enough of a workout that it's amazing there was ever a second one: nine of twelve starters failed to finish a Gulf Stream thrash in menacing easterlies. The winning yacht, *Vamarie*, completed the 184-mile ordeal in fifty-two hours, under the command of Vadim Makaroff.

174

In those years, each race was a separate entity. There was no agreement among the sponsoring yacht clubs on how a race should be run or even what handicapping rule should be used. For example, up to 1940, when most of the nation and the other Florida yacht clubs were racing under the CCA rule, the St. Petersburg Yacht Club kept to its own formula, which ignored hull shape altogether.

The St. Pete rule—hardly one of the great achievements in ocean-racing mathematics—measured only the working sail area, took the square root of this number, then cranked in some prop and rig corrections. What came out was a rating in feet; and the scratch boat, presumably the one with the most sail area, gave each competitor twenty minutes for each foot of rating. One respected reporter of the scene decried such a parochial rule for its "complete arbitrariness," which he attributed to the "general cockeyedness" of the St. Petersburg Yacht Club.

Although the rest of the world was at war in 1940, yacht racing continued in the United States, which was still officially neutral. This was the year that *Good News*—a radical design by Olin J. Stephens II with a J-boat-style duralumin mast, a thing which had never been seen before on an ocean racer, and with a tab on the rudder's trailing edge, which Stephens had previously designed into *Vim*—made her auspicious debut. *Good News,* a keel/centerboarder called, predictably, a "mechanical marvel," won the prestigious St. Petersburg-Havana race in a quick contest that saw *Tioga* (better known later as *Ticonderoga*) set the course record in sailing the 284 miles in nineteen hours and thirty-six minutes. Robert Johnson had commissioned *Good News* to replace *Stormy Weather,* the boat that brought him the previous three Miami-Nassau victories. The new owner of *Stormy Weather,* William H. Labrot, proved that *Stormy* still knew the way to Nassau in 1940; earlier that winter she did it again, beating the fleet and Johnson's new mechanical marvel in the process. Superboats, then as now, are sometimes brought up short by their slightly older sisters.

At the finish of 1940's Havana Race, there was more talk than usual about uniting the autocratic yacht clubs and their various races so that a circuit winner could be named. Writing in *Yachting,* Alfred Loomis, a keen observer, commented: "There are those who contend that southern waters are the finest there are for ocean racing and who in the present trend toward winter vacations foresee a day when the St. Petersburg-Havana and Miami-Nassau race will be but a nucleus for a long winter's schedule. The arrival of that day will be speeded, say they, if a uniform rule, such as the Cruising Club's, is adopted in the South—for then a man will know the probabilities in advance and can race around the coast with the hope of evening up old scores."

It was an obviously good idea, but it took the energies of two men, Lew McMasters of St. Petersburg and Arthur Bosworth of Miami, who inaugurated the Nassau Race in '34, to unite the independent Florida yachting establishment. After a few phone calls and letters, a rating system was agreed upon—CCA—and a point system and schedule were finalized. The dates of the races were compressed so that the entire series could be sailed without taking an impossibly long winter vacation.

Actually, Bosworth's and McMasters's interest in all this was not merely the greater glory of the sport. The two men, involved in mortgage investment and real estate, respectively, figured that they could buck up a bearish real estate market—gone flat during the Great Depression and kicked while it was down by the Recession of '37 —by selling property to yachtsmen. Bosworth and McMasters were bullish on sailors.

Even chambers of commerce chipped in money for the SORC over the years, for the greater glory of the sport and for other reasons, and saw their faith rewarded. Some other places and yacht clubs, meanwhile, welcomed the SORC fleet—with its rumpled rich, merely rumpled female racer chasers and strong, young winch grinders with large appetites for everything—with the same cheer and good fellowship that might meet a weekend outing of the Hell's Angels. If you've ever wondered why the fleet doesn't race to Venice, Florida, or Lucaya in the Bahamas any more, there are reasons.

Dennis Conner's Stinger, *the one-tonner that won the 1975 Southern Ocean Racing Conference.*

The first SORC was sailed in 1941 and resulted in a tie between the yachts *Stormy Weather* and *Gulfstream,* owned by Dudley Sharp. There was not another SORC for six years. The circuit resumed in 1947. It has sailed every winter since, in one form or another, attracting an international array of sailors and characters to its challenges and entertainments.

In that first Nassau Race after the war, the weather, which had been merely bad, turned rotten. On Thursday night, February 13, 1947, the thirty-six-foot cutter *Windy,* one of three Cuban yachts making that country's debut in this particular race, was in New Providence Harbor, twenty-five miles from Nassau. With her helmsman lashed to the wheel, a sea broke aboard, parting the mainsheet and carrying off the doghouse, along with two of the crewmen inside. It took some terribly long moments for the remaining crew to rerig the mainsheet. Finally, they turned back and recovered one crew member, but the other man, a professional hand, was never found.

For the Cubans, the 1947 SORC began in tragedy but ended in jubilation as the Cuban yacht *Ciclon,* sailed by Mario Muñoz Bustamente, won the race home. *Ciclon*'s strong finish in the Havana Race and consistent performance throughout the series brought her the (Florida) Governor's Cup, emblematic of overall SORC honors. In other SORC years, with nothing quite so personal to celebrate, Señor Bustamente was the perfect host. But in that year of his own boat's triumph, Bustamente outdid himself. So much so that the next race to Key West was canceled as a result of what was described as the "hospitality" of the Cubans.

Among Cuban contributions to 1950s Florida ocean racing was the infamous welcome-to-our island party, a full-tilt shore leave that will be part of the folklore of yachting forever. Old-timers, those who survived such carousing, still get a youthful, full-of-themselves grin when recounting Havana anecdotes and perhaps reflecting close mouthed on things they'll never tell anyone.

The years of nautical decadence came to an end in 1960 when one F. Castro decided that imperialists aboard yachts were no longer welcome in Havana. Because of the Cuban revolution, there was no race in 1958. But it was tried again the next year, sailing to a much-subdued and socialistically righteous Havana. The race was finally abandoned because it was "not a social success," as one reporter put it. The Havana Race was replaced by the St. Petersburg-Fort Lauderdale Race, which is the best ocean race in America and probably one of the top five fleet tests in the world. In the détente of recent years, there has been talk of reviving the Havana Race, a move which, if successful, would be the first known example of yachting diplomacy.

Innovation is the essence of the SORC. Sailmakers, equipment manufacturers, yacht designers—the established, soon-to-be-established, and never-to-be-heard-from-again—are all aboard for the circuit's business and ego possibilities. And the yachting press from around the world eats it all up in ravenous bites. The SORC is one of the most analyzed and photographed sailing events in the world, along with the America's Cup and perhaps the Admiral's Cup. In the beginning, this was so because the magazines had little else to write about at a relatively inactive time of the year. Another reason was that, like sailors, yachting reporters enjoy a February holiday in Florida too, so they hyped the event appropriately to

justify their expense accounts and to insure themselves a place in the sun the following winter. But after a time, the SORC, which was first a real estate promotion, then a media event, became a true wintertime world series for the elite of ocean racing.

The Southern Circuit launched the career of Charlie Morgan. In a St. Petersburg gin mill, the brash young Morgan was sounding off to Jack Powell and company that he could design a boat faster than the several SORC world beaters that were then under discussion. Powell, tired of such arrogance from a man who didn't have a single design to his name, dared Morgan to do just that. The result was the ultralight (for its day), homely (for any day) speedster *Paper Tiger*. This forty-footer was one of the first-ever one-off fiberglass yachts, a light hull reinforced with a welded-steel spine that made it extremely strong for its weight. (It is interesting to note that the '77 circuit's wonderboat—*Imp*—was built around an aluminum birdcage structure, similar to that of *Paper Tiger,* which was hailed in 1961 as "revolutionary.")

Morgan launched an impressive business and racing career with *Paper Tiger's* 1961 SORC victory. He went on to design the twelve-meter *Heritage,* and also to build her sails and take her helm in a southern assault on the 1970 America's Cup. Along the way, he created Morgan Yachts and, recently, Heritage Yachts, a company which offered a lot of boat for very little bucks ($30,000 for a one-tonner). Apparently, it was too little bucks for, most recently, Morgan filed a Chapter XI in behalf of Heritage.

In 1973, the candidate for SORC notoriety, if not fame and fortune, was the diminutive Dr. Jerry Milgram, a professor of ocean engineering at MIT. Milgram, dressed in high-topped black sneakers—what are called "felony shoes" in the ghetto—baggy pants and a rumpled shirt, looked like the poor boy at the yacht-club party.

Milgram's SORC contender was in his own image—homely. It was the cat-rigged ketch *Cascade,* which caused the rule makers to drag out their calculators and play them like pinball machines. *Cascade* had two masts with two large mainsails and no headsails, thus, no rated sails in front of the mast. She did have some devious spinnakers, which were not flown from a pole and thus were not rated like spinnakers, and some strange sails that flew in front of the masts but were not genoas. Milgram wasn't sure what they were either, and he would command his crew: "Trim the reacher or whatever the hell you call that thing!" *Cascade* was rated for 325 square feet of sail, while the one-tonners she sailed against boat for boat averaged about 550 square feet.

Cascade first made her presence felt the summer before the '73 SORC in the New York Yacht Club Cruise, earning two firsts and three seconds before breaking a mast. Then she rated 22.8. Before the SORC, the rule makers penalized her 10 percent to 24.7. Milgram countered by cutting four feet from each mast, dropping the rating lower than the original to 22.7.

Milgram's beast began to roar in the Lauderdale Race with second place overall, but he was penalized for a rule infraction. Then she won the overall prize in the fastest and last Lucaya Race. Next was another overall win in the Lipton Cup. For good measure, *Cascade* appropriated the overall honors in the Nassau Race. Only an eightieth placing in the Nassau Cup Race and the penalty from the Lauderdale Race kept the maverick cat from dominating the whole shebang. The next time the Technical Committee met, oddly enough, the day of the cat had ended.

Although it often seems that way, the Southern Circuit is not just for trade people. The reputation of many a Corinthian has been made and lost in this arena. The 1966 circuit brought the world that Good Ol' Southern Boy with the Big Ol' Southern Mouth, Ted Turner, who sailed a Cal 40, *Vamp X,* to overall honors. Turner, now an Atlanta TV tycoon and owner of that town's two terrible professional teams, the baseball Braves and the basketball Hawks, almost won it again in 1969 with his converted twelve-meter, *American Eagle,* until she was dismasted in the Nassau Race following an unscheduled meeting with the bottom. His most recent accomplishment, of course, was winning the 1977 America's Cup with *Courageous.*

Turner was twenty-seven when he won the SORC, and he ushered in a new era in ocean racing. A successful dinghy sailor at college and then in FDs, he sailed his big machines just like dinghies. Sheets were never cleated; sails were called constantly; and crew weight was always where it should be and let sleep be damned. His favorite phrase in describing his success was that it was done with a "full-court press." The working press found him "breezy and confident" in 1966. Today they find him a full-blown gale.

He was not that way following his America's Cup summer with *Mariner.* After the summer of his discontent (1974), Turner commissioned a Frers yacht named *Tenacious,* which he brought to the 1975 SORC. He wanted a victory in the SORC badly. There were six races—"six bullets," as Turner put it endlessly. That year, he and his merry band of men, and an occasional woman, won their class without losing a race. The "mouth of the South" had returned.

The handsome Turner, father of five, looks like a movie star. He is the only yacht racer to expound upon his philosophy of life to the housewives of America on the Mike Douglas TV show. There is a definite showbiz quality about Turner and the yachts he sails, and an unusual number of beautiful people make up his entourage.

Among them is the able-bodied seaperson Frederique Dargon, who has been known to grind a winch or two on an assortment of Turner's yachts, and to grind the teeth of every able-bodied seaman who has had the pleasure of seeing her sunning on the foredecks of the Turner flotilla. Frederique is into brown skin and rarely into bathing suits. Frederique is French, and she speaks the King's English about as well as Charo of the talk shows, with whom she shares other attributes. When Hugh Hefner invented women, Frederique is what he had in mind. "An awesome package," is how Hood Sails' own Bill Rudkin once put it.

In the 1976 SORC, Turner was again sailing *Tenacious,* despite the fact that at the conclusion of the previous year's series he had greeted overall winner Dennis Conner with a bottle of Mount Gay and, on the spot, bought his one-tonner *Stinger* for $75,000. Turner then shipped *Stinger* to Australia to compete in level racing down under, keeping the red *Tenacious* as his circuit steed. On the last leg of the Ocean Triangle Race from Palm Beach to Miami, *Tenacious,* although in the lead, lost the breeze. Up came the smaller yacht *Rattler,* power reaching under spinnaker, bringing along the building breeze. *Tenacious* soon got the same wind, but not before *Rattler* stuck her bow a few feet from the big red yacht's stern and locked on. Like racing cars drafting, the bigger, faster *Tenacious* literally sucked *Rattler* along.

Aboard *Rattler* was part of the Hood factory team, Robbie Doyle and Phil Steggall, along with Graham Hall, sailing coach of the Naval Academy. The tiny Kiwi Steggall went to the bow to communicate the meanderings of *Tenacious,* then reeling like a drunk trying to escape a mugger. Steggall sounded a lifeguard's whistle on the bow so *Rattler*'s helmsman could keep in sync with the evasive weaving of *Tenacious.* One toot told *Rattler*'s helmsman to go up. Two, down.

Steggall's music was working, and working on Turner's nerves as well, so crew members from *Tenacious* removed the whistles from the life rings and started tooting back, which quickly confused the issue. Even so, the smaller *Rattler* hung on like a pilot fish to a shark.

After some five hours of this, drastic measures were called upon. The fair Frederique removed her top and, to heighten the effect, climbed the backstay hand over hand. *Rattler* and crew wobbled a bit but stayed fast, perhaps because now there was even more reason to maintain close formation. The floor show had begun.

"Listen, girl," came a shout from the cockpit of *Tenacious,* "if you really want to help us, remove your gear." In a moment, Frederique was the way God made us all—except that He made her much better. Once again Frederique played Jane, shinnying up the backstay. There was a stampede aboard *Rattler* as the Tarzans, including the off-watch, rushed to the foredeck and fired away with Instamatics.

With the bow down under the weight of the audience, *Rattler* mushed to a halt. *Tenacious* broke free and sailed home first to the finish. However, *Rattler* still got the corrected-time vic-

tory and her crew got some treasured Koda-chromes. There goes another maxim: anatomy isn't always destiny.

In addition to tactics that Arthur Knapp and Bob Bavier never even thought of, recent SORC campaigns have been notable for leaps (some would say dives) of sailing technology and/or rule-beating finesse. The 1978 series carries on the tradition. In hull shape, 1978 is the year of the dagger-board yacht. Both from a hydrodynamic point of view and because of a loophole in the IOR—closed somewhat this year—such yachts are faster than their keel-encumbered sisters, upwind and down.

Draft is controlled in the rule. Beyond a certain point, an unbearable penalty is assessed. All designers go to the limit, because—keel or dagger board—draft has the greatest effect on upwind performance. With the dagger board, however, the rule gives—or at least gave—more draft for the rating. With this edge, the upwind performance of such yachts was enhanced. When sailing downwind, the dagger board is raised, as it is in a dinghy, which significantly decreases wetted surface and thus friction between the hull and the water.

Recently the rule makers, recognizing the inequity, upped the rating of the dagger-board yacht so that draft is considered in much the same manner as it is for the keelboat. This rule went into effect as of January 1. Every designer we talked to felt that such amendments, although an improvement, do not go far enough. Parity has not yet been reached.

Why is a dagger board hydrodynamically superior to a keel? Shape can be optimized with the dagger board because it does not have the additional requirement of carrying any—or at least much—ballast. (The dagger board's only weight requirement is that it be heavy enough to sink. Some designers do put ballast in the board to lower the center of gravity of the yacht, however slightly.) The keel, however, carries thousands of pounds of lead ballast and requires many more compromises in design to support its heavy burden. Also, the recent rule change focuses primarily on the dagger board's upwind advantage, ignoring the downwind side of the equation. As

The Southern Ocean Racing Conference, a series of six races, has evolved into the national championship for offshore yachts. Here one of several divisions gets underway at the start in a recent Southern Circuit.

the board is retracted when sailing downwind, wetted surface is decreased, which is most advantageous in light-air sailing.

Expect further rating increases for such yachts the next time the rule makers get together. It is interesting to note that every two-tonner hoping to challenge or defend the Canada's Cup this summer on the lakes will use a dagger board. So as not to alter the rule *after* the designs of these yachts were finalized—the kind of thing that makes designers and owners grumpy—the rule was frozen before the recent depth correction went into effect. This automatically gives such yachts at least ½-foot advantage (in the eyes of the rule) over any keelboat, a substantial edge in such keen competition. Of the four Canada's Cuppers turning up at the SORC for the summer-long battle on the lakes— *Evergreen, Mia, Black Majic, Agape*—all use dagger boards.

Except for speed, the only other advantage

to a dagger board is the fact that it can be raised to make the hull shoal-draft, which is a boon to cruising. Only a masochist, however, would want to seriously cruise such racing machines as these. The dagger board requires a huge, unsightly housing, or trunk, in the center of the cabin, which effectively divides the yacht in half and also competes for space with the mast step. As a result, masts are being stepped on deck, hardly the safest place.

Dagger-board yachts like the new generation of Canada's Cuppers represent an extreme in yacht design. (*Mia*, with her lovely teak decks and relatively warm cabin, is perhaps the only exception.) They are as high-tech and hybrid as the modern twelve-meter. And when their moment in a competitive limelight is past, they are absolutely useless for anything else. Unless you have an almost unlimited supply of after-tax dollars, and can afford a big-deposit, little-return yacht, avoid rushing to buy one.

Forgetting about dollars altogether, which you must do anyway these days to sail successfully in the SORC, there are real doubts about the self-righting capabilities of such yachts in the event of a knockdown. Most dagger-board yachts must carry their ballast internally in the bilges, (which accounts for the fatter bilges). Internal ballasting gives these hulls a higher than normal center of gravity, decreasing overall stability and perhaps compromising their ability to self-right.

Before the recent Sydney-Hobart Race, the Cruising Yacht Club of Australia (CYCA) questioned the self-righting capabilities of such hulls and decided to submit what it termed "suspect" yachts to some tests before permission to race would be granted. Using such things as foretriangle height, I-measurement, sailing length, rating and depth—all from the IOR certificate—a test weight was determined. Then the CYCA proposed that, with sails furled and board up, the yacht be hauled over on its side and this weight affixed to the top of the mast. After that, "a positive righting ability [must be displayed by the yacht] by moving upward in a righting direction."

There was much objection to this, especially by New Zealand yachtsmen, who seem to favor these boats, probably because New Zealand's own Bruce Farr has done wondrous things with ultralight dagger-board boats. While this controversy was ranging, the Offshore Racing Council (ORC) was holding its annual meeting in London. Several expensive phone calls were placed and a compromise—of sorts—was worked out. Internally ballasted yachts had to submit to a computer screening. If this test were failed, then changes would have to be made to the yacht to pass the computer test. Otherwise, the physical test, described above, had to be passed. No yachts failed the computer screening. This ruling went into effect for the world on January 1, 1978.

Wide, flat transoms are becoming popular for offshore racing yachts, and they seem to be bringing up the rear of most hulls at the SORC. Keeping the transom wide—to a lesser degree what Britton Chance tried in his ill-fated, twelve-meter *Mariner*—moves a yacht's quarter wave aft. This artificially increases a boat's sailing length.

Sailing length is also increased by the flatness of the stern and its width. At speed with crew weight aft, the transom quickly becomes immersed, which has the same effect of increasing the sailing length. However, since a boat is measured without crew and in bow-down trim, the extra sailing length introduced by crew weight on one of these hulls does not fully enter the rating equation.

All designers are going this route. It is faster, relatively inexpensive and aesthetically very pleasing, especially in the cases of yachts designed by Ron Holland—*Aries* and *Marionette*, for example. The point of departure, however, occurs when the wide, flat transom is used on ultralight displacement boats (ULDB) such as those favored by Bruce Farr. Rule makers—designers like Olin Stephens and Gary Mull, who don't like light boats and thus don't draw them —upped the rating of some Farr designs about .34 feet. The transom of the Farr-designed *Mr. Jumpa*, with its pornographic illustration of frogs doing what frogs occasionally do, is a perfect example, although the illustration has little redeeming social value.

The boat expected to trip the light fantastic at this SORC was *Circus Maximus*, designed by the creative Yves-Marie Tanton. She is sixty-six feet overall, sixty one feet on the water, a pencil-thin twelve feet three inches in beam, and draws nine feet. Her hull was cold-molded using the WEST System (Wood Epoxy Saturation Technique), which brings wood as close as it can get to glass. The hull alone weighs a feathery forty-two hundred pounds and the boat's total displacement is twenty-one thousand pounds. Long, thin, light and deep are not attributes that please the rule, so *Circus Maximus* was saddled with an "X-rating" of 69.9. For purposes of comparison, the seventy-eight feet Ondine, seventy-three feet on the water, rates 70. The owners of *Circus* were more interested in a fast boat than in giving any bows and scrapes to the rule.

Despite what she costs in rating, *Circus* was easy on the pocketbooks of her owners, John Raby and Don Ritter, more often seen racing powerboats. Light boats require less building material, and thus cost less. All up, this maxiboat priced out at less than many custom two-tonners, under $200,000.

No one disputes the performance of ULDBs downwind. Their dominance of the TransPac sleigh-ride proves this. Upwind they are suspect, however, because light weight gives rise to excessive pitching. Since her owners anticipate worldwide competition (*Circus Maximus* means "great circle"), Tanton attempted to maximize her upwind performance by installing a water tank on the top of the keel to add ballast.

Kindly put: *Circus Maximus* has not set the SORC afire. One problem is that the special water tank has been broken. The keel also seems to lack lateral area, causing excessive leeway. This is further aggravated by a rudder that is overly balanced and delivers a lee helm. Such things can be modified or fixed, so *Circus Maximus* should not be counted out after one series.

With radical boats, it takes time to learn their idiosyncrasies. No longer can a Grand Prix ocean racer be taken off the shelf, put in the water, then sailed off to beat the world's best. Proof of this is the performance of such boats as the two-year-old *Love Machine* and the new *Williwaw*, which Dennis Conner has been sailing since the fall, drilling the crew and fine-tuning the boat.

The smaller one-tonners aren't immune to calorie counting either. The Farr one-tonner *Mr. Jumpa*, and *Rogue's Roost*, designed by Bill Cook while associated with Bruce Kirby, Inc., are also extremely light. For example, *Rogue's Roost*, a keelboat that won the Boca Grande Race, displaces seventy-five hundred pounds, which is about half of what the '73 SORC overall winner, the Ranger one-tonner *Muñequita*, displaced.

As mentioned before, light and long ring up some funny numbers from the IOR formula. This is much more important for level racers than for maxi-yachts. To satisfy the all-important equation, both Farr and Cook traded in headsail area. The rule recognizes that headsails are much more effective than the mainsail. This is why ⅞ and even ¾ rigs are being seen.

According to Cook, whose one-tonner has a ¾ rig, there is an ancillary benefit to this setup. With a light boat, it is often (more often) neces-

sary to reduce the heeling moment by spilling wind at the top of the rig. Mast bend at the top most effectively accomplishes this. The non-masthead rig, with only the backstay reaching the top of the spar, is easily bent, conforming handily to the desired shape.

With lower-aspect-ratio headsails, like those on the one-tonners, winches are getting smaller, and fewer. Smaller because headsails are smaller, but also because, when the boat is ultralight, it is more easily driven and sheets actually don't pull as hard on blocks and winches. The lack of winches—an advantage to the light weight of the boat and the heavy weight of the owner's pocketbook—means that sheet stoppers are seen everywhere.

If you had the hydraulics concession for this year's SORC, you'd be a rich man. And Tim Stearn, the man who gave the world the Twinstay, had it. Hundreds of oily pounds of hydraulic fluid were bending masts, tensioning vangs, raising dagger boards and, for all we know, cooking stew in the galley when off watch in this year's SORC. The hydraulic controls on at least one yacht, *Evergreen,* are mounted on a center console and resemble a moog synthesizer. Not only does this setup look like that computerized musical wonder, it sounds like it too. When mast tension is hydraulically released, a screeching harmonic is given off, sounding a little like the theme from *Close Encounters. . . .*

Mast sections are getting frightfully small on the new generation of ocean racers. The minimal mast is especially evident on the Canada's Cuppers. Like their hulls, the masts of the Grand Prix yachts are on the edge. In the first race, some were apparently over the edge as a half-dozen of the magic wands succumbed to gravity in what was not a particularly rough race. (This was the one thing that kept hydraulics expert Tim Stearn from becoming a rich man; many of the masts that failed were of his design and manufacture.)

An extreme example of the minimal mast is found on the yacht *Evergreen,* which uses a three-quarter-ton mast section in a two-tonner and supports it all—hopefully—with four sets of spreaders, running backstays, a jackstay and a cat's cradle of other stays near the gooseneck, which were jury-rigged because the hydraulically controlled mast ram (moving the mast fore and aft at the deck partners) was declared unkosher. It is fortunate that Tim Stearn, the designer of this sophisticated lash-up, is in residence on *Evergreen* as principal helmsman. For all that, the mast developed some compression bumps and hollows in the first race. With the new rigs, timing while tacking is as important for the man working the running backstays and the hydraulic controls as it is for the helmsman, grinders and tailers. Faulty timing accounted for more than one lost mast.

A small mast section is desirable in the ocean racer because it decreases air disturbance in the inherently ineffectual mainsail. With a smaller mast, there is less windage behind it, and this allows the wind to meet the mainsail closer to the mast. A smaller section is also more readily bent and shaped, which allows a flatter mainsail, helpful in upwind sailing as it decreases weather helm.

The trend toward the minimal mast began in 1976 with *Williwaw*. The rig was designed by Tim Stearn and sailmaker Lowell North. They used a one-ton section on a two-tonner and strengthened it with costly carbon fiber. *Williwaw*'s spar was smaller and lighter but sufficiently strong.

For masts, carbon fiber is verboten this year, so other means were employed to keep spars in the sky. A more creative use of aluminum has helped. Traditionally, the walls of a mast have been the same thickness. Now they show variable thickness with more aluminum at the extremities, where the greatest loading occurs. There is a trade-off, however, because despite the smaller section there is more material (internally), and more rigging and spreaders, making the mast heavier. A heavier mast increases pitching. Up to a point, however, the decrease in windage, as it affects the mainsail, is more important than a slightly heavier spar and the increased windage of several sets of spreaders.

Shrouds put most of the load on a mast, about 55 percent for a boat with ordinary (wide) spreader lengths and up to 75 percent for a narrow yacht or one with short spreaders. With the smaller mast sections, spreaders are doing more of the work. This is why we are seeing three- and even four-spreader rigs. Multispreader rigs reduce strain on the mast and on the base of the spreader.

This year's SORC fleet continues a seventies trend to increasingly higher technology in materials, systems and the engineering of rigs, sail plans and hulls. It reminds you of the space program, and it produces the same ambiguous answers to the question, What does it all mean? Who wants to cruise on one of these boats? Who wants to live on Mars? The apologists for the space program assure us that their *Star Wars* technology eventually finds a prosaic place for itself in our own backyards. The yachting technologists, busy beating one another and the IOR rule with successive triumphs of science, make the same vague connection between their floating test beds and tomorrow's family yachts.

The connection is there, but it's not the reason for the circuit's superboats. The technology race in sailing has become an end in itself, a thing that many people find disturbing. What does it all mean? It may mean that tomorrow's cruising yacht will have a thinner but stronger aluminum mast; it definitely means that the vital competitive tradition of the SORC is alive and well in a different form.

Let de Boat Walk

by **BOB PAYNE**

All sports, like life, need comic relief. Just to show that they had a sense of humor, some of the world's top sailors decided one year to see how well they could work a Bahamian sloop. Bob Payne, a contributing editor for Sail Magazine, *went along and this is what happened.*

SOMETIME during the Southern Ocean Racing Conference (SORC), a story started going around that after the final race in Nassau, Ted Hood, Lowell North and Ted Turner would race each other in workboat-style Bahamian sloops. Trying to imagine such an event is like trying to imagine Jack Nicklaus and Arnold Palmer teeing off against each other at miniature golf, or race-car driver A. J. Foyt taking on all comers at a go-cart track, but by the time the SORC fleet reached Nassau, the story had been confirmed and the list of participants expanded to include Tom Blackaller, Dennis Conner and Buddy Melges. After two days of racing, the three best finishers would sail against three top Bahamian skippers.

The second day of racing begins sunny with a breeze. The Reverend McPhee is in danger of being late for church when I arrive at the *Thunderbird* to find him reminding Captain Bullet that the new mast—fifty-seven feet of varnished spruce—cost $8,000. Apparently, Captain Bullet

is a driver. The *Thunderbird* is one of six boats being used in the regatta. The reverend owns her. By hinting to him that I could make her a star, I sail as part of her crew.

This morning, most of the crew seem to be suffering from the aftereffects of Saturday Night Fever. One man is drinking from a pint bottle wrapped in a brown paper bag. Another is having trouble getting his eyeballs to do what he tells them to do. At least we are better off than the *Southern Cross,* whose captain has had to send a press-gang down Bay Street.

Each U.S. helmsman sails each boat once. I ask the *Thunderbird* crew what they thought about the helmsmen they had aboard yesterday—Blackaller, Conner, Turner. It is only Turner about whom they have anything to say. Turner, who introduced himself with: "Anybody here play baseball?" Turner, who brought them a quart of rum. Turner, who made the old *Thunderbird* strut like a spring chicken. What they say is: "Dat Turner, he one stubborn mon."

From what I saw yesterday, it takes a stubborn man to skipper a workboat-style Bahamian racing sloop. Although the fat, deep-draft, twenty-eight-foot hull supports an enormous mainsail on spars that resemble telephone poles, it carries very little permanent ballast. Ballast used to be provided by lumber and chickens and maybe a new cast-iron bell for the church. Now it is provided by as many as twenty-two men, most of whom spend the balance of their time sitting out over the water on a hiking board called a pry. All these men think they know more about sailing than anyone else on board. Which is why every time there is a decision to be made the skipper receives twenty-one usually conflicting opinions. These opinions are not sealed in a neat white envelope and dropped into a suggestion box. They are delivered simultaneously at full volume and are accompanied by ten-foot strings of four-letter words and racial slurs. The best workboat skippers are those with an enormous capacity for ignoring people.

The *Thunderbird* has probably had more skippers and won more races than any other workboat in Nassau. That is because she is thirty-four years old. To the uninitiated eye, she is nearly identical to her much younger competitors, but even her crew admits she is heavy and slow. Now, her chief claim to fame is that she is the only "work" boat in the fleet who has ever done an honest day's work. The others were born to race.

At a quarter until eight, Buddy Melges arrives. He is a stocky man flushed pink from yesterday's sun. "I'm looking for today's winner," he says. "Is this the *Thunderbird*?" Right away the crew likes his style. "Welcome aboard, captain," somebody says. The man with the paper sack offers Melges a drink. He takes a swallow, rubs his hands together, then—sounding like a Midwestern high-school coach—he says: "All right men, we have a race to win. Let's go get 'em."

We have thirteen men aboard, which is a half dozen less than we should have, but about a hundred yards off the dock two decide the boat isn't big enough for them both. A quick shouting match—about what, I am not able to discover—ends in one pulling his broad-brimmed hat tight over his head and, still holding it with both hands, stepping over the side. He does it with all the dignity of a retired gentleman exiting from a bus, except that he steps into ten feet of water. As we sail for the start, I watch him dog-paddle for shore.

The race starts from anchor. Our start is terrible. The problem is that the *Thunderbird* is prone to drag. To stop her, we put out so much scope I begin to suspect our strategy is to pull ourselves to the windward mark. Only what happens is that when the gun goes off and the other boats are up and away, we still have two hundred feet of line out. Despite protests from Melges and half the crew, the other half sets the main. (It takes half the crew to do almost everything because there is not a winch on any of the boats.) We sail past the anchor until the boat is brought up short like a dog on a choke chain. And then the confusion begins.

Despite our start, we are moving well and, by the first mark, have overtaken Conner, who never does seem to get the hang of sailing these things. From the look in his eyes, he seems to be yearning for a simpler time when all he had to do was start *Courageous* in the America's Cup. The first solid water sloshing across the decks and out the scuppers like Niagara South has washed away the effects of last night. Melges is beginning to be peppered with conflicting advice on how to get more drive out of the old bird. A few of our best voices are exchanging obscenities with Conner's crew. And above it all is the constant cry of "Out on de pry, out on de pry."

My job is to ride the pry. I am one of four. We scoot in and out as if we are a variegated tango team practicing steps we learned from Arthur Murray. Everyone is shouting commands, but the words come out so rapidly that most of them sound like a foreign language. I do understand "Hang on, honky." The rules say a boat has to finish with the number of crew she started with, but I've already been told that if I fall off, they will leave me and deny that I was ever on board. Riding the pry, I soon learn, is an art which consists mostly of convincing yourself that if you go, the man in front goes with you. I hold on to the man in front of me as if we are in love and want to be married. Somebody in the afterguard says we are not moving in and out fast enough. The man holding me—he is a two-hundred-pounder with such a death grip that I occasionally look over my shoulder to see if he has died and rigor mortis has set in—has an answer for him: "You sail de boat. We'll sail de pry."

Buddy Melges is traded for Ted Hood. Church over, the Reverend McPhee has joined us too. Hood is leading the series and our crew has high hopes of what he can do for the *Thunderbird,* but they don't warm to him the way they did to Melges. He doesn't take part, for instance, in the general discussion about our dragging anchor. We are still discussing it when the gun goes off, resulting in the same kind of start we had with Melges.

It is marvelous to watch a dozen people telling Ted Hood how to sail a boat. We are beginning to appear low of the mark, and some of them, including the reverend, who looks like he is going to jump up and grab the tiller any minute, want him to come up in the puffs. "Let de boat walk, mon, let de boat walk," they say. Like a good workboat skipper, Hood ignores them.

It is equally marvelous to watch the crew take exception to almost every suggestion the reverend makes. If he says tack now, they all say wait a minute. If he says wait a minute, they all say tack now. "You got to understand, Rev. we been sailing dis boat a lot more dan you. We know what make him go." It strikes me that this kind of racing isn't so much different from the SORC.

We finish fifth, Hood's worse race of the series, but about average for the *Thunderbird.* The crew—ever optimistic—blames our poor showing on Hood's refusal to "let de boat walk."

After Hood is Lowell North. Our terrible starts have taken on an aura of tradition. On the way to the weather mark, we notice Turner's boat is aground. A few minutes later, she is gone, turned over, sunk. The *Thunderbird* crew finds this enormously funny. "Dat mon don't listen even when dey tell him where de reefs are." We are now in fifth place.

North is enthusiastic. "Out on the pride, out on the pride," he keeps shouting. We veterans on the pry snicker among ourselves. How can a man claim to be a good sailor and not even know the word is *pry.* I am beginning to feel at home on the end of this long plank. Or, at least, fear for my life and dignity has been replaced by worries about splinters and blisters.

On the final downwind leg, we are not un-

reasonably far behind the fourth-place boat. North thinks we ought to try something. Below are a dozen bags of sand used to supplement the permanent ballast. "Let's dump some sand," he says. The inevitable arguing begins. The reverend thinks it is a good idea but wants Bullet to say which bags go. Bullet, who is up forward fiddling with the whisker pole, seems to be ignoring him. "Let's dump the sand," North repeats. The discussion continues. I tell him I'll do it except that there seems to be some argument. "Dump it," he says. "You can be done before they are through arguing." Another good workboat captain.

After the third race, we break for lunch. We anchor near the starting line and the skippers are taken ashore so that they can be told what everybody already knows. Hood is first overall, Melges second, then North, Blackaller, Turner and Conner. A launch comes around to deliver boxes of Kentucky Fried Chicken. It is compliments of the Bahamian government, who has sponsored the regatta as part of a program to focus international attention on sports in the islands. An empty box goes over the side. "Hey mon," somebody says. "Dat's against de law. Pollution makes de tourists stay away." Soon there is a whole flotilla of red and white boxes running before the wind.

The wind has freshened. The reverend thinks it's a good idea to refill the sandbags. Three Americans, two men and a woman, are riding by in a dinghy. He talks them into taking him ashore for sand. When they return, the woman and one of the men climb aboard. The reverend has invited them to race. Their names are Jack and Marita.

The final race of the afternoon will be Bahamian skippers against U.S. skippers. Since Bahamian skippers are not allowed to race their own boats, for this race we get Captain Greene from the *Mona Lisa.* Bullet stays aboard as an adviser. Because of Turner's accident, there are only five boats for the race. North and Melges decline to race, because they have plans to catch. So Tom Blackaller joins Hood in challenging the Bahamians.

We get our best start of the day, but the old

Thunderbird just can't fly any more and we are soon in our accustomed last place. Hood and Blackaller are in front. The leading Bahamians tack. Hood, figuring the locals know which way to go, tacks to cover. Blackaller goes his own way and crosses the finish line first. Hood is second.

But the drama is not over. At least not for the crew of the *Thunderbird.* Still competitive in spirit if not in fact, we start talking about dumping the sand again. Captain Greene gives the order. Marita, who is standing in the waist-deep hold, passes the bags up. Bullet is at his usual downwind post, sitting on the whisker pole. "No more sand," he says. "De boat get cranky."

As he says it, we roll the lee rail under. The whisker pole jumps out of its slot, sending Bullet flying aft. In a domino effect, half the crew ends up in the water, streamed out along the lee rail. As I am swept over the side, I grab the block for the jibsheet and will myself to hold on. It takes me a few seconds to realize that the reason I can't get back aboard is that somebody is holding onto my ankles.

We all manage to get back aboard somehow, possibly because we know that since we are in last place anyway there is no compelling reason for the boat to go back and get us, but one man has a chunk of skin the size of a hamburger pattie missing from the back of his hand. He says it is just a scratch.

An hour after the finish, it is impossible to tell the winners from the losers. The beach in front of Fort Montagu is thronged with hundreds of people. I am drinking straight rum from a Coke can somebody has cut the top out of. The police band is high-stepping it toward the awards platform. A shoeless, shirtless army of children have fallen in behind them, playing imaginary instruments and keeping perfect time to the beat. Blackaller, a Star sailor, is in the crowd. "Nothing like this happens when you win the Bacardi Cup," he says.

The Ultimate Marathon

by JOANNE A. FISHMAN

If you measure races by their scope, breadth and length, then the Whitbread is king. Four legs, the shortest being almost six thousand miles; more than four months at sea; for a variety of reasons, the least of which is financial reward: all these are part of the Whitbread experience. In the end, though, the salient act, in a contest as grueling as the Whitbread, is a matter, as one skipper put it, of overcoming not the unconquerable sea but oneself.

SOMEWHERE in the North Atlantic, a fleet of twenty-nine yachts is coursing southward in the first leg of the ultimate nautical marathon, the third Whitbread Round the World Race. By now, the leaders of the flotilla that set out eight days ago from Portsmouth, England, should have encountered the brisk northerly winds known as the Portuguese trades and will be sweeping down the coast of the Iberian Peninsula toward the Canary Islands. Before the boats sail back into Portsmouth harbor roughly seven months from now, they and their crews will have been pushed to their uttermost limits to cross more than twenty-seven thousand miles of ocean as fast as possible through some of the worst weather in the world.

Anyone who goes to sea under sail must cope with the unpredictability of water and wind.

But in racing around the world, a sailor must also cope with every extreme of weather—from the heat and the patience-grinding calms of the Doldrums in the Atlantic between Africa and South America to the storms and cold and ice of the Southern Ocean on the edges of Antarctica, all the while running against the clock and the calendar.

Those who venture to the bottom of the world also encounter a challenge that few sailors ever brave, the Roaring Forties, that legendary stretch between forty degrees and fifty degrees south latitude that is the only part of the globe where no land interrupts the passage of the wind around the circumference of the earth. There, gales howl over vast stretches, pushing up mountainous seas. There, too, sailors face a nerve-racking passage among treacherous icebergs, the misery of frostbite and the bone-chilling discomfort of working and sleeping in wet clothes, sometimes for weeks on end.

Why do they do it? What makes those wealthy enough to indulge themselves in nearly any way they please focus their energies on the Whitbread, rearranging their lives to compete in a race that requires nearly a year's preparation and another seven months to sail and whose only material award is a modest trophy? And why do other sailors scramble to go along with them?

Peder Lunde, skipper of the fifty-seven-foot Norwegian entry *Berge Viking,* must have pondered this when 150 people applied to crew for him, for he had them all psychoanalyzed to determine their motives and compatibility. (While crew berths on the top yachts are highly selective, one skipper, Leslie Williams, of *F.C.F. Challenger,* a British entry, helped underwrite his venture by selling ten berths at £7,000 [$12,700] a head.)

The lure of the Whitbread is essentially basic—man pitting himself against the forces of nature, but on a global scale. Cornelis van Rietschoten, a Dutch investment banker who won the 1977–78 race on corrected time (based on a handicap rating that takes into account boat size, shape and speed potential) in his ketch *Flyer* and now hopes his new seventy-six-foot boat of the same name will be the first over the finish line, recently explained it this way: "You don't go into this race for the glory of it. You must do it just for yourself. In this material world, this is something that just comes down to you and the elements. In the process, I've learned a lot about myself."

For Roy Mullender, a retired British Royal Navy commando, the navigator aboard the new *Flyer* in a series of tune up races, the magic, the pure joy of sailing to the limit, was epitomized one evening after leaving the Roaring Forties on the way up from Cape Horn during the 1977–78 Whitbread.

"We were running with the mainsail and boomed-out genoa," Mullender recalled. (A genoa is a large foresail that overlaps the mainsail.) "We had about twenty knots of wind over the deck and we were surfing continuously in long bursts. But it was a clear night, with enormous stars up there. The sails were lit by the moon behind me. We had the boat's stereo speakers on and Rachmaninoff's Second Piano Concerto was quietly playing behind me. The boat was under fingertip control. Let her go half a degree the wrong way, and she would break loose and be in awful trouble. We were sailing right on the edge. It was absolute perfection."

The first global circumnavigation was launched in the name of economic competition on a September morning 362 years ago, when Ferdinand Magellan left Spain with a fleet of five ships and 265 men to find the inside track to fortune, the westward route to the Spice Islands. Though he was not among the eighteen who survived the three-year-long voyage (he was killed in the Philippines during a skirmish with natives), Magellan's success in finding the western passage established for once and all that the earth's shape is round.

Profit was still the motive of circumnavigation under sail in the nineteenth century when sleek clipper ships raced between ports in England, the United States, China and Australia, and the first to arrive reaped the highest financial rewards for their cargoes of tea, nitrates, coal and spices. For those who race in the Whitbread, there is no monetary award, only a fifteen-inch-high sterling-silver trophy in the form of a steering compass for the winner on corrected time, and a handful of lesser trophies in other categories.

Today's Whitbread yachts, even with their superbly engineered hulls and onboard computers, are not going to find it easy to beat the pace set by the old clipper ships, whose larger size and sail capacity sped them along the seas. In 1854, the clipper *Lightning* set the existing record of sixty-three days from Liverpool to Melbourne, matched later that year by the *James Baines* and four years after that by *Thermopylae* both on the second half of the circumnavigation.

Racing around the world for the sheer unremunerated thrill of it began only thirteen years ago, inspired by the epic solo voyages of Sir Francis Chichester, the first yachtsman to sail alone around the world (he made the journey in 226 days, with only one stop, aboard the fifty-three-foot *Gipsy Moth IV*) and Sir Alec Rose, who made two stops in the thirty-four-foot *Lively Lady* before returning to England after nearly a year en route.

With the exploits of Chichester and Rose followed closely in the British press, the first and only single-handed round-the-world race was declared shortly thereafter by the *Sunday Times* of London and a £5,000 ($12,000) prize offered. There was no formal start. Instead, boats simply

The sixty-eight-foot French ketch Kriter, *skippered by Alain Gliksman, sails past brooding Cape Horn during the first twenty-seven thousand-mile Whitbread Round the World Race held in 1973–74.*

had to leave from any port in the British Isles between June 1 and October 31, 1968, and return to the same or another port in Britain. Of the nine boats that started, all English-owned, only Robin Knox-Johnston's thirty-two-foot ketch *Suhaili* fulfilled all the conditions of the race, finishing in 313 days, nonstop. Five other yachts were badly damaged, and a sixth was found adrift and abandoned in the Atlantic.

England's prestigious Royal Naval Sailing Association organized the next global race, bringing in Whitbread & Company, a brewery, as the sponsor. Unlike the calamitous race for lone crewmen, the Whitbread was carefully plotted, with safety a prime consideration. The RNSA specifies that the race—which is held every four years—is for fully crewed monohulled yachts carrying a minimum of five persons. As a safety measure, all boats are required to radio their positions twice a week to race headquarters in Portsmouth. Though the reports are often a blend of fact and fantasy as the skippers try not to let one another know exactly where they are and what progress they have made, the accounts are must listening on all boats.

The RNSA also imposes three mandatory layovers, to give the boats a chance to replenish supplies, make repairs and give the crews some time for rest and recreation. The race is thus divided into four legs with the shortest being almost six thousand miles long, or twice the length of the next longest yacht races, such as the Cape Town to Rio Race and the TransPac Race, from California to Hawaii. At each stop, the boats are logged in by representatives of the Royal Naval Sailing Association, assisted by a race committee drawn from local yacht clubs.

The first leg is Portsmouth to Cape Town,

followed by Cape Town to Auckland, New Zealand, then Auckland to Mar del Plata, Argentina, and, finally, Mar del Plata to Portsmouth. Boats are expected to set sail from Cape Town around October 31, from Auckland about December 26, from Mar del Plata around February 23, 1982, and to complete the course toward the end of March. For the larger and faster boats, layovers between legs can be as long as a month, while the smaller, slower boats may spend only two weeks in a port. A date for the start of each leg following the first is determined after 70 percent of the fleet has completed the previous stretch. A straggler arriving after the next leg has already begun can start out on its own, but its standing in that leg is still calculated as it would have been had it left with the rest of the fleet.

In the first Whitbread, held in 1973–74, seventeen boats started and fourteen finished, with Raymon Carlin of Mexico winning with his sixty-five-foot ketch *Sayula II*. Three crewmen from three other boats were swept into the sea and drowned. The next Whitbread drew fifteen entries, all of which finished without loss of life. To date, the fastest round-the-world aggregate time posted by a yacht—the seventy-seven-foot ketch *Great Britain II*—has been 134 days, twelve hours. This was nine hours longer than the record for circumnavigation under sail set in 1976, also by *Great Britain II*, during the one-stop Financial Times Clipper Race. But this record is expected by many to be broken in the race now under way, possibly by the new *Flyer*, because of the improvements in sail and hull technology in the intervening years.

The fleet for this third Whitbread is drawn from fourteen countries, with the smallest boat the forty-three-foot British yacht *Bubblegum* and the largest, also British, the eighty-foot *F.C.F. Challenger*. For the first time, the United States is represented—by *Alaska Eagle*, a sixty-five-foot sloop owned and skippered by Neil Bergt, an Anchorage industrialist who bought, modified and refitted van Rietschoten's old *Flyer* at a cost of more than $1.3 million. In keeping with the current vogue, most yachts are sloop-rigged (single-masted, with fore-and-aft sails), with nearly half of them designed and built specifically for

this race. Among the French entries are *Euromarché*, sailed by Eric Tabarly, a national hero for his yachting victories, and two boats sponsored by wineries, the *Charles Heidsieck III* and *Kriter 9*. There are also such avowedly pan-European entries as *Traite de Rome*, which flies the flag of the European Economic Community (from whose inaugurating treaty it takes its name), and *European University Belgium*, named for its Brussels sponsor.

The top-seeded boats, in addition to van Rietschoten's new *Flyer*, include *Ceramco New Zealand*, skippered by Peter Blake, and *Alaska Eagle*. A late entry, *United Friendly*, the old *Great Britain II*, must also be considered a contender because of its record-setting pace in earlier global races and the experience and talent of its skipper and previous owner, Chay Blyth, who only two weeks before the start of the race agreed to take over command of the seventy-seven-foot sloop, now owned by Cecelia Unger, a Swedish yachtswoman, who will be on board for the race.

The role of women has increased considerably since the first Whitbread. And as women have become more competitive and skilled in yacht racing, they have moved out of the galley to trim sails and take the helm. In the first race, Zara Pascoli, whose husband, Erik, skippered the Italian yawl *Tauranga*, became the first woman to race around the world. The best-known woman in the second contest was England's Clare Francis, a noted long-distance sailor who had skippered the sixty-five-foot ketch *ADC Accutrac* around the world. Including Cecelia Unger of Sweden, eleven women signed up for the current race. The only American is Debbie Scalin, a twenty-three-year-old Texan who is aboard the sixty-five-foot South African entry *Xargo III*. Gaye Sarma, a twenty-seven-year-old English nurse, is serving as medical officer aboard *Traite de Rome*. And three French women, all veterans of transatlantic crossings, signed on to crew on *Fernanda*, a seventy-foot ketch. One of the three, Florence Sote, twenty-two, is serving as sailmaker.

"I couldn't sleep one night last October," said Neil Bergt during an interview earlier this summer at the New York Yacht Club. "I went into my library and started reading about the Whitbread race again. I've always had an intense desire to do this race. Then it dawned on me about four in the morning that this was the time."

Bergt, who started out as an Alaskan bush pilot, made the fortune that is enabling him to fulfill his dream by building a small airline into a $160 million conglomerate, Alaska International Industries. He said he found it easier to put a $20 million offshore drilling rig into operation in the Arctic than to ready a boat for the Whitbread, because there are "so many little pieces that have to be dealt with."

Although the forty-five-year-old Bergt has done some racing in the eight years since he took up the sport, he is not considered in the mainstream of yacht racing. But his twelve-man crew is a seasoned one that includes two veterans of the last Whitbread race. When asked what there is in his background that makes him think he can win the Whitbread, the soft-spoken entrepreneur took a puff of his cigar and set his jaw firmly before replying, "Because I'm a winner."

Later, thinking of his friends' and business associates' reactions to his adventuring, Bergt let out a hearty laugh and said, "They all look at me like I've gone absolutely bananas. This is absolutely the most frivolous thing I've ever done. But I'm going to do the Whitbread—and then go back to work."

For thirty-two-year-old Peter Blake, "this is the last time." A mechanical engineer from New Zealand, Blake crewed in both previous races, but this time around, he is skippering his own yacht, *Ceramco New Zealand,* a new sixty-eight-foot aluminum sloop designed by a countryman, Bruce Farr, and sailed by an all-Kiwi crew. The yacht is something of a national effort, having been underwritten in large measure by the New Zealand ceramics company whose name it bears and by 500 shareholders, including old-age pensioners, amateur sailors and even an elementary-school class, each of whom paid $500 for the privilege. In addition, 150 New Zealand companies donated products or sold them at cost. Even the government cooperated, by exempting Blake from paying sales taxes on donated items.

Discussing the Whitbread course, Blake pointed out that, from England south to Gibraltar, the winds are most likely to be between the southwest and northwest—"nothing too severe at this time of year." From Gibraltar, the fleet will pick up northeasterly trade winds past the Canary Islands to about six hundred miles north of the equator. Off the African coast, the boats will hit the Doldrums, a belt of calms that stretches nearly across the Atlantic. Here, said Blake, the challenge is "to waffle your way across maybe four hundred miles of very variable conditions."

South of the equator, he said, the yachts will encounter the southeasterly trade winds and then can expect to spend the next couple of weeks tacking into the wind most of the way to Cape Town.

The next leg, Blake noted, "is down to iceberg country, about fifty-five degrees south latitude. It's very cold, and traditionally the wind is from behind, from the west." The winds there are usually gale force, thirty-five to forty-seven knots, but often reach storm force, forty-eight to sixty-three knots, and sometimes go higher, to hurricane force. This is when safety harnesses are constantly worn by crewmen on deck and tethered by cables to the rail or deck. At night, the temperature on deck drops to fourteen degrees Fahrenheit. The water temperature, said Blake, "is nearly zero, with a lot of ice and snow. It gets so cold that the sails freeze solid. All the lines have snow and slush on them and all the metalwork, as well as the spinnaker pole, has an ice covering." The living quarters below decks are heated, but other areas, such as the bow, where the sails are stowed, also are covered with ice.

In the last Whitbread, Blake recalled, the boat on which he crewed broke its mast in the middle of the Atlantic. "We were lucky to have a wealthy enough backer, so we jury-rigged a mast and pulled into port, had a new one flown to us and were away again." As Blake pointed out, the availability of the right backup gear, particularly for the rigging and sails, can sometimes be crucial in such a long race. Some skippers, like

Bergt and van Rietschoten, are sending a container loaded with spare parts and supplies ahead to each stopover point.

Because frostbite has been a problem in the past, Blake, like most other skippers, has equipped his crew with specially designed foul-weather gear to help retain body heat and reduce the dangers of hypothermia. Nevertheless, between the condensation and the water on the deck, he admitted, "you end up getting wet in the end and not being able to dry anything, and you've just got to put up with it. You get into your sleeping bag wet because you haven't any more dry clothes and shiver for a couple of hours before gradually becoming warm again. Then you've got to go back up on deck again."

But it's there, at the bottom of the world, from South Africa to New Zealand and then on to South America and around Cape Horn, where *Ceramco* is designed to fly. And it is there too, on this long stretch of gale winds and mountainous seas, where this race is likely to be won or lost. Running before big seas, *Ceramco* is designed to plane, almost like a surfboard. "It's quite thrilling," Blake said.

Thrilling, but dangerous.

In the official Whitbread program for an earlier race, Robin Knox-Johnston, the solo circumnavigator, described in this way the sensation of planing before the huge waves of a following sea in the Roaring Forties:

"As the slope of the waves picks up the stern, there is a tremendous feeling of a giant hand urging the boat forward. The bow wave grows higher and spreads out, the boat starts to hum like a tube train, but the sound is only dimly heard because of the noise of the water and the spray. Knuckles whiten as everyone grips onto anything firm, because although a boat flying down a big wave provides the most exhilarating sensation, it only requires . . . a small yaw [analogous to a car skid] or the slightest lapse of concentration on the part of the helmsman for the boat to broach or swing round broadside in front of the wave, in which case, the oncoming wave . . . rolls onto the boat and swamps it completely."

Once a boat has started planing, Knox-John-ston observed, "it is as committed as a cyclist coming down a steep hill on a bicycle without brakes. There is no way the boat can be stopped until the wave finally overtakes it, and then there is only a brief respite before the next wave comes along and the experience is repeated. This sort of sailing requires skill and nerve, and the crew who combine both will put many miles between themselves and their competitors by keeping sails up and hanging on."

For many sailors, the Southern Ocean holds a fascination all its own. The sea is alive with seals, occasional penguins and great whales, seventy feet long. Here, too, a thousand miles from land, one finds albatross, birds with a wingspan of up to seven feet across. And at night there is the awesome phenomenon known as aurora australis, the Antarctic's version of the northern lights.

"It's like shimmery green curtains of light from one end of the sky to the other," explained Peter Blake. "People would stay up all night to watch it, if they were allowed to."

But amid this hypnotic meteorological display and the thrills of high-speed sailing lurk serious dangers. Sophisticated electronic equipment now is making it possible to detect some approaching problems. Most of the yachts in this Whitbread are equipped with newly developed navigation systems which pick up signals from orbiting satellites that can tell a navigator precisely where he is anywhere in the world. And most have weather-facsimile machines on board that print out satellite photographs of the weather. Although the satellite photos cover an area as great as three thousand square miles, a different weather system rolls through every three or four days, so skill in forecasting on the part of a skipper or navigator can provide a tactical advantage.

One problem modern instrumentation has not been able to eliminate is the danger of icebergs. "You're allowed to use radar or sonar," Blake observed, "but we feel the large icebergs, which radar would pick up, are no danger, as a rule, because you can see them. It's the ones the size of a small house that float with one foot above the water showing—the ones you can't really see—that are the problems. We keep an iceberg watch all the time."

Roy Mullender pointed out during a prerace interview aboard *Flyer,* on which he serves as navigator, that those who have competed in the past two Whitbread races are well aware that "we haven't had the worst weather that can be produced by any means. Sooner or later, we're going to get a real gale"—Force 12 winds, reaching sixty to seventy knots or more, and blowing from the south.

"This means that it's coming from ice no more than a couple of hundred miles away, and you've just got to survive," Mullender said. "The enormous seas and the intense cold slow people down. They may not be able to do things quickly enough to safeguard the ship. With Force 12 blowing for two days in the open ocean, you will get eighty-foot seas. They're rogues or freaks, but they exist."

Because of the rapid technological development of yacht construction in recent years and the discovery of new materials and building methods, racing yachts have generally become lighter. Weight alone does not necessarily make a boat stronger, but the stresses on a light boat are greater because the lighter the boat, the faster it is capable of going. Driving a boat hard into high seas is something akin to repeatedly driving a car into a brick wall. If you go fast enough, you will smash it to bits. Much of the skill in steering an ocean-racing yacht is knowing how hard to push a boat to reach its top speed without breaking it into pieces.

Roy Mullender recalled facing such a dilemma in the Tasman Sea during the Financial Times Clipper Race. The wind was shifting and he found the boat starting to head into thirty-five-foot breaking waves. "I thought I would smash the boat up if I carried on, so I slowed her down [by shortening the sails] to about 60 percent of what she was capable of and she just rode through the night beautifully. At the same time, I didn't know whether I was just being scared or whether I was being a good seaman."

The first light of dawn showed that his nearest rival had caught up during the night. "Some of the crew were looking at me and saying, 'Hell, the old man's scared.' But it was only four hours later that their rudder fell off," Mullender recounted.

Cornelis (Conny) van Rietschoten, a rangy fifty-five-year-old Dutchman with Delft blue eyes is a man of singular purpose. Particularly in a race as arduous as the Whitbread, preparation becomes the key to morale, safety and, ultimately, victory. From the day last spring when his new boat, believed to coast $1.5 million, was launched at Wolter Huisman's yard in the Netherlands, van Rietschoten has worked at tuning it. He sailed *Flyer* across the Atlantic to Marblehead, Massachusetts, to check out the sails. While he was on the East Coast, he competed in the five-hundred-mile Annapolis-to-Newport Race, winning on elapsed time. And then he kept adjusting the rig on the three-thousand-mile jaunt back to England, where the tune-up continued in a further series of races.

A seventy-six-foot aluminum sloop, *Flyer* is the newest in a series of maxis, ocean racers built to the maximum length allowed under the International Off shore Rule, the handicap system under which the Whitbread is raced. Created on the drawing board of German Frers, a highly respected Argentine designer, *Flyer* has a rig that is a little shorter than most maxis—it stretches 105 feet above the water—and a keel that's a little longer. While this might make *Flyer* a touch slower than other maxis, it also gives the boat more stability, which over the long haul is likely to prove more important.

Flyer's instrument panel in the cockpit resembles that of an airplane, with digital readouts continually blinking at the helmsman. The numbers provide a barrage of information, including the speed of the boat through the water and the speed it is making toward its destination (which is not necessarily the same thing, because the boat may be tacking upwind or affected by currents). Another set of numbers tells the helmsman how close the boat is sailing up to its maximum performance, determined from the speed profile given in a boat's handicap rating. The on-board computer system also gives the speed and direction of the true wind and the apparent wind, the latter a combination of the true wind and the wind created by the boat's movement through the water.

When all this sophisticated electronic equipment fails to help him move his boat as fast as he would like, Conny van Rietschoten resorts to more primitive methods. He tosses coins into the sea, "for luck, to bring wind." Who's to say if such tribute influences the gods? But it can be reported from personal observation that during last June's Annapolis-Newport tune-up race, when van Rietschoten tossed several Dutch guilders into a flat sea on two different occasions, the wind subsequently picked up.

To carry it along, *Flyer* has twenty-seven sails on board, some weighing several hundred pounds, and every time the wind velocity changes five knots or so, the jib is likely to be changed to keep the boat moving at top speed. The sails are controlled by the crew with the aid of fifteen winches, several of which are almost a foot in diameter.

In the past year, fast-paced technology has challenged the longtime dependence on sails made of Dacron, a woven polyester. Now many of the leading ocean-racing yachts carry headsails made of Mylar, a polyester film that is bonded to Dacron, and mainsails that combine Mylar and Dacron with Kevlar, another synthetic fiber that is as strong as steel.

Yet the enormous sails used to drive a maxiboat have to be able to withstand great pressure without losing their shape and must be easy to handle as well as exceptionally durable. Only two of *Flyer*'s headsails are coated with Mylar, both for use in light air. To use Mylar for heavier sails would make them too stiff to handle. Instead, the rest of the sails are made of a soft Dacron weave that is cut into narrow panels.

As Chris Bouzaid, president of Hood Sailmakers in Marblehead, Massachusetts, sailmaker for 60 percent of the Whitbread fleet, explained it during one of *Flyer*'s shakedown cruises, such sails are more expensive because more sewing time is required to stitch the panel. The resulting tight weave adds longevity and makes handling easier.

During the long weeks at sea, each boat competing in the Whitbread must be totally self-sufficient, so crew selection is crucial. *Flyer*'s crew of fifteen from eight countries includes Patrick Antelme, a chef borrowed from a Parisian restaurant who is said to work wonders with freeze-dried foods. Another vital crew member is Julian Fuller, a thirty-year-old doctor from Cape Town, and veteran sailor, who has taken a one-year sabbatical from his residency to join *Flyer*. According to Fuller, dampness and the severe cold in the Southern Ocean, which limits bathing to once a week, make infection the most common medical problem at sea. Consequently, he has stocked *Flyer* with a wide range of antibiotics as well as assorted pills and creams, and large bottles of 1,000-unit tablets of vitamin C, which crew members are urged to take daily. Fuller is also prepared for surgical emergencies, with two complete sterile suture packs on board. And he has brought along a complete dental set that will enable him to do everything from setting temporary fillings to coping with any crowns that might fall out.

Being prepared for medical emergencies not only makes good sense, but in this race it can also save a skipper from losing time, and possibly the race, by having to bring an injured crewman into port.

Grant Dalton, a sailmaker from New Zealand, is equipped to make whatever sail repairs are necessary on board. The boat's main salon is designed to be turned into a sail loft simply by moving a section of the dining table and inserting a sewing machine.

Behind the table is the galley, which in addition to a stove and double sink has a freezer, powered by the boat's generator, capable of holding enough food to feed fifteen people for thirty-five days.

There are two enclosed crew quarters, each with four bunks, down aft, meaning that all but the two watch captains work on the hot-bunk principle, one shift falling into beds the previous shift has warmed. The navigator and the skipper have their own cabins, both loaded with electronic gear, in the stern. *Flyer* also has a drying locker for wet clothes and a head, or toilet. But at sea, ablutions are usually performed on a small platform behind the stern, using buckets of salt water.

Life aboard any racing boat revolves around the watch system. On *Flyer*, the crewmen are divided into two six-man watches, each with its own leader who is responsible for the yacht's operation when the skipper is not on deck. During the day, there are two six-hour watches, and the rest of the twenty-four hours are broken into four-hour watches. The only personnel not on the watch system are the skipper, the navigator and the cook.

While on watch, each crewman has an assigned station on deck and specific responsibilities during each change of sail. The crew also constantly inspects for chafe, one of the biggest problems in long-distance sailing. Sails rub on the rigging and worn spots have to be patched before entire sails tear. Chafe also occurs on the wire halyards that are used to hoist and hold up the sails, and that can spell disaster in a strong wind if they break. When their watches end, *Flyer*'s crewmen sleep, read or listen to music on the two tapes each of them has been allowed to bring on board.

Van Rietschoten is a calm, unflappable skipper who never shouts at his crew, but he is strong on discipline. Roy Mullender, the navigator, thinks *Flyer* is even more formal a boat than the two British military yachts on which he has sailed. "But that's the right way to do it," he says.

At sea, *Flyer* is a teetotal ship, but in port it's another story. It is van Rietschoten's style to treat his crew royally ashore. On the eve of each leg of the race, he believes in giving his crew a good party so they have something pleasant to remember during the long journey to the next port. And during stopovers between legs of the race, van Rietschoten has planned special outings as a break from the shipboard routine. During their stay in Cape Town, for instance, he plans to charter a plane and take his crew to a game preserve.

While some yachts have a happy hour every evening to alleviate the tensions of the race, *Ceramco*'s Blake says he too, believes in running a dry ship. However, if there has been an unusually difficult sail change or a dangerous task up in the mast, Blake has been known to offer his crewmen cups of coffee laced with rum.

Most skippers agree that crews must be compatible as well as disciplined in order to overcome what Mullender refers to as "the rat-in-the-box syndrome."

"For every species," says the navigator, "fed into their genes is a demand to have a certain amount of space around them. If you attempt to reverse that, you are playing with an important part of man's fiber. To be shut up in a small boat for any length of time eventually will lead to people behaving irrationally. This means that people will think they're being perfectly normal and the other guy is off his nut, when in fact, it's they themselves who are at fault. But you can't tell them that. I don't know if anyone knows how to cope with this, but it helps to know this state of affairs exists."

What holds a crew together then? "Attitude" is Mullender's answer. People just learn to shrug off the difficult moments and "do what needs to be done. And we spend a lot of time laughing. This is Conny's approach: let's win, but let's have fun doing it."

Van Rietschoten views compatibility as a combination of organization and discipline. During a tune-up race he noted that, while a skipper has to discipline the others, "it all starts with yourself. You show to the others you are not afraid, that you can handle it. There are many moments during a race like this when people are scared. But you have to show there's not time to be scared. There are many things you don't like, but you overcome them. You do this all the time in your life, you overcome problems. But this is not just another problem. This is the most difficult thing to master."

When, someday next March or April, the Whitbread yachts begin to sail back into Portsmouth harbor, their skippers may have mastered themselves and their crews, but not the sea, never the sea, which mariners learn time and again, can never be fully conquered, only survived.

The Story of Grimalkin

by JOHN ROUSMANIERE

The 1979 Fastnet Race, which ran 605 miles from Cowes around Fastnet Rock and back to Portsmouth, has become synonymous with nautical disaster. As the opening line of this story presages, the outcome for Grimalkin *was not simply ominous, it was a poignant tale of human nature—first failing, then stubbornly hanging on and defeating terrible odds.*

THE abandonment of *Grimalkin* was also the abandonment of high hopes. David Sheahan, her owner, was one of thousands of middle-class people who were attracted to the sport of ocean racing, looking for escape from the pressures of organized, professional life ashore. Fastnet Race fleets had doubled in size since the late 1960s, and the sport boomed everywhere as more disposable income and leisure time became available to an increasing number of people. Away from land for several days at a time, fighting the weather and the sea in relatively small sailboats, men and women could regain touch with the satisfactions of working together in a natural environment—satisfactions that were a part of normal everyday existence before work became stratified, individualized and air-conditioned.

The virtues of the discomfort of an ocean-racing yacht—wet clothes, lack of sleep, bunk sharing and the constant pressure to outrace frequently invisible competitors—are difficult to explain yet addictive. For the men and women who keep returning to the Fastnet and other long-distance races until they are on the verge of old age, the lure is not the hope of winning trophies. Perhaps the sport provides a means of rediscovering some lost part of their primitive nature, unsullied by civilized life. In the 1970s, yachting went through a technological revolution as space-age materials and electronic instruments found their way into boats that were becoming increasingly fast and difficult to sail well. Many younger sailors seemed to respond to these challenging developments with the enthusiastic delight of race-car drivers and mechanics first encountering turbocharged engines, and the satisfactions of sailing in an ocean race may have been less important in their minds to the pleasures of winning. Yet for most of the twenty-seven or so people in the 1979 Fastnet Race, the attractions of the sport were the same ones that had encouraged ninety men to sail in nine yachts in the first Fastnet Race, in 1925.

Like a great many of the people in the 303 boats that started the Fastnet Race on August 11, David Sheahan had only recently discovered ocean racing. An accountant in his early forties, he had raced in dinghies and other day-sailing boats for many years before buying *Grimalkin*. Thirty feet long, she was almost the minimum size for most of the important distance races sailed off England, but she had a pedigree. Her designer was Ron Holland, in the past five years probably the most successful architect of ocean-racing yachts. She was built of fiberglass by the distinguished English firm of Camper and Nicholsons. Her shape, construction, rigging and equipment were as modern as those of most of her competitors. Sheahan did his best to supplement his boat's inherent speed and strengths with careful organization for the many races he entered. Some boat owners set aside the conscious, orderly sides of their natures when they make the transition from work to pleasure, but he approached yachting with the same attention to detail that he showed in his profession.

The six-page memorandum that Sheahan sent to his crew before the Fastnet Race began with a description of the course. The race would start in the early afternoon on August 11 off the Royal Yacht Squadron, at Cowes, on the Isle of Wight. The course was 605 miles long: from Cowes down the southwest coast and around Land's End; across the Western Approaches and around Fastnet Rock, which lies eight miles off the southwest tip of Ireland; then back to England and around the Isles of Scilly and on to the finish at Plymouth. *Grimalkin* would sail in Class V, reserved for the smallest boats, and she might be at sea for more than six days.

Sheahan then reported that the safety gear, which included a rubber life raft inflatable by a CO_2 cartridge, flares and equipment to aid in the rescue of crew members who had gone overboard, would be examined by Camper and Nicholsons. They would also make a repair to the yacht's rudder. He planned to carry six gallons of diesel fuel, enough to run the engine for twenty-four hours in order to charge batteries and "to give ourselves a safety margin in case of problems." And, he wrote, "The insurance of the boat and its contents [i.e., the crew] has been extended to take in this race, which is beyond our normal cruising [*sic*] limits." *Grimalkin* never went on cruises, and her normal insurance applied only near her home waters, on the Solent near Hamble. Sheahan then discussed safety. Although the first-aid kit would be "upgraded to a more suitable level for this event," each crew member was responsible for his own special medication. He recommended that each make an appointment for a prerace dental checkup and flatly reported that nobody on board had special medical training.

Since space was limited in the little boat (food would be stored in clothing lockers), everybody was expected to bring aboard only one duffel of sailing clothes. Shore clothes, Sheahan ironically noted, would not be necessary, "as we will break with our normal tradition and not dress for cocktails or dinner."

As for provisions, Sheahan expected the crew to share equally in the cost of food, for which he and a crew member, Gerry Winks, would shop. Although he had increased *Grimalkin*'s water capacity to twenty-five gallons, Sheahan wrote, washing and cooking would be done in seawater, and to provide a reserve for emergencies, freshwater consumption would be limited to three gallons a day. He asked the crew to notify him if there were special dietary problems.

Continuing with his concern about emergencies, Sheahan noted that he planned to talk daily over marine radio with his wife, who would be able to transmit any messages to families. "It might not always be possible," he cautioned, "so make sure that your family, etc., don't worry unduly if there is no news to pass on."

Taking almost an entire page, Sheahan detailed the crew assignments. He would be skipper and navigator; Gerry Winks would be second in command; Mike Doyle would back Sheahan up "to insure that in all circumstances we have a navigator"; his seventeen-year-old son, Matthew, would be in charge of the foredeck and sail changes; Nick Ward would trim the spinnaker; and Dave Wheeler would help Matthew on the foredeck. They would all take turns steering and cooking. *Grimalkin*'s watch system, described in the memorandum in a two-page chart, had two men on deck at all times. Each of the five men who stood watch (Sheahan would be busy navigating) would alternate four hours on deck and four hours below, and during the race each would take one twelve-hour period off the watch schedule to cook.

Sheahan ended his memorandum with instructions to be aboard *Grimalkin* at 8:00 A.M. on the eleventh and with a final reminder: "We have maintained a high standard of personal safety on board, let's retain it for this event."

Although no skipper preparing for the Fastnet Race should have been unaware of the potential for bad weather—strong winds often are as much a part of sailing off the English coast as light winds are prevalent on Long Island Sound in America—Sheahan's relative lack of experience may have made him more cautious than many Fastnet Race veterans. The previous three races, in 1973, 1975 and 1977, had been sailed in light winds and calms in which the main worry had been food and water shortage, not first-aid equipment.

Safety harnesses that restrain crew members from being flung overboard, life jackets and life rafts, fire extinguishers, first-aid kits, emergency rations—all were required of Fastnet Race entrants by the sponsor, the Royal Ocean Racing Club (RORC). Yet a man who worries about whether his crew will suffer toothaches is not a man to take chances. The RORC did not require Sheahan to carry a radio transmitter. A receiver capable of picking up marine weather broadcasts was the only radio that *Grimalkin* and most of the other Fastnet entrants had to have aboard. (The exceptions were the fifty-seven boats in the Admiral's Cup competition, which were required to carry transmitters. In 1979, the Admiral's Cup, an international championship for ocean races sailed biennially in Fastnet Race years, included three-boat teams from nineteen nations, among them the United States, Poland, Hong Kong, Brazil, Ireland, Australia and Great Britain.) Even though he was not required to do so, Sheahan equipped *Grimalkin* with three very high-frequency (VHF) marine radio transmitters and receivers, two of which were powered by the boat's battery, and one of which could be used in a life raft if necessary.

Sheahan also went beyond the regulations to equip his boat with jackwires along the decks and in the cockpit (in nautical parlance, *jack*

means "utility"). In rough weather, his crew could hook the snap hooks at the end of the six-foot tethers on their safety harnesses to these wires so they would be securely attached to the boat as they worked on deck or sat in the cockpit. The racing regulations required only that *Grimalkin* be equipped with lifelines running fore and aft two feet above each rail, suspended on stainless-steel posts called stanchions. Both the stanchions and lifelines were vulnerable to damage by a broken mast or by a man thrown against them, and Sheahan felt that, in the worst possible situation, the jackwires were more dependable restraints against a man's being flung into the sea.

David Sheahan's concern for safety may have been motivated by knowledge that his crew was, in a way, flawed. Gerry Winks, the first mate, was arthritic, and Nick Ward, the sail trimmer, was an epileptic. Neither case was serious, and with the proper medication the two men were able to lead normally active lives. Yet doctors had advised Winks not to sail. He ignored that advice. At age thirty-five, Gerry Winks aspired to being a successful yachtsman with all the eagerness of a young boy hoping to score goals in a soccer World Cup. His spare time was devoted to boats: sailing in them, reading about them in books and yachting magazines, planning for the day when he could be skipper of his own ocean racer in a Fastnet Race. "The Fastnet is either the beginning or the end," he told his wife before setting out in *Grimalkin*. "I'll know myself as a racing yachtsman after this." If he proved himself by meeting his own high standards in this race, he would try to join the crew of a larger boat, and then onwards until he could afford his own yacht—regardless of doctor's orders. But until then, he would do his best to help David Sheahan win in *Grimalkin*.

When Nick Ward was sixteen, he suffered a neurological attack that left him partially paralyzed. Technically an epileptic, he had little or no feeling in his left side, although he was able, with medication, to stay active, ride his bicycle and continue sailing dinghies. He took waterfront jobs in boatyards, marinas and chandleries, and by the time he was twenty-four, he had helped deliver many yachts across the English Channel and the Bay of Biscay and had endured bad weather offshore. His knowledge, experience, seriousness and intensity made him a valued member of racing crews. David Sheahan sought him out and asked him to come aboard *Grimalkin* for the 1979 racing season. His only failing afloat was clumsiness in the galley. While cooking during a race in the Channel, he allowed a plastic spatula to melt in a frying pan. Sheahan, who knew the importance of barracks humor to a group of men under pressure, turned the incident into a running joke, announcing in the pre–Fastnet Race memorandum that Ward was scheduled to take the first tour as cook just after the start "whilst we still have a packed lunch," and labeling the new spatula "The Nick Ward Memorial."

Grimalkin's crew members were in high spirits when they boarded her at Hamble, near Southampton, early in the warm, sunny morning of August 11. They stowed their seabags and cast off the dock lines, and as *Grimalkin* made her way under power out toward Cowes, they sang loudly and waved cheerily to friends on the pier. Margaret Winks, Gerry's wife, was there to send them off, and the possibility of danger never crossed her mind as she watched the boat and her crew head off into the light southwest breeze.

Class V was the first group to start from the line that extended from transits on the castlelike clubhouse of the Royal Yacht Squadron to an outer distance buoy over one mile out in The Solent, the narrow body of water that separates the Isle of Wight from the English mainland. Fifty-eight boats crossed the line in Class V, while the 245 larger boats in Classes O, I, II, III and IV, and a flock of photographer, press and spectator boats swarming about, somehow avoided collision. A strong tidal stream pushing the boats toward and over the starting line further confused the situation. Sheahan was not intimidated. *Grimalkin* had an excellent start and held her own against larger boats as she tacked to windward, working her way toward the Needles, the chalk cliffs that guard the west end of the Solent.

The southwest wind held steady for the next two days, rarely blowing less than ten or more than fifteen knots as the massive fleet of racing yachts sailed as closely as they could in its direction, first on one tack and then, after a wind shift of a few degrees, on another. The sea was calm and the only discomfort was the minor annoyance of living in a world that was tilted twenty degrees. *Grimalkin* encouraged her crew by continuing to sail near boats ten to fifteen feet longer and potentially much faster as most of the huge fleet sailed close along the English shore to try to avoid strong contrary currents. David Sheahan endured the bout of seasickness that often afflicts even highly experienced offshore sailors on their first day or so at sea. When he recovered, he used one of the radios to call a marine operator, who connected him to his home telephone, and he told his wife that they were comfortable and sailing fast.

Like most of the Fastnet Race entries, *Grimalkin*'s crew depended for weather forecasts on the British Broadcasting Corporation's four times daily shipping bulletin on the long-range Radio 4. The forecasts had been almost exactly the same since Friday: southwesterlies of Force 4 to Force 5, with the chance of a Force 7 or Force 8 gale near Fastnet Rock on Monday, the thirteenth. In the Beaufort scale of wind and sea conditions, used by most seamen and yachtsmen to describe the weather, Force 4 ("Moderate Breeze") is an average of eleven to sixteen knots of wind (one knot is equal to 1.1 miles per hour), so the lower ranges of the forecast certainly were correct; only occasionally did the fleet feel the seventeen to twenty-one knots of wind of Force 5 ("Fresh Breeze"). Force 7 ("Moderate Gale") and Force 8 ("Fresh Gale") encompass wind strengths of between twenty-eight and forty knots, which every sailor in *Grimalkin* and her competitors must have experienced at least once in their sailing careers, and, which, probably, they all desired for at least part of this Fastnet Race.

The forecasts duly came at 12:15 A.M., 6:25 A.M., 1:55 P.M. and 5:50 P.M., and the wind and the barometer held steady at the relatively high pressure of 1020 millibars (30.1 inches), yet the thick fog that shrouded the boats most of Sunday was not evidence of the kind of stable fair weather that those indicators normally point to. The fog cleared away Sunday night and was replaced just after dawn on Monday by a flat calm. The air sat motionless between thick puffy clouds and a greasy sea undulating monotonously to the rhythms of the ground swell that rolls in soundlessly from the Atlantic. The ground swell is propelled by the southwesterlies that are ubiquitous except when a cell of low atmospheric pressure, called a depression, sweeps east from America to cancel out the effects of the great, stable Azores high-pressure system. *Grimalkin* rolled uncomfortably in these waves as her crew looked aloft for any indication of wind in the sails. After several hours, a breeze filled in quickly from a new direction—the northeast—and her crew soon had *Grimalkin* decked out in a spinnaker to take advantage of the new wind from astern. As she cleared Land's End and stuck her bow out into the Western Approaches, she was propelled at eight knots, almost twice the speed she had been making on the two-day, 210-mile leg into the wind down from Cowes.

Once again, the thirty-footer was staying even with larger boats, and her crew had every reason to feel satisfied. But for those who looked up into the western sky early Monday afternoon, there were other things to think about. The clouds were darkening to the point where Nick Ward thought them "terrific." The barometer had dropped slightly, to 1010 millibars (29.8 inches), and, with the strengthening wind that was slowly veering from northeast to east to southeast, there was reason to suspect that some bad weather was on the way. Yet the 1:55 P.M. BBC shipping bulletin for sea area Fastnet was: "southwesterly, Force 4 or 5, increasing 6 or 7 for a time, veering westerly later. Occasional rain or showers." That said only that a depression would be passing through with no more wind than had previously been forecast, but with a shift in wind direction to the west. Despite the clouds and the ground swell, which seemed to be growing higher, there was little in the wind or over the radio frequencies to cause even the most cautious sailor to consider turning back and heading for a protected harbor.

By late Monday afternoon, the wind had shifted to the southwest and had increased to twenty knots, with occasional puffs of twenty-five. *Grimalkin*'s crew doused her spinnaker, and, heading west-northwest toward Fastnet Rock, she burst over and sometimes through the swells at exhilarating speeds, under mainsail and genoa jib. At 5:50 P.M., the precise yet sympathetic voice of the BBC announcer presented the shipping bulletin, the relevant part of which was, "Mainly southerly 4 locally 6, increasing 6 locally gale 8, becoming mainly northwesterly later." He also located a depression two hundred and fifty miles west of the Fastnet area that the British meteorological office expected to pass to the north.

The six men in *Grimalkin* were not surprised by this news, for it was not the first mention of a Force 8 gale. Yet a forecast two hours later from another source painted a new and much more worrisome picture. At about 8:00 P.M., a French-language broadcast anticipated a Force 8 to Force 10 gale, with stronger gusts. Called a "Whole Gale" or "Storm" in the Beaufort scale, Force 10 conditions are considerably more severe than Force 8. Force 10's forty-eight- to fifty-five-knot winds are some twenty knots stronger, and its thirty-two- to forty-foot waves are as much as twice as high. Most significant is the violence of Force 10 waves. The description in the Beaufort scale is: "Very high waves with long overhanging crests. The resulting foam in great patches is blown in dense white streaks along the direction of the wind. On the whole, the surface of the sea takes a white appearance. The tumbling of the sea becomes heavy and shocklike. Visibility affected."

The maelstrom described in those five sentences and phrases is entirely more vicious than a Force 8 sea, in which there are "Moderately high waves of greater length [than Force 7 waves]; edges of crests begin to break into spindrift. The foam is blown in well-marked streaks along the direction of the wind." Force 10 is to Force 8 what stomach cancer is to gallstones.

David Sheahan and his crew knew the difference between Force 10 and Force 8, and the French broadcast worried them. *Grimalkin,* it seemed, was now heading straight into a major storm. Another Fastnet Race boat, later remembered as *Pegasus,* also heard the forecast, and her crew called the Land's End coast guard station over her marine radio to ask if the French had been correct. By the rules of yacht racing, this was illegal, since *Pegasus* was soliciting outside help, but the action is understandable given the circumstances. The coast guards' response was that the BBC forecast was the correct one. Overhearing both the question and the answer, *Grimalkin*'s crew breathed more easily. Yet the barometer had dropped to 995 millibars (29.4 inches), the wind had increased to thirty knots, the waves were building in size, and the boat was beginning to pound uncomfortably. The sun set at 8:26, its rays mostly hidden by low scuddy black clouds flying over water now broken by spray and whitecaps.

David Sheahan could not know that the French forecast had been accurate. *Grimalkin* was about to rendezvous with a compact, violent storm that had traveled over five thousand miles in four days to sweep across the Western Approaches during the precise hours when those waters would be crowded with small racing yachts.

"Depressions are born, reach maturity, and then decline and die," the English weather specialist Ingrid Holford writes in *The Yachtsman's Weather Guide.* "They travel in their youth and stagnate in their retirement; some are feeble from birth and never make a mark on the world, while others attain a vigor which makes them remembered with as much awe as a hurricane." This storm had already made its mark.

The storm was born in the northern Great Plains of the United States, where hot air over baking wheat fields frequently tangles with cold Canadian air to produce tornadoes and violent thunderstorms. Often, these tiny, vicious depressions do their worst damage immediately and are quickly gone, their energy dissipated in wind, rain and hail. But this storm had a force that kept it alive long after it dropped over an inch and a half of rain on Minneapolis, Minnesota, on Thursday, August 9. From there, it headed east across northern Lake Michigan, upstate New York, and New England. Its greatest effects were to its south. On Friday, sixty-knot wind gusts blew the roof off a tollbooth on the New Jersey Turnpike and knocked down power lines and tree limbs, one of which killed a woman walking in Central Park, in New York City. That afternoon, severe wind and rain squalls swept across Connecticut and into Narragansett Bay, in Rhode Island, where the twelve-meter yacht *Intrepid* was practicing for the 1980 America's Cup trials. One of her wire jib sheets broke and hit a crew member with such force that he thought his arm was broken. Nearby, seventy-eight boats competing in the world championship of the J-24 sailboat class were swept by unpredictable, violent gusts from the southwest and northwest. Three boats were knocked over until their masts touched the water. The boats finished the race under a black sky and made it safely into the protected harbor of Newport just before the coast guard issued an alert warning all sailors to seek shelter. Sheets of rain drenched the town, and a fifty-knot wind broke windows and threatened to blow over a large waterside tent. One sailor, Mary Johnstone, thought that this thirty-minute period of rain and wind was as wild as some of the hurricanes she had experienced during her many years of living in New England. That night, northwest squalls swept across the crowded harbors of the islands off southern New England, and dozens of yachts containing vacationers dragged their anchors. Moving east at speeds as high as fifty knots, the swirling cell of violent air was over Halifax, Nova Scotia, at about the time the Fastnet Race started on Saturday, and was in the open Atlantic a day later.

So small and fast moving was the storm that meteorologists had difficulty keeping a precise track of it, and some of the weather maps compiled every six hours by the United States National Weather Service show it only as an area of low pressure and not as a distinct depression encircled by isobars, or lines of equal barometric pressure. The weather map published in British newspapers over the August 11–12 weekend identified the depression as "Low Y" that would "move quickly east and deepen" to cause the Force 7 winds predicted for Monday.

In meteorologists' terminology, this was a "shallow" depression with an atmospheric pressure of about 1008 millibars (29.8 inches) at the lowest. A "deep" depression might have a pressure of less than 995 millibars (29.4 inches). Differences in atmospheric pressure are what create weather and, in particular, wind. Hot air and damp air are less dense than cool air and dry air. The less dense air has a lower pressure than the dense air and creates depressions in the atmosphere in the way a prolonged rainfall creates valleys and basins in a beach. Into these depressions pours cooler, more dense air from surrounding high-pressure hilltops or plateaus: the deeper the depression, the steeper the slope of the hill; the steeper the slope, the faster the air moves and the more wind there is.

Due to the earth's rotation, this flow of air from high to low pressure is not straight. The Coriolis effect curves the flow to the right, or counterclockwise, in the Northern Hemisphere and to the left in the Southern Hemisphere. In the Northern Hemisphere, air flows toward the center of a depression in the same way that water drains out of a sink, spinning in a counterclockwise direction as it works its way to the center. The deeper the depression, the more rapid the spin. The flow takes a different compass direction at each point on the spiral. To the north of a depression, the wind blows from the northeast; to the west, from the northwest; to the east, from the southeast; and to the south, from the southwest.

Depressions, unlike sinks, are usually in motion, being pushed from west to east by the prevailing westerlies created by the spin of the earth. A phenomenon of depressions is that when they move slowly they are relatively benign, but when they move rapidly they may be more dangerous than the differences of atmospheric pressure indicate. To put it another way, a fast-moving shallow depression may be more violent than a slow-moving deeper depression. Another phenomenon of depressions, especially the fast-moving ones, is that the winds on their lower half—the southern part of a depression moving east—may well be more violent than those on the upper half. In fact, sailors often speak of a storm's "dangerous quadrant," its lower right-hand area. As people in New Jersey, New York and Rhode Island already knew, the winds in the lower half of this particular fast-moving depression were exceedingly violent.

Between midday Sunday (as *Grimalkin* sailed down the English Channel in the fog) and midday Monday (when the northeast wind filled in after the calm), the depression traveled east-northeast at a speed of between twenty and forty knots, covering over eight hundred miles. To its south was the great Azores high, a mass of air with relatively high atmospheric pressures in the range of 1017 to 1034 millibars (30.0 to 30.5 inches). Air flowed down the slopes of this nearly stationary mid-Atlantic mound into the valleys of the low-pressure areas around it. The Coriolis effect of the spin of the earth redirected this air to the right, so that to the north of the Azores high a southwest wind was helping to push Low Y toward the northeast.

Conspiring with the high was a large depression of low-pressure air to the north that stretched almost one thousand miles from the latitude of Greenland to the latitude of northern Ireland. The depression had left the coast of Canada on Friday morning, the tenth, and had lumbered across the Labrador Banks, absorbing along the way two smaller depressions that had moved down from Greenland. On Sunday morning, August 12, the center of this depression was located about three hundred and fifty miles southwest of Reykjavik, Iceland. Called "Low X" on British weather maps (since it had been spotted earlier than the depression called Low Y), it had an atmospheric pressure of 990 millibars (29.2 inches) and perhaps a bit less in its center. The outer isobar of Low X, 1016 millibars (30.0 inches), stretched across the mid-Atlantic Ocean between the latitudes of fifty and sixty degrees north. The wind there also blew from the southwest.

Low Y had hitchhiked east on the westerlies of the Azores high and Low X. Born at the latitude of forty-five degrees, the depression had not moved south of forty-three nor north of forty-seven degrees during its quick trip across eastern American and the western Atlantic, and it would have made its European landfall in the Bay of Biscay if another factor had not appeared.

This factor was offered by Low X. Instead of continuing on its easterly course, Low X stopped moving. While it stalled for two days off the west coast of Iceland, Low Y overtook it and moved into the quadrant where southerlies and not westerlies blew. In the predawn hours of Monday, August 13, the dangerous little depression changed course and headed northeast, at first aimed west of Ireland on the well-worn path of many previous depressions. Once weather satellites had a look at it and computers could digest the limited amount of information that was radioed from a few ships in mid-Atlantic, the British forecasters realized at around noon on Monday that Low Y, swinging around Low X, would sweep across southern Ireland and the Western Approaches that night.

Unfortunately, the meteorological office came to this conclusion too late to provide a gale warning for the 1:55 P.M. BBC Radio 4 shipping bulletin, upon which almost all the Fastnet Race sailors depended for their afternoon weather forecast. The forecasters did, however, issue for special broadcast a warning of an imminent Force 8 gale for southern Ireland and the Fastnet area ("imminent" meaning within the next six hours), and for a Force 8 gale expected soon at Lundy, the island at the mouth of the Bristol Channel and one hundred miles northeast of Land's End ("expected soon" meaning from six to twelve hours after the forecast).

Made even more violent by cold air sweeping down into it from Low X, the depression slowed down and deepened on Monday afternoon, and the 5:50 shipping bulletin reported that it was about two hundred and fifty miles west of Fastnet Rock with a barometric pressure of 998 millibars (29.5 inches). Again too late for the shipping bulletin, which would not come on the air again until 12:15 A.M., the meteorological office at 6:05 P.M. released a new warning of imminent Force 8 increasing to Force 9 gales in the Fastnet area. If they had continuously monitored BBC's Radio 4, or if they had been within the limited range of and had been listening to one of four coastal radio stations using special frequencies, the sailors would have heard these gale warnings. But being human, they relied upon scheduled and predictable sources of information, and most of them had neither the time nor the inclination to monitor radios continuously. Furthermore, radios can be a drain on batteries that must also be used to provide power for navigation lights. (In the United States, many areas are covered by continuous marine weather forecasts, which are repeated every few minutes on special frequencies.)

At 8:50 P.M., the meteorological office issued revised gale warnings for mainland Ireland: the imminent Force 9 winds would veer from southwest to west. The area that most concerned any racing sailors who heard the warnings was not mentioned again in new gale warnings until 10:45: "Fastnet: southwest severe gale Force 9 increasing storm Force 10 imminent."

During its weather forecast that evening, BBC television showed a satellite picture of the Atlantic Ocean west of Ireland. The photograph was dominated by a clearly defined swirl of clouds curving north about three hundred miles southwest of Ireland. This was the front of the depression. Erroll Bruce, an experienced ocean-racing sailor who was sitting out this Fastnet Race, took one look at the picture and telephoned his business partner Richard Creagh-Osborne to say, "They're in for it."

David Sheahan required neither a gale warning nor the satellite picture to come to the same conclusion. Between 9:00 and 10:00 P.M., the wind built rapidly while the barometer plummeted, and by 11:00 P.M. *Grimalkin* was sailing at six knots under her tiny storm jib alone. Even a reefed mainsail was too much sail for this Force 8 wind. Soon water started to come on deck while heavy rain drove down continuous and cold. The crew sealed off the cabin by placing the wooden slats, called washboards, in the companionway hatch, and rather than go below—where equipment, food, clothing and bedding were flying everywhere as the boat rocked and rolled —all six men sat in the cockpit, their safety harnesses firmly hooked to the jackwires that Sheahan had so carefully installed. Gerry Winks steered *Grimalkin* on port tack out into the blackness of the Western Approaches, holding a course about 20 degrees off the rhumb line of 330 degrees to Fastnet Rock—and (though they did not know it) almost directly into the path of the dangerous quadrant of the depression. On starboard tack, heading south instead of northwest, they would have been steering away from the storm but also from Fastnet Rock. Storm or no, this crew would continue toward their objective until the boat ceased making headway.

Gerry Winks tired quickly. At 3:00 A.M., exhausted and shivering, he went below, where dry clothes and some food took the edge off his hypothermia, the dangerous loss of body heat that comes from prolonged exposure to cold air or water. At the helm, Nick Ward thought that the high, steep waves and powerful wind were part of a scene from a surrealistic film. No sail was possible, and they were unable to stay on course under bare poles. David Sheahan wondered out loud what they should do to try to cope with the seas ("these blocks of flats but three times as wide," Nick Ward called them). They eventually decided to run before it, effectively abandoning the race, with the wind and the waves on their stern, towing ropes overboard to try to keep their speed down. Yet even with six hundred feet of line dragging over the stern, *Grimalkin* was barely in control. She surfed wildly down the faces of the waves, like an elevator cut loose from its cable, and threatened to pitchpole, or somersault over her bow. She once accelerated to over twelve knots and, tilting forward until she was almost vertical, plunged down the face of a huge wave. Ward at the helm and Mike Doyle, sitting next to him, frantically looked to port and starboard for a flat spot to aim for, a landing field on which to level out, but all around was broiling white foam and ahead was a black wall—the back of the next wave rising out of the narrow trough. *Grimalkin* stuck her bow ten feet into the wall until her entire foredeck was buried three feet deep. The wall parted, and she shook off the tons of water and surfed off on another wave.

At least six times between 3:00 and 5:00 A.M., *Grimalkin* spun broadside to the faces of such waves and was caught under the curl and rolled until her mast was in the water. Each time, all six men were thrown out of the cockpit and left dangling by their safety-harness tethers in the water or wrapped around the lifelines and backstay. A 150-pound man generates a force of more than three thousand pounds when he is thrown twelve feet. The safety harnesses and jackwires withstood those loads, but the men themselves took a fearful beating.

On the fifth knockdown, Ward, who was still steering, was thrown entirely across the cockpit, over the lifelines and into the water with his left leg tangled in the harness tether. As David and Matthew Sheahan dragged him aboard, Ward felt an unfamiliar sensation: his left leg hurt. He had not felt pain in that limb since the neurological attack eight years earlier. The leg, he decided, must have been broken when he hit the lifelines. He half sat, half lay in the cockpit while some of the men around him tensed themselves against the pounding waves and the driving wind simply to remain aboard a yacht that fell out from under them every time a wave passed.

David Sheahan slid open the companionway hatch and went below to radio for help. He reported their assumed position to *Morningtown,* the RORC's escort yacht, and he hoped that she would send it on to the coast guards. He soon reported to the men in the cockpit that spotter airplanes and helicopters were on the way. Mike Doyle attempted to light flares, but he was unfamiliar with the ignition procedure and they merely fizzled into the sea.

Sheahan came back on deck just in time to be slung into the lifelines when *Grimalkin* was knocked flat once again. When the weight of her keel rolled her back upright, he lay in the cockpit, his head badly cut. The crew helped him below, where his son, Matthew, sprayed antiseptic into the wound. Seeing that the cabin was almost totally wrecked—the radios, chart table, engine housing and companionway ladder were destroyed—they returned to the cockpit, which, though exposed, seemed safer than the shattered interior. In their inflated life jackets and safety harnesses, the six men huddled together for warmth and protection. Nick Ward's leg was causing him great pain, and Sheahan and Winks

Dismasted, its hull battered and its lifelines cut, the abandoned Grimalkin *rolls aimlessly amidst the wreckage left by Fastnet's Force 10 winds.*

were dazed and frequently unconscious from their injuries and from hypothermia. Eventually, Winks was lowered to the cockpit sole, where, at the others' feet, he had some degree of refuge.

The next knockdown was the worst. *Grimalkin* was capsized, rolled right over by a giant breaker. David Sheahan was trapped under the cockpit as the boat lay upside down. To free him, his crew cut his safety-harness tether, and when the boat finally righted herself after half a minute or more, he drifted away helplessly, never to be seen again.

Grimalkin was dismasted in the capsize and her broken mast and rigging and boom now cluttered her deck. The five survivors dragged them-

selves back through the lifelines and rigging into the cockpit, where Nick Ward collapsed. Gerry Winks rolled, unconscious, on top of him.

Matthew Sheahan, Mike Doyle and Dave Wheeler talked over their situation and decided that *Grimalkin* was not safe. She was half full of water and wallowing dangerously, and in the gray morning light the seas seemed even more violent than they had before dawn. The skipper, Matthew's father, had been swept away to a sure death before their eyes, and their shipmates lay unconscious at their feet. They pulled the rolled-up, uninflated life raft out from its storage locker under the cockpit sole, pulled the line that triggered the CO_2 bottle and watched the bundle of rubber raft inflate. A close look convinced them that if Winks and Ward were not dead, they soon would be, and that in either case they could never be dragged into the raft. Taking off their safety harnesses, they climbed gingerly into the life raft and pushed themselves away. The time was about 8:00 A.M.

The life raft turned out to be not much more reassuring than *Grimalkin* had been. Almost covered by the canopy, the three young men could barely see outside, and could only await help as they bailed out water thrown in by the waves. Yet rescue was only an hour in coming. A Sea King helicopter hovered overhead and dropped a wet-suited airman on a wire. As the airman in the water secured one man at a time in a harness, the winchman aloft let out slack in the wire and the pilot backed the helicopter downwind and rose well above the waves to stay away from the salt spray that might clog its turbines. When the airman in the water waved an "all ready," the pilot, flying blind because he could not see the raft, moved the machine slowly forward under instructions from the winchman in the cabin. The pilot elevated and dropped his helicopter in tune with the steep waves monotonously rolling down at him from the horizon, all the while following the winchman's instructions: "Six feet left, four forward . . . right over." The winchman pushed a button and *Grimalkin*'s survivors were fished out of the sea, one by one.

With all three yachtsmen on board, the Sea King set off in search of another life raft. When two survivors of a yacht named *Trophy* had been lifted aboard, the helicopter swung east. A few minutes later, the five exhausted, cold men were in the sick bay of the Royal Naval Air Station at Culdrose.

Neither *Grimalkin* nor the half-dead men in her cockpit received any grace after being abandoned by the others. She was rolled over once again. Nick Ward regained consciousness to find himself underwater, his arms and legs tangled in stays and lines, his head being banged by the hull. He struggled to the surface, untangled himself and painfully crawled up into the boat through a gap left in the lifelines by the destruction of two stanchions. From the cockpit, he saw

Gerry Winks dragging overboard. Wrapping Winks's tether around a winch, he slowly winched his shipmate aboard. Winks was still alive. Using artificial respiration, Ward pumped water out of and breathed air into Winks's lungs, but the combined effects of the cold, exhaustion and his own physical disability were fatal. Winks whispered, "If you see Margaret again, tell her I love her," and died.

Twenty-four-year-old Nick Ward was now alone with a dead man in a wrecked boat in a gale, without either a life raft or a functioning radio. His leg pained him and was possibly fractured, and his back and shoulders ached from the beating that he had taken. His only course of action was to try to keep *Grimalkin* afloat and to hope for rescue. He staggered below, where everything was either shattered or afloat in the water. Even moving around in the cabin was dangerous, since the floorboards were floating, and loose food, broken crockery and pieces of equipment continued to fly about as the boat rolled. David Sheahan had set aside four buckets for emergencies, but three had disappeared during the knockdowns and capsizes, leaving only the smallest for Ward to bail with. He established a schedule of one hour for bailing and thirty minutes off for rest in a wet and sometimes half-submerged bunk.

The bailing seemed to make no progress. He wondered if the transducer, the speedometer sensor projected through the hull, had fallen out. More likely, the gallons of water that had accumulated in shelves, drawers, sleeping bags and clothing were now dripping down into the bilge.

Whatever emotions he felt were focused on survival. His shock at Gerry Winks's death and the horror of realizing that he had been left behind by his shipmates were, he decided, subordinated to the energy he needed to survive. His great frustration was that the three who had abandoned *Grimalkin* were not on board to help him save her and, when the storm had subsided, to sail her to port under an emergency rig. Except for the small transducer hole, the hull seemed sound enough, and, Ward thought, there was a way to step a jury mast once the wind and sea calmed. But he could never do it alone. He held no personal grudge against the three. Rather, he was angry at them for giving up on the boat.

To gain better access to the bilge, he ripped out two bunks and tossed sails and equipment forward into a pile. Rummaging through the debris in the lockers, he found some milk. He could not, however, locate his medicine, which he was meant to take every four hours. The doctors had said that he could do without it for perhaps a day, but no longer. He had last taken the medicine Monday night, nearly twelve hours before.

As Ward tried to keep to his schedule, estimating time because his watch had stopped, the sky cleared to an almost cloudless, cold blue. The wind had shifted into the northwest and was chilling. It continued to blow very hard until midafternoon. The waves, which more than the wind had caused the capsizes, lengthened out. They were just as high as the night before, if not higher, but they were much less steep. Where they had broken and fallen on *Grimalkin* with fearful regularity, they now rolled under her relatively harmlessly. Nick Ward bailed and napped, bailed and napped all afternoon.

Sometime around 6:00 P.M., he heard an airplane pass close overhead. By the time he had scrambled into the cockpit, the plane had disappeared. To avoid a recurrence of that disappointment, he remained in the cockpit, securing his weary, hurting body next to Gerry Winks's corpse with his safety harness and the mainsheet.

Another yacht soon appeared out of the waves. Ward was able to attract her attention with blasts on a foghorn. Although they had no transmitter, her crew fired off several flares that attracted the attention of a third yacht, which radioed a request for assistance. As dusk began to fall over the Western Approaches, Nick Ward saw a helicopter come at him rapidly from the east. The helicopter swung up and hovered forty feet overhead, and a man dropped quickly from the door on its right side onto the dismasted *Grimalkin*'s deck. Weeping with relief, Ward helped the airman secure Winks's body to the harness. After the corpse was hauled into the helicopter, the harness dropped down again. Talking barely coherently, Ward told the airman to wait. "I must get my clothes from below," he said. But the airman told him it was too late, that *Grimalkin* was sinking. As they were hauled through the air to the helicopter, Nick Ward looked down at the now truly abandoned sloop and quietly thanked her for providing refuge. He also thought how sad it was that nobody had stayed behind to help him keep her afloat.

Freedom of the Dream

by ROGER VAUGHAN

Fingers, the persona used by the gifted writer Roger Vaughan, lived through the fury of Fastnet aboard Kialoa, *a luckier ship than* Grimalkin. *While capturing the immensity of the storm as it beat upon him and his shipmates, Vaughan manages to transcend it effectively with thoughts about courage, racing and deeper human needs that only the gale force winds could satisfy.*

THE ferocity of the storm began to take its toll even on *Kialoa*. Radio reports had indicated all kinds of trouble developing behind us, and occasionally word would be passed to the deck from Christie Steinman, the navigator, about the increasing number of boats, planes and helicopters responding to distress calls. No one thought seriously about turning around to help. We were probably a hundred miles ahead (south) of the yachts that needed help most. Even at twelve knots, it would be eight hours before we could arrive on their scene.

Probably is the key word. Boats in an ocean race rarely know the positions of more than a half-dozen competitors, and those are usually boats of their own size and speed. It is difficult to imagine how 303 sailboats that all start within an hour of one another and that are all going to the same place can so quickly lose track of one another. But they do. With perfect visibility a boat is hull down at fifteen miles. The ocean seems to consume boats. Electronics solves the problem. The boats with those passenger-jet navigation areas know exactly where they are and where they want to go and why, and how the stock market closed as well. And radio communication is excellent. But boats in ocean races don't keep their radios on simply because they don't want to talk to each other. Loose talk afloat is for Sunday powerboaters and commercial fishermen. Sailors don't fraternize on the radio. For sailors, fraternizing on the radio is like being loud at a golf match, intoxicated in public. For all their technological warfare and systemized big-business approach, most people who go ocean racing really like being at sea. They like it for old-fashioned reasons: communing with nature, getting away from the hustle and bustle of land, breathing the best-smelling air in the world, showing a little courage in a primal form. They don't want the damn phones ringing. Had they wanted to talk with anybody who isn't on the boat, they would have invited them along. Nor do they want to give away their positions. They are racing.

In some races radio talk among boats is illegal. Certainly, it was against the rules for boats on Admiral's Cup teams to compare notes during races. If not, it would have been a battle of radios, not boats. And in the Fastnet Race, the British decided to shut down all those passenger-jet navigation areas in the interest of fairness to the less-well-equipped boats. For people who enjoy lukewarm beer, who wash their hair bent double in bathtubs, and who have made *sorry* into their national word, it was consistent thinking. Radio direction finders were allowed, a concession of dubious worth. RDFs have a reputation just slightly above life rafts in terms of effectiveness. On aluminum boats, they don't work at all. Recording depth finders were allowed. Fortunately.

Most boats were proceeding around the course by dead reckoning (DR), a time-honored system by which one keeps periodic records of the compass course steered, boat speed, wind speed and direction, sea state, current set, the altitude of passing birds, and whatever else might seem helpful, all modified by a critical seat-of-the-pants factor. Based on these data, little *x*'s are penciled on the chart and then connected like numbers in a children's puzzle. Instead of a moose in the woods, what materializes is history: the course the boat has followed up to its present position. More or less. Using DR is like playing piano. If you don't practice, you get rusty. Navigators used to the electronic game are not good dead reckoners. Theoretically, star and sun sights can be taken with the sextant for more accurate navigation. But this was the British Isles, where the sun shines only when it is not on duty in southern California, where the skies are cloudy many a day.

Christie sat below for six or seven hours during the storm watching the depth recorder. By comparing its ups and downs with water depths shown on the chart, she could tell more or less when we passed over two big underwater banks on the way to Bishop Rock, our southern turning mark. More or less. Our distance to the right (west) of Bishop Rock was very imprecise. Like *Kialoa,* a lot of boats had only a vague idea of their positions. By the time boats in trouble went for their loran sets, the instruments might have been broken or shorted out. When it was time to give the rescue service

a position, it was very vague indeed. Too vague.

We knew only vaguely where we were, and even more vaguely where boats in trouble were. And we were starting to get very busy ourselves. At first, we sat on deck encouraging the helmsman when he made a particularly adroit move to avoid a wave that looked certain to nail us. Driving was exhausting. The helmsman needed encouragement. He faced painfully into blowing scud that stung like sand, looking for the optimum path through confused seas that lifted us up and up, and either rolled under us or struck us full force. The helmsman would yell a warning the moment he knew he had been beaten by one of the monsters. We would double our grip and tuck our heads in as thousands of gallons of solid water tried to batter us off the deck. We listened to gear straining, watched it work as the loads increased, felt the awesome forces tearing at the boat in a dozen directions at once from the sudden braking action of her bow slugging into a wave, or from waves falling on us broadside at the same time that heavy gusts struck. It didn't seem possible that gear and vessel could bear such loads in combination with the terrible shocks they were receiving. One had to marvel at *Kialoa*'s performance, and also hope it was not short-lived.

The outhaul was the first to go. This was a piece of three-quarter-inch braided Dacron line rigged through a sheave at the end of the boom to the number 3 reef cringle of the shortened sail. Its job was to stretch the foot of the sail taut along the boom. It had been chafing in the sheave, out of sight of our constant inspection for chafe, and it parted with the sound of a rifle shot.

The crew was so attuned to the possibility of gear failure that we all jumped at once, like sprinters coming off the blocks. Speed is of the essence when gear fails, because the failure usually places an overload on other gear, with a potential domino effect. In this case, the reef cringle was also tied around the boom to hold it down, but now the mainsail had inched forward along the boom in puckers, putting great strain on small reef lines that went through lightly reinforced grommet holes in the sail itself. The whole middle of the sail could have been torn apart. Four men did a quick job reaving a new line and taking tension. They would get better at it. That outhaul would part twice more before the night was over.

As the positions got shuffled around on the rail, Fingers found himself sitting next to the running backstay wires. Two multistrand stainless wires were attached to the mast at heights of forty and sixty-six feet. They were joined together about eight feet off the deck by a metal plate from which a block was hung. Another wire of equal strength dead-ended on the deck, passed up through the block, ran back to the deck through another block and aft to a large winch. This was the running backstay, whose job was to support the middle of the huge mast, keep it from collapsing forward from the strain of headsails, especially staysails, which do not hoist to the masthead. And it was a small staysail that was helping pull *Kialoa* through the night at twelve knots.

As reluctant as he was to move, since any movement was accomplished with great effort and discomfort, Fingers moved. There are certain unwritten rules of behavior that one has to believe in. Like really making sure that the oven has been turned off before leaving the house. Like getting up in the night to check an anchor line at the slightest suspicion of slippage. Like staying outside the "V" ("the slingshot") formed by a line or cable under tension. Like keeping one's distance from any heavily tensioned member of the rig unless performing a specific job. Bruce Kendall was very nearly killed a few years before when one of *Kialoa*'s big spinnaker guy wires snapped. The boat was racing in smooth water in Block Island Sound and took a big knockdown with the spinnaker set. Bruce was on the weather rail trying to organize the disaster party when the guy parted. Quick reflexes and some luck saved his life. He ducked, and the recoiling wire lashed him across the top of the head instead of the forehead or temple. It took eighty stitches to close him up. He had to wear a baseball batting helmet on the boat for two years. He still has a bump on his scalp that itches when someone asks him about it.

Fingers grabbed the running backstay wire and tested it. It was under big tension. He moved. Ten minutes later, the block hanging from the metal plate exploded.

Several of the crew scrambled. The staysail was quickly lowered to take forward pressure off the mast. The main was trimmed to bring pressure aft. The deck lights came on. The mast was wobbling like it might have been made of plastic or hard rubber. It was a frightening sight to see the 1,073-pound, ninety-five-foot column of extruded, welded aluminum so out of control. Disaster seemed imminent. It felt like an awful loss of balance at a critical moment—catching an edge while streaking down a mountain on skis; stubbing a toe while crossing hurriedly against a flashing don't-walk sign in bad traffic. There didn't seem to be any way the mast could take such a whipping for very long without coming down.

From the number of eyes darting glances aloft, it was a general expectation. For a moment after the failure, there was disorientation. There was so much wind and sea noise to cut through. It was difficult to see. Then we knew it was the runner. But where had it broken? Aloft, in the mast? On deck? Was it the wire? The wire was tested for 12,500 pounds, the block for 28,000. We were lucky it was the block, which turned out to have suffered a crystallized weldment. If it had been the wire to the mast, it would have taken hours to repair. And someone would have had to ascend that wobbly stick to do it. But one of the crew quickly scrambled to leeward and retrieved the metal plate, which was swinging around wildly. We got a line from the deck to the plate for temporary relief to the spar. It was done with one eye for the job and one eye for the mast. If the mast did fall, there was no predicting which direction it would go. The thought made the back of Fingers's neck prickle.

By the time a new block was attached to the plate and the wire reassembled, an hour had passed. But the mast was still standing. That was an immense credit to Hood Yacht Systems, which engineered and built it. But the boat was being sailed gingerly during that period. We spent an hour at half speed. Because it was thought the mast might have sustained serious damage, the staysail was not raised again. Without it, we were two knots slower. But our priorities had shifted quite properly from racing to win, to racing to finish. Down one notch. It would cost us.

With the boat back on course and the crisis settled for the moment, we once again clipped onto the weather rail and huddled together, each of us privately assessing his personal discomfort, measuring energy reserves, checking endurance levels and wondering how much worse it would get before it got better.

Fingers took a look around him and really observed the night for the first time. Since he stepped on deck, his attention had been buried in one job or another. He had seen the storm only peripherally. Now with time on his hands, he focused on it and wondered if it was a dream.

Unlike the claustrophobic, ominous feel of most storms, this one presented the striking contrast of clear skies alight with a full complement of stars. Occasional clusters of low, fast-moving fleecy clouds would pass through. The moon was high, three-quarters full and brilliant, illuminating the steep seas with cold, eerie light. When clouds masked it, its beams peeked through to dapple small patches of ocean with pure pounded silver. Astern, the Big Dipper was full to brimming.

It roared a special kind of beauty, this night. Beauty of the sort that cuts deep, leaves marks. Fingers had always relied upon the sea to restore him, and the sea had never let him down. He lived by it, fished and dreamed upon it, planned and schemed beside it. It nurtured him like a great mother. For him, its beauty would never be surpassed. He knew that. But this night something shook him besides the howling gusts and their driven volleys of water that pressed his soaked inner garments against his chilled skin. Fingers sensed something. He was not a churchgoer, but at sea his agnosticism always faltered. At sea was when the concept of cosmic unity was most difficult to deny. This night it was impossible. Fingers felt out there, connected, wide open, hitched for a moment to a bit of business that is

the stuff of man's greatest fantasy. Awed, Fingers concentrated, engraving silver blue images on his brain.

Kialoa was reaching at ten knots under reefed main only. Her fine racing bow sliced into the seas, carving off hunks of ocean that were splattered to either side as foam and heaved high into the air and blown into the sails. The water was thick with globs of phosphorescence that would stick on the sail and glow for a moment, or speed off to leeward on the wind like sparks from spent fireworks. From her mad dash through the storm, *Kialoa* was leaving a swath of pure white foam astern fully two hundred yards long that shimmered like a snowfield in the moonlight. Fingers yearned to watch *Kialoa* pass from a nearby vantage point. We must be a sight, he thought.

In the glow of the red deck lights, crewmen moved to and fro, glistening wet in their bulky, white foul-weather suits, moving awkwardly in slow motion, like space travelers caught in a hostile, topsy-turvy environment. Faces, even bodies, were indistinguishable. Names that some had written on their jackets in marking pencil were fragile reminders of life on earth.

Fingers was fatigued, cold. It had been better with work to do. Now, there was nothing to do but sit on the hard, nonskid aluminum deck and endure, a necessary and essentially thankless task, complicated by discomfort and a nagging desire to use a recrimination or two. Endurance was such a head game.

He thought a lot about turning the corner, arriving at Bishop Rock on the southwest tip of the treacherous Scilly Islands, leaving it to port, then easing the sheets and heading downwind back to England. Turning the corner. It had a nice ring to it. But how long would it be? Three hours? Four? Six? The storm had hit *Kialoa* about seventy-five miles northwest of the Bishop. How long had it been since then? Fingers had lost track of time. He would try and get a position, talk to Christie. It would help to know how long one had to bang his head against the wall. Because thinking about turning the corner would pull him through; turning the corner (ahh), running off, rum and Cokes, soothing tokes.

To pass the time, he began a serious search for Bishop Rock. Serious, but impossible. Visibility was good, if one could focus properly between clouds of wind-driven spray, and if the boat was on top of a wave at those moments and not down in the trough putting a thirty-foot wall between him and the Bishop. The Bishop wasn't helping, with its stingy two white flashes every fifteen seconds. Maybe the Scilly Islanders had extinguished the light, or hung lanterns from the necks of meandering cows, as they once did to lure cargo-laden sailing ships to their doom during storms. The islanders would murder the survivors, then loot the vessels. But he continued to search with diligence. What else was there to do? Better an impossible task at hand than rerunning old Clint Eastwood movies, or dwelling on the problems with his woman (the fifteen-year hitch), or other troublesome alternatives that were lying in ambush. So he searched, and thought about his small herd of sheep and his cats and dogs, about taking piano lessons again and laying in wood for winter, about his woman (in spite of himself) and playing pool at Duffy's Putnam County roadhouse. Occasionally a passage from a familiar piece of music would passed through his head, providing a welcome sound track. Wagner and Beethoven were best for this night.

Nothing really distracted him from the extraordinary hardness of the cold deck, or the discomfort of the water that sneaked through gaps in his foul-weather armor and trickled against his skin. He made himself take deep breaths, and from time to time he flapped his elbows vigorously like an aroused penguin. He checked, and realized he was functioning. He looked around, and found that several of his fellows were lapsing into a head-down body slump that announced they were temporarily taking their leave, entering mental hibernation, checking out, sorry about that . . . They weren't responding to the various calls to attention for this little job or that. Fingers seized upon this forfeited energy, picked it up and swallowed it like Popeye devours spinach, and with the same empowering result. It wasn't a trait he was especially proud of—energy leeching. So be it. Since he

had come on board, he had been laying back, playing new boy on a new boat, taking it slow, doing a set of dinner dishes (for twenty!) because he believed new boys should do that sort of thing. But now he began running around in his customary fashion, hell this was a boat like any other, just a big bastard, responding to jobs three people away from him.

When there was help needed aft to dig the storm sails out of the bottom of a cockpit locker, he was there. When the bulky number 5 jib was ordered forward, he grabbed the huge, heavy thing and struggled forward with it, dragging and rolling it along the slanting deck like a huge beanbag chair filled with lead shot. Halfway forward he slipped, and he and the sail slid down the deck until his safety harness went taut. Cursing, he struggled to his knees. A large body loomed over him. It was Alastair, one of the Kiwis. Alastair reached down and grabbed the bag by the neck and picked it up. "No shortcuts, mate," Alastair said, and moved forward with the burden.

Stuart Williamson was thinking about his garden. He was estimating six more hours to the corner, and the thought seriously dismayed him. He was cold. He worked to displace his mind, and it ended up in his garden. When I get home, he thought, I will garden. And he thought about old sticks and dirt and compost being fed into the shredder, watching happily as the shredder spewed out a soft pile of fine organic material that the seedlings would treasure. It was better than thinking about what would happen if the mast broke.

Stuart was a flier, and he was comparing flying in bad weather with his current discomfort. Lurching and bumping through the air versus this. About the same. A wing could fall off, the engine could stall, but then the mast could go too. Better chance of survival on the ocean, probably, but until the wing fell off, flying was warmer, and drier. If only he could stay as warm and dry as he was at home he would like ocean racing a lot better. Stuart counted the positive aspects, and was glad this weather hadn't hit at the start of the Transatlantic Race that he had recently completed on *Kialoa.* That would have meant nine days to go. Nine days! The worst. For sure the mast would have gone, and he might never have gotten warm again.

Stuart allowed himself to dwell on a favorite puzzle: why he went ocean racing time after time. Why anybody did. Why he had been a regular on *Kialoa* for ten years. Why he had spent all that money on plane tickets, all those weeks beating his head against the bulkhead and freezing his ass when he could have been touring Spain (*olé!*) or planting shallots. He had never been in a sport where more people who swore they would never go again kept showing up. Take the Sydney-Hobart Race. Now, there was a monster outing. Long, cold and always an unpleasant surprise, a storm, dead calm and always totally unpredictable and unexpected until it was right on top of you. Sydney-Hobart. It had a nice ring to it. A trip to Australia. He could understand why people did it once. But twice, three times, six times? Jesus. Was it masochism?

Maybe it was latent heroism. When Stuart got home, people said they had prayed for him. People he hadn't heard from in years wrote him admiring letters. Stuart was astounded. "I would have had to burn my house down with me in it to get that kind of response," Stuart said.

There was no sport quite like it, Stuart knew that. No one waved the yellow flag if there was a wreck and oil got on the track, or if it began to rain. You started and you kept going. Dates for races were set months (years) in advance, weather be damned. One could count the ocean-race cancellations over the years on half the fingers of one hand. He knew that the idea of living through it was important; there was something about the sea and man.

Walking through Cowes, the night before the start of the race, we had passed a pink-and-white tent from which music emanated. A hand-written sign nailed to a post announced Film—7:00 P.M. It was just after the appointed hour, so we squeezed into the tent in time to see the film Qantas Airlines produced about the 1977 Sydney-Hobart Race. They had picked a good year for filming. A bad storm struck the fleet, disabling dozens of boats. A hero helicopter pilot had flown a dauntless cameraman close by the mast tips of floundering yachts, and some of the resulting footage was spectacular. The film also captured the very moment a 180-degree wind shift struck *Kialoa* at twenty-five knots, showing her heads-up reaction as she doused sails and regrouped and was back on course in less than twenty minutes. She went on to win.

"During that film was the only time I've had a strong insight into why I do it," Stuart said. "There was one shot that got to me. It was after the storm had passed and *Kialoa* was sailing about three miles off this huge vertical headland in about twenty knots of breeze, looking beautiful and white against a smoothly textured sea and the dark cliffs. Then the camera zoomed back and we got smaller and smaller, less and less significant as true perspective was gained, and it took my breath away—I said, 'That's me! I'm there!' "

A still photograph of *Kialoa* against that Tasmanian headland hangs in Stuart's house in California. It is by far his favorite because it best fulfills his fantasy, expresses the freedom of the Dream: "It has something to do with the infiniteness of water, its vastness; it doesn't inhibit vision."

The Dream again. To compare the Dream to the reality, one condenses the reality into the photograph for more favorable measurement. The mysterious chill of a real landfall (the return from limbo) is underpainted for maximum romantic satisfaction in the literature of the sea: *Moby-Dick, Two Years Before the Mast, Captains Courageous, The Nigger of the Narcissus*. There is heavy romance in those pages, of course, but after a while one has to admit how outweighed it is by the pain and suffering, the cracked and bleeding hands and the scurvy, the madness and cruelty, the plank walking and keelhauling, the flogging and fighting. Listen to poet John Masefield:

Then the dead men fouled the scuppers and
   the wounded filled the chains,
and the paint-work all was spatter-dashed with
   other people's brains.
She was boarded, she was looted, she was
   scuttled till she sank,

And the pale survivors left us by the medium
of the plank
>> from "A Ballad of John Silver"

Or this from Masefield:

Your nose is a red jelly, your mother's a
toothless wreck.
And I'm atop of you, banging your head upon
the dirty deck;
And both your eyes are bunged and blind like
those of a mewling pup,
For you're the juggins who caught the crab
and lost the ship the Cup
>> from "Evening—Regatta Day"

Or perhaps that *is* the grim stuff of romance —the sharing, by one's very presence on the ocean in a situation of stressful threshold exploration, of all that pain and suffering, of all the blood that has run in all the scuppers, of hanging it out (primal courage) in the name of that ancient and ghastly and heroic and undeniably seductive tradition of the sea and man.

There is the occasional shot of pure bliss too. What Stuart calls "the total body charge" one receives when everything is perfect, when all is right with the world. "The guns!" Stuart says, exulting, "the guns!" closing his eyes the better to hear them again, the better to hear the highly polished brass cannons whose lovely voices are reserved for the first three boats that cross the finish line, throaty voices that never fail to rattle the stomach and stop the heart for at least one beat.

"In 1971 we did the Tasman Sea Race," Stuart says. "We were first to finish, first on corrected time and set a new course record. The whole race was sailed in perfect weather. We never needed foul-weather gear. To make the finish line at the end, we had to execute a jibe in heavy going. It was perfect. The chute never so much as trembled. When the gun went off, it brought tears to our eyes. Twenty cases of beer were waiting for us at the dock."

But ocean racing mimics life. Pure bliss is a great rarity. The pictures help sustain it, of course, help make it possible to come to terms with the stranger need for one's fair share of abuse.

PART III

THE ART OF SAILING

"Of all the living creatures upon land and sea, it is ships alone that cannot be taken in by barren pretences, that will not put up with bad art from their masters."

—Joseph Conrad from *Mirror of the Sea.*

The Fine Art of Sailing

by JOSEPH CONRAD

The aristocratic Pole turned master of English prose, Joseph Conrad, sailed the world until he was in his forties. Then he retired to write some of the most profound and complicated stories in world literature. But Conrad was always a sailor and in his book, Mirror of the Sea, *he shared his knowledge and wisdom. Here are his observations on what constitutes the "art" of sailing.*

THE other year, looking through a newspaper of sound principles, but whose staff *will* persist in "casting" anchors and going to sea "on" a ship (ough!), I came across an article upon the season's yachting. And, behold! it was a good article. To a man who had but little to do with pleasure sailing (though all sailing is a pleasure), and certainly nothing whatever with racing in open waters, the writer's strictures upon the handicapping of yachts were just intelligible and no more. And I do not pretend to any interest in the enumeration of the great races of that year. As to the fifty-two-foot linear raters, praised so much by the writer, I am warmed up by his approval of their performances; but, as far as any clear conception goes, the descriptive phrase, so precise to the comprehension of a yachtsman, evokes no definite image in my mind.

The writer praises that class of pleasure vessels, and I am willing to endorse his words, as any man who loves every craft afloat would be ready to do. I am disposed to admire and respect the fifty-two-foot linear raters on the word of a man who regrets in such a sympathetic and understanding spirit the threatened decay of yachting seamanship.

Of course, yacht racing is an organized pastime, a function of social idleness ministering to the vanity of certain wealthy inhabitants of these isles nearly as much as to their inborn love of the sea. But the writer of the article in question goes on to point out, with insight and justice, that for a great number of people (twenty thousand, I think he says) it is a means of livelihood—that it is, in his own words, an industry. Now, the moral side of an industry, productive or unproductive, the redeeming and ideal aspect of this bread winning, is the attainment and preservation of the highest possible skill on the part of the craftsmen. Such skill, the skill of technique, is more than honesty; it is something wider, embracing honesty and grace and rule in an elevated and clear sentiment, not altogether utilitarian, which may be called the honor of labor. It is made up of accumulated tradition, kept alive by individual pride, rendered exact by professional opinion, and, like the higher arts, it is spurred on and sustained by discriminating praise.

218

This is why the attainment of proficiency, the pushing of your skill with attention to the most delicate shades of excellence, is a matter of vital concern. Efficiency of a practically flawless kind may be reached naturally in the struggle for bread. But there is something beyond—a higher point, a subtle and unmistakable touch of love and pride beyond mere skill; almost an inspiration which gives to all work that finish which is almost art—which *is* art.

As men of scrupulous honor set up a high standard of public conscience above the dead-level of an honest community, so men of that skill which passes into art by ceaseless striving raise the dead-level of correct practice in the crafts of land and sea. The conditions fostering the growth of that supreme, alive, excellence, as well in work as in play, ought to be preserved with a most careful regard lest the industry or the game should perish of an insidious and inward decay. Therefore I have read with profound regret, in that article upon the yachting season of a certain year, that the seamanship on board racing yachts is not now what it used to be only a few, very few, years ago.

For that was the gist of that article, written evidently by a man who not only knows but *understands*—a thing (let me remark in passing) much rarer than one would expect, because the sort of understanding I mean depends so much on love; and love, though in a sense it may be admitted to be stronger than death, is by no means so universal and so sure. In fact, love is rare—the love of men, of things, of ideas, the love of perfected skill. For love is the enemy of haste; it takes count of passing days, of men who pass away, of a fine art matured slowly in the course of years and doomed in a short time to pass away, too, and be no more. Love and regret go hand in hand in this world of changes swifter than the shifting of the clouds reflected in the mirror of the sea.

To penalize a yacht in proportion to the fineness of her performance is unfair to the craft and to her men. It is unfair to the perfection of her form and to the skill of her servants. For we men are, in fact, the servants of our creations. We remain in everlasting bondage to the pro-

ductions of our brain and to the work of our hands. A man is born to serve his time on this earth, and there is something fine in the service being given on other grounds than that of utility. The bondage of art is very exacting. And, as the writer of the article which started this train of thought says with lovable warmth, the sailing of yachts is a fine art.

His contention is that racing, without time allowances for anything else but tonnage—that is, for size—has fostered the fine art of sailing to the pitch of perfection. Every sort of demand is made upon the master of a sailing yacht, and to be penalized in proportion to your success may be of advantage to the sport itself, but it has an obviously deteriorating effect upon the seamanship. The fine art is being lost.

The sailing and racing of yachts has developed a class of fore-and-aft sailors, men born and bred to the sea, fishing in winter and yachting in summer; men to whom the handling of that particular rig presents no mystery. It is their striving for victory that has elevated the sailing of pleasure craft to the dignity of a fine art in that special sense. As I have said, I know nothing of racing and but little of fore-and-aft rig; but the advantages of such a rig are obvious, especially for purposes of pleasure, whether in cruising or racing. It requires less effort in handling; the trimming of the sail planes to the wind can be done with speed and accuracy; the unbroken spread of the sail area is of infinite advantage; and the greatest possible amount of canvas can be displayed upon the least possible quantity of spars. Lightness and concentrated power are the great qualities of fore-and-aft rig.

A fleet of fore-and-afters at anchor has its own slender graciousness. The setting of their sails resembles more than anything else the unfolding of a bird's wings; the facility of their evolutions is a pleasure to the eye. They are birds of the sea, whose swimming is like flying, and resembles more a natural function than the handling of man-invented appliances. The fore-and-aft rig in its simplicity and the beauty of its aspect under every angle of vision is, I believe, unapproachable. A schooner, yawl or cutter in charge of a capable man seems to handle herself as if endowed with the power of reasoning and the gift of swift execution. One laughs with sheer pleasure at a smart piece of maneuvering, as at a manifestation of a living creature's quick wit and graceful precision.

Of those three varieties of fore-and-aft rig, the cutter—the racing rig *par excellence*—is of an appearance the most imposing, from the fact that practically all her canvas is in one piece. The enormous mainsail of a cutter, as she draws slowly past a point of land or the end of a jetty under your admiring gaze, invests her with an air of lofty and silent majesty. At anchor a schooner looks better; she has an aspect of greater efficiency and a better balance to the eye, with her two masts distributed over the hull with a swaggering rake aft. The yawl rig one comes in time to love. It is, I should think, the easiest of all to manage.

For racing, a cutter; for a long pleasure voyage, a schooner; for cruising in home waters, the yawl; and the handling of them all is indeed a fine art. It requires not only the knowledge of the general principles of sailing, but a particular acquaintance with the character of the craft. All vessels are handled in the same way as far as theory goes, just as you may deal with all men on broad and rigid principles. But if you want that success in life which comes from the affection and confidence of your fellows, then with no two men, however similar they may appear in their nature, will you deal in the same way. There may be a rule of conduct; there is no rule of human fellowship. To deal with men is as fine an art as it is to deal with ships. Both men and ships live in an unstable element, are subject to subtle and powerful influences, and want to have their merits understood rather than their faults found out.

It is not what your ship will *not* do that you want to know to get on terms of successful partnership with her; it is, rather, that you ought to have a precise knowledge of what she will do for you when called upon to put forth what is in her by a sympathetic touch. At first sight the difference does not seem great in either line of dealing with the difficult problem of limitations. But the difference is great. The difference lies in the spirit in which the problem is approached. After all, the art of handling ships is finer, perhaps, than the art of handling men.

And, like all fine arts, it must be based upon a broad, solid sincerity, which, like a law of nature, rules an infinity of different phenomena. Your endeavor must be single-minded. You would talk differently to a coal heaver and to a professor. But is this duplicity? I deny it. The truth consists in the genuineness of the feeling, in the genuine recognition of the two men, so similar and so different, as your two partners in the hazard of life. Obviously, a humbug, thinking only of winning his little race, would stand a chance of profiting by his artifices. Men, professors or coal heavers, are easily deceived; they even have an extraordinary knack of lending themselves to deception, a sort of curious and inexplicable propensity to allow themselves to be led by the nose with their eyes open. But a ship is a creature which we have brought into the world, as it were, on purpose to keep us up to the mark. In her handling, a ship will not put up with a mere pretender, as, for instance, the public will do with Mr. X, the popular statesman; Mr. Y, the popular scientist, or Mr. Z, the popular—what shall we say?—anything from a teacher of high morality to a bagman—who have won their little race. But I would like (though not accustomed to betting) to wager a large sum that not one of the few first-rate skippers of racing yachts has ever been a humbug. It would have been too difficult. The difficulty arises from the fact that one does not deal with ships in a mob, but with a ship as an individual. So we may have to do with men. But in each of us there lurks some particle of the mob spirit, of the mob temperament. No matter how earnestly we strive against each other, we remain brothers on the lowest side of our intellect and in the instability of our feelings. With ships it is not so. Much as they are to us, they are nothing to each other. Those sensitive creatures have no ears for our blandishments. It takes something more than words to cajole them to do our will, to cover us with glory. Luckily, too, or else there would have been more shoddy reputations for first-rate seamanship. Ships have no ears, I repeat, though, indeed, I think I have known ships who really seemed to have had eyes, or else I cannot understand on what ground a certain one-thousand-ton bark of my acquaintance on one particular occasion refused to answer her helm, thereby saving a frightful smash to two ships and to a very good man's reputation. I knew her intimately for two years, and in no other instance either before or since have I known her to do that thing. The man she had served so well (guessing, perhaps, at the depths of his affection for her), I have known much longer, and in bare justice to him I must say that this confidence-shattering experience (though so fortunate) only augmented his trust in her. Yes, our ships have no ears, and thus they cannot be deceived. I would illustrate my idea of fidelity as between man and ship, between the master and his art, by a statement which, though it might appear shockingly sophisticated, is really very simple. I would say that a racing-yacht skipper who thought of nothing else but the glory of winning the race would never attain to any eminence of reputation. The genuine masters of their craft—I say this confidently from my experience of ships—have thought of nothing but of doing their very best by the vessel under their charge. To forget one's self, to surrender all personal feeling in the service of that fine art, is the only way for a seaman to accomplish the faithful discharge of his trust.

Such is the service of a fine art and of ships that sail the sea. And therein I think I can lay my finger upon the difference between the seamen of yesterday, who are still with us, and the seamen of tomorrow, already entered upon the possession of their inheritance. History repeats itself, but the special call of an art which has passed away is never reproduced. It is as utterly gone out of the world as the song of a destroyed wild bird. Nothing will awaken the same response of pleasurable emotion or conscientious endeavor. And the sailing of any vessel afloat is an art whose fine form seems already receding from us on its way to the overshadowed Valley of Oblivion. The taking of a modern steamship about the world (though one would not minimize its responsibilities) has not the same quality of intimacy with nature, which, after all, is an

indispensable condition to the building up of an art. It is less personal and a more exact calling; less arduous, but also less gratifying in the lack of close communion between the artist and the medium of his art. It is, in short, less a matter of love. Its effects are measured exactly in time and space as no effect of an art can be. It is an occupation which a man not desperately subject to seasickness can be imagined to follow with content, without enthusiasm, with industry, without affection. Punctuality is its watchword. The incertitude which attends closely every artistic endeavor is absent from its regulated enterprise. It has no great moments of self-confidence, or moments not less great of doubt and heart searching. It is an industry which, like other industries, has its romance, its honor, and its rewards, its bitter anxieties and its hours of ease. But such seagoing has not the artistic quality of a single-handed struggle with something much greater than yourself; it is not the laborious, absorbing practice of an art whose ultimate result remains on the knees of the gods. It is not an individual, temperamental achievement, but simply the skilled use of a captured force, merely another step forward upon the way of universal conquest.

Every passage of a ship of yesterday, whose yards were braced round eagerly the very moment the pilot, with his pockets full of letters, had got over the side, was like a race—a race against time, against an ideal standard of achievement outstripping the expectations of common men. Like all true art, the general conduct of a ship and her handling in particular cases had a technique which could be discussed with delight and pleasure by men who found in their work not bread alone, but an outlet for the peculiarities of their temperament. To get the best and truest effect from the infinitely varying moods of sky and sea, not pictorially, but in the spirit of their calling, was their vocation, one and all; and they recognized this with as much sincerity, and drew as much inspiration from this reality, as any man who ever put brush to canvas. The diversity of temperaments was immense among those masters of the fine art.

Some of them were like Royal Academicians

of a certain kind. They never startled you by a touch of originality, by a fresh audacity of inspiration. They were safe, very safe. They went about solemnly in the assurance of their consecrated and empty reputation. Names are odious, but I remember one of them who might have been their very president, the P.R.A. of the seacraft. His weather-beaten and handsome face, his portly presence, his shirtfronts and broad cuffs and gold links, his air of bluff distinction, impressed the humble beholders (stevedores, tally clerks, tidewaiters) as he walked ashore over the gangway of his ship lying at the Circular Quay in Sydney. His voice was deep, hearty, and authoritative—the voice of a very prince among sailors. He did everything with an air which put your attention on the alert and raised your expectations, but the result somehow was always on stereotyped lines, unsuggestive, empty of any lesson that one could lay to heart. He kept his ship in apple-pie order, which would have been seamanlike enough but for a finicking touch in its details. His officers affected a superiority over the rest of us, but the boredom of their souls appeared in their manner of dreary submission to the fads of their commander. It was only his apprenticed boys whose irrepressible spirits were not affected by the solemn and respectable mediocrity of that artist. There were four of these youngsters: one the son of a doctor, another of a colonel, the third of a jeweler; the name of the fourth was Twentyman, and this is all I remember of his parentage. But not one of them seemed to possess the smallest spark of gratitude in his composition. Though their commander was a kind man in his way, and had made a point of introducing them to the best people in the town in order that they should not fall into the bad company of boys belonging to other ships, I regret to say that they made faces at him behind his back, and imitated the dignified carriage of his head without any concealment whatever.

This master of the fine art was a personage and nothing more; but, as I have said, there was an infinite diversity of temperament among the masters of the fine art I have known. Some were great impressionists. They impressed upon you

the fear of God and Immensity—or, in other words, the fear of being drowned with every circumstance of terrific grandeur. One may think that the locality of your passing away by means of suffocation in water does not really matter very much. I am not so sure of that. I am, perhaps, unduly sensitive, but I confess that the idea of being suddenly spilled into an infuriated ocean in the midst of darkness and uproar affected me always with a sensation of shrinking distaste. To be drowned in a pond, though it might be called an ignominious fate by the ignorant, is yet a bright and peaceful ending in comparison with some other endings to one's earthly career which I have mentally quaked at in the intervals or even in the midst of violent exertions.

But let that pass. Some of the masters whose influence left a trace upon my character to this very day, combined a fierceness of conception with a certitude of execution upon the basis of just appreciation of means and ends which is the highest quality of the man of action. And an artist is a man of action, whether he creates a personality, invents an expedient, or finds the issue of a complicated situation.

There were masters, too, I have known, whose very art consisted in avoiding every conceivable situation. It is needless to say that they never did great things in their craft; but they were not to be despised for that. They were modest; they understood their limitations. Their own masters had not handed the sacred fire into the keeping of their cold and skillful hands. One of those last I remember specially, now gone to his rest from that sea which his temperament must have made a scene of little more than a peaceful pursuit. Once only did he attempt a stroke of audacity, one early morning, with a steady breeze, entering a crowded roadstead. But he was not genuine in this display which might have been art. He was thinking of his own self; he hankered after the meretricious glory of a showy performance.

As, rounding a dark, wooded point, bathed in fresh air and sunshine, we opened to view a crowd of shipping at anchor lying half a mile ahead of us perhaps, he called me aft from my station on the forecastle head, and, turning over and over his binoculars in his brown hands, said: "Do you see that big, heavy ship with white lower masts? I am going to take up a berth between her and the shore. Now do you see to it that the men jump smartly at the first order."

I answered "Aye, aye, sir," and verily believed that this would be a fine performance. We dashed on through the fleet in magnificent style. There must have been many open mouths and following eyes on board those ships—Dutch, English, with a sprinkling of Americans and a German or two—who had all hoisted their flags at eight o'clock as if in honor of our arrival. It would have been a fine performance if it had come off, but it did not. Through a touch of self-seeking, that modest artist of solid merit became untrue to his temperament. It was not with him art for art's sake: it was art for his own sake; and a dismal failure was the penalty he paid for that greatest of sins. It might have been even heavier, but, as it happened, we did not run our ship ashore, nor did we knock a large hole in the big ship whose lower masts were painted white. But it is a wonder that we did not carry away the cables of both our anchors, for, as may be imagined, I did not stand upon the order to "Let go!" that came to me in a quavering, quite unknown voice from his trembling lips. I let them both go with a celerity which to this day astonishes my memory. No average merchantman's anchors have ever been let go with such miraculous smartness. And they both held. I could have kissed their rough, cold iron palms in gratitude if they had not been buried in slimy mud under ten fathoms of water. Ultimately they brought us up with the jibboom of a Dutch brig poking through our spanker—nothing worse. And a miss is as good as a mile.

But not in art. Afterwards the master said to me in a shy mumble, "She wouldn't luff up in time, somehow. What's the matter with her?" And I made no answer.

Yet the answer was clear. The ship had found out the momentary weakness of her man. Of all the living creatures upon land and sea, it is ships alone that cannot be taken in by barren pretenses, that will not put up with bad art from their masters.

Navigation

by **CARLETON MITCHELL**

Although newly developed navigation systems exist which pick up signals from orbiting satellites and can tell a navigator precisely where he is anywhere in the world, the practice of navigation always will remain an art. Carleton Mitchell, who has won the Southern Ocean Racing Conference and the Bermuda Race on numerous occasions, here gives the finest account we have read of the origins of this art. This selection is excerpted from his marvelous book Passage East, *which is based on a 1952 race across the North Atlantic Ocean on Mitchell's fifty-seven-foot yawl called* Caribbee.

NO aspect of the sailor's world is more mysterious to the landsman than the practice of navigation. To find a precise point in a trackless waste seems neither art nor science, but magic. Yet in no other sphere of progress has the continuity of development been so clearly based on the heritage of the past, nor has the accumulated knowledge been so universally shared by men of all races, creeds and nations.

The word *navigation* stems from the marriage of a Latin noun and verb: *navis,* a ship, and *agere,* to move or direct. Its progress has been essential to the development of every maritime civilization. In Europe, the first glimmerings of scientific navigation began with the introduction of the compass, although men had already made long voyages without its aid. There is considerable evidence that an expedition of Phoenicians circumnavigated Africa six hundred years before the birth of Christ. There is also evidence the Greek Pythias of Marseilles reached Iceland and beyond two hundred years later. Meanwhile, the Polynesians found their way from island to island in the vast reaches of the Pacific by crude but accurate diagrams of the stars, and Norsemen regularly traded across the breadth of the North Atlantic by computing latitude from the length of the sun shadow cast along an oarsman's thwart by the gunwale of the ship.

There is much mystery surrounding the origin of the compass. It was long believed to have been invented in China and brought to Europe by Marco Polo about 1260; other theories credited it to the Chinese, but held it was the Arab pilots of the Mediterranean who introduced it to Italy. Yet evidence seems to indicate the compass might be a European development. The Greek philosopher Thales is reputed to have been familiar with the magnetic properties of iron ore, and known that particles orient themselves along a north-south line. According to Charles L. Petze, Jr., in *The Evolution of Celestial Navigation,* the Norwegians were using this principle aboard ship to establish direction in the eleventh century A.D., and about 1200 "the poet Guyot de Provins described a compass used by mariners in place of the Pole Star when the latter was obscured by storm or fog. Hugo de Bercy, in 1248, wrote that the construction of the compass had been changed, the needle 'now being' supported on two floats in a glass cup." In 1269 appeared a description of a pivoted compass complete with lubber's line, a circle divided into four quadrants of ninety degrees and a form of pelorus for taking bearings—all common to the most modern instruments.

Equally obscure is the origin of those other adjuncts of basic navigation, the lead and the log, the first to tell men how much water lay under the keel, the second how fast and how far the ship had traveled. The lead might well have been the first aid man ever developed in his questing across the surface of the sea. In its earliest form, it must have been a rock at the end of a twisted vine, lowered over the side of Neolithic rafts when drifting toward an unfamiliar shore. As metals were discovered, they replaced the stone, until finally lead was available, and used so universally its name became synonymous with the ancient device.

The development of the log was more complicated, being based on accurate units of time and distance. The navigators of the Middle Ages estimated progress by eye, watching bubbles and weed drift past. Later, bits of wood were thrown over from the bow and timed by sandglass as they passed two observers on deck; the interval required to pass indicated the speed of the vessels. Beginning in the sixteenth century, a line was attached to the bit of wood, and it was timed as it floated astern: the origin of the chip log, standard aboard sailing ships for the next three centuries. The chip was a wooden triangle weighted at the bottom to keep it upright in the water. It was attached to a bridle, in turn attached to a length of line knotted every 47 feet 3 inches. The chip was lowered over the taffrail. Floating vertically, it remained relatively motionless while the ship moved ahead. A sailor stood by with a 28-second sandglass. When the last grain ran through, the line was stopped and the knots counted, the theory being that the propor-

tion of 47 feet 3 inches is to 28 seconds as a sea mile of 6,080 feet is to 1 hour. Thus, if a ship ran out seven knots in the line in 28 seconds, she was covering seven miles in an hour, so the term *knot* came into universal use as a definition of speed: one nautical mile per hour. Even after the modern rotating log was generally adopted—a dial aboard ship which recorded distance by counting the revolutions of a spinner towed astern, utilizing the same principle as the automobile speedometer—the term *knot* remained. Yet curiously although the phrase "knots per hour" was used regularly in the old journals by the finest sailors the world has ever known, today it is considered by some a landlubber's expression.

Thus, the simplest implements of voyaging are compass, lead and log. With these, men still find their way for long distances in many parts of the world, practicing a type of navigation more art than science, dead reckoning. *Dead* is a contraction and corruption of *deduced,* where the ship's position is a matter of deduction after consideration of all possible variables—compass error, current, leeway and even the human fallibilities of the helmsmen.

But even as sailors groped along by dead reckoning, gradually accumulating the knowledge that resulted in charts so others following might have some idea of what lay ahead, learned men were working to transform navigation into a science. Hipparchus in 130 B.C. had prepared a calendar and tables of astronomical phenomena, but these were forgotten during the Dark Ages. Of direct interest to medieval navigators, the *Toledan Tables* of Arzachel appeared in 1080 and the *Alfonsine Tables* in 1252, while Roger Bacon added his *Opus Majus* in 1267, first using the term *almanac* to describe tables giving data on the apparent motions of heavenly bodies. After 1500, books of tables and manuals of navigation appeared with increasing frequency, spurred by the invention of the printing press.

Concurrently ran the development of instruments for measuring the altitudes of the heavenly bodies: sun and stars, moon and planets. The earliest appears to have been the astrolabe, a circular disk marked in degrees and equipped with a suspension ring and movable sighting vane. In use, the instrument was held by the ring and allowed to swing free like a plumb bob. The vane was then moved until it pointed directly at the body being observed, and the altitude read off the scale. The astrolabe was known to astronomers long before the beginning of the Christian era, but was never satisfactory at sea. Still, it was used by Columbus and Vasco da Gama to determine latitude on their voyages of discovery, two of the most important in history.

In more general vogue were the cross-staff and quadrant, the latter the direct ancestor of the sextant. The former consisted of a wooden staff along which vertical crosspieces could slide; altitude was determined by sliding the crosspiece until the observer could see the heavenly body on the line of the upper arm and the horizon on the lower. The angle was then shown on a scale along the central staff. This too was unsatisfactory, as it required simultaneous judgment of two widely separated objects. The quadrant was simply an arc marked in degrees, with a movable arm to point at the sun or star while holding the base level with the horizon.

The sextant, although not unlike some forms of quadrants in appearance, was the first device that permitted the heavenly body being observed to be "brought down" to the horizon by a system of reflecting mirrors. This eliminated the need for guesswork and permitted a degree of accuracy impossible with any previous instrument. Oddly, the sextant was invented at practically the same time on both sides of the Atlantic: by Thomas Godfrey, a Philadelphia glazier, in 1730, and by John Hadley, an English scientist, in 1731. Unable to decide who was first, the Royal Society made equal awards to both.

During the same fateful years, the other requirement for scientific navigation was being fashioned by an obscure Yorkshire carpenter, John Harrison. In 1714 the British Parliament had passed an act offering a reward of "£10,000 for a method that would give the longitude with an accuracy of 1 degree on a voyage to any of the West Indian islands and return, £15,000 for an accuracy of 40 minutes of longitude in arc, and £20,000 for an accuracy of 30 minutes." Man had long been able to determine with fair accuracy

his latitude, the distance north or south of the equator, but had no satisfactory method of calculating longitude, the distance east or west of a given point. But if the exact altitude of sun or star could be made with the knowledge of the exact time at some given point on the earth's surface, such as the Royal Observatory at Greenwich, a simple calculation would show the difference in time—readily converted into distance—between the two places. Harrison's invention, the chronometer, was the answer. In 1736, his first version, an unwieldy mechanism weighing sixty-five pounds, was carefully laid on pillows in the great cabin of H.M.S. *Centurion* for a voyage to Lisbon. Its error was only 3 minutes of longitude. Harrison was awarded £500 and retired to perfect a smaller and more rugged version. After much difficulty, including the opposition of the Astronomer Royal, his "Harrison Number 4" finally proved itself beyond any question. Taken from England to Barbados and return in 1764 on a voyage lasting 154 days, the timekeeper gained only fifty-four seconds over its rate, an error equal to 13.5 minutes of longitude.

Within four years, the modern age of navigation had begun. In 1768, Captain James Cook left Plymouth for the Pacific in the *Endeavour* to observe a predicted transit of the planet Venus, in order to secure data to calculate more precisely the distance from the earth to the sun. Aboard were not only the compass, lead and log of previous voyagers, but chronometer, sextant and even a *Nautical Almanac* from the Royal Observatory which had been established at Greenwich. During his voyage, the observations made and recorded daily in the ship's log read like those of any modern ship not equipped with the electronic inventions of the last two decades.

Landsmen probably do not realize that for smaller vessels there has been no basic advance in navigation since that first voyage of Cook, with the possible exception of radio reception as a check on the timekeeper, and establishment of lines of position. Loran, radar, automatic position-computers and all the other gadgets are for large steamers and ships of war, not anachronistic little vessels of wood and canvas. Instruments

Carleton Mitchell's thirty-eight-foot yawl **Finisterre,** *the only yacht to have won the Bermuda Race three times.*

have been improved, tables have been made more complete and simpler to use, yet the tools and techniques are essentially those of two centuries ago. And let fog or storm hide the sun and stars, and even sextant and chronometer become useless, forcing the sailor still farther back down the ladder of centuries. Navigation is then no longer a science but an art, and a prayerful one at that.

Thus still, for the small-boat sailor, a landfall at the end of a long passage has a quality of suspense, of thanksgiving, and will continue to so long as little ships sail the seas.

Below the surface of the sea lies a world of filtered sunshine paling into impenetrable darkness, of deadening cold and intolerable pressure, of vast areas and utter silence. Mountains far more majestic than the Andes or Himalayas rise mile after mile to terminate in peaks under the keels of passing ships; gorges infinitely greater than the Grand Canyon groove the rocky floor. Through the mountains and the valleys and "the dark unfathomed caves" move types of life inconceivably more numerous and varied in form than the denizens of the land, engaged in a struggle for existence incomparably more fierce.

For centuries, men sailed the oceans with no comprehension of what lay beyond the coastal shallows, their probing limited to depths which could be reached by weights attached to a few hundred feet of rope. Gradually, knowledge accumulated, but even today the ocean abyss is the earth's last frontier, likely to remain inviolate in the foreseeable future. "Could the waters of the Atlantic be drawn off so as to expose to view this great sea-gash which separates continents, and extends from the Arctic to the Antarctic, it would present a scene the most rugged, grand, and imposing," wrote Matthew Maury. "The very ribs of the solid earth, with the foundations of the sea, would be brought to light, and we should have presented to us in one view, in the empty cradle of the ocean, 'a thousand fearful wrecks,' with that array of dead men's skulls, great anchors, heaps of pearl and inestimable stones, which, in the poet's eye, lie scattered on the bottom of the sea, making it hideous with sights of ugly death."

But despite fluctuations of the ocean's level —from 600 feet above its present height during the Ordovician period, 350 million years ago, when the North American continent was reduced to a group of scattered islands, to recessions when trees grew on the floor of the Baltic and a land bridge extended from Alaska to Siberia—it is doubtful if the waters of the Atlantic or any other ocean will be "drawn off." Thus, man will never see a panorama as rugged and fantastic as could exist on any dead world in the far reaches of the universe.

Yet modern oceanography is making possible some idea of the vastness of the ocean in relation to the land, and glimmerings of the hidden contours lying between the continents. First, it is necessary to understand that 70 percent of the surface of planet Earth is covered by water, making it more properly planet Ocean, as has been suggested. This vast sheet of water has been calculated as having a volume of some 300 million cubic miles. And while the mean depth of the oceans of the world is about 13,000 feet, the average height of the land is only about 2,800 feet. Thus, if a celestial bulldozer could shove all the land into the water, and somehow complete the job of spreading the earth evenly into the crevices until the central core was a perfectly smooth ball, and ocean 8,000 feet deep would roll unbroken around this planet.

Like so many other steps in man's technical progress, the means of determining the depths of the ocean came as a result of trying to achieve something else. In the early days of navigation, measuring the water under the keel of a ship was a laborious process of lowering weights attached to ropes. The difficulties can be imagined. During an Antarctic expedition in 1839, Sir James Clark Ross pieced together a line of 3,600 fathoms and made the first successful sounding of the ocean abyss, reaching bottom at 2,425 fathoms. Yet by 1854, when Maury brought together all known records, there were only 180 soundings of the Atlantic depths. Maury was responsible for many more, substituting strong twine for

Carleton Mitchell won the Southern Ocean Racing Conference three times, in 1952 and 1953 with Caribbee, *a fifty-seven-foot Rhodes design; and again in 1956 with* Finisterre, *a thirty-eight-foot Sparkman and Stephens design.*

The first surprise was the unevenness of the ocean bottom. It had long been envisioned as an almost level plain, a characterless expanse covered by mud and sediment. Immediately, the fallacy, of this concept became apparent as soundings accumulated in the hydrographic offices of the world faster than they could be recorded on charts. Then swiftly followed comprehension of how much greater were the variations than comparable ones on land: the mountains higher, the valleys deeper, the escarpments steeper, the canyons more complex. Vast ranges of mountains appeared, mountains which if bathed in sunshine and capped by snow would surpass anything visible in majesty and beauty—yet their slopes were wrapped in eternal darkness and quiet, and subjected to pressure sufficient to crush any terrestrial life. . . . And systems of rivers as defined and complicated as the Mississippi Basin, buried far beneath any explicable rise of the bottom, or fall of the sea. . . . And trenches so deep, Mount Everest, symbol to man of virtually unconquerable height, could be dropped in and still be buried by a mile of water.

With the knowledge came a new concept of the hidden world of the sea, a division into three major classifications: the *shelf,* the *slope* and the *abyss.* To put it another way: the continental shallows, the pillars supporting the land masses, and the floor of the sea itself, the basalt crust over the flaming core of planet Earth. Of the flooded areas of the world, 7 percent is shelf, 15 percent slope and 78 percent abyss.

Of these it is easiest to visualize the shelf, the gently sloping shoulders of continents and islands, presently drowned extensions of land which have alternately been flooded and exposed during past geological ages. Generally speaking, the characteristics of a coast below water are similar to the visible part coming down to the tide line. This is understandable when it is remembered our present shores are being swallowed by the rising level of the sea at a rate of eight inches per century, as glaciers and the polar ice pack melt in the current warm cycle of the earth. In ages to come, it is predicted, the level of the ocean will rise from 100 to 200 feet, transforming much of our present coastal coun-

rope, and in 1870 Lord Kelvin introduced his deep-sea sounding machine of wire on a geared drum. Until World War I, when the submarine menace forced development of underwater listening devices, no better way of finding depth was invented. But antisubmarine research resulted in "sonic sounding," a method of transmitting a sound from the ship and measuring the time of the echo from the bottom in terms of the velocity of sound through seawater, some 4,800 feet a second. Continuous soundings could thus be recorded on lengths of graph paper, accurately depicting every hill and valley of the seafloor below. For the first time, man could have some understanding of the hidden depths.

tryside into shelf, and completely altering the maps of the world.

In all oceans, the average shelf width is 30 miles, and its outer depth 72 fathoms, giving it a gradient of 15 feet in a mile, an incline barely perceptible to the eye. Here live almost all the plants and animals of the sea which humans know or use for food. For as plant life is unable to survive in the rarefied atmosphere of higher altitudes, so it cannot live in the depths of the sea. Below 200 feet, plant life is scarce, although in some areas of exceptionally clear water plants find enough sunlight to manufacture food in depths of 600 feet.

At a usual depth of between 360 and 480 feet begins the slope, the suddenly steepening descent of the bottom toward the floor of the sea. The average slope extends down to some 12,000 feet, but can drop as deeply as 30,000 feet. Thus, the slope is a series of terrific escarpments, towering pillars of rock buttressing the islands and the continents. These vast cliffs are deeply grooved by canyons and gorges far greater than anything above the surface of the sea, just as the escarpments themselves dwarf anything beheld by the eyes of men. For the slope marks the part of this planet which does not belong to man, an alien and eerie void of eternal darkness, pressures up to seven tons per square inch and animals that feed only on other animals.

At the base of the slope, the floor of the sea becomes less steep. Beyond extends the abyss, the very name a frightening symbol of the unknown, the "bottomless gulph" of the ancient cosmogonies. In the vastness and the silence and the stillness—far below the reach of the most savage waves which lash the surface—dwell creatures strange and terrible, moving blindly across canyons of the greatest magnificence, their being only suspected by men above. Here for hundreds of miles may extend a range of mountains, there a drowned river system, here strange isolated peaks with flattened tops, there a gorge gaping even deeper into the core of the earth, here a level plain. . . . All hidden by utter and complete darkness, dead and soundless in a living world, part of the immutable secret of the universe. . . .

Strangely, the greatest depths of the ocean do not lie far from shore, but at the bases of some of the most precipitous mountain ranges which thrust above the surface. The deepest discovered chasm is the trench which winds across the Pacific past the Marianas, the Bonin Islands and along the steep shore of Japan, an awesome abyss attaining 35,640 feet. In the Atlantic the greatest depth is close to the north shore of Puerto Rico and the Virgin Islands, where the Brownson Deep descends to 30,250 feet. It is thought by many geologists these depths are part of nature's universal scheme of compensation: that at the bases of great mountains there is a fault in the earth's crust to balance the height above.

Another feature of the abyss is the sediment, the gradual accumulation of erosion and decay through the eons. There are places where it is many miles in depth, others where submarine currents have swept the rock bare, but seismic echo-soundings show that in general several thousand feet of sediment cover the floor of the ocean. Yet some scientists estimate as little as one inch might accumulate in twenty-five hundred years, a process so leisurely as to further remind man of his status on even his own planet, that minute speck in space.

On *Caribbee,* we had one knowledge not shared by the sailors of old: a comprehension of the nature of the abyss, of the dimension below the surface. Bermuda itself we could visualize as the only exposed peak of a mighty system of mountains thrusting up from the floor of the Western Atlantic Basin. As we sailed north and east, we moved over lesser peaks dropping down to hills and valleys, then reached the slope off Newfoundland, a fantastic escarpment towering out of the abyss. As we wondered what the weather gods above might have in store, below the depths were rising from 2,247 fathoms to 1,565 to 1,291 to 1,008. Then suddenly, in the space of a few miles, came the gigantic lift: 1,000 fathoms rising to 500, to 200, to less than 100, and we were over the Grand Banks, part of the continental shelf, a vast drowned plateau spreading like a fan under the sea, one of the widest shelf areas of the world.

And beyond the banks to the east Flemish Cap, a flattish hillock separated by a valley nearly 100 miles wide, but not very deep as submarine valleys go. Then another slope, the final plunge into the abyss separating the continents of North America and Europe. Far from traveling over a level and featureless plain, then, we were crossing some of the most awesome geological heritages of the genesis of planet Earth: a vast river system, not unlike the Mississippi, extending south from Greenland and deeply etching the floor of the sea with canyons and gorges and the arms of many tributaries; and beyond, the Mid-Atlantic Ridge—the greatest mountain range of this world, a complex of peaks and valleys winding down the center of the ocean from Iceland to Antarctica, 10,000 miles long and 500 miles wide, mostly lying 9,000 feet deep, but with one of its visible manifestations, Mount Pico in the Azores, towering 7,613 feet above the surface and plunging 20,000 feet below.

And beyond the sheer rock cliffs of the ridge, the lesser peaks diminish into hills, gradually merging into one of the rare plains of the ocean, the Eastern Atlantic Basin, a fairly level floor covered deeply with sediment, its vast expanse broken only by small knolls believed to be volcanic in origin. Then again the rise of the slope, this one supporting the Isles of Britain, the shelf beyond dipping down into the shallow sluice called the English Channel and rising again to the continent of Europe itself.

So man has added a new dimension to his knowledge: the dimension of depth. To the ancients, the sea itself was the limiting boundary. The Greeks called it *Oceanos Potamos,* the "Ocean River," conceiving it as a stream flowing endlessly around the rim of the world. Any human who attempted to penetrate its mysteries would pass into darkness and finally plunge into the abyss, from which there could be no return. To the real hazards of the sea were added the terrors of the imagination.

Yet men quested. Today the abyss is a definable scientific term. Perhaps in some future age, when sails and their use are as forgotten as the ox cart, humans will roam the floor of the sea. Only then will man's conquest of his planet be complete. Thus, the ocean is the ultimate challenge, as it was the first.

Less Weight and More Speed

by MEADE GOUGEON and TYRUS KNOY

Meade Gougeon built and sailed his first boat at the age of ten. He now is a boat builder in Bay City, Michigan, who, along with his brothers, developed the revolutionary WEST (Wood Epoxy Saturation Technique) system of construction. Gougeon also is known for his skills as a "hardwater" sailor with his high performance ice boats. Here, in an excerpt from his book Sailboat Design *written with journalist Ty Knoy, Gougeon provides valuable insight into the mechanical princples of the centers of gravity, balance and effort and the way they affect sailboat performance.*

LITTLE progress in speed under sail was made in the two centuries following Columbus's voyage to America. Many contend that the art even slid backward in those years, roughly 1500 to 1700.

To be fair, though, one must realize that speed was not the first concern of builders and mariners. Columbus's voyage was at the beginning of an era in which ships were venturing on vast oceans. Destinations were only vaguely known and weather along the routes was often fierce, always unpredictable.

If one keeps these things in mind and also realizes that a voyage to "the New World" took sixty or seventy days, probably ten times the average length of voyages between port calls around Europe, one can forgive the ugly, tublike vessels. Ships probing the New World needed a huge capacity for provisions, and they needed heavy timbers in their frames to withstand the seas.

In short, the overriding concern during the explorations was just getting there and getting back, and speed was given little thought. An analogy is with the space voyages of today. For all of today's thousands of people working on the space program, just making the journey is the thing. No one is complaining—yet—that a trip to the moon takes three or four days each way.

The beginnings of colonization made voyages to the New World more common, but still there was no great improvement in speed. Nor, apparently, was there much improvement in navigation: 128 years after Columbus, the beloved *Mayflower* inadvertently established the colony of Massachusetts when she took sixty-six days to cross the Atlantic and miss her mark by over five hundred miles (she had set sail from Southampton for Virginia, but ended up in Cape Cod Bay).

But eventually a situation arose that put a premium on pure speed. The time was roughly 225 years after Columbus, the place was the English colonies on the eastern coast of North America, and the situation was a trade restriction imposed by the English on their colonies. In a policy designed to improve the financial position of the mother country, the English limited the amount of trade with countries other than England the colonists could engage in.

The result, of course, was smuggling. As happens with trade restrictions, prices of contraband goods were driven so high that profits were high enough to cover high risks. The only problem was getting the contraband past the Royal Navy a reasonable amount of the time. Since it was impractical for a smuggler to arm his ship and shoot it out, the answer to the problem was speed. Thus, in the early 1700s, in clandestine shipyards, in makeshift ports and anchorages all the way from Massachusetts to Georgia, the Americans began to earn the reputation they enjoy to this day of being the builders and sailors of the fastest sailing machines in the world.

Colonial smugglers were able to take advantage of several unhappy features of English warships, among them square rigging, which has little ability to go to windward; high freeboard and high structures above deck, both of which caused windage and further cut down ability to windward; extremely heavy construction, which increased weight; heavy armament (up to three gun decks, each with a score or more of cannon), which again increased weight; and heavy ballasting, tons upon tons of rocks and/or pig iron in the bilge, necessary to counterbalance the topheaviness caused by the first four features, but further increasing all-up weight.

It would be charitable to describe these ships as slow and lumbering. Yet they suited the unimaginative naval tactics of the time—two lines of these floating forts would simply drift up to each other and blast away. Such craft, however, were ill-suited for pursuit of the ships that were developed by the colonists.

The economics of smuggling worked on the side of the colonists. Since the margin of profit on cargo was so high, it was not necessary for smuggling ships to carry big loads to have a lucrative run. This important fact had two effects: smuggling ships were much lighter than Royal Navy ships of comparable dimensions; and the hulls of the smuggling ships could be designed for speed with little regard for capacity of the

hold. In other words, the hulls could be long and thin, with great dead rise (*V*-like bottom) and long, sharp bows and sterns.

Of course, long, sharp hulls were nothing new when the colonists began building ships—hulls of the cogs and caravels were long and sharp. But the configuration had been forgotten for several hundred years. The colonists revived the design and eventually carried it to a greater extreme.

Another economic fact of smuggling worked in favor of speed: smuggling ships were subject to a high rate of loss, and therefore they were cheaply built. And being cheaply built, they were of light construction, with the result that all-up weight was less than it would have been with the English standard of construction.

But the crowning feature, which practically became standard on all medium-size American ships and has been standard on American yachts for decades, was that the schooners were, for the most part, fore-and-aft rigged. Most were schooners; some were sloops.

A sloop in colonial America was the same thing as a sloop today. It is a craft with a fore-and-aft rig on a single mast. (In the days of the smugglers though, the sails were gaff-rigged.)

The schooner, according to American tradition, was invented at Gloucester, Massachusetts, in 1713. This may or may not be true, depending on how you define a schooner. Today, a vessel is designated a schooner only on the basis of its rig, and the rig was not invented in 1713. It was in use in Holland at least a century earlier. Today's definition, which we will use, is a vessel with at least two masts, the forward mast being the same height or shorter than the other mast(s), *and* all masts being rigged with fore-and-aft sails. There are many variations within this definition.

Most schooners of the colonial period and of the early years of the Republic were two- or three-masted. In addition to the fore-and-aft sails, most of the early schooners also carried a small, square-rigged topsail above the gaff on the mainmast, and sometimes on the foremast also. These topsails were used for running (with the wind), but not for beating (against the wind). It is an important point that these topsails, yardarms and all, were on halyards and were lowered to the deck and stowed when the schooner was beating. The yardarms of square-rigged ships were permanently fastened to the masts and were not set up to be lowered.

Why is it important that the topsail yardarms of schooners could be lowered? It has to do with weight distribution.

We have already established that square-riggers tended to be heavier than fore-and-aft riggers, and it should need no explaining that it takes more power—more wind or more sails or both—to move a heavy ship at a given speed than it does to move a lighter one. But of as much importance as the amount of weight is the consideration of where the weight is located.

Any object has a center of gravity (CG), and for ships, it is best that the center be somewhere near the waterline. In fact, the lower the CG is, the less likely the ship is to get knocked down or to turn turtle.

Assume for a moment that there is a vessel that has a CG right at the waterline. That CG can be lowered (with respect to the hull) by adding weight (ballast) below the waterline. The CG of that same vessel will be raised by adding weight above the waterline.

If the CG is very much above the waterline, the vessel would be almost as likely to sail upside down as right side up.

Of course if one must add say, one hundred pounds on deck, which is ten feet above the waterline, this can be counterbalanced by putting another 100 pounds in the bilge, if the bilge is ten feet below the waterline. Then the ship will be as stable as it ever was, but it will be a total of two hundred pounds heavier.

But here is the hooker. Suppose one puts a weight (a yardarm, for instance) up on the mast one hundred feet above the waterline and that yardarm weighs one hundred pounds. Now to counterbalance the weight of that yard, one cannot put just one hundred pounds in the bilge ten feet below waterline; one must put in one thousand pounds. The reason is that the yardarm, while weighing only one-tenth of what the ballast does, has ten times the leverage of the ballast. The result is that the all-up weight is in-creased eleven hundred pounds to accommodate a simple yardarm. If one multiplies this by the dozens of yardarms, rigging hardware (iron in those days), etc., one can understand why square-riggers were such heavy beasts.

Sweden, while preparing for her invasion of Germany during the Thirty Years' War, had a sad experience with a warship that was built and fitted without enough regard for weight distribution.

In August 1628, amid cheers of thousands gathered at the quay of the Royal Palace, a 180-foot galleon sailed out into Stockholm's harbor on a Sunday afternoon.

The ship was the *Vasa*. She was on her maiden voyage with dozens of wives and children of her officers aboard for a parade cruise around the harbor. Less than a mile from her berth, while sailors high in the rigging were still breaking out sails, *Vasa* rolled to port and did not recover. Cheers along the harbor changed to gasps of horror as sailors aboard waited breathlessly for the next wave. When it came, it heeled *Vasa* even farther. Solid water began cascading through gunports. In a few minutes, she filled, and her ballast, which was not heavy enough to keep her upright, was nonetheless heavy enough to take her to the bottom in a hundred ten feet of water off Beckholmen. Some fifty lives were lost before rescue boats could get out. *Vasa*'s bulk was raised (1959–61) and is now a permanent museum at Djurgarden, on the harbor.

Not many ships have been out of balance so badly as to suffer the fate of *Vasa,* but there are records of plenty that were balanced poorly enough so that their rigs had to be reduced from what was originally put on them.

Fore-and-aft rig involves less weight aloft on any given size vessel than does square-rig. On colonial sloops and schooners, there were long, heavy gaffs aloft, but that was about all except for the masts themselves. Over the years, the gaffs gradually became shorter and shorter. Today, the gaff rig has all but been eliminated by the wide popularity of the Marconi sail, an invention of the twentieth century.

After the American Revolution, schooners became increasingly popular as legitimate com-

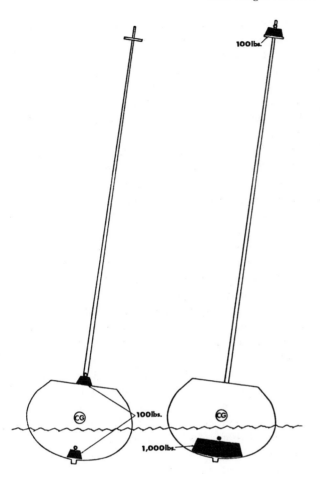

WEIGHT ALOFT REDUCES SPEED. Weight aloft indirectly cuts heavily into a boat's potential for speed, because weight aloft must have heavy ballast for counterbalance. In the cutaway end view at left, a deck weight of 100 pounds is counterbalanced by a mere 100 pounds of ballast because the weights are an equal distance from the vessel's center of gravity. In the drawing at right, the 100 pounds that was on deck has been moved high up into the rigging. Now a much heavier ballast weight is required as a counterbalance. If the 100 pounds is ten times as far from the center of gravity as the ballast, then ten times as much ballast, or 1,000 pounds, will be required because the weight aloft has ten times the leverage of the weight below. The 100 pounds on deck forces the ship designer to increase the all-up weight only 200 pounds, but the 100 pounds aloft forces an increase of 1,100 pounds. The added displacement and wetted surface slows the ship.

mercial vessels, particularly as coasters, fishing boats, pilot boats and Great Lakes boats. Fore-and-aft riggers, being more weatherly, are much more manageable in constricted waters, and they were labor savers. It takes only half a dozen men to sail a large schooner, whereas it takes four or five times that many to run a square-rigger. Fore-and-afters are run almost entirely from the deck. Square-riggers have to have dozens of men ready to scurry up into the rigging to trim sails every time the ship changes course or to furl or unfurl sail if the wind velocity changes.

The only trouble with fore-and-afters from a commercial sailing point of view is that they cannot be scaled up indefinitely. The sails become impractically large on masts of about one hundred feet or over. There have indeed been some very large boats rigged fore-and-aft. Masts of the America's Cup boats before World War II, for instance, were considerably more than one hundred feet, and all were fore-and-aft rigged, but these boats were backed by hundreds of thousands of dollars, a good part of it spent on maintaining crews that could handle such acreages of sail, and another good part of it spent on designing, building and maintaining spars and standing rigging that could withstand the pressures. Even so, those monstrosities had to high-tail it into port if the wind got anywhere above a fair breeze. They could not sail under all conditions of wind and sea without great risk of having their rigging either damaged or demolished.

Americans, until after World War I, put a lot of sail on their vessels. On schooners, the boom of the aftermost sail extended far past the stern rail, and the headsail invariably was on a stay that ran to a bowsprit, far overboard of the bow.

Clipper ships were the epitome of stacking canvas on square-riggers. In addition to spankers and a dozen or more studding sails and staysails, the last of the clippers carried square sails six high on three different masts.

The reason for the large sail plans on this side of the Atlantic is that Americans, from the beginning, have tended to design for average conditions of weather. Europeans, on the other hand, designed for extreme conditions, and their sail areas tended to be smaller. For runs to the

West Indies, the most common passage for American smugglers, the average conditions were light to moderate winds.

With all sails set, American schooners moved along well in light air and reached hull speed[1] in moderate wind. If the wind became stronger, sail had to be reduced, because the sails began developing power that the hulls couldn't handle. The excess power, which had no release through an increase in speed, was a threat. It made the boat less controllable and it threatened damage to the rigging.

Beginning about 1900, sailing craft began to appear that blew the hull-speed formula to pieces. Yachting in the late 1800s operated within the hull-speed formula, and some yachting circles today (most ocean racing and the America's Cup races, for instance) that are tied to heavy-displacement hulls must still operate within it. In these circles, the objective is faster acceleration to hull speed and designing rigs to reach hull speed in lighter and lighter air.

Reaching hull speed in light air is a two-part thing. The first part is power, which concerns the rigging, and the second part is resistance, which concerns the hull. In closed-course races, where marks must be rounded frequently, one might also add a third part, handiness, which concerns hardware for handling lines to set sails. This third part, though critical in closed courses, is of far less importance in ocean racing, where points of sailing are infrequently changed.

Increasing power of sail, up through World War I, was mostly a matter of figuring ways to put

up and to handle more and more sail. Before then, there were few dramatic improvements in rigging, except to make it bigger. However, there were two significant developments: the introduction of cotton sailcloth in the early 1800s, and the sewing of sails so that seams were parallel, rather than perpendicular, to the flow of the air.

Before 1800, linen was used as sailcloth. Linen has a lot of stretch, which doesn't matter much for square-riggers but is a definite aerodynamic disadvantage for fore-and-afters. Linen also "leaks" air through its loose weave, and that is a disadvantage to either type of rig.

Hand-woven cotton sails appeared in the first decade of the 1800s, but they were not widely accepted at first, partly because they were very expensive. During the war of 1812, ships of both the United States and England were still carrying linen sails. At that time, in light air, it was common practice to haul buckets of water aloft to dampen the linen, thereby shrinking the weave and cutting down on the leakage of air.

Cotton sails leaked less and held their shape far better than linen. Many privateers of the War of 1812 used cotton, and it was generally conceded that vessels with cotton sails, all else being equal, were faster.

By about 1830, the introduction of the power loom made cotton cheap enough so that it was competitive with linen; and the power loom also improved cotton as a sailcloth because the fibers could be woven much tighter than they ever were woven by hand. The tight weaving reduced the leakage almost to zero, and it also resulted in sails that would fairly well hold the shape to which they were sewn. This quality of cotton became especially important in the 1900s when the science of aerodynamics was applied to sail design.

Seaming sails horizontally, parallel with air flow, was the invention of Nathanael G. Herreshoff. The horizontal sewing increased power because it cut down the interruption in the flow of air across the sail.

The matter of resistance to reaching hull speed is a complicated subject, mainly because resistance is not the only factor a designer must

---

[1]The formula here is: $1.25 \times \sqrt{\text{LWL}} = $ hull speed. LWL is length on the waterline (in feet), and hull speed is the theoretical maximum in knots. According to the formula, a hull of 36 feet LWL can go no faster than 7.5 knots, a hull of 100 feet no faster than 12.5 knots. The formula is fairly accurate for old-time vessels today whose hulls are of the deep-displacement type. The formula was probably worked out, originally, from observation. The modern, scientific explanation has to do with the building up of the bow wave and the quarter wave. At or near the hull speed, according to the explanation, these two waves begin operating in tandem and cause a great hollow (and therefore suction) at the stern. In the final days of commercial sailing and the early days of yachting, hull speed was a very real limitation. On many types of boats today (scows, trimarans, catamarans, etc.), the formula is meaningless. In fact, the formula would have been meaningless to Polynesians of a thousand years ago. At that time, they were sailing catamarans far above "hull speed."

consider when laying down the lines of a hull. If it were, all hulls, below the waterline, would be approximately the shape of half a fish, cut lengthwise. Such a shape would have the least resistance to water.

However, in designing a sailing hull, the designer must consider steering, lateral resistance (the thing that keeps the hull from slipping sideways when power is not directly in line with the desired direction of travel—and that's most of the time, in a sailboat), righting moment (a factor involving the interrelation of the center of gravity and the center of buoyancy, which keeps the hull from turning onto its side), and the effect that waves have on everything else.

But for a moment, let us consider hull design only in regard to resistance. The terms we must use are *wetted surface* and *fluid flow.*

A solid object passing through water is hampered by friction, and the friction is between the water and the surface of the object. If the speed remained the same, and the object remained the same proportionate shape, but became larger, friction would increase as the area of the surface (wetted surface).

Now, suppose the object is a proposed boat hull—or, rather, the portion of the hull that is going to be below the waterline. Assume the displacement will be five tons. We are talking, of course, only about displacement hulls, which remain at a constant draft, and not about planing hulls. Into what shape can we mold the bottom to present the least amount of surface to the water around it? The answer is a sphere, completely submerged.

Of course, a sphere is an absurdity as a shape for a boat bottom, but one thing we know is that wetted surface will increase (though displacement remains constant) the more we depart from the shape of a sphere.

The nearest thing to a sphere that would be remotely practical as a configuration for a boat bottom is, perhaps, a hemisphere (flat side up). For least wetted surface, this would beat anything except something nearer to a sphere.

Fluid flow around a hemisphere is not smooth, however, so it is necessary to compromise wetted surface further to obtain a fluid-dynamic shape. This is simply a matter of drawing out the hemisphere into an oblong shape. The precise shape is not a subject within the scope of this essay, so let us just say that the shape would closely resemble the bottom half of a rainbow trout or a salmon, minus fins, tail and gills.

With the hypothetical displacement of five tons, the whole problem of fluid flow can be visualized as follows: every time the boat moves its own length, it must take apart and put back together five tons of water. The trick is to move this mass of water no more than is necessary, and the best way is to move it out at right angles to the path of the hull, and back in, also at right angles. In addition, the acceleration and deceleration of the mass along these right angles should be even. If one imagines a fish passing through water, and then thinks of the motion of the water only as motion at right angles to the fish's line of travel, it may help in visualizing the desired effect.

The idea of building ship bottoms to the general shape of fish goes back a long way. Drawings of designers five and six centuries ago occasionally have sketches of fish superimposed on sketches of hulls. Though designers today are not apt to put an overlay of a fish on their blueprints, their science of fluid dynamics leads them still to shapes approximating those of fish.

Up through the commercial sailing era, ship underbodies resembled the fish configuration, but with something extra added. The extra was a long, straight keel. Though hulls were rounded smoothly, fore and aft and up and down, the planking was also built down to this keel.

The long keel probably hurt fluid flow very little, but it did increase wetted surface considerably. Still, this modification of the fish configuration was necessary to reduce leeway. It increased lateral resistance.

The Americans, though they built long, thin hulls, still used the long keels. In the early 1800s, certain builders began putting in a protruding keel, a heavy board on edge that protruded below the planking all along the bottom of the hull. This was simply a matter of letting the keel-board stick out below the point of the lowest plank, and part of the keel thus became, in effect, a long fin that ran the length of the bottom. The schooner yacht *America* had such a fixture on her bottom. The obvious advantage is that a greater area of lateral resistance is afforded so that dead rise can be reduced and beam can be slightly increased. The extra beam would make the hull somewhat stiffer[2] and power would be increased, especially in working to weather.

Through the 1700s and early 1800s, keels were gradually shortened, lengthwise, and hull design began moving in the direction of what we now call "cutaway ends." In other words, they began moving more toward the fish shape.

This cutting away of ends reduces lateral resistance and therefore increases leeway, but this problem was solved for a lot of boats with the invention of the centerboard.

The centerboard came into common use in the United States in the first half of the nineteenth century, and it became practically standard equipment on all sloops and schooners operating in coastal waters, in rivers and on the Great Lakes. During the lumbering boom of the 1800s, nearly every sailing vessel in the Great Lakes was rigged with a centerboard, or drop keel, as it was called then.

The centerboard is simply a fin that can be lowered into the water, right through the bottom of the boat. Like centerboards on sailboats today, a cabinet was built up from the hole to a level higher than the waterline, but in the 1800s it was much more difficult to seal the base of these cabinets to the bottom of the hull than it is with today's methods. In the 1800's some of the centerboards went through a notch in a plank beside the keel.

The centerboard solves all problems of leeway, and the rest of an underbody can be molded without regard to it. The reason centerboarders became so popular on rivers and coastal waters is that the board, being retractable, enables the

[2]"Tenderness" and "stiffness" are opposites. A boat is said to be tender if it has little resistance to heeling. It is said to be stiff if it has great resistance to heeling. Hulls that are of wide beam are generally very stiff, while narrow hulls are generally tender, especially in low angles of heel, though if they are heavily ballasted they become progressively stiffer as the angle of heel is increased.

boat to operate in shallow waters. For a commercial vessel, the centerboard hull has another advantage in that there is a lot of lateral resistance even when the hull is empty and riding high.

Centerboards were apparently something new in the early 1800s, but the idea of a retractable fin was not. A century or two before, the Dutch began using leeboards, a pair of fins that swung up and down from pins at the rail, one on either side of the boat. These Dutch craft were flat bottomed and of shallow draft because they had to operate in shallow canals on the way out and the way back in from sea. When in deep water, the leeboards were lowered. They extended well below the bottom of the hull. Centerboards operate exactly the same way, except that they operate through a hole in the center of the hull.

Occasionally, even today, you see a sailing boat with leeboards. They are still quite common in the Netherlands, but for some reason they never caught on in other parts of the world. The most common application of leeboards in the United States today is on canoes. A canoe rigged with a sail will invariably have leeboards to provide lateral resistance.

The use of a fin (centerboard, leeboards or nonretractable fin) frees a designer to follow the fish form and lay out a hull with more consideration for fluid flow and wetted surface. Many sailboats of the 1880s and 1890s had underbodies that were basically fish shaped, but with fins protruding from or through the bottom. Such configurations are very popular today.

One thing that cannot be ignored in hull design, fin or no fin, is stability. We touched on this subject earlier in discussing weight distribution and the effect it had on the center of gravity. But center of gravity (CG) is only one of the factors of stability. The other factor is center of buoyancy (CB).

In any vessel, the CG is that point at which it is balanced in all directions. If the boat were floating in space and then someone spun it, in any direction, it would rotate around the CG. The CG never shifts within a boat unless weight is redistributed.

When a boat is in water, gravity pulls it

downward. If the weight of the boat is five tons, the gravity exerts a force of five tons, and one may view this force as being straight down along a vertical line that passes through the CG. Straight down means straight down with respect to the earth, *not* with respect to the boat. It matters not if the boat is heeled to one side or the other, or is down at the bow or the stern. Put the boat in any position you like—sixty degrees over or knocked flat or upside down—and the gravity is still pulling straight down through the CG.

Buoyancy, of course, is the counterforce to gravity. Buoyancy is water pressure pushing up on the hull, and if gravity is pulling the hull downward with a force of five tons, then buoyancy is pushing it upward with a force of five tons. All of the force of buoyancy may be viewed as operating on a central point within the hull, and this point is called the center of buoyancy. And all the force may be said to operate straight up along a vertical line through the CB—straight up with respect to the earth, *not* with respect to the boat.

Now, if you take a boat that is sitting perfectly still on a day without wind and in water without waves, the boat will be sitting upright and the vertical lines through the CG and the CB will be one and the same. Suppose you could take the mast in your fingers and tip it to one side, then let it go. The boat would rock a few times, but it would soon settle back to an upright position.

What has happened is that you have moved the center of buoyancy to the side to which you tipped the boat. But the center of gravity remained in the same place. The CB had moved away from the CG. And when you let go the mast, the force acting through the CB pushed the low side up, working against the CG, which pushed the high side down. When the boat had settled back to an upright position, the CG and the CB had realigned themselves.

We have established that the CB moves within the hull, while the CG does not. Is there any way of expressing the nature of the CB's movement? Yes. The center of buoyancy is always at the volumetric center of the displacement of the hull.

Take the boat from the example above, put it in any position you like and then imagine that the water freezes. Pull the boat out and there will be a hole in the ice where the hull was. This hole is the displacement of the hull, and the center of the volume of this hole is the CB for that position of the boat. Obviously, the shape of the hole will change for every angle of the hull; therefore the CB moves with every change of angle of the hull.

Of course, there is an exception to all this: a hull with a perfectly round bottom. With such a bottom, the shape of the hole would always be the same, regardless of the position of the hull, and of course the CB would not move. That is why round-bottom boats are unstable—a canoe, for instance. Canoe bottoms are not perfectly rounded, but they come fairly close.

A rowboat, on the other hand, with a wide, flat bottom and sharp, angular bilges to near-vertical sides, tends to be very stiff. Tip a rowboat even slightly to one side and the sharp bilge moves down into the water as the bilge on the other comes to the surface. The CB moves instantly well over to the low side, creating tremendous righting arm.[3]

For such stability, the penalty is, of course, resistance and therefore decreased speed. A rowboat-type hull has several times the wetted surface and a much less smooth fluid flow than a canoe of approximately the same capacity.

It may appear from these two extreme examples—rowboat versus canoe—that one cannot have it both ways, that low resistance and high stability are incompatible. This is somewhat true, but a lot of things have happened, many of them in the last hundred years, to bring stability and low resistance together in the same vessel.

One thing that improves stability, as we have already mentioned, is getting weight down low, or in other words, lowering the CG. As was men-

[3]Righting arm is the horizontal distance between the CB and the CG. If the force of buoyancy is five tons, then righting moment is five foot-tons if the centers are one foot apart horizontally, ten foot-tons if the centers are two feet apart and so on. In other words, righting moment is the product of the force of buoyancy (a constant) and the length of the righting arm (a variable). When the boat is upright, there is no righting moment because the centers are vertically aligned and the variable is zero.

tioned earlier, square-riggers had the problem of heavy rigging, requiring heavy ballasting as a counterweight, which increased displacement and therefore increased wetted surface.

The French, in years gone by, were always fond of designs with low centers of gravity. During their centuries of war with England, they occasionally captured an English warship, and, of course, the English captured some of theirs. When either side captured a ship, it usually put the vessel into service in its own navy.

Along toward the last of the rivalry, the English ships were very heavily armed. They often had three and sometimes four decks, all bristling with heavy cannon. When the French got hold of one of these vessels, they very often altered it to make its center of gravity lower. Upon capturing a three- or four-deck vessel, they would run it into a shipyard, remove the guns from the upper deck and then cut the whole ship down by one deck before putting it back into service. The French were quite willing to sacrifice some firepower to gain stiffness, speed and maneuverability.

On smaller vessels, the Americans went a long way in bringing down centers of gravity with their fore-and-aft rigs and low-profile hulls.

The biggest breakthrough in stability, however, was the introduction of outside ballasting and its eventual evolution to the uncapsizable hull.

Earlier in this essay we explained that it takes one hundred pounds ten feet below the CG to counter one hundred pounds ten feet above the CG, and one thousand pounds ten feet below the CG to counter one hundred pounds at one hundred feet above the CG, and so on. In that discussion, it was assumed that ten feet was the very bottom of the bilge and that ballast could be placed no farther below the CG than that.

But suppose you weighed all of this ballast and then had a foundry cast that weight in iron or lead to a shape that could be bolted along the bottom of the keel, *outside* the hull. Assume that the gain in depth of the ballast is two feet. Then the ballast would have twelve feet of leverage, rather than ten, and the boat would either become more stable or the amount (weight) of the

ballast could be reduced by $1/5$. Because just as the weight of a yardarm has more effect as it is raised farther and farther aloft, the weight of ballast has more effect as it is placed farther and farther down.

The English were the first to put outside ballast on ships. Two schooners were built for the Admiralty in 1796 with short sections of pig iron bolted along their keels. The schooners were designed by Samuel Bentham, and in addition to the innovation in ballast, they also had other new features, such as iron windlasses and winches and geared steering.

Neither vessel was particularly successful, and outside ballasting never caught on in commercial or naval warships. The gears and the winches caught on, however, and such devices regularly replaced rope-tackle steering mechanisms and capstans on sailing ships built afterward.

Deep ballasting did catch on in yachting, and it was designed into many yachts, both large and small, along toward the end of the nineteenth century. It first appeared on the America's Cup defenders in designs by Edward Burgess, the Boston designer of the 1880s. From deeper and deeper ballasting, the uncapsizable hull evolved.

The whole trick to building a sailboat that is uncapsizable is to get the center of gravity below the center of buoyancy. Recall for an instant the discussion of the rowboat (flat-bottom) and the way the center of buoyancy moves to the low side when the boat is heeled. Now suppose that there is an iron fin running three feet deep beneath the keel of this rowboat and that there is a heavy weight welded to the very bottom of this fin. Further suppose that this weight is heavy enough so that the CG of the total boat is two feet under the water. Where does the CG go when the boat is heeled?

As we have said before, it stays in the same place, with respect to the boat. But with respect to the vertical of the earth, it moves over beneath the high side of the boat. In other words, the CG and the center of buoyancy move in opposite directions. And the greater the angle of heel, the farther the CB and CG move apart, creating even

One of the world's fastest boats, the powerful catamaran Kriter III, *cuts through the sea.*

more leverage to pull the hull back upright. Even if the boat were upside down, with the CG perfectly aligned over the CB, the very slightest nudge to misalign the two centers would cause the boat instantly to flop back upright. (For the sake of this example, think of the rowboat as completely decked and with all hatches closed.)

Of course, a rowboat-type hull with a weighted keel would be tremendously stiff. Because the horizontal distance between the CG and the CB would build up so fast, the slightest angle of heel would give the two opposing forces tremendous leverage to right the boat.

Now let us go to the other extreme by taking the weighted iron fin off the rowboat-type hull and putting it on a canoe-type hull (also a hypothetical decked vessel). The canoe would then be uncapsizable, just like the rowboat, but the canoe, instead of being stiff, would be very tender. In other words, it would have little righting moment at low angles of heel, but the righting force would build up as the angle of heel increased.

The reason for the tenderness is that on round bottoms, the center of buoyancy moves very little toward the low side. The lever arm between CB and CG, in the case of the canoe, is increased mostly by the moving of the CG toward the high side. At low angles of heel, this distance is not building up very fast. At steep angles of heel, a powerful righting moment builds because the two centers are far apart.

Modern keel yachts are generally somewhere between the two extremes, neither hard bilges (as the rowboat type) nor uniformly rounded bilges. Hot racing boats generally have higher initial stability, so that they will sail more nearly upright (and therefore develop more power in the sails). Cruising sailboats, on the other hand, will generally be more tender, so that the rolling motion in seas will be less jerky. With less stiffness, the boat will not be quite as fast as it might have been, but it will be much more comfortable.

The Aerodynamics of Sails: Nature as a Guide

by DR. MANFRED CURRY

Dr. Manfred Curry, a German scientist and dinghy sailor, wrote a book called Yacht Racing: The Aerodynamics of Sails *that, when it was published in 1925, proved prophetic. Curry was the first to discover how and why sails really work and he foretold the superiority of wing sails to soft sails, the superior form of the high aspect ratio sails, and also defined the slot effect between the jib and mainsail. Here is his classic statement on using nature as a guide.*

IF we observe the great difference of type in our modern sails, if we listen to the varied opinions on their efficacy, we cannot escape the conclusion that our technical knowledge is too limited to permit one to speak with absolute authority as to the correct and best form of racing sail. When one sees that the same boat, under similar conditions, sometimes sails better than at other times, one comes gradually to the conclusion that, inasmuch as the hull has not changed, the set and form or cut of the sail must be more or less decisive in determining its efficiency. As only *one* form of sail can be correct and not, as is so often held, a different form of sail for every type of boat, we must deal first and foremost with this vital problem. In the following, I am adhering to the process of thought developed, step by step, in my observations and experiments on this important subject.

As a starting point, nature should give us an indication in which direction we should undertake our researches, uninfluenced by current opinions or theories. It is astonishing that it has not been recognized that the sail is, and should be, precisely nothing more nor less than a great *bird's wing,* which moves the slender hull through the water. If we are persuaded that the sail should correspond to the wing of a bird, and that the requisites for both are the same, it behooves us to study this natural sail in all its intrinsic details.

But first we shall ask ourselves, To what extent can we speak of a likeness or similarity in the process of operation of a sail and those of a wing? To answer this question, we shall compare the soaring bird and the sailing boat. Both move at a given angle to the wind by means of a certain power, the force called into action by the pressure of the wind, whereby only that component force that acts at right angles to the surface comes into consideration. The other component force parallel to and along the surface in the opposite direction to propagation acts as a retarding factor in the form of surface and form friction and must be overcome. As nature has endowed the bird with wings of such favorable

The twelve-meter yachts **Freedom** *and* **Enterprise,** *practicing off Newport, R.I., illustrate Manfred Curry's prophetic observation that "the sail is precisely nothing more nor less than a great bird's wing, which moves the slender hull through the water."*

form that a large pressure is created, called the "up drive," which enables the bird to hold itself in the air, we must by constructive means, through the form and cut of the sail, endeavor to attain a maximum pressure and at the same time a minimum retarding action or component. The pressure or component force at right angles to the sail can again be resolved into two components, one of which is directed forward—the other component acts at right angles to the lateral plane of the boat. How far we may follow the construction of a bird's wing in making a sail, the closer observation of the wing and of its operation will reveal.

It would be a mistake to try to deduce any principles alone from the airplane or even birds in flight without a previous study of the bird's wing, because not only would one fail to recognize readily the peculiarities which cannot be utilized for a sail, but also one would fall into the same error that led airplane constructors to depend on large motors instead of improved wing design. Much more instructive is the observation of soaring flight, which has, from the very beginning, followed new paths of research in the development of airplane surfaces.

It may also be interesting to study the peculiarities of the free flight of gliders, though this may not be absolutely necessary. The flying of gliders has developed into a sport, and planes have been built which fly for several hours—*without motors.*

We shall first treat of the flight of birds and observe nature in her minute accuracy. When we observe the various good flyers among birds, we should not commit the error of including the "air acrobats," such as swallows; rather should we direct our observations to those species that conquer the atmosphere by soaring and achieve a great "up drive" without a stroke of the wings. To these belong the albatross, the gull and the buzzard. How is it possible, we may ask, for them to soar freely in the air—one over land, one over sea, the gull over land and sea; to play with the third dimension without a stroke of the wing? The secret, so long concealed, lies in the wind, which, though it may have only a small velocity near the earth's surface, almost always increases

in velocity at greater heights. Another factor is the direction of the wind and—last but not least —the extremely favorable form of the wing, which enables these birds to perform such feats.

Let us state briefly here the physical laws by which the action of the wind on a plane surface is governed and upon which in part the flight of man, on sea and in the air, depends:

1. Whether a plane is moved against the air or whether the air, in the form of wind, blows against the plane, the effect is the same. The requisite air pressure or density, which renders it possible for a bird or airplane to float or soar freely in the air, is not obtained until the wing is struck by air that has attained a certain (high) speed. This speed, at which the air becomes dense enough to float the bird or plane, can be attained in two ways. Either the plane moves against the air or the air moves against the plane —the result being the same in either case according to the above principle of relativity. To the former category belong gliding flight as, for instance, the gliding of a bird from the top of a tree to the ground, whereby height, which is essential here, is sacrificed—conversion of potential into kinetic energy; and also the ascent of an airplane, the speed of which is accelerated by the propeller until it is borne up by its planes, whereby no initial height need be sacrificed. The work done by the motor is transformed into work against the air, which is in turn imparted to the wings or planes and makes ascent possible. To the second category belongs the bird or glider sailing or soaring against the wind.

2. The pressure or resistance increases as the square of the velocity and directly as the area of the surface; for flat surfaces according to the formula:

$$A = 0.13 \cdot F \cdot v^2 \cdot \sin a.$$

That is, a plane surface of one square meter, which, moved at uniform speed in a direction at right angles to its surface, covers in one second a distance of one meter, will develop a resistance of approximately .13 kilogram. By this formula, we can calculate the resistance A of the air against a surface of F square meters area that is inclined at an angle of opposition *a** to its direction of propagation and is moved at a uniform speed of v meters per second against the air.

A second favorable factor for flight is that the wind has not, as is commonly supposed, an exactly horizontal direction, but blows at an angle of about four degrees upward.

Finally, the bird is aided by the peculiar action or operation of its wings, a factor of greatest moment in our ensuing investigations.

If we observe gulls against the sun, as they soar along easily over the water, the shadows in their wings show that these are being continually pulled and turned. They are evidently seeking by this means to catch and utilize every puff of wind in its constantly varying direction. And we also observe that birds, under ordinary circumstances, fly upward never *with* the wind, but always *against* it.

We observe that there is considerable difference in the length of these wings. The longer the wing, the better soarer is the bird. To the albatross, for example, nature has given remarkably long, narrow wings—up to a span of nearly ten feet—which, in spite of their small area, have to bear up a comparatively large body, often without any movement of the wings and on the lightest breeze. In spite of the hindrance such long wings may be to the bird in its nest or when they are folded on the body, nature provides them. She might even make them longer, if a longer lever arm were feasible. At all events, she appears to lay special stress on a large proportion of length to breadth.

Then there is the thickness of the fore edge of the wing, which entirely contradicts all earlier views on air resistance; to this we shall return in our later observations.

All wings have a certain degree of *arching*—slight in those of swift-flying birds, greater in those of our slow flyers, which fact should surely demand our further consideration and careful

*I prefer the nomenclature "angle of opposition" to that used in the technique of flying "angle of incidence," as the latter is employed in physics—in the theory of light—to denote the angle, which the direction of the ray makes with the normal to the surface.

study. And not only birds show an arching in their wings; in the vegetable kingdom also there are to be found winged seeds, such as *Zanonia* seeds, whose wings are arched, that they may sail off on the wind.

After these general observations, let us turn to some phenomena, seldom observed by sailors, which should illustrate what has just been mentioned and are investigated in part in the treatise "Vogelflug" ("Bird Flight") by Lilienthal, one of the first pioneers in this field.

The striking thing about these phenomena is the greater lifting power of an arched or vaulted surface in comparison to that of a plane surface of the same area. Let us recall a few examples from everyday life which certainly everybody has noticed but on which few have expended much thought.

An umbrella held horizontally, that is, with its stock upright, will, even in horizontal motion, exercise an upward pull.

The family wash flapping in the wind is lifted, in consequence of its involuntary vaulting or arching, above the horizontal. An accustomed sight to the sailor, so natural that it remains unobserved, is the flapping sail.

Flapping is due to the action of a force that is called forth by the arched surface. The belly of the sail is pulled by this force in the direction of its arching, which manifests itself in a lateral motion. As it is blown out beyond its natural limit, not only the belly but the whole sail is pulled over to the other side, whereupon the same process is repeated. This alternate play, which occurs with great rapidity, gives us the flapping sail. But let it be noted that the shaking of the leech of a drawing sail has another cause, to be discussed later.

A last example: a spoon passed through a cup of coffee or a spoon oar dragged through the water in the direction at right angles to its arching tends to evade the path prescribed and to turn off in the direction of its arching without offering greater direct resistance to the motion imparted.

The accompanying drawings, wherein the forces acting on plane and arched surfaces are represented graphically, give us an explanation

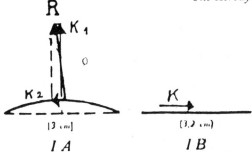

Forces acting on arched and plane Surface.

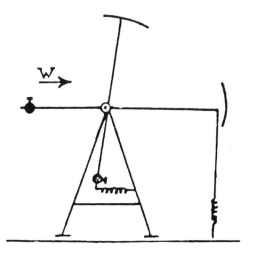

tendency* *against* the wind—in the direction of flight. It can be resolved into two components, a vertical one K_1 and a horizontal one K_2, the latter directed forward—against the wind; this horizontal component acts in the opposite direction both to the front or form and to the friction resistance and can neutralize both. Hence, a properly arched surface will, in a sufficiently strong wind, both rise and, on the assumption that it is correctly balanced, move forward *against* the wind, as is confirmed by the flight of birds. This forward movement is favored by the upward direction of the wind, if not caused by it—see footnote.

This advantage of arching becomes more pronounced when the wind hits the plane at an angle from below or when the plane is moved against the wind in an inclined position. The arched surface develops more than double the force of the plane surface in this position.

Now we come to the question as to how much the plane should be arched. To determine the arching which a bird's wing has in the act of soaring in the wind, one loads its hollow surface with sand until the weight equals half that of the bird. This done, the wing, which naturally must be fresh and untreated, regains the form—a slightly enlarged arching, which it has in the air. The measurement of the wing arching of good flyers shows an average depth of curvature of $\frac{1}{15}$, that is $\frac{1}{15}$ of the breadth of the wing at the point of deepest arching; of less rapid flyers $\frac{1}{10}$ to $\frac{1}{12}$. To make the matter clearer, experience with kites may be recalled. A kite with a flatly stretched surface rises notably badly; also the cord to which it is attached makes an angle with the ground of much less than ninety degrees. On the other hand, a kite with a loose, bellying surface reaches a much greater height, and its cord forms an angle of almost ninety degrees with the ground, the kite soaring approximately perpendicularly overhead. In favorable cases, the cord may be observed to cross this perpendicular, which means that the kite is then soaring against the wind at a speed greater than the velocity of

for these phenomena. The first measurements on surfaces were made by O. Lilienthal with the primitive apparatus shown in the sketch below.

The parallelogram of forces for the arched surface will certainly be a surprise to the layman. On the plane surface held in a horizontal position appears a force K acting in the direction of the wind which tends to move the plane in that direction. It is the resultant or sum of two retarding or obstructive forces that act in one and the same direction. The one is called the form or front resistance, which is called forth by the form of the surface, that is, by the volume of air displaced by it; the other the friction, surface or skin resistance, which is caused by the friction of the air particles that adhere to the sides of the surface.

On the other hand, for the arched surface the resultant force R is directed *upward*, with a

*This is a moot point, the most recent view being that the forward tendency of this force is due to the upward trend of the wind—of four degrees near the surface of the earth.

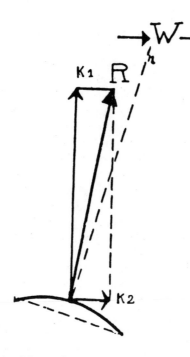

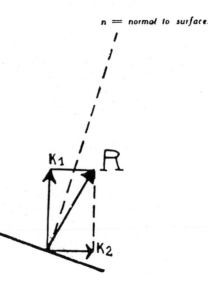

n = normal to surface.

the wind itself. As the pull of the cord gives us an idea of the magnitude of the force developed by the kite, its inclination determines the *direction* of that force.

The following further experiment with kites is of special interest: let two kites rise, one having a loose covering, which will be blown out by the wind into an *arched* surface, the other a *stiff arched* surface. To our surprise, the latter will soar considerably higher and more perpendicularly than the former; that is, it will exert a greater pull. A comparison here with the boat's sail is of great importance, for thereby it is confirmed that the stiffening of the sail with battens is fully justified.

In experiments of recent date, the flow of the air is made visible by filling it with smoke, but the flow may even be seen in dusty air exposed to the rays of the sun; the surface is then moved through the air and the flow with its various eddies is recorded photographically.

In the upper drawing, we observe that the lines of flow or the air paths (and by air paths we understand the paths of its single particles) are broken and torn asunder by the plane and that eddies are formed. An eddy has motion, that is, kinetic energy, which is developed at the cost of another source of energy. Consequently, every eddy, whether in the air or water, means loss of energy to the moving plane.

It is different in the case of arched surfaces; here the lines of flow are not *torn* but *bent;* this is equivalent to a gain of energy: a downward acceleration is imparted to the surface by the air, that is, the surface itself is lifted or forced upward to a greater degree. In the case of a plane surface, this lifting tendency is more or less paralyzed by the formation of eddies with their capricious effect—arbitrary rotation. The process of eddy formation is the same in water, and, truly, this is the principal reason why the sharp-cornered form of the boat's hull has been abandoned for the rounded one in most of our racing types.

The next important factor is the *relation of length to breadth* in the wing. The following experiment should give us an idea of the influence of this relation on the carrying power—the attain-

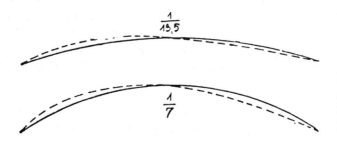

ment of high pressure: a rectangular plane, whether flat or arched, does by no means behave similarly when placed at the same angle of inclination lengthwise or sidewise to the wind. It develops a higher pressure, when its longer edge is cutting the wind—at one and the same angle of inclination. Moreover, a peculiar humming is distinctly audible from plane 1, which is nothing else than the noise produced by the eddies formed on the edge facing the wind, a phenomenon that is less pronounced on plane 2. Larger eddies, which contain more energy, that is, revolve faster, arise in the former position of the plane. This means that more energy is lost than when the rectangle is held lengthwise to the wind, where, it is true, many eddies form, but

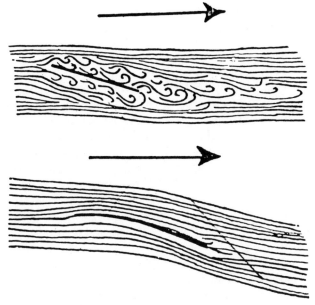

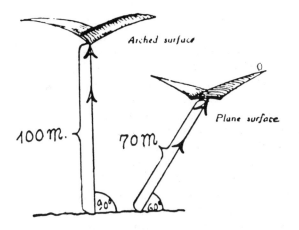

these are of both smaller and weaker structure.

With regard to the general form of birds' wings, we can discern the presence, in most of them, of small "taking-off" points on their rear edge. These "taking-off" points are the tips of the feathers, beginning, where their rigid portions terminate, by means of which the wings when spread fanlike are stiffened. It is conceivable that these points possess a property similar to that exhibited by such points in the flow or discharge of electricity. The jagged or indented form resulting from these "taking-off" points is characteristic of the wings of all birds and is not alone confined to the rear contour of the wing but also to be traced in the feathers that project laterally. This peculiarity of structure is also observable in the wings of many butterflies, bats

and flying squirrels, as also in the fins of fish. It is quite possible that the object of these indentations lies in the formation of small, weak eddies instead of the larger, stronger ones, which would otherwise appear on the rear edge of every wing.

Perhaps it is not superfluous to note here a further observation I have made. All birds have little downy feathers on the underside of the wing near the fore edge, that is, just in front of the point or line of its largest curvature. When one blows on the underside of the wing from the rear, these feathers erect themselves. Experiments on models constructed similarly to the wing of a bird, with the greatest curvature in the fore third of the surface, have shown that, when these models are inclined at certain angles to the wind, a large eddy is formed under the fore edge, which in the technique of flying has been given the name of the "ram" or "Aries" eddy. This eddy revolves at its greatest distance from the surface in the direction of the wind, then turns up toward the arched surface and finally passes along it in the opposite direction—that of flight. The flow of the eddy along the surface—in the direction of flight—would, therefore, be obstructed more or less by the downy feathers just mentioned that consequently tend to erect themselves against that current; or, in other words, the bird is facilitated in its flight by this forward-driving force thus imparted to its wings.

To ascertain the action of this eddy, I have held various wings horizontally in a wind current, employing the so-called blizzard which barbers use for drying the hair. It appears that, in a weak current, the feathers, which are arranged in the form of a large "pocket" on the underside of the wing just behind its fore edge, begin to tremble; in a stronger current, they erect themselves at an angle of about forty-five degrees to the current. This pocket may even be observed on large birds in flight, it being especially noticeable on gulls as they follow in the wake of a ship, soaring for minutes without a stroke of the wing. The opening of the feather pocket is aided by the anatomical structure of the fore edge of the wing and by these downy feathers projecting from its skin; if this sinewy skin is hit lightly, the pocket opens automatically. The pressure of the wind, which is brought to bear on the wing of a soaring

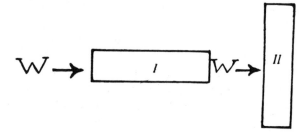

bird, acts on this sinew and thus might tend to open the pocket.

If we peel off the skin on the fore edge of the wing with a knife, we discover two muscles; the one stretches the skin, thus closing the pocket; the other contracts it, thus releasing the tension and opening the pocket.

The proof of a forward air current along the wing was established by Gustav Lilienthal in 1913. He fastened little bannerets onto the underside of birdlike planes, which he caused to fly in a circle. The experiment confirmed that the current of air flowed not at all points along the surface from the front to the rear as one might

suppose, but, even at a considerable distance from the fore edge, from the rear toward the front. Lilienthal was of the opinion that this current of air is utilized as a forward-driving force by the bird. Furthermore, he established the fact that this eddy does not become pronounced till a speed of five meters per second is reached, which is the average minimum speed of birds.

To summarize, my experiments have confirmed that not only do the separate feathers erect themselves, but there is often a regular "pocket" exactly where the principal eddy strikes the wing; further, that this pocket is opened partly by the air current flowing forward along the surface near the fore edge of the wing and partly by the anatomical structure both of pocket and fore edge of wing.

Now the greater the arch of the wing and the smaller the angle of opposition, the larger the eddy produced and the farther back it strikes the wing. Accordingly, the pocket on wings of greater arch is farther back from the fore edge than it is on wings of smaller arch. Nature, in fact, operates so exactly, that in one and the same wing she gives the pocket such a form, that it is developed to the greatest degree and placed farthest back at the point of deepest arching, gradually decreasing in size and approaching the fore edge of the wing as we proceed from the body toward its flatter outer end.

Before I draw from all these considerations those conclusions, which have a bearing on the form of a sail, or attempt to confirm their correctness from the knowledge we possess of the most effective forms of sails, I desire to state briefly the various characteristics of birds' wings, airplanes and boat sails. Why one may not adhere *strictly* to the form of a bird's wing, so well planned by nature, will be discussed later.

In the first place, the wing, even that of the best soarers among birds, is intended not only for soaring, but also for the stroke of the wing, for which the motion of the tip of the wing is more rapid than its portion nearer the body, and thus the pressure of the air that is brought to bear on its various parts differ. In order to protect the wing from breaking and also that it may adhere to the body when not in use—when the bird is in its nest—nature has invested it with great elasticity.

It is not only the whiplike elasticity of the whole wing but also the give of its rear outer portion when pressure is brought to bear on it, which has led to the false conception that is still stubbornly maintained in most yachting circles, namely, that the upper part of the sail should swing out, that is, that the give of the gaff or of the top of a Marconi mast is a favorable factor. This is a gross error, which has only persisted because few sailors have taken the pains to look into the matter, thinking it simpler to accept the old, though unproved point of view. We only need to wave a fan or a piece of paper through the air, first with the outer edge giving way to the pressure of the air and then with the edge stiffened so that it cannot give, and we notice at once that the stiff surface offers a greater resistance than the supple one does. Experiments in the wind tunnel have supported this theory.

In the case of the bird, the tip of the wing bends upwards on the downward stroke, in order to avoid too great a *strain* on its weakest part and to spare the muscles *expenditure of energy*—necessary in consequence of its long lever arm. Further, however, we must realize that the tip of the wing gives *only on the downward stroke* and that in soaring it always retains its normal form.

The wing of a bird is necessarily of light structure; for nature to make it stiff and unbending would be, aside from the above considerations, most difficult. But this need not be so with the sail; by means of stays and battens the essential stiffness or rigidity may be achieved without any material increase in weight, which in the case of a boat is of little moment.

The conclusion is that to win *increased power*, the sail should be constructed rigidly, so as to prevent any sagging or giving of its upper and rear portions.

Finally, we should not attempt to follow those lines which insure the birds longitudinal and lateral stability and play important roles for the bird, but not for the boat. For example, the fore edge of the bird's wing is inclined more and more backward toward its tip, which appears to have led yacht designers, especially the Swedes,

to give the mast a considerable rake aft. This backward inclination of the wing has the single purpose of insuring the bird the necessary longitudinal stability. It is marked with swallows, which have a special claim on it on account of their acrobatic air stunts. The give of the tip of the wing answers the same purpose. Airplanes rigged with such wings proved especially stable, but they lacked the greater carrying capacity.

It is also surprising that arching has an unfavorable influence on stability; wherefore airplane builders are accustomed to avoid extreme arching. This might suggest that the sail could be cut with a somewhat larger belly.

In other respects the sail should correspond to nature.

To the limit consistent with stability, the relation of length to breadth shown in bird's wings should be followed in designing sails. As yet this limit is far from having been reached, for the center of gravity even of our Marconi sails lies, with few exceptions, not much higher than that of gaff-rigged sails.

A thick opposing surface to the wind is not harmful. Therefore a thick mast may be used, if by some means the transition from mast to sail can be effected in the form of a *uniform* curve.

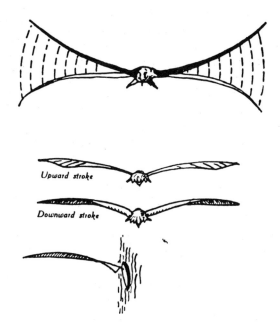

Upward stroke

Downward stroke

The modern device of inserting battens in a sail and letting them project slightly aft—out of the pockets—reminds one of the "taking-off" points of the bird's wing, and they may possess a small advantage.

The *S*-shaped contour of the fore edge of the wing, from the point where the wing projects from the body, deserves notice and is evidently to be accounted for by its junction with the body and the action of the muscles. More important is the fact that the wing presents a remarkably smooth surface to the wind, over which it can glide with minimum friction. The advantage gained in stiffening the sail by inserting as many battens as possible is confirmed empirically, especially on the wind.

Finally, it may interest the yachtsman to know that there are sea animals that actually sail, a species of jellyfish (*Siphonophora*). Although they are old Phoenicians compared to our luxurious yachts, it is amusing to observe how they can tack and jib, reciprocally blanket one another, and one may even imagine a regatta. I had an opportunity to watch these animals, which sail the Mediterranean to the number of millions, off the Italian and African coasts, day after day, and to study their manner of life.

When we observe the animal closely, we can imagine that we have a little model boat before us. Its body can be compared best to that of the scow. Of a finger's length, the flat body, which lies almost entirely on the water, is rounded off evenly fore and aft. Under the water, the animal possesses a number of feelers, which are used to capture food as well as to steer, and even, when held lengthwise, to serve as centerboards. The sail consists of a transparent, arched membrane, which crosses the body diagonally and, in tacking, arches itself in the direction of the wind—to leeward.

These little fairy sailors, with their bluish, shimmering wings, proceed in great squadrons over the endless surface of the water. In the wake of one another, abreast one another, mutually blanketing one another, these miniature navigators beat against the wind in long tacks. And when in their midst one looks at them from a skiff, one might imagine oneself a judge in a small-boat regatta; an uncommonly amusing sight! Only that, in a storm, no judges' boat comes to the rescue of the overturned, and the poor helpless creatures soon lie keel up, blowing hither and thither on the water—dead. These animals know what fate awaits them, and they avoid sea paths dangerous to them, often fleeing to the shelter of islands, where one may find hundreds collected behind protecting rocks, some with flapping sails, apparently anchored, others maneuvering desperately in order to remain protected from wind and wave. If they do not succeed and are caught by a wave and overturned or driven ashore, then boat and rigging are lost, and they dry up in a few minutes on the hot strand.

On Sails

by TED HOOD

Ted Hood is one of the dominant influences on the sport of sailing because he is the complete sailor. The head of Hood Enterprises based in Marblehead, Massachusetts, he not only is one of the world's foremost sailmakers but also makes sailcloth, builds spars and designs hulls and rigs. Then he takes the helm of his own boat, the latest in a series with the name of Robin, *and wins races. In 1974, he won the Southern Ocean Racing Conference and later that year skippered* Courageous *to a successful defense of the America's Cup. His discussion "On Sails," taken from* Racing With Cornelius Shields and the Masters, *is a classic explanation of sail trim as well as how to win races.*

BEFORE I begin this discussion of sail trim, among other things, I would like to make one specific note on articles in sailing books. If the authors of the books, and I mean all of them, could remember all of the things they have written while they are out racing, they would all do very well. Racing is always doing the fewest wrong things and most of the right things, rather than doing anything perfectly.

Sailing will continue to be more of an art than a science, no matter how many technical advances are made in sailcloth, hull construction or rigging. The proper setting and trimming of sails will also be one of the most important aspects of this art.

A mainsail serves two purposes. It provides lift when you are sailing to windward and it provides drag when sailing off the wind.

The main lifts like a kite as you beat to windward. The air passes over the sail to create areas of differing pressure: higher pressure on the windward side and lower pressure on the leeward side of the sail. The lift is transferred to the hull and the boat moves forward. The proper shape of the sail, along with the velocity of the wind and the sea conditions, determines the speed of the boat.

Sailing downwind, the main is no longer important for providing lift, as the force that drives the boat is the drag of the sails in the wind. The main stops the flow of the wind and the boat moves forward, so the area of the main is most important downwind. Its shape is far less important, except when reaching off the wind, when a full draft is helpful.

One of the most important steps in sail control is attaching the sail to the spars. The main is fastened along the mast and the boom and attached at the tack, clew and head. The tack should be attached so that the foot of the main lies parallel to the boom. After the sail is hoisted, look for wrinkles radiating from the tack. If you

Ted Hood, sailmaker, yacht designer and successful ocean racing skipper, defended the America's Cup with **Courageous** *in 1974.*

use a flexible fiberglass batten in the top pocket, since it is the most sensitive. The thin or most flexible end of the batten should always head forward in the pocket.

The mainsheet, vang, outhaul, traveler, Cunningham and leech lines are all used to control the shape and position of the main. The line should be trimmed so that it presents a smooth, efficient contour without wrinkles or hard, flat spots.

The draft of the main is important for power. The following are a few general guidelines which, while good points to begin with, are not meant as definitive statements on trim for maximum performance under all possible conditions.

In light winds, from zero to ten knots, the main should be full and baggy. The draft should be deep and about 50 percent back from the luff. Tighten the leech line a bit and slack the Cunningham and outhaul to obtain the desired draft. Going to windward, the boom should be on the centerline of the boat, with the sheet eased and the traveler to windward. Of course, this varies with the rig and aspect position (length of the boom). Off the wind, use the vang only to steady the boom but don't tighten it so much that it flattens the sail and overtrims the top of the main.

In moderate winds, from ten to eighteen knots, the main still should be fairly full with the draft relatively deep and about 45 percent back from the luff going to windward. Put firm tension on the Cunningham and outhaul. Tighten the leech line only enough to stop the flutter between the battens. Zip in or tie in the reef along the foot of the sail if a flatter sail is desired. The boom should be just to leeward of the centerline with the sheet taut; ease the traveler to leeward to ease weather helm or to tighten a sloppy leech.

Heading off the wind, the sail should be bagged out by easing on the outhaul, Cunningham and leech lines. Let out the foot zipper or flattening reef. Strap the vang down only enough to take the twist out of the leech. Too much tension on the vang only flattens the sail, which is quite undesirable.

Heavy air, over eighteen knots, requires sev-

see them, the tack is too tight and must be raised. The clew also should be attached so that the sail is parallel to the boom. If wrinkles appear at the clew after hoisting, raise the clew also, but use strong fittings as the clew is under great strain. The headboard should lie snugly against the mast. It should not fall away from the spar or jam tightly against the track. In either of these cases, wrinkles will reach into the sail much like those from the clew or tack. If the headboard falls away from the mast, add an extra slide near the top of the headboard or to the halyard. If it is too tight, rework the masthead so the halyard has a fair lead. The leech line should be led forward along the boom through several sail slide grommets and tied on itself with a rolling hitch, where it can be adjusted even when the boom is outboard.

The battens also are important, as they support the roach and help to shape the sail. Always eral major changes. The main should be flattened and the draft reduced by one-half to three-quarters and adjusted to keep the draft from moving aft. Tighten the Cunningham and outhaul completely. Tighten the leech line only enough to stop the flutter between the batten pockets. The boom may have to be well to leeward with the mainsheet strapped in tightly. The sail may even have to be luffed in puffs to ease the helm. If the wind really builds, the sail may have to be reefed to balance the helm and keep the boat on its feet.

Off the wind in heavy air still requires easing the Cunningham and outhaul, and using only enough vang to keep the extreme twist out of the leech. The reefs, if any, should also be taken out.

There are three basic rules to keep in mind. First, as the wind increases, the draft of the mainsail is pushed aft and your controls must adjust for this. Second, going to windward, the main should be flattened and the draft prevented from moving aft as the wind increases. Third, when off the wind the main should be bagged and made as full as possible.

Tension along the luff, foot and leech of the mainsail controls its shape and draft. Tightening any one of those will have several effects. Cloth from other areas of the sail (the draft) will move toward the tight area. The opposite side of the sail will loosen and the sail will flatten. For example, if the Cunningham is pulled tight, the luff will stretch. The draft of the sail will move forward, toward the luff. The whole sail will be flattened and the leech will be freed.

The boom vang acts as an auxiliary mainsheet to control draft and twist when off the wind, as the mainsheet doesn't have much downward force with the boom end outboard. Without the vang, the sail will twist off at the top, easing the leech and riding the boom up in the air.

The Cunningham allows a main to be built with the maximum luff length and still be tensioned without violating the measurement rules. The sail is hoisted to its limits and then tensioned within those limits. The Cunningham consists of a simple cringle placed twelve to eighteen inches above the tack along the luff of the sail. A line is dead-ended at or below the tack and run up through the cringle and back down. To tighten the luff, the line is tightened, bringing the Cunningham cringle down toward the tack.

The mainsheet and the traveler are really a matched pair of controls and should be adjusted together. In partnership, they control the position of the boom athwartship and the tension along the leech, which, in turn, controls the twist.

Going to windward, the boom is usually inboard, very close to the centerline of the boat. The mainsheet and the traveler should be adjusted together to maintain this position. The tension of the mainsheet and the position of the traveler can be infinitely adjusted to adapt the mainsail to changes in wind velocity. Mainsheet tension directly affects the leech. The greater the tension, the tighter the leech. This relationship is one that should be the subject of many experimental practice sessions in tuning your boat.

Where most boats will have only one, or perhaps two mainsails and a storm trysail, the same boat might have several varieties of headsails.

The genoa is a headsail that overlaps the mainmast and is used primarily sailing to windward. For ease of description, they are usually numbered, with the largest a number 1, the next number 2, and so on. The weights of fabric also are used, as there might be a six-ounce number 1 for general use as well as a three-ounce number 1 for lighter air.

The reacher is a high-clewed full-cut genoa used for reaching or for light-air windward work with or without a staysail double-head rig. The drifter is a genoa made of light cloth to be used in drifting conditions. The windseeker or windfinder is a superlight headsail usually smaller than the drifter, used in flat calm conditions to keep steerage and headway.

The jib is a headsail that doesn't overlap the mainmast. A storm jib is a small jib made of very strong fabric designed for storm conditions.

Most genoas are described by sailmakers and sailors using the IOR dimensions along the luff and the LP. The LP is the luff perpendicular; the distance between the luff of the sail and the clew along a line perpendicular to the luff. The

LP is used along with the fore-triangle base (J) or spinnaker-pole length (SPL) to derive a percentage overlap for a headsail. A 150-percent genoa might have an LP either one-and-one-half times the length of the J or of the SPL, whichever is longer.

When measuring headsails, the area is considered to be the luff length times the LP, divided by two. There is no credit for leech hollow or penalty for extra round in the foot.

The headsail, especially the genoa, must be considered both as a single airfoil and as a part of the total sail plan as it relates to the mainsail.

Like the main, the headsail is an airfoil creating areas of higher and lower pressure as the wind flows over it. The difference in pressure again produces lift, as in the main. Because of this airfoil role, the shape of the headsail is very important.

There are four primary shape considerations: first, the leading edge; second, the position of maximum draft; third, the shape of the leech; and fourth, the overall uniformity of shape.

The leading edge should present a smooth, flat entrance to the wind. This allows the sail to be sheeted close inboard and increases the pointing ability of the boat. The angle of attack (the angle at which the sail meets the apparent wind) should allow the sail to luff evenly from head to tack. Since the apparent wind is farther aft at the head than at the tack, the sail must be able to compensate for this.

The draft of the sail should be between 33 and 45 percent back from the luff and vary from full to flat fore and aft while remaining nearly uniform from head to foot. The draft also must be adjustable to make up for wind and sea conditions. A light-air sail should be fairly full with its greatest draft nearly 40 percent back from the luff, while a heavy-air jib should be very flat with its maximum draft about 33 percent back from the luff.

The after portion of the sail should be flat and not hook to windward. The leech also should be about the same distance from the shrouds from the deck to the upper spreaders.

Overall, the shape should be smooth and uniform. The draft should be nearly equal throughout with no hard spots or areas where the sail is overly full or flat.

The aerodynamic interaction of the headsail and the mainsail is almost as critical as the shape of the sail itself. The genoa and the mainsail create a slot when they are properly trimmed. The air that is funneled through this slot accelerates and produces a larger area of lower-pressure air on the leeward side of the main. This increases the lift of the sail plan and increases the power of the boat.

The shape of the slot is important to get the most from the two sails. If the slot is too wide, the effect is lost. If it is too narrow, the air slams into the leeward side of the main and backwinds the sail excessively, decreasing its effectiveness. Some backwinding is often desirable. A properly trimmed genoa leech should parallel the mainsail's leech, making the slot a uniform width from top to bottom. This requires constant attention and trimming to achieve the potential of the boat's sails and rig and is often the major cause of a boat's speed to windward.

The shape of the headsail is controlled much like the shape of the mainsail. The controls include luff tension, sheet lead position and sheet tension.

Luff tension affects the position and depth of the draft in the sail, much like the Cunningham on the mainsail. Often maximum-size headsails are built with Cunninghams to adjust draft. Tightening the luff of the headsail moves the draft forward; easing it moves the draft aft.

The correct sheet lead position is as important for the headsail as the mainsheet and traveler adjustments are for the mainsail. The position of the lead controls the tension in the leech and foot as well as the relative angle of attack of the luff. The position can move fore and aft and also athwartship. The lead position athwartship is termed the sheeting angle and is measured from the centerline of the boat, with the tack of the sail as the apex of the angle. The angle should be from 6 to 10 degrees, depending on the velocity of the wind. A good general rule of thumb for the lead position is: inboard in light air and outboard in heavy air. The main thing is to watch the slot and make sure it isn't too narrow, with the lead too far inboard; or too wide, with the lead too far outboard.

The fore and aft position is equally important. If the lead is too far aft, the sheet will pull the foot too tight, making the sail luff aloft much before it luffs near the deck. If the lead is too far forward the opposite will occur, and the sail will luff much sooner down low than aloft as the boat heads up. The entire sail should break into a luff at the same time when the lead is in the proper position fore and aft. Remember that both the fore and aft and the athwartship positions will vary as one or the other is changed, and they also will vary as the luff tension is changed. Trimming the headsail is a full-time job.

Sheet tension is the other method of adjusting shape. The best advice, until you have experimented with your own boat, is to avoid either extreme of trimming too hard or easing too much. Overtrimming stalls the air in the slot and distorts the shape of the headsail. Too much ease will decrease the boat's pointing ability.

Different headsails and conditions require varying trimming techniques for top performance. The best way to accumulate the data you need to make the right decisions is to practice. Here is a suggested routine.

Start on a day with a light to moderate wind, between five and ten knots apparent wind. Hoist the headsail with the minimum tension, just enough to eliminate the wrinkles along the luff. Set the initial sheeting angle at about seven degrees, and the fore and aft position to put the lead at a point that is a natural extension of the leech. Sheet the sail in close to the shroud and bring the boat up into the wind. Watch the point at which the sail luffs first. If it luffs aloft first, move the lead forward an inch or two; if it luffs down low first, move the lead aft a couple of inches. Keep adjusting until the sail luffs evenly from tack to head.

Now look up the leech from the clew. The sail should be an equal distance from the shrouds from deck to spreaders. If it is farther away at the spreaders than at the deck, move the lead forward. If it is farther away from the shrouds at the deck, move the lead aft.

Move to the transom or the stem (whichever gives you the best view) and look at the slot. With the main trimmed correctly, the leeches of the two sails should be parallel and the slot should be a uniform width from deck to masthead.

If the wind built up to, say, fifteen knots, the sail would appear fuller, without any change in trim. The draft would have moved aft, giving the sail a rounder appearance rather than the flat entry and leech that make for a powerful sail. Looking up the leech, the sail will appear to have moved away from the spreaders more than from the chain plates at the deck. To get the sail back to optimum shape, the luff must be tightened, with the halyard or the Cunningham. The sheet may have to be trimmed harder and the lead moved forward slightly to complete the job. The leech should then be back in its proper place.

As the wind continues to build, the sail will reach a point at which the leech cannot be trimmed back into place. That is the time to change to the number 2 and start the process all over again.

It should be obvious by now that there is an amazing amount of detail to manage aboard a modern racing boat. I think that is one reason why a skipper cannot do it all himself. If he is steering the boat in a tough situation, he needs a right-hand man to assist him by taking care of sail trim, tactical considerations and all the other things that must be taken care of to eliminate mistakes. All the twelve-meter campaigns have taught us the importance of the number-two man. He might not be able to order the correct sail change or adjustment, but he will remember it and remind the proper person to make or prepare for a sail-evolution adjustment. He will make sure that no one is missing anything. He may not say, "You do this and you do that," but he will say, "Don't forget that," and "Shouldn't we be doing this?" He is like a copilot in an aircraft running down a mental checklist.

Another important aspect of offshore racing is navigation. Good and precise navigation, along with proper observation of the racing rules and the regatta requirements, can mean the difference between a win and a loss.

The 1973 One-Ton Cup is a fine case in

point. Rounding one mark in the wrong direction lost the world championship for Doug Peterson and *Ganbare.* Even if everything is set up well and the boat is moving fast, the smallest miscalculation in the navigation or tactics department can lose the race or the series.

Referring back to the selection and setting of sails, a truly competitive boat should have one man with the sole duty of calling the trim of the sails. Unless you have an experienced crewman who really knows the boat and its sails, you can't really use effectively the eighteen bags of sails that many one-tonners carry. You will never have the right one up at the right time and rarely make the correct change early enough.

For example, think of how many times a boat will go around the windward mark and the call for the spinnaker goes up. Before the chute is set and drawing, people will be rushing around to set the staysail. As soon as the staysail goes up, the spinnaker collapses and the boat loses its drive. It takes half an hour for the staysail, working perfectly, to make up for that collapse. The sail-trim specialist could have prevented that mistake.

Let's put this into some logical form. Imagine that you are the skipper of a thirty- to forty-foot offshore racing boat. There are many questions that you should be asking yourself as you prepare for the start of a day race around a triangular course.

Is the wind dying or coming up? This determines whether you would use a heavy genoa or a lighter one. It is better to be overpowered than underpowered, especially around the buoys. If the wind is dying, you might want to start overpowered, because there is nothing worse than getting caught in a leftover slop with lighter air and too small a sail. The loss in changing can be too costly. So, make sure that you can reef the main and start with the larger headsail, because it is always easier to take a reef out than put one in after the start.

The above plan can be modified somewhat if you are quite sure of the wind direction. If the weather leg is very short, it is better to start with a large genoa and lug it through the windward work so the larger sail is up for the reaching leg.

As you sail to windward, the trimmer should be directing action with a crewman assigned to each control. It is surprising to see the number of people who are really geared up for racing, having traveled a long distance and spent a lot of money to prepare for racing, get lazy on the boat. The crew shouldn't just sit on the rail and observe the competition, they should each have a task to perform, perhaps with a sheet in hand, because sheets should never be cleated. There is no point in running about making a lot of commotion for no reason, but there are many jobs that can be done if a man knows what his duty includes. This is especially true in light air and drifting conditions. On a puffy day, the crew won't have time to uncleat and cleat a sheet for adjustment on each puff. The sails must not be cleated, but trimmed constantly, whether with a large coffee grinder or with a small sheet winch. If you are going to race, then race seriously,

When you arrive at that weather mark, don't be too anxious to hoist the spinnaker. The skipper or helmsman should call the shots because he is the only one in a position to really see and feel all the factors involved. Whether you ease to round or hoist a spinnaker at the mark, wait for the skipper to give the commands. So often there are close calls as the ascending chute nearly fouls the mark, or the genoa as it is eased almost brushes the mark. No one on the boat can judge the proper timing as well as the helmsman. He has the feeling of the boat and knows what chances he can take at any given moment.

As you go off the wind, it is important to have the sail trimmer pay close attention to easing the sails to increase draft, to trimming the spinnaker and staysails and to ordering changes in the sails as the conditions require. The helmsman should be able to concentrate on sailing the boat, confident that the crew will monitor all the variations in wind and tactical considerations.

The people on the foredeck must be prepared for a quick tack at the mark, setting the spinnaker gear up to allow for this. As soon as the command for the chute hoist is given, the sail should go up rapidly and be trimmed immediately. The first thing to do is to get the guy and sheet manned as the sail goes up. Someone always seems to be playing with the topping lift, fiddling with the foreguy or working with the inner end of the pole before the spinnaker is even full. First things should come first. Someone should be calling the spinnaker trim to the winch crankers, who can't see anything most times because of the mainsail and jib. Otherwise, you may end up sailing along for a minute or more with the chute overtrimmed, and the foredeck crew taking care of the small details, ignoring the major ones. What's the difference if the pole isn't at the right height? That's a small thing compared to having the sheet eased properly and the sail doing its job.

Sometimes there are certain details that must be attended to right away. If it is a dead run, the pole must come back early, and if it is rough going, the vang should be set as soon as possible to prevent a flying jibe. The main also wants to go out fairly soon, but the most important thing is to get the spinnaker up and drawing at the earliest moment. The outhaul, Cunningham and traveler can all wait until the chute and even a staysail are up and drawing right, unless there are enough crew to do it all at once.

It really is a matter of organization, with each man knowing his job. It also is a matter of having one man calling the shots and the crew cooperating with him. Too many people making too many different decisions can spoil an operation. This often occurs with too many competitive sailors on one boat. It turns into a load of indians with no chief.

Well, let's say we have sailed the reaching leg and are now at the jibe mark. If the next leg is a run, we should be ready with the shooter or blooper. This is a hybrid combination of spinnaker and reacher tacked to the stemhead with about a two-foot pennant, the halyard eased from five to ten feet, and the sheet led to the end of the main boom. The mainsail is dropped about halfway or more. The shooter makes up for the loss in area of the modern high aspect main by putting up about two-and-a-half times the area of the main. It also steadies the boat on a run by rolling the opposite direction from the spinnaker. You can use it to sail by the lee much more effectively than the usual staysail.

Since this is a triangular race, the run to the finish is nearing its end and the race is about to be won by your boat and your crew and you, because you were better prepared, made fewer mistakes and kept the goal of the race in mind throughout.

The winning of the race is always the long-term goal of the sailmaker, yacht designer and the sailor, but there are other rewards as well. I like to sail and was sailing long before I ever made a sail or designed a boat. I have always liked to race and to sail. I also try to keep that pleasure separate from the business side of things. If I had more time and money, I would spend more time racing than I do working in the industry. The men who have the knowledge, money and time to race continuously are very hard to beat.

It is getting harder and harder to win races because of new talent, better boats and keener competition. I can remember when I could do well in a race with three couples and an extra crew, but you can't do that anymore. To just finish in the top ten these days, you need a top crew on a hot boat with the best equipment and then practice to develop teamwork and expertise. Skippers are always looking for one-design small-boat sailors to crew, steer and trim sails on offshore racing boats, because the one-designers know competition.

There have been a lot of so-called improvements during the past ten to fifteen years that are what I would call detriments to progress. The constant trend toward stripped-down racing machines continues moving toward extremes which I think could be bad for the sport. It is a case of history repeating itself. The designers of the old J-boats kept making them lighter and lighter until the boats would last only a year or so. Then some sort of scantling rules were developed to prevent that. I see the same progression developing with offshore boats today. Competition is getting so wicked that someone will end up building a boat like a model airplane—just a framework covered with fabric and doped tightly. We should try to stop this trend before too many good skippers give up and leave the sport.

What I am describing has nothing to do with what design rule is in effect. It happens that the IOR is the one we are using at present, but the same things would happen under the CCA or the RORC. As long as racing competitors become more fanatically dedicated to winning, extremes of design will continue to develop. In the 1930s, the Cruising Club was initiated because people were tired of having to race in six-meters, R-boats, Q-boats and the like. They decided to take up cruising boats and establish a less fanatical category of racing. This kind of movement is presently taking place in California and other areas. People who enjoy racing, but not in the superrace category, are finding alternate rules and races. The one-ton level-rating class is a supertype strictly devoted to racing. A boat capable of winning in the class can't have much going for it in the way of cruising ability or comfort.

I really enjoy designing boats—it's a fun thing. I designed my first boat when I was about fifteen. It was a small dinghy, and after I built it, I made a sail for it. I guess that was my initiation into the business end of sailing. Designing is strictly an after-hours hobby for me, in spite of its relationship to my primary business.

The first major boat I designed was a center-board Finnesterre type in 1959. It is still my most successful boat—at least it won more races in a season than any of my other designs. I try to make the design hobby self-supporting by selling the boats after I use them for a couple of years. Then I do another design in a short time to try to offset any loss. Furthermore, if I went to a major designer for a boat, all the other designers in the area would ask why I didn't come to them. All designers are potential customers for a sailmaker.

I also like to experiment with the rigs of the boats. The rig relates to the sails and vice versa, each affecting the other a great deal. Adaptations of the rig in conjunction with sail changes can make a tremendous difference in the performance of the boat.

It is still a thrill to watch a boat of mine go into the water for the first time, even though I already have an idea for another one as soon as the first is off the drawing board. It is always a problem trying to improve the next design. If you design both a new rig and hull, you really don't know if you will have a better boat or not. If you keep one constant, then you have a basis for comparison.

It is extremely difficult to compare the performance of one boat with another. Out on the racecourse, a slight difference in wind conditions, different helmsmen and different sails make comparison literally impossible. Everyone seems to jump to conclusions when a boat is performing a bit better. They might have the right reason, but more often they are wrong, since pinpointing what makes the difference is too complicated.

Tank testing is undoubtedly the best way to compare one hull with another, if you have the time and the money for it. When all is said and done, it is the designer's feel for the data of tank testing, his original ideas of design, comments of others and last-minute practical considerations that finalize his design decisions.

Despite my comments in this chapter on sailing as a science, it is good boats with good sails, good crews and good luck that win races. As I said earlier, sailboat racing continues to be more of an art than a science, and let's hope it always remains so!

Formula for Success

by DR. STUART WALKER

Dr. Stuart Walker, who long has been a leading competitor in the Soling Class, is best known for his superb instructional books. "Formula for Success" is excerpted from Wind and Strategy, *the definitive study on the character of the wind as it applies to the racer. Here is his masterful piece on the strategic implications of wind shifts when racing to windward.*

*No one surely pays his debt
As wet to dry and dry to wet.*

THE management of wind shifts to windward and to leeward is the major strategic determinant of success in sailboat racing. No amount of understanding will permit the correct prediction of a wind shift on every occasion, however. Therefore it is essential to establish certain rules which, if followed *when there is doubt,* will result in the greatest frequency of success referable to the majority of competitors. Consistent and reproducible success in each race relative to the majority, not occasional victory in a single race, is the determinant of series success.

Risks are inherent in sailboat racing and therein lies the excitement. If the outcome were predictable and dependent entirely upon boat speed, few would participate. Two major circumstances exist which, dependent upon the nature of the wind shift, require totally opposite solutions. If the shift is an oscillating one, the immediately desirable tack is the one away from the direction of shift; if the shift is a persistent one, the immediately desirable tack is the one toward the direction of shift. If the shift is an oscillating one and a series of shifts is expected to follow, the ideal course is close to the rhumb line, avoiding the laylines to the last possible moment. If the shift is a persistent one, the ideal course is directly to the layline in the direction of the shift and a tack toward the mark along the new layline. Risk is inherent in the inability of the helmsman to recognize in a given instance whether a given shift is persistent (will persist for the remainder of the beat or run) or is oscillating (will be succeeded by one or more additional shifts in the opposite direction prior to the completion of the beat). And risk is inherent in the inability of the skipper to recognize whether a series of oscillating shifts may not have some persistent tendency to deviate from the previously determined median (i.e., whether a persistent shift is superimposed upon the oscillations). Oscillating shifts may be ignored with little loss; persistent shifts cannot be.

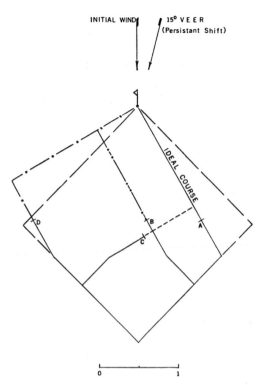

INITIAL WIND | 15° VEER (Persistant Shift)

IDEAL COURSE

D   B   A
C

0   1

Conservatism—Tacking Halfway

Often, a single persistent shift is evident during a given beat which, with or without associated oscillating shifts, is clearly decisive. The less experienced the fleet, the more likely becomes the possibility of a big win by a boat which alone takes the ideal course toward such a persistent shift. In large fleets of competent helmsmen, success is more likely to derive from a conservative course on each beat, one which minimizes the possibility of loss rather than maximizes the possibility of gain. In some racing areas, the only shifts are oscillating ones, or there is a clearly predictable persistent shift which most boats can be expected to handle correctly. Strategy in these areas is predetermined. In other areas, such as Long Island Sound and the Chesapeake, persistent shifts are frequent and difficult to predict. In these circumstances, it is essential that beats be sailed conservatively in a manner consistent with an accurate assessment of the inherent possible gains or losses.

The principles governing the risks are as follows:

1. The least gain or loss by one boat relative to another resulting from a given shift occurs when each is on the rhumb line, and the greatest gain or loss from a given shift occurs when each is farthest from the rhumb line (closest to the opposite laylines).
2. The maximum gain or loss occurs when one boat on the tack toward the shift reaches the new layline (the layline after the shift) at the time of the shift and the other is on the opposite old layline.
3. The greater the shift, the lesser the distance that must be sailed toward it to achieve the maximum gain, i.e., the sooner the new layline is reached. In a thirty-degree shift, the new layline is reached by a boat continuing halfway to the original layline. In such a shift, a boat proceeding beyond halfway loses progressively. A forty-five-degree shift means that boats are on the layline at the start or at the leeward mark and all boats proceeding toward the shift are overstanding. In such a shift or even a slightly lesser shift, the preferred initial tack is *away* from the shift, as boats on this tack will be ahead and to leeward on the major tack just below the layline.
4. A smaller shift results in a lesser gain or loss and justifies a closer approach to the layline. It is never justifiable to sail all the way to the layline without tacking, however, as on the final approach tack the advantageous position for any subsequent shift is ahead and to leeward, below the layline.

The diagram indicates the relative gains or losses of boats assuming four different courses which subsequently experience a fifteen-degree persistent shift. Boat A sails the ideal course: she proceeds toward the shift and receives it precisely when she reaches the new layline. Boat D sails the worst possible course, proceeding from the start directly toward the port-tack layline away from the shift. Boat B sails a compromise course—toward the shift initially but back toward the rhumb line (and away from the shift) when halfway to the layline. Boat C also sails a compromise course but in the opposite direction: away from the shift initially and back toward the rhumb line when halfway to the layline. If we presume the weather leg to be 1.5 miles in length, the maximum gain possible from a fifteen-degree persistent shift—the difference between the lengths of the courses sailed by boats A and D—is .37 miles. If the boat sailing away from the shift initially (boat C) takes a conservative tack back when halfway to the layline, she reduces her loss by 33 percent to .25 miles. Relative to another conservative boat which tacks back halfway after initially sailing toward the shift (boat B), boat C's loss is reduced to .17 miles. The loss incurred by the boat which proceeds toward the shift initially but tacks back (boat B) relative to boat A, which continues to the new layline, is but .11 miles.

The boat that tacks back from her initial tack halfway to the layline reduces her chance of loss to almost all other boats. If she has selected the appropriate tack toward the shift, she gains less than she would have had she continued to the new layline and less than boats who continue beyond her toward that new layline. But she gains on all other boats, all those who sail away from the shift and all those who tack back from the advantageous tack sooner than she. She will also gain or lose relatively little to any boats which continue the initial tack beyond the new layline and thus overstand. As only a few boats will continue beyond her to the new layline (and not beyond), she will gain on the vast majority of the fleet. If she has selected the tack away from the shift, she will lose progressively the farther she continues that tack. She will reduce her loss dramatically as soon as she tacks back (if the shift has yet to arrive). If she tacks back when halfway to the layline, she will have reduced her loss relative to the few boats which continue toward the shift and reach the new layline by 33 percent. She will gain relative to all boats continuing on the tack away from the shift and reduce her loss relative to boats which tack back early from the tack away and those which tack back early from the tack toward the shift. A boat which continues all the way to the new layline on the preferred tack can only gain approximately $\frac{1}{10}$ of a mile on a boat on the same initial tack which tacks back

halfway, but she can lose $\frac{3}{8}$ of a mile to a boat which has sailed to the new layline on the opposite tack if the shift goes the other way.

Even when a helmsman is quite confident that he is sailing in the right direction toward a persistent shift, there is so little to be gained and so much to be lost by continuing beyond halfway to the layline that it is rarely justified. When he is anything less than confident that he is sailing toward a shift (and shifts are likely), he is assuming an intolerable risk to continue beyond halfway. Most persistent shifts are less than thirty degrees, and therefore halfway is unlikely to result in overstanding. If greater shifts are probable, proceeding even halfway to the layline before tacking is unwarranted. In series racing, one is bound to be on the wrong side of the course occasionally. More is sometimes lost by continuing too far in the wrong direction on one beat in one race than is gained by continuing beyond halfway in all the others.

Follow the Leader

If a persistent shift occurs, or some boats receive an oscillating or geographic shift which others do not, alertness to the position and headings of one's competitors is essential. Some competitors, advertently or otherwise, will obtain an advantage from such shifts. The difference between recovery and disaster may then depend upon how soon the advantage is detected and how soon those who gain are followed (or proceeded). Any continuance of a tack away from a progressive persistent shift increases the loss, so that an immediate response is essential.

Alertness is thus the secret of success. Just after the start, one must get his head out of the bilge and his eyes off the compass to watch the boats going off on the opposite tack. It is easy to see a shift developing once out on the course after the fleet spreads out but difficult to detect it in the melee of the start and the confusion of involvement with neighboring boats. A good solution is to tack toward the middle of the course after the start, on port from the port end, or on starboard from the starboard end, of the line.

This avoids excessive movement away from a shift in either direction. Port tack provides the real advantage, a break away from the pack and a good view of boats moving in either direction. Once on port, a move to follow a shift on either side of the course can readily be accomplished. The theme of the first part of the initial weather leg must be: get out where you can see and cover.

Successful racing to windward in persistent shifts or in oscillating shifts on short legs depends upon observing the progress of one's competitors early in the leg. If boats on the same tack are pointing higher, tack; if boats on the opposite tack are pointing lower, i.e., greater than ninety degrees to one's own course, tack. This technique results in sailing a lifted tack compared to the opposition early in the leg and covers the opponents who are most likely to gain subsequently. If course alterations by competitors are detected immediately, first-leg disasters can be avoided.

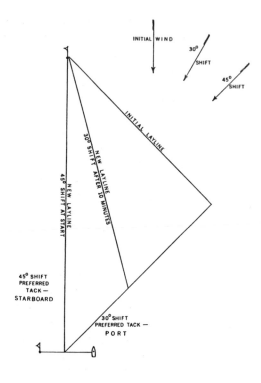

Ahead and to Leeward Near the Layline

Two of the most important tactical principles of windward sailing are in direct conflict when a major persistent shift appears. If the theoretically ideal "inside, to windward of the fleet" position is sought and is achieved on the layline, it is impossible simultaneously to adhere to the principle of "keeping to leeward near the layline." If the persistent shift is large or progressive, particularly if it occurs early in the leg, or if any oscillating shift appears subsequently, boats "ahead and to leeward" may have the greater advantage.

Strategic advantage is determined by the position of the boat relative to the "new" layline, the layline at the termination of the leg. If the tack toward the persistent shift results in overstanding, then the attempt to sail toward the shift has been carried to excess and boats on the layline to leeward ("ahead and to leeward") have gained more. If the tack toward the persistent shift is terminated short of the layline, boats on the layline to windward ("inside and to windward") have gained more. In a persistent shift, the boat which tacks precisely on the new layline

gains the most. This position is difficult to gauge from afar, and there is never any means of recouping the loss from the windward-overstanding position. When in doubt, therefore, an early tack to leeward of the layline is most appropriate. From this position, a further lift (and persistent shifts are likely to progress) will bring the boat up to the layline (while a header from a superimposed oscillation will bring all boats to weather down in line astern). The leeward position also provides the tactical advantage of the lee-bow effect and makes it extremely difficult for a competitor to get past.

At the start of a beat before the fleet has spread out to opposite sides of the course, a marked shift of thirty to forty-five degrees may be best managed by remaining in the lee bow ("ahead and to leeward") of the fleet position. The lifted tack is then the major tack, and the greatest likelihood of gain will be acquired in this position whether the lift progresses or the old wind (a header) returns. If a persistent shift appears after the fleet is farther out on the leg, boats to leeward of the rhumb line are positioned far below the new layline. They are then best advised to comply with the standard recommendation to "tack for the new wind" toward the persistent shift before their loss becomes even greater. Crossing the "fan" of lifting boats at its base will reduce the loss to the least possible. Boats already well out on the side of the course from which the persistent shift appears should tack for the mark immediately they perceive the shift. If they continue toward the shift, they are likely to end up overstanding and will in any case relinquish all the advantages of the "ahead-and-to-leeward" position (which they could have had) as they sail down the major tack near the layline.

The immediate, reflexive response of any sailor who perceives a new wind that will cause a significant persistent shift should be to tack immediately toward that wind. Such a tack achieved ahead of the competition may provide victory if it positions the boat inside and to windward of the fleet but to leeward of the layline—the ideal position from which to manage the sea-breeze "fan," or the bend in the river or the refracted wind near the shore. But if such a tack positions the boat on the layline (or beyond it), or if the shift progresses so that at the termination of the leg the boat is above the layline, then all boats to leeward will gain and those ahead and to leeward will win. Go for the new wind—but don't go too far!

One condition modifies this general rule. If the layline lies along the edge of a zone of persistent geographic shift (near a shore, for instance) or a zone of new wind development (the sea breeze progressing under an offshore-weather-system wind), it is essential to sail well into the shifted wind before tacking even at the risk of overstanding. Tacking early to insure an "ahead-and-to-leeward" position may in these circumstances result in the leeward boat's sailing out of the shift, unable to lay the mark which the windward boat lifts up to lay easily. The fundamental rule when two winds are present simultaneously, of course, is to seek advantageous position in whichever wind is operative at the next mark.

Summary

If an understanding of wind conditions permits an accurate prediction of a persistent shift, an immediate tack should be taken in the direction from which it is expected. The strategy of the beat will be to sail toward the expected shift and a race-winning advantage may be obtained. If the airflow is unstable and oscillating shifts are to be expected, the race should be sailed in accordance with the principles governing the management of oscillating shifts, and the strategy of the beat will be to keep to the lifted tack. Persistent shifts due to the development of ocean sea breezes, channeling or refraction are often accurately predictable as to both location and time. Unfortunately, in many areas and in many races, persistent shifts (which may or may not be associated with oscillating shifts) cannot be accurately predicted. In many racing areas, a persistent shift in either direction is possible but unpredictable. In most racing areas the timing of a persistent shift is uncertain and the likelihood of its appearance during a particular beat is undeterminable. In *these* circumstances, a "formula for success" is needed which will provide the least possibility of major loss and the maximum possibility of gain regardless of the direction, time or location of a persistent shift.

The possibility of strategic gain is directly proportional to the possibility of strategic loss. The farther one sails from the rhumb line or the farther one separates from the remainder of the fleet, the greater is the possibility of gain and the greater is the possibility of loss. Ultimately, the risks taken should be equated to the need. What placing in the race is sufficient to series victory? How many places must be gained to achieve that placing? Can the single place to be gained by a particular course of action justify the possible loss of several places which may result? Separation from the rhumb line and the fleet should be sufficient to accomplish the task at hand. When in the lead, no separation is justified; when far back in the fleet, a single tack to the layline is appropriate. Don't be greedy; take what you've got when you've got it. Tack back whenever the fleet to weather falls in line astern *and* whenever the fleet to weather starts to lift. On the first beat,

A FORMULA FOR SUCCESS
(particularly applicable to large fleets)

STARTING

In light air:

(1) Start at the end of the line and/or away from other boats—on starboard from the port end, tacking to port from the starboard end—moving away from the fleet and away from the rhumb line.

(2) Continue the tack until a return tack toward the rhumb line to cover will provide clear air across the mass of the fleet.

In moderate air:

(1) Start at one end of the line but close to other boats—on starboard from the starboard end, on port or tacking to port (as soon as possible) from the port end—moving toward the rhumb line.

(2) Continue the starboard tack from the starboard end or the port tack from the port end until upwind of the opposite end of the line. From this vantage point evaluate the distribution and heading of the competitors to determine the tack on which to continue.

In heavy air:

(1) Start away from other boats, usually at a moderate distance from the upwind end of the line or in the middle of the line when the favored side of the course is in doubt (to avoid the necessity of an early tack)—moving at maximum speed—to obtain clear air away from the rhumb line.

(2) Continue the initial tack until the majority of the fleet is on the opposite tack or until halfway to the layline.

EARLY IN THE WINDWARD LEG

In all winds:

(1) Watch other boats (and other wind indicators) at the extremities of the course to detect the appearance of a persistent shift.

(2) Watch the compass to determine whether a shift beyond the range of previous oscillations is occurring.

(3) Tack immediately toward any persistent shift revealed by (1) or (2).

LATER IN THE WINDWARD LEG

If no persistent shift has appeared:

(1) Tack back toward the rhumb line at or prior to the halfway position to the layline.

(2) Assume such a tack back toward the rhumb line so as to be ahead and to leeward of the majority of competitors who were previously on the same tack (between them and the rhumb line).

(3) Tack back toward the same layline or continue across the rhumb line so as to be astern and to windward or dead to windward of the majority of competitors.

(4) Continue to cross from side to side of the rhumb

line, keeping nearer to the rhumb line than the majority of the competitors (or significant competitors).

(5) Keep alert to the possibility of a persistent shift (watch other boats and compass) and tack toward it immediately after its detection.

and to leeward of the majority of competitors on or near the layline.

(2) Keep alert to the possibility of a persistent shift occurring in a zone at or just beyond the layline and assume or continue the tack toward it (if the windward mark lies within it) overstanding slightly if necessary to reach it.

LATE IN THE WINDWARD LEG

Near the layline: (1) Tack so as to be ahead

set your sights on fifth or sixth so as to avoid first-leg disasters—the major determinant of race disasters. On subsequent beats and runs, pick the advantageous side of the course and sail slightly, but only slightly farther, to the preferred side of the course than the competition. Once in good position, let your opponents make the mistakes. Sail fast and conservatively. The risk of loss may outweigh the chance of gain if the strategic decision is in doubt.

Racing

by **UFFA FOX**

Uffa Fox was a leading English yacht designer as well as sailor. "Racing," which is an excerpt from According to Uffa, is notable—aside from Fox's succinct and charming style—for giving one of the finest explanations of sail handling techniques. It reflects the wisdom gained by years of sailing and observation.

HAVING learned to sail and handle a boat, the earlier you can start racing the better. Once you race, every fault is pointed out in the way the other boats sail away from you, and when you do anything well, this too is revealed as you start sailing away from the rest of the fleet. Cruising men, on the other hand, try to avoid everything. They give other craft a good wide berth and so do not learn to handle their boats in an exact manner. When we drive a car along our roads, we miss other cars by inches all day long. In a day's drive, we learn to steer and handle a car with great exactness; so it is with sailing a race. When we are on the port tack, we have to give way to starboard tack boats; if we touch the mark on rounding, we are disqualified and have to retire, yet, if we leave the mark ten yards wide, we have to sail this ten yards back again. As we are rounding marks and buoys throughout the race—possibly rounding ten different marks—if we give each mark a ten-yard

berth and have to sail the same ten yards back again, we have made the race two hundred yards longer for ourselves. We can never win a race doing this. We also learn to judge with great exactness the speed and the ability of our boat.

In the five minutes before the race starts, we are maneuvering our vessel in close proximity to the others under the watchful eye of a sailing committee. Once the five-minutes signal is made, we come under the racing rules and can be disqualified for any breach of the rules. When, finally, the starting gun has gone, we attempt to cross the line in the best position with full way on, within a second or so of gunfire. Because we are attempting to get the utmost out of our boat, we watch every cloud, every squall and every shift of wind; for races that take hours to sail are often won by seconds. Time and time again, only thirty seconds divide the first six boats.

Therefore, though a man may take up sailing in order to go cruising, it will be well for him to race for a season early in his sailing career. It will teach him perfection in the handling and sailing of his craft; which will stand him in good stead when he goes cruising. It is frequently the cruising man who has raced who makes his harbor without any trouble; whereas a man who has only cruised goes about things in a much more slovenly manner, for he has not

Close quarters—Three Shields Class sloops approach the mark in a race on Long Island Sound.

the exactness and the skill found in racing men.

Through my life, I have taken part in almost every sport. When you are boxing, you are either giving punishment to another man, receiving it yourself or by skillful footwork avoiding it; when you are cross-country running, you have all the physical joy of running a little faster than the other man; he does not touch or harm you—you are just running, it is a pure test of physical strength and so brings great joy into your heart. So it is in sailing a race; you sail your boat without touching another and derive a great deal of pure joy from the boat's speed through the water with her sheets trimmed to perfection and the steersman interfering with her as little as possible. Generally speaking, a man derives his greatest pleasure from his day's work; he is either sad

that it has not been done to his satisfaction, or full of joy because it has been done well that day. We get all this joy endeavoring to sail to perfection throughout a race.

Nothing is perfect in this world and we can never sail a perfect race; but if we make only one mistake—providing it is not a fatal one—we should come in first. Two mistakes make us second and three mistakes bring us into third place.

As we race our sailing vessel, we should try to sail clear of the fleet, as then we are not interfered with by other boats and only then can we give all our thoughts and energies to our own—to the trim of her sheets, the flaws of wind, the squalls and lulls, the different run in the tide and the hundred and one little things around us all day long. Whenever I race, I try to get off on my own, away from the fleet, where I have only my own vessel, her sails, rig and crew to consider.

A great many people try to win races by spoiling tactics such as interfering with another vessel's wind. These people do not aim at sailing their own boat fast but try to stop other people sailing theirs fast. Of course, when in close company with another vessel, we at all times possible try to sit on her wind, keeping our own free. But generally a race is more fun clear of the fleet, where you can devote all your energies and thought to your own boat, which is quite enough to occupy any brain.

There are many rules which must be obeyed, and if you break any, you are out of the race. In most sports there are referees or umpires, but in yacht racing you are your own judge. Because of this, you must pay very strict attention to the rules, for although you can now break them unobserved through being clear of the fleet, you cannot escape from your own conscience and you would have no satisfaction in winning a race knowing you had broken a rule in order to do so.

Sailing races have been arranged for hundreds of years and they still take place without a referee or umpire. This tells us of the honesty of sailing people and long may it continue.

All racing in Great Britain is under the control of the Royal Yachting Association and international racing under the International Yacht Racing Union, which has from the very beginning met in London under the wing of our Royal Yachting Association. This shows that all countries look upon Britain as being fair-minded, and also that the RYA is a very important body, so all taking part in yacht racing should join it and give it added strength and encouragement by their

A fleet of eleven-and-one-half-foot Interclub Class dinghies bear down on the starting line in frostbite races on Long Island Sound.

membership. As well as this, you should join the club under whose burgee you propose to do your greatest amount of racing.

Before we can race, we must study the RYA racing rules. Until 1959, these were all based on the international rule of the road at sea. Then, in 1959, an American set of rules came in; and now the racing man has to know two sets of rules. Whenever he meets a vessel—trading or cruising, or a racing vessel before or after her race and not actually racing—he has to conform to the Rule of the Road at Sea to avoid an accident and the risk of paying a damage claim. And he must also know the new Racing Rules. When racing in 1959 in The Solent, we came upon twelve boats sailing exactly the same course, and we had to give way to only one of them, because this racer had taken down her racing flag: to my mind a most stupid situation.

The Racing Rules demand that ten minutes before the start a warning gun should be fired to draw attention to the class flag that has been broken out at that moment. Remember, it is the flag that is the signal—the gun or horn or other noise is only to draw attention to the flag. Five minutes later, exactly to the second, the Blue Peter is broken out and the second gun fired—the five-minute signal. Now all in this class come under the Rules of Racing, for although there is no proper course, as all the boats are darting and weaving to and fro like swallows in an endeavor to make the best start, the rules must be obeyed. Five minutes later, the Blue Peter and the class flag are hauled down. This is the signal to start, and attention is drawn to it by the starting gun. As we all know, guns sometimes misfire, and that is why it is most important to look at the flags, for these are the signals.

Away we go on our course. For five minutes, we have maneuvered hoping that we should start across the line in the best position—sometimes to windward, sometimes to leeward, sometimes in the middle of the line—and cross it with full way on so that we pull right ahead of the fleet. But as all the rest are bent on doing the same thing, it is extremely difficult and needs very exact timing and a great understanding of our boat and of the virtues and flaws in our crew. For

if we have a bad crew, we have to make our start with a minimum of turns and a minimum of action on the crew's part.

So off we go, round the course full of hope.

Hard-Weather Racing

When racing in strong breezes and heavy winds, we must always carry more sail to windward than our boat can really stand. There are many reasons for this. Although she is overcanvased in the squalls, sometimes wallowing, and so slowed up, there are many lulls between them and in these she will be traveling at her top speed. And if we are skillful, we can also keep our vessel on her feet and traveling at her top speed through the squalls, which is where we gain on those who do not know. Here where we must use every ounce of wind pressure to keep up our speed, it is particularly important to be able to adjust our sails quickly and easily so that we do not lose way. When I discovered that I had to ease a great deal of sheet off to get any relief from the pressure of wind, my mind traveled back over the years to a cruise to the Bermudas where dinghies with a crew of six carry as much sail as our six-meters—450 square feet—in a brisk breeze. The reason they could carry all this sail was that their main booms were well up on the mast high above the tack, which meant that the outer end of the mainsail could not lift, and that the whole sail swung out in one plane when the sheet was eased, like a door on its hinges. So a great deal of pressure was eased out of it swiftly with the minimum of sheet, and as well as this, there was much less strain on the mainsheet. We tried such a boom, but with the small mainsails allowed by our rules, we could not afford the loss of efficiency caused by this boom. When it was to windward of the loose-footed mainsail, it had its deepest flow at half its width, instead of at one-third from the luff, which it has when the flow is controlled by the curved mainsail foot attached to the boom. When the boom was to leeward, the mainsail at this point was absolutely flat with no flow at all. Then we tried a split-wishbone boom curved on either side of the sail; but although this was better, the flow was still too far aft, as it

With a fresh breeze and sparkling waters, the crew in this Tempest Class sloop works upwind.

always is in a loose-footed mainsail. Finally, I invented the wire kicking-strap, which was attached to the boom and mast so that it made an angle of forty-five degrees to the mast, and this, by preventing the boom from lifting, gave us instant relief on easing away the least bit of the mainsheet. It put a great deal of strain on the main boom, but this short spar could stand it: and so the kicking-strap was invented and has been a boon to sailing men ever since.

Another great help was a wide mainsheet horse, as this pulled the outer end of the main boom down to the desired angle and eliminated a great twist from the sail. With the final lead of the mainsheet led from the center of the boom down on deck, it acted in a smaller way as an extra kicking-strap. So these things enabled us to carry more sail than we had carried to windward before.

In this way, we carried the extra sail that these *V*-sectioned boats needed to lift them out and set them planing over the surface of the sea, and the newly developed seagoing planing hull caused me to develop a new technique of sailing —that of playing the mainsheet in and out as you do a heavy game fish on a light line. And this, in turn, put more zip and zest into sailing, so that today's standard of sailing is far above that of thirty years ago.

Light-Weather Racing

When there is hardly a wag of wind, you put up your ghosting sails—the lightest ones you have, though not always the largest. For though the material in the sails is light, once it exceeds a certain area the bulk is so great that the light air cannot move it. Now, with your ghosting headsail up, you start the difficult job of making your boat travel fast with hardly a breath of wind.

The great thing to do is to keep the boat moving through the water. Never attempt to sail really tight up on the wind but keep her footing as fast as possible, so that you will often be sailing, not close hauled, but one point free of this, covering a greater distance, searching for more wind. When you go on to the other tack, do this as quietly and slowly as you can, as it is surprising how long a boat will carry her way with gentle use of the rudder. In the old days, the big five—*Britannia, Westward, White Heather, Lulworth* and *Shamrock*—in light airs and the smooth water that went with them, were allowed to shoot dead into the eye of the wind when going through it for almost a quarter of a mile before they were thrown over on the other tack; for once these long, shapely vessels had gathered energy, they maintained it a long while under these conditions.

In light airs move quietly yet firmly about the decks, handle all sails as peacefully as possible and use the minimum amount of helm—and so build up and keep the energy of your vessel as high and long as possible.

Now, we can see that though in easy weather conditions with a moderate breeze of fifteen miles per hour the new entry is on an equal footing with the experienced seaman, this is not so in the difficult conditions brought about by light airs or strong winds. It is in these extremes of weather that the wisdom gained by years of sailing and seamanship tells. To sail without wind is as difficult as it is to skate without ice, yet the expert often seems to sail without wind; so we all should at all times try to understand the ways of wind and sea.

The Heavies-North, Turner, Hood and Melges

by DENNIS CONNER

What makes a winning skipper? It's a subject Dennis Conner has given considerable thought over the past twenty years or so. And, judging from laurels garnered —including a record four victories in the SORC, an Olympic medal and two Star Class world titles—he has found the answer. In this selection from No Excuse to Lose, *Conner, who defended the America's Cup in 1980 with the twelve-meter yacht* Freedom, *analyzes the winning characteristics of the four sailors he admires the most on the race course—Ted Hood, Lowell North, Buddy Melges and Ted Turner. He then offers valuable advice on preparing a winning boat.*

I have sailed with and against the best in twelve-meters, ocean racers and small boats, and I think I have learned something from each person. What is interesting is that although each is especially good at one particular thing—leadership, boat preparation, helmsmanship—they all have this in common: when they get up in the morning and look at themselves in the mirror, they all have the self-confidence to be able to say realistically, "I'm the best."

When I was growing up in San Diego, I and everybody else knew that Paul Elvstrom was the best sailor in the world. A Danish sailmaker and boatbuilder, Elvstrom has won four Olympic gold medals, two Star World Championships, two Soling World Championships, a Half Ton World Championship and lord knows how many other major championships in other classes. Business and health problems have kept him from racing much since the early 1970s, and it may be that he is burned out. But in the fifties and sixties, he was the god of yacht racing.

We all knew this, but we had trouble figuring out where Lowell North stood until somebody once decided that if Elvstrom was the god, Lowell must be the pope—which is why some of Lowell's friends and employees refer to him casually as "the Pope." I think that now Lowell must be the best all-round sailor in the world. I have lived near him all my life and have raced against him in Stars and with him in my ocean racers *Stinger* and *Carpetbagger.* I have come to know his strengths and weaknesses pretty well.

Lowell is a trained engineer now in his late forties who became interested in the technical side of sailing about twenty-five years ago. He started his own sail loft, which has since grown to a multi-million-dollar international organization of seventeen lofts. His early racing interest was in Stars, in which he has won an Olympic gold medal and four world championships. He also won the 1964 bronze medal in Dragons. In the early 1970s, he became interested in ocean-racing boats, particularly level-rating "Ton"

Lowell North, founder and chairman of North Sails, is four-time Star Class world champion as well as an Olympic gold medalist.

boats, and he won the 1975 One Ton Worlds in *Pied Piper* and the 1976 SORC and Two Ton Worlds in *Williwaw.* He discovered about that time that he liked crewing, which enabled him to concentrate on all the details that keep racing through his mind without having to worry about steering. He crewed for Robbie Haines in a Soling in the 1976 Olympic trials, and they finished second. When he was named skipper of the new Sparkman & Stephens twelve-meter *Enterprise,* he brought Malin Burnham aboard to steer upwind while he worked on tactics and sail trim. That he was dropped as skipper and *Enterprise* was not selected to defend does not change my mind about Lowell's ability.

Fascination with details is Lowell's strong point. Like myself, he probably does not think of himself as endowed with a great deal of natural sailing ability, but he and I both know that natu-

ral ability isn't everything. Practice, not natural ability, teaches you how to round a mark properly and how to trim a sail. Lowell is a fanatic about boat preparation and equipment. You always know that he will have lighter, more sophisticated gear than you will because he has put so much time and effort into doing things just right. For instance, with *Pied Piper* he was the first person to put a hydraulic cylinder on a headstay, to permit changing an ocean-racing boat's balance by moving the top of the mast fore and aft. By letting the pump out, he could move the masthead aft and give the boat some necessary weather helm in light beating conditions. Then on a hard reach, he could shorten the headstay by pumping the cylinder up, moving the rig forward and relieving the weather helm. When most people saw this, they thought it was dangerous and unseaworthy, even though it was rigged only on a small one-tonner. But by the next SORC, forty-foot two-tonners had the gear and *High Roler,* my forty-six-footer, had one in 1977.

Though it's very hard to understand how anybody could beat Lowell on anything but talent in a small-boat race, he does have a weakness when it comes to big boats. He is a shy man who does not like to tell people what to do, so he may not have great leadership ability, which may have been his biggest problem on *Enterprise.* But he is changing as he becomes more confident in groups of people and as he gains ocean-racing experience.

For contrast, take Ted Turner. By 1977, when he was thirty-seven, he had won two SORCs, a world ocean-racing championship and any number of distance races. He had done well in small boats, too, in 5.5-meters and Flying Dutchmen, and he won the 1977 Congressional Cup match-racing series and the 1977 America's Cup. Ted's strong point is neither innate ability nor attention to detail and preparation—it is his enthusiastic competitiveness and leadership ability. He drives himself and his crew as hard as men can be pushed. This skill is really important in adversity, whether it is keeping *Mariner*'s crew together through the disastrous 1974 campaign, or driving *American Eagle* through two broken masts and any number of blown-out sails, or winning the 1977 America's Cup in an old boat, *Courageous.*

This combativeness can be good some of the time and bad some of the time. Ted has a tendency to think only of the battle and not the war. This may mean grinding down one opponent on a corner of a course while he forgets about the rest of the fleet. It may also mean steering for a dozen hours straight until he collapses with exhaustion. His kind of aggressive leadership works well when times are tough, but it can be counterproductive when things are going well. Ted did well early—winning his first SORC when he was twenty-six—because he sailed so much harder than anybody else. Of course, now that other people sail just as hard, it's more difficult for him to win.

Ted's charisma often leads people to underestimate his sailing ability. He is a good upwind helmsman, but he is one of the very best at downwind sailing. He seems to have a natural feel for driving off in puffs and heading up in lulls, and he has an excellent touch at choosing jibing angles and finding wind. His small-boat experience must help him here, but I know a lot of one-design sailors who don't have his feel downwind.

Ted Hood is very much like Lowell North in that he is an introvert and an extremely talented sailmaker and technical man. He is also limited as a leader. On one SORC, he didn't even tell his crew where the boat would be docked. With a lot of people around, he does very little talking. Sometimes instead of saying something, he will simply shrug his shoulders. In *Courageous,* I never did know if this shrug meant no and he didn't want to hurt my feelings by saying it, if it meant yes, or if he didn't care. My approach to sailing is based on having a lot of quiet talk between the important people in the cockpit, but it just didn't seem to work with him.

Hood is in his late forties, like North, and is also an engineer. He was one of the first sailmakers to start working with Dacron cloth back in the early 1950s, and he also invented the crosscut spinnaker. His technical and business expertise in sailing is enormous: he makes sailcloth, cuts sails, builds masts and rigging, and designs and

Dennis Conner, skipper of the 1980 America's Cup defender Freedom, *an Olympic medalist and three-time winner of the Southern Ocean Racing Conference.*

builds boats at his yard in Marblehead, Massachusetts. If there is a professional in sailing, he's Ted Hood. He has made sails for most American twelve-meters and has designed two of them, *Nefertiti* and *Independence,* unsuccessful contenders in 1962 and 1977. As a sailor, he has won an SORC, a Bermuda Race and many ocean races in New England, where he is as much "the Pope" of sailing as Lowell is in California. He was one of the first Americans to become interested in level racing, and he was sailing one-tonners in Europe long before they became popular in North America. And, of course, he won the America's Cup in 1974.

The following story says a lot about Ted Hood. In the 1974 SORC, he was sailing one of his one-tonners, a boat that was no better than anybody else's. Before the start of the St. Petersburg-Fort Lauderdale Race, all the weathermen were predicting that the southerly would veer to the southwest. So we in *Carpetbagger* and almost everybody else got on the port tack after leaving Tampa Bay and footed for the header out into the Gulf of Mexico. Instead of footing, Hood and Ted Turner, in his one-tonner *Lightnin'*, stayed high. Each had obviously decided that the other boat was the one to beat. Turner gradually pulled away from *Robin Too II* (Hood names all his own boats *Robin* or something derived from that name) and Hood tacked. Turner, relying on the weather forecast, kept on going on port, and Hood, confident of his own experience and intuition, kept on going on starboard. The wind backed to the east, *Robin Too II* finished one hour and three-quarters ahead of *Lightnin'* and won the race, with Turner tenth overall. Hood won the circuit. Hood's self-confidence also appeared when he disobeyed Bob McCullough's instructions to use a North mainsail in the first race of the 1974 America's Cup. That confidence may not be obvious when you meet him, but it's there.

It is not surprising that these three talented men—North, Turner and Hood—were racing against each other in twelve-meters in the 1977 America's Cup summer, but there is one other man who is probably their superior in small boats. Buddy Melges grew up racing scows on the small lakes of Wisconsin, won three Mallory Cup North American sailing championships, took the bronze medal in the Flying Dutchman in 1964 and totally dominated the Soling fleet at the 1972 Olympics. Like North and Hood, he is a good technical man. He makes sails and builds boats, and is extremely talented with arrangements for sail-handling gear. Unlike them, he is a warm and outgoing man who deals well with people. I have never heard anybody say something bad about him. Melges exudes a positive attitude that is one of the reasons why he is so successful, along with hard work and obvious natural talent at steering a boat and at spotting wind shifts. Unfortunately, he has never chosen to prove himself in America's Cup, Congressio-

nal Cup or offshore racing. This may be because his business is in small boats, but I think it may also be because he knows what kind of sailing he enjoys. If I were to have a sailing hero now, he would be Buddy Melges.

Lowell North, Ted Turner, Ted Hood and Buddy Melges—they are the best sailors in North America and perhaps the world. But just a cut below them are a handful of other very talented men. One is Bill Buchan, a quiet, dedicated Seattle sailor who has won two Star Worlds, who does well in ocean racing and who was tactician in *Intrepid* in 1974. Another—and an entirely different kind of person—is Tom Blackaller, a loud, aggressive and charming guy from San Francisco who has won a Star Worlds and several international match-racing series in six-meters. In ocean racing, Dick Deaver and O. J. Young have to be considered in almost the same breath as North and Hood. Deaver is a sailmaker from Southern California who is particularly good at getting on an unfamiliar boat and making it go well. He did this in the 1976 One Ton Worlds and won. Young is a New Orleans boatyard owner who has won an SORC, in *Muñequita* in 1973, and a Three-Quarter-Ton Worlds, in 1974 (with Deaver on board). They are both talented, competitive guys who attract loyal crews; and, though their technical ability may not be that of Hood or North, if you give them a good boat and good equipment, they will do well in any series.

The quality that links all of these sailors (and myself) is a winning self-image. They know they are the best men for the job of winning sailboat races, and most of them keep looking for more sailboat races to win. They have the self-confidence to know when to ask for help from experts and to know that playing the percentages is better than taking chances. They are talented, competitive men but intelligent enough to realize that skill and drive are not enough. They have to work hard too.

I think it all comes down to a statement: "Give yourself no excuse to lose."

Turner and Jobson in Conversation

by TED TURNER and GARY JOBSON

Ted Turner is America's most recognized sailor, probably because he owns a successful cable news network and half of the Atlanta's pro sport francises. But behind the roaring mouth and all the outrageous publicity, there lies a dedicated and talented sailor who has excelled in a variety of competetive situations. In the following selection from THE RACING EDGE, Turner and his America's Cup tactician, Gary Jobson, talk about racing, rules and what makes a great skipper.

I *hear you talking to reporters a lot about why we complete in sailing and other sports. What do you think is the value of competition, particularly in sailing?*

I would just say that we have a need to compete. It's as natural as sleeping or eating. We have a need to excel. And sailing is very good at bringing it out.

What challenges you to win? Of all the people I've ever sailed with, I've never seen anybody as strong-willed to win on the racecourse. What is that?

I've got a larger dose of motivation than most people have. Some people are born fleet of foot, make great runners. When basic characteristics were doled out, I got more than my share of competitiveness. That's probably all. In fact, it may not be all that healthy.

Some people say that competition can bring out the worst in people, and others that competition can bring out the best.

I would say there are a lot of people who get more enjoyment and camaraderie and friendship out of sailing competitively than in sailing just for relaxation. But the competition ought to be kept in perspective. Sailing is sport—at least, it's supposed to be. It ought to be fun. That doesn't mean you can't give it everything you have; but when poor sportsmanship and skinning the edges of the rules and so forth fall into it, as they have in certain areas, that's not good. Sailboat racing ought to be fun.

Do you think the key to success in sailing is persistence—just plugging away at it? Some people sail for forty years and never get in the top half of the fleet.

I'd say that's one of the qualities you have to have to win in anything. You have to be persistent and you have to be dedicated. You have to be hardworking. I've never run into the guy who could win at the top level in anything today and didn't have the right attitude, didn't give it everything he had, at least while he was doing it; wasn't prepared and didn't have the whole program worked out. On the other hand, you have to have the ability and you've got to have good sense. And that's true in every aspect of life. Sailing is a brains game to a large degree, as well as physical. And you've got to be able to figure

278

out what's going wrong and correct it. To get to the top, you have to have the ability and the attitude, I'd say.

Do you think physical conditioning plays an important part in it?

Certainly in certain areas of sailing it does. In sailing a boat like the Shields, the skipper could be a one-legged man and do all right. But when you're sailing something like a Flying Dutchman or a Finn or a 470, any of the high-performance boats, certainly you have to be in tremendous physical shape—quick and agile. Also when you're sailing on a large boat such as a twelve-meter, you have to have quick hands. And you have to be strong, maybe up to a football or basketball level of physical conditioning. If you're navigating, the biggest physical strain is the cranking of a backstay, although on *Courageous* that was no small job either.

Where do you think you can find the best competition in sailing?

It's all over the place. Take Atlanta, for instance. Sailing up on the lakes in Atlanta, you normally have light air, pretty shifty, and some of the sailors who sail up there, primarily every weekend, could blow the brains off a lot of the great guys, say from Buzzards Bay or San Francisco. It's always difficult to go into any club, whether it's Barnegat Bay or wherever, and go against the locals, since they know the tidal conditions and everything. So I'd say that the competition is good and interesting just about everywhere in the country.

Who would you say are some of the great yachtsmen of the day?

You're talking about big-boat sailors? Small-boat sailors? There are just so many. You know, a lot of sailors don't get the recognition that you do sailing big boats because I guess the newspapers and magazines like to write about the bigger boats. Well, elephants get a lot more attention than the ants do.

There are a lot of guys sailing small boats who never leave their own classes but would be excellent on the big-boat circuit if they had the desire or the money or the opportunity to get into it. So I really think it's hard to choose, though some obviously come to mind right away:

Paul Elvstrom and Buddy Melges; those two would be a couple of the absolute greatest. There are lots of other ones—Peter Commette and John Bertrand—younger guys. And you have older ones, like Bus Mosbacher. There would be literally hundreds of them, if you researched it, and most of the young guys I don't even know.

There are a lot of fellows around who take a lot from the sport, but not that many who are returning a lot. Who are some of the people who seem to balance between the two?

Anyone who has been active in helping out on the regional level and at the national level. I really believe that the USYRU [United States Yacht Racing Union] and USISA [United States International Sailing Association] have a lot of fine people who have helped out, in the Olympic effort and so forth. And once again, the list of people without whose work sailing couldn't take place is really endless. It includes committee people at every level, class presidents and officers, local commodores at yacht-racing associations, vice-commodores of the local yacht clubs . . .

What are the great offshore races in the world? Which would you rank as, say, the top five or six?

I prefer courses that keep the fleet fairly close together, so that fluky weather conditions are minimized. A point-to-point race over a wide expanse of ocean—the Bermuda or Honolulu race, for example—can be a challenge, but it is not as true a test of sailing ability as the St. Petersburg-Fort Lauderdale Race, say, or even the Miami-Nassau Race, in which you have two marks that you have to turn. That keeps the fleet pretty much on the same course. I would say that the Fastnet Race is probably the most competitive one in the world.

How about the Mackinacs?

They're great too. All the big-name races are great, because they attract top-level competition. I like the Hobart Race too, because the coasts of Australia and Tasmania keep the fleet fairly close together.

This may be a good time to say that I enjoy fleet racing actually more than match racing. It's always really interesting when the boats are closely matched and the crews and skippers are evenly matched in ability. But match racing just isn't as challenging, on the average, as racing against a twenty- or thirty-boat fleet. If you're a little faster than the other guy, it's no contest. In a fleet race, a guy that's a little bit slower, for whatever reason, does have an outside chance. In a match race, he really doesn't, since he's always being covered.

What was the roughest race you've been on?

Obviously, the Chicago-Mackinac, which you just mentioned, would be a candidate. It can be nasty and cold on the lakes, even in summer. The Sydney-Hobart Race, with those southerly busters coming up from the South Pole, that's really rough, and the Transatlantic Race, with the westerly gales, can be pretty bad, even though the wind is primarily behind you. The Lauderdale race is another one, if a norther comes through in the winter—or any SORC [Southern Ocean Racing Conference] race when a real bad cold front comes through, which is fairly often.

I haven't been with you when it's really rough— blowing sixty—but I've been with you at the point where safety becomes a factor. You want to hold the chute as long as you can, but then it starts blowing just too hard for the chute, so you take it down a little early. Where do you draw the line?

Fortunately, I always have pretty strong boats. I have not allowed myself to get caught up in the craze for light boats and equipment. When the wind starts to really come on, it's better to be prepared than to have to go right to the edge. In other words, once you've gotten down to your storm canvas, you may not be going very fast, but there's not much that can go wrong. You're not likely to lose your rig if you've got a good stick in the boat. Incidentally, we discovered in the Sydney-Hobart Race on the *Pied Piper* that a great storm rig, fast as the devil for downwind running in extremely heavy air and heavy seas, is a mainsail—a genoa—winged out to windward and a reacher out to leeward. That's a heck of a good rig if you have a double-grooved headstay, as most boats do now. The boat was much more controllable than it was with a spinnaker, and we were going, I think, just as fast, maybe faster,

because we weren't yawing or rolling as much.

The most frightening time for me, and I think when you get into the most trouble, is when you have a spinnaker up going downwind in marginal conditions. The wind is strong, and the seas are running pretty rough. You never know when you're going to wipe out. Upwind it's not that bad, because no matter how hard it blows, all you have to do is put on smaller sails. It's uncomfortable changing them, but once you are down to the right canvas, the reaching is not a problem—up to fifty or sixty knots, I think.

When you're going downwind in that kind of breeze, do you ever sail by the lee?

By the lee in heavy wind is pretty dangerous. And in the kind of winds we're talking about, you can't fly a blooper because the bloopers are basically light and they'll blow out. Your blooper usually blows out just about the time you really need it.

Let's face it, though: only 2 or 3 percent of sailboat racing is done in winds over thirty to thirty-five knots. You're not going to win much by being a great sailor in winds over thirty knots.

When do you set aside the pushing hard and racing hard and start thinking about safety? When the crew can no longer handle it, or when you're afraid the boat's not going to be able to handle it, or a combination of both?

The roughest conditions I've encountered were during winter cruises when we were shorthanded, when I first started ocean racing. I used to go out with crews that were not experienced, and you get in a lot of trouble there, but over the last ten years we've always had a large-enough and competent-enough crew, so I've never had to worry much about the safety of the crew. We take all the precautions on that. For instance, the guys we haul aloft are normally extremely competent and experienced. They have enough sense to know when they can go up, but if I thought it was really dangerous, I'd just get by without replacing a halyard. I have to say, I've never been out in the kind of breaking seas— eighty- or a-hundred-knot weather—that Adlard Coles writes about. That might be something you encounter once every twenty-five years or something. I've been racing for thirty years, and I've never been out in eighty-knot winds, except in small-boat racing when a line squall would come—you know, sort of Bam! and over you'd go.

Do you remember when the seventy-knot line squall came through right after one of the America's Cup trial races?

Yeah, but we had the sails down—

We were towing.

The committee called that off—wisely, or it would have had two twelve-meters towed in without their spars. The spars probably would have been blown over, with the sails blown out completely or else flogged to ribbons.

When was the first time you aspired to win the America's Cup? Is it something you always wanted to do?

I think the first time was when I was in college at Brown. I had the good fortune to watch the first twelve-meter defense, in 1958, and I remember the boats: *Columbia* and *Sceptre*. I was out there watching the first race. We were on a sailboat about thirty feet long, owned by the family of a friend of mine. We were near Castle Hill, and they towed the boats by—both white, if I remember. The crews were all big, muscular men, with their matching shirts on. I'm sure that at the time I didn't just decide I was going to go out and win the cup, but I was pretty impressed. At the time, I had never sailed on anything bigger than a Y Flyer or a Lightning.

I remember when I thought Lightnings were like J-boats. I was ten years old and I was sailing a Penguin. I thought, Boy, if I ever get a Lightning, that would really be out of sight! And then when I did, I really enjoyed it. Lightnings are a lot of fun.

In fact, I enjoyed every boat I ever sailed. It doesn't really matter what size boat you're sailing. The sport is the same, whether it's a Penguin or an Interclub dinghy or a Laser or a twelve-meter or a Class A offshore racer. Same wind, same waves, same principles; just a lot less agony and grief in a smaller boat.

Some people think that the best big-boat sailors are the ones who have gone through the fire in small boats first.

Absolutely. I say that a good small-boat background is essential, starting with dinghies and then on to a little sloop, with spinnaker and so forth. I mean, to go straight into big boats without sailing small boats at least a number of years would be like trying to go to college without having gone to high school.

Do you think it's good to stay in touch with small boats when sailing big ones?

It's good if you have the time to do it. If you ask me, sailing is so much fun that it's best to do it in all sizes of boats. The average weekend sailor might be able to make a couple of big-boat races a year or something like that. The rest of the time, he's sailing in his own club on small boats. Of course, most people sail small boats and don't really get a chance to race offshore, because of the time and money involved.

A couple of years ago, before I bought the baseball team, I got a Y Flyer again, and I had as much fun sailing that as I do the bigger boats. The only reason I'm not sailing every weekend in small boats right now is simply because I don't have the time. But they're just as much fun as the big boats, maybe more.

The main thing is to buy a boat you can afford to campaign in a first-class manner. There's nothing sadder than to see a guy with a boat for which he can't afford first-class equipment because the boat's too large. It's like buying a bigger house than you can afford to maintain. If you want a big boat, the thing to do is check out a used one, particularly in one-design. Normally, all it will need is sails and maybe a few more fittings and so forth. You just have to be sure to weigh it to make sure it's not too heavy.

One thing, though. Whatever size boat, it's important to race a high-performance boat if you want to raise your level of racing. Low-performance boats teach tactics, since they are relatively close in speed; high-performance boats teach good boat-handling techniques, and that is how to improve most quickly. If you want to be really good, you need to be in a high-performance or Olympic-class boat.

I have tended to sail the highest-performance type of boat I could, and I think it's been a major factor in my success as a sailor. I started in a Penguin, which was good experience because it requires good balance or you capsize.

After several years, I got into the Y Flyer, another relatively high-performance boat. And I really started making progress when I got into the Flying Dutchman, which in the sixties was probably the hottest boat around. My keelboat sailing began in a 5.5-meter, which was definitely the most sophisticated small keelboat ever built.

These days 470s are excellent. So are Lasers and Finns. And there are a number of other boats in the high-performance class: the Thistle, 505, and Scows.

Ted, there really isn't that much match racing going on in this country, or in fact the world. Is this what makes the America's Cup so interesting?

Well, the biggest challenge of the America's Cup is to get *into* the America's Cup—figuring out how to get a berth. But of course the fact that the boats are so large and expensive is the reason it gets the publicity. And it does attract the best sailors. You know, the level of racing in the America's Cup has improved. So much time and money is devoted to it that you can reach a level of performance, with the practice and continual working on the sails, that is pretty impressive. You have sailmakers sailing on the boats and working on the sails daily.

Still, I would say that going to the Olympics and winning a gold medal is a far greater challenge than defending the America's Cup, because, first of all, there's a lot more people you're competing against. There was a total of, I think, only seven boats in the entire America's Cup, whereas in the Finn class at the Olympics there are probably five to six hundred sailors who try for a slot, and those are the finest sailors. Then too, the Olympic sailor is a much younger fellow, because of the physical demands of boats like 470s, for example. It's just not a boat that somebody in his forties would be sailing. On the other hand, you're going to have a basically older group in the America's Cup anyway, because of the complexity and the money and experience required. . . .

The average age on Courageous *was thirty-three, and that was young compared with a lot of the twelve-meter campaigns of the past.*

I think we had the youngest afterguard in history. . . .

How do you put your crews together? What do you look for; what are the qualities for a successful crew?

Of course, the nature of the crew depends on the size of the boat. As the boat gets bigger, you have more of a division of labor. An FD crewman, for example, has to be as skillful a sailor as there is. He's got to be the spinnaker man, the jib man, the hiking man, the tactician, the navigator. The helmsman just hangs on and tries to keep the boat going fast through the waves.

Of course, on a Laser or Finn, you are the crew. When I sailed a Finn and wasn't doing well, everybody used to say I cussed my crew. I'd talk to myself: "You stupid son-of-a-gun, you. You can hike out harder." You know—when they're going by on both sides. I found I really enjoyed sailing on two- and three-man boats more because I like the camaraderie of having somebody along.

Now, when you get on a bigger boat, the crew becomes more of an organizational deal. On a twelve-meter, you have one guy who is the tactician, one guy who is bowman and so on down the line, with eight guys leaning over the side and a guy trimming the jib. In a way, it becomes simpler. On a twelve, you can take somebody who really doesn't know that much about tactics but is a good, strong, willing worker, and he can be a very important addition to the crew just by grinding. On a big boat, you also need to consider getting a group of guys who will get along with one another, especially if you're going to stay together for more than one series. Your greatest premium, though, is on organization and recruiting, just like it is in basketball and baseball. Having the experience to know what kind of equipment to get and who to put your money on.

Another thing on that. From the skipper's standpoint, and even from every crew member's, you have to be extremely tolerant when you are on an offshore boat, because people are going to make mistakes, and the more people the more mistakes. The chance for mistakes is about equal to the number of the crew squared, so every additional crew member increases that percentage quite a bit. I personally enjoy the camaraderie and the challenge of the larger group, but there are a lot of people who don't want to bother with that. I know some trememdous sailors who are not really good on large boats—not because they don't have the ability to sail them, but just because they find it difficult getting along with all those people. They can't put up with the hollering when somebody makes a mistake; they simply like to do things independently. This is one of the great things about sailing: there's room for all kinds of people.

About three hundred people have asked me, "How do you get on a twelve-meter crew?"

One way is to buy your way on. But you've got to be good then. I'd say to sail on a twelve-meter you need to be a good small-boat sailor—not necessarily a skipper, but you need to have both small-boat experience, and a lot of it, and the big-boat experience too. Most basic of all, it's good to find out who has twelve-meter aspirations, from both a syndicate and a skippering standpoint, and to get to know those people, since they pick the crew.

What were some of the qualities that helped Courageous *to win in '77?*

It's like any successful operation. It was very soundly structured and planned from the bottom up. But I would say from an overall planning and preparation standpoint, our two competitors were ahead of us. Even though our planning was excellent, theirs was certainly more lavish. In other words, they both had decided that a newer design would be faster—which is always a gamble, but usually a sound one. Normally, there is some progress in yacht design, so normally, the best new twelve-meter is a little better than the old one.

But *Courageous* was all we could get. We couldn't have gotten a new boat unless, of course, I'd wanted to sell everything I had and put it all into a twelve-meter, which I didn't do. Even as it was, I had to put up an awful lot of money to get *Courageous* because of the financial difficulties we had in campaigning the two boats [*Mariner* and *Valiant*], which is always more difficult than just campaigning one, and also because of the poor showing that we had on *Mariner*. [Turner was replaced as the skipper of *Mariner* in

1974.] Normally, when you get clobbered as badly as we did on *Mariner*, then draw a slow twelve-meter like *Valiant*, it can't help hurting your chances quite a bit of getting another shot at it. But it turned out okay after all. I gambled that *Courageous* would be competitive, and she has turned out to be that and more. However, I don't think the basic hull was significantly faster than *Independence* or *Enterprise*.

Then, after getting the boat, I did the best I could at putting together the most mature and experienced crew I possibly could. Since the other two boats were already under way and they had already begun to select their crews before I even had a boat, they had the first- and second-round drafts and we drafted third. But there were still quite a few good guys available in the third draft. We had a couple of rookies, but also plenty of experience.

In your case, Gary, I knew you'd be super if you had a chance to get to know what I expected of you and we had a chance to get on the same wavelength. Sailing the circuit together on *Tenacious*, which wasn't a twelve-meter but was about the same size and speed, we almost had match-racing experience, particularly in the good racing we had against *Running Tide*. That was hours and hours of just sailing along and working on trying to catch or pass them or stay ahead of them, and it was very, very close. Then the Congressional Cup, with nine tough match races.

Much of the rest of the crew, as you'll recall, had sailed with me on *Mariner* and *Valiant* before, so they knew what was expected and what it was going to take to win. It helped also that we gave everyone jobs to do early on, so they could perfect their areas, and I think everyone did perfect his area. As problems arose with our sails and so forth, we sat down, and, luckily, we had brilliant people—brilliant, dedicated people—in every area, who had, I think, more responsibility, certainly, than Ted Hood tended to give his group. Hood kept rotating people around, and I don't think they achieved anything like the level of performance on *Independence* that we did, though had the boat been faster they might have. They seemed to have guys doing the same jobs pretty much, but they did have some problems. I remember they fired some people early on.

When we got to Newport, if I remember, we had some sickness, and we brought in a couple of tremendous substitutes. You've got to have a good bench to win in anything. But other than that, I don't think we changed the crew from the first day of the summer until the last day, though of course we had tryouts for a couple of positions up in Marblehead before coming down.

I'd say we put in eight or nine hours a day every day in practice, and we were deadly serious about what we were doing, but what with the length of the campaign, I tried to keep it as light as possible, so we didn't burn ourselves out. We had plenty of energy left—emotional energy as well as physical—for a good push at the end.

I remember once in the middle of everything just taking a sail and having lunch at Block Island.

That day *Independence* broke down. Ordinarily, I don't find it beneficial just to go out and sail by yourself. It's like playing tennis by yourself; you can knock a ball up against the wall and get a little exercise doing it, but it's a pretty low-key workout. But we'd been working extremely hard, so at that point we just cruised over to Block Island. We did some tacking and jibing drills on the way over. I think we changed sails at the time just to practice, but we went the straight line. A lot of guys had never been to Block Island, and we went ashore, had lunch for an hour, then sailed back.

What about your own frame of mind, as skipper? How would you assess your emotions at the time of the America's Cup, aside from just being up for the competition?

I was ready. With all the big-boat experience that I had had in messing around with *American Eagle* and doing a lot of sailing in larger boats, one-tonners and larger, I learned plenty. You know—sailing *American Eagle* ten thousand miles and then the disastrous *Mariner* campaign, when we learned how to eat humble pie. But that in itself is something you need to learn, because in twelve-meter racing you need to have a lot of humility. You're not sailing your own boat; you're working for a committee, the New York Yacht Club selection committee, and you're working for your syndicate. So you have to be a little bit of a politician, in the better sense of the word. You have to be a gentleman, and you have to do what is expected of you on the water as well as off. I mean, going around and writing *turkey* with a grease pencil on another guy's boat, like they do in the Finn class, doesn't make sense in a twelve. If they found out who did it, you'd be taking a walk down the dock the next day. You ought to be a gentleman and make the yacht club and your competitors happy to have known you. Good sportsmanship and reasonable standards of conduct are important.

What did defending the cup mean to you in the end, after it was all over?

Like any international-championship regatta, particularly the first time, it's a tremendous experience. I remember when I first went to the Lightning Internationals up in Buffalo. I was so impressed just to be there and meet all the real big cheeses in it. So there was excitement and elation and satisfaction at having accomplished what we set out to do, and reaching what is certainly one of the great pinnacles in yacht racing.

And there was a sense of relief, too, that it was over. I spent all year getting ready for those cup races. When we went to Newport and when we were up there sailing, I wiped almost everything out of my mind, just about every waking moment, except for maybe a couple of hours in the evening when I'd relax and watch a ball game.

It kept building up day after day. . . .

The pressure was intense for the summer. Everyone was trying so hard to do a perfect job, so there was a sense of relief that it was over and we could all go home to our regular careers, which seemed like they would almost be vacations. I know that every man in the crew, including myself, felt the strain. Those races last so long. When you're behind, you keep trying to tack to get away, for hours and hours, and it's so hard to do that it feels like somebody has taken a whip and beaten you on the back.

And there was a lot of work even when we weren't racing or practicing. We'd watch Ted Hood when he was sailing against *Enterprise*—we watched both Hood and North to see how they were reacting when they raced against each other. We checked their sails and how they were tacking, looking for the good things they were doing and for the chinks in their armor. . . .

I think knowing your competition is a very important thing.

It's certainly important in the America's Cup, or any match race. A lot of it is psychological. I think our good start in June gave us a leg up and gave our crew a sense of elation and optimism, whereas a sense of gloom and defeatism crept into the other two boats. It was important that we maintained this edge, though we came close to losing it in July.

Somebody said to me after it was over, "You guys were so good. Did you ever make mistakes?" So I told him about the first time against *Independence*, when we were up there with all of our people green and went into that tacking duel. Those kids cleaned our clocks. Losing track of where the trim tab was was kind of fun.

That was my fault. I locked the rudder one way and the trim tab the other.

We just stopped—had to take two tacks right at the mark.

Everything is great when you're winning, but when you lose and come back, that's the toughest thing. What's the secret there? We lost five in a row to Enterprise, *yet we came back to beat them.*

In my mind, we were losing in July primarily because we just had not gotten our light-air mainsail. We were using a mainsail that was a cut-down sail from *Independence*. It was a fine sail in a breeze, but it was not up to it in light air— a little short on the foot, and it had a relatively small roach. The other boats had high-roach mains. When we finally got our high-roach main, we were never defeated. Another thing. The amount of tacking we did in June and early July broke down the jibs. Those sails have only so many races in them, and all that tacking shortens the life of the sail to probably half of what it would be on an ocean race. When we got new sails, we won that big last race against *Enterprise*.

So I think the main reason for our defeat in July was sails—the fact that our sails were just worn out. Now, I think it's important to say here again how close the boats were. I mean, when we

would swap jibs with *Independence*, they would beat us with a good jib. And we would beat them when the sails were changed the other way. It was that close; it was so close because the basic boat speed of all three boats through the water was just about even. This is why we have to give so much of the credit for our victory to Robbie Doyle, for recutting the sails, and also to L. J. Edgcomb and Stretch Ryder, who helped him. Having new sails was one thing, but the shape that Robbie built into them made a big difference. He was constantly recutting all our sails. And I think it was the consensus of experienced men on the selection committee, who were close to the racing, that our sails were superior.

Would you say our ability to change jibs quickly was one of our major keys to success on Courageous?

Absolutely. We had the right jibs and we had the right system and the right personnel to change them. You have to have all three. And then we had spent the time to know which ones to use under which circumstances. The right sails, the right people, the right system and the experience to know which one should be up when. I think that particularly helped us against *Enterprise*, because I think *Independence* certainly had the right sails and knew which ones to have up. They didn't change as often as we did, but they had the system. I think maybe they didn't have as much confidence in their personnel as we did to make the changes in critical situations. And if you'll remember, Robbie Doyle, God bless his soul, didn't have as much confidence in our ability to do it as we did. But we never had a major foul-up, to my knowledge, changing a jib. We changed them a lot. We practiced it a lot, too. We practiced it because there's no room for error changing jibs on a seventy-foot boat while tacking.

As far as practicing, you had everybody following the same routine, a set routine, even on nonrace days.

It's just like in baseball: you're so much better off with a set lineup than you are changing things around, because you just can't get too proficient in what you're doing—particularly on a large boat, but even on a small one. And the more people involved, the more you have to integrate. Any one person failing to do his job in a tack or a jibe causes the jibe or tack to miscarry. Had a sail change been wrong, we could have ended up with a sail in the water, and it would have cost us the race. Just the slightest little fitting going—remember when we lost the backstay?—that's the end of the race. Your crew has to have every single, possible maneuver or circumstance, fore and aft, down to where you don't even think about what it is when it occurs, because usually when something busts or breaks or miscarries, you don't have time. You've got to have it all planned out. And you practice so that after a while nobody even has to say anything.

How do you integrate new crew? We got a new crew—two or three guys—and then you had everybody stand in their positions and sort of run through the deck for the different things, plus a disaster drill.

I try to take the experienced, qualified guys, who have sailed on the boat before, and put them in all the key positions. In offshore racing, you usually just go reaching off for hours at a time, and you have plenty of time to talk things over and straighten things out. But when you go around the buoys, as we did at Newport in the du Pont series, you have no margin for error. We had a very competent crew, and except for a couple, everyone in it had practiced on the boat before. We got around the course, but not without a few fire drills, considering that it was blowing twenty to thirty the whole time.

What do you think of the trend in offshore racing toward one-design sailing—the J-24, the New York 40s, Aphrodite 101?

This whole sport has grown so much, and there's room for so many different games. Perhaps in the future, one-design offshore classes will become predominant. And I don't think that's necessarily a bad thing. As I remember sailing in one-design classes, you spend more time and effort tuning up than you do in a custom boat, because in a custom boat you think, Well, the boat's good or it isn't good. But when you're sailing week in and week out against boats of the same type, you do anything for an edge.

In Lasers, I remember, they took them apart, trying to find something. So the one-design rules have to be awfully good, and the competition is bound to get more arduous. It's

going to make better sailors of the people who are racing the boats, if they can stand losing without having an alibi.

I remember you saying that you believe a lot of people would rather race by rating.

There are a lot of people who like to race by rating, I'm sure, because the sting of defeat is not so great. You always have oodles of excuses, you know: small boat, not my weather, and so on. I would say that handicap offshore racing is a relatively low level of competition, compared with one-design.

Do you think the boatbuilders are setting up a market for one-design?

Absolutely. Having been in the boat business, I know the best thing in the world a boatbuilder can do is establish a proprietary product like the Laser. That way, all he has to do is maintain the same standards for all boats. And he can charge whatever he wants, because no one's competing with him in the same marketplace. They make money on that sort of thing, whereas in building Lightnings or Flying Dutchmans or a class that anyone can build, there's no money in it at all, and there's no promotional budget available, no marketing, no advertising—not even any dealers usually, since there's no room for a dealer markup. This makes it very, very difficult to buy a new custom ocean racer. You have to go to a designer and you have to get a builder, and you don't know what it's going to cost and you don't know whether it's going to be good or not, because you're building a new design. If you buy a J-24, you know what you get; or a Laser, Windsurfer, Sunfish or Hobie Cat.

So offshore racing is dominated by the proprietary products. They're also easier to buy and sell.

Let's talk a little about mental preparation. How do you psych yourself?

I stay psyched up all the time. My two sports teams play every day, and I take the role of underdog, so for me it's nothing to be psyched. At least when we're racing, it's only once every two weeks or once a weekend.

How about for the circuit? When do you start getting ready mentally?

For races like the Southern Ocean Racing

Conference, I don't get ready until I get down there, the day before the race. Having an excellent crew and an excellent captain helps, so I stay away from the details and concentrate on the competiton.

Do you get nervous before you go out racing?

I used to get tremendously nervous; not as much anymore. Let's face it: I'm fidgety and high-strung. Years ago I used to have a bad case of nerves, and a lot of times I would clutch up. I can remember sailing in a boat one time and my foot started shaking uncontrollably, so I almost fell out of the hiking straps. It was a Sears semifinals, and I had to pass a boat to win. I didn't.

I guess I was so intense in sailing that I clutched there more than in any other area. It's one of the worst habits you can have, because if you're going to clutch in a tight sailing situation, then you will in other situations too—in an automobile, for example, when another car is coming at you.

There are a lot of guys who have that problem. How can you overcome that?

You have to work hard on it, the same way you work on quitting smoking or biting your fingernails. It doesn't hurt either to tell yourself that this race is not that important, that you're going to have a good time. But the real solution is confidence, and that comes with experience and hard work. Then, once you overcome the problem in sailing, it will be a lot easier to overcome it in other areas as well.

What are the important factors a sailor should weigh in looking toward the next year's campaign or the next two years'?

It depends on the sailor's budget, the amount of time he can devote to his racing, how important it is to him in the overall scheme of things. If he is a beginner, he could be shooting to be in the top half of his local fleet the next year, and if he has been down at the bottom, that's a very worthwhile and interesting goal. I don't think you ought to set unrealistically high goals for yourself. It's disappointing if you don't make them.

So you should set a goal. . . .

You don't really have to, but I think it's always more fun to have something in mind that you want to accomplish. If you don't have a goal, it's harder to achieve something.

And your goals—how do you go about planning them each year?

I sit down and think about a year in advance as to what events we're going to attend. After the America's Cup, though, it was a pretty easy year. You build up to it, and then it's best, I think, to take a little time off to yourself. Relax a bit.

How long can you compete for? Some athletes go for a year at a time, then rest. What about you, and other sailors?

It depends on the situation. You have to pace yourself. Sailing is so varied that it's like comparing a sprinter and a marathon runner. You have to pace yourself so that you'll peak when it's most important, and that varies with the type of event you're in.

What about the question of how much time to devote to sailing? Some people seem to get hooked on the sport and lose a sense of proportion. They allow it to rule their lives.

It can be a problem. I would have to say that your business comes first. If you want to give your full time to sailing, you can sail twelve hours a day, three hundred sixty-five days a year, and you can compete in a regatta somewhere every weekend. It's a great field to be in, even though I would caution young people who are thinking about it. It's not as much fun when you do it for a living as when you do it for a hobby. I think if you asked anyone over forty who has spent his career in it—particularly in the racing area (I'm not talking about yacht brokerage)—you'll find a lot of heartaches.

So if it's not going to be your vocation, then you shouldn't give it more importance than it really has. One of the unhealthy things today, I think, is that many people spend more time playing than working. I've spent a lot of time sailing, but I've spent a lot more time working, and had I not been successful in business, I could never have achieved success in sailing. It took money, and that came from my business. Your career provides for your sailing, so your career should come first.

I find that sailing is great, but a big part is getting around and meeting people and seeing different places.

I'd never been to Mackinac Island, for example, before we raced there last summer.

You have the best of all worlds. You're really more like a teacher—a teacher and coach—particularly since so many of your goals have already been achieved. I think that's great. You don't have to prove anything; you can go out and really enjoy it. Share your knowledge with others.

That kind of life is a lot more interesting than that of a sailmaker, who is dealing with all the customers who'd like to blame the fact that they're not winning on their sailmaker. You can get out and race, and somebody's going to be last; you can't blame that on the sails.

One last question. What do you see for the future of twelve-meter racing?

I'd like to see a twelve-meter world championship held the year before the America's Cup —a fleet race off Newport. It would be a great opportunity for yachtsmen from all over the world to get together and exchange ideas. And it would have to make the America's Cup a better competition.

PART IV

BEFORE THE WIND

"I saw that Jesús was lost to me. He was no longer a waiter, nor just another Brazilian with just another wisp of mustache. . . . He was breathing deeply as if inhaling some powerful elixir, his attention shifted from the sail to the sea, to the horizon . . . I saw that Jesús had left his apron-bound soul and transcended all the heritage of a puny physique and complete ignorance of power. He was a conquerer now, a guide through the little-known. He was, in these moments of rising speed and spirit, a swashbuckler, an intrepid mariner, and a paladin all in one."
—Ernest K. Gann from *Song of the Sirens*.

The Sirens

by **HOMER**

One of the world's most famous voyages was made (at least in legend) by the ancient Greek hero, Odysseus, whose wanderings on his way home from the Trojan War provided Homer with the theme for his second great epic poem, The Odyssey. *In the following selection, Book XII, Odysseus encounters first the Sirens, who try to bewitch him, then the horrific dilemma of Scylla and Charybdis.*

NOW, after the ship had left the stream of the river Oceanus, and was come to the wave of the wide sea, and the isle Aeaean, where is the dwelling place of early Dawn and her dancing grounds, and the land of sunrising, upon our coming thither we beached the ship in the sand, and ourselves too stepped ashore on the sea beach. There we fell on sound sleep and awaited the bright Dawn.

So soon as early Dawn shone forth, the rosy-fingered, I sent forth my fellows to the house of Circe to fetch the body of the dead Elpenor. And speedily we cut billets of wood and sadly we buried him, where the furthest headland runs out into the sea, shedding big tears. But when the dead man was burned and the arms of the dead, we piled a barrow and dragged up thereon a pillar, and on the topmost mound we set the shapen oar.

Now all that task we finished, and our coming from out of Hades was not unknown to Circe, but she arrayed herself and speedily drew nigh, and her handmaids with her bare flesh and bread in plenty and dark red wine. And the fair goddess stood in the midst and spake in our ears, saying:

"Men overbold, who have gone alive into the house of Hades, to know death twice, while all men else die once for all. Nay come, eat ye meat and drink wine here all day long; and with the breaking of the day ye shall set sail, and myself I will show you the path and declare each thing, that ye may not suffer pain or hurt through any grievous ill-contrivance by sea or on the land.

So spake she, and our lordly souls consented thereto. Thus for that time we sat the livelong day, until the going down of the sun, feasting on abundant flesh and on sweet wine. Now when the sun sank and darkness came on, my company laid them to rest by the hawsers of the ship. Then she took me by the hand and led me apart from my dear company, and made me to sit down and laid herself at my feet, and asked all my tale. And I told her all in order duly. Then at the last the lady Circe spake unto me, saying:

"Even so, now all these things have an end; do thou then hearken even as I tell thee, and the god himself shall bring it back to thy mind. To the Sirens first shalt thou come, who bewitch all men, whosoever shall come to them. Whoso draws nigh them unwittingly and hears the sound of the Sirens' voice, never doth he see wife or babes stand by him on his return, nor have they joy at his coming; but the Sirens enchant him with their clear song, sitting in the meadow, and all about is a great heap of bones of men, corrupt in death, and round the bones the skin is wasting. But do thou drive thy ship past, and knead honey-sweet wax, and anoint therewith the ears of thy company, lest any of the rest hear the song; but if thou thyself art minded to hear, let them bind thee in the swift ship hand and foot, upright in the mast-stead, and from the mast let rope-ends be tied, that with delight thou mayest hear the voice of the Sirens. And if thou shalt beseech thy company and bid them to loose thee, then let them bind thee with yet more bonds. But when thy friends have driven thy ship past these, I will not tell thee fully which path shall thenceforth be thine, but do thou thyself consider it, and I will speak to thee of either way. On the one side there are beetling rocks, and against them the great wave roars of dark-eyed Amphitrite. These, ye must know, are they the blessed gods call the Rocks Wandering. By this way even winged things may never pass, nay, not even the cowering doves that bear ambrosia to Father Zeus, but the sheer rock evermore takes away one even of these, and the Father sends in another to make up the tale. Thereby no ship of men ever escapes that comes thither, but the planks of ships and the bodies of men confusedly are tossed by the waves of the sea and the storms of ruinous fire. One ship only of all that fare by sea hath passed that way, even Argo, that is in all men's minds, on her voyage from Aeetes. And even her the wave would lightly have cast there upon the mighty rocks, but Hera sent her by for love of Jason.

"On the other part are two rocks, whereof the one reaches with sharp peak to the wide heaven, and a dark cloud encompasses it; this never streams away, and there is no clear air about the peak neither in summer nor in harvest tide. No mortal man may scale it or set foot thereon, not though he had twenty hands and feet. For the rock is smooth, and sheer, as it were polished. And in the midst of the cliff is a dim cave turned to Erebus, towards the place of darkness, whereby ye shall even steer your hollow ship, noble Odysseus. Not with an arrow from a bow might a man in his strength reach from his hollow ship into that deep cave. And therein dwelleth Scylla, yelping terribly. Her voice indeed is no greater than the voice of a newborn whelp, but a dreadful monster is she, nor would any look on her gladly, not if it were a god that met her. Verily she hath twelve feet all dangling down, and six necks exceeding long, and on each a hideous head, and therein three rows of teeth set thick and close, full of black death. Up to her middle is she sunk far down in the hollow cave, but forth she holds her heads from the dreadful gulf, and there she fishes, swooping round the rock, for dolphins or sea dogs, or what so greater beast she may anywhere take, whereof the deep-voiced Amphitrite feeds countless flocks. Thereby no sailors boast that they have fled scatheless ever with their ship, for with each head she carries off a man, whom she hath snatched from out the dark-prowed ship.

"But that other cliff, Odysseus, thou shalt note, lying lower, hard by the first: thou couldest send an arrow across. And thereon is a great fig tree growing, in fullest leaf, and beneath it mighty Charybdis sucks down black water, for thrice a day she spouts it forth, and thrice a day she sucks it down in terrible wise. Never mayest thou be there when she sucks the water, for none might save thee then from thy bane, not even the Earth-shaker! But take heed and swiftly drawing nigh to Scylla's rock drive the ship past, since of a truth it is far better to mourn six of thy company in the ship, than all in the selfsame hour."

So spake she, but I answered, and said unto her: "Come I pray thee herein, goddess, tell me true, if there be any means whereby I might escape from the deadly Charybdis and avenge me on that other, when she would prey upon my company."

So spake I, and that fair goddess answered me: "Man overbold, lo, now again the deeds of war are in thy mind and the travail thereof. Wilt thou not yield thee even to the deathless gods?

As for her, she is no mortal, but an immortal plague, dread, grievous, and fierce, and not to be fought with; and against her there is no defense; flight is the bravest way. For if thou tarry to do on thine armor by the cliff, I fear lest once again she sally forth and catch at thee with so many heads, and seize as many men as before. So drive past with all thy force, and call on Cratais, mother of Scylla, which bore her for a bane to mortals. And she will then let her from darting forth thereafter.

"Then thou shalt come unto the isle Thrinacia; there are the many kine of Helios and his brave flocks feeding, seven herds of kine and as many goodly flocks of sheep, and fifty in each flock. They have no part in birth or in corruption, and there are goddesses to shepherd them, nymphs with fair tresses, Phaethusa and Lampetie, whom bright Neaera bare to Helios Hyperion. Now when the lady their mother had borne and nursed them, she carried them to the isle Thrinacia to dwell afar, that they should guard their father's flocks and his kine with shambling gait. If thou doest these no hurt, being heedful of thy return, truly ye may even yet reach Ithaca, albeit in evil case. But if thou hurtest them, I foreshow ruin for thy ship and for thy men, and even though thou shouldest thyself escape, late shalt thou return in evil plight with the loss of all thy company."

So spake she, and anon came the golden-throned Dawn. Then the fair goddess took her way up the island. But I departed to my ship and roused my men themselves to mount the vessel and loose the hawsers. And speedily they went aboard and sat upon the benches, and sitting orderly smote the gray seawater with their oars. And in the wake of our dark-prowed ship she sent a favoring wind that filled the sails, a kindly escort—even Circe of the braided tresses, a dread goddess of human speech. And straightway we set in order the gear throughout the ship and sat us down, and the wind and the helmsman guided our barque.

Then I spake among my company with a heavy heart: "Friends, forasmuch as it is not well that one or two alone should know of the oracles that Circe, the fair goddess, spake unto me, therefore will I declare them, that with foreknowledge we may die, or haply shunning death and destiny escape. First she bade us avoid the sound of the voice of the wondrous Sirens, and their field of flowers, and me only she bade listen to their voices. So bind ye me in a hard bond, that I may abide unmoved in my place, upright in the mast-stead, and from the mast let rope-ends be tied, and if I beseech and bid you to set me free, then do ye straiten me with yet more bonds."

Thus I rehearsed these things one and all, and declared them to my company. Meanwhile our good ship quickly came to the island of the Sirens twain, for a gentle breeze sped her on her way. Then straightway the wind ceased, and lo, there was a windless calm, and some god lulled the waves. Then my company rose up and drew in the ship's sails, and stowed them in the hold of the ship, while they sat at the oars and whitened the water with their polished pine blades. But I with my sharp sword cleft in pieces a great circle of wax, and with my strong hands kneaded it. And soon the wax grew warm, for that my great might constrained it, and the beam of the lord Helios, son of Hyperion. And I anointed therewith the ears of all my men in their order, and in the ship they bound me hand and foot upright in the mast-stead, and from the mast they fastened rope-ends and themselves sat down, and smote the gray seawater with their oars. But when the ship was within the sound of a man's shout from the land, we fleeing swiftly on our way, the Sirens espied the swift ship speeding toward them, and they raised their clear-toned song:

"Hither, come hither, renowned Odysseus, great glory of the Achaeans, here stay thy barque, that thou mayest listen to the voice of us twain. For none hath ever driven by this way in his black ship, till he hath heard from our lips the voice sweet as the honeycomb, and hath had joy thereof and gone on his way the wiser. For lo, we know all things, all the travail that in wide Troyland the Argives and Trojans bare by the gods' designs, yea, and we know all that shall hereafter be upon the fruitful earth."

So spake they uttering a sweet voice, and my

heart was fain to listen, and I bade my company unbind me, nodding at them with a frown, but they bent to their oars and rowed on. Then straight uprose Perimedes and Eurylochus and bound me with more cords and straitened me yet the more. Now when we had driven past them, nor heard we any longer the sound of the Sirens or their song, forthwith my dear company took away the wax wherewith I had anointed their ears and loosed me from my bonds.

But so soon as we left that isle, thereafter presently I saw smoke and a great wave, and heard the sea roaring. Then for very fear the oars flew from their hands, and down the stream they all splashed, and the ship was holden there, for my company no longer plied with their hands the tapering oars. But I paced the ship and cheered on my men, as I stood by each one and spake smooth words:

"Friends, forasmuch as in sorrow we are not all unlearned, truly this is no greater woe that is upon us, than when the Cyclops penned us by main might in his hollow cave; yet even thence we made escape by my manfulness, even by my counsel and my wit, and someday I think that this adventure too we shall remember. Come now, therefore, let us all give ear to do according to my word. Do ye smite the deep surf of the sea with your oars, as ye sit on the benches, if peradventure Zeus may grant us to escape from and shun this death. And as for thee, helmsman, thus I charge thee, and ponder it in thine heart seeing that thou wieldest the helm of the hollow ship. Keep the ship well away from this smoke and from the wave and hug the rocks, lest the ship, ere thou art aware, start from her course to the other side, and so thou hurl us into ruin."

So I spake, and quickly they hearkened to my words. But of Scylla I told them nothing more, a bane none might deal with, lest haply my company should cease from rowing for fear, and hide them in the hold. In that same hour I suffered myself to forget the hard behest of Circe, in that she bade me in nowise be armed; but I did on my glorious harness and caught up two long lances in my hands, and went on to the decking of the prow, for thence methought that Scylla of the rock would first be seen, who was to bring woe on my company. Yet could I not spy her anywhere, and my eyes waxed weary for gazing all about toward the darkness of the rock.

Next we began to sail up the narrow strait lamenting. For on the one hand lay Scylla, and on the other mighty Charybdis in terrible wise sucked down the salt seawater. As often as she belched it forth, like a cauldron on a great fire she would seethe up through all her troubled deeps, and overhead the spray fell on the tops of either cliff. But oft as she gulped down the salt seawater, within she was all plain to see through her troubled deeps, and the rock around roared horribly and beneath the earth was manifest swart with sand, and pale fear gat hold on my men. Toward her, then, we looked fearing destruction; but Scylla meanwhile caught from out my hollow ship six of my company, the hardiest of their hands and the chief in might. And looking into the swift ship to find my men, even then I marked their feet and hands as they were lifted on high, and they cried aloud in their agony, and called me by my name for that last time of all. Even as when a fisher on some headland lets down with a long rod his baits for a snare to the little fishes below, casting into the deep the horn of an ox of the homestead, and as he catches each flings it writhing ashore, so writhing were they borne upward to the cliff. And there she devoured them shrieking in her gates, they stretching forth their hands to me in the dread death struggle. And the most pitiful thing was this that mine eyes have seen of all my travail in searching out the paths of the sea.

Now when we had escaped the Rocks and dread Charybdis and Scylla, thereafter we soon came to the fair island of the god; where were the goodly kine, broad of brow, and the many brave flocks of Helios Hyperion. Then while as yet I was in my black ship upon the deep, I heard the lowing of the cattle being stalled and the bleating of the sheep, and on my mind there fell the saying of the blind seer, Theban Teiresias, and of Circe of Aia, who charged me very straitly to shun the isle of Helios, the gladdener of the world. Then I spake out among my company in sorrow of heart:

"Hear my words, my men, albeit in evil

plight, that I may declare unto you the oracles of Teiresias and of Circe of Aia, who very straitly charged me to shun the isle of Helios, the gladdener of the world. For there she said the most dreadful mischief would befall us. Nay, drive ye then the black ship beyond and past that isle."

So spake I, and their heart was broken within them. And Eurylochus straightway answered me sadly, saying:

"Hardy art thou, Odysseus, of might beyond measure, and thy limbs are never weary; verily thou art fashioned all of iron, that sufferest not thy fellows, foredone with toil and drowsiness, to set foot on shore, where we might presently prepare us a good supper in this seagirt island. But even as we are thou biddest us fare blindly through the sudden night, and from the isle go wandering on the misty deep. And strong winds, the bane of ships, are born of the night. How could a man escape from utter doom, if there chanced to come a sudden blast of the South Wind, or of the boisterous West, which mainly wreck ships, beyond the will of the gods, the lords of all? Howbeit for this present let us yield to the black night, and we will make ready our supper abiding by the swift ship, and in the morning we will climb on board, and put out into the broad deep."

So spake Eurylochus, and the rest of my company consented thereto. Then at the last I knew that some god was indeed imagining evil, and I uttered my voice and spake unto him winged words:

"Eurylochus, verily ye put force upon me, being but one among you all. But come, swear me now a mighty oath, one and all, to the intent that if we light on a herd of kine or a great flock of sheep, none in the evil folly of his heart may slay any sheep or ox; but in quiet eat ye the meat which the deathless Circe gave."

So I spake, and straightway they swore to refrain as I commanded them. Now after they had sworn and done that oath, we stayed our well-built ship in the hollow harbor near to a well of sweet water, and my company went forth from out the ship and deftly got ready supper. But when they had put from them the desire of meat and drink, thereafter they fell a weeping as they thought upon their dear companions whom Scylla had snatched from out the hollow ship and so devoured. And deep sleep came upon them amid their weeping. And when it was the third watch of the night, and the stars had crossed the zenith, Zeus the cloud gatherer roused against them an angry wind with wondrous tempest, and shrouded in clouds land and sea alike, and from heaven sped down the night. Now when early Dawn shone forth, the rosy-fingered, we beached the ship, and dragged it up within a hollow cave, where were the fair dancing grounds of the nymphs and the places of their session. Thereupon I ordered a gathering of my men and spake in their midst, saying:

"Friends, forasmuch as there is yet meat and drink in the swift ship, let us keep our hands off those kine, lest some evil thing befall us. For these are the kine and the brave flocks of a dread god, even of Helios, who overseeth all and overheareth all things."

So I spake, and their lordly spirit hearkened thereto. Then for a whole month the South Wind blew without ceasing, and no other wind arose, save only the East and the South.

Now so long as my company still had corn and red wine, they refrained them from the kine, for they were fain of life. But when the corn was now all spent from out the ship, and they went wandering with barbed hooks in quest of game, as needs they must, fish and fowls, whatsoever might come to their hand, for hunger gnawed at their belly, then at last I departed up the isle, that I might pray to the gods, if perchance some one of them might show me a way of returning. And now when I had avoided my company on my way through the island, I laved my hands where was a shelter from the wind, and prayed to all the gods that hold Olympus. But they shed sweet sleep upon my eyelids. And Eurylochus the while set forth an evil counsel to my company:

"Hear my words, my friends, though ye be in evil case. Truly every shape of death is hateful to wretched mortals, but to die of hunger, and so meet doom is most pitiful of all. Nay come, we will drive off the best of the kine of Helios and will do sacrifice to the deathless gods who keep wide heaven. And if we may yet reach Ithaca, our own country, forthwith will we rear a rich shrine to Helios Hyperion, and therein would we set many a choice offering. But if he be somewhat wroth for his cattle with straight horns, and is fain to wreck our ship, and the other gods follow his desire, rather with one gulp at the wave would I cast my life away, than be slowly straitened to death in a desert isle."

So spake Eurylochus, and the rest of the company consented thereto. Forthwith they drave off the best of the kine of Helios that were nigh at hand, for the fair kine of shambling gait and broad of brow were feeding no great way from the dark-prowed ship. Then they stood around the cattle and prayed to the gods, plucking the fresh leaves from an oak of lofty boughs, for they had no white barley on board the decked ship. Now after they had prayed and cut the throats of the kine and flayed them, they cut out slices of the thighs and wrapped them in the fat, making a double fold, and thereon they laid raw flesh. Yet had they no pure wine to pour over the flaming sacrifices, but they made libation with water and roasted the entrails over the fire. Now after the thighs were quite consumed and they had tasted the inner parts, they cut the rest up small and spitted it on spits. In the same hour deep sleep sped from my eyelids and I sallied forth to the swift ship and the sea banks. But on my way as I drew near to the curved ship, the sweet savor of the fact came all about me; and I groaned and spake out before the deathless gods:

"Father Zeus, and all ye other blessed gods that live for ever, verily to my undoing ye have lulled me with a ruthless sleep, and my company abiding behind have imagined a monstrous deed."

Then swiftly to Helios Hyperion came Lampetie of the long robes, with the tidings that we had slain his kine. And straight he spake with angry heart amid the Immortals:

"Father Zeus, and all ye other blessed gods that live forever, take vengeance I pray you on the company of Odysseus, son of Laertes, that have insolently slain my cattle, wherein I was wont to be glad as I went toward the starry heaven, and when I again turned earthward from the firmament. And if they pay me not full atonement for the cattle, I will go down to Hades and shine among the dead."

And Zeus the cloud gatherer answered him, saying: "Helios, do thou, I say, shine on amidst the deathless gods, and amid mortal men upon the earth, the grain giver. But as for me, I will soon smite their swift ship with my white bolt, and cleave it in pieces in the midst of the wine-dark deep."

This I heard from Calypso of the fair hair; and she said that she herself had heard it from Hermes the Messenger.

But when I had come down to the ship and to the sea, I went up to my companions and rebuked them one by one; but we could find no remedy, the cattle were dead and gone. And soon thereafter the gods showed forth signs and wonders to my company. The skins were creeping, and the flesh bellowing upon the spits, both the roast and raw, and there was a sound as the voice of kine.

Then for six days my dear company feasted on the best of the kine of Helios which they had driven off. But when Zeus, son of Cronos, had added the seventh day thereto, thereafter the wind ceased to blow with a rushing storm, and at once we climbed the ship and launched into the broad deep, when we had set up the mast and hoisted the white sails.

But now when we left that isle nor any other land appeared, but sky and sea only, even then the son of Cronos stayed a dark cloud above the hollow ship, and beneath it the deep darkened. And the ship ran on her way for no long while, for of a sudden came the shrilling West Wind, with the rushing of a great tempest, and the blast of wind snapped the two forestays of the mast, and the mast fell backward and all the gear dropped into the bilge. And behold, on the hind part of the ship the mast struck the head of the pilot and brake all the bones of his skull together, and like a diver he dropt down from the deck, and his brave spirit left his bones. In that same hour Zeus thundered and cast his bolt upon the ship, and she reeled all over, being stricken by the bolt of Zeus, and was filled with sulphur, and lo, my company fell from out the vessel. Like seagulls they were borne round the black ship upon the billows, and the god reft them of returning.

But I kept pacing through my ship, till the surge loosened the sides from the keel, and the wave swept her along stripped of her tackling, and broke her mast clean off at the keel. Now the backstay fashioned of an oxhide had been flung thereon; therewith I lashed together both keel and mast, and sitting thereon I was borne by the ruinous winds.

Then verily the West Wind ceased to blow with a rushing storm, and swiftly withal the South Wind came, bringing sorrow to my soul, that so I might again measure back that space of sea, the way to deadly Charybdis. All the night was I borne, but with the rising of the sun I came to the rock of Scylla, and to dread Charybdis. Now she had sucked down her salt seawater, when I was swung up on high to the tall fig tree whereto I clung like a bat, and could find no sure rest for my feet nor place to stand, for the roost spread far below and the branches hung aloft out of reach, long and large, and overshadowed Cha-rybdis. Steadfast, I clung till she should spew forth mast and keel again; and late they came to my desire. At the hour when a man rises up from the assembly and goes to supper, one who judges the many quarrels of the young men that seek to him for law, at that same hour those timbers came forth to view from out Charybdis. And I let myself drop down hands and feet, and plunged heavily in the midst of the waters beyond the long timbers, and sitting on these I rowed hard with my hands. But the father of gods and of men suffered me no more to behold Scylla, else I should never have escaped from utter doom.

Thence for nine days was I borne, and on the tenth night the gods brought me nigh to the isle of Ogygia, where dwells Calypso of the braided tresses, an awful goddess of mortal speech, who took me in and entreated me kindly. But why rehearse all this tale? For even yesterday I told it to thee and to thy noble wife in thy house; and it liketh me not twice to tell a plain-told tale.

Call Me Ishmael

by HERMAN MELVILLE

The opening line of **Moby Dick** *is one of the most famous in all fiction. The chapter it introduces is Melville's summary statement on what drives and draws men to sail the seas. A later chapter, "The Mast-head," reveals the mystical side of Melville's hero, Ishmael, and explains why the oceans inspire meditation.*

CALL me Ishmael. Some years ago—never mind how long precisely—having little or no money in my purse, and nothing particular to interest me on shore, I thought I would sail about a little and see the watery part of the world. It is a way I have of driving off the spleen, and regulating the circulation. Whenever I find myself growing grim about the mouth; whenever it is a damp, drizzly November in my soul; whenever I find myself involuntarily pausing before coffin warehouses, and bringing up the rear of every funeral I meet; and especially whenever my hypos get such an upper hand of me, that it requires a strong moral principle to prevent me from deliberately stepping into the street, and methodically knocking people's hats off—then, I account it high time to get to sea as soon as I can. This is my substitute for pistol and ball. With a philosophical flourish Cato throws himself upon his sword; I quietly take to the ship.

There is nothing surprising in this. If they but knew it, almost all men in their degree, some time or other, cherish very nearly the same feelings towards the ocean with me.

There now is your insular city of the Manhattoes, belted round by wharves as Indian isles by coral reefs—commerce surrounds it with her surf. Right and left, the streets take you waterward. Its extreme downtown is the Battery, where that noble mole is washed by waves, and cooled by breezes, which a few hours previous were out of sight of land. Look at the crowds of water gazers there.

Circumambulate the city of a dreamy Sabbath afternoon. Go from Corlears Hook to Coenties Slip, and from thence, by Whitehall, northward. What do you see? Posted like silent sentinels all around the town, stand thousands upon thousands of mortal men fixed in ocean reveries. Some leaning against the spiles; some seated upon the pierheads; some looking over the bulwarks of ships from China; some high aloft in the rigging, as if striving to get a still better seaward peep. But these are all landsmen; of weekdays pent up in lath and plaster—tied to counters, nailed to benches, clinched to desks. How then is this? Are the green fields gone? What do they here?

But look! here come more crowds, pacing

straight for the water, and seemingly bound for a dive. Strange! Nothing will content them but the extremest limit of the land; loitering under the shady lee of yonder warehouses will not suffice. No. They must get just as nigh the water as they possibly can without falling in. And there they stand—miles of them—leagues. Inlanders all, they come from lanes and alleys, streets and avenues—north, east, south, and west. Yet here they all unite. Tell me, does the magnetic virtue in the needles of the compasses of all those ships attract them thither?

Once more. Say, you are in the country; in some high land of lakes. Take almost any path you please, and ten to one it carries you down in a dale, and leaves you there by a pool in the stream. There is magic in it. Let the most absent-minded of men be plunged in his deepest reveries—stand that man on his legs, set his feet a-going, and he will infallibly lead you to water, if water there be in all that region. Should you ever be athirst in the great American desert, try this experiment, if your caravan happen to be supplied with a metaphysical professor. Yes, as every one knows, meditation and water are wedded forever.

But here is an artist. He desires to paint you the dreamiest, shadiest, quietest, most enchanting bit of romantic landscape in all the valley of the Saco. What is the chief element he employs? There stand his trees, each with a hollow trunk, as if a hermit and a crucifix were within; and here sleeps his meadow, and there sleep his cattle; and up from yonder cottage goes a sleepy smoke. Deep into distant woodlands winds a mazy way, reaching to overlapping spurs of mountains bathed in their hillside blue. But though the picture lies thus tranced, and though this pine tree shakes down its sighs like leaves upon this shepherd's head, yet all were vain, unless the shepherd's eye were fixed upon the magic stream before him. Go visit the Prairies in June, when for scores on scores of miles you wade knee-deep among tiger lilies—what is the one charm wanting?—Water—there is not a drop of water there! Were Niagara but a cataract of sand, would you travel your thousand miles to see it? Why did the poor poet of Tennessee, upon suddenly receiv-

ing two handfuls of silver, deliberate whether to buy him a coat, which he sadly needed, or invest his money in a pedestrian trip to Rockaway Beach? Why is almost every robust healthy boy with a robust healthy soul in him, at some time or other crazy to go to sea? Why upon your first voyage as a passenger, did you yourself feel such a mystical vibration, when first told that you and your ship were now out of sight of land? Why did the old Persians hold the sea holy? Why did the Greeks give it a separate deity, and make him the own brother of Jove? Surely all this is not without meaning. And still deeper the meaning of that story of Narcissus, who because he could not grasp the tormenting, mild image he saw in the fountain, plunged into it and was drowned. But that same image, we ourselves see in all rivers and oceans. It is the image of the ungraspable phantom of life; and this is the key to it all.

Now, when I say that I am in the habit of going to sea whenever I begin to grow hazy about the eyes, and begin to be overconscious of my lungs, I do not mean to have it inferred that I ever go to sea as a passenger. For to go as a passenger you must needs have a purse, and a purse is but a rag unless you have something in it. Besides, passengers get seasick—grow quarrelsome—don't sleep of nights—do not enjoy themselves much, as a general thing—no, I never go as a passenger; nor, though I am something of a salt, do I ever go to sea as a commodore, or a captain, or a cook. I abandon the glory and distinction of such offices to those who like them. For my part, I abominate all honorable respectable toils, trials, and tribulations of every kind whatsoever. It is quite as much as I can do to take care of myself, without taking care of ships, barques, brigs, schooners, and whatnot. And as for going as cook—though I confess there is considerable glory in that, a cook being a sort of officer on shipboard—yet, somehow, I never fancied broiling fowls—though once broiled, judiciously buttered, and judgmatically salted and peppered, there is no one who will speak more respectfully, not to say reverentially, of a broiled fowl than I will. It is out of the idolatrous dotings of the old Egyptians upon broiled ibis and roasted river horse, that you see the mummies of those creatures in their huge bakehouses the pyramids.

No, when I go to sea, I go as a simple sailor, right before the mast, plumb down into the forecastle, aloft there to the royal masthead. True, they rather order me about some, and make me jump from spar to spar, like a grasshopper in a May meadow. And at first, this sort of thing is unpleasant enough. It touches one's sense of honor, particularly if you come of an old established family in the land, the Van Rensselaers, or Randolphs, or Hardicanutes. And more than all, if just previous to putting your hand into the tar pot, you have been lording it as a country schoolmaster, making the tallest boys stand in awe of you. The transition is a keen one, I assure you, from a schoolmaster to a sailor, and requires a strong decoction of Seneca and the Stoics to enable you to grin and bear it. But even this wears off in time.

What of it, if some old hunks of a sea captain orders me to get a broom and sweep down the decks? What does that indignity amount to, weighed, I mean, in the scales of the New Testament? Do you think the archangel Gabriel thinks anything the less of me, because I promptly and respectfully obey that old hunks in that particular instance? Who ain't a slave? Tell me that. Well, then, however the old sea captains may order me about—however they may thump and punch me about, I have the satisfaction of knowing that it is all right; that everybody else is one way or other served in much the same way—either in a physical or metaphysical point of view, that is; and so the universal thump is passed round, and all hands should rub each other's shoulder blades, and be content.

Again, I always go to sea as a sailor, because they make a point of paying me for my trouble, whereas they never pay passengers a single penny that I ever heard of. On the contrary, passengers themselves must pay. And there is all the difference in the world between paying and being paid. The act of paying is perhaps the most uncomfortable infliction that the two orchard thieves entailed upon us. But *being paid*—what will compare with it? The urbane activity with which a man receives money is really marvelous, considering that we so earnestly believe money to be the root of all earthly ills, and that on no account can a moneyed man enter heaven. Ah! how cheerfully we consign ourselves to perdition!

Finally, I always go to sea as a sailor, because of the wholesome exercise and pure air of the forecastle deck. For as in this world, head winds are far more prevalent than winds from astern (that is, if you never violate the Pythagorean maxim), so for the most part the commodore on the quarterdeck gets his atmosphere at second-hand from the sailors on the forecastle. He thinks he breathes it first; but not so. In much the same way do the commonalty lead their leaders in many other things, at the same time that the leaders little suspect it. But wherefore it was that after having repeatedly smelled the sea as a merchant sailor, I should now take it into my head to go on a whaling voyage; this the invisible police officer of the Fates, who has the constant surveillance of me, and secretly dogs me, and influences me in some unaccountable way—he can better answer than anyone else. And, doubtless, my going on this whaling voyage, formed part of the grand program of Providence that was drawn up a long time ago. It came in as a sort of brief interlude and solo between more extensive performances. I take it that this part of the bill must have run something like this:

Grand Contested Election for the Presidency of the United States.
WHALING VOYAGE BY ONE ISHMAEL.
BLOODY BATTLE IN AFFGHANISTAN.

Though I cannot tell why it was exactly that those stage managers, the Fates, put me down for this shabby part of a whaling voyage, when others were set down for magnificent parts in high tragedies, and short and easy parts in genteel comedies, and jolly parts in farces—though I cannot tell why this was exactly; yet, now that I recall all the circumstances, I think I can see a little into the springs and motives which, being cunningly presented to me under various disguises, induced me to set about performing the part I did, besides cajoling me into the delusion that it was a choice resulting from my own unbiased free will and discriminating judgment.

Chief among these motives was the overwhelming idea of the great whale himself. Such a portentous and mysterious monster roused all my curiosity. Then the wild and distant seas where he rolled his island bulk; the undeliverable, nameless perils of the whale; these, with all the attending marvels of a thousand Patagonian sights and sounds, helped to sway me to my wish. With other men, perhaps, such things would not have been inducements; but as for me, I am tormented with an everlasting itch for things remote. I love to sail forbidden seas, and land on barbarous coasts. Not ignoring what is good, I am quick to perceive a horror, and could still be social with it—would they let me—since it is but well to be on friendly terms with all the inmates of the place one lodges in.

By reason of these things, then, the whaling voyage was welcome; the great floodgates of the wonder world swung open, and in the wild conceits that swayed me to my purpose, two and two there floated into my inmost soul, endless processions of the whale, and, midmost of them all, one grand hooded phantom, like a snow hill in the air.

It was during the more pleasant weather, that in due rotation with the other seamen my first masthead came round.

In most American whalemen the mastheads are manned almost simultaneously with the vessel's leaving her port; even though she may have fifteen thousand miles, and more, to sail ere reaching her proper cruising ground. And if, after a three, four, or five years' voyage she is drawing nigh home with anything empty in her —say, an empty vial even—then, her mast-heads are kept manned to the last; and not till her sky-sail poles sail in among the spires of the port, does she altogether relinquish the hope of capturing one whale more.

Now, as the business of standing mastheads, ashore or afloat, is a very ancient and interesting one, let us in some measure expatiate here. I take it, that the earliest standers of mastheads were the old Egyptians; because, in all my researches, I find none prior to them. For though their progenitors, the builders of Babel, must doubtless, by their tower, have intended to rear the loftiest masthead in all Asia, or Africa either; yet (ere the final truck was put to it) as that great stone mast of theirs may be said to have gone by the board, in the dread gale of God's wrath; therefore, we cannot give these Babel builders priority over the Egyptians. And that the Egyptians were a nation of masthead standers is an assertion based upon the general belief among archaeologists, that the first pyramids were founded for astronomical purposes: a theory singularly supported by the peculiar stairlike formation of all four sides of those edifices; whereby, with prodigious long upliftings of their legs, those old astronomers were wont to mount to the apex, and sing out for new stars; even as the lookouts of a modern ship sing out for a sail, or a whale just bearing in sight. In Saint Stylites, the famous Christian hermit of old times, who built him a lofty stone pillar in the desert and spent the whole latter portion of his life on its summit, hoisting his food from the ground with a tackle; in him we have a remarkable instance of a dauntless stander-of-mastheads; who was not to be driven from his place by fogs or frosts, rain, hail, or sleet; but, valiantly facing everything out to the last, literally died at his post. Of modern standers-of-mastheads we have but a lifeless set; mere stone, iron, and bronze men; who, though well capable of facing out a stiff gale, are still entirely incompetent to the business of singing out upon discovering any strange sight. There is Napoleon; who, upon the top of the column of Vendôme, stands with arms folded, some one hundred and fifty feet in the air; careless, now, who rules the decks below; whether Louis Philippe, Louis Blanc, or Louis the Devil. Great Washington, too, stands high aloft on his towering mainmast in Baltimore, and like one of Hercules' pillars, his column marks that point of human grandeur beyond which few mortals will go. Admiral Nelson, also, on a capstan of gunmetal, stands his masthead in Trafalgar Square; and even when most obscured by that London smoke, token is yet given that a hidden hero is there; for where there is smoke, must be fire. But neither great Washington, nor Napoleon, nor

Nelson, will answer a single hail from below, however madly invoked to befriend by their counsels the distracted decks upon which they gaze; however, it may be surmised, that their spirits penetrate through the thick haze of the future, and descry what shoals and what rocks must be shunned.

It may seem unwarrantable to couple in any respect the masthead standers of the land with those of the sea; but that in truth it is not so, is plainly evinced by an item for which Obed Macy, the sole historian of Nantucket, stands accountable. The worthy Obed tells us, that in the early times of the whale fishery, ere ships were regularly launched in pursuit of the game, the people of that island erected lofty spars along the seacoast, to which the lookouts ascended by means of nailed cleats, something as fowls go upstairs in a hen house. A few years ago this same plan was adopted by the Bay whalemen of New Zealand, who, upon descrying the game, gave notice to the ready-manned boats nigh the beach. But this custom has now become obsolete; turn we then to the one proper masthead, that of a whaleship at sea.

The three mastheads are kept manned from sunrise to sunset; the seamen taking their regular turns (as at the helm), and relieving each other every two hours. In the serene weather of the tropics it is exceedingly pleasant—the masthead; nay, to a dreamy meditative man it is delightful. There you stand, a hundred feet above the silent decks, striding along the deep, as if the masts were gigantic stilts, while beneath you and between your legs, as it were, swim the hugest monsters of the sea, even as ships once sailed between the boots of the famous Colossus at old Rhodes. There you stand, lost in the infinite series of the sea, with nothing ruffled but the waves. The tranced ship indolently rolls; the drowsy trade winds blow; everything resolves you into langor. For the most part, in this tropic whaling life, a sublime uneventfulness invests you; you hear no news; read no gazettes; extras with startling accounts of commonplaces never delude you into unnecessary excitements; you hear of no domestic afflictions; bankrupt securities; fall of stocks; are never troubled with the thought of what you shall have for dinner—for all your meals for three years and more are snugly stowed in casks, and your bill of fare is immutable.

In one of those southern whalemen, on a long three or four years' voyage, as often happens, the sum of the various hours you spend at the masthead would amount to several entire months. And it is much to be deplored that the place to which you devote so considerable a portion of the whole term of your natural life, should be so sadly destitute of anything approaching to a cozy inhabitiveness, or adapted to breed a comfortable localness of feeling, such as pertains to a bed, a hammock, a hearse, a sentry box, a pulpit, a coach, or any other of those small and snug contrivances in which men temporarily isolate themselves. Your most usual point of perch is the head of the t'gallant mast, where you stand upon two thin parallel sticks (almost peculiar to whalemen) called the t'gallant crosstrees. Here, tossed about by the sea, the beginner feels about as cozy as he would standing on a bull's horns. To be sure, in coolish weather you may carry your house aloft with you, in the shape of a watch coat; but, properly speaking, the thickest watch coat is no more of a house than the unclad body; for as the soul is glued inside of its fleshly tabernacle, and cannot freely move about in it, nor even move out of it, without running great risk of perishing (like an ignorant pilgrim crossing the snowy Alps in winter); so a watch coat is not so much of a house as it is a mere envelope, or additional skin encasing you. You cannot put a shelf or chest of drawers in your body, and no more can you make a convenient closet of your watch coat.

Concerning all this, it is much to be deplored that the mastheads of a southern whaleship are unprovided with those enviable little tents or pulpits, called *crow's nests,* in which the lookouts of a Greenland whaler are protected from the inclement weather of the frozen seas. In the fireside narrative of Captain Sleet, entitled "A Voyage among the Icebergs, in Quest of the Greenland Whale, and Incidentally for the Rediscovery of the Lost Icelandic Colonies of Old Greenland"; in this admirable volume, all standers of mastheads are furnished with a charmingly circumstantial account of the then recently invented *crow's nest* of the *Glacier,* which was the name of Captain Sleet's good craft. He called it the *Sleet's crow's nest,* in honor of himself; he being the original inventor and patentee, and free from all ridiculous false delicacy, and holding that if we call our own children after our own names (we fathers being the original inventors and patentees), so likewise should we denominate after ourselves any other apparatus we may beget. In shape, the Sleet's crow's nest is something like a large tierce or pipe; it is open above, however, where it is furnished with a movable side-screen to keep to windward of your head in a hard gale. Being fixed on the summit of the mast, you ascend into it through a little traphatch in the bottom. On the after side, or side next the stern of the ship, is a comfortable seat, with a locker underneath for umbrellas, comforters, and coats. In front is a leather rack, in which to keep your speaking trumpet, pipe, telescope, and other nautical conveniences. When Captain Sleet in person stood his masthead in this crow's nest of his, he tells us that he always had a rifle with him (also fixed in the rack), together with a powder flask and shot, for the purpose of popping off the stray narwhales, or vagrant sea unicorns infesting those waters; for you cannot successfully shoot at them from the deck, owing to the resistance of the water, but to shoot down upon them is a very different thing. Now, it was plainly a labor of love for Captain Sleet to describe, as he does, all the little detailed conveniences of his crow's nest; but though he so enlarges upon many of these, and though he treats us to a very scientific account of his experiments in this crow's nest, with a small compass he kept there for the purpose of counteracting the errors resulting from what is called the "local attraction" of all binnacle magnets; an error ascribable to the horizontal vicinity of the iron in the ship's planks, and in the *Glacier's* case, perhaps, to there having been so many broken-down blacksmiths among her crew; I say, that though the captain is very discreet and scientific here, yet, for all his learned "binnacle deviations," "azimuth compass observations," and "approxi-

mate errors," he knows very well, Captain Sleet, that he was not so much immersed in those profound magnetic meditations, as to fail being attracted occasionally towards that well replenished little case bottle, so nicely tucked in on one side of his crow's nest, within easy reach of his hand. Though, upon the whole, I greatly admire and even love the brave, the honest, and learned captain; yet I take it very ill of him that he should so utterly ignore that case bottle, seeing what a faithful friend and comforter it must have been, while with mittened fingers and hooded head he was studying the mathematics aloft there in that bird's nest within three or four perches of the pole.

But if we southern whale-fishers are not so snugly housed aloft as Captain Sleet and his Greenland-men were; yet that disadvantage is greatly counterbalanced by the widely contrasting serenity of those seductive seas in which we southern fishers mostly float. For one, I used to lounge up the rigging very leisurely, resting in the top to have a chat with Queequeg, or anyone else off duty whom I might find there; then ascending a little way further, and throwing a lazy leg over the topsail yard, take a preliminary view of the watery pastures, and so at last mount to my ultimate destination.

Let me make a clean breast of it here, and frankly admit that I kept but sorry guard. With the problem of the universe revolving in me, how could I—being left completely to myself at such a thought-engendering altitude—how could I but lightly hold my obligations to observe all whaleships' standing orders, "Keep your weather eye open, and sing out every time."

And let me in this place movingly admonish you, ye shipowners of Nantucket! Beware of enlisting in your vigilant fisheries any lad with lean brow and hollow eye; given to unseasonable meditativeness; and who offers to ship with the Phaedon instead of Bowditch in his head. Beware of such one, I say: your whales must be seen before they can be killed; and this sunken-eyed young Platonist will tow you ten wakes round the world, and never make you one pint of sperm the richer. Nor are these monitions at all unneeded. For nowadays, the whale fishery furnishes an asylum for many romantic, melancholy, and absentminded young men, disgusted with the carking cares of earth, and seeking sentiment in tar and blubber. Childe Harold not unfrequently perches himself upon the masthead of some luckless disappointed whaleship, and in moody phrase ejaculates:

> Roll on, thou deep and dark blue ocean, roll!
> Ten thousand blubber-hunters sweep over thee in vain.

Very often do the captains of such ships take those absentminded young philosophers to task, upbraiding them with not feeling sufficient "interest" in the voyage; half-hinting that they are so hopelessly lost to all honorable ambition, as that in their secret souls they would rather not see whales than otherwise. But all in vain; those young Platonists have a notion that their vision is imperfect; they are short-sighted; what use, then, to strain the visual nerve? They have left their opera glasses at home.

"Why, thou monkey," said a harpooneer to one of these lads, "we've been cruising now hard upon three years, and thou hast not raised a whale yet. Whales are scarce as hen's teeth whenever thou art up here." Perhaps they were; or perhaps there might have been shoals of them in the far horizon; but lulled into such an opiumlike listlessness of vacant, unconscious reverie is this absentminded youth by the blending cadence of waves with thoughts, that at last he loses his identity; takes the mystic ocean at his feet for the visible image of that deep, blue, bottomless soul, pervading mankind and nature; and every strange, half-seen, gliding, beautiful thing that eludes him; every dimly-discovered, uprising fin of some undiscernible form, seems to him the embodiment of those elusive thoughts that only people the soul by continually flitting through it. In this enchanted mood, thy spirit ebbs away to whence it came; becomes diffused through time and space; like Wickliff's sprinkled pantheistic ashes, forming at last a part of every shore the round globe over.

There is no life in thee, now, except that rocking life imparted by a gently rolling ship; by her, borrowed from the sea; by the sea, from the inscrutable tides of God. But while this sleep, this dream is on ye, move your foot or hand an inch; slip your hold at all; and your identity comes back in horror. Over Descartian vortices you hover. And perhaps, at midday, in the fairest weather, with one half-throttled shriek you drop through that transparent air into the summer sea, no more to rise forever. Heed it well, ye pantheists!

Bad Prospects

by RICHARD HENRY DANA, JR.

In 1834 Richard Henry Dana, Jr. left Boston on the brig Pilgrim, *rounding Cape Horn to California, returning on the ship* Alert, *then doubling the Horn and reaching Boston on September 20, 1836. His "two years before the mast" opened his eyes to the life of the nineteenth-century seaman and made him a vocal champion of sailors' rights. Here he records how the* Alert *weathered the storms and the captain kept his crew in line.*

THERE began now to be a decided change in the appearance of things. The days became shorter and shorter; the sun running lower in its course each day, and giving less and less heat, and the nights so cold as to prevent our sleeping on deck; the Magellan Clouds in sight on a clear, moonless night; the skies looking cold and angry; and, at times, a long, heavy, ugly sea setting in from the southward told us what we were coming to. Still, however, we had a fine strong breeze, and kept on our way under as much sail as our ship would bear. Towards the middle of the week, the wind hauled to the southward, which brought us upon a taut bowline, made the ship meet, nearly head-on, the heavy swell which rolled from that quarter; and there was something not at all encouraging in the manner in which she met it. Being still so deep and heavy, she wanted the buoyancy which should have carried her over the seas, and she dropped heavily into them, the water washing over the decks; and every now and then, when an unusually large sea met her fairly upon the bows, she struck it with a sound as dead and heavy as that with which a sledgehammer falls upon the pile, and took the whole of it upon the forecastle, and, rising, carried it aft in the scuppers, washing the rigging off the pins, and carrying along with it everything which was loose on deck. She had been acting in this way all of our forenoon watch below; as we could tell by the washing of the water over our heads, and the heavy breaking of the seas against her bows, only the thickness of a plank from our heads, as we lay in our berths, which are directly against the bows. At eight bells the watch was called, and we came on deck, one hand going aft to take the wheel, and another going to the galley to get the grub for dinner. I stood on the forecastle, looking at the seas, which were rolling high, as far as the eye could reach, their tops white with foam, and the body of them of a deep indigo blue, reflecting the bright rays of the sun. Our ship rose slowly over a few of the largest of them, until one immense fellow came rolling on, threatening to cover her, and which I was sailor enough to know, by the "feeling of her" under my feet, she would not rise over. I sprang upon the knight-heads, and, seizing hold of the fore-stay, drew myself up upon it. My feet were just off the stanchion when the bow struck fairly into the middle of the sea, and it washed the ship fore and aft, burying her in the water. As soon as she rose out of it, I looked aft, and everything forward to the mainmast, except the longboat, which was griped and double-lashed down to the ringbolts, was swept off clear. The galley, the pigsty, the hen coop and a large sheep pen, which had been built upon the fore-hatch, were all gone in the twinkling of an eye—leaving the deck as clean as a chin new reaped—and not a stick left to show where anything had stood. In the scuppers lay the galley, bottom up, and a few boards floating about—the wreck of the sheep pen—and half a dozen miserable sheep floating among them, wet through, and not a little frightened at the sudden change that had come upon them. As soon as the sea had washed by, all hands sprang up out of the forecastle to see what had become of the ship; and in a few moments the cook and Old Bill crawled out from under the galley, where they had been lying in the water, nearly smothered, with the galley over them. Fortunately, it rested against the bulwarks, or it would have broken some of their bones. When the water ran off, we picked the sheep up, and put them in the longboat, got the galley back in its place, and set things a little to rights; but had not our ship uncommonly high bulwarks and rail, everything must have been washed overboard, not excepting Old Bill and the cook. Bill had been standing at the galley door, with the kid of beef in his hand for the forecastle mess, when away he went, kid, beef, and all. He held on to the kid to the last, like a good fellow, but the beef was gone, and when the water had run off we saw it lying high and dry, like a rock at low tide—nothing could hurt *that.* We took the loss of our beef very easily, consoling ourselves with the recollection that the cabin had more to lose than we; and chuckled not a little at seeing the remains of the chicken pie and pancakes floating in the scuppers. "This will never do!" was what some said, and everyone felt. Here we were, not yet within a thousand miles of the latitude of Cape Horn, and our decks swept by a sea not one-half

so high as we must expect to find there. Some blamed the captain for loading his ship so deep when he knew what he must expect; while others said that the wind was always southwest off the Cape in the winter, and that, running before it, we should not mind the seas so much. When we got down into the forecastle, Old Bill, who was somewhat of a croaker—having met with a great many accidents at sea—said that if that was the way she was going to act, we might as well make our wills, and balance the books at once, and put on a clean shirt. " 'Vast there, you bloody old owl; you're always hanging out blue lights! You're frightened by the ducking you got in the scuppers and can't take a joke! What's the use in being always on the lookout for Davy Jones?" "Stand by!" says another, "and we'll get an afternoon watch below, by this scrape"; but in this they were disappointed; for at two bells all hands were called and set to work, getting lashings upon everything on deck; and the captain talked of sending down the long topgallant masts; but as the sea went down towards night, and the wind hauled abeam, we left them standing, and set the studding sails.

The next day all hands were turned-to upon unbending the old sails, and getting up the new ones; for a ship, unlike people on shore, puts on her best suit in bad weather. The old sails were sent down, and three new topsails, and new fore and main courses, jib, and fore-topmast, staysail, which were made on the coast and never had been used, were bent, with a complete set of new earings, robands, and reef points; and reef tackles were rove to the courses, and spilling lines to the topsails. These, with new braces and clew lines fore and aft, gave us a good suit of running rigging.

The wind continued westerly, and the weather and sea less rough since the day on which we shipped the heavy sea, and we were making great progress under studding sails, with our light sails all set, keeping a little to the eastward of south; for the captain, depending upon westerly winds off the Cape, had kept so far to the westward that, though we were within about five miles of the latitude of Cape Horn, we were nearly seventeen hundred miles to the westward of it. Through the rest of the week we continued on with a fair wind, gradually, as we got more to southward, keeping a more easterly course, and bringing the wind on our larboard quarter, until—

Sunday, June 26, when, having a fine, clear day, the captain got a lunar observation, as well as his meridian altitude, which made us in latitude forty-seven degrees fifty minutes south, longitude one hundred thirteen degrees forty-nine minutes west. Cape Horn bearing, according to my calculations, east-southeast half east, and distant eighteen hundred miles.

Monday, June 27. During the first part of this day, the wind continued fair, and, as we were going before it, it did not feel very cold, so that we kept at work on deck in our common clothes and round jackets. Our watch had an afternoon watch below for the first time since leaving San Diego; and, having inquired of the third mate what the latitude was at noon, and made our usual guesses as to the time she would need to be up with the Horn, we turned in for a nap. We were sleeping away "at the rate of knots," when three knocks on the scuttle and "All hands, ahoy!" started us from our berths. What could be the matter? It did not appear to be blowing hard, and, looking up through the scuttle, we could see that it was a clear day overhead; yet the watch were taking in sail. We thought there must be a sail in sight, and that we were about to heave to and speak her; and were just congratulating ourselves upon it—for we had seen neither soil nor land since we left port—when we heard the mate's voice on deck (he turned in "all standing," and was always on deck the moment he was called) singing out to the men who were taking in the studding sails, and asking where his watch was. We did not wait for a second call, but tumbled up the ladder; and there, on the starboard bow, was a bank of mist, covering sea and sky, and driving directly for us. I had seen the same before in my passage round in the *Pilgrim*, and knew what it meant, and that there was no time to be lost. We had nothing on but thin clothes, yet there was not a moment to spare, and at it we went.

The boys of the other watch were in the tops, taking in the topgallant studding sails, and the lower and topmast studding sails were coming down by the run. It was nothing but "hail down and clew up," until we got all the studding sails in, and the royals, flying jib, and mizzen-topgallant sail furled, and the ship kept off a little, to take the squall. The fore and main topgallant sails were still on her, for the "old man" did not mean to be frightened in broad daylight, and was determined to carry sail till the last minute. We all stood waiting for its coming, when the first blast showed us that it was not to be trifled with. Rain, sleet, snow, and wind enough to take our breath from us, and make the toughest turn his back to windward! The ship lay nearly over upon her beam-ends; the spars and rigging snapped and cracked; and her topgallant masts bent like whipsticks. "Clew up the fore and main topgallant sails!" shouted the captain, and all hands sprang to the clew lines. The decks were standing nearly at an angle of forty-five degrees, and the ship going like a mad steed through the water, the whole forward part of her in a smother of foam. The halyards were let go, and the yard clewed down, and the sheets started, and in a few minutes the sails smothered and kept in by clew lines and buntlines. "Furl 'em, sir?" asked the mate. "Let go the topsail halyards fore and aft!" shouted the captain in answer, at the top of his voice. Down came the topsail yards, the reef tackles were manned and hauled out, and we climbed up to windward, and sprang into the weather-rigging. The violence of the wind, and the hail and sleet, driving nearly horizontally across the ocean, seemed actually to pin us down to the rigging. It was hard work making head against them. One after another we got out upon the yards. And here we had work to do; for our new sails had hardly been bent long enough to get the stiffness out of them, and the new earings and reef points, stiffened with the sleet, knotted like pieces of iron wire. Having only our round jackets and straw hats on, we were soon wet through, and it was every moment growing colder. Our hands were soon numbed, which, added to the stiffness of everything else, kept us a good while on the yard. After we had got the sail hauled upon the yard, we had to wait a long time for the weather earing to be passed; but there was no fault to be found, for French John was at the earing, and a better sailor never laid out on a yard; so we leaned over the yard and beat our hands upon the sail to keep them from freezing. At length the word came, "Haul out to leeward," and we seized the reef points and hauled the band taut for the lee earing. "Taut band—knot away," and we got the first reef fast, and were just going to lay down, when—"Two reefs! two reefs!" shouted the mate, and we had a second reef to take in the same way. When this was fast, we went down on deck, manned the halyards to leeward, nearly up to our knees in water, set the topsail, and then laid aloft on the main topsail yard, and reefed that sail in the same manner; for, as I have before stated, we were a good deal reduced in numbers, and, to make it worse, the carpenter, only two days before, had cut his leg with an axe, so that he could not go aloft. This weakened us so that we could not well manage more than one topsail at a time, in such weather as this, and, of course, each man's labor was doubled. From the maintopsail yard, we went upon the main yard and took a reef in the mainsail. No sooner had we got on deck than—"Lay aloft there, and close-reef mizzen-topsail!" This called me; and, being nearest to the rigging, I got first aloft, and out to the weather earing. English Ben was up just after me, and took the lee earing, and the rest of our gang were soon on the yard, and began to fist the sail, when the mate considerately sent up the cook and steward to help us. I could now account for the long time it took to pass the other earings; for, to do my best, with a strong hand to help me at the dog's ear, I could not get it passed until I heard them beginning to complain in the bunt. One reef after another we took in, until the sail was close-reefed, when we went down and hoisted away at the halyards. In the meantime, the jib had been furled and the staysail set, and the ship under her reduced sail had got more upright and was under management; but the two topgallant sails were still hanging in the buntlines, and slatting and jerking as though they would take the masts out of her. We gave a look aloft, and knew that our work was not done yet; and, sure enough, no

sooner did the mate see that we were on deck than—"Lay aloft there, four of you, and furl the topgallant sails!" This called me again, and two of us went aloft up the fore rigging, two more up the main, upon the topgallant yards. The shrouds were now iced over, the sleet having formed a crust round all the standing rigging, and on the weather side of the masts and yards. When we got upon the yard, my hands were so numb that I could not have cast off the knot of the gasket if it were to save my life. We both lay over the yard for a few seconds, beating our hands upon the sail, until we started the blood into our fingers' ends, and at the next moment our hands were in a burning heat. My companion on the yard was a lad (the boy, George Somerby) who came out in the ship a weak, puny boy, from one of the Boston schools—"no larger than a spritsail-sheet knot," nor "heavier than a paper of lampblack," and "not strong enough to haul a shad off a gridiron," but who was now "as long as a spare topmast, strong enough to knock down an ox, and hearty enough to eat him." We fisted the sail together, and, after six or eight minutes of hard hauling and pulling and beating down the sail, which was about as stiff as sheet iron, we managed to get it furled; and snugly furled it must be, for we knew the mate well enough to be certain that if it got adrift again we should be called up from our watch below, at any hour of the night, to furl it.

I had been on the lookout for a chance to jump below and clap on a thick jacket and sou'wester; but when we got on deck we found that eight bells had been struck, and the other watch gone below, so that there were two hours of dog watch for us, and a plenty of work to do. It had now set in for a steady gale from the southwest; but we were not yet far enough to the southward to make a fair wind of it, for we must give Tierra del Fuego a wide berth. The decks were covered with snow and there was a constant driving of sleet. In fact, Cape Horn had set in with good earnest. In the midst of all this, and before it became dark, we had all the studding sails to make up and stow away, and then to lay aloft and rig in all the booms, fore and aft, and coil away the tacks, sheets, and halyards. This was pretty tough work for four or five hands, in the face of a gale which almost took us off the yards, and with ropes so stiff with ice that it was almost impossible to bend them. I was nearly half an hour out on the end of the fore yard, trying to coil away and stop down the topmast studding-sail tack and lower halyards. It was after dark when we got through, and we were not a little pleased to hear four bells struck, which sent us below for two hours, and gave us each a pot of hot tea with our cold beef and bread, and, what was better yet, a suit of thick, dry clothing, fitted for the weather, in place of our thin clothes, which were wet through and now frozen stiff.

This sudden turn, for which we were so little prepared, was as unacceptable to me as to any of the rest; for I had been troubled for several days with a slight toothache, and this cold weather and wetting and freezing were not the best things in the world for it. I soon found that it was getting strong hold, and running over all parts of my face; and before the watch was out I went to the mate, who had charge of the medicine chest, to get something for it. But the chest showed like the end of a long voyage, for there was nothing that would answer but a few drops of laudanum, which must be saved for an emergency; so I had only to bear the pain as well as I could.

When we went on deck at eight bells, it had stopped snowing, and there were a few stars out, but the clouds were still black, and it was blowing a steady gale. Just before midnight, I went aloft and sent down the mizzen-royal yard, and had the good luck to do it to the satisfaction of the mate, who said it was done "out of hand and shipshape." The next four hours below were but little relief to me, for I lay awake in my berth the whole time, from the pain in my face, and heard every bell strike, and, at four o'clock, turned out with the watch, feeling little spirit for the hard duties of the day. Bad weather and hard work at sea can be borne up against very well if one only has spirit and health; but there is nothing brings a man down, at such a time, like bodily pain and want of sleep. There was, however, too much to do to allow time to think; for the gale of yesterday, and the heavy seas we met with a few days

before, while we had yet ten degrees more southing to make, had convinced the captain that we had something before us which was not to be trifled with, and orders were given to send down the long topgallant masts. The topgallant and royal yards were accordingly struck, the flying jibboom rigged in, and the topgallant masts sent down on deck, and all lashed together by the side of the longboat. The rigging was then sent down and coiled away below, and everything made snug. There was not a sailor in the ship who was not rejoiced to see these sticks come down; for, so as the yards were aloft, on the least sign of a lull, the topgallant sails were loosed, and then we had to furl them again in a snow squall, and *shin* up and down single ropes caked with ice, and send royal yards down in the teeth of a gale coming right from the South Pole. It was an interesting sight, too, to see our noble ship dismantled of all her top-hamper of long tapering masts and yards, and boom pointed with spear head, which ornamented her in port; and all that canvas which, a few days before, had covered her like a cloud, from the truck to the water's edge, spreading far out beyond her hull on either side, now gone; and she stripped like a wrestler for the fight. It corresponded, too, with the desolate character of her situation—alone, as she was, battling with storms, wind, and ice, at this extremity of the globe, and in almost constant night.

Friday, July 1. We were now nearly up to the latitude of Cape Horn, and having over forty degrees of easting to make, we squared away the yards before a strong westerly gale, shook a reef out of the foretopsail, and stood on our way, east by south, with the prospect of being up with the cape in a week or ten days. As for myself, I had had no sleep for forty-eight hours; and the want of rest, together with constant wet and cold, had increased the swelling, so that my face was nearly as large as two, and I found it impossible to get my mouth open wide enough to eat. In this state, the steward applied to the captain for some rice to boil for me, but he only got a "No! d——you! Tell him to eat salt junk and hard bread, like the rest of them." This was, in truth, what I expected. However, I did not starve, for Mr.

Brown, who was a man as well as a sailor, and had always been a good friend to me, smuggled a pan of rice into the galley, and told the cook to boil it for me, and not let the "old man" see it. Had it been fine weather, or in port, I should have gone below and laid by until my face got well; but in such weather as this, and shorthanded as we were, it was not for me to desert my post; so I kept on deck, and stood my watch and did my duty as well as I could.

Saturday, July 2. This day the sun rose fair, but it ran too low in the heavens to give any heat, or thaw out our sails and rigging; yet the sight of it was pleasant; and we had a steady "reef-topsail breeze" from the westward. The atmosphere, which had previously been clear and cold, for the last few hours grew damp, and had a disagreeable wet chilliness in it; and the man who came from the wheel said he heard the captain tell "the passenger" that the thermometer had fallen several degrees since morning, which he could not account for in any other way than by supposing that there must be ice near us; though such a thing was rarely heard of in this latitude at this season of the year. At twelve o'clock we went below, and had just got through dinner when the cook put his head down the scuttle and told us to come on deck and see the finest sight that we had ever seen. "Where away, Doctor?"[1] asked the first man who was up. "On the larboard bow." And there lay, floating in the ocean, several miles off, an immense irregular mass, its top and points covered with snow, and its center of a deep indigo color. This was an iceberg, and of the largest size, as one of our men said who had been in the Northern Ocean. As far as the eye could reach, the sea in every direction was of a deep blue color, the waves running high and fresh, and sparkling in the light, and in the midst lay this immense mountain island, its cavities and valleys thrown into deep shade, and its points and pinnacles glittering in the sun. All hands were soon on deck, looking at it, and admiring in various ways its beauty and grandeur. But no description can give any idea of the strangeness, splendor, and, really, the sublimity, of the sight.

[1] The cook's title in all vessels.

Its great size—for it must have been from two to three miles in circumference, and several hundred feet in height—its slow motion, as its base rose and sank in the water, and its high points nodded against the clouds; the dashing of the waves upon it, which, breaking high with foam, lined its base with a white crust; and the thundering sound of the cracking of the mass, and the breaking and tumbling down of huge pieces; together with its nearness and approach, which added a slight element of fear—all combined to give to it the character of true sublimity. The main body of the mass was, as I have said, of an indigo color, its base crusted with frozen foam; and as it grew thin and transparent towards the edges and top, its color shaded off from a deep blue to the whiteness of snow. It seemed to be drifting slowly towards the north, so that we kept away and avoided it. It was in sight all the afternoon; and when we got to leeward of it the wind died away, so that we lay to quite near it for a greater part of the night. Unfortunately, there was no moon, but it was a clear night, and we could plainly mark the long regular heaving of the stupendous mass, as its edges moved slowly against the stars, now revealing them, and now shutting them in. Several times in our watch loud cracks were heard, which sounded as though they must have run through the whole length of the iceberg, and several pieces fell down with a thundering crash, plunging heavily into the sea. Towards morning a strong breeze sprang up, and we filled away, and left it astern, and at daylight it was out of sight. The next day, which was—

Sunday, July 3, the breeze continued strong, the air exceedingly chilly, and the thermometer low. In the course of the day we saw several icebergs of different sizes, but none so near as the one which we saw the day before. Some of them, as well as we could judge at the distance at which we were, must have been as large as that, if not larger. At noon we were in latitude fifty-five degrees twelve minutes south, and supposed longitude eighty-nine degrees five minutes west. Towards night the wind hauled to the southward, and headed us off our course a little, and blew a tremendous gale; but this we did not mind, as there was no rain nor snow, and we were already under close sail.

Monday, July 4. This was "Independence Day" in Boston. What firing of guns, and ringing of bells, and rejoicings of all sort, in every part of our country! The ladies (who have not gone down to Nahant for a breath of cool air and sight of the ocean) walking the streets with parasols over their heads, and the dandies in their white pantaloons and silk stockings! What quantities of ice cream have been eaten, and how many loads of ice brought into the city from a distance, and sold out by the lump and the pound! The smallest of the islands which we saw today would have made the fortune of poor Jack, if he had had it in Boston; and I dare say he would have had no objection to being there with it. This, to be sure, was no place to keep the Fourth of July. To keep ourselves warm, and the ship out of the ice, was as much as we could do. Yet no one forgot the day; and many were the wishes and conjectures and comparisons, both serious and ludicrous, which were made among all hands. The sun shone bright as long as it was up, only that a scud of black clouds was ever and anon driving across it. At noon we were in latitude fifty-four degrees twenty-seven minutes south, and longitude eighty-five degrees five minutes west, having made a good deal of easting, but having lost in our latitude by the heading off of the wind. Between daylight and dark—that is, between nine o'clock and three—we saw thirty-four ice islands of various sizes; some no bigger than the hull of our vessel, and others apparently nearly as large as the one that we first saw; though, as we went on, the islands became smaller and more numerous; and at sundown of this day a man at the masthead saw large tracts of floating ice, called "field ice," at the southeast. This kind of ice is much more dangerous than the large islands, for those can be seen at a distance, and kept away from; but the field ice, floating in great quantities, and covering the ocean for miles and miles, in pieces of every size—large, flat, and broken cakes, with here and there an island rising twenty and thirty feet, as large as the ship's hull—this it is very difficult to sheer clear of. A constant lookout was necessary; for

many of these pieces, coming with a heave of the sea, were large enough to have knocked a hole in the ship, and that would have been the end of us; for no boat (even if we could have got one out) could have lived in such a sea; and no man could have lived in a boat in such weather. To make our condition still worse, the wind came out due east, just after sundown, and it blew a gale dead ahead, with hail and sleet and a thick fog, so that we could not see half the length of the ship. Our chief reliance, the prevailing westerly gales, was thus cut off, and here we were, nearly seven hundred miles to the westward of the cape, with a gale dead from the eastward, and the weather so thick that we could not see the ice with which we were surrounded until it was directly under our bows. At 4:00 P.M. (it was quite dark) all hands were called, and sent aloft, in a violent squall of hail and rain, to take in sail. We had now all got on our "Cape Horn rig"—thick boots, sou'westers coming down over our neck and ears, thick trousers and jackets; and some with oilcloth suits over all. Mittens, too, we wore on deck, but it would not do to go aloft with them, as, being wet and stiff, they might let a man slip overboard, for all the hold he could get upon a rope: so we were obliged to work with bare hands, which, as well as our faces, were often cut with the hailstones, which fell thick and large. Our ship was now all cased with ice—hull, spars, and standing rigging; and the running rigging so stiff that we could hardly bend it so as to belay it, or, still less, take a knot with it; and the sails frozen. One at a time (for it was a long piece of work and required many hands) we furled the courses, mizzen-topsail, and foretopmast staysail, and close-reefed the fore and main topsails, and hove the ship to under the fore, with the main hauled up by the clewlines and buntlines, and ready to be sheeted home, if we found it necessary to make sail to get to windward of an ice island. A regular lookout was then set, and kept by each watch in turn, until the morning. It was a tedious and anxious night. It blew hard the whole time, and there was an almost constant driving of either rain, hail, or snow. In addition to this it was "as thick as muck," and the ice was all about us. The captain was on deck nearly the whole night, and kept the cook in the galley, with a roaring fire, to make coffee for him, which he took every few hours, and once or twice gave a little to his officers; but not a drop of anything was there for the crew. The captain, who sleeps all the daytime, and comes and goes at night as he chooses, can have his brandy and water in the cabin, and his hot coffee at the galley; while Jack, who has to stand through everything, and work in wet and cold, can have nothing to wet his lips or warm his stomach. This was a "temperance ship" by her articles, and, like too many such ships, the temperance was all in the forecastle. The sailor, who only takes his one glass as it is dealt out to him, is in danger of being drunk; while the captain, upon whose self-possession and cool judgment the lives of all depend, may be trusted with any amount, to drink at his will. Sailors will never be convinced that rum is a dangerous thing by taking it away from them and giving it to the officers; nor can they see a friend in that temperance which takes from them what they have always had, and gives them nothing in the place of it. By seeing it allowed to their officers, they will not be convinced that it is taken from them for their good; and by receiving nothing in its place, they will not believe that it is done in kindness. On the contrary, many of them look upon the change as a new instrument of tyranny. Not that they prefer rum. I never knew a sailor, who had been a month away from the grog shops, who would not prefer a pot of hot coffee or chocolate, in a cold night, to all the rum afloat. They all say that rum only warms them for a time; yet, if they can get nothing better, they will miss what they have lost. The momentary warmth and glow from drinking it; the break and change which it makes in a long dreary watch by the mere calling all hands aft and serving it out; and the simply having some event to look forward to and to talk about—all give it an importance and a use which no one can appreciate who has not stood his watch before the mast. On my passage out, the *Pilgrim* was not under temperance articles, and grog was served out every middle and morning watch, and after every reefing of topsails; and though I had never drunk rum before, nor desire to again, I took my allowance then at the capstan, as the rest did,

merely for the momentary warmth it gave the system, and the change in our feelings and aspect of duties on the watch. At the same time, as I have said, there was not a man on board who would not have pitched the rum to the dogs (I have heard them say so a dozen times) for a pot of coffee or chocolate; or even for our common beverage—"water bewitched and tea begrudged," as it was.[2] The temperance reform is the best thing that ever was undertaken for the sailor; but when the grog was taken from him, he ought to have something in its place. As it is now, in most vessels, it is a mere saving to the owners; and this accounts for the sudden increase of temperance ships, which surprised even the best friends of the cause. If every merchant, when he struck grog from the list of the expenses of his ship, had been obliged to substitute as much coffee or chocolate as would give each man a potful when he came off the topsail yard on a stormy night, I fear Jack might have gone to ruin on the old road.[3]

But this is not doubling Cape Horn. Eight hours of the night our watch was on deck, and during the whole of that time we kept a bright lookout: one man on each bow, another in the bunt of the fore-yard, the third mate on the scuttle, one man on each quarter, and another always

[2] The proportions of the ingredients of the tea that was made for us (and ours, as I have before stated, was a favorable specimen of American merchantmen) were a pint of tea and a pint and a half of molasses to about three gallons of water. These are all boiled down together in the "coppers," and, before serving it out, the mess is stirred up with a stick, so as to give each man his fair share of sweetening and tea leaves. The tea for the cabin is, of course, made in the usual way, in a teapot, and drunk with sugar.

[3] I do not wish these remarks, so far as they relate to the saving of expense in the outfit, to be applied to the owners of our ship, for she was supplied with an abundance of stores of the best kind that are given to seamen; though the dispensing of them is necessarily left to the captain. And I learned, on our return, that the captain withheld many of the stores from us, from mere ugliness. He brought several barrels of flour home, but would not give us the usual twice-a-week duff, and so as to other stores. Indeed, so high was the reputation of "the employ" among men and officers for the character and outfit of their vessels, and for their liberality in conducting their voyages, that when it was known that they had the *Alert* fitting out for a long voyage, and that hands were to be shipped at a certain time—a half hour before time, as one of the crew told me, sailors were steering down the wharf, hopping over the barrels, like a drove of sheep.

standing by the wheel. The chief mate was every-where, and commanded the ship when the captain was below. When a large piece of ice was seen in our way, or drifting near us, the word was passed along, and the ship's head turned one way and another; and sometimes the yards squared or braced up. There was little else to do than to look out; and we had the sharpest eyes in the ship on the forecastle. The only variety was the monotonous voice of the lookout forward—"Another island!" "Ice ahead!" "Ice on the lee bow!" "Hard up the helm!" "Keep her off a little!" "Stead-y!"

In the meantime the wet and cold had brought my face into such a state that I could neither eat nor sleep; and though I stood it out all night, yet, when it became light, I was in such a state that all hands told me I must go below, and lie by for a day or two, or I should be laid up for a long time. When the watch was changed, I went into the steerage, and took off my hat and comforter, and showed my face to the mate, who told me to go below at once, and stay in my berth until the swelling went down, and gave the cook orders to make a poultice for me, and said he would speak to the captain.

I went below and turned in, covering myself over with blankets and jackets, and lay in my berth nearly twenty-four hours, half asleep and half awake, stupid from the dull pain. I heard the watch called, and the men going up and down, and sometimes a noise on deck, and a cry of "ice," but I gave little attention to anything. At the end of twenty-four hours the pain went down, and I had a long sleep, which brought me back to my proper state; yet my face was so swollen and tender that I was obliged to keep my berth for two or three days longer. During the two days I had been below, the weather was much the same that it had been—head winds, and snow and rain; or, if the wind came fair, too foggy, and the ice too thick, to run. At the end of the third day the ice was very thick; a complete fog bank covered the ship. It blew a tremendous gale from the eastward, with sleet and snow, and there was every promise of a dangerous and fatiguing night. At dark the captain called all hands aft, and told them that not a man was to leave the deck that night; that the ship was in the greatest danger, any cake of ice might knock a hole in her, or she might run on an island and go to pieces. No one could tell whether she would be a ship the next morning. The lookouts were then set, and every man was put in his station. When I heard what was the state of things, I began to put on my clothes to stand it out with the rest of them, when the mate came below, and looking at my face, ordered me back to my berth, saying that if we went down, we should all go down together, but if I went on deck I might lay myself up for life. This was the first word I had heard from aft; for the captain had done nothing, nor inquired how I was, since I went below.

In obedience to the mate's orders, I went back to my berth; but a more miserable night I never wish to spend. I never felt the curse of sickness so keenly in my life. If I could only have been on deck with the rest, where something was to be done and seen and heard, where there were fellow beings for companions in duty and danger; but to be cooped up alone in a black hole, in equal danger, but without the power to do, was the hardest trial. Several times, in the course of the night, I got up, determined to go on deck; but the silence which showed that there was nothing doing, and the knowledge that I might make myself seriously ill, for no purpose, kept me back. It was not easy to sleep, lying as I did with my head directly against the bows, which might be dashed in by an island of ice, brought down by the very next sea that struck her. This was the only time I had been ill since I left Boston, and it was the worst time it could have happened. I felt almost willing to bear the plagues of Egypt for the rest of the voyage, if I could but be well and strong for that one night. Yet it was a dreadful night for those on deck. A watch of eighteen hours, with wet and cold and constant anxiety, nearly wore them out; and when they came below at nine o'clock for breakfast, they almost dropped asleep on their chests, and some of them were so stiff that they could with difficulty sit down. Not a drop of anything had been given them during the whole time (though the captain, as on the night that I was on deck, had his coffee every four hours), except that the mate stole a potful of coffee for two men to drink behind the galley, while he kept a lookout for the captain. Every man had his station, and was not allowed to leave it; and nothing happened to break the monotony of the night, except once setting the maintopsail, to run clear of a large island to leeward, which they were drifting fast upon. Some of the boys got so sleepy and stupefied that they actually fell asleep at their posts; and the young third mate, Mr. Hatch, whose post was the exposed one of standing on the forescuttle, was so stiff, when he was relieved, that he could not bend his knees to get down. By a constant lookout, and a quick shifting of the helm, as the islands and pieces came in sight, the ship went clear of everything but a few small pieces, though daylight showed the ocean covered for miles. At daybreak it fell a dead calm, and with the sun the fog cleared a little, and a breeze sprung up from the westward, which soon grew into a gale. We had now a fair wind, daylight, and comparatively clear weather; yet, to the surprise of everyone, the ship continued hove to. "Why does not he run?" "What is the captain about?" was asked by every one; and from questions it soon grew into complaints and murmuring. When the daylight was so short, it was too bad to lose it, and a fair wind, too, which every one had been praying for. As hour followed hour, and the captain showed no sign of making sail, the crew became impatient, and there was a good deal of talking and consultation together on the forecastle. They had been beaten out with the exposure and hardship, and impatient to get out of it, and this unaccountable delay was more than they could bear in quietness, in their excited and restless state. Some said the captain was frightened —completely cowed by the dangers and difficulties that surrounded us, and was afraid to make sail; while others said that in his anxiety and suspense he had made a free use of brandy and opium, and was unfit for his duty. The carpenter, who was an intelligent man, and a thorough seaman, and had great influence with the crew, came down into the forecastle, and tried to induce them to go aft and ask the captain why he did not run, or request him, in the name of all hands, to make sail. This appeared to be a very

reasonable request, and the crew agreed that if he did not make sail before noon they would go aft. Noon came, and no sail was made. A consultation was held again, and it was proposed to take the ship from the captain and give the command of her to the mate, who had been heard to say that if he could have his way the ship would have been half the distance to the cape before night—ice or no ice. And so irritated and impatient had the crew become, that even this proposition, which was open mutiny, was entertained, and the carpenter went to his berth, leaving it tacitly understood that something serious would be done if things remained as they were many hours longer. When the carpenter left, we talked it all over, and I gave my advice strongly against it. Another of the men, too, who had known something of the kind attempted in another ship by a crew who were dissatisfied with their captain, and which was followed with serious consequences, was opposed to it. Stimson, who soon came down, joined us, and we determined to have nothing to do with it. By these means the crew were soon induced to give it up for the present, though they said they would not lie where they were much longer without knowing the reason.

The affair remained in this state until four o'clock, when an order came forward for all hands to come aft upon the quarterdeck. In about ten minutes they came forward again, and the whole affair had been blown. The carpenter, prematurely, and without any authority from the crew, had sounded the mate as to whether he would take command of the ship, and intimated an intention to displace the captain; and the mate, as in duty bound, had told the whole to the captain, who immediately sent for all hands aft. Instead of violent measures, or, at least, an outbreak of quarterdeck bravado, threats, and abuse, which they had every reason to expect, a sense of common danger and common suffering seemed to have tamed his spirit, and begotten in him something like a human fellow feeling; for he received the crew in a manner quiet, and even almost kind. He told them what he had heard, and said that he did not believe that they would try to do any such thing as was intimated; that they had always been good men—obedient, and knew their duty, and he had no fault to find with them, and asked them what they had to complain of; said that no one could say that he was slow to carry sail (which was true enough), and that, as soon as he thought it was safe and proper, he should make sail. He added a few words about their duty in their present situation, and sent them forward, saying that he should take no further notice of the matter; but, at the same time, told the carpenter to recollect whose power he was in, and that if he heard another word from him he would have cause to remember him to the day of his death.

This language of the captain had a very good effect upon the crew, and they returned quietly to their duty.

For two days more the wind blew from the southward and eastward, and in the short intervals when it was fair, the ice was too thick to run; yet the weather was not so dreadfully bad, and the crew had watch and watch. I still remained in my berth, fast recovering, yet not well enough to go safely on deck. And I should have been perfectly useless; for, from having eaten nothing for nearly a week, except a little rice which I forced into my mouth the last day or two, I was as weak as an infant. To be sick in a forecastle is miserable indeed. It is the worst part of a dog's life, especially in bad weather. The forecastle, shut up tight to keep out the water and cold air; the watch either on deck or asleep in their berths; no one to speak to; the pale light of the single lamp, swinging to and fro from the beam, so dim that one can scarcely see, much less read, by it; the water dropping from the beams and carlines, and running down the sides, and the forecastle so wet and dark and cheerless, and so lumbered up with chests and wet clothes, that sitting up is worse than lying in the berth. These are some of the evils. Fortunately, I needed no help from any one, and no medicine; and if I had needed help, I don't know where I should have found it. Sailors are willing enough, but it is true, as is often said, no one ships for nurse on board a vessel. Our merchant ships are always undermanned, and if one man is lost by sickness, they cannot spare another to take care of him. A sailor is always presumed to be well, and if he's sick he's a poor dog. One has to stand his wheel, and another his lookout, and the sooner he gets on deck again the better.

Accordingly, as soon as I could possibly go back to my duty, I put on my thick clothes and boots and sou'wester, and made my appearance on deck. I had been but a few days below, yet everything looked strangely enough. The ship was cased in ice—decks, sides, masts, yards, and rigging. Two close-reefed topsails were all the sail she had on, and every sail and rope was frozen so stiff in its place that it seemed as though it would be impossible to start anything. Reduced, too, to her topmasts, she had altogether a most forlorn and crippled appearance. The sun had come up brightly; the snow was swept off the decks and ashes thrown upon them so that we could walk, for they had been as slippery as glass. It was, of course, too cold to carry on any ship's work, and we had only to walk the deck and keep ourselves warm. The wind was still ahead, and the whole ocean, to the eastward, covered with islands and field ice. At four bells the order was given to square away the yards, and the man who came from the helm said that the captain had kept her off to north-northeast. What could this mean? The wildest rumors got adrift. Some said that he was going to put into Valparaiso, and winter; and others, that he was going to run out of the ice, and cross the Pacific, and go home round the Cape of Good Hope. Soon, however, it leaked out, and we found that we were running for the Straits of Magellan. The news soon spread through the ship, and all tongues were at work talking about it. No one on board had been through the straits, but I had in my chest an account of the passage of the ship *A. J. Donelson,* of New York, through those straits a few years before. The account was given by the captain, and the representation was as favorable as possible. It was soon read by everyone on board, and various opinions pronounced. The determination of our captain had at least this good effect, it gave us something to think and talk about, made a break in our life, and diverted our minds from the monotonous dreariness of the prospect before us. Having made a fair wind of it, we were going off at a good rate, and leaving the thickest of the ice behind us. This, at least, was something.

Having been long enough below to get my hands well warmed and softened, the first handling of the ropes was rather tough; but a few days hardened them, and as soon as I got my mouth open wide enough to take in a piece of salt beef and hard bread I was all right again.

Sunday, July 10. Latitude fifty-four degrees ten minutes, longitude seventy-nine degrees seven minutes. This was our position at noon. The sun was out bright; and the ice was all left behind, and things had quite a cheering appearance. We brought our wet peajackets and trousers on deck, and hung them up in the rigging, that the breeze and the few hours of sun might dry them a little; and, by leave of the cook, the galley was nearly filled with stockings and mittens, hung round to be dried. Boots, too, were brought up; and having got a little tar and slush from below, we gave them thick coats. After dinner all hands were turned to, to get the anchors over the bows, bend on the chains, etc. The fish tackle was got up, fish davit rigged out, and after two or three hours of hard and cold work both the anchors were ready for instant use, a couple of kedges got up, a hawser coiled away upon the fore hatch, and the deep-sea lead line overhauled and made ready. Our spirits returned with having something to do; and when the tackle was manned to bowse the anchor home, notwithstanding the desolation of the scene, we struck up "Cheerily, men" in full chorus. This pleased the mate, who rubbed his hands and cried out, "That's right, my boys; never say die! That sounds like the old crew"; and the captain came up, on hearing the song, and said to the passenger, within hearing of the man at the wheel, "That sounds like a lively crew. They'll have their song so long as there're enough left for a chorus!"

This preparation of the cable and anchors was for the passage of the straits; for, as they are very crooked, and with a variety of currents, it is necessary to come frequently to anchor. This was not by any means a pleasant prospect; for of all the work that a sailor is called upon to do in cold weather, there is none so bad as working the ground tackle. The heavy chain cables to be hauled and pulled about decks with bare hands; wet hawsers, slip ropes, and buoy ropes to be hauled aboard dripping in water, which is running up your sleeves and freezing; clearing hawse under the bows; getting under way and coming to at all hours of the night and day, and a constant lookout for rocks and sands and turns of tides—these are some of the disagreeables of such a navigation to a common sailor. Fair or foul, he wants to have nothing to do with the ground tackle between port and port. One of our hands, too, had unluckily fallen upon a half of an old newspaper which contained an account of the passage, through the straits, of a Boston brig, called, I think, the *Peruvian,* in which she lost every cable and anchor she had, got aground twice, and arrived at Valparaiso in distress. This was set off against the account of the *A. J. Donelson,* and led us to look forward with less confidence to the passage, especially as no one on board had ever been through, and we heard that the captain had no very satisfactory charts. However, we were spared any further experience on the point; for the next day, when we must have been near the Cape of Pillars, which is the southwest point of the mouth of the straits, a gale set in from the eastward, with a heavy fog, so that we could not see half the ship's length ahead. This, of course, put an end to the project for the present; for a thick fog and a gale blowing dead ahead are not the most favorable circumstances for the passage of difficult and dangerous straits. This weather, too, seemed likely to last for some time, and we could not think of beating about the mouth of the straits for a week or two, waiting for a favorable opportunity; so we braced up on the larboard tack, put the ship's head due south, and stuck her off for Cape Horn again.

Sharks in the Boatyard

by JACK LONDON

Novelist Jack London loved to sail. His success as a writer allowed him the luxury of designing and building his own yacht, with the fond hope of circling the globe. Predators, as the title says, lurk not only at sea, but can strike before the maiden launching. With good humor London accepted the imperfections of his dream boat and made a good story out of it.

"To build," says Dr. Johnson, "is to be robbed." He was speaking of houses; but his epigram is equally true of boats. To have a yacht built to order is more trouble than an ocean cruise. The ship chandlers and mechanics are more inimical than gales.

The famous Jack London, an author who had been a working seaman and was about to become a yachtsman, found this out the hard way in 1907. He and his wife, Charmian, had decided to circumnavigate the earth in their own little ship. They spent infinite pains and three times as much money as they possessed getting their dream boat constructed. And when, at long, painful last, the fifty-five-foot Snark *was launched, nothing about her was right!*

Just the same, the Londons, with a yachtsman friend and three paid hands, sailed from San Francisco to the Solomon Islands, where the cruise had to be abandoned because of illness. Here is the anguished (and expensive) birth of the Snark—in the London manner.

THE *Snark* is a small boat. When I figured $7,000 as her generous cost, I was both generous and correct. I have built barns and houses, and I know the peculiar trait such things have of running past their estimated cost. This knowledge was mine, was already mine, when I estimated the probable cost of the building of the *Snark* at $7,000. Well, she cost thirty thousand. Now don't ask me, please. It is the truth. I signed the checks and I raised the money. Of course, there is no explaining it. Inconceivable and monstrous is what it is, as you will agree, I know, ere my tale is done.

Then there was the matter of delay. I dealt with forty-seven different kinds of union men and with one hundred and fifteen different firms. And not one union man and not one firm of all the union men and all the firms ever delivered anything at the time agreed upon, nor ever was on time for anything except payday and bill collection. Men pledged me their immortal souls that they would deliver a certain thing on a certain date; as a rule, after such pledging, they rarely exceeded being three months late in delivery. And so it went, and Charmian and I consoled each other by saying what a splendid boat the *Snark* was, so stanch and strong; also we would get into the small boat and row around the

Snark and gloat over her unbelievably wonderful bow.

"Think," I would say to Charmian, "of a gale off the China coast and of the *Snark* hove to, that splendid bow of hers driving into the storm. Not a drop will come over that bow. She'll be as dry as a feather, and we'll be all below playing whist while the gale howls."

And Charmian would press my hand enthusiastically and exclaim: "It's worth every bit of it—the delay and expense and worry and all the rest. Oh, what a truly wonderful boat!"

Whenever I looked at the bow of the *Snark* or thought of her watertight compartments, I was encouraged. Nobody else, however, was encouraged. My friends began to make bets against the various sailing dates of the *Snark.* Mr. Wiget, who was left behind in charge of our Sonoma ranch, was the first to cash his bet. He collected on New Year's Day, 1907. After that the bets came fast and furious. My friends surrounded me like a gang of harpies, making bets against every sailing date I set. I was rash, and I was stubborn. I bet, and I bet, and I continued to bet; and I paid them all. Why, the womenkind of my friends grew so brave that those among them who never bet before began to bet with me. And I paid them, too.

"Never mind," said Charmian to me; "just think of that bow and being hove to on the China Seas."

"You see," I said to my friends, when I paid the latest bunch of wagers, "neither trouble nor cash is being spared in making the *Snark* the most seaworthy craft that ever sailed out through the Golden Gate—that is what causes all the delay."

In the meantime, editors and publishers with whom I had contracts pestered me with demands for explanations. But how could I explain to them, when I was unable to explain to myself, or when there was nobody, not even Roscoe, to explain to me? The newspapers began to laugh at me and to publish rhymes anent the *Snark*'s departure with refrains like "Not yet but soon." And Charmian cheered me up by reminding me of the bow, and I went to a banker and borrowed five thousand more. There was one recompense for the delay, however. A friend of mine, who happens to be a critic, wrote a roast of me, of all I had done, and of all I ever was going to do; and he planned to have it published after I was out on the ocean. I was still on shore when it came out, and he has been busy explaining ever since.

And the time continued to go by. One thing was becoming apparent, namely, that it was impossible to finish the *Snark* in San Francisco. She had been so long in the building that she was beginning to break down and wear out. In fact, she had reached the stage where she was breaking down faster than she could be repaired. She had become a joke. Nobody took her seriously; least of all the men who worked on her. I said we would sail just as she was and finish building her in Honolulu. Promptly she sprang a leak that had to be attended to before we could sail. I started her for the boatways. Before she got to them she was caught between two huge barges and received a vigorous crushing. We got her on the ways, and, partway along, the ways spread and dropped her through, stern first, into the mud.

It was a pretty tangle, a job for wreckers, not boat builders. There are two high tides every twenty-four hours, and at every high tide, night and day for a week, there were two steam tugs pulling and hauling on the *Snark.* There she was, stuck, fallen between the ways and standing on her stern. Next, and while still in that predicament, we started to use the gears and castings made in the local foundry whereby power was conveyed from the engine to the windlass. The castings had flaws; they shattered asunder, the gears ground together, and the windlass was out of commission. Following upon that, the seventy-horsepower engine went out of commission. This engine came from New York; so did its bedplate; there was a flaw in the bedplate; there were a lot of flaws in the bedplate; and the seventy-horsepower engine broke away from its shattered foundations, reared up in the air, smashed all connections and fastenings, and fell over on its side. And the *Snark* continued to stick between the spread ways, and the two tugs continued to haul vainly upon her.

"Never mind," said Charmian, "think of what a stanch, strong boat she is."

"Yes," said I, "and of that beautiful bow."

So we took heart and went at it again. The ruined engine was lashed down on its rotten foundations; the smashed castings and cogs of the power transmission were taken down and stored away—all for the purpose of taking them to Honolulu where repairs and new castings could be made. Somewhere in the dim past, the *Snark* had received on the outside one coat of white paint. The intention of the color was still evident, however, when one got it in the right light. The *Snark* had never received any paint on the inside. On the contrary, she was coated inches thick with the grease and tobacco juice of the multitudinous mechanics who had toiled upon her. Never mind, we said; the grease and filth could be planed off, and later, when we fetched Honolulu, the *Snark* could be painted at the same time she was being rebuilt.

By main strength and sweat we dragged the *Snark* off from the wrecked ways and laid her alongside the Oakland City Wharf. The drays brought all the outfit from home, the books and blankets and personal luggage. Along with this, everything else came on board in a torrent of confusion—wood and coal, water and water tanks, vegetables, provisions, oil, the lifeboat and the launch, all our friends, all the friends of our friends, and those who claimed to be their friends, to say nothing of some of the friends of the friends of the friends of our crew. Also there were reporters and photographers and strangers and cranks and, finally and over all, clouds of coal dust from the wharf.

We were to sail Sunday at eleven, and Saturday afternoon had arrived. The crowd on the wharf and the coal dust were thicker than ever. In one pocket I carried a checkbook, a fountain pen, a dater, and a blotter; in another pocket I carried between one and two thousand dollars in paper money and gold. I was ready for the creditors, cash for the small ones and checks for the large ones, and was waiting only for Roscoe to arrive with the balances of the accounts of the hundred and fifteen firms who had delayed me so many months. And then—

And then the inconceivable and monstrous happened once more. Before Roscoe could arrive there arrived another man. He was a United States marshal. He tacked a notice on the *Snark*'s brave mast so that all on the wharf could read that the *Snark* had been libeled for debt. The marshal left a little old man in charge of the *Snark* and himself went away. I had no longer any control of the *Snark* nor of her wonderful bow. The little old man was now her lord and master, and I learned that I was paying him $3 a day for being lord and master. Also, I learned the name of the man who had libeled the *Snark.* It was Sellers; the debt was $232, and the deed was no more than was to be expected from the possessor of such a name. Sellers! Ye gods! Sellers!

But who under the sun was Sellers? I looked in my checkbook and saw that two weeks before I had made him out a check for $500. Other checkbooks showed me that during the many months of the building of the *Snark,* I had paid him several thousand dollars. Then why in the name of common decency hadn't he tried to collect his miserable little balance instead of libeling the *Snark?* I thrust my hands into my pockets and in one pocket encountered the checkbook and the dater and the pen, and in the other pocket the gold money and the paper money. There was the wherewithal to settle his pitiful account a few score of times and over—why hadn't he given me a chance? There was no explanation; it was merely the inconceivable and monstrous.

To make the matter worse, the Snark had been libeled late Saturday afternoon; and though I sent lawyers and agents all over Oakland and San Francisco, neither United States judge, nor United States marshal, nor Mr. Sellers, nor Mr. Sellers's attorney, nor anybody could be found. They were all out of town for the weekend. And so the *Snark* did not sail Sunday morning at eleven. The little old man was still in charge, and he said no. And Charmian and I walked out on an opposite wharf and took consolation in the *Snark*'s wonderful bow and thought of all the gales and typhoons it would proudly punch.

"A bourgeois trick," I said to Charmian, speaking of Mr. Sellers and his libel; "a petty trader's panic. But never mind; our troubles will cease when once we are away from this and out on the wide ocean."

And in the end we sailed away on Tuesday morning, April 23, 1907. We started rather lame, I confess. We had to hoist anchor by hand, because the power transmission was a wreck. Also, what remained of our seventy-horsepower engine was lashed down for ballast on the bottom of the *Snark*. But what of such things? They could be fixed in Honolulu, and in the meantime think of the magnificent rest of the boat! It is true the engine in the launch wouldn't run, and the lifeboat leaked like a sieve; but then they weren't the *Snark*; they were mere appurtenances. The things that counted were the watertight bulkheads, the solid planking without butts, the bathroom devices—they were the *Snark*. And then there was, greatest of all, that noble, wind-punching bow.

We sailed out through the Golden Gate and set our course south toward that part of the Pacific where we could hope to pick up the northeast trades. And right away things began to happen. I had calculated that youth was the stuff for a voyage like that of the *Snark*, and I had taken three youths—the engineer, the cook, and the cabin boy. My calculation was only two-thirds off; I had forgotten to calculate on seasick youth, and I had two of them, the cook and the cabin boy. They immediately took to their bunks, and that was the end of their usefulness for a week to come. It will be understood from the foregoing that we did not have the hot meals we might have had, nor were things kept clean and orderly down below. But it did not matter very much anyway, for we quickly discovered that our box of oranges had at some time been frozen; that our box of apples was mushy and spoiling; that the crate of cabbages, spoiled before it was ever delivered to us, had to go overboard instanter; that kerosene had been spilled on the carrots, and that the turnips were woody and the beets rotten, while the kindling was dead wood that wouldn't burn, and the coal, delivered in rotten potato sacks, had spilled all over the deck and was washing through the scuppers.

But what did it matter? Such things were

mere accessories. There was the boat—she was all right, wasn't she? I strolled along the deck and in one minute counted fourteen butts in the beautiful planking ordered specially from Puget Sound in order that there should be no butts in it. Also, that deck leaked, and it leaked badly. It drowned Roscoe out of his bunk and ruined the tools in the engine room, to say nothing of the provisions it ruined in the galley. Also, the sides of the *Snark* leaked, and the bottom leaked, and we had to pump her every day to keep her afloat. The floor of the galley is a couple of feet above the inside bottom of the *Snark*; and yet I have stood on the floor of the galley, trying to snatch a cold bite, and been wet to the knees by the water churning around inside four hours after the last pumping.

Then those magnificent watertight compartments that cost so much time and money—well, they weren't watertight after all. The water moved free as the air from one compartment to another; furthermore, a strong smell of gasoline from the after compartment leads me to suspect that some one or more of the half-dozen tanks there stored have sprung a leak. The tanks leak, and they are not hermetically sealed in their compartment. Then there was the bathroom with its pumps and levers and sea valves—it went out of commission inside the first twenty hours. Powerful iron levers broke off short in one's hand when one tried to pump with them. The bathroom was the swiftest wreck of any portion of the *Snark*.

And the ironwork on the *Snark*, no matter what its source, proved to be mush. For instance, the bedplate of the engine came from New York, and it was mush; so were the casting and gears for the windlass that came from San Francisco. And finally, there was the wrought iron used in the rigging that carried away in all directions when the first strains were put upon it. Wrought iron, mind you, and it snapped like macaroni.

A gooseneck on the gaff of the mainsail broke short off. We replaced it with the gooseneck from the gaff of the storm trysail, and the second gooseneck broke short off inside fifteen minutes of use, and, mind you, it had been taken from the gaff of the storm trysail, upon which we would have depended in time of storm. At the present moment, the *Snark* trails her mainsail like a broken wing, the gooseneck being replaced by a rough lashing. We'll see if we can get honest iron in Honolulu.

Man had betrayed us and sent us to sea in a sieve, but the Lord must have loved us, for we had calm weather in which to learn that we must pump every day in order to keep afloat, and that more trust could be placed in a wooden toothpick than in the most massive piece of iron to be found aboard.

As the stanchness and the strength of the *Snark* went glimmering, Charmian and I pinned our faith more and more to the *Snark*'s wonderful bow. There was nothing else left to pin to. It was all inconceivable and monstrous, we knew, but that bow, at least, was rational. And then, one evening, we started to heave to.

How shall I describe it? First of all, for the benefit of the tyro, let me explain that heaving to is that sea maneuver which, by means of short and balanced canvas, compels a vessel to ride bow on to wind and sea. When the wind is too strong or the sea is too high, a vessel of the size of the *Snark* can heave to with ease, whereupon there is no more work to do on deck. Nobody needs to steer. The lookout is superfluous. All hands can go below and sleep or play whist.

Well, it was blowing half of a small summer gale, when I told Roscoe we'd heave to. Night was coming on. I had been steering nearly all day, and all hands on deck (Roscoe and Bert and Charmian) were tired, while all hands below were seasick. It happened that we had already put two reefs in the big mainsail. The flying jib and the jib were taken in, and a reef put in the forestaysail. The mizzen was also taken in. About this time, the flying jibboom buried itself in a sea and broke short off. I started to put the wheel down in order to heave to. The *Snark* at the moment was rolling in the trough. She continued rolling in the trough. I put the spokes down harder and harder. She never budged from the trough. (The trough, gentle reader, is the most dangerous position of all in which to lay a vessel.) I put the wheel hard down, and still the *Snark* rolled in the trough.

Eight points was the nearest I could get her to the wind. I had Roscoe and Bert come in on the mainsheet. The *Snark* rolled on in the trough, now putting her rail under on one side and now under on the other side.

Again the inconceivable and monstrous was showing its grisly head. It was grotesque, impossible. I refused to believe it. Under double-reefed mainsail and single-reefed staysail the *Snark* refused to heave to. We flattened the mainsail down. It did not alter the *Snark*'s course a tenth of a degree. We slacked the mainsail off with no more result. We set a storm trysail on the mizzen and took in the mainsail. No change. The *Snark* rolled on in the trough. That beautiful bow of hers refused to come up and face the wind.

Next we took in the reefed staysail. Thus, the only bit of canvas left on her was the storm trysail on the mizzen. If anything would bring her bow up to the wind, that would. Maybe you won't believe me when I say it failed, but I do say it failed. And I say it failed because I saw it fail and not because I believe it failed. I don't believe it did fail. It is unbelievable, and I am not telling you what I believe; I am telling you what I saw.

Now, gentle reader, what would you do if you were on a small boat rolling in the trough of the sea, a trysail on that small boat's stern that was unable to swing the bow up into the wind? Get out the sea anchor. It's just what we did. We had a patent one, made to order and warranted not to dive. Imagine a hoop of steel that serves to keep open the mouth of a large, conical, canvas bag, and you have a sea anchor.

Well, we made a line fast to the sea anchor and to the bow of the *Snark,* and then dropped the sea anchor overboard. It promptly dived. We had a tripping line on it, so we tripped the sea anchor and hauled it in. We attached a big timber as a float, and dropped the sea anchor over again. This time it floated. The line to the bow grew taut. The trysail on the mizzen tended to swing the bow into the wind, but, in spite of this tendency, the *Snark* calmly took that sea anchor in her teeth and went on ahead, dragging it after her, still in the trough of the sea. And there you are. We even took in the trysail, hoisted the full mizzen in its place, and hauled the full mizzen

The lure of the boatyard.

hot meal that should have awaited us, but to skate across the slush and slime on the cabin floor, where cook and cabin boy lay like dead men in their bunks, and to lie down in our own bunks, with our clothes on ready for a call, and to listen to the bilge water spouting knee high on the galley floor.

In the Bohemian Club of San Francisco, there are some crack sailors. I know, because I heard them pass judgment on the *Snark* during the process of her building. They found only one vital thing the matter with her, and on this they were all agreed, namely, that she could not run. She was all right in every particular, they said, except that I'd never be able to run her before it in a stiff wind and sea. "Her lines," they explained enigmatically, "it is the fault of her lines. She simply cannot be made to run, that is all."

Well, I wish I'd only had those crack sailors of the Bohemian Club on board the *Snark* the other night for them to see for themselves their one, vital, unanimous judgment absolutely reversed. Run? It is the one thing the *Snark* does to perfection. Run? She ran with a sea anchor fast for'ard and a full mizzen flattened down aft. Run? At the present moment, as I write this, we are bowling along before it, at a six-knot clip, in the northeast trades. Quite a tidy bit of sea is running. There is nobody at the wheel, the wheel is not even lashed and is set over a half-spoke weather helm. To be precise, the wind is northeast; the *Snark*'s mizzen is furled, her mainsail is over to starboard, her headsheets are hauled flat; and the *Snark*'s course is south-southwest. And yet there are men who have sailed the seas for forty years and who hold that no boat can run before it without being steered. They'll call me a liar when they read this; it's what they called Captain Slocum when he said the same of his *Spray.*

As regards the future of the *Snark,* I'm all at sea. I don't know. If I had the money or the credit, I'd build another *Snark* that *would* heave to. But I am at the end of my resources. I've got to put up with the present *Snark* or quit—and I can't quit. So I guess I'll have to try to get along with heaving the *Snark* to stern first. I am waiting for the next gale to see how it will work. I think

down flat, and the Snark wallowed in the trough and dragged the sea anchor behind her. Don't believe me. I don't believe it myself. I am merely telling you what I saw.

Now I leave it to you. Who ever heard of a sailing boat that wouldn't heave to?—that wouldn't heave to with a sea anchor to help it? Out of my brief experience with boats I know I never did. And I stood on deck and looked on the naked face of the inconceivable and monstrous—the *Snark* that wouldn't heave to. A stormy night with broken moonlight had come on. There was a splash of wet in the air, and up to windward there was a promise of rain squalls; and then there was the trough of the sea, cold and cruel in the moonlight, in which the *Snark* complacently rolled. And then we took in the sea anchor and the mizzen, hoisted the reefed staysail, ran the *Snark* off before it, and went below—not to the it can be done. It all depends on how her stern takes the seas. And who knows but that some wild morning on the China Sea, some graybeard skipper will stare, rub his incredulous eyes, and stare again at the spectacle of a weird, small craft, very much like the *Snark,* hove to stern first and riding out the gale?

P.S. On my return to California after the voyage, I learned that the *Snark* was forty-three feet on the waterline, instead of forty-five. This was due to the fact that the builder was not on speaking terms with the tape line or two-foot rule.

The Story of Sailing

by JAMES THURBER

One of America's best-loved and most pungent humorists and illustrators, James Thurber has a talent for not only making people laugh, but making a telling point—in some cases by reductio ad absurdum. *The art of rigging a ship is, as Thurber shows very economically, an evolution from classical simplicity to egocentric complexity, or, as it's often called—progress.*

PEOPLE who visit you in Bermuda are likely to notice, even before they notice the flowers of the island, the scores of sailing craft which fleck the harbors and the ocean round about. Furthermore, they are likely to ask you about the ships before they ask you about the flowers, and this, at least in my own case, is unfortunate, because although I know practically nothing about flowers, I know ten times as much about flowers as I know about ships. Or at any rate, I did before I began to study up on the subject. Now I feel that I am pretty well qualified to hold my own in any average discussion of rigging.

I began to brush up on the mysteries of sailing a boat after an unfortunate evening when a lady who sat next to me at dinner turned to me and said, "Do you reef in your gaff-topsails when you are close-hauled or do you let go the mizzen-top bowlines and crossjack braces?" She took me

for a sailor and not a landlubber, and of course I hadn't the slightest idea what she was talking about.

One reason for this was that none of the principal words (except *reef*) used in the sentence I have quoted is pronounced the way it is spelled: *gaff-topsails* is pronounced "gassles," *close-hauled* is pronounced "cold," *mizzen-top bowlines* is pronounced "mittens," and *crossjack braces* is pronounced "crabapples" or something that sounds a whole lot like that. Thus, what the lady really said to me was, "Do you reef in your gassles when you are cold or do you let go the mittens and crabapples?" Many a visitor who is asked such a question takes the first ship back home, and it is for these embarrassed gentlemen that I am going to explain briefly the history and terminology of sailing.

In the first place, there is no doubt but that the rigging of the modern sailing ship has become complicated beyond all necessity. If you want proof of this, you have only to look up the word *rigging* in the *Encyclopædia Britannica.* You will find a drawing of a full-rigged modern ship and under it an explanation of its various spars, masts, sails, etc. There are forty-five different major parts, beginning with *bowsprit* and going on up to *davit topping lifts.* Included in between are, among others, these items: the fore-topmast

323

staysail halyards (pronounced "fazzles"), the topgallant mastyard-and-lift (pronounced "toft"), the mizzen-topgallant braces (pronounced "maces"), and the fore-topmast backstays and topsail tye (pronounced "frassantossle"). The tendency of the average landlubber who studies this diagram for five minutes is to turn to *Sanscrit* in the encyclopedia and study up on that instead, but only a coward would do that. It is possible to get something out of the article on rigging if you keep at it long enough.

Let us creep up on the formidable modern sailing ship in our stocking feet, beginning with one of the simplest of all known sailing craft, the Norse Herring Boat. Now when the Norse built their sailing boats, they had only one idea in mind: to catch herring. They were pretty busy men, always a trifle chilly, and they had neither the time nor the inclination to sit around on the cold decks of their ships trying to figure out all the different kinds of ropes, spars and sails that might be hung on their masts. Each ship had, as a matter of fact, only one mast. Near the top of it was a crosspiece of wood and on that was hung one simple square sail, no more complicated than the awning of a cigar store. A rope was attached to each end of the crosspiece and the other ends of these ropes were held by the helmsman. By manipulating the ropes, he could make the ship go ahead, turn right or turn left. It was practically impossible to make it turn around, to be sure, and that is the reason the Norsemen went straight on and discovered America, thus proving that it isn't really necessary to turn around.

As the years went on and the younger generations of Norsemen became, like all younger generations, less hardworking and more restless than their forebears, they began to think less about catching herring and more about monkeying with the sails of their ships. One of these restless young Norsemen one day lengthened the mast of his ship, put up another crosspiece about six feet above the first one and hung another but smaller sail on this new crosspiece, or spar (pronounced, strange as it may seem, "spar"). Thus was the main topsail born.

After that, innovations in sails followed so fast that the herring boat became a veritable shambles of canvas. A Norseman named Leif the Sailmaker added a second mast to his ship, just in front of the first one, and thus the foremast came into being and with it the fore mainsail and the fore topsail. A Turk named Skvar added a third mast and called it the mizzen. Not to be outdone, a Muscovite named Amir put up a third spar on each of his masts; Skvar put up a fourth; Amir replied with a fifth; Skvar came back with a sixth, and so it went, resulting in the topgallant foresail, the top-topgallant mizzen sail, the top-top-topgallant main topsail, and the tip-top-topgallant-gallant mainsail (pronounced "twee twee twee twa twa").

Practically nobody today sails a full-rigged seven-masted ship, so that it would not be especially helpful to describe in detail all the thousands of different gaffs, sprits, queeps, weems, lugs, miggets, loords (spelled "leewards"), gessels, grommets, etc., on such a ship. I shall therefore devote what space I have left to a discussion of how to come back alive from a pleasant sail in the ordinary twenty- or thirty-foot sailing craft such as you are likely to be "taken for a ride" in down in Bermuda. This type of so-called pleasure ship is not only given to riding on its side, due to coming about without the helmsman's volition (spelled "jibe" and pronounced "look out, here we go again!"), but it is made extremely perilous by what is known as the flying jib, or boom.

The boom is worse than the gaff, for some people can stand the gaff (hence the common expression "he can stand the gaff"), but nobody can stand the boom when it aims one at him from the floor. With the disappearance of the Norse herring fisherman and the advent of the modern pleasure-craft sailor, the boom became longer and heavier and faster. Helmsmen will tell you that they keep swinging the boom across the deck of the ship in order to take advantage of the wind, but after weeks of observation it is my opinion that they do it to take advantage of the passengers. The only way to avoid the boom and have any safety at all while sailing is to lie flat on your stomach in the bottom of the ship. This is very uncomfortable on account of the hard boards and because you can't see a thing, but it is the one sure way I know of to go sailing and come back in the boat and not be washed up in the surf. I recommend the posture highly, but not as highly as I recommend the bicycle. My sailing adventures in Bermuda have made me appreciate for the first time the essential wonder of the simple, boomless bicycle.

Christmas with Cyrano

by WILLIAM F. BUCKLEY, JR.

William F. Buckley, Jr.'s erudition, wit and pungent political views are known to millions through television, books, newspaper and magazine articles. Buckley finds refuge from his prodigious schedule on his boat Cyrano, *a name perfectly suited to the verbal genius of its owner. Here in Buckley style is* Cyrano's *maiden cruise.*

WHEN I first saw *Cyrano* I was undecided whether to let Pat aboard. Better to wait until after the renovations? . . . I knew that on examining it, she would pronounce it a lost cause, even as I might do on first seeing a room or a house before such transformations as she can visualize. But I did let her see the boat, and it was as I had thought: *Cyrano* would *never* do. I bought it anyway. Ned Killeen, the broker in the transaction, had himself once owned a shipbuilding yard, and volunteered to take a leave of absence and serve as my agent for the purpose of effecting the alchemy; later he became the boat's captain for three years. Our initial sail was memorable.

We would begin the little cruise by sailing the boat from the yard at Fort Lauderdale where it had been rebuilt, down to Miami—a four-hour sail. Pat brought along her matronly, endearing, spartan, humorous, arthritic mother, Babe Tay-

lor. Christopher and Danny were about sixteen, and my sister Priscilla and Reggie were there— and off we went.

To reach the harbor of Fort Lauderdale from the boatyard, one has to proceed along a canal about fifty feet wide for about one mile; then through the harbor and out to sea. Mrs. Taylor was comfortably installed in a deep deck chair in the covered cockpit section, and I was at the wheel. About a quarter of a mile down the canal, suddenly the engine stopped. I roared out to Ned, and he tore down to the engine room. Two long minutes later he came up, his Douglas Fairbanks moustache twitching, and explained that the drive shaft had been frozen by the octopus action of electric wires that had wound round it. Why had the wires wound round it? Because they had not been properly tied down, said Ned, a little defensively—and the revolving motion of the drive shaft had caused one of those knobbly protuberances on the shaft to snag a wire and, like a propeller on a fishing line, others with it, all those fine threads finally bringing the stainless-steel shaft to a halt. How many of the other electrical wires? *Every wire in the boat,* Ned finally forced himself to say, his voice now a sort of whiskey-falsetto.

We were, then, without engine, sail or electrical power; floating without steerageway down a narrow canal with traffic of every kind barreling past us. I called Danny and told him and Christopher to jump into the whaler, which is the ship's dinghy, start the outboard engine and tow *Cyrano* back to the yard. They did so eagerly, and Christopher gave a powerful yank on the starter. So powerful that the forty-horsepower outboard, which had not been properly secured, leaped up from the transom and dove to the bottom of the canal.

At just this moment, a sight-seeing boat with about a hundred people on it trolled by. One of the tourists recognized me and shouted my name in greeting. In the general clamor, the pilot of the boat slowed; and then reversed his engines to permit his guests to take a picture of Mr. Buckley and his friends cruising peacefully aboard his yacht. No one had any reason to suspect that Mr. Buckley and his friends and his yacht weren't going anywhere at all for the simple reason that there was nobody around to push them. They must have thought it genial of me to stop my boat to allow the whole world all the leisure they wanted to take our picture. Noblesse oblige. Under the strain of posing unself-consciously for a dozen cameras, it was difficult to continue with our war game. But Ned finally volunteered to row the dinghy to the far bank and then to run back to the boatyard to get the yard tender to tow us in. *Don't let that electrician go home,* I growled.

A half hour later, the electrician, who moonlighted for the yard—his regular job was to install navigational gear for National Airlines —not only volunteered genially to sail with us to Lauderdale, which would give him the necessary time to splice together the forty or fifty severed lines, but to lend us his own beloved thirty-horsepower outboard, provided we would agree to treat it as one of the family. Pat contributed the observation that unless I agreed to treat it much better than one of the family, the engine was surely doomed. He had meanwhile pulled the wires out of the way of the drive shaft, so we were at least able to start our engine, and now, as we slid down the canal, every half hour or so an additional electrical installation would begin to work as, on his back, the electrician worked chirpily away in what

proved to be dreadfully uncomfortable weather with heavy swells.

We could not get stability from our sails because the wind was from the south, and Mrs. Taylor began to vomit regularly, causing Pat, who has never quite believed that I don't secretly control a weather switch, to stride back from time to time to the wheel to accuse me of *deliberately* trying to kill her mother. Suddenly the wind swung right around, and we quickly lifted the mainsail. Ned proudly fastened a brake strap to the drive shaft, to prevent the propeller from turning unnecessarily while the engine was turned off. An hour or so later, Christopher and the very young first mate began to lower the dinghy, the electrician's precious family outboard attached thereto, into the water, so that it would be readily available to us on coming into the harbor in Miami. At this operation, they were unskilled, with the result that the flowing water suddenly caught the edge of the dinghy, swamped it—and the second outboard flew out into the water.

Without a second's hesitation, the young mate dove overboard. "Keep your eyes on him!" I shouted to Christopher, tossing over the life ring. I then started up the motor and slipped the boat into gear. Mrs. Taylor roused herself from her comatose state to point out in a weak voice that smoke was coming up from directly under her. "Great God!" said Ned, shouting to me to put the gear back into neutral. He had forgotten to loose the strap. He disappeared below, and in due course told me I was free to engage the gear. We hauled up into the wind, dropped the sail and in ten minutes were abeam of the mate, who said proudly he was certain he was still swimming directly over the outboard engine.

The electrician, smoked out from his ghetto below by the drive-shaft fire, was marvelously stoical about the separated member of his family, but took careful bearings—depth of water, bearing on points of land, etc.—and said that the next day, in the daylight, he would venture out with his son and try to find the motor with a scuba outfit; and so we resumed our way, dropping anchor in Biscayne Bay forty-five minutes later, feeling as if we had crossed the ocean. Ned hung out a kerosene anchor light of which he was very proud, fastening it on the headstay, and Mrs. Taylor began to revive as her daughter and friends began to joke about our maiden voyage. She did not, however, say anything; until, finally, she looked at me and said, "Bill, dear, is there supposed to be a fire up there?"—pointing to the bow of the boat.

The kerosene light, for reasons unknown, had fallen into the collapsed genoa below, which was now beginning to light up like a bonfire. Ned Killeen rushed forward with a fire extinguisher. The electrician, who had finally emerged sweatily from his completed task, a Coke and a sandwich in his hand, continued eating. "You know," he said, "I've been doing marine electrical work for years, but this is the first trip I've ever taken except on my fishing dinghy. Is it always like this?"

I knew she would be the first to speak, even though I'm fast at the draw . . . "Yes," said Pat, calm as Ethel Barrymore. "Oh, yes. In fact, tonight was one of the more *peaceful* sails we've ever *had.*"

But you move quickly to other extremes (as even Pat would agree). A few weeks later, we cruised over Christmas, our first prolonged family experience with *Cyrano.* I wrote about that cruise at sufficient length to convey at once some of the properties of cruising . . . on *Cyrano* . . . in the Caribbean . . . with me.

Friday, December 19. We arrived at Antigua airport, and that was an achievement. J. K. Galbraith says you shouldn't use pull unless you need to. Well, I needed to get to Antigua because I decided to go there for Christmas aboard *Cyrano*—that was two months ago—only to find all the airlines booked solid for December 19 and for a day or two bracketing that day. I tried everybody I knew—or almost everybody I knew—and finally got Mrs. Julie Nicholson, who with her husband and family dominate Antigua more firmly than Horatio Nelson ever did, to help. She and her husband are yacht and charter brokers, and can get you a ticket from anywhere to anywhere, anytime. It was only ordained that we

should make a stop at San Juan. There, waiting for us, were the three Finucanes, who had come in from Los Angeles, joining three Buckleys and Danny, and the seven of us arrived at Antigua. At the dockside was our own Captain Ned Killeen, and a half dozen partygoers, at the center of whom was Mrs. Nicholson herself, who greeted me warmly, and, as I slipped away in the tender, demanded to know what comes after *Gaudeamus igitur.* My memory failed me, and I felt dreadful, after all the Nicholsons had done for me. However, I did not forget to bring her Barricini chocolates and ribbon candy, which you must not forget to do if ever you find yourself coming from where you can get Barricini chocolates and ribbon candy to Antigua at Christmastime. I have made a mental note to let Mrs. Nicholson know what comes after *Gaudeamus igitur* as soon as I find out. Let us therefore rejoice. What *would* follow naturally from that? At this point, I could only think: *Quam ad Antiguam pervenimus.*

Saturday, December 20. Cyrano is nowadays based in St. Thomas, and it was Ned Killeen's idea that it would make for a pleasant cruise if he "deadheaded" Cyrano to Antigua, permitting us to cruise downwind back to St. Thomas. *To deadhead* means to take a boat without payload. It took him two long nights, into mid-morning, to ferry *Cyrano* 220 miles from St. Thomas to Antigua. Ned likes daytime landfalls. I like nighttime landfalls. Ned usually prevails. Ned always prevails when I am not aboard. Interesting thought. How much should we charge charterers to deliver them *Cyrano* in Antigua, should they so desire it? Ned suggests $200 for the two days, which is less than one half the $265 per day that we get for the use of *Cyrano;* but his point is that at $100 per day we are not actually losing money, and a little noblesse oblige on the high seas is always in order. I say something dour about how I wish the bankers would show a little noblesse oblige and acquiesce in the arrangement.

My beautiful *Cyrano.* Built in the Bahamas, in Abaco, to an old fishing-boat design. Sixty feet long, fifty-four feet at the waterline, with an extraordinary eighteen feet of bowsprit (which I reduced to twelve after Captain Crunch, by going under the fixed bridge, allowed me to start *ex nihilo*), seventeen and one-half feet of beam, tapering back to about thirteen feet at the transom, where two stout davits hold up the tender. Acres and acres of deck space. And below, an upright piano which Art Kadey, the previous owner and skipper, banged away at to the great delight of his passengers over the three years between the construction of the boat and my purchase of her.

What was needed, I thought on first looking the boat over, was a great deal of impacted luxury, plus complete instrumentation and rerigging for ocean passages. The latter was obvious enough: running backstays, loran, radar, automatic pilot; that kind of thing. The former is, I think, less obvious. I had done a fair amount of chartering, not a great deal. But I had come to a few conclusions. They are:

1. Sleeping quarters should be small and public quarters large. One needs in sleeping cabins only privacy and room to turn around in.

2. Every room should have a port, which should be situated at about eye level when your head is down on the pillow. Why not? All my life I have been on steamships which require that, in order to see through the port—presumably there for you to see through—you stand on tiptoe, which is hard to do while going to sleep. I got my ports. Three of them on the starboard side, one for each of the cabins, and three of them on the port side in the saloon—all of this *in addition* to the picture windows.

3. Color, color and more color. More boats are ruined by monochromatic dullness than by careless seamanship. So every room was decorated by my wife in a chintz of different color, of congruent patterns; so that we have the red cabin, the yellow cabin and the green cabin, a green carpet, and a glazed cotton print for the settee and couches, a pattern taking off, in reds and blues, on an old Spanish sailing map.

4. Chairs, settees and couches must be *comfortable*. I rebuilt the main settee three times, so as to make it, finally, slope back steeply enough and extend out far enough to make sitting in it truly comfortable for the slouchers of this world —who are my friends and clients. Opposite it, two club chairs, facing my three ports. Wall-to-

wall carpeting is right for a boat; kerosene and electric torches, of course. Then I persuaded my friend Richard Grosvenor, the excellent New England artist who teaches at St. George's School, to do three original oil paintings of boat scenes which exactly fit the principal exposed areas I wired to receive them. So that every picture is lit as in an art gallery, the three little overhead lights providing plenty of illumination for the entire saloon, unless you want to read, in which case you snap on one of the other lights. But with the oil paintings alone, the saloon now lights up in color and comfort, a beautiful room designed for total relaxation. When you are under way in a breeze, the seas sometimes rise up, covering the ports completely for whole seconds at a time. (Sometimes the moonlight comes in to you right through the water.) Abaft the piano is the bar and refrigerator which the former owner so thoughtfully installed to keep charterers from having to go back and forth to the galley quarters, a whole engine room away.

5. The deck area should be—well, perfect. There was no deckhouse. I had one designed and built, with two six-and-a-half-foot-long, four-foot-wide cushions, usable as berths, on either side. Between them, the companionway and then a well, where your feet can dangle while you navigate over a luxuriously large area (larger than a standard card table), or look into your radar screen or check your depth finder or a supplementary compass, and where you can even steer the ship electrically. That is, when you want to come forward from the wheel, to get out of the rain.

Stepping aft, six or seven feet, an enormous settee. Once again, the accent on comfort. In the Mediterranean, many boats have main cockpit settees on which you can sprawl out in any direction. The trick was to accomplish this and also convert the new deckhouse into dining quarters for fair weather. Castro Convertible came to the rescue—by the adaptation of its essential mechanism that permits the raising of a table. Then a custom-built tabletop which exactly fits the arc of the settee, so that when you are not eating, the table sinks down and three tailored cushions exactly cover the area, which now merges with the settee, giving you an enormous area of about four feet by twelve feet in which four or five people can stretch out and read or merely meditate on the splendid achievements of the settee designer. At mealtimes, remove the three cushions, pull a lever—and (presto) a perfectly designed table rises elegantly into place, around which eight people can sit. At night, you can close off the entire area with canvas, giving you something of the feel of a large Arabian tent.

6. The crew must have living space. Under existing arrangements, it is never necessary for guests to occupy the old dining quarters in the after section. There the crew has its privacy, adjacent to the captain's cabin, the main navigational table, the galley and the lazaret.

7. Noise. Somebody, somewhere along the line, told me that the biggest, most expensive, generators make the least noise. Ned came up with an Onan so noiseless you can hardly tell if it's on or off. It provides all the power you need, including 110-volt AC outlets. And finally,

8. Coolness. I know it is costly and difficult to install. Even so, air-condition, or die. I reason as follows. If you live in the Caribbean the year round, perhaps you can get used to hot temperatures. But if you only *visit* the Caribbean, you get hot in the middle of the day—just as you can get hot in the middle of Long Island Sound in the middle of the summer. Turn on your air conditioner and life changes for you; or it does for me, anyway. I shall never be without my air conditioner. If the bankers one day descend on me, I shall go on national TV and deliver a Checkers speech about my air conditioner. They will never take it from me.

I am staring at the chart as we cruise out of the tight little entrance to English Harbor. "What do you say we go to Nevis?" I suggest to Ned. Nevis is about forty-five miles west, and it is already noon. The wind is as it should be, east-northeast. Ned, so wise, so seasoned, suggests that perhaps we would be better off just going west along the coastline of Antigua, instead of striking out for so distant a goal so late in the day. I am glad I gave in.

Sunday, December 21. I said I was glad I gave in, and I suspect that I gave the impression that

where we did spend the night, which was in Mosquito Bay in Antigua, was unique. Not really. It is a very pretty cove (there are no mosquitoes on it, by the way), shallow, and if you want to know when the tide changes, it changes exactly when it changes in Galveston, Texas, for heaven's sake; and not even Ned knew instinctively how to figure *that* one out. I mean, if the *Tide Book* says: "*see* Galveston, Texas," and you find that the tide begins to ebb at Galveston, Texas, at 1900, at what time does it begin to ebb at Mosquito Bay, Antigua? You will immediately see that conflicting hypotheses are plausible. You may find yourself reasoning that when it is 7:00 P.M. at Galveston, the tide also begins to change at Mosquito Bay: which means you have to figure out the time zone for Galveston. Well, figure Galveston is two hours behind New York and we are one hour ahead of New York; ergo, it changes at Mosquito Bay at 10:00 P.M. Right? Not necessarily. Maybe it means that just as when it is 7:00 P.M. local time at Galveston the tide changes, so when it is 7:00 P.M. local time at Mosquito Bay, the tide changes—what's implausible about that?

The time has come to note a further complication, which is that when I sail *Cyrano* in the Caribbean, I go on what we call Buckley Watch Time, the only eponymous enterprise I have ever engaged in. What you do is tell all hands on board to move their clocks up by one hour. The practical meaning of it all is that you can start the cocktail hour as the sun is setting and eat dinner one hour later, at eight o'clock. Otherwise, you start drinking at six o'clock and eat dinner at seven. The former offends the Calvinist streak in a Yankee; the latter, the Mediterranean streak in a yacht owner. Anyway, in order to avoid digging into the fine print of the *Tide Book*, we decide to fasten on the fact that, after all, the tide here is less than one foot anyway; so we throw out the hook 150 yards from the beach rather than crawl up further, as we might have done if we had been absolutely sure that Galveston had another hour or so to go before the ebb began. No matter. The sunset was beautiful, we swam, ate—ate very well, thanks to Rawle, a native of St. Vincent who is a superb cook, and who has the prestige of a real-life shipwreck under his belt. Then we played 21, and I won consistently. The tape-player is the arena of a subtle contest between the generations. When one of *us* goes by it, we glide into the tape cavity something melodic. When one of the seventeen-year-olds goes by, quite unobtrusively he, or she, will slip in The Cream or The Peanut Butters, or whoever. I acknowledge to myself that the war will be formally declared by about tomorrow, lunchtime. ("Will you please get those screaming banshees off the air, children?" "Mother, can we put on something that isn't Marie Antoinette?") I am right. We go to bed, and my wife and I can see, outside our porthole, the full moon and the speckly light it casts on the waters—our waters, because there is no one else in sight.

Monday, December 22. I must make myself plain. I am glad I took the advice that we make the shorter rather than the longer run to Nevis, because I know enough now about other people to know what suits the general taste in a cruise. I am accustomed to a more spartan schedule, which, however, is not what cruising-chartering is about. I remember, in talking with Art Kadey, the disbelief with which I heard him say that the typical charterer travels approximately four hours every *other* day! I thought that (and still do) rather on the order of spending a fortnight at your fishing lodge and going out to fish only every other day. It takes time to adapt, if you have raced a boat in ocean races, accustomed to day and night running. Some come easily to the change, and indeed find it easy to oscillate from furious, implacable racing, day after day—week after week, in such as the Transatlantic or Trans-Pac race to Honolulu—to strolling about for a few hours on the same boat you often race, going perhaps no further than ten or fifteen or twenty miles in a single day. Moreover, *Cyrano* takes long sails in stride. She is a shoal-draft boat, built for the Bahamas. She hasn't even a centerboard —merely a long keel stretching the entire length of the hull to a distance of five and one-half feet from the waterline. The result is a certain stodginess in coming about, as any boat has that isn't equipped with ballet shoes; but with that great beam and with whatever it is the designer did to effect those numinous lines, she achieves a glori-

ous seakindliness that makes ocean sailing dry, fast and stable.

It isn't easy for everybody to relax on a boat. I adore my boat: and every boat I have ever had. But I feel, somehow, that I am always, in a sense, on duty; that I must be going from here to there, and if there is a little bad weather or whatever, well, isn't that a part of the general idea? The point, as Ned and others have patiently explained to me, is that there is the wholly other use of a boat, the use which is absolutely ideal for charterers, and that is the totally comfortable, totally unstrained cruise. So that if you decide this morning to go from Antigua to Nevis but the wind isn't right, why you simply go somewhere else! You don't have any obligations to meet the New York Yacht Club Squadron at Nevis at 1700, and nobody will tell the commodore if, instead, you ease off to St. Kitts—I mean, some people come to total relaxation in boats more easily than others, and they do not feel any constraint to harness their boats to an instrumental objective, like getting from here to exactly there, and There had better be a good distance away from Here in order to give you the feeling that you have accomplished a good run and earned the quiet hours of anchorage. All I say is: there are those of us who are driven, and if you are one of those, you will have to speak firmly to Ned. To say nothing of your wife.

St. Kitts is absolutely ravishing. We arrive rather late and do not disembark, simply because we cannot be bothered to register the boat. Why, oh why, don't the islands issue a triptyque, or whatever the Europeans called that document with all the coupons that they used to issue which facilitated car travel in postwar Europe. Hunting down the immigrations and customs officer, giving him (on one occasion, at Virgin Gorda, *six* copies of the crew and passenger list). Why not a bond that every boat owner could buy, the possession of which would grant free passage everywhere during a season, with a severe penalty if you are caught smuggling, or whatever, guaranteed by the bonder? How easy everything would be if I were given plenipotentiary power over these matters.

The run to St. Bartholomew (St. Barts) is

quite long—forty miles or so—and I suggest to Ned that we take off early, at nine o'clock, and sail under the great rock which they call the Gibraltar of the Caribbean. "Surely you mean after the crew has breakfast?" says Ned. "What the hell," say I, "why not get started under power, and *then* have breakfast?" We weigh anchor and proceed, and two days later I notice in the ship's log the stern entry, "Got under way before the crew had breakfast." A brilliant day, strong winds just abaft the beam, poor Christopher is seasick, the only time during the whole trip, but by two o'clock we have pulled into the exemplary little harbor, so neat, so thoroughly landlocked, so lackadaisical, where the rum is cheaper than the water and the rhythm of life is such that the natives never go to work before breakfast, and not always after breakfast.

Tuesday, December 23. The proposal is to make a short run for St. Barts, which my materialistic family favors, sight unseen, because the guidebook says that the prices there are even a little bit less than those at St. Maarten. The sail is a mere fifteen miles. We considered dropping by St. Mart and then proceeding four or five miles west to Anguilla, perhaps to decolonize it, now that history has taught us how easy it is to do. But the iron schedule (we must relinquish the boat to charterers in four days) makes this imprudent. I feel very keenly the loss, inasmuch as during the few months of Anguilla's independence, when the rebel government took a full page ad in the *New York Times* asking for contributions to revolutionary justice, I slipped the government a five-dollar bill in the mail and got back a handwritten letter of profuse gratitude from the prime minister. (Another day.)

The idea is to spend a relaxed few hours at St. Mart, and then make the longish (one hundred-mile) sail to the Virgins, touching in at Virgin Gorda. St. Mart is half Dutch (the lower half) and half French. A very large harbor, almost the size of Provincetown, with beaches and calm and lots of picturesque boats. We swim and water ski, and then head out for dinner at the Little Bay Hotel, which is a Hilton type, with casino, triple-air-conditioned bar, so-so restaurant and higher

than so-so prices. We did not get to gamble because the casino opened at 9:00 P.M. and we forgot that Buckley Watch Time wiped out the gambling hour we had counted on; so we went back to *Cyrano* and started out.

I took the watch until 0200, along with Bill Finucane, Pat's exemplary sister, while my wife and her brother-in-law played gin rummy and the boys and my niece lazed about on deck forward, discussing no doubt the depravities of their elders. I felt constrained (I am that way on a boat) to go forward every twenty minutes or so to make an aesthetic point—single out the moon, for instance, which was about as easy to miss at this point as the sun at dawn—and say casually, "Have you noticed the moon?" The kids are so easy to ambush, because it never fails that they will look up from their conversation, stare about, focus eventually on the moon, and say, finally, "Huh?"

It was an uneventful overnight journey, except that at 3:00 A.M. I was roused from my cabin by my wife, who reported that my apprehensive brother-in-law desired me personally to confirm that the lights off at one o'clock were not (*a*) an uncharted reef, (*b*) an unscheduled island, or (*c*) a torpedo coming at us at full speed. I came on deck and peered out at the lights of what appeared to be a tanker going peacefully toward whatever it was going peacefully toward. A good chance, though, to show off my radar, which immediately picked it up at six and one-half miles away, heading toward, approximately, Morocco. I went back to sleep, and awoke when Ned at the wheel was past the famous Anegada Passage, down which the Atlantic often sweeps bustily into the Caribbean, but which on this passage had acted like a wall-to-wall carpet; and now we were surrounded by tall, hilly islands, such that by contrast we felt almost as though we were going through a network of rivers, calm, warm, but with breeze enough (finally) to sail. And we put in, at eleven, at Spanish Town, in order to regularize ourselves with the government of the British Virgins, which, on Christmas Eve, was most awfully obliging, after the first mate and I completed the six forms registering the names and affirming the nonsubversive intentions of the tired but happy crew and passengers of the schooner *Cyrano.*

Wednesday, December 24. We head now for a bay, particularly favored by Ned, in Virgin Gorda. Getting there is a minor problem, requiring a certain concentration so as to avoid Colquhoun Reef. In nonnavigational language, you proceed like up, over, down, back and up, so as to avoid the long reef. Look it up in any of the books or guides, and it is abundantly charted. The rewards are great, because after you nestle down there you see along the reef, a few hundred yards away from the anchorage, the beautiful blues and greens you have been missing thus far, where the water was deep. It is strictly Bahamian here. They say, by the way, that the Virgins are vastly to be preferred to the Bahamas "from the water level up." This is shorthand to communicate the following: The islands are infinitely more interesting in the Antilles—the Virgins, the Windwards and the Leewards. Every island is strikingly interesting and different, both topographically and culturally. St. Kitts, for instance, has Mt. Misery, an enormous volcano rising to forty-three hundred feet. Nothing of the sort happens in the Bahamas, where the islands are almost uniformly low. But the Bahamian waters are uniquely splendid in coloration. The sandbars and reefs, which are so troublesome to the navigator, repay the bother to the swimmer and to anyone who just wants to look. Anyway, Virgin Gorda is that way, and on shore is the Drake's Anchorage hostelry, which just that morning had changed hands. The previous owner of the little bar and inn had sold out to—would you believe it?—a professor at MIT. The bar and dining room were Somerset Maugham-tropical, and were all dressed up for Christmas. The talk was of the necessity to persuade somebody to come down and take over the exciting underwater tours of the departing owner, who specialized in taking adventurous spirits for scuba diving in the Anegada Passage to poke about the wrecks at Horseshoe Reef, not all of which have, by any means, reposed there since the eighteenth century. The flagpole at the hostelry is the corroded aluminum mast of the *Ondine,* which foundered there just a few years ago.

Having reconnoitered, we went back to *Cyrano,* at that point almost alone in the anchorage, just in time to see a smallish sloop come gliding toward us, brazenly avoiding the circumnavigatory imperatives of the guidebooks, treating the reef we had given such studied berth to as familiarly as if it were the skipper's bathroom. We watched in awe as a dignified lady with sunbonnet directed the tiller to conform with the directions given by the angular, robust old gentleman up forward handling the anchor. The landing was perfect, the motor never having been summoned to duty, and they lodged down, fifty yards away from us. I discreetly manned the binoculars, peeked for a while and said to my companions, "By George, I do believe that is Dr. Benjamin Spock."

I know the gentleman slightly, having sparred with him here and there in the ideological wars. I wondered what, under the circumstances, would be an appropriate way to greet him. I thought of sending Ned over to his sloop, instructed to say, "Dr. Spock, compliments of *Cyrano,* do you happen to have anything on board for bubonic plague?" But the spirit of the season overcame me, and instead I wrote out an invitation, "Compliments of the military-industrial complex, Mr. and Mrs. William F. Buckley, Jr. would be honored to have the company of Dr. and Mrs. Benjamin Spock and their friends for Christmas cheer at 6:00 P.M." The good doctor rowed over (I knew, I *knew* he wouldn't use an outboard) to say Thanks, how was I? Mrs. Spock wasn't feeling very well, please forgive them, they were pulling out anyway within the hour, come back soon, once you've sailed the Virgins you can never sail anywhere else; and rowed back. We struck out in the glasshopper (all-glass dinghy) with the kids to explore the reef, which they did for hours on end. I returned to *Cyrano* (I enjoy skin diving, but a half hour of it is fine by me), mounted the easel and acrylic paint set Bill brought me for Christmas and set about industriously to document, yet again, my lack of artistic talent. The girls were working on the decorations, and by the time the sun went down we had a twinkling Christmas tree on deck and twinkling lights along the canvas of the dodger;

the whole forward section was piled with Christmas gifts and decorations, and when we sat down for dinner, with three kerosene lights along my supper table, the moon's beam, lambent, aimed at us as though we were the single target of the heavens, Christmas music coming in from the tape-player, the wine and the champagne and the flambéed pudding successfully passed around, my family there, and friends, I persuaded myself that nowhere on that evening, at that time of day, could anyone have asked for any kinder circumstances for celebrating the anniversary of the coming of the Lord.

Thursday, December 25. Intending to go to a church service on Christmas Day at Road Town, the capital of the British Virgins, we pull out earlyish, on the assumption that there is a Mass at noon. We arrive at 11:45 and come in European style at the yacht basin. European-style, by the way, involves dropping an anchor, sometimes two, about thirty yards ahead of where you intend finally to position your boat. Then you back up toward the pier (usually stone or concrete) while someone up forward, the anchor having kedged, is poised to arrest your backward movement by snubbing up on the anchor line the moment you give the signal. You back up the boat to about ten feet from the landing. At the right moment, you toss out the port stern line diagonally, and the starboard stern line ditto. Obliging passersby secure these lines on the pier, and you have—you can readily see—a very neat situation. The stern lines are acting as, in a way, spring lines, restricting the boat's sideward movement, sideward being where other boats are lined up, leaving, very often, no more than a few inches of sea room. Then, when you are safely harnessed, you motion to the gentleman on the foredeck to ease the line to the anchor, while the two gentlemen aft take up on *their* lines, bringing the stern of *Cyrano* gently aft until the davits are hanging quietly over the pier. You have now only to take a step over the taffrail, touch down easily on the ground and, without equilibratory gyration (something you should practice), stroll on toward the nearest *taverna.* I don't know why the custom isn't more widespread in American harbors, the economy of space and motion being so very obviously advantageous. Of course, you need to have a sheer situation off the pier, which isn't always the case, for instance, in many New England snuggeries. But even when there is water, the habit is not practiced by American yachtsmen. So much is it the drill in, for instance, Greece, that pleasure craft of any size carry gangways that extend from the transom to the pier, including stanchions and lifelines to serve as bannisters for milady to hang on to as she descends daintily to earth. I remember a year ago in the Aegean seeing a hedonistic triumph called the *Blue Leopard,* an enormous yawl which, miraculously, ejected its gangway—it would appear electrically—from just beneath the deck level where it is stowed, like the dictation slide that pulls out of a desk—right down onto the pier? No, dear. To six inches above the pier, contact with which it was protected from by two special halyards which quickly materialized and were quickly attached to the far corners. The purpose? Why, to spare the *Blue Leopard* the fetid possibility that a restless rat might, seeking a tour of the Aegean, amble up the companionway, it being acknowledged that healthy rats tend to board a floating ship.

We linger only an hour or so. The gentleman who owns the bar, the Sir Francis Drake Pub, is moved by the spirit of the season and does not charge you—Merry Christmas!—for your first drink, and we feel rather sneaky ordering only a single round and then returning to *Cyrano* for lunch. Christmas lunch. Rawle could give us anything, beginning with lobster Newburgh and ending with Baked Alaska. We settle on a fish chowder, of which he is surely the supreme practitioner, and cheese and bacon sandwiches, grilled, with a most prickly Riesling picked up at St. Barts for peanuts. Then we wander off to the Fort Burt Hotel, which is built around the top of the old fort, providing a 300-degree view of the harbor and adjacent islands. There is another hotel there, dubbed the Judgment Day Hotel, which has not been completed, even though it has been abuilding, lo, these many years, and is therefore the butt of many local jokes, seniority going to the one about how it will finally open only on Judgment Day. The attitude toward progress in the Antilles is ambivalent. On the one hand, the natives recognize that "progress" is both ineluctable and commercially desirable. On the other hand, the agents of progress are the presumptive disrupters of the natural order, and when bad fortune befalls them—as with the builder of the phantom hotel —the natives take pleasure in their fugitive alliance with adversity.

Off we go, to swim and to spend the night off Norman Island, which is reputedly the island Robert Louis Stevenson described when he wrote *Treasure Island*. It is, needless to say, just like any other island (except that it lies adjacent to fascinating grottos, complete with bats, into which you row wide-eyed). On the other hand, needless to say, like the other islands it too is captivating: a beach; a fine, protected cove. I remember a few years ago when, intending to pleasure him, I took Christopher, at fourteen and having done exceptionally well at school, with me cross-country, to San Francisco and Los Angeles, where I was to record television programs. My son was the prodigy of the McLuhanite dogma, but I was determined *not* to raise my voice in criticism—he was at my side (*a*) because I adored him, and (*b*) because I sought concrete expression of my admiration of his academic work. But finally—after *four* hours of flight, during which, earphones glued on, Christopher merely stared at the ceiling, even as his overworked father fussed fetishistically with briefcases and papers—I lost control, turned on him and said, acidly, or better, acidulously (if the word has uses, let it now pull its oar):

"Christopher, just out of *curiosity*, have you *ever* read a book?"

He moved his right hand slowly, with that marvelous impudence the rhythm of which comes so naturally to the goddamn kids, dislodging his right earphone *just* enough to permit him to speak undistracted, but not so much as to cause him to lose the musical narrative of whatever rockrolling fustian he was listening to, and replied in Peter Fonda-drawl, "Yeah. *Treasure Island.*"

Back went the earphones. The eyes did not need to revert to the ceiling of the plane. They had never left it.

It was our final night aboard *Cyrano* and we felt, although we did not sentimentalize on it, the little pang one always feels on approaching the end—of anything. The night was fine. Calm, peaceful. The moon made its appearance, though later; grudgingly, it seemed. I think we all lingered more than usual before going below.

Friday, December 26. We stopped at Trunk Bay, St. John, to skin dive. St. John is the island most of which was given by the U.S. government to the Rockefellers, or vice versa, I forget which. In any case, you must drop your anchor well out in the cove, because the lifeguards do not permit you to come too close. In fact, when you come in on the beach with your dinghy, you are required, if you have an outboard motor, to anchor it fifty yards from the beach and off to the right, away from the swimmers. If you don't have an outboard, you may beach your dinghy. But if you do beach your dinghy, you may not attach its painter (the boat word for the leash of a dog or tether of a horse) to the palm tree up from the beach, because you will be told that people might stumble over it, which indeed people might do if they are stone-blind. Then you walk to the east side of the beach, put on your face mask and fins and follow the buoys, ducking down to read, underwater, marvelously readable descriptions of flora, fauna and fish, the reading matter engraved on stone tablets which tilt up at a convenient angle and describe the surrounding situation and the fish you are likely to come across.

The tablets I saw did not describe the barracuda that took a fancy to me, whose visage was fascinatingly undistinguishable from Nelson Rockefeller's, but then my eye mask was imperfectly fitted. We got back to *Cyrano* and sailed on down past the Rockefeller Hotel at Caneel Bay, to Cruz Bay, where we officially reentered the United States of America. Embarrassing point. My wife thought, it being the day after Christmas and all, that it would be pleasant if I took to the lady who transacts these official matters a bottle of cheer. I went to her with Ned at my side, and found her wonderfully efficient and helpful. She completed the forms and then, rather like Oliver Twist making time with the headmaster, I surfaced a bottle of Ron Ponche, and, with a flourish or two, presented it to her, trying to look like Guy Kibbee playing Santa Claus. She smiled benignly and then explained that she could not, under The Rules, accept such gifts. I was crestfallen, embarrassed, shaken, and returned feistily to my wife to say, "See, that's what you get trying to bribe American authorities." To which she replied, "Trying to bribe them to do what?" Which stumped me, and I took a swig of the rejected Ron Ponche, which tasted like Kaopectate, perhaps explaining the lady's rectitude.

We travel under power to St. Thomas, a mere couple of hours. Yacht Haven at St. Thomas might as well be Yacht Haven at Stamford, Connecticut, where *Cyrano* would spend next summer. Hundreds of boats, harried administrators, obliging officials giving and taking messages, paging what seemed like everybody over the loudspeaker, connecting pallid, sleepy Northeasterners with their snowflaked baggage and then with wizened boat captains. Only the bar, which opens at 8:00 A.M., made it obviously other than Yacht Haven, Stamford; and, of course, the weather. About eighty-two degrees, and sun, sun, sun: we had not been without it, except for an hour or two on either side of a squall, during the entire idyllic week. A charter would board the next afternoon, and the preparations were accordingly feverish. The adults obliged by taking a couple of rooms at the Yacht Haven Hotel. The boys stayed on board to help. We had yet to consummate a dinner cruise around the harbor, and our scheduled guests were my libel lawyer in New York, Mr. Charles Rembar, his wife and son. They arrived (an hour late—a serious matter, inasmuch as they had not been indoctrinated in Buckley Watch Time), and we slid out in the darkness (the moon would be very, very late) and cruised about, under power this time, bounding off the lights of the five great cruise ships that lined the harbor and its entrance. St. Thomas is not unlike Hong Kong at night, except, of course, that its hills are less high. But the lights are overwhelming, and the spirit of Christmas was everywhere, so that we cruised gently in the galaxy, putting down, finally, the anchor; had our dinner, pulled back into the slip, said our good-byes and left my beautiful *Cyrano,* so firm and reliable, so strong and self-assured, so resourceful and copious, and made our way back, in stages, to New York, where, for some reason—obscure, after the passage of time—our ancestors left *their* boats in order to settle down there, so that their children's children might dream, as I do, of reboarding a sailing boat and cruising the voluptuous waters that Columbus hit upon in his crazy voyage five hundred years ago, because he did not have Ned aboard to tell him when enough was enough.

About Figaro

by WILLIAM SNAITH

William Snaith, winner—among other races—of the Bermuda-Copenhagen event, was a literate lover of sailing. He used sophisticated references to raise the following discussion of his boat Figaro *to a universal level. In fact, Snaith was a brilliant writer who happened to be a sailor, weaving his words into gemlike phrases as deftly as he rode the wind.*

IT is hard to stay gloomy aboard *Figaro,* although events conspire to peg our spirits at the nadir. It is not too farfetched to imagine she exudes happiness, an invisible elixir distilling from her woodwork, making short work of the glums. She's just the opposite of the craggy manors that lady writers of Gothic novels discover on Cornish cliffs or isolated moors in Devon or Transylvania. Whereas these haunted bits of architecture inject their inhabitants with broody gloom, *Figaro* does what she can to chase the blues. Besides, I really don't believe the average man has the stomach for protracted gloom unless he be one who looks for it around every corner like Schopenhauer or wallows in it like Hamlet. Most of us would incline toward hedonism or one of its jolly subdivisions. Unhappily, the events of life intrude and no matter how we stuff the mattress with down, a few nails from the fakir's cot show up in our bed of pleasure.

In response, therefore, to *Figaro*'s magic elixir and my own brighter instincts, I awoke after the long and lonely night of wondering and reached eagerly for lightheartedness. From my first waking moment, I felt sure the right decision would be made. That conviction persists despite a look out of the companionway. We are in the murky first ring of a watery purgatory. Somewhere nearby is Vergil waiting to guide us deeper or else the Flying Dutchman ready to rattle his chains. We must elude them both.

Figaro sails in an eerie environment, a world of curdled gray mist. At times, the coils of curd thicken and a deeper murk settles around her. Suddenly the layers thin and the boat sails in a strangely pale crepuscular light. Each droplet in this thinner mist hangs separately against the washed-out yellow eye of the sun; a scummy cataract of varying density veils its burning stare. The chalky green face of the ocean is seen in a short radius around the boat, its heaving surface broken by small, tumbling crests. The waves come out of the mist suddenly, invisible until they are almost on the boat and then as quickly disappear ahead; a rush of energy, hurrying toward an undisclosed rendezvous. Only the bow wave roils the even pattern of the oncoming seas as it falls back diagonally across their path. The churned air imprisoned in foaming bubbles breaks out and hisses in rage as the bubbles clutch fruitlessly at the hull slipping by. Then with a last crackle, no longer sounding angry, like the ultimate gush of gas escaping from stirred champagne or of Alka-Seltzer, the wave expires quietly into the mist, leaving a wake discernible to no one but the two Mother Carey's chickens who have decided to be companions to this voyage. The bow plunges steadily on as though it, and not we, knows where we are going. It is not precisely the morning for hornpipes and chanteys.

As the morning moves on, the weather looks as though it will break clear, even a suspicion of frosty blue tints the muddy blanket overhead. But then the boat enters another area of heavy fog, the sea disappears, all but the bubbles. The bow can no longer be seen, but its wave is still heard in tempo with the rise and fall as it plunges on somewhere ahead. *Figaro* carries on steadfastly, unshaken by the lack of visibility. I cannot say as much for myself; blind Polyphemus at the mouth of the cave, wondering from which corner the assailant will come.

My son MacLeod stands at the wheel. His watch captain, Bobby Symonette, sits under the dodger smoking a Montecristo No. 1, the size which lasts longer. An unfailing rule on all my *Figaro*s gives the man smoking a good cigar the right to enjoy it under the dodger (except in the case of alarums and excursions). I think it a crime against civilized behavior to let a cigar burn like a torch, hot and hard in the wind. The fact of my liking cigars must have a great deal to do with this sensitivity. Cleody, on the other hand, who does not smoke cigars, feels the rule to be outrageous, especially in view of the fact that Bobby can make the enjoyment of a cigar last more than one hour. To Cleody's mind, this is one hell of a long time to devote to civilities while other men stand out in the wet and cold. In spite of his voiced protest, he steers cheerfully.

I am not the one to thwart the authority of the man in charge, especially in a rule of my own making, so I sit down alongside Bobby and accept a cigar. After carefully lighting up, I ask, "Do you think we can count on catching enough rainwater on the way across to piece out our supply?"

"It's a thought. We've never gone across when we did not have our share of rain. We might as well put it to use."

"I am thinking that way. If we wash in seawater, don't shave, boil as many things as we can in half seawater, except for coffee and soup, we could make it across with water to spare. If we catch rain in addition, we will have built-in insurance."

Monk Farnham, from a position in the galley aft, says, "It sounds good to me."

During the lunch break, at the change of watch, the first time we are all together, I broach the idea to the whole crew. I tell them about the rain catcher made for just such a contingency. It is especially fitted to the boat, a suspended, fabric, bathtublike gizmo lying in the waterway, the tops fastened between the rail and the handgrabs on the cabin top. It is fitted with a spout at the bottom so we can pour off into containers. Knud Reimers, the other watch captain, is a Swedish citizen. He likes the idea of coming home in a sailboat. It is the true Viking (he pronounces it "wicking") return; the only honorable return is to stand up in a boat or be prone on a shield. Once the older and, by inference, wiser men are agreed, the young unhesitatingly go along with the idea. They put their faith in us; we have placed ours in the boat. She has become more than a thing; she is entrusted with our lives. We are committed.

Everyone goes enthusiastically topside to see how the rain catcher fits. We dig it out of its bag. A shock-odor of creosote hits us in the nose, so strong that were it not for the damp sea air our eyes would smart. The cloth is fiberglass. It must still be curing. The smell is so strong we decide to leave it on deck spread out on the cabin housetop to let it air. We are convinced that now having awakened the chemical beast, if we dared put it back in the bag, it would creep in the night.

We are surrounded by fog. The rain catcher and ourselves are soon as wet as if we had been dipped.

Figaro never falters through all this. She plunges along as though she did not have grievously wounded tanks in her vitals and as if the souls on board did not secrete little quaverings of their own. Seeing or not, oblivious of the threat of oncoming or overtaking vessels, she sails on. Occasionally, an out-of-sync wave catches her bow and a shattering of spray shoots diagonally across her deck. Shaking off the water through her freeing ports, she picks up her rhythm as though nothing happened. She's one hell of a boat. How can anything bad happen to you when you are in her!

That's a good question, friend, a real measure of the mythic trust one puts in a creature-thing. Anyway, that's what it is all about and how it stands. We are physically sound, perhaps a bit bruised in spirit, and committed to some two weeks of racing in the open Atlantic. While the crew do not show it, there must be an underlying unease, like that running through an army that has crossed a Rubicon by forced march and wonders if its baggage train will catch up. We have placed our reliance in one another and in the boat. If ever a boat is capable of putting out magic, we could sure as hell use some of it now.

A sport is something special in order to offset an image, which, to the uninitiated, must appear to be an idiot's delight. For those not hooked on ocean racing, yachtsmen must seem to be a web-footed, secular subsection of the Penitentes, a strange order of devotees, each man serving as his own Torquemada and his own subject for trial by water. He allows himself to be torn from his normal habitat and defenses; his usual bodily functions, habits and schedules are upset and in a restlessly rocking shelter at that.

This little vessel, the repository of our faith, in whose fortitude we believe, despite her seeping innards, is the only heroine in an otherwise all-male cast and blessed with a man's name at that—Figaro. Like all beauties who quicken subjective response, she can be given dimensions. Instead of the standard breasts, beam and buttocks, we count her vital statistics as forty-six-foot overall, thirty-two feet six inches on the waterline with a beam of twelve feet. She is a centerboarder and a yawl. Designed by Olin Stephens of Sparkman & Stephens and built in eighteen long months by Joel Johnson, a fine crafts-

man in Black Rock, Connecticut, in itself a muddy backwater which somehow finds its way into Long Island Sound. She is double planked with Honduras mahogany over ⅜-inch Oregon spruce. Her keelson is white oak, a massive timber, personally selected by Joel. He used a hand adze to achieve the finished shape. It was a great sight to see Joel standing astride the balk and taking off long slivers and short as accurately and fine as with a plane. One rarely sees that sort of skill and craftsmanship anymore. Just to see it is a privilege. Unhappily, the balk lay too long in the building shed during the protracted building period while wonders took place above. It checked badly, being very green in the beginning, and did not dry well. Right after launching, we had trouble with the nagging leaks until another craftsman stopped them. Now the water comes in only at the stuffing box, and that too will be cured. Originally, *Figaro* drew four feet six inches with her board up. With her bronze board down, she drew another three feet six inches. I changed her draft and ballast for this race, but that story deserves a separate telling later on.

Her layout is quite conventional, with her galley aft. The main saloon is handsome. It is paneled in Brazilian rosewood; the forward-bulkhead paneling frames an open fireplace with a white overmantel. This is shaped like a truncated obelisk. It is of white formica into which nautical decorations in imitation of scrimshaw were cut. As part of the decorations, I included a line from Samuel Pepys' *Diary,* "My Lords in discourse discovered a great deal of love to this Ship." Even in her building days, I sensed she would be that kind of boat. I did these engravings myself and have the calluses to prove it. Oval escutcheons on which gimbaled oil lamps are mounted are done in the same technique.

This saloon holds four berths, two regular uppers and two in-extension transoms under which are the wounded and bleeding water tanks. A cabin forward is separated from the saloon by the head on the port side and two hanging lockers across the passageway to port. The roller-coaster movement of this forward cabin is exaggerated when the boat is banging into a head sea. When we are at sea, its use is normally reserved for the ship's acknowledged "Iron Guts."

But a boat should be more than a sterling example of the boat-builder's art and man's desire to embellish her with decorations. Obviously, she means a special thing to the man who sails her. She has the ability to surcharge each event with a special aura, a release of spirit, a feeling of safety and a sense of fellowship.

Consider a single instance when the boat becomes the only secure center of your suddenly changed world—a North Atlantic storm (there is a 75-percent chance of encountering one in a crossing). The usual cyclone system, not a cyclone but the pattern associated with a low-pressure area, lasts an average of two to three days in its coming and going, during which unhappy time a thought threatens to overwhelm all other ideas. It is the question buried in one's mind or expressed to a companion alongside: "How the hell did I get myself into this?" Like as not, the storm will leave bone-tiring repairs in its wake. Yet, if the boat and company are proper, it somehow adds up to a rewarding experience.

Not the least of the various magics which take place is the bond created between a man and the boat in which he sails. It is not necessarily that between a man and a thing. After a time at sea, a boat becomes more than a clever assemblage of insensible matter. I think of a boat as a creature-thing. For me, she is infused with a persona, hovering on the edge of animation. It should not be difficult to understand how a yacht can become imbued with anima and personality. After all, it is a shelter and shield, however frail, and each yacht develops attributes and characteristics peculiar to herself in the way she meets the conditions and hazards of a passage. She can be cranky or sea-kindly, but in the end, the man and boat are made partners in the presence of the antagonist, the sea. To one degree or another, this bond is shared by all who sail in her and is not the sole privilege of the man who pays her yard bills, although somewhere within the Judeo-Christian ethic the idea persists that the degree of love is directly related to the amount of oneself and of one's wealth given. However

painful this way to or from love may seem, especially to a man paying alimony, or yard bills, there is no doubt whatever that the bond between the boat and the owner-skipper increases when the burden of a decision which involves his faith in the boat is placed upon him.

Even while the man who sails in her responds to her anima, this creature-thing somehow becomes adapted to his bent and temperament though cherishing idiosyncrasies of her own. Chameleonlike, she takes on the coloration of her owner's needs. Each man uses his boat in his own way to fill certain wants. There are as many roads to Nirvana as boats and men. Nowhere does this show up as precisely as in choosing a name for the darling of his heart. Linguistics and semantics have become important analytical tools in philosophy and behavioral sciences. The choice of a boat's name is the semantic key to his dream, a revealing decision; the clues to his attitude are as clear as the strewn shreds in a paper chase.

The names fall into easily identifiable categories. As an instance, *Mother's Mink* and *String of Pearls* betray certain uxorious guilt feelings. *Press on Regardless, September Song, Last Chance,* speak of the quiet perturbation in the face of onrushing years. *Atomic, Hurricane, Leopard* (usually found on racers) vie with the names chosen for automobiles by automakers in the hunt for virility symbols and a wish-fulfilling longing to identify with tearing power and force. Of quite another order is the desire to relate to the beauty and poetry of the sea. One could let go in Mailerian hyperbole or choose a stanza from a Masefield poem which would dramatically fill a transom and provide inspiring reading for those behind. But timidity, inhibitions and age-old models intrude. A popular device whereby to capture the sea's magic is to choose a name with the prefix *sea*. The waters abound with *Sea Winds, Sea Stars, Sea Witches,* etc. It is my presumption that there are as many names starting with *Sea* in *Lloyd's Register of Yachts,* as listings of *Martinez* in the Madrid phone book, or in the Manhattan directory, for that matter.

In another reaching out for identity with beauty, we encounter *Aphrodites, Apollos,* and

The forty-six-foot yawl Figaro, *named by owner William Snaith after his dog that, in turn, had been named after Beaumarchais' Figaro—"a lively scamp thumbing his nose at the establishment around him, left, right and center."*

*Circe*s, and for those who wish on a star, there is an *Orion, Vega* or *Arcturus*.

A whole other order of boat names belongs to the dedicated family men. Their boat transoms carry conjunctive family names such as *Joanted* or hyphenated as in *Mar-jac-lou*. It is the bridegroom's last epithalamic song or else a sneaky way to involve the whole family in a sport for which they have little stomach and less enthusiasm.

I do not intend to denigrate any man's choice of name for his ark of dreams but rather to confirm the notion that there is a boat for all seasons in men.

I have made a brief résumé of the origins of boat names because it now falls on me to reveal how I chose the name for my own heart's delight. I have known privilege, joy, rage and frustration as the owner of a string of boats called *Figaro 1* through *Figaro 5*. On the face of it, this redundant choice paints me as an unimaginative clod or one with dynastic dreams. I must profess, "It is not so." My first boat bore the name *Cleody-Skipper,* named for my two eldest sons, MacLeod and Shepperd (Skipper). With the birth of our third son, Jonathan (Jocko), reason returned. The addition of one more child-inspired suffix seemed an empty game. I came to see the shortcomings of the practice. The first seizure on acquiring a new boat is poetic, an anodyne perhaps for signing the check. But my new boat had a smallish transom, incapable of carrying a reasonable stanza in Coast Guard-approved letter size. I did own a beloved dog named Figaro. Immediately one is repelled. What manner of man would exalt a dog over his children or give a dog's name to a thing of beauty like a sailboat (even if the dog is lit by a beauty of his own and if the genus name is that of God spelled backward). It is a tangled tale requiring some explanation. The secret lies in the answer to the question, How did my dog get his name?

A phenomenon that I recognize but can never quite explain is the fact that I instinctively find myself thinking at cross-purposes to any establishment with which I have contact, be it institutional, political, social or esthetic. As an instance: I am emotionally and actively dedicated to contemporary art. I am the head of a leading design firm. For several years running, my paintings had been hung in the Whitney Museum Annual of American Paintings (a practice now discontinued). I was protected from what was happening around me for a time by my recognition of two older polarities of genius—Picasso and Klee. But one day, looking past these two, I wrote a critically polemic book bemoaning certain onrushing antihuman trends. In this, I took my stand alongside Ortega y Gasset and other distinguished voices against the spoilers of the human spirit. But, unlike them, I fell from institutional grace.

In another instance, as a minority liberal ideologue in a tory stronghold, I served for several years as Democratic Party chairman in my town but finally gave way to the fact that I had little admiration or stomach for politics and for several of my party's candidates (and even less for others).

In these various ways, I find myself closer to the quaking edge than the quivering epicenter of a whole order of establishments. It is not by plan —it just turns out that way. It is obvious that being a temperate rebel, never having learned either to make my peace or take to the outer barricades, I have wound up in a mild limbo with undefined geographical borders. There is no home for such.

There may be something in all of the foregoing which harks back to my never-waning admiration for Beaumarchais's antic scamp Figaro— not just for the embellishments added by Mozart and Rossini, but for the character himself.

It is him, the essence of that character, for whom my dog was named and whom my various *Figaro*s honored—a lively scamp thumbing his nose at the establishment around him, left, right and center.

This explanation for my repetitious selection should be enough, but even while recognizing the dangers of "He doth protest too much," there is a very sound, if entirely different, reason for the reiteration. We live in a confused and overly communicated-to world, wandering at a loss in the midst of a traumatic identity crisis. We are witness to the loss of self in the lonely crowd.

It is comforting in all this to hold on to a sense of continuity, a something that belongs to you and to which you belong. It may be minimal, but, nevertheless, it is reassuring to be part of a continuing stream, even if it is only the name for boats. This should not be confused with the hollowness of dynastic dreams or substitute clutchings for immortality. Choices like this begin and end with you. This minimal symbol of continuity may be a poor thing, but while it lasts, it is all your own.

Having thus introduced you into one of the pothering muddles that confound and confuse a yachtsman's heart and mind, I can speak glowingly of my joy, rage, frustration in the ownership of my *Figaro*s all in one breath. It is because my normally happy involvement with boats is complete. It is my form of Zen. Beginning with the passive enjoyment of the beauty of sail to the active excitements of competition and through this latter into the theory and self-inflicted practice of do-it-yourself yacht design, I have been enthralled by boats in their many aspects. Through boats, I have made lasting friendships with men who sail with me and whom I sail against.

A boat designed to cock-a-snook must be saucy, pert and nimble on her heels. *Figaro* is all of that and more. She is reliable and gives off confidence that she will take you out and bring you back safely.

The Hunting of Hewlish

by SAM NICHOLSON

In an antiseptic future dominated by computers and robots, sailing, as Sam Nicholson portrays it in this story for Omni, *is an anachronism. The following dialogue defines its meaning for the hero:*

"What is this satisfaction for which you roughen and abuse your body?"

"The freedom of direction, without robot interference . . .

"How strange! I thought you would say the beauty of the boats fascinated you."

"The aliveness of the boats. My own aliveness. It's a feeling Terra lost many centuries ago."

But maybe it's not lost entirely . . .

SIBYL stood at the vast, blue-tinted window, swept aside the gossamer draperies with both arms and gloated over the blue Azorean Sea; over floating gardens, lily-padding in clusters; over helix-caged towers like the one in which she was so luxuriously installed.

"Oh, Roxanne, come and see!" she called to her twin sister.

Roxanne tied the jeweled belt of her chatoyant silk dressing gown and stepped to the window. The girls were blondes of rare beauty, not identical, but complementary.

"What shall we do first?" Sibyl asked, smiling.

"Go hunting, of course," replied Roxanne. "What else is there to do at a holiday resort?"

"Whom shall we hunt?"

"The wealth of the galaxy has come for the regatta."

"Oh, I'm bored with wealth. We don't need wealth."

"We'll need it later."

"We'll hunt it later. Who else is here?"

"The rulers of the galaxy."

"We'll hunt rulers when we're ready to mate."

"You're very difficult today, Sibyl. There's no other prey than wealth and status."

"Nonsense. If we look, we'll find exciting prey."

They stood shoulder to shoulder, hand in hand, and watched the scene. Far below, gleaming white sails fluttered at an edge of the floating platform. The sails tightened, skimmed like low-soaring birds over the deep blue Terran waves.

"How beautiful!" Roxanne exclaimed.

"From here, yes. A wretched sport. One climbs into a narrow shell that dips and tilts—and the sun inflames the skin—and the salt foam stings the eyes—and one must grasp horrid, wet ropes."

"We've never hunted sailors."

"That's true. But let's hunt them on land."

"A hunt is a hunt, dear Sibyl. Shall we share or divide our prey?"

"Sailors are not wealthy men. Even a whole one apiece will scarcely make the hunt worth the effort."

"How can you be so stupid? Sailing is a wealthy sport."

"And therefore, dear Roxanne, the sportsmen are poor."

Sibyl turned with a flouncing of lace and sank into the soft cushions nested on the opalescent floor. She picked up a crystal cube and pressed it.

An inner wall of the room became a viewing screen. Rainbows pinwheeled into infinity as a voice asked, "Animal, Vegetable or Mineral?"

"Animal."

"Primates or nonprimates?"

"Primates."

"Human or subhuman?"

"Human."

"Terran or Galactic?"

"Hold!"

The pinwheels froze. Sibyl called to Roxanne. "Come and help me. How do I answer? There are sailors on all the water planets."

Roxanne swung from the window and sat beside her sister. "Well, do we want to hunt Galactics?"

"I really can't like Galactics. They're either the wrong shape or too knobby or wear their ears and eyes at disconcerting angles."

"Then you know the answer."

Sibyl restarted the pinwheel and said, "Terran."

The voice intoned, "Name the categories, from the greater to the lesser."

Sibyl sighed and said carefully, "Human sports. Sailing. The Atlantic Rift Regatta. Now inform."

The pinwheels gave place to a panorama of the sailcraft now jostling for position beyond the starting buoys for the first race.

"Oh, drat," said Sibyl. "I programmed wrong. These are only the boats."

"You should have continued the categories and said, 'Teams.' Now you'll have to begin all over again."

"I won't. I hate voice programming. It was my worst subject at school. Roxanne, dear, begin all over again for me."

"No. Let's watch the boats. How else can one hunt sailors?"

Sibyl leaned back against the cushions, one arm curved over her head. "I wonder. Does passion-rose scent go with satin?"

"The boats are very beautiful."

Sibyl's smooth, curling lashes sank to rest on her cheeks, and she slept.

The race took all afternoon to sail the ancient Olympic circle. Roxanne followed the maneuvers closely. When the race was over, she softly ordered the screen, "Hold for further category."

The three-dimensional scene froze in its exuberance of sail and spray. Roxanne looked at her sister. Sibyl's face was peaceful, her eyes still shut.

"Teams," Roxanne murmured to the cube. "Today's winner. Now inform."

A sailboat flashed onto the screen and froze for a moment while the voice said, "Name, *Terran Hope.*" Another flash, and a grizzled, still-handsome old salt stood there, a broad smile on his face and a sharp squint to his eyes. The voice said, "Name, Captain Mack."

"Truly a brave breed," Roxanne observed, "to court wind erosion of the flesh and solar burning."

One after another the *Terran Hope*'s crewmen were displayed on the screen, until a firm-jawed young man looked into the recording lens. They scrutinized his handsome face. He had a serious countenance and was frowning slightly, as if resenting the necessity of facing the throng of reporters gathered for the regatta.

The voice intoned, "Name, Hewlish."

Roxanne gasped, "Hold!" She studied the young man, then said, "Clear!"

The screen resumed being a wall. Roxanne jumped up. Sibyl stirred and opened her eyes drowsily. "Where are you going?"

"Hunting. Will you come?"

"Beating the bushes isn't my style."

"No, dear Sibyl. You're the python coiled on a limb above the water hole."

"The regatta teams will be at tonight's ball. Good hunting, sister."

Roxanne left the room and entered her dressing alcove.

Sibyl lay dreamily winding a blonde curl around one pearly finger. "Hewlish—the hunting of Hewlish."

The sailcraft bobbed in their slots about the yacht basin, prows to the pier and stern lines to buoys aft. The sails had been taken down and stowed away, carefully, and the masts were but skeletons of glory.

The sailors were still leaving the boats. Only Captain Mack and young Hewlish remained aboard the *Terran Hope.*

The skipper eased the tension of the jibstay, walked lithely aft to the cockpit, where Hewlish was sitting, and grunted, "Coming ashore? We won't be altering anything for tomorrow's race."

"I'll stay awhile, captain. I'm enjoying the sea, wringing my holiday of every drop."

"You're fatigued."

"I'm enjoying that too."

"As you like."

Captain Mack turned toward the bow again, but stopped. A slim, white-cloaked girl, sun cowled and gloved, was standing on the pier. Under the cloak, her daytime suit clothed her in gold from her cushioned soles to her throat.

She spoke in a low voice. "Captain Mack, congratulations. I'm Roxanne. May I come aboard?"

"Sorry, no."

"Why not?"

"To be frank, I know about you and your sister. The huntresses. The *Hope*'s win today gives us honor, not wealth."

"I'm not hunting now. I'm curious. What is this satisfaction for which you roughen and abuse your body?"

Hewlish had come forward from the cockpit. "The freedom of direct action, without robot interference." He spread out his palms. "These hands haul the sails."

"Thus you've bruised and wounded them."

"And toughened them."

"How strange! I thought you would say the beauty of the boats fascinated you."

"The aliveness of the boats. My own aliveness. It's a feeling Terra lost many centuries ago. Look at you, Roxanne—cosseted, eating what robots give you, making up deficiencies with pills instead of with air and sunlight. A huntress? I pity the fool who lets you catch and bleed him!"

"But I'm not hunting now. I don't understand the aliveness of sailing. Can you explain it?"

"It can't be explained, only experienced."

"Take me sailing."

Captain Mack growled, "Ask at the other boats."

"No. I expect to be drenched, buffeted, bruised and salt stung. The only compensation will be the undergoing of the frightful ordeal with the winners."

"You'll get seasick too," the skipper grumbled.

"What is seasickness?"

Captain Mack smiled. "Want to sail, hey? Come here at 0900 hours tomorrow. Hewlish and I will take you for a short run before the wind freshens."

"Thank you. I'll be here."

She bowed and walked away, swiftly and gracefully.

Hewlish asked, "Why did you do that?"

"To get rid of her. She'll forget and oversleep. Huntresses don't rise early."

"Why would men pay to have her? Sex is free, reciprocal."

"It's not payment on demand. The men enjoy—and bestow, endow."

"What for? It doesn't seem logical."

"It's not. It's a primitive magic—a bewitchment. Stay clear of Roxanne and Sibyl, Hewlish, or before you know it, you'll be without a credit to your name."

"Heed your own warning, skipper. You were the one who invited her aboard."

"She won't come. Don't sit here wondering about her. There'll be plenty of women at the ball tonight."

The first-race ball was past its full tide and on the ebb when Captain Mack arrived, clad in his dress uniform. He sauntered around the circumference of the great circular hall, smiled benevolently at the dancers, bowed here and there to acquaintances and finally set his course for the tables in the refreshment bay.

Alone at a near table sat Hewlish, correctly but not festively attired. He beckoned the captain to join him.

Captain Mack seated himself and said, "I thought you'd have paired off and been gone by now."

"Pairing seemed too routine—too cut and dried. The women seemed dull. I suppose it's their contrast to Roxanne."

"What could you see of Roxanne? Just a shadowed face inside a hood."

"Well, I can't get her out of my mind. Maybe it was her voice, or her manner."

"So you've been waiting for her?"

"She didn't come. I don't know what I've been waiting for. When did you get here?"

"Just now—to be courteous to the regatta committee. I'm singleminded about regattas. Women don't interest me when I'm competing. All I think about is winning."

"The winning boat will have to compete on Trivector. A shallow, rocky sea, and the three moons play havoc with the tides. The Trivec scouts are here."

"Let 'em scout. Could you crew out there for the *Hope?*"

Hewlish drew a deep breath. "No. I can't get dispensation. You're lucky, being retired and rich enough to ride your hobby."

They sat for a moment. Then Hewlish asked, "Shall I program a drink?"

"Not for me, thanks. You're not drinking either?"

"I don't like robot bartenders. The customer has nothing to say. I developed a bartender that was viable along six categories, but the chief ordered the brain for a political unit."

They continued to sit. At last Hewlish came to life. "There she is! No—there's something different—"

Captain Mack glanced at the satin-gowned blonde who was approaching the refreshment area, gracefully fending off dance bids. He said, "That's Sibyl."

"Have you met both girls?"

"Seen 'em, not met 'em. On my last transit, before I retired from the starship service. They like to hunt in space. Spearing fish in a barrel, that's what it is."

Sibyl approached their table. Both men rose. She smiled. "Captain Mack? And this must be Hewlish. Are you waiting for Roxanne?"

The three sat down, and Sibyl continued, "Roxanne wouldn't come. She says she has to get up early and sail. Ridiculous, isn't it?"

Captain Mack growled, "So you're hunting alone."

Sibyl shrugged languidly. "I ought to be. It's no fun without Roxanne. I'm rather sad, really. Twins sometimes are only half people when they're alone."

"You and Roxanne will have to take separate paths when you mate," Hewlish said by way of rejoinder.

"Oh, I never think of it. Roxanne keeps reminding me. I'm bored with hunting, but I really don't want a change."

"A change from what? What are you?" Hewlish asked.

"I don't know. What are you—I mean, when you're not sailing?"

"My job is to develop increasingly complicated robots. I sail to use my human muscles and skills—to know uncertainty, decisions, fatigue."

"What horrid things to know! And you must be very clever otherwise, making robots. You make me feel so stupid. Memorizing all those category responses!"

"Galactic knowledge now encompasses several classes of what, for all practical purposes, are infinities. No single master computer can do the sorting and reassigning. The human brain is still the most economical computer. The least it can do is the preliminary indexing. What's so difficult about responding to Animal, Vegetable, Mineral?"

"Because I never can remember how to program for fish or birds, or flyovers or hats, or why air, water and transportation are Mineral."

"The logic is very sound. Is air Animal? Or Vegetable?"

"But I'm not logical."

"Of course you are! Every human being is logical."

"Oh, dear me, Hewlish, no!" Sibyl laughed, in light musical tones that charmed more than her gown. "I loathe boats and robots, yet I'm amusing myself at a ball with a sailing captain and an expert robotist."

"Would you like to dance?" Hewlish suggested.

"Oh, yes, if you'd be so kind. Just one dance, before I return to Roxanne."

The couple rose and joined the dancers waiting for the next configuration.

"Young fool!" Captain Mack muttered. "That's the last I'll see of him tonight."

But Hewlish returned alone after the configuration. He said, "Her helix cab was on standby at the flyover platform."

"You didn't ask her to pair?"

"Well, no, I couldn't, somehow. She was gracious, but not interested. That is, when we were dancing, I thought she was interested—and then I decided she wasn't—and then I just wanted time to stop because she was so lovely—and so fragrant—and her voice was like music. She's—"

"Bewitching," Captain Mack completed the thought. He stood up. "I've made my appearance. I can go back to the tower and take off these confounded ceremonials."

Hewlish rose also. Captain Mack said, "Plenty of girls—ready, willing and able."

"Yes, but Sibyl makes the whole routine seem—routine."

When Captain Mack and Hewlish arrived at the *Terran Hope* the next morning, Roxanne was waiting in the cockpit. She was wearing a black jacket, thick black gloves, black waterproof trousers and boots, and a close-fitting black cap.

"Do we sail the circle?" she asked.

"Today's race is to be from buoy to buoy through the channels," said Captain Mack, tightening the jibstay. "We'll take a look at the course."

Roxanne watched them rig the sails, which fluttered and whipped in the breeze.

"Back sail! Cast off!"

Hewlish jumped to the pier, released the bowline and jumped back, giving the boat a vigorous shove. Captain Mack continued to warp the boat out of the slot with the boat hook. When she was clear, they hauled the sails over, she caught the wind, and the hull pivoted against the rudder.

"How marvelous!" Roxanne squealed. "No power unit needed at all!"

"The wind is power," Hewlish said. "Human muscles are power."

The *Hope* glided on even keel. In the narrow channels, the breeze shifted, died, gusted again, and the boat tacked one way and then another.

Roxanne said critically to Hewlish, who was hauling the jib, "I perceive you sail by the rule book, not by the boat."

"What do you mean?"

"Always at the same moment you follow the mainsail. You don't feel what the boat wants to do."

"You think you know better than I do?"

"I think I sense the boat better."

"We won without you yesterday."

"You were sailing an open circle. In a channel the wind comes trickily. Give me the rope."

Captain Mack warned. "The boat is too light with only three aboard. She'll heel over when the wind freshens."

"Not completely over," Roxanne answered. "I observed during the race yesterday that, when the sails lay over, the wind spilled out and the boat righted."

Roxanne took the line in her gloved hands. Whether it was a new breeze, or a quicker response, the *Hope* glided more easily.

After the last channel, when they were proceeding across the open sea, the rising wind came strongly and pulled the sail away from Roxanne.

"On the rail!" roared Captain Mack.

Hewlish took hold of the jib line, close-hauled the sail and jumped to join Roxanne, who was clinging for dear life to the tilted rail.

"How exciting!" she chirped. "Much better than hunting!"

Lower rail plowing a furrow of foam, they flew over the water and gained the lee of the mooring basin.

"Oh, I'm drenched!" Roxanne complained, cajoling attention. "And salt stung and sun inflamed! But I've never been happier." She sprang to the pier. "Thank you, Captain Mack. Remember what I told you, Hewlish."

She ran joyfully away.

Hewlish said to the skipper, "The nerve of her! She can't really handle a jib."

"Naturally—she lacked muscle power."

"I mean, in the channel. It was just beginner's luck."

"She seems to have an intuition about boats."

"But sailing has definite physical laws."

"So has singing or playing an instrument."

"Captain, are you saying the girl sails better than I do?"

"No, Hewlish. Calm down, man."

"Roxanne's too slow changing tack. She continually plays the sail."

"Yes. Forget it."

"Do you want to replace me as jibman?"

"No, what's the matter with you?"

"Well, the boat did sail better. Maybe just the weight distribution when she moved forward to take the jib—"

"Will you forget it? We've got a big race this afternoon."

"Sure, sure. It's just—well—"

That afternoon, Sibyl and Roxanne sank onto their cushions and programmed the channel regatta. Roxanne said, "Sibyl, you must be ready to dress and helix to the mooring basin. After the race Hewlish will need consolation."

"You're certain they'll lose?"

"Thanks to my newly discovered sailing talent, yes. I've shaken Hewlish's confidence—and Captain Mack's confidence in him. At crucial moments, they'll hesitate. That's the time for you to move in."

"He may turn to Captain Mack instead of to me."

"I'll come with you and divert Captain Mack."

"Even so"—Sibyl looked sulky—"Hewlish isn't real prey."

"Does he bore you because he's not wealthy?"

"No. He's not wealthy because he doesn't prey on others. He's clever, yet honest."

"Dear Sibyl, you're giving this young man much unaccustomed thought."

"Hewlish is incomplete—and interesting. He'll be wealthy, in time. He'll sail better, in time. Who knows where his inventive mind will take him, in time? His life journey makes him interesting. Later he'll be boring."

"All the more reason to hunt him now."

"Is it? When one sets out to shear a sheep, one chooses a full-grown beast with a thick coat, not a young lamb with little to give and an honest nature to be hurt."

"To me, Hewlish seemed stubborn and disagreeable."

"You upset and confused him."

"I set him up for you. Don't you want to console him?"

"I suppose I do. I don't want him to lose the final race tomorrow."

"Then come and watch the results of my handiwork today. I've never known you to be so difficult."

The *Terran Hope* made a good start in the race but somehow lost her speed. She fell off on the tacks and was sluggish around the buoys, and her flying dash to the finish pulled her only to a third place.

Hewlish was crestfallen and would not follow the rest of the crew ashore.

Captain Mack said, "Don't take it so hard. With a first and a third, we're still leading. Tomorrow we'll win."

"It's the circle again. True, I'm more used to the circle."

"Of course you are. Come ashore—to the casino, perhaps."

They secured the gear, adjusted the mooring lines and stepped ashore.

Two familiar sun-cloaked figures greeted them. "Ah, Captain Mack," said Roxanne, "now you must walk the gardens with me and explain the race in detail. I shall scold you properly for losing the current at the second buoy."

"They set the buoy in the riptide. Whether from ignorance or devilment," said Captain Mack, "we'd better not inquire," and he followed Roxanne.

Hewlish said to Sibyl, "May I escort you to your helix, or will you follow your sister?"

"Neither. I don't know what to do."

"About what?"

"Roxanne. She's so mischievous."

"Mischievous, indeed! I wish she had never come aboard. Let me tell you—"

Sibyl glanced around uncertainly. "Must we talk standing here?"

"No—that is—may I escort you to the pavilion?"

"Oh, yes. You must be hungry after the long sail."

"I'm disgusted with myself. I don't want to look at food."

"You'll have to, in the pavilion. Besides, you'll have to program for me. Food categories bewilder me."

They crossed a flower-bordered lawn and entered the pavilion. The robot maître d'hôtel flipped the number thirty-three, and the number over a corresponding table lit up.

"Oh, I'd prefer a window table," Sibyl said.

"The robot is programmed for the convenience of the serving wagons."

"Let's step aside then. Others can take the middle tables."

Hewlish looked curiously at Sibyl. "Do you often circumvent robots?"

"Doesn't everyone? Step aside, Hewlish, and let this other couple have the table."

Hewlish stepped aside. One after another, he bowed four couples ahead of them, until a window table lit up and Sibyl swept triumphantly past the robot maître d'hôtel.

As they seated themselves, Sibyl said, "Program for me, dear Hewlish."

"Sibyl, the food categories are simple. Breakfast, Lunch, Tea, Dinner." He reached to the center of the table and turned the order unit toward them. "Which would you like?"

"Tea—but I want pancakes."

"Pancakes are a Breakfast category."

"No. Breakfast pancakes have syrup. I want pancakes with jam."

"With Tea you can have waffles with jam."

"But I want pancakes. Sometimes Roxanne and I program both Breakfast and Tea, and I use her jam pot with my pancakes. But she really doesn't like my syrup on her waffles."

"Discard the waffles and syrup."

"Well, yes, but food wasting is the worst crime in the galaxy. I'd be arrested if I left food in a public place."

"Are you hinting that I should eat the waffles and syrup?"

"Would you, dear Hewlish?"

"No, I would not. What a selfish question! I don't understand why men endow you with riches."

"Neither do I. But I did hope you'd endow me with pancakes. You said you design the robots."

"Yes—which is why I can't see how you acquired a taste for an unprogrammed combination."

"Oh, but Roxanne and I had parents! Parents make all the difference. The four of us could program for six dishes and divide and share and combine as we wished, and not a morsel was wasted."

"Was your mother as giddy as you?"

"Oh, yes. Papa said that coming home was like stepping onto a carousel. He never understood why Roxanne and I left home to seek adventure, but Mama wished us good hunting."

"Will you ever say something amusing to me, Sibyl?"

"Not while I'm hungry."

"I veto the pancakes. Choose a viable category."

"You choose first."

Hewlish programmed firmly, "Dinner. Meat—steak. Vegetable—potato crisps. Vegetable—mixed salad. Beverage—coffee. Now serve."

He looked inquiringly at Sibyl. She said, "The steaks are always small. You didn't program a dessert. You really could eat a dessert, don't you think."

"Like waffles and syrup?"

She smiled a slow, dazzling smile. "It would make me so happy."

He programmed the pancakes and waffles.

He scarcely tasted his dinner, so bewitched was he by her childish glee over the pancakes and jam. Before he realized how hungry he had been, the steak was gulped down, and the waffles followed just as quickly.

"I'm glad you suggested the pavilion," he said. "I feel much better."

Sibyl smiled to herself. "What else shall I suggest?"

"We could dance more than one dance at tonight's ball, though I would have to leave early. Tomorrow—" He stopped as if an electric shock had gone through him. "I forgot. The race—the defeat—everything. I forgot!"

"It's well forgotten. The defeat was my sister's doing."

"Captain Mack would rather have her handling the jib."

"I daresay he would. And she'd put him on the rocks fast enough. How could you let such mischief destroy your self-confidence? Forget today."

"I can never forget it."

"But, dear Hewlish, you just forgot it completely."

"That was only because you were here—because you—" He paused. "Do you always keep the carousel turning?"

"It's fun, isn't it? Why stop it? When shall we meet at the ball tonight?"

"Just to dance?"

"What else does one do at a ball?"

"One pairs. If you're a huntress, you must pair."

"But I'm not hunting. Shall we meet at the same refreshment table, about nine o'clock?"

"Eight o'clock."

"Very well. Now you may see me to my helix."

Meanwhile, Roxanne had been at the Sail Club with Captain Mack, scanning racks of cassettes.

"The whole sail theory, if you're interested," he said gruffly.

"I am. Such a vast array makes me feel very ignorant. I was impertinent to poor Hewlish today."

"Yes. Upset him considerably. Hope he settles down tomorrow."

"Oh, he'll regain his confidence by then." Roxanne looked at the racks. "Sailing is a weighty matter."

"Do you read?"

"Yes. I was lucky in my schooling. My parents believed reading was a good mental discipline."

"In that case, I can lend you a book that will be much less burden than cassettes on the same matter. But I'm keeping you late. Will you dine with me?"

"Yes, thank you. But only a brief meal. I'm eager to begin reading."

"Excuse me. You'll take good care of the book, won't you? Books are expensive and hard to replace. From observing you on my last space cruise, I did not suppose you even knew the alphabet."

Roxanne laughed. "Did you observe us? Sibyl and I were quite awed by your authority. It's nice to find you human."

"If I may say so, Roxanne, you're far more likable when you're not hunting."

"I enjoy being myself. How and when did it happen that literacy became the opposite of pleasure?"

"The perfection of voice programming and cassettes, I suppose, made literacy unnecessary to the lazy mind—and most human beings are lazy. Fortunately. If sailing were easy, the sport would be cluttered by robot minders and button pushers, as it was in the Early Atomic Age, when modern civilization began.

"But you'll find the history of the Sail Reform Movement in the book," he went on. "A fair breeze and human brain and muscle—there's the real sport."

"It's all very exciting," Roxanne agreed.

When Sibyl returned from the ball at midnight, Roxanne was reading Captain Mack's book.

"You're taking great pains for my sake," said Sibyl.

"Captain Mack is no fool. By tomorrow, my homework must be thoroughly done."

"You underestimate my own powers with Hewlish."

"Never. You danced closely, I assume. He was dizzied by your touch, your perfume, your inconsequential, hypnotic chatter. Did you pair?"

"I think Hewlish is worth more than pairing. It would be fun to direct an inventive mind."

"Why, Sibyl! Would you mate with him?"

"I don't know. It would be so permanent. He's so serious. He'd never leave me while the offspring were young."

"An advantage, surely? Nursery robots are tiresome. Remember ours? Papa and Mama were very useful."

Sibyl sighed. "But I do love luxury. How much would you let me take, Roxanne? Your jewels are grander than mine."

"Now here's a sisterly act. You leave me hunting alone and empty my jewel cases as well."

"Yes. And when you mate with a rich oligarch, I shall expect magnificent presents. Our parents endowed us unequally with brains, and it's only fair that your abundance should make up for my lack."

Roxanne laughed and returned to reading the book.

The third and final race was the closest of all. The other boats, with few chances of winning the regatta, determined to spoil the day for the *Terran Hope.* Soon the protest flag was straining from her mast top as foul after foul blocked her progress.

Sibyl and Roxanne were watching the race on the viewscreen.

"How unfair!" said Sibyl. "A protest does no good from a tenth place."

"But the fouls only increase the crew's angry efforts."

"How do you know?"

"I know."

Never before had the *Terran Hope* been so tightly hauled. Never had she sailed so close to

the wind. Her opponents fell off to leeward, and she outsailed them easily, racing between the orange finish buoys with a clear victory.

"They've won! Come, Sibyl," Roxanne said, standing up. "Now we can claim our prey."

Our? Sibyl wondered.

This time the *Terran Hope* was not so easily approached. The pier was crowded with well-wishers, regatta committeemen and Trivec officials who had come to offer the formal challenge.

Sibyl and Roxanne waited until the ceremonies were completed and the crowd was thinning. Hewlish saw them and went up to them. They congratulated him, and Roxanne strolled toward the boat.

Hewlish said to Sibyl, "Roxanne must feel foolish, doubting my abilities."

"We both are pleased you won. But the victory has agitated you. I doubt that uncertainty, decisions and fatigue are as pleasant as you boasted."

"They're pleasant to experience and overcome. The reliving of them is unpleasant—the thought of how near we came to failure. That's why I'm glad to see you, Sibyl. With you, I can remember the victory and forget the anxiety."

"Victory soon erases anxiety. Will you dance with me at tonight's ball?"

"Will you pair afterward?"

"Hewlish, I like you too much. I don't want to pair with you as I'd pair with prey. You're too fine and honest. I wish the holiday could go on forever."

"It can—as long as your nonsensical carousel keeps turning. Will you mate with me? I have little wealth, but you'd share it equally, such as it is."

"Oh, I accept you, dear Hewlish! I'm sorry you're not yet rich, but I'll never find a mate more clever or sensible."

Hewlish put his arms around her, pulled off her sunhood, kissed her smooth lips, and laid his cheek against her glossy hair.

She gently freed herself. "We must dine and dress for the victory ball."

"A victory within and beyond a victory!" Hewlish exulted.

Roxanne had been talking to Captain Mack. They saw Hewlish embrace Sibyl, and the skipper scowled. "She caught him. I knew it. Poor fool!"

"I fear it's Sibyl who's caught," said Roxanne. "She spoke of wanting to mate with him. Not a brilliant match, but she was bored and restless. What was I to do?"

"Is Hewlish your doing?"

"I chose him, yes. Sibyl never has had my zest for the chase. Her nature is softer, more attuned to mating. I'll miss her dreadfully, of course."

"You made a good team, that's for sure. The old one-two," Captain Mack said with gusto. "A man never knew whether he was coming or going. You'll need a change of pace, Roxanne."

"Later. When I start hunting again. Now I'm fascinated by sailing."

"Don't hand me that sludge, girl. I'm not Hewlish."

"Exactly. Hewlish crewed for the *Terran Hope*. You own her. I'm studying your book. I hope you'll find a crew place for me if I follow you to Trivector."

"Hmm. You're not strong enough for jibman."

"Sailing skill is needed more in the light, shifting breezes than in the steady winds. I could be jibman when it pleased you, and rail crew at other times."

"I demand concentration in the regattas. You'd have to give up hunting."

"How could I hunt? When I sail, my face will be sun reddened and ugly, my hands will bruise, my arm muscles will enlarge into unsightly lumps. A ruined huntress, I fear. But the Trivector race—oh, I would give up much—everything —to win aboard the *Terran Hope*."

"And then?"

"I don't know. Why do you ask?"

"Because I'm a lonely man. I never mated when I was in the starship service, because I would seldom have seen my mate or offspring. I didn't mate when I retired, because I met no woman who shared my passion for the sea." He paused. "Can a huntress understand that a man might have a passion for anything except—passion?"

"A huntress, of all people, knows that a man's passion is but an inner room of his heart. It must be approached by the right avenue, and there are as many avenues as there are men. Which is the fun of the hunt."

"I'll grant you all that, Roxanne, but we are still talking about two different things. Your hunt ends in a mutual passion for each other. My yearnings have been toward a mutual passion for the sea."

"And for each other," Roxanne insisted gently.

"Yes, yes, of course," the captain agreed, "but my nature is such that I cannot separate the two."

"I think the sea is such a mistress," said Roxanne, "that she floods a man's heart and must be included."

"I perceive clearly that she has flooded *your* heart, Roxanne. I'm fairly well off," he went on. "I won't pair with you, wily Roxanne, because you'd rob me and walk away. But mating is a legal and permanent commitment. You couldn't rob me without robbing yourself."

"I've never robbed anyone, Captain Mack."

"As if bewitchment wasn't robbery of a man's senses and, afterward, of everything else he possessed!"

"Now here's an odd proposal," Roxanne retorted. "The man distrusts me and yet would mate with me."

"I don't distrust your sailing. That's genuine enough to make young Hewlish green with envy. Nor do I distrust your ability to keep a mate amused, if you kept your part of the bargain."

"I've never broken faith either."

"Perhaps you think I'm too old for mating, but I'm capable of it, never doubt!"

"Never for a second would I doubt," said Roxanne, laying her hand on the captain's sleeve. "I'm happy and honored to accept your offer. You'll be a handsome mate and a wonderful sire for our offspring."

"Lucky little bastards," said Captain Mack, grinning.

The Chains of Possession

by ERNEST K. GANN

Novelist Ernest K. Gann has had a lifelong affair with ships and the sea. Here, in the person of a poor Brazilian waiter, Jesús, whose boat is really a balsa raft, Gann illustrates what the sailing passion is all about.

THERE is a unique softness about an English afternoon, and in the early fall the high northerly latitude permits the light to remain long into the evening. It is the mellow light rendered so truly in the paintings of Turner and Constable, and it creates an ambience of tranquility and stolid confidence in man's place on earth.

It was in this luminous atmosphere with the lavender of evening just arrived that for the last time I observed the *Albatros* putting out to sea.

We had been outward bound for Portugal from Germany and had reached the English Channel when I received a radio message telling of the sudden death of my father. We had made at once for the nearest port, which was Cowes. Atcheson had taken over command, and now, still stunned by the loss of a man I had so loved and admired, I stood very much alone on a pier watching the anchor chain slithering through the hawse. The *Albatros* was nearly half a mile offshore, yet I could see figures moving about her decks. It was as if I was observing them from another world, and since I knew them so well, it was easy to recognize them as individuals. Hekka appeared from the after deckhouse for a moment and then vanished somewhere below. Post was in her usual place at the helm. Ptacnik came out of his galley and strolled aft to her. I was certain they would be discussing stores versus menus. Forward, I could see Dawson's white-thatched head moving about the anchor winch and Cox was easily identified because of his size. With them was Lauritzen, a charming Dane who had joined us in Copenhagen. Gillette was hosing the Solent mud from the chain as it rose. That was all. They were going to be on the short-handed side if they encountered any rough weather, but Atcheson was a shrewd commander and would not be lured into trusting the Bay of Biscay.

The wind was light and in my direction, so I could hear the anchor winch. From such a distance, its multiple parts did not clank together in their usual fashion but tinkled, as if suiting their truly raucous character to my diminutive vision of the ship. How small she was, I thought, and yet how long she had been the boundaries of my world.

I tried to turn away. I would leave this scene and step into the nearby pub and have a gin or two until the ferry came to take me on the first leg of my journey back to the United States. But

I could not turn away, because I knew this would be the last time I would see the *Albatros* as mine again. What sentimental foolishness! I condemned to hell the unknown romanticist who originated the ridiculous fancy that a man might fall in love with a thing. And what else was a vessel but a thing? Yet long before my time, men ensnared by this same suspect fetish had lavished both affection and fortune on ships in which to sail the seas. So doughty and yet so amorous a man as Nelson referred to his great, ungainly flagship *Victory* as his "little darling." Drake was nearly maudlin about his awkward, roly-poly little *Golden Hind.* There had been legions of sailors great and unknown who had been compelled to express their devotion in words or print, and it seemed they became all the more eloquent when parted from their favorites. It was as if they lived.

Few men go about publicly proclaiming their wives as faithless whores, extravagant bitches or foul-mouthed shrews, even when these things are true and when, in desperation, the man resolves he can no longer endure his marriage. And no more will a man speak ill of his vessel, though he may own but the smallest piece of her. Only *after* the inevitable parting might he concede that the craft which had held his affection was actually a bit on the lethargic side, or she might have a cranky way of bashing her occupants about, or was ravaged with disease, or had a mind of her own when maneuvering.

I was as guilty as any other sailor. Here I stood in a sentimental funk watching the *Albatros* as if she was the most perfect vessel ever created.

At the age of twelve, I had felt the same way about the *Diver,* which was the second craft I had ever commanded and which I proposed to finance by raising Indian artifacts and perhaps even treasure from the bottom of a Minnesota lake. Now, with memories of my father so vivid before me, I wondered how he must have truly regarded the *Diver,* because it was he who had lent me the fifty dollars for her original charter, accepting as security my vow that I would stay out of mischief that summer and perform brilliantly in school the following semester. He lost on both counts.

The *Diver* was sixteen feet in length and of open-launch design. Amidships there was a small one-cylinder engine which made a very satisfying racket when I could finally persuade it to function. The *Diver* leaked in an extraordinary number of places even for a lapstreak boat, and I soon discovered she was a beast to row. Yet when the summer ended and I returned the boat to her rightful owner, I did so in the manner of a benefactor. "This boat," I stated authoritatively, "can go just about anywhere in the whole world. You should have seen her in that storm last week. And, why I could row her clean across the lake without getting tired if I just wanted. Sure the engine needs some fixing, but once you get it started, mister, it just never wants to quit."

It had also been my indulgent father who had financed the little *Caroline,* because he believed some further seafaring could only improve a young man. But he was suspicious of sailboats in Lake Michigan, and so the *Caroline* was strictly a motor cruiser. And still I came to love her.

They were hoisting the main on the *Albatros* now. What an aesthetic mistake I had made in changing the cut of her main from gaff to Marconi. But the sail was of course much easier to handle and apparently we had suffered little loss in speed.

Go away, wench. I can very well get along without you.

There was the *Don Quixote* in Spain. We had sailed together in the Balearic Islands for a time and I had never known a clumsier vessel. She was thirty feet long and double-ended and her engine was a single-cylinder Bolander diesel of unknown vintage. From the first, I regarded the engine as senile, but it was not only because of its age that I so rarely employed it. It was located in the small midships cabin and thus occupied the only shelter in the *Don Quixote.* Starting the engine was a nervous business which you commenced by lighting off a blowtorch and directing the flame upon the cylinder head for several minutes. The blowtorch was kept on a shelf between the bilge frames, and beside it was a wine bottle filled with ether alcohol. When you supposed the cylinder had reached easy combustion temperature, you turned off the blowtorch, opened a cup valve on top the cylinder and poured a jigger of the ether alcohol therein. Assuming nothing had gone wrong, such as spilling too much of the highly explosive mixture in the bilge, you at once grasped the heavy flywheel in both hands and swung it with all your might. If the engine failed to fire after three spins of the flywheel, you waited until your heartbeat and breathing subsided and started all over again with blowtorch and wine bottle.

The exhaust of *Don Quixote*'s engine was short, so it would not interfere with passage of the sail across deck, and it was aimed straight up in the air. As a consequence, it blew the most perfect smoke rings I have ever seen, and sometimes I would start the engine in port just so visitors could admire the display.

Yet the principal reason I avoided starting the engine was the terrible vibration which accompanied its cruising power. The *Don Quixote* was steered with a tiller, and the only possible place for the helmsman was to sit on a little deck at the extreme after end of the hull. Here the vibration was such that I often feared for my sacroiliac and the entire world became a blur. Conversation was discouraging because everyone whimpered. The violent shuddering imparted a plaintive vibrato to the voice, and everyone aboard sounded as if he had just been cruelly beaten. For these reasons, I normally chose the lesser of two evils and sailed the *Don Quixote*.

I had never been shipmates with a lateen sail, and so I asked Xavier, who owned the *Don Quixote,* to instruct me in its time-honored ways. Xavier had left the sea, having found an easier way of life selling "Spanish" knickknacks to tourists. But he did know his craft, and once he had convinced himself that I would not deliberately stand her into peril, he left his sister's ninth son, Oresté, as my crew and returned to his busy shop.

The ninth son was much too small for his job, yet his willingness and utter devotion to the vessel made it impossible to contemplate replacing him. He was very old, as the youth of Spain may sometimes be, and he told me that he had fourteen years of life on earth, which I knew was a lie because Xavier had said that he was not yet twelve. Except that he smoked the blackest, foulest-smelling cigarettes I had ever seen whenever his hands were momentarily idle, Oresté was a comfortable companion and possessed a rarity among human senses, for he knew instinctively when another human being was in the mood for idle conversation. At all other times he kept absolute silence.

I was disappointed in the lateen rig mainly because it was impossible to sail the *Don Quixote* single-handed with such gear and also because I saw how coming about in rough seas was a dangerous affair for the crew. It was necessary for one man to be forward and ready to push the base end of the boom around to the opposite side of the mast after we passed through the eye of the wind. During this operation, the boom end would acquire a bucking motion in response to the seas and there were times when Oresté, because of his light weight, was nearly catapulted overboard. Other lateen-rigged boats rarely bothered to transfer the boom when coming about and simply allowed it to press against the mast, making two fat balloons of the sail. But the *Don Quixote* flatly refused to sail under such casual treatment, and so Oresté was kept very busy. He pretended that he heard my cautions when he went forward, and once I hurt his feelings by pleading with him to use a safety line about his waist. Suddenly his black eyes burned with scorn, he turned his pockmarked little back on me and remained sullen for the rest of the day.

In time, I became accustomed to the *Don Quixote*'s casual ways, and every day, it seemed, she provided new cause for amusement. So there was continual pleasure in our relation and soon I was infatuated, as a man may become when a woman gives him frequent cause for smiling. I knew this was a dangerous stage, because overexposure to the pleasant may find a man in love.

I escaped entrapment by the *Don Quixote* only because we lived together for barely a month and because I remembered a similar affair with an enchanting craft known as the *Butterfly*.

Jesús was her true owner and he kept her in Fortaleza, Brazil.

I first met Jesús in a breeze-swept open-sided cantina on the beach. It was the coolest place in Fortaleza and hence regularly patronized by crews of airplanes who were about to fly the South Atlantic or had just done so. Jesús was one of the waiters in the cantina and spoke a brand of English which was distinctly his own yet quite understandable. The word *nice* was a special favorite of his and he employed it to cover a multitude of queries and replies. He was a young man with a wispy trace of moustache, eyelids that always drooped as if to protect his eyes from the actinic blaze of the Brazilian sun, and a shriveled arm which must have been with him at birth. When I asked him where I might rent a boat, he insisted I take his very own, which he called the *Butterfly*.

The working conditions for waiters in Brazil were agreeably loose, so Jesús whipped off his apron and, taking me by the arm, led the way to a dilapidated taxi. Once inside, he settled back into the seat and sighed contentedly. "My boat," he announced, "is nice and far from here."

Suddenly I realized we had embarked upon a journey, for Brazilians of Jesús' economic status rarely splurged on taxis. He knew the driver, a morose man whose name was Fernando, and who was called *the* Fernando because of his perpetual gloom. Such was his local fame that if you were dejected you were said to be "in a Fernando."

I had supposed we were in for a long ride to find Jesús' boat, but we had careened along hardly three miles before we turned toward the ocean and came to an open stretch of beach. The Fernando set his jaw and his throttle at full power. We left the last hint of roadway and charged a series of sand hummocks as if our taxi was a fullback and the goal was the sea. Neither the Fernando nor Jesús ceased his excited chattering, though at times all three of us were bounced into a weightless condition. When I was certain the taxi must collapse on the very next hummock, we tumbled off it and there was the foaming ocean. And there was the *Butterfly*. I could not be sure if Jesús was joking or was sim-

ply a scoundrel who wanted to get away from his work at my expense.

"Look!" he said. "How nice?" What he was pointing at was a collection of logs lying in the sand.

There was a tin shanty farther up the beach which now exploded a cluster of people. Several children ran toward us screaming in their naked delight. There were three men, one very old, and two women. "My family," Jesús explained, just before he was engulfed by their affections. Finally, when the initial excitement of our arrival had subsided, I was escorted to Jesús' "boat."

It was not a boat at all, but a raft made up of balsa logs about twelve inches in diameter. It was some twenty feet long and protruding from the sand on each side were two leeboards made of a heavy, close-grained wood which I could not identify. There was a mast also lying in the sand and a sail of musty-looking cloth was wrapped around it. There was a short, very thick and heavy oar which Jesús explained fitted in a sort of slot at the stern of the raft and was used for steering.

I tried to hide my disappointment, for I realized now that Jesús really did intend us to go sailing in this collection of flotsam and that his interest was only for my welfare. He was almost pathetically eager to assemble the functional components of his craft and enlisted his entire family as well as the Fernando in the project.

I studied the water-soaked logs and guessed they must weigh a ton. The *Butterfly!* What an ill-chosen name. Even if we could drag her down to the water, she must submerge in the first wave and never be seen again. And I had always been an indifferent swimmer.

The Fernando took off his shoes and socks and rolled up his pants in the best beach-holiday tradition. I had no choice but to do the same, and together with all of Jesús' relatives we hauled the *Butterfly* down to the sea. Now, at least, she did bear some vague resemblance to a seagoing craft, for she had a mast supported by two shrouds of frayed rope, a woven fiber bench for the helmsman, and a leeboard on each side.

The naked children squealed with continuous rapture, and it was a launching amid such gaiety I instantly ceased to care if this clumsy thing ever got beyond the first line of breakers.

The beach sloped gently and soon the Fernando dropped behind because the water had reached the height of his rolled pants. With him, we left two of the smallest children and then the women when the water became knee deep, and then we paused while Jesús and I boarded the *Butterfly*. After waiting alertly for a smooth between breakers, Jesús shouted, the men and remaining boys gave a great shove on the *Butterfly*'s stern, and we glided into deep water. Jesús immediately hoisted sail and I was soon reminded that the quality of a vessel may no more be judged by appearance than that of a man or a woman.

At first, while we were still only a little way offshore, the breeze held light and we glided rather sluggishly over the sea. I took the helm and studied the sail, which was made of coffee and flour bags sewn together with heavy twine. Poor Jesús. There was a hole the size of a football halfway up the leech of his sail, and I could see streaks of the glittering sea through many of the seams joining the various bags. My compassion increased as I saw into his eyes and realized that here was a moment which far transcended what little financial reward he would receive from my few hours' rental of his awkward craft. For I was smiling and he was too innocent to detect the hypocrisy behind my lips. He could not suspect that I wanted to come about at once, head for the beach and make a quick end of my disappointment.

"Nice?" he asked softly.

"Nice," I agreed, because it is a waste of breath to disagree with those who are content with next to nothing.

Now we were beginning to catch the offshore wind and the cerulean blue surface of the sea began to shiver. Diminutive popcorn wavelets blossomed all about and when we left the shoreside haze the horizon became sharp-etched against the burning sky. It was only a modest wind, yet the *Butterfly* suddenly changed character. She was a Jekyll and Hyde boat. She shuddered as if to shake off her resemblance to a stray logjam. She emerged from her cocoon and became an entirely new individual. In a remarkable act of levitation, she climbed right out of the water so that barely the bottom third of the logs was submerged. In seconds, we were gliding along at an easy ten knots with the wind and seas full on our beam. After a few seconds more, I was certain we were doing fifteen knots, then even faster.

Jesús beckoned toward the horizon and I eased the *Butterfly* gingerly into the wind. I sheeted home the boom until it was most inboard of the logs; and the pitiful sail, in defiance of all formal aerodynamics, drove us ever faster. Not one of the bags which composed the sail panels had the same degree of stretch, so that each ballooned in its own way. I could not see the lee side of the sail, but it must have achieved a sort of cobbled surface, and all of the straining seams now passed bright sunlight.

The *Butterfly*'s deck, if it could be called that, had been awash since we first boarded her; now the top surface of the logs began to dry in the sunlight and only occasionally did we take dollops of spray aboard. Although I could sense very little increase in the wind, I was astonished to see our hull speed continuously increasing. I could think of no other comparable sensation except iceboating, and I was quite certain Jesús would have comprehension trouble if I told him that his *Butterfly* sailed like a boat on a frozen lake.

Whatever explanation I might have attempted would have made little difference, for now I saw that Jesús was lost to me. He was no longer a waiter, nor just another Brazilian with just another wisp of moustache. He squatted easily with his heels jammed into the division between the two highest logs and his bare feet curving over the lowest. A small religious medallion dangled from his neck, glistening when it caught the sun, and his head was thrown back in such a way that I marveled at his suppleness. I saw that he was breathing deeply, as if inhaling some powerful elixir, his attention shifted from the sail to the sea, to the horizon, and to a frigate bird which now joined our headlong flight across the wind. I saw that Jesús had left his apron-bound soul and transcended all the heritage of a puny

Sunset at sea.

physique and complete ignorance of power. He was a conquerer now, a guide through the little-known. He was, in these moments of rising speed and spirit, a swashbuckler, an intrepid mariner and a paladin all in one.

I could not decide if it was Jesús' personal triumph or the tremendous exhilaration of the *Butterfly*'s grace and speed which so made me want to cheer. We were skimming over a brilliant sea which itself was dancing with life, and the sense of escape from all natural burdens was intoxicating. I doubted that many scientifically designed catamarans or trimarans had sailed faster, and certainly we would have soon left any two-million-dollar America's Cup contender far over the horizon.

Jesús turned to look at me questioningly and I hoped that if he had suspected my smile before, he would now see that it was genuine. "Nice?" he asked.

"Nice."

Sailing the *Butterfly* became such an inner compulsion that I soon found myself trying to rearrange plans so that I would have at least a day or two in Fortaleza. But with all my plotting, I managed no more than half a dozen sails in the *Butterfly* before I had to leave. Each time was a repeated delight and each time the routine was the same.

I would seek out Jesús at the cantina and then we would find the Fernando, who would be slumping in his taxi as morose and angry at the world as ever. A half smile for me, then some clearing of his eyes at his first abuse of the engine. The wild ride to the beach greatly stimulated the Fernando, and he would change by the time of our usual launching and become positively ecstatic.

Moments later, I could watch Jesús undergo his metamorphosis as the *Butterfly* picked up her skirts, and all was as it should be in God's world.

Eventually, I learned that the *Butterfly* was not at all exceptional to the coast of Brazil and that her type was generally used for swift transport to the fishing grounds, where the sail was doused and the crew went to work on a stable platform. Therefore, like all truly fine sailing craft, her design developed from regional neces-

sity and many years of practical experience. She was a workboat at heart and not some plastic confection designed by men more concerned with dainty interiors than nautical ability. Her initial clumsy appearance and apparent great weight were, of course, a deception. In the water, the balsa logs were curved fore and aft in just the right way and there was no comparison in their weight displacement with any other natural material.

The *Butterfly*'s speed was due to her remarkable lightness, which was matched only by her financial burden. Once I asked Jesús to make an estimate of her price and he said his uncle had built her somewhat smaller than the rafts actually used for fishing and therefore could use logs that were in little demand. Jesús' mother had sewn the sail and he had gathered the material from innumerable contributors, so the actual cost was nothing. He had had to buy the sisal rope for the shrouds, sheet, halyard and anchor, and this had come to six dollars. His uncle had not charged anything at all for his labor, but he obtained the balsa logs in trade for a superior pig which would have brought some eight to ten dollars on the market. The total worth of the *Butterfly* then was about sixteen dollars, which we agreed was a considerable investment.

My infatuation with the *Butterfly* was such that I tried desperately to think of a way we could see more of each other. But I could not conceive of her performing anywhere along the Atlantic coast of the United States with the possible exception of Florida. The same was true of the Pacific coast, for the *Butterfly* could not sail in her customary environment anywhere north of San Diego, where there was rarely enough wind. At last, I was forced to concede that the *Butterfly* was a siren inherently incapable of being transplanted. To the South Seas or the Hawaiian Islands perhaps, but along my chill native shores she would soon wither and die of neglect. So we parted and I felt her loss for a long time.

I raise my arm slowly. It is an attempt to wave as if I am merely wishing bon voyage to my shipmates. The September dusk has settled over the Solent now and the *Albatros* is already gathering way. In a few minutes, she must disappear around the point stretching north from this ferry landing and I will be left even more wretched. Then I will not wait until she is entirely gone from view. Somewhere I once heard that was bad luck. And I will not have any misfortune harm that assembly of steel and wood and rope and canvas which is more than a thing, which is in truth an inexhaustible fountain of adventure for those who dare to drink. Of all my sirens I am now certain there will never be another like the *Albatros,* if only because she is the most demanding.

Go! I will not weep.

THE RECORDS

THE AMERICA'S CUP: Record of Matches

	WINNING AMERICAN DEFENDER			CHALLENGER				
Year	Yacht	Owner	Skipper	Yacht	Country	Owner	Skipper	Won-Lost record
1870	Magic	Franklin Osgood	Andrew Comstock	Cambria	England	James Ashbury	J. Linnock	1–0
1871	Columbia	Franklin Osgood	Nelson Comstock	Livonia	England	James Ashbury	J. R. Woods	2–1
	Sappho	William Douglass	Sam Greenwood					2–0
1876	Madeleine	John S. Dickerson	Josephus Williams	Countess of Dufferin	England	Major Charles Gifford Syndicate	J. E. Ellsworth	2–0
1881	Mischief	Joseph R. Busk	Nathaniel Clock	Atalanta	Canada	Alexander Cuthbert	Alexander Cuthbert	2–0
1885	Puritan	J. Malcolm Forbes Syndicate	Aubrey Crocker	Genesta	England	Sir Richard Sutton	John Carter	2–0
1886	Mayflower	General Charles Paine	Martin Stone	Galatea	England	Lieutenant William Henn, R. N.	Dan Bradford	2–0
1887	Volunteer	General Charles Paine	Henry Haff	Thistle	Scotland	James Bell Syndicate	John Barr	2–0
1893	Vigilant	C. Oliver Iselin Syndicate	William Hansen	Valkyrie II	England	Earl of Dunraven	William Cranfield	3–0
1895	Defender	C. Oliver Iselin Syndicate	Henry Haff	Valkyrie III	England	Earl of Dunraven	William Cranfield	3–0
1899	Columbia	J.P. Morgan Syndicate	Charles Barr	Shamrock I	Ireland	Sir Thomas Lipton	Archie Hogarth	3–0
1901	Columbia	J. P. Morgan Syndicate	Charles Barr	Shamrock II	Ireland	Sir Thomas Lipton	E. A. Sycamore	3–0
1903	Reliance	C. Oliver Iselin Syndicate	Charles Barr	Shamrock III	Ireland	Sir Thomas Lipton	Robert Ringe	3–0
1920	Resolute	Henry Walters Syndicate	Charles Francis Adams	Shamrock IV	Ireland	Sir Thomas Lipton	William Burton	3–2
1930	Enterprise	Winthrop Aldrich Syndicate	Harold Vanderbilt	Shamrock V	Ireland	Sir Thomas Lipton	Ned Heard	4–0
1934	Rainbow	Harold Vanderbilt	Harold Vanderbilt	Endeavour	England	T.O.M. Sopwith	T.O.M. Sopwith	4–2
1937	Ranger	Harold Vanderbilt Syn.	Harold Vanderbilt	Endeavour II	England	T.O.M. Sopwith	T.O.M. Sopwith	4–0
1958	Columbia	Henry Sears Syndicate	Briggs Cunningham	Sceptre	England	Hugh Goodson	Graham Mann	4–0
1962	Weatherly	Henry D. Mercer	Bus Mosbacher	Gretel	Australia	Frank Packer Syndicate	Jock Sturrock	4–1
1964	Constella-tion	W. S. Gubelman & Eric Ridder	Robert Bavier	Soverign	England	James J. A. Boyden	Peter Scott	4–0
1967	Intrepid	Intrepid Syndicate	Bus Mosbacher	Dame Pattie	Australia	Emil Christensen Syndicate	Jock Sturrock	4–0

1970	Intrepid	Intrepid Syndicate	Bill Ficker	Gretel II	Australia	Frank Packer Syndicate	Jim Hardy	4–1
1974	Courageous	Courageous Syndicate	Ted Hood	Southern Cross	Australia	Alan Bond	Jim Hardy	4–0
1977	Courageous	Kings Point Fund Syndicate	Ted Turner	Australia	Australia	Alan Bond	Noel Robbins	4–0
1980	Freedom	Maritime College Foundation	Dennis Conner	Australia	Australia	Alan Bond	Jim Hardy	4–1

THE BERMUDA RACE

Year	Yacht	LOA	Owner
1906	Tamerlane	38 ft.	Frank Maier
1907	Dervish	85 ft.	H. A. Morss
1908	Verona	65 ft.	E. J. Bliss
1909	Margaret	93 ft.	George S. Runk
1910	Vagrant	76 ft.	H. S. Vanderbilt
1923	Malabar IV		John G. Alden
1924	Memory		R. N. Bavier
1926	Malabar IVV		John G. Alden
1928	Rugosa II		Russell Grinnell
1930	Malay		R. W. Ferris
1932	Malabar X		Rod Stephens, Jr.
1934	Edlu		R. J. Schaefer
1936	Kirawan		R. P. Baruch
1938	Baruna		H. C. Taylor
1940–44	(cancelled)		
1946	Gesture		A. H. Fuller
1948	Baruna	71.2 ft.	Henry C. Taylor
1950	Argyll	56.6 ft.	William T. Moore
1952	Carina	46 ft.	Richard S. Nye
1954	Malay	39.6 ft.	D. D. Strohmeier
1956	Finisterre	38.6 ft.	Carleton Mitchell
1958	Finisterre	38.6 ft.	Carleton Mitchell
1960	Finisterre	38.6 ft.	Carleton Mitchell
1962	Nina	58.8 ft.	DeCoursey Fales
1964	Burgoo	37.7 ft.	Milton Ernstof
1966	Thunderbird	40 ft.	T. V. Learson
1968	Robin	52 ft.	Ted Hood
1970	Carina	48.3 ft.	Richard S. Nye
1972	Noryema	48.1 ft.	R. Amey
1974	Scaramouche	54.6 ft.	Chuck Kirsch
1976	Running Tide	60 ft.	Al Van Metre
1978	IOR Division: Acadia	51 ft.	Burt Keenan
	MHS Division: Babe	39.9 ft.	Arnold Gay
1980	IOR Division: Williwaw	48 ft.	Seymore Sinett
	MHS Division: Holger Danske	42 ft.	John Wilson

THE SOUTHERN OCEAN RACING CONFERENCE

1941	Tie, Stormy Weather, William Labrot, and Gulf Stream, Dudley Sharp.
1947	Ciclon, A. Gomez-Mena and M. Bustamente.
1948	Stormy Weather, Fred Temple.
1949	Tiny Teal, Palmer Langdon and Richard Bertram.
1950	Windigo, Walter Gubelmann.
1951	Belle of the West, Will Erwin.
1952	Caribbee, Carleton Mitchell.
1953	Caribbee, Carleton Mitchell.
1954	Hoot Mon, Worth Brown, Lockwood Pirie and Charles Ulmer.
1955	Hoot Mon, Brown, Pirie and Ulmer.
1956	Finisterre, Carleton Mitchell.
1957	Criollo, Luis Vidana.
1958	Ca Va, J. W. Hershey and Bus Mosbacher, Jr.
1959	Callooh, Jack Brown and Bus Mosbacher, Jr.
1960	Solution, Thor Ramsing.
1961	Paper Tiger, Jack Powell.
1962	Paper Tiger, Jack Powell.
1963	Doubloon, Joe Byars.
1964	Conquistador, Fuller E. Callaway III.
1965	Figaro IV, William Snaith.
1966	Vamp X, Ted Turner.
1968	Red Jacket, Perry Connolly.
1969	Salty Tiger, Jack Powell and Wally Frank.
1970	American Eagle, Ted Turner.
1971	Running Tide, Jakob Isbrandsten.
1972	Condor, Hill Blackett.
1973	Munequita, Jack Valley and Click Shreck.
1974	Robin Too II, Ted Hood.
1975	Stinger, Dennis Conner.
1976	New boat division: Williwaw, Seymore Sinett. Old boat division: Saudade, Bill Pascoe.
1977	New boat division: Imp, David Allen. Old boat division: Running Tide, Al Van Metre.
1978	New boat division: Williwaw, Seymore Sinett and Dennis Conner. Old boat division: Immigrant, Bill McAteer.
1979	Williwaw, Seymore Sinett and Dennis Conner.
1980	Acadia, Burt Keenan.
1981	Intuition, Pat Malloy.
1982	Retailiation, Dennis Conner, David Fenix, Tom Whidden.

THE FASTNET RACE

Year	Yacht	Owner	Nationality
1925	Jolie Brise	Lt. Cmdr. E. G. Martin	Britain
1926	Ilex	Royal Engineer YC	Britain
1927	Tally Ho	Lord Stalbridge	Britain
1928	Nina	Paul Hammond	United States
1929	Jolie Brise	Robert Somerset	Britain
1930	Jolie Brise	Robert Somerset	Britain
1931	Dorade	Rod Stephens	United States
1933	Dorade	Rod and Olin Stephens	United States
1935	Stormy Weather	P. LeBoutillier	United States
1937	Zeearend	C. Bruynzeel	Netherlands
1939	Bloodhound	Isaac Bell	Britain
1947	Myth of Malham	Capt. J. H. Illingworth, R.N.	Britain
1949	Myth of Malham	Capt. J.H. Illingworth, R.N.	Britain
1951	Yeoman	O. A. Aisher	Britain
1953	Favona	Sir Michael Newton	Britain
1955	Carina	Richard S. Nye	United States
1957	Carina	Richard S. Nye	United States
1959	Anitra	S. Hansen	Sweden
1961	Zwerver	W.N.H. van der Vorm	Netherlands
1963	Clarion of Wight	D. Boyer and D. Miller	Britain
1965	Rabbit	R. E. Carter	United States
1967	Pen Duick III	Eric Tabarly	France
1969	Red Rooster	R. E. Carter	United States
1971	Ragamuffin	S. Fischer	Australia
1973	Saga	E. Lorentzen	Brazil
1975	Golden Delicious	P. Nicholson	Britain
1977	Imp	David Allen	United States
1979	Tenacious	Ted Turner	United States
1981	Regardless		Ireland

TRANSPAC
1906–1979
(The Honolulu Race)

Year	Yacht	Owner	Class
1906	Lurline	H. H. Sinclair	
1908	Lurline	H. H. Sinclair	
1910	Hawaii	Syndicate	
1912	Lurline	A. E. Davis	
1923	Diablo	A. R. Pedder	
1926	Invader	Don M. Lee	
1928	Teva	C. W. Stose	
1930	Enchantress	Morgan Adams	
1932	Fayth	Wm. S. McNutt	
1934	Manuiwa	H. G. Dillingham	A
	Burrapeg	W. E. Candy	B
	Queequeg	B. M. Varney	C
1936	Navigator	G. H. Singer, Jr.	A
	Dorade	James Flood	B
	Flying Cloud	J & J McNabb	C
1939	Fandango	E. W. Pauley	A
	Zoe H.	Ray K. Person	B
	Blitzen	R. J. Reynolds	C
1941	Escapade	D. W. Elliott	
1947	Chubasco	W. L. Stewart, Jr.	A
	Dolphin II	Frank Morgan	B
	Suomi	J. Arvid Johnson	C
1949	Flying Cloud	Jay A. Quealy, Jr.	A
	Kitten	Fred W. Lyon	B
	Sea Witch	Alex McCormick	C
1951	Fair Weather	Fred J. Allen	A
	Chiriqui	Tucker McClure	B
	Sea Witch	A. L. McCormick	C
1953	Chubasco	W. L. Stewart III	A
	Chiriqui	Tucker McClure	B
	Staghound	Ira P. Fulmor	C
1955	Constellation	Frank Hooykaas	A
	Kawamee	W. W. Valentine	B
	Nalu II	Peter Grant	C
	Staghound	Ira P. Fulmor	D
1957	Nam Sang	Louis Statham	A
	Legend	Charles Ullman	B
	Nalu II	Peter Grant	C
	Altura	Hugh J. Jacks	D
1959	Constellation	Sally Blair Ames	A
	Chubasco	Arnold Haskell	B
	Nalu II	Peter Grant	C
	Debit	Theodore Stephens	D
1961	Nam Sang	A. B. Robbs, Jr.	A
	Ichiban	George Sturgis	B
	Nalu II	Peter Grant	C
	Vamanos	Robert Taylor	D
1963	Orient	Tim Moseley	A
	Legend	Charles Ullman	B
	Mistress	Aldo Alessio	C
	Islander	Earl Corkett	D
1965	Kialoa II	John B. Kilroy	A
	Rascal	Wm. H. Wilson	B
	Psyche	Don Salisbury	C
	Misty	Ed Spaulding	D
1967	Audacious	Al Cassel	A
	Simoon	Stan Williams and John Hall	B

	Holiday Too	Robert M. Allen, III	C
	Intrepid	Barry A. Berkus	D
1969	Concerto	John J. Hall	A
	Salacia	Thos. C. Corkett	B
	Argonaut	Mortimer Andron	C
	Esprit	Geo. W. Phillips, Jr.	D
1971	Windward Passage	Robert Mark Johnson	A
	Encore	Dick Blatterman and Bill Lawhorn	B
	Argonaut	Jon Andron	C
	Dakar	Wm. V. Goodley, MD	D
1973	Warrior	Al Cassel	A
	Improbable	D. W. Allen	B
	Blue Streak	G. L. Myers	C
	Chutzpah	Stuart Cowan	D
1975	Sunset Boulevard	John Calley	A
	Blue Streak	James A. Lyman	B
	Mamie	Milton Smith	C
	Chutzpah	Stuart M. Cowan	D
1977	Kialoa	Jim Kilroy	A
	Scaramouche	Robert Alexander	B
	Ariana	George Thorson	C
	Vivant	S. Alexander/Finn Bevin/Phillip Rowe	D
1979	Jader	John Galanis, Charter	A
	Arriba	Dennis Choate	B
	Secret Love	Bradley Herman	C
	Brown Sugar	Ulf Werner	D

THE TAHITI RACE

Year	Yacht	Owner
1925	Mariner	L. A. Norris
1953	Mistress	Walter Johnson
1956	Jada	William Sturgis
1961	Athene	James Wilhite
1964	Rascal	William Wilson
1968	Aranji	Henry W. Wheeler
1970	Widgeon	Norm Bacon
1972	Pen Duick III	Eric Tabarly
1974	Sorcery	Jacob D. Wood
1976	Bravura	Irving Loube
1978	Sorcery	Jacob D. Wood

THE ADMIRAL'S CUP NATIONAL TEAM RACES

1957	Britain
1959	Britain
1961	United States
1963	Britain
1965	Britain
1967	Australia
1969	United States
1971	Britain
1973	West Germany
1975	Britain
1977	Britain
1979	Australia
1981	Britain

THE LITTLE AMERICA'S CUP
(International Catamaran Challenge Trophy Match)

Year	Yacht	Country	Races Won	Skipper
1961	Hellcat II	Britain	4	Rod MacAlpine-Downie
	Wildcat	United States	1	Bob Harris
1962	Hellcat I	Britain	4	MacAlpine-Downie
	Beverly	United States	1	Van Allen Clark
1963	Hellcat III	Britain	4	MacAlpine-Downie/Reg White
	Quest	Australia	0	J. Muns/G. Anderson
1964	Emma Hamilton	Britain	4	Reg White/B. Holloway
	Sealion	United States	1	Bob Smith
1965	Emma Hamilton	Britain	4	R. White
	Quest II	Australia	1	L. Cunningham/J. Buzaglo
1966	Lady Helmsman	Britain	4	R. White
	Gamecock	United States	2	R. Shields/J. Bonney
1967	Lady Helmsman	Britain	4	P. Schneidau/R. Fisher
	Quest III	Australia	2	L. Cunningham
1968	Lady Helmsman	Britain	4	R. White
	Yankee Flyer	United States	3	Greer Ellis
1969	Opus III	Denmark	4	Friedricksen/Wagner-Schmitt
	Lady Helmsman	Britain	3	R. White
1970	Quest III	Australia	4	Bruce Proctor/Graham Candy
	Sleipner	Denmark	0	Wagner-Schmitt/Klaus Anton
1972	Quest III	Australia	4	
	Weathercock	United States	0	C. Millican/J. Evans
1974	Miss Nylex	Australia	4	Bruce Proctor/G. Ainslie
	Miss Stars	New Zealand	0	B. DeThier/B. Hende
1976	Aquarius V	United States	4	R. Harvey/A. Kozloff
	Miss Nylex	Australia	3	Bruce Proctor/G. Ainslie
1977	Patient Lady III	United States	4	D. MacLane/S. Banks
	Nicholas II	Australia	0	L. Cunningham/G. Candy
1978	Patient Lady IV	United States	4	D. MacLane/Banks
	Miss L	Italy	0	Franco Pivoli/A. Guilandi
1980	Patient Lady V	United States	4	D. MacLane/Banks
	Signora G	Italy	0	Franco Pivola

UNITED STATES MEN'S CHAMPIONSHIP

1952	Yacht Racing Association of Long Island Sound—Cornelius Shields, Cornelius Shields, Jr., William LeBoutillier.
1953	Gulf Yachting Association—Eugene H. Walet III, John Ryan, Ralph Christman, Eugene H. Walet II.
1954	Gulf Yachting Association—Eugene H. Walet III, Allen McClure, Jr., Gilbert Friedrichs, Jr.
1955	Pacific International Y. A.—William Buchan, Jr., William Buchan, Sr., Ron McFarlane.
1956	Y.R.U. of Massachusetts Bay—Ted Hood, Bradley P. Noyes, Charles Pingree.
1957	Y.R.U. of Massachusetts Bay—George D. O'Day, David J. Smith, Charles A. Forsberg.
1958	Texas Yachting Association—Robert Mosbacher, George C. Francisco III, C. B. Masterton.
1959	Inland Lake Y. A.—Harry C. (Buddy) Melges, Jr., John B. Shethar, Jr., Richard Reynolds.
1960	Inland Lake Y. A.—Harry C. Melges, Jr., John B. Shethar, Jr., Edward Smith, Mrs. Harry C. Melges, Jr.
1961	Inland Lake Y. A.—Harry C. Melges, Jr., Dr. A. R. Wenzel, John B. Shethar, Jr.
1962	Inland Lake Y. A.—James S. Payton, Peter Barrett, Chuck Miller.
1963	Y.R. A. of San Francisco Bay—James DeWitt, Jocelyn Nash, Jacob Van Heeckeren.
1964	Gulf Yachting Association—G. Shelby Friedrichs, Jr., B. Tommy Dreyfus, Ray Troendle, Sr.
1965	Y.R.A. of Long Island Sound—Cornelius Shields, Jr., Dr. George Brazil, Jr., Craig Walters.
1966	Y. R. A. of Long Island Sound—William S. Cox, Thomas Hume, Robert Barton.
1967	Barnegat Bay Y.R.A.—Clifford W. Campbell, Howard Wright, Ann Campbell.
1968	Southern Massachusetts Y.R.A.—James H. Hunt, Bourne Knowles, Joshua Hunt.
1969	Y.R.A. of Long Island Sound—Graham M. Hall, John Luard, Jack G. McAllister.
1970	Florida Sailing Association—Dr. John W. Jennings, James L. Pardee, Barbara Pardee.
1971	Texas Yachting Association—John Koluis, Bill Hunt, Scott Self.
1972	Florida Sailing Association—Edwin H. Sherman, Jr., Harvey A. Ford, Hubert Rutland III.
1973	Florida Sailing Association—Dr. John W. Jennings, James L. Pardee, Barbara Pardee.
1974	Y. R. A. of San Francisco Bay—Vann Wilson, N. Russell, F. Thomson.
1975	Y.R.A. of Long Island Sound—Christopher W. Pollak, Lisa Hamm, Elliam Ehrhorn.
1976	Southern California Y.A.—David Crockett, Sid Exley, Kurt Nicolai.
1977	Texas Y. A.—Marvin Beckman, Curt Oetking, Tommy Sims.
1978	Texas Y. A.—Glenn Darden, Kelly Gough, Jay Raymond.
1979	Texas Y. A.—Glenn Darden, Kelly Gough, Scott Young.
1980	Southern California Y. A.—Dave Ullman, Bill Herrschaft, Paul Murphy.
1981	Texas Y. A.—Mark Foster. Chuck Wilk, Scott Young.

UNITED STATES WOMEN'S CHAMPIONSHIP

1924	Ruth Sears, Cohasset YC.
1915	Ruth Sears, Cohasset YC.
1926	Jessie Bancroft, Cohasset YC.
1927	Lorna Whittelsey, Indian Harbor YC.
1928	Lorna Whittelsey, Indian Harbor YC.
1929	Frances Williams, Cohasset YC.
1930	Lorna Whittelsey, Indian Harbor YC.
1931	Lorna Whittelsey, Indian Harbor YC.
1932	Clair Dinsmore, Edgartown YC.
1933	Ruth Sears, Cohasset YC.
1934	Lorna Whittelsey, Indian Harbor YC; Myrtle Whittelsey, Mrs. DeBoise, Kitty Kunhardt.
1935	Frances McElwain, Cohasset YC; Pamela Anderson, Norma Anderson.
1936	Frances McElwain, Cohasset YC; Katherine Johnson, Joan Chapin.
1937	Frances McElwain, Cohasset YC; Katherine Johnson, Frances Williams, Joan Chapin Waters.
1938	Frances McElwain, Cohasset YC; Katerine Johnson Fisher, Joan Chapin Waters, Barbara Benson.
1939	Sylvia Shethar, American YC; Gwendolyn Shethar, Rosamund Corwin, Elizabeth Richards.
1940	Sylvia Shethar, American YC; Rosamund Corwin, Elisabeth Richards.
1941	Lois Macintyre, Riverside YC: Mrs. Frederick Allen, Charlotte Maher, Mrs. Carleton Marsh.
1942–45	No contest.
1946	Virginia Weston Bease, Edgartown YC; Adelaide Wolstanholme, Honora Haynes, Mary Edmonds.
1947	Sylvia Shethar Everdell, American YC; Rosamund Corwin, Lois Shethar, Allegra Knapp Mertz.
1948	Aileen Shields, Larchmont YC: Grace Emmons, Margot Gotte, JoAnne Sandborn.
1949	Jane McL. Smith, Portland YC; Jane Hughes, Dana Smith, Martha Soule.
1950	Allegra Knapp Mertz, American YC; Rosamund Corwin, Carol Walter, Beverly Compton.
1951	Jane Smith, Seal Harbor YC: Molly Shaw, Polly Hessenbrunch, Anne Rockefeller.
1952	Pat Hinman, Manhasset Bay YC; Toni Monetti, Gwen Van Hagen, Mrs. George Hinman.
1953	Judy Webb, Riverside YC; Barbara Sheldon, Sandra Gill, Jill Ayers.
1954	Allegra Knapp Mertz, American YC; Beverly Compton, Ellen Kelly.

1955	Toni Monetti, Manhasset Bay YC; Chris Drake, Frances Macy, Jill Thomson.
1956	Mrs. Glen Lattimore, Fort Worth Boat Club; Diane McFarland, Rose Rector, Jane Mooney.
1957	Jane Pegel, Chicago YC; Machael Sennot Roche, Judy Gayle Nye.
1958	Nancy Underhill Meade, American YC; Rosamund Corwin, Gwendolyn Everett.
1959	Allegra Knapp Mertz, American YC; Rosamund Corwin, Betty Duncan, Cindy Matthews.
1960	Pat Duane, Delray Beach YC; Nancie Pearce, Rose Marie Altemus.
1961	Timothea Schneider, Seawanhaka YC; Deborah Read, Sara Glenn.
1962	Susan Sinclair, Noroton YC; Alexandra Falconer, Carolyn McCurdy.
1963	Allegra Knapp Mertz, American YC; Lois Shethar Smith, Betty Duncan, Lucia Elmore.
1964	Jane Pegel, Lake Geneva YC; Marnie Frank, Nancy Frank.
1965	Timothea Schneider Larr, Seawanhaka YC; Sarah Glenn Mayer, Patience Outerbridge.
1966	Jerie Clark, Corinthian YC of Seattle; Mary Anne Easter, Renate McVitti.
1967	Mrs. William Foulk, Jr., Indiana Harbor YC; Mrs. Albert Preston, Jr., Mrs. Aubrey Whittemore, Sue Ann Shay.
1968	June Methot, Monmouth Boat Club; Bette Power, Dede Heron.
1969	Jan O'Malley, Mantoloking YC; Patricia O'Malley, Jacqueline Hart.
1970	Jan O'Malley, Mantoloking YC; Patricia O'Malley, Connie Blaise.
1971	Sylvia Shethar Everdell, Duxbury YC; Pamela O'Day, Mrs. Horace Sawyer, Jr. Mrs. David Fogg.
1972	Sally Lindsay, Dinghy Club; Alix Smullin, Nancy Hearne
1973	Timothea Schneider Larr, Seawanhaka Corinthian YC; Shelia McCurdy, Mrs. Geegie Miller.
1974	Debora Freeman, Beachwood YC; Lynn Campbell, Jennifer Valdes.
1975	Cindy Batchelor, Pettipaug YC; Nan Hall, Carmen Wetmore, Cara Worthington.
1976	Ellen Gerloff, Galveston Bay C.A.; Ruth Maudlin, Jane Baldridge, Rita Matthews.
1977	Cindy Stieffel, Bay Waveland YC; Amy Chapman, Judy McKinney.
1978	Bonnie Shore, Ida Lewis YC; Yvonne Burns, Bea Grimmitt, Nancy Kaull.
1979	Allison Jolly, St. Petersburg YC; Susan Blaketer, Janice Robertson, Sue Reischmann.
1980	Judy McKinney, Bay Waveland YC; Charlotte Gordon, Amy Chapman.
1981	Ann Boyd Sloger, Charleston, S.C.; Janet Scarborough, Carolyn Simmons, Cathy Christman.

UNITED STATES CHAMPIONSHIP OF CHAMPIONS

1976	Clark Thompson, Jr., Doug Johnston, Lawrence Daniel (spring), (Ensign Class). Tom Ehman, Major Hall (fall), (Flying Scot).
1977	Tom Linskey, Jeff Lenhart (Buccaneer).
1978	Tom Linskey, Neal Fowler (Taser).
1979	Hobie Alter, Jr., Paula Alter (Hobie 18).
1980	Dave Ullman, Jim Linskey (Lido 14).
1981	John Koluis, Chuck Wilk, Mark Foster (J 24).

UNITED STATES WOMEN'S CHAMPIONSHIP: DOUBLE- AND SINGLE-HANDED.

1974	Nell Taylor, Lisa Coughlin, Branford, Conn. (double-handed). Jane Pegel, Williams Bay, Wisc. (single-handed).
1975	Nell Taylor, Sally Lindsay, Branford, Conn. (double-handed). Single-handed not completed.
1976	Diane Greene, Jennifer Lawson, Annapolis, Md. (double-handed). Kristina Saltmarsh, South Dartmouth, Mass. (single-handed).
1977	Jan O'Malley, Pat O'Malley, Mantoloking, N.J. (double-handed). Poppy Truman, Berkeley, Calif. (single-handed).
1978	Sandy Ray, Carol Hayes, Westport, Conn. (double-handed). Meredith O'Dowd, Riverside, R.I., (single-handed).
1979	Nell Taylor, Charlotte Lewis, Marion, Mass. (double-handed). Betsy Glenitis, Bricktown, N.J. (single-handed).
1980	Anne Preston, Nelle Alexander, Watertown, Mass. (double-handed) Lynne Jewell, Plymouth, Mass. (single-handed).
1981	Martha Staskweaths, Sara Deadrick, Newport, R.I.; (double-handed) Betty Glenitis; Bricktown, N.J. (single-handed).

UNITED STATES SINGLE-HANDED SAILING CHAMPIONSHIP

1962	Peter J. Barrett, Madison, WI.
1963	Henry Sprague III, Newport Beach, Ca.
1964	Robert Andre, San Diego, Ca.
1965	Colin Park, Vancouver, B.C.
1966	Norman D. Freeman, Ithaca YC, N.Y.
1967	Charles Barthrop, U. S. Merchant Marine Academy, Kings Point, N.Y.
1968–69	Gordy Bowers, Jr., Minnetonka YC, MN.
1970–71	Robert P. Doyle, Harvard University YC, Cambridge, MA.
1972	Craig Thomas, Corinthian YC, Seattle, Wa.
1973	Jim Hahn, U. S. Naval Sailing Association, Annapolis, MD.
1974	Carl Buchan, Seattle YC, Seattle, WA.
1975	Roger Altrueter, Inter-Collegiate Y.R.A., Marblehead, MA.
1976	Jim Reynolds, Island Heights, N.J.
1977	Dave Chapin, Springfield, Il.
1978	Shawn Kempton, Ocean Gate, N.J.
1979	Peter Commette, Bay Head, N.J.
1980	Shawn Kempton, Ocean Gate, N.J.
1981	Steve Lowery, Annapolis, MD.

UNITED STATES ONE TON CHAMPIONSHIP

1972	Lightnin' (Sparkman & Stephens), Vincent Monte-Sano.
1973	Ganbare (Peterson), Douglas Peterson.
1974	Lightnin' (Sparkman and Stephens), Ted Turner.
1975	Pied Piper (Peterson), Lowell North, Dick Jennings.
1977	America Jane III (Kaufman), George Tooby.
1978	Scalawag (Farr), John Kilroy, Jr.
1979	Firewater (Cook), Bob Barton.
1980	Rush (Nelson-Marek), Kris Hicks.
1981	no contest.

UNITED STATES THREE-QUARTER TON CHAMPIONSHIP

1974	Kermit (Mortan), Robert M. Wohlfarth.
1975	Swampfire (Mull), W. Reese/O. J. Young.
1976	Vanpire (Mull), Dan W. Van Heeckeren.
1977	Cold Gold II (Irwin), O. H. Rodgers/T. Dudinsky.
1978	Chocolate Chips (Graham & Schlageter), D. Porter/R. Lester.
1979	Ciao (Graham & Schlageter), P. Laitala/Ward.
1980	no contest.
1981	Mandala (O. H. Rodgers), John Zaren.

UNITED STATES HALF TON CHAMPIONSHIP

1972	Scampi IV (Scampi), Ragge Hakanson.
1973	First Morning (Norlin), Deane Tank, Robert Barton.
1974	Animal Farm (Wylie), W. N. Carter, C. N. Corlett.
1975	Crackers (Wylie), Grant Crowley.
1976	Mouth (Peterson), O. J. Young.
1977	Petrified (Burns), Philip McGinn.
1978	OOOH NO!! (Peterson), James Jacobitz.
1979	Boomerang (Mull), Charles and John Tompkins.
1980	Toy Boat (Graham & Schlageter), Ron Lester/Tim Boehlke.
1981	Toy Boat (Graham and Schlageter), Ron Lester/Tim Boehlke.

UNITED STATES QUARTER TON CHAMPIONSHIP

1971	Tigermoth (Creekmore), Lee Creekmore.
1972	Dulcinea (Ranger 23), O. J. Young.
1973	Dark Star (Fino), Ben Hall.
1974	El Principio (Peterson 25), Lowell North.
1975	Truckin Machine (Kiwi), J. E. R. Chilton III.
1976	Why Why (Farr), John T. Potter.
1977	Fun (Davidson), Clay Bernard.
1978	Blivit (Nelson), Dave Neal.
1979	Summertime Dream (Schumacher), Carl Schumacher.
1980	Summertime Dream (Schumacher), Carl Schumacher.
1981	no contest.

UNITED STATES MINI-TON CHAMPIONSHIP

1978	Sauerkraut (Kelley), Mike McKillip.
1979	Mr. Bill's Dog (Kelley), Mike McKillip.
1980	Mr. Bill's Dog (Kelley), Mike McKillip.
1981	no contest.

UNITED STATES TWO TON CHAMPIONSHIP

The United States Two Ton Championship has been held only once, in 1975, and was won by Aggressive II (King), owned by David Gamble/Frank Piku.

UNITED STATES YOUTH SAILING CHAMPIONSHIP

1973	Peter Commette, Middletown, N.J. (single-handed). Terry Neff, Kevin Gaughan, Oyster Bay, N.Y. (double-handed).
1974	Chris Maas, Seattle, WA. (single-handed). Robert Whitehurst, Thomas Whitehurst, Pensacola, FL. (double-handed).
1975	Carl Buchan, Seattle, WA. (single-handed). Robert Whitehurst, Thomas Whitehurst, Pensacola, FL. (double-handed).
1976	Stuart Neff, Oyster Bay, N.Y. (single-handed). Peter Melvin, David Woolsey, Lighthouse Point, FL. (double-handed).
1977	Kelly Gough, Dallas, TX (single-handed). Peter Melvin, David Woolsey, Lighthouse Point, FL. (double-handed).
1979	Kevin Kempton, Ocean Gate, N.J. (single-handed). Gerald Braun, Tom Tompkins, Marblehead, MA. (double-handed).
1980	Russ Silvestri, Tiburon, CA. (single-handed). Allen Lindsey, Peter Lindsey, Miami, FL. (double-handed).
1981	John Shadden, Ron Rosenberg, Long Beach, CA. (double-handed). Charlie McKee, Seattle, WA. (single-handed).

UNITED STATES JUNIOR SAILING CHAMPIONSHIP

1921	Pleon YC: R. S. Thayer, E. K. Kepner, A.G. Wood, Jr.
1922	Larchmont YC: Arthur Knapp, Jr., George R. Hinman, Sterling Van B. Kryder.
1923	Duxbury YC: Raymont Hunt, Baldwin Robinson, Marshall Dwinnell.
1924	Pleon YC: H. B. Thayer, Jr., F.W. Andres, P.H. Rice.
1925	Duxbury YC: Raymont Hunt, Marshall Dwinnell, Edmund Kelley, Jr.
1926	Duxbury YC: John S. Wilbor, Edmund Kelley, Jr., Bertram Currier.
1927	Chatham YC: C. Ashley Hardy, Jr., Louis McClennen, Howland Hirst.
1928	Beverly YC: William B. Cudahy, Sterling Adams, Pierce Archer, Jr.
1929	Bar Harbor YC: William Cudahy, Michael Cudahy, Townsend Munson.
1930	Vineyard Haven YC: William S. Cox, Angelo Smith, Jr., Thomas Jackson.
1931	Beverly YC: Michael Cudahy, Henry Chatfield, Virginia Hoyt.
1932	Eastern YC: Chandler Hovey, Jr., Albert Goodhue, Jr., George Poor.
1933	Vineyard Haven YC: Frank B. Jewett Jr., Theodore Robie, Lane Fuller.
1935	Vineyard Haven YC: John Ware, Jr., Edward Robie, John Willis.

1936	Vineyard Haven YC: John Ware, Jr., Edward Robie, John Willis.
1937	Pequot YC: Charles Stetson, Robert Gordon, William Watkins.
1938	Pequot YC: Robert Gordon, Howland Hayes, Roderick McNeil, Jr.
1939	Annisquam YC: Richard Mechem, Frederick Norton, Jr., John Lowe.
1940	Eastern YC: Robert Coulson, David Loring, Clinton McKim.
1941	Eastern YC: Robert Coulson, Clinton McKim, Paul Webster.
1942–45	No contest.
1946	Stage Harbor YC: William McClay, H. T. Woodland, Jr. Andrew Griscom.
1947	Buzzards YC: Michael Jackson, Nicholas Baker, Allen Chase.
1948	Vineyard Haven YC: Douglas Cassel, Robert Billings, James Norton.
1949	Cohasset YC: Kingsley Durant, Francis Cahouet, Edward Bursk, Jr.
1950	Pleon YC: Stephen Smithwick, George Stephenson, Nelson Aldrich, Jr.
1951	Rocky Point S.C.; George Reichelm, James Blattman, William Osgood III.
1952	Indian Yarbor YC: Martin Purcell, Constance Neher, Carolyn Neher.
1953	Sandusky S. C.: Dave Ortmann, Ellen Seaman Forbes Hotchkiss.
1954	Kingston YC: Harry Jemmett, Henry C. Connell, Barry Gilbert.
1955	Royal Canadian YC: A. R. Lennox, D. Day, P. Carver.
1956	Seattle Corinthian YC: Alan Holt, Fred Ray, Stephen Banks.
1957	Pequot YC: John Merrifield, Peter Clark, Thomas Munnell.
1958	Noroton YC: Kevin Jaffe, Carolyn McCurdy, Peter Wilson.
1959	Hudson YC: John Welch, Barbara Thomas, Ian Ritchie.
1960	Royal Vancouver YC: David Miller, Colin Park, Kenneth Baxter.
1961	Pleon YC: Steven Wales, Lee Harris, Tex Mason, Reennie Greenlaw.
1962	Newport Harbor YC: Henry Sprague III, George Twist, Bill Symes.
1963	Milford YC: Whit Batchelor, John Cordes, Dave Brown.
1964	Corinthian YC: Robert Doyle, Robert McCann, Joan Thayer.
1965	Corinthian YC: Robert Doyle, Robert McCann, Bruce Atkins.
1966	Monmouth Boat Club; Robert Held, Robert McCutcheon, David Allen.
1967	Southern YC: John Dane III, John Cerise, Mark LeBlank, Bill Smith.
1968	Galveston Bay C.A.: John Kolius, Jay Williams, Dan Williams.
1969	Noroton YC: Manton Scott, Christopher Wilson, Steven Heath.
1970	Houston YC: Dan Williams, Clark Thompson Jr., Ed McFarlan.

1971   Annapolis YC: Charlie Scott, John Becker, Ed Holt.

1972   Houston YC: Clark Thompson, Jr., Paul Thompson, Glen Brown.

1973   Houston YC: Glen Brown, Paul Thompson, Paul Wells.

1974   Minnetonka YC: Tom Burton, Chris Thompson, Fritz Van Nest.

1975   Coconut Grove S.C.: Mike Alexander, Reid Hutchinson, Fred Hutchinson.

1976   Potomac River S.A.: Andrew Menkart, Jeff Stamper, Berkeley Sherving, Chris Mason.

1977   Buckeye Lake YC: Will Petersilge, Dan Roshon, Dan Dressel.

1978   Pymatuning YC: Mark Thompson, Mike Wereley, George LeBrun.

1979   American YC: Bill Lynn, Tom Mundinger, Bobby Capita.

1980   Long Beach YC: John Shadden, Mike Pickney, Bobby Frazier.

1981   Richmond YC: John Kostecki, Albert Boyce, Mark Hempstead, Rand Arnold.

UNITED STATES JUNIOR SINGLE-HANDED SAILING CHAMPIONSHIP

1974   Huron-Portage YC: Richard Lyons.
1975   Ocean Gate YC: Shawn Kempton.
1976   White Rock Boat Club: Scott Young.
1977   Stockton YC: Paul Yost.
1978   St. Petersburg YC: Richard Merriman.
1979   Coconut Grove S.C.: Baird Lobree.
1980   San Diego YC: Brian Ledbetter.
1981   Coconut Grove S.C.: Louis Verloop.

UNITED STATES JUNIOR DOUBLE-HANDED SAILING CHAMPIONSHIP

1975   White Rock Boat Club: Dan Hathaway, Scott Young.

1976   Shrewsbury Sailing & YC: Chris Loyd, Mark Perkins.

1977   Cohasset YC: Brian Keane, Stephen Higginson.

1978   Long Beach YC: John Shadden, Peter Frazier.

1979   Alamitos Bay YC: John Shadden, Steve Rosenberg.

1980   St. Petersburg YC: Mike Funsch, Mark Shepard.

1981   St. Petersburg YC: Mike Funsch, Mark Shepard.

SINGLE-HANDED TRANSATLANTIC RACE

Year	Winner	Yacht	LOA	Starters	Time
1960	Francis Chichester (Britain) (Britain)	Gipsy Moth III	39 ft.	5	40 days, 11 hours
1964	Eric Tabarly (France)	Pen Duick II	45 ft.	16	27 days, 3 hours
1968	Geoffrey Williams (Britain)	Sir Thomas Lipton	56 ft.	35	25 days, 20 hours
1972	Alain Colas (France)	Pen Duick IV	70 ft.	52	21 days, 13 hours
1976	Eric Tabarly (France)	Pen Duick VI	73 ft.	126	20 days, 12 hours
1980	Phil Weld (USA)	Moxie	50 ft.	90	17 days, 23 hours

WHITBREAD ROUND THE WORLD RACE

Year	Yacht	Country	Skipper	Starters	Elapsed Time (hours)	Corrected Time (hours)	Corrected Time (days)
1973–74	Sayula II	Mexico	Ramon Carlin	17	3657.2	3204.5	134
1977–78	Flyer	Netherlands	Cornelis van Rietschoten	16	3269.5	2857	119
1981–82	Flyer	Netherlands	Cornelieus Van Rietschoten	29	2886.3	2857.01	119

RETURN TO
JOHN OLIVER LIBRARY
530 EAST 41st AVE,
VANCOUVER, B.C.